Scientific Foundations of Cognitive Theory and Therapy of Depression

Scientific Foundations of Cognitive Theory and Therapy of Depression

David A. Clark

and

Aaron T. Beck,

with

Brad A. Alford

John Wiley & Sons, Inc.

New York • Chichester • Weinheim • Brisbane • Singapore • Toronto

Copyright © 1999 by John Wiley & Sons, Inc. All rights reserved.

Published simultaneously in Canada.

Library of Congress Cataloging-in-Publication Data:

Clark, David A., 1954–
    Scientific foundations of cognitive theory of depression / David A. Clark, Aaron T. Beck, Brad A. Alford.
        p.   cm.
    Includes bibliographical references and index.
    ISBN 0-471-18970-7 (cloth : alk. paper)
    1. Depression, Mental.   2. Cognitive therapy.   3. Affective disorders.   I. Beck, Aaron T.   II. Alford, Brad A.   III. Title.
    RC537.C53   1999
    616.85'270651—dc21   98–44674

Printed in the United States of America.
10 9 8 7 6 5 4 3 2 1

Preface

ONE IN five Americans will suffer from some form of mental illness during his or her lifetime. The personal, economic, and social costs of mental illness are immense, with the economic impact of affective disorders alone estimated at $44 billion (1990) in terms of both direct and indirect health costs (P. Greenberg, Stiglin, Finkelstein, & Berndt, 1993). Thus research into the causes, persistence, and treatment of mental illness represents a major challenge facing the scientific community.

Affective disorder is one of the most common forms of mental illness with estimated lifetime prevalence rates of 13% and 21% for men and women, respectively (Kessler et al., 1994). Depression can take a chronic and recurring course, causing significant impairment in social, occupational, and personal functioning. Epidemiological and family studies suggest that depressive disorders are on the rise especially among young adults (Klerman & Weissman, 1989). Thus research into the nature and treatment of these disorders is particularly important to any national mental health research strategy.

Since its emergence in the early 1960s, Aaron T. Beck's cognitive theory and therapy has become one of the most widely accepted of the contemporary psychological theories and treatments of depression. Hypotheses derived from cognitive theory have been tested in hundreds of empirical studies (Haaga, Dyck, & Ernst, 1991), and his therapy has been evaluated in dozens of clinical outcome trials (Dobson, 1989). The application of cognitive therapy has been well documented in the publication of treatment manuals such as *Cognitive Therapy of Depression* (A. Beck, Rush, Shaw, & Emery, 1979), *Anxiety Disorders and Phobias: A Cognitive Perspective* (A. Beck & Emery with Greenberg, 1985), *Cognitive Therapy of Personality Disorders* (Beck, Freeman & Associates, 1990), and *Cognitive Therapy of Substance Abuse* (A. Beck, Wright, Newman, & Liese, 1993) as well as numerous chapter contributions in various edited volumes. The cognitive theory of depression, on the other hand, has not been presented in this unified manner. Instead, descriptions of the model can be found in various chapters, usually in reference to specific psychological problems such as substance abuse, panic disorder, or personality disorders.

The purpose of this book is to present the most current treatise on Beck's cognitive theory of depression and its scientific foundations. To evaluate the scientific status of this theory, it is necessary to consider its relevance to the clinical phenomena under consideration, in this case depression, and its account of the experimental findings. We chose to focus exclusively on depression in this work because of the significant mental health problem posed by affective disorders. We anticipate that later volumes will deal with the scientific basis of the cognitive theory of anxiety and other disorders.

The book is divided into two main sections. The first four chapters focus on a presentation of the clinical phenomena of depression and the current version of cognitive theory. Chapter 1 discusses the features and issues associated with depression that must be explained by any theoretical account of these disorders. Chapter 2 describes the historical development of cognitive theory noting its origins in laboratory experimentation and clinical observation of depression. Chapter 3 presents the theoretical assumptions that provide a foundation for cognitive theory and also introduces some of the general criticisms of the scientific basis of the cognitive model. Chapter 4 describes the most current version of the cognitive formulation of depression that has been refined and expanded in response to the wealth of experimental research on the cognitive basis of depression as well as insights gained from the theory's application to an increasing range of psychological problems.

The second section of this book (Chapters 5–10) is devoted to an evaluation of the empirical status of the descriptive and vulnerability hypotheses of the cognitive theory of depression. Chapters 5, 6, and 7 present a comprehensive review and critique of the descriptive hypotheses; whereas Chapters 8, 9, and 10 review the level of empirical support for the vulnerability hypotheses of the cognitive model. The final chapter of this book summarizes the extant findings on the cognitive basis of depression and suggests issues that will require the attention of future researchers.

In 1967, the first detailed description of the cognitive theory of depression was published in *Depression: Causes and Treatment* by one of us, Aaron T. Beck. The basic concepts of the theory laid out in that volume still provide the foundation for the cognitive model 30 years later. As well as describing the first systematic investigations of the theory, the 1967 work contributed to a paradigmatic shift in theory, research, and treatment of depression that resulted in a vigorous and widespread research initiative on the cognitive basis of depression. The present book is intended to provide a comprehensive and critical update of developments in cognitive theory and research on depression that have occurred since the initial publications in the 1960s.

We gratefully acknowledge partial support for preparation of this manuscript from the Social Sciences and Humanities Research Council of Canada and the Foundation for Cognitive Therapy. We are grateful to Willem Kuyken for his valuable comments on an earlier draft of this manuscript. We are indebted to Barbara Marinelli for her invaluable assistance in coordinating the communication and seemingly endless flow of manuscripts among us. We also thank Murray Linton and Tim Cannon for their assistance and technical advice on word processing and file transfer programming. I (DAC) am grateful to the graduate students, faculty, and the Chair of the Department of Psychology, University of New Brunswick for creating an environment that is conducive to the pursuit of scientific interests. Finally I (DAC) would especially like to express appreciation to my wife (Nancy) and daughters (Natascha and Christina) for the constant encouragement and understanding they expressed toward me while I was involved in writing this book.

DAVID A. CLARK
AARON T. BECK

Contents

CHAPTER 1

Depressive Symptoms and Disorders: Diagnostic and Conceptual Considerations

DEPRESSION IS the second most common psychological disorder, annually afflicting nearly 100 million people worldwide (Gotlib & Hammen, 1992). Depending on how depression is defined and assessed, lifetime prevalence rates for diagnosable major depressive disorder range from 2.6% to 12.7% in men, and 7% to 21% for women (Kessler et al., 1994; M. Weissman, Bruce, Leaf, Florio, & Holzer, 1991). The 1994–1995 National Population Health Survey revealed that 5.6% of Canadians over 18 years of age experienced a major depressive episode in a previous 12-month period (Beaudet, 1996). In their review of 20 studies conducted since 1980, Wittchen, Knauper, and Kessler (1994) concluded that the lifetime prevalence of major depression falls between 15% and 18%. Milder subclinical forms of depressive disorder involving too few symptoms to meet diagnostic criteria for caseness are even more common, with prevalence rates significantly higher than for major depressive disorder (Barrett, Barrett, Oxman, & Gerber, 1988; K. Wells et al., 1989). In fact, most people can attest to feelings of sadness or dysphoria that emerge as a normal human response to the frustrations, failures, and losses occurring in daily life.

Because depressed mood or dysphoria is a universal experience that falls within the normal spectrum of emotion, most people fail to appreciate the serious personal, social and economic costs associated with the more severe clinical forms of depression. Presence of a depressive disorder or even a few depressive symptoms has been associated with significant reductions in physical and social functioning (Spitzer et al., 1994;

K. Wells et al., 1989). As well, individuals with just a few depressive symptoms appear to be at higher risk for the development of a subsequent more severe depressive episode (Crum, Cooper-Patrick, & Ford, 1994; Horwath, Johnson, Klerman, & Weissman, 1992; K. Wells, Burnam, Rogers, Hays, & Camp, 1992). When one also considers that rates of depression appear to be on the rise especially among younger age groups 15–45 years of age (Cross-National Collaborative Group, 1992; Klerman & Weissman, 1989; Wittchen et al., 1994), it is little wonder that the diagnosis and treatment of this disorder represents one of the most important challenges facing mental health researchers and clinicians today.

In this chapter, we deal with six issues that are crucial to our understanding of depressive phenomena. Although we will not be covering all the issues important in depression research, nevertheless these six topics deal with fundamental aspects of depression that must be addressed by any theoretical model of the phenomena. These issues all deal with depression at the descriptive level and have resulted in a considerable body of empirical research. The six areas of inquiry are (a) the *Diagnostic and Statistical Manual of Mental Disorders* (*DSM-IV*; American Psychiatric Association [APA], 1994) and core symptoms of depression, (b) diagnostic heterogeneity and depressive subtypes, (c) the continuity versus discontinuity of disorders, (d) the comorbidity of depression, (e) the course of clinical depression, and (f) negative consequences or outcomes associated with depression.

This chapter is not intended to provide a comprehensive review of depression since this can be found in textbooks on psychopathology (e.g., Beckham & Leber, 1985; Maser & Cloninger, 1990; Paykel, 1992). Rather, we want to focus on important conceptual issues that must be addressed by any theory of depression. In subsequent chapters, we evaluate Beck's cognitive theory of depression in terms of its ability to adequately account for the issues and features of depression highlighted in this chapter. Let us begin then with a discussion of what is considered the cardinal manifestation of clinical depression, major depressive disorder.

CORE SYMPTOMS OF DEPRESSION

DYSPHORIA AND LOSS OF INTEREST

If there is one set of symptoms that psychologists and psychiatrists consider prototypic of clinical depression, it would have to be that of *major depressive episode*. According to *DSM-IV* (American Psychiatric Association, 1994), a diagnosis of major depressive episode can be made only if five or more symptoms from Criterion A are present for at least two weeks. The list of possible symptoms includes depressed mood, loss of interest or pleasure, weight or appetite gain or loss, insomnia or hypersomnia, psychomotor agitation or retardation, fatigue or loss of energy, sense of worthlessness or excessive guilt, reduced concentration or indecisiveness, and recurrent thoughts of death or suicidal ideation. In addition, depressed mood or loss of interest or pleasure must be present in order to make a diagnosis of major depressive episode, and the symptom presentation must cause clinically significant distress or impairment in social, occupational, or other areas of daily functioning. Major depression would be ruled out if the symptoms were associated with a mixed episode of mania and depression, were caused by the direct physiological effects of drugs or a medical condition, or were better accounted for by bereavement.

Several features of these symptom criteria are worth noting. First, *DSM-IV* considers depressed mood and loss of interest or pleasure to be core symptoms of major depression. To qualify for a diagnosis of major depression, individuals must present with one or both of these symptoms. Coyne (1994b) noted that the sustained mood disturbance in major depression can be met by either sad mood or apathy (i.e., loss of interest or pleasure in most activities). Studies have found that either of these two symptoms occur in practically all cases of clinically significant depression (A. Beck, 1967; Depression Guideline Panel, 1993). Analysis of 40,000 questionnaires collected during the 1992 and 1993 National Depression Screening Day revealed that "having difficulty doing things that one did in the past" and "no longer enjoying the things one used to do" were among the top five most prevalent symptoms in subjects reporting some level of depression ("Study Results," 1994). Coyne (1994b) noted that 10% to 15% of severely depressed patients may deny feelings of sadness and only meet mood criteria on the basis of loss of interest or pleasure. However, Buchwald and Rudick-Davis (1993) found that loss of interest was present in only 75% of outpatients meeting criteria for *DSM-III* major depressive episode. Bech (1992) stated that the mood disturbance in major depression is not simply a feeling of sadness but includes feelings of apprehension, hopelessness, and helplessness. We can conclude from this that a sustained negative mood disturbance is a core defining characteristic of clinical depression and that it involves either severe dysphoria and/or loss of pleasure or anhedonia.

SOMATIC VERSUS SUBJECTIVE SYMPTOMS IN DEPRESSION

A second characteristic of the *DSM-IV* criteria for major depression is the strong emphasis on the biological or somatic symptoms of depression and the relative neglect of the subjective experience of the disorder (Gotlib & Hammen, 1992). Seven of the Criterion A symptoms refer to the somatic, motivational, or behavioral features of depression (i.e., diminished interest, weight loss, insomnia, psychomotor agitation, fatigue, inability to concentrate, and suicidality), whereas only two symptoms, depressed mood and feelings of worthlessness, refer to the subjective aspects of depression. But is this emphasis on somatic and behavioral symptoms supported by the empirical evidence?

Numerous studies have found that the more subjective symptoms of depression such as depressed mood, hopelessness, and feelings of worthlessness or self-dislike are as critical or even more central to the definition of major depression than the biological symptoms such as weight loss and insomnia (A. Beck, 1967; Coulehan, Schulberg, Block, & Zettler-Segal, 1988; D. Goldberg, Bridges, Duncan-Jones, & Grayson, 1987; Lovibond & Lovibond, 1995; "Study Results," 1994). On the other hand, anhedonia, or loss of interest or pleasure, has consistently emerged as a defining symptom feature of depression (see reviews of L.A. Clark & Watson, 1989, 1991b).

In our own research on a large sample of psychiatric outpatients (52% had a clinical depression) and nonclinical subjects, we found that the cognitive and subjective symptom items of the Beck Depression Inventory loaded uniquely on a depression factor; whereas the biological symptoms such as weight loss, loss of libido, and loss of appetite failed to produce significant factor loadings (D.A. Clark, Steer, & Beck, 1994; Steer, Clark, Beck, & Ranieri, 1995). However, in a study of symptom frequency in outpatients with major depressive episode, Buchwald and Rudick-Davis (1993) found that sleep disturbance, loss of energy, and appetite disturbance occurred in over 80% of cases; whereas psychomotor disturbance and feelings of worthlessness were present in less than 70% of the depressed patients. Coryell et al. (1995) recently reported 6-year follow-up data on individuals with an untreated major depressive disorder. For this group, anhedonia, fatigue, trouble concentrating, guilt, and insomnia were reported by at least 50% of the sample.

Together, these findings indicate that there is some disagreement in the nosological literature on the centrality of the biological symptoms for a diagnosis of depression. Alternatively, somatic symptoms such as weight loss, insomnia, poor appetite, and psychomotor retardation may be indicative of an endogenous or melancholic subtype of depression (APA, 1994; Blazer et al., 1988; Grove et al., 1987; Rush & Weissenburger, 1994); or at least some of these symptoms, such as insomnia, may simply be indicative of depression severity (Casper et al., 1985; D.A. Clark, Beck, & Beck, 1994). At the very least, the strong emphasis on biological symptoms and the relative neglect of subjective symptoms in the *DSM-IV* diagnostic criteria for major depressive episode may represent an imbalance or bias that is not warranted by the findings from descriptive symptom studies of depression. As discussed in later chapters, the cognitive model considers the subjective symptoms such as a negative view of self, world, and future critical defining features of depression (A. Beck, 1963, 1967).

THE DURATION AND IMPAIRMENT CRITERIA

The mere presence of depressive symptoms is not sufficient for a diagnosis of major depression. There must also be evidence of a sustained mood disturbance (i.e., present every day or nearly every day for at least 2 weeks) which causes clinically significant distress or impairment. The impairment criteria was added to *DSM-IV* because of concerns that too many cases of *DSM-III-R* major depression were only mildly symptomatic and so not responsive to antidepressant medication (Coyne, 1994b). Thus both the duration and impairment criteria are included to assist in distinguishing major depression from minor subclinical forms of depression.

The importance of the duration criteria is supported by studies indicating that major depression tends to take a chronic, recurring course in a majority of patients seeking treatment (Coryell, Endicott, & Keller, 1991; Gotlib & Hammen, 1992; Keller, Shapiro, Lavori, & Wolfe, 1982; K. Wells et al., 1992). In the *DSM-IV* mood disorders field trial, 68% of the major depressive sample presented with a recurrent depressive condition (Keller et al., 1995). The recurrent nature of depression suggests that the course of the disorder may be important in differentiating clinical from nonclinical states. Coyne (1994b) has argued that duration is an important factor in diagnosable depression because subclinical depressive and dysphoric states tend to be briefer and more transient than major depressive episodes.

Moreover, the presence of a depressive disorder, or even a few depressive symptoms, is associated with significant and persistent impairment in social and occupational functioning in both the acute and follow-up period as indicated by increased family dysfunction, reduced social activities, an increase in days lost from work, reduced annual income, decline in job status, poorer work performance, reduced educational attainment, and increased financial dependency (Broadhead, Blazer, George, & Tse, 1990; Hays, Wells, Sherbourne, Rogers, & Spritzer, 1995; Kessler, Foster, Saunders, & Stang, 1995; Mintz, Mintz, Arruda, & Hwang, 1992; M. Weissman et al., 1991; K. Wells et al., 1989). These findings suggest that the duration and impairment criteria of *DSM-IV* may be important characteristics of diagnosable major depression. However, two qualifications are in order. First, there is no evidence that assessment of impairment can be done reliably and accurately by clinicians who depend entirely on the patient's self-report. Individuals may find it more difficult to judge the degree of interference that depressive symptoms cause in their life compared with reporting on the mere presence or absence of symptoms. And second, it is still not clear that inclusion of the impairment criteria will eliminate cases of mild depression. It has been shown that even minor subclinical forms of depression can cause significant impairment in social and occupational functioning (Broadhead et al., 1990; Hays et al., 1995). Thus the clinical utility of the impairment criteria in *DSM-IV* major depressive episode remains to be seen.

This brief discussion of the diagnostic criteria of *DSM-IV* major depressive episode leads us to the first characteristic of depression that must be addressed by any theory of the disorder:

ISSUE 1: *Clinically significant depression is characterized by a sustained disturbance in mood involving behavioral inhibition, subjective negativity and, in more severe cases, disturbance in somatic functioning.*

HETEROGENEITY OF DEPRESSION

There is considerable symptom variability in the depressive experience, prompting depression researchers to acknowledge that diagnosable clinical depression consists of a heterogeneous set of disorders. Over the years, numerous classification schemes have been proposed in an effort to identify reliable and valid subtypes of depression. Some of these schemes have generated a considerable amount of research attention such as the endogenous-reactive, neurotic-psychotic, and primary-secondary distinctions as well as Winokur's Iowa classification system (see Gotlib & Hammen, 1992; Grove & Andreasen, 1992; Leber, Beckham, & Danker-Brown, 1985). In this chapter, however, we focus on four subtypes of depression that appear in *DSM-IV* as valid or provisional diagnostic categories; bipolar disorders, dysthymia, minor depressive disorder, and mixed anxiety-depressive disorder.

BIPOLAR DISORDER

One of the most widely accepted diagnostic distinctions in psychiatric nosology centers on whether depression occurs with or without a period of mania. *DSM-IV* follows this tradition, drawing a sharp distinction between unipolar depression or major depressive disorder which occurs without mania, and bipolar disorder which can take the form of alternating periods of depression and mania or hypomania. *DSM-IV* makes a further distinction between bipolar I disorder and bipolar II disorder. The primary focus in bipolar I disorder is on the manifestations of mania. It is diagnosed when there has been one or more manic or mixed episodes with or without a previous major depressive episode (*DSM-IV*, APA, 1994).

Mania is described as a distinct period of abnormally elevated mood lasting at least one week and characterized by at least three of the following symptoms; inflated self-esteem, decreased need for sleep, more talkative than usual, flight of ideas, distractibility, increase in goal-directed activity, or excessive involvement in pleasurable activities. These symptoms must also be sufficiently severe to cause marked impairment in social and occupational functioning. In hypomania, these same symptom criteria are present except that the duration is shorter (at least 4 days) and the disturbance, though representing a change in functioning, is not so severe as to cause significant impairment in function. For a mixed episode, criteria are met for both a manic and major depressive episode nearly every day over at least a one-week period. A diagnosis of bipolar II disorder is made when one or more major depressive episodes occurs in the presence of at least one hypomanic episode. In bipolar II disorder, there has never been a full-blown manic or mixed episode.

Considerable empirical evidence has accumulated over the years to support the diagnostic validity of the unipolar-bipolar distinction. For example, there is evidence that, compared with unipolar depression, bipolar disorder has a stronger and/or different genetic basis (Suinn, 1995), occurs at a younger age, is equally prevalent in men and women, is much less common in the general population, may have shorter acute episodes but a higher relapse rate, and has a worse overall outcome during the posttreatment follow-up period (Depue & Monroe, 1978a; J. F. Goldberg, Harrow, & Grossman, 1995; Leber et al., 1985; Perris, 1992; M. Weissman et al., 1991; Winokur, Coryell, Keller, Endicott, & Leon, 1995). However, it has been more difficult to find consistent differences in depressive symptomatology, personality, occurrence of life events, biological variables and response to treatment (Fabrega, Mezzich, Mezzich, & Coffman, 1986; Khouri & Akiskal, 1986; Perris, 1992). Thus the distinction between unipolar and bipolar disorder is based primarily on the differential course associated with each disorder rather than on symptomatic or etiologic distinctives. Although this represents a departure from the usual *DSM* approach to differential diagnosis, the weight of the empirical evidence remains with those advocating the unipolar-bipolar distinction.

DYSTHYMIC DISORDER

In *DSM-IV*, chronic, mild depressive states are represented under the category of dysthymia. The essential characteristics of this disorder are (a) chronicity—depressed mood lasting more days than not for at least a 2-year period; (b) mild clinical presentation—presence of at least two symptoms comprising either poor appetite or overeating, insomnia or hypersomnia, low energy or fatigue, low self-esteem, poor concentration or difficulty making decisions, or feelings of hopelessness; (c) absence of recovery—in the preceding 2 years, no evidence of a symptom-free period for longer than 2 months; (d) major depressive episode not present during the first 2 years of the disturbance; and (e) clinically significant distress or impairment in social, occupational, or other important areas of functioning. Dysthymia as a chronic, subsyndromal state refers to a dispositional tendency toward dysphoria and so the concept has links to the European notion of the depressive personality (Akiskal, 1983) and the *DSM-II* concept of depressive neurosis (Phillips, Gunderson, Hirschfeld, & Smith, 1990). As noted by Akiskal, the person with dysthymia is characteristically "gloomy, introverted, brooding, overconscientious, incapable of fun and preoccupied with personal inadequacy" (p. 11).

There can be little doubt that there is a subgroup of patients whose depression is not self-limiting but rather follows a chronic, sometimes lifelong course (Akiskal, 1983; Gold, 1990). Chronic depressions account for 25% to 40% of patients presenting for treatment of depression in psychiatric settings (Kocsis & Frances, 1987; M. Weissman, Leaf, Bruce, & Florio, 1988), although the lifetime prevalence rates of dysthymia (3%–6%) tend to be lower than the 5% to 17% reported for major depressive disorder (Kessler et al., 1994; M. Weissman et al., 1988, 1991). There is also empirical evidence that compared with episodic major depression, dysthymia is characterized by lower levels of social adjustment, higher levels of chronic strain, poorer prognosis, more depressive personality traits, and more melancholic symptoms (D. N. Klein, Taylor, Dickstein, & Harding, 1988; K. Wells et al., 1992). In the *DSM-IV* mood disorders field trial, cognitive and social/motivational symptoms were more common in dysthymia than the vegetative and psychomotor symptoms (Keller et al., 1995).

A number of problems are apparent with the diagnosis of dysthymia. First, the diagnostic boundaries between major depression and dysthymia are "fuzzy" making it difficult for the clinician to arrive at a differential diagnosis. Kocsis and Frances (1987) noted that the severity criteria for *DSM-III* dysthymia (3 out of 13 depressive symptoms) were too close to that of a major depression episode (4 out of 6 symptoms), thereby possibly inflating the number of double depressions (individuals with major depression superimposed on dysthymia). It is clear that major depression and dysthymia are related, and possibly overlapping, conditions given evidence of a common genetic basis, high comorbidity rate (i.e., double depression), a substantially elevated risk for subsequent major depression among dysthymics, and the fact that the defining symptoms for each disorder are practically identical (Akiskal, 1983; Hirschfeld, 1994; D. N. Klein, Clark, Dansky, & Margolis, 1988; D. N. Klein, Taylor, et al., 1988; D. N. Klein et al., 1995; Lewinsohn, Rohde, Seeley, & Hops, 1991; K. Wells et al., 1992). Keller et al. (1995), for example, found that of the 190 individuals in the *DSM-IV* mood disorders field trial who met diagnostic criteria for dysthymia, 62% also met criteria for a current major depressive episode and 79% a lifetime diagnosis of major depression.

A second problem noted for dysthymia is the probable heterogeneity of chronic depression. Akiskal (1983) distinguished between two types of chronic depression, the first labeled character-spectrum disorders and the second subaffective dysthymic disorders. The character-spectrum dysthymia is primarily a characterological pathology with poor response to medication treatment, absence of melancholic symptoms, substance abuse, and high rates of familial alcoholism. The subaffective dysthymic disorders are characterized by a greater emphasis on frequent episodes of subclinical endogenous depressions with personality disturbances playing a secondary role. These patients showed a better response to biological treatment, had symptoms characteristic of primary affective disorders, and had personalities that resembled the depressive personality typology. There is some empirical support for Akiskal's distinction between the two types of chronic depression (see Phillips et al., 1990). *DSM-IV* allows for a distinction between early-onset dysthymia (onset before 21 years of age) and late onset disorder (onset after 21 years of age) because early-onset dysthymia is considered to be most similar to a depressive personality disorder.

A third problem centers on disagreement over the *DSM-III* decision to place dysthymia within the Axis I disorders rather than within Axis II as a depressive personality disorder (Kocsis & Frances, 1987). Whether one considers dysthymia an Axis I or II disorder depends on which characteristics of the disorder are emphasized. Those who focus on the early-onset and chronic nature of the disorder are more likely to view dysthymia as a type of personality disorder, whereas those who emphasize the subaffective symptoms are more likely to view it as an Axis I disorder. Phillips et al. (1990) more recently argued for retaining dysthymia on Axis I and the creation of a category called depressive personality disorder on Axis II. Pepper et al. (1995) found that a significantly higher proportion of patients with early-onset dysthymia had a comorbid Axis II personality disorder (60%) than did patients with episodic major depression (18%), again suggesting a strong link between dysthymia and characterological disorders.

Kocsis and Frances (1987) have also argued that the *DSM* criteria for dysthymia may have poor content validity. They suggest that the somatic and vegetative symptoms are overrepresented and the cognitive and functional symptoms underrepresented. Descriptive cross-sectional studies have tended to support this criticism with evidence that cognitive, social, and motivational symptoms predominate in dysthymia more than the somatic and vegetative symptoms (Keller et al., 1995; Kocsis & Frances, 1987). *DSM-IV* has recognized this controversy by offering a list of alternative criteria that emphasizes the social, cognitive, and motivational symptoms. However, these are found in the provisional appendix and are intended for research purposes only. Despite the controversy over the nature, diagnosis, and relationship of dysthymia to other Axis I and II disorders, a significant number of individuals present with a chronic unremitting form of subclinical affective disturbance.

Minor Depressive Disorder

A new diagnostic category, Minor Depressive Disorder, was introduced in *DSM-IV* as one of the provisional criteria sets that did not have sufficient empirical support for its inclusion as an official category but nonetheless deserved further study. The symptom features and duration are identical to that of major depressive episode with the exception that fewer symptoms are needed to meet diagnostic criteria (2 out of 9 with 1 of the 2 being depressed mood or loss of interest or pleasure). Exclusionary criteria include a past episode of major depression or dysthymia. In addition, the significant distress or impairment criterion found in major depression has been omitted.

The importance of minor depression can be seen in the prevalence of depressive symptoms and their clinical significance. Some depressive symptoms, such as dysphoria, thoughts of death, and change in sleep and appetite, are quite common, with lifetime prevalence rates of 20% to 30% in the general population. Other symptoms, such as psychomotor slowness or loss of interest, are much less frequent (M. Weissman et al., 1991). Community studies indicate that the presence of a few depressive symptoms that are not sufficient to meet criteria for major depression can be found in 9% to 24% of the population, depending on whether interviews or screening questionnaires are utilized (Boyd & Weissman, 1981; Horwath et al., 1992). In primary care settings, the prevalence of subthreshold depression is even more common with rates ranging from 27% to 50% (Crum et al., 1994; Duer, Schwenk, & Coyne, 1988; Schulberg et al., 1985). In their review of depression research in adolescence, Compas, Ey, and Grant (1993) estimated point prevalence rates of 15% to 40% for adolescents with significant depressed mood, with 5% to 6% of these adolescents having anxious and/or depressed symptoms in the clinical range but only 1% to 3% meeting diagnostic criteria for a depressive disorder.

Minor depression or presence of a few depressive symptoms is associated with significant long-term impairment in social and occupation functioning, decrease in well-being, increased utilization of health care services, and more disability days from work (Broadhead et al., 1990; Hayes et al., 1995; J. Johnson, Weissman, & Klerman, 1992; Spitzer et al., 1994). Duer et al. (1988) found that physical symptoms, chronic health conditions, recent life events, and deficiencies in social support were all significantly higher in family practice patients with elevated levels of self-reported depressive symptoms. Moreover, there is evidence that minor depression is a variant of affective disorder. Individuals with subthreshold or minor depression are at a substantially higher risk for developing a subsequent major depression (Crum et al., 1994; Horwath et al., 1992; K. Wells et al., 1992) and show a family history of depressive episode (Sherbourne et al., 1994). Zonderman, Herbst, Schmidt, Costa, and McCrae (1993) found that elevated self-reported depressive symptoms predicted the occurrence of clinical depression as well as other psychiatric diagnoses as determined from hospitalization records taken during a 12-year follow-up period. However, Keller et al. (1995) found that only 6% of their sample of depressed patients met *DSM-IV* criteria for minor depression, calling into question the need for an additional diagnostic category. These results appear contrary to the findings of other studies, especially those conducted in primary care settings suggesting the need for a diagnostic category that captures the large number of individuals presenting with subthreshold depressive states and who are at higher risk for developing a subsequent major depressive episode.

MIXED ANXIETY-DEPRESSIVE DISORDER

A final depression category, mixed anxiety-depression, has again been introduced in the provisional diagnostic section of *DSM-IV.* This category is intended to identify individuals with only a few depressive and anxious symptoms that are not sufficient in frequency or severity to meet diagnostic criteria for an anxiety or depressive disorder. The symptoms must persist for at least one month and involve a dysphoric mood with four or more of the following symptoms:

- Difficulty concentrating.
- Sleep disturbance.
- Fatigue or low energy.
- Irritability.
- Worry.
- Being easily moved to tears.
- Hypervigilance.

- Anticipating the worst.
- Hopelessness.
- Low self-esteem or feelings of worthlessness.

In addition, the symptoms must cause significant distress or functional impairment, with exclusionary criteria being a previous episode of major depression, dysthymia, panic disorder, or generalized anxiety disorder.

Empirical support for this diagnostic category is still in the preliminary stage. In their review of community, psychiatric, and primary care studies, Katon and Roy-Byrne (1991) concluded that a large subgroup of individuals have a mixture of anxious and depressive symptoms that are not sufficient to meet caseness for an anxiety or depressive disorder. Furthermore, this subthreshold anxiety and depression is associated with decrements in social and occupational functioning, and places individuals at higher risk for a more severe major depressive or anxiety disorder. A *DSM-IV* field trial for mixed anxiety-depression was recently conducted with 666 patients drawn from five primary care medical sites and two psychiatric outpatient facilities (Zinbarg et al., 1994). Analysis of self-report and interview symptom measures revealed a significant number of patients with subdefinitional threshold affective symptoms. These cases, diagnosed Anxiety NOS and Depression NOS under *DSM-III-R* criteria, showed a symptom profile of nonspecific anxious and depressive symptoms. They were best discriminated from subjects with no psychiatric diagnosis by general distress, or negative affect symptoms rather than more specific anxiety or depressive symptoms. Furthermore, there was some evidence that this milder, nonspecific mixed anxiety-depression took a chronic course and was associated with significant impairment in functioning. Based on these findings, the authors proposed the current *DSM-IV* diagnostic criteria for mixed anxiety-depression. The relation between this milder, mixed disturbance and syndromal anxiety or depression is currently unknown.

We have discussed four subtypes of affective disorder that, along with major depressive disorder, have a varying amount of empirical support in the research literature. Regardless of which system of subclassifying depression is accepted, depression is not a unitary construct. The cognitive model recognizes this symptom and diagnostic diversity in depression, but considers a core cognitive dysfunction evident to a greater or less degree in all types of depression (Haaga et al., 1991). This, then, brings us to the second characteristic of depression that must be addressed by any theory of the disorder:

ISSUE 2: *Depression consists of a heterogeneous group of disorders that vary in severity, chronicity, and clinical presentation.*

DIMENSIONAL VERSUS CATEGORICAL PERSPECTIVES ON DEPRESSION

One debate at the core of any conceptualization of psychopathology is whether psychological disturbance varies in degree or in kind. Researchers in depression have been particularly divided on this issue, with some advocating a dimensional or continuum view of depression, and others advancing a categorical or discontinuous perspective on depressive states. The dimensional viewpoint argues that depression lies on a continuum of severity, with normal depressed mood and minor depressive states at one end of the pole and the more severe clinical states, such as major depressive episode, at the other end. Thus the nonclinical, milder states of depression form a continuum with clinical, diagnosable depression, differing only in the severity and persistence of the depressive symptomatology. The categorical perspective, on the other hand, argues that clinical or diagnosable depression is qualitatively different from subthreshold depression and normal dysphoria.

Both of these views have far-reaching implications for how depression research is conducted. Those adopting a dimensional view argue that research on milder depressive states in nonclinical samples, or on subjects who report an increase in depressive symptoms on self-report depression measures, may be of relevance to clinical depression (A. Beck, 1991; Flett, Vredenburg, & Krames, 1997; Seligman, 1978; Vredenburg, Flett, & Krames, 1993). Researchers holding a categorical viewpoint argue that research on nonclinical subjects who produce elevated scores on self-report depression measures is of questionable relevance or generalizability to clinical depression. A reason cited for the lack of relevance is the postulated discontinuity between clinical and nonclinical depression (Coyne, 1994b; Coyne & Downey, 1991; Depue & Monroe, 1978b; Gotlib & Hammen, 1992).

EVIDENCE FOR DISCONTINUITY

Several reasons are cited by those who hold the categorical position. One of the most compelling arguments for discontinuity is the apparent difference in incidence or prevalence rates between mild depression or dysphoria, as assessed by self-report depression measures like the Beck Depression Inventory, and the rates of diagnosable depression obtained with diagnostic interview schedules (Coyne, 1994b; Flett, Vredenburg, et al., 1997; Vredenburg et al., 1993). Coyne (1994b), in particular, has argued forcefully that high scores on self-report depression measures are not necessarily indicative of major depression (see also Compas et al.,

1993). He contends that depression scores may also be elevated for other reasons such as the presence of physical symptoms, side effects of medication, high negative affectivity or neuroticism, or other psychopathological states such as anxiety or substance abuse. Coyne (1994b) cites a number of studies in which the majority of subjects having elevated scores on the Beck Depression Inventory (BDI) or Center for Epidemiologic Studies Depression Scale (CES-D) were found not to have a diagnosable depression when followed up with a clinical interview (Coyne, Schwenk, & Smolinski, 1991; Deardorff & Funabiki, 1985; Fechner-Bates, Coyne, & Schwenk, 1994; Myers & Weissman, 1980; Oliver & Simmons, 1984). Gotlib and Hammen (1992) noted that most people who show mild, transient symptoms of depression following a stressful experience do not become clinically depressed.

Coyne (1994b) stated that one reason for the low positive predictive value found for measures like the BDI and the CES-D is the differential base rates for depressive symptoms and disorders in the normal population. Whereas some depressive symptoms, such as sadness or dysphoria, are relatively common, rates of diagnosable depression are comparatively quite rare. Thus self-report measures consistently overestimate depression in the normal population resulting in high sensitivity but low specificity. Furthermore, a number of correlational and factor analytic studies have found that depression measures correlate very highly with measures of negative affect and other psychological states (i.e., anxiety, anger) prompting some to conclude that self-report depression measures may be assessing general nonspecific distress or negative affectivity rather than specific depressive states (L.A. Clark & Watson, 1991b; Feldman, 1993; Gotlib, 1984; Meites, Lovallo, & Pishkin, 1980).

More recently Flett, Vredenburg, et al. (1997) questioned whether the high false positive rates for self-report depression measures can be taken as evidence for the underlying discontinuity of dysphoria and diagnosable depression. They noted that a high false positive rate is not unique to self-report depression measures but instead is a general feature of psychopathological self-report measures. High rates of false positive have been reported for questionnaire measures of eating disorders, panic disorder, psychosis proneness, obsessive-compulsive disorders, and personality disorders. In addition, Flett and his colleagues argue that the discrepancy between self-reports and diagnoses may be due to methodological problems with the instruments themselves. Thus they conclude that the high false positive rate for self-report depression measures may be due to limitations in self-report symptom methodology and so cannot be assumed to be a demonstration of discontinuities in the construct under investigation, in this case depression.

A second source of evidence cited for discontinuity is the apparent distinctiveness in symptom presentation between diagnosable depression and milder states of nonclinical or "normal" depression. Depue and Monroe (1978b), for example, concluded from their review of the few studies available at that time, that behavioral, somatic anxiety, and the other somatic symptoms of depression best distinguished diagnosable depression from normal depression and unhappiness (see also Coyne & Gotlib, 1983). Nonclinical depression, or dysphoria, on the other hand, was best characterized by unhappiness, sadness, and loneliness. L.A. Clark and Watson (1991b) also concluded that milder nonclinical states of depression may be primarily characterized by the more general nonspecific symptoms of negative affectivity (i.e., a state of worry, unhappiness, distress, anger, tension, low self-worth) whereas diagnosable depression is distinguished by symptoms considered specific to depression such as anhedonia, loss of interest and pleasure, or low positive affect (i.e., loss of pleasurable engagement). In the Buchwald and Rudick-Davis (1993) study, patients with major depressive episode (MDE) were distinguished from the non-MDE patients by the vegetative symptoms of depression as well as loss of energy and thinking difficulties. The non-MDE subjects reported at least two weeks of sadness or loss of interest but failed to present with at least four other depressive symptoms in order to meet diagnostic criteria. As noted previously, Zinbarg et al. (1994) found that patients diagnosed with a *DSM-III-R* diagnosis of depression NOS (patients with subdefinitional threshold affective symptoms) were characterized by elevated scores on a negative affect scale but not on the anhedonia/low positive affect, subjective anxiety, or physiological arousal scales.

In a community study of adolescents, Gotlib, Lewinsohn, and Seeley (1995) found that individuals with diagnosable depression were distinguished from participants with high CES-D scores but no depressive disorder (false positives) by anhedonia, weight change, sleep difficulties, indecisiveness, and suicidal ideation. In their review paper, Compas et al. (1993) concluded that the presence of somatic and vegetative symptoms in adolescents with depressive disorders distinguished them from adolescents with merely depressive symptoms or a dysphoric mood state.

Empirical evidence for a distinctive symptom profile for clinical versus nonclinical depression has been inconsistent at best. Vredenburg et al. (1993) highlighted a number of specific methodological problems with the early empirical studies cited by Depue and Monroe (1978b). Other studies like those of Zinbarg et al. (1994) and Buchwald and Rudick-Davis (1993) may not be particularly relevant to this issue because their symptom comparisons were made on clinical samples only rather than between clinical and nonclinical groups. Flett, Vredenburg, et al. (1997), in a detailed and thoughtful critique of this literature, concluded that the bulk of the evidence comparing symptom presentation at varying levels of depression favors the continuity position. For example, although Gotlib et al. (1995) did report symptom differences between the diagnosed depression and the false positive groups, Flett, Vredenburg, et al. reanalyzed the information provided in this study and found a substantial degree of similarity in the rank order of the nine depressive symptoms of the two groups. As described under "Evidence for Continuity," some studies have found considerable similarity in symptom expression between clinical and nonclinical depression.

A third argument for discontinuity centers on whether the correlates or risk factors of dysphoria and diagnosable depression are different. The following factors appear to differ between nonclinical and clinical depression: (a) poverty increases the risk for dysphoria and depressive symptoms but not major depressive episode; (b) minor and major life events both appear related to increases in depressive symptoms, but only severe, relatively infrequent life events that require long-term adjustment are associated with diagnosable depression; (c) chronic stressors such as unemployment or caring for a handicapped child are associated with depressive symptoms but not depressive disorder; and (d) gender differences are apparent with twice as many women suffering major depression as men, whereas elevated scores on self-report depression measures assessing dysphoria fail to show this gender difference (Coyne, 1994b; Coyne & Downey, 1991).

The study by Lewinsohn, Hoberman and Rosenbaum (1988) deserves special mention because it has been frequently cited (i.e., Gotlib & Hammen, 1992) as providing strong empirical evidence for differential correlates or risk factors for depressive symptoms and disorders. In this study, 998 community adults returned a mail-out battery of self-report measures at Time 1 and then completed a diagnostic clinical interview 8 months later at Time 2. Individuals were considered to have a depressive disorder if they met Research Diagnostic Criteria for major, minor, or intermittent depressive disorder based on the SADS clinical interview at Time 2. Demographic, symptom, life event, social support, cognition, and attributional variables were correlated with Time 1 CES-D scores and a dummy variable indicating whether or not a subject had diagnosable depression at Time 1. Age, sex, and past history of depression had a stronger association with a diagnosis of depression at Time 2, whereas the cognition and attribution variables had a stronger relationship with CES-D scores. The authors concluded that although diagnosable depression and depressive symptoms as measured by elevated CES-D scores have a common core of nonspecific negative affect, each "also carries with it unique characteristics" (p. 261).

There are, however, a number of problems with this study. First, the authors' conclusions are based on subjective judgments of differences in the magnitude of the correlations rather than on statistical tests to determine whether the differences in the correlates of CES-D scores and diagnosis are indeed significant. This subjectivity allows greater opportunity for bias to enter into the interpretation of the results. For example, four out of the five attribution correlations were below .30 indicating that these variables had little association with either depression scores or diagnosis. Age correlated −.14 with depression diagnosis and −.09 with CES-D scores. We question whether this difference is as meaningful as the authors seem to think. Second, the authors provided no adjustment for Type I error rate. With less than half of the correlations with CES-D and depression diagnosis different, it is difficult to know the extent to which the differences that did emerge were simply due to chance. At the very least, the authors have overinterpreted the differences and underestimated the considerable degree of similarity in the social correlates of dysphoria and diagnosable depression.

Flett, Vredenburg, et al. (1997) also raised statistical problems with studies that compare correlations with continuous (e.g., CES-D) versus dichotomous (e.g., presence versus absence of diagnosable depression) criterion variables. Differences between the correlates of continuous and dichotomous variables could be due to lower statistical power because of the restricted range of the dichotomous variable, measurement error (i.e., structured diagnostic interviews can have interrater variability), or the need to use different statistical procedures with dichotomous variables. They conclude, "These statistical differences make it exceedingly difficult to draw conclusions about the continuity issue in terms of the correlates of distress versus depression" (Flett, Vredenburg, et al., 1997, p. 407).

Finally, a number of additional arguments have been made by advocates of discontinuity: (a) differential rates of duration exist, with dysphoria and depressive symptoms being more transient and less persistent than diagnosable depression; (b) diagnosable depression is associated with greater functional impairment in daily living than nonclinical and minor depression; and (c) depressive symptoms as measured by self-report measures predict other psychiatric disorders in addition to depression suggesting that nonclinical depressive states may be more accurately characterized as a general vulnerability factor (Coyne, 1994b; Tennen, Hall, & Affleck, 1995; Zonderman et al., 1993).

Evidence for Continuity

Support for the continuity or dimensional perspective on psychological disorders such as depression comes from two general avenues. First, criticisms have been raised with categorically based classification schemes, such as *DSM,* which attempt to define the distinct attributes of disorders so that diagnostic boundaries can be established between cases and noncases, or between various types of disorders. These criticisms have led to proposals for a more dimensional approach to psychiatric classification. And second, empirical studies have investigated the relationship between levels of depression severity (mild, moderate, or severe) or have compared clinical and nonclinical depressive states. These studies, then, provide the empirical basis for the dimensional viewpoint.

In a review and critique of current psychiatric classification, L.A. Clark, Watson, and Reynolds (1995) discuss three issues that challenge a categorical view on psychopathology. First, they state that the high rate of comorbidity across Axis I disorders complicates the establishment of distinct categories of disorder. They note that in depression, 75% of cases involve some degree of comorbidity making the occurrence of pure cases of depression quite rare. Second, the considerable degree of within-category heterogeneity again threatens categorical diagnoses. In major depression, patients must have either sad mood or loss of interest plus any four of the remaining symptoms. This means that individuals with different clinical presentation can nonetheless meet diagnostic criteria for major depression. L.A. Clark et al. (1995) note that the attempt to deal with this heterogeneity by creating subtypes ends up more closely resembling a dimensional rather than a categorical classification scheme. This is nowhere more apparent than with depression, where we see the introduction in *DSM-IV* of subtypes such as dysthymia, adjustment disorder with depressed mood, minor depressive disorder, recurrent brief depressive disorder, mixed anxiety-depressive disorder, and depressive personality disorder. And third, the authors point out that the large number of atypical and subdefinitional threshold cases calls into question the validity of a categorical classification (see also H. Eysenck, Wakefield, & Friedman, 1983). This was evident in the study by Zinbarg et al. (1994), which had no difficulty in identifying a large number of primary care and outpatients who were diagnosed with depression NOS (i.e., presence of a few depressive symptoms that falls short of diagnostic criteria).

The dimensional perspective on depression also has support from a number of empirical studies. Flett, Vredenburg, et al. (1997) concluded from their review of this literature that there is considerable empirical support for phenomenological (i.e., similar symptom presentation) and etiologic (i.e., minor depression confers greater risk for subsequent major depression) continuity in depression. The difficulty in consistently finding distinct subtypes of depression is also consistent with the continuity viewpoint. However, Flett and colleagues acknowledge that recent psychometric studies of self-report depression measures indicate that the items may not assess the full range of depressive symptom expression nor do they all necessarily follow a continuous distribution with increasing levels of severity. This body of data may be the strongest empirical support for discontinuity in depression (see Santor, Ramsay, & Zuroff, 1994; Santor, Zuroff, Ramsay, Cervantes, & Palacios, 1995). In this section, we present a brief summary of the empirical evidence for continuity. The reader is referred to Flett, Vredenburg, et al. for a more detailed discussion.

As noted, studies have found that individuals with minor depression or a few depressive symptoms are at higher risk for developing a subsequent major depressive episode (Crum et al., 1994; Gotlib et al., 1995; K. Wells et al., 1992) although they seem to be at higher risk for developing other psychiatric disorders as well (Gotlib et al., 1995; Zonderman et al., 1993). Horwath et al. (1992), for example, found that more than 50% of first-onset cases of major depression have had a prior history of depressive symptoms. G.W. Brown, Bifulco, Harris, and Bridge (1986) in a one-year follow-up study of a community sample of inner London working-class women with at least one child living at home, found that presence of subclinical anxious and/or depressive symptoms did predict a subsequent depressive disorder. However, the authors also found that low self-esteem, ongoing life difficulties, and severe life events were significant predictors of depression onset and so raised the possibility that depressive symptoms predict depressive disorder mainly through their association with ongoing difficulties and severe matching life events. Flett, Vredenburg, et al. (1997) referred to this as etiologic continuity and concluded that it has substantial support in the empirical literature.

Second, presence of a few depressive symptoms is associated with considerable functional impairment that appears to differ from major depression only in degree rather than kind (Broadhead et al., 1990; Spitzer et al., 1994; K. Wells et al., 1989). In a longitudinal community study of adolescents, Gotlib et al. (1995) found that subjects with elevated self-report depression scores but no diagnosable depression (false positives) did not differ significantly from individuals with diagnosable depression on most variables of psychosocial functioning (i.e., on 14/20 variables). The two groups did differ on internalizing and externalizing psychopathology, suicidal ideation, physical health and illness, self-esteem, and social support of friends.

Third, in another study, individuals with subthreshold depression were found to have a 41% rate of family history for depression, which is only slightly lower than the 59% rate found for individuals with major depression (Sherbourne et al., 1994). The authors concluded that subthreshold depression appears to be a variant of affective disorder.

Fourth, it is not at all clear that minor depressive states or depressive symptoms are more transient than major depressive disorders. Katz and Yelin (1993) assessed depressive symptoms in 822 rheumatoid arthritis patients over a 4-year period using the Geriatric Depression Scale. Presence of depressive symptoms in one year greatly increased the probability of depressive symptoms in future years, with a person with depressed symptoms in 1986 six times more likely to report depressive symptoms in 1990 than nondepressed individuals. As noted, the persistence of depressive symptoms can be seen in the Zonderman et al. (1993) study where the presence of depressive symptoms constituted a significant risk factor for depressive and other psychiatric disorders over a 12-year follow-up period. Also, Gotlib et al. (1995) found that adolescents with a diagnosable depression and those with an elevation in self-reported depressive symptoms but no diagnosable disorder failed to differ in the duration of their depressive symptoms. Coyne, Gallo, Klinkman, and Calarco (1998) found that their sample of distressed primary care patients had elevated scores on the Hamilton Rating Scale of Depression that remained relatively unchanged over a 4.5-month period. These findings support Flett, Vredenburg, et al.'s (1997) contention that mild subclinical depressive states are not always brief and transient, and that those associated with a persistent mood disturbance of at least 2 weeks' duration are more similar to major depression than subclinical depression without persistent sadness or dysphoria.

A fifth consideration is the degree of similarity in symptom presentation between clinical and nonclinical depressive states. By definition, individuals with diagnosable depression will have a greater number of depressive symptoms at higher levels of severity or intensity than individuals with subthreshold depression. However, it has not been consistently shown that major depression has unique symptom characteristics that distinguish it from subthreshold depression. Many studies have found more similarities than differences in the symptoms reported by those with clinical and nonclinical depressive states (e.g., Fechner-Bates et al., 1994; M. Weissman, Prusoff, & Pincus, 1975). In the factor analytic studies of the BDI and Beck Anxiety Inventory (BAI) referred to earlier, we found that the structure of self-reported anxiety and depressive symptoms was very similar in a large sample of primarily anxious and/or depressive disorder outpatients and a sample of nondepressed college students (D.A. Clark, Steer, et al., 1994; Steer et al., 1995). Cox, Borger, Enns, and Parker (1997) compared the covariance matrices of 101 adult outpatients with *DSM-IV* major depression and 175 dysphoric undergraduate students (BDI score greater than 9) on the BDI and the *DSM-IV* Based Depression Scale (DDS). The pattern of correlations for both the DDS and BDI were virtually identical in both samples. The clinical sample did report significantly higher endorsement of suicidal ideation items, although 57% of the dysphoric students reported at least moderate levels of distress and lifestyle interference. The authors concluded that the symptom and impairment differences between their samples was more quantitative than qualitative in nature.

Finally, severity of depression has been found to be an important factor in determining the nature and course of depression (Goethe, Fischer, & Wright, 1993; Gold, 1990). Severity and number of depressive symptoms are significantly related to the onset of future depressive episodes (e.g., Lewinsohn et al., 1988; Zonderman et al., 1993) and to relapse rates (Coryell et al., 1991). In a study of depressed psychiatric inpatients, depressed and nondepressed medical patients, and nondepressed healthy controls, self-report and clinician rating scales of anxious and depressive symptoms showed a linear progression in symptomatology that depended on the level of severity (D.A. Clark, Cook, & Snow, 1998). Thus depressed psychiatric inpatients scored highest on all the symptom scales, followed by the depressed medical patients, then the nondepressed medical patients, and finally the nondepressed normal controls. This was found for the negative affect, depressotypic cognition, anhedonia, neurovegetative, and low positive affect symptom measures. These results support the continuity model in postulating symptom intensity or severity as an important variable in depression. In fact, it is incumbent on the advocates of discontinuity to ensure that symptom differences between clinical and nonclinical states is not due simply to a continuous variation in symptom severity.

IMPLICATIONS OF THE CONTINUITY/DISCONTINUITY DEBATE

We have provided an extended discussion of the continuity versus discontinuity debate in depression. Not only is this issue fundamental to our understanding of psychopathology in general and depression in particular, but it determines how we diagnosis, assess, and conduct research on depression. Those who assume the discontinuity of disorders will feel more comfortable with categorical classification systems such as *DSM-IV*. They will consider structured clinical interview schedules that require one to count the number of criterion symptoms present based on dichotomous ratings of the presence or absence of symptoms as the only true and valid method for assessing clinical disorders. And they will abhor research involving the administration of continuous symptom measures to nonclinical samples, claiming that it has no relevance to true clinical depression.

But as we have seen, the case for the discontinuity of depression is not convincing. There is now a considerable amount of empirical support for the continuity or dimensional view of depression. No doubt, the moderate standpoint adopted by Flett, Vredenburg, et al. (1997) is more in tune with reality. They advocate a complex view in which depression may show continuity in some spheres but discontinuity in other domains. As discussed in Chapter 4, the cognitive model takes a strong dimensional perspective on depression (see also A. Beck, 1991). The model assumes that psychopathological states represent extreme or excessive forms of normal cognitive, emotional, and behavioral functioning. As is evident in our presentation of the empirical research on the cognitive model, we include studies on depressed mood in normals, subclinical or analogue depression samples, and clinically depressed patient groups because we concur with Flett, Vredenburg, et al. (1997) that there is substantial evidence in favor of the continuity of depression at least at the phenomenological and etiologic levels:

ISSUE 3: *Depressive states vary on a continuum of severity with milder, nonclinical affective symptoms at one end and the more severe clinical affective disorders at the other end.*

COMORBIDITY AND DEPRESSION

The importance of depression as a serious and pervasive psychological condition is also evident in its high rate of co-occurrence with other types of psychiatric and medical conditions. Referred to as comorbidity, researchers are just beginning to understand the frequency and diagnostic significance of comorbid conditions. Depressive disorders can be found in alcohol and drug abuse, anxiety disorders, eating disorders, somatization disorder, personality disorders, and chronic medical disorders to name but a few conditions (Canadian Mental Health Association, 1995; Depression Guideline Panel, 1993).

Maser and Cloninger (1990) argued that the term *comorbidity* should be reserved for the co-occurrence of syndromes or disorders, and should not be applied to the co-occurrence of symptoms. Within the co-occurrence of disorders, however, there are different types of comorbidity. There is pathogenic comorbidity in which two disorders have a common underlying etiology, or prognostic comorbidity in which one disorder can develop into a second disorder (Kendall & Clarkin, 1992; Maser & Cloninger, 1990). Our discussion in this section focuses on diagnostic comorbidity or the cross-sectional co-occurrence of two disorders in the same individuals.

Comorbid rates among disorders are very influenced by the characteristics of the diagnostic classification system. Although anxiety and depression have a high comorbidity rate, this was unrecognized in *DSM-III* because of the use of diagnostic hierarchical exclusionary criteria. In *DSM-III*, depression occupied a higher position than anxiety disorders. Consequently, patients who met diagnostic criteria for depression and anxiety were only diagnosed as depressed. With *DSM-III-R* and then *DSM-IV*, the rates of comorbid conditions have steadily increased because of (a) decreased emphasis on hierarchical exclusionary criteria, (b) an increase in possible diagnoses, (c) overlapping nonspecific symptom criteria across different disorders, (d) a tendency to lower the threshold for some diagnoses, and (e) defining different diagnostic categories from a single continuum of pathology (Frances, Widiger, & Fyer, 1990; Maser & Cloninger, 1990).

COMORBIDITY OF ANXIETY AND DEPRESSIVE DISORDERS

As noted, the existence of "pure" depressive states may be quite rare, with up to 75% of depressed patients showing comorbidity with other psychiatric conditions (Canadian Mental Health Association, 1995; L.A. Clark et al., 1995). However, it is the comorbidity between anxiety and depressive disorders that has received most of the empirical attention because roughly 50% of clinically depressed or anxious individuals may have a coexisting anxious or depressive disorder (L.A. Clark, 1989). Numerous studies have demonstrated a high comorbidity rate for anxiety and depression depending on sample characteristics (i.e., community, outpatient, or inpatient samples) and whether comorbidity estimates are based on current or lifetime diagnoses (for reviews, see Alloy, Kelly, Mineka, & Clements, 1990; Brady & Kendall, 1992; T.A. Brown & Barlow, 1992; L.A. Clark, 1989). In the Philadelphia Center for Cognitive Therapy outpatient sample, 37% to 42% of patients with a principal diagnosis of major depression and 29% to 47% with dysthymia met diagnostic criteria for a secondary anxiety disorder, the most common being generalized anxiety or social phobia (D.A. Clark, Beck, et al., 1994; Sanderson, Beck, & Beck, 1990). A comorbid depressive disorder was evident in 58 (37%) patients with panic disorder and 40 (51%) individuals with generalized anxiety disorder (D.A. Clark, Beck, et al., 1994). However, T.A. Brown and Barlow (1992) reported much lower comorbidity rates for depression among their outpatients with a principal diagnosis of panic disorder (16%), generalized anxiety (29%), or social phobia (20%), although 45% of a small sample of patients with major depression ($n = 11$) were comorbid for generalized anxiety (Di Nardo & Barlow, 1990).

Much lower comorbidity rates for anxiety and depression are found when a different diagnostic classification of depression is used such as the Research Diagnostic Criteria (Rohde, Lewinsohn, & Seeley, 1991). Based on the NIMH Epidemiologic Catchment Area (ECA) study, Regier, Burke, and Burke (1990) reported lifetime prevalence rates for comorbid anxiety of 43% for those with affective disorders, and a rate for comorbid depression of 25% for individuals diagnosed with a principal anxiety disorder. Results from the more recent National Comorbidity Survey revealed that 79% of individuals with lifetime disorders were comorbid for two or more disorders (Kessler et al., 1994). Comparable high rates of comorbid anxiety and depression have also been found among children and adolescent clinical samples (Brady & Kendall, 1992). In fact, anxiety and depression comorbidity may be the highest among severely disturbed groups such as psychiatric inpatients.

A number of studies have reported high correlations between measures of anxiety and depression, prompting some researchers to conclude that these symptom measures do not assess distinct anxiety and depression constructs but rather a single common general distress or negative affect dimension (e.g., L.A. Clark & Watson, 1991a; Dobson, 1985; Feldman, 1993; Gotlib, 1984; Ollendick & Yule, 1990). Other studies, though, have shown that self-report measures like the BDI and BAI can distinguish between anxiety and depression (D.A. Clark, Beck, & Stewart, 1990; D.A. Clark, Steer, et al., 1994; Cox, Swinson, Kuch, & Reichman, 1993; Lovibond & Lovibond, 1995; Steer et al., 1995). One reason posited for the high comorbidity of anxiety and depression as well as the high correlation between anxiety and depression symptom measures is the overlap in many of the symptoms (and consequently item overlap) that define these two syndromes (Brady & Kendall, 1992; L.A. Clark, 1989; Gotlib & Cane, 1989). Thus research into the common and distinct symptoms of anxiety and depression has gained added significance for the diagnosis and assessment of these disorders.

Common and Specific Symptoms of Depression

Symptoms such as irritability, restlessness, difficulty concentrating, fatigability, insomnia, crying, general distress, decreased activity, poor social skills, helplessness, worry, and low self-efficacy have been considered common to both anxiety and depression by at least some researchers (Alloy et al., 1990; L.A. Clark, 1989). More recently, L.A. Clark and Watson (1991a) proposed a tripartite model of anxiety and depression. They described a state/trait concept of high negative affect (NA) characterized by

(a) feelings of distress, fear, hostility, nervousness, or worry, (b) negativistic appraisals of self and others, (c) somatic complaints, (d) negative cognitions, and (e) diverse personality traits such as low self-esteem, pessimism, and trait anxiety. In their proposal, high NA was considered a common symptom feature of both anxiety and depression (see also L.A. Clark, Watson, & Mineka, 1994).

According to the tripartite model, depression is distinguished by symptoms of anhedonia and low positive affect (PA), the latter being defined as a loss of pleasurable engagement with the environment, disinterest, low motivation, and social withdrawal (Tellegen, 1985; Watson & Kendall, 1989). Anxiety, on the other hand, is distinguished by symptoms of heightened physiological arousal such as heart palpitations, shortness of breath, dizziness, trembling, and the like (L.A. Clark et al., 1994). L.A. Clark and Watson (1991b) contend that symptom measures of anxiety and depression could improve on their low discriminant validity by including more items that assess either physiological hyperarousal or PA, respectively.

Mineka, Watson, and Clark (1998) offered a revision to the tripartite model that recognizes that each psychological syndrome contains both common and specific symptom components. The common component in anxiety and depression is NA, a pervasive higher-order factor that accounts for the overlap among disorders. Anhedonia or low PA is a unique feature of depression; however, contrary to the original model, anxious arousal is no longer considered characteristic of all anxiety disorders but rather is a unique symptom feature of panic disorders. Every other anxiety disorder, with the exception of generalized anxiety disorder (GAD), will have unique symptom features that can be distinguished from anxious arousal. Two implications of this more integrative model is the recognition that the size of the common and specific symptom components of different anxiety disorders could vary considerably, and, that in the end, symptom specificity must be considered in relative rather than absolute terms. That is, given the problems inherent with *DSM* diagnostic classification, it is unlikely that any symptom will be unique to any particular disorder.

Numerous studies have found support for the tripartite model with NA being the common factor to both anxiety and depression, low PA specific to depression, and physiological hyperarousal specific to anxiety (e.g., Jolly, Dyck, Kramer, & Wherry, 1994; Watson, Clark, & Carey, 1988; Watson et al., 1995). However, some inconsistent findings have also been reported. In some studies, a hierarchical model has been supported with NA a common higher-order factor and anhedonia (depression) and physiological hyperarousal (anxiety) as lower-order factors (D.A. Clark, Steer, et al., 1994; Steer et al., 1995), whereas other studies have supported a nonhierarchical model with NA, low PA (depression), and physiological hyperarousal (anxiety) distinct or orthogonal first-order dimensions (Joiner, 1996; Joiner, Catanzaro, & Laurent, 1996; Jolly & Dykman, 1994). Burns and Eidelson (1998) found that the tripartite model did not fit any of the covariance matrices derived from self-report symptom measures based on large samples of mood and anxiety disorder outpatients. Furthermore, physiological hyperarousal has not always been found to be specific to anxiety (D.A. Clark et al., 1998; Lonigan, Carey, & Finch, 1994), and low PA and anhedonia symptom items have emerged with significant loadings on a general NA dimension (D.A. Clark et al., 1998; Watson et al., 1995). This led to questions about the specificity of PA, whereas the inconsistent findings with physiological hyperarousal support the revision offered by Mineka et al. (1998).

The comorbidity of anxiety and depression is an important clinical issue because findings indicate that the co-occurrence of anxiety and depression may be associated with more severe psychological distress, increased chronicity, poorer response to treatment, and poorer psychosocial outcome (Bronisch & Hecht, 1990; D.A. Clark et al., 1990; Hecht, von Zerssen, & Wittchen, 1990; Kessler et al., 1994). However, the issue of comorbidity is also important to the cognitive model. Cognitive theory postulates that anxiety and depression can be distinguished by their cognitive content, with thoughts of personal loss and failure specific to depression, and cognitive content involving physical or psychological threat and danger specific to anxiety. As discussed in later chapters, empirical support for cognitive content-specificity has been found in a number of studies (for reviews, see D.A. Clark & Beck, 1989; Haaga et al., 1991; see also A. Beck, Brown, Steer, Eidelson, & Riskind, 1987; D.A. Clark, Beck, et al., 1994):

ISSUE 4: *Depressive symptoms and disorders show considerable covariation with other psychological conditions, especially anxiety and its disorders.*

THE COURSE OF CLINICAL DEPRESSION

DURATION OF DEPRESSIVE EPISODES

Depressive disorders are best characterized as chronic disabling conditions that take a self-limiting episodic course. Most individuals recover from an acute episode of unipolar major depression, either with or without treatment (Coryell et al., 1995). The typical major depressive episode lasts from 3 to 11 months (Gotlib & Hammen, 1992), although 60% of cases recover within 6 months of the onset of depression (Coryell & Winokur, 1992). Kendler, Walters, and Kessler (1997) reported that the median *DSM-III-R* major depressive episode was 42 days for the 235 twins who met diagnostic criteria in their population-based twin registry study. Within 90 days, 75% of the sample had recovered, whereas only 2.2% had not recovered by the end of one year. In their 6-year follow-up of 313 treated and 234 untreated individuals with major depressive disorder, Coryell et al. (1995) found that median episode duration for the untreated individuals was 12 weeks compared with 42 weeks for the treated subjects. Although most individuals with major depression or other psychiatric disorders do not seek professional treatment (Diverty & Beaudet, 1997; Kessler et al., 1994), the results of the Coryell et al. study indicate that individuals with a more persistent and disabling depression may be overrepresented in clinical samples.

RELAPSE AND RECURRENCE RATES

Most individuals with an initial episode of major depression will experience a recurrence of the disorder even though they may have recovered from the initial episode. In fact, there is growing recognition that major depression takes a recurring course in most individuals who seek treatment for their disorder.

In the *DSM-IV* mood disorders field trial, 68% of subjects had a recurrent depressive condition (Keller et al., 1995). In the 6-year follow-up study conducted as part of the National Institute of Mental Health Program on the Psychobiology of Depression–Clinical Studies, 234 individuals who had an untreated major depressive disorder were found to have a mean number of 2.2 depressive episodes (Coryell et al., 1995). However compared with the study's probands who sought treatment for their depression, the untreated depressed group had milder and shorter-lived depressions that selectively caused impairment in marital and interpersonal relationships but resulted in little impairment in occupational or educational attainment. Keller et al. (1982) found that 25% of patients treated for major depression relapsed in the first 12 weeks after recovery. Moreover, a smaller group of patients (25%) will experience six or more episodes throughout their lifetime (Angst, 1986). In their retrospective study, Keller et al. (1995) found that 66% of treated patients with recurrent major depression experienced intermittent depressive symptoms between episodes, whereas the remainder reported full interepisode recovery. In a review article, Keller (1994) concluded that the predicted median length of time for being well after an episode of major depression is 20 months and the probability of maintaining a state of recovery for 5 years is only 22%. Thus multiple and recurring episodes of major depression are common, with the highest rate of relapse occurring in the first six months after recovery.

Several variables significantly predict relapse in major depression: (a) increased number of previous depressive episodes, (b) age of onset under 40 years, (c) severity of depression at worst episode, (d) presence of dysthymia, (e) presence of minor depression, and (f) an episode of depression during adolescence (Compas et al., 1993; Coryell et al., 1991; Keller et al., 1982). Belsher and Costello (1988) concluded from their review of the literature that (a) within 2 years of recovery, 50% of unipolar depressed patients will relapse, (b) the longer you stay well, the less likely you are to relapse in the future, (c) recent stressors and absence of social support both increase risk of relapse, (d) history of depressive episodes increases relapse, (e) persistent neuroendocrine dysregulation after recovery increases probability of relapse, and (f) maintenance treatment with antidepressant medication can reduce risk of relapse. Early onset, persistent low-grade depression, stressful environment, and a history of recurrence increase one's risk for further episodes of depression.

Chronic Depression

Between 15% and 25% of individuals with major depression fail to recover within the usual time period, although most of these individuals (75%) were found to eventually recover during a 5-year follow-up (see Gotlib & Hammen, 1992). Factors that appear to be related to chronicity include (a) older age at onset, (b) presence of psychotic features, (c) a major depression superimposed on dysthymia, (d) early onset dysthymia, (e) possibly a variety of adverse stressful circumstances and reduced social resources, (f) greater severity and longer duration of episode, (g) higher neuroticism and poorer ego resilience, and (h) possibly the inadequate provision of treatment (Coryell & Winokur, 1992; Gotlib & Hammen, 1992; K. Wells et al., 1992). Although not all these factors have been investigated or been found significant across studies, each has some empirical support as a possible predictor of chronicity in depression.

Summary

Major depression is a self-limiting condition that often takes a persistent and recurring course. A number of clinical, psychological and social factors have been proposed as having an impact on the course of major depression. Because research on maintenance factors in depression requires large samples and moderately long follow-up periods, most of the findings are based on the large-scale NIMH research projects.

As discussed in subsequent chapters, cognitive theory proposes that some individuals may possess a cognitive vulnerability that increases their risk for unipolar depressive episodes. Unless this underlying vulnerability is dealt with effectively in the course of treatment, the theory proposes that a recurring depressive episode is even more likely because an initial depression may prime the prepotent depressogenic cognitive structures. In later chapters, we discuss possible cognitive processes that may influence the course of depression as well as the empirical support for cognitive predictors of relapse and recurrence in major depression:

ISSUE 5: *Depressive disorders are self-limiting conditions that often take a persistent and recurring course.*

OUTCOME IN MAJOR DEPRESSION

A final feature of depression that must be considered by any model or theory concerns the negative consequences or outcomes associated with having an episode of major depression. In this section, we consider two important outcomes that have been associated with depression—suicide and psychosocial functioning.

SUICIDE

Depression is a life-threatening condition because of its association with an increased risk for suicide. Suicide is the ninth leading cause of death in the United States, occurring in approximately 11 deaths per 100,000 (Resnik, 1980). Presence of a psychiatric illness is a significant risk factor for suicide, with 90% of individuals who commit suicide found to have a psychiatric condition at the time of death. Depression, alcoholism, and schizophrenia are the leading psychiatric disorders associated with risk for suicide (Barraclough, Bunch, Nelson, & Sainsbury, 1974).

The link between depression and suicide is especially strong with 40% to 70% of suicide victims estimated to have an affective disorder (Brent, Kupfer, Bromet, & Dew, 1988). However, follow-up studies indicate that the lifetime probability of suicide in depressed patients appears to be approximately 15%. Based on the NIMH ECA study, J. Johnson et al. (1992) found that a significant number of suicide attempts were associated with presence of a depressive disorder (23%) or even subclinical depression (25.8%). Thus although presence of an affective disorder or even depressive symptoms is associated with a significant risk for suicide or suicide attempts, obviously it is a minority of individuals with depression who eventually commit suicide.

The low base rate for suicide has made it difficult to study risk factors because even if predictors are found that yield low false-positive and false-negative rates, the extremely low base rate results in more false-positives than true-positives (Goldstein, Black, Nasrallah, & Winokur, 1991). With this caution in mind, a number of variables have emerged in studies of risk factors for suicide among depressed patients. Possible risk factors in some of the studies include (a) male gender, (b) suicidal ideation at admission, (c) number of previous suicide attempts, (d) unipolar depressive disorder, (e) social isolation, (f) longer duration of depressive episode, and (g) hopelessness (Goldstein et al., 1991; Hawton, 1992).

Of particular interest to the cognitive model of depression is the link found between hopelessness, suicidal intent, and committed suicide. Hopelessness has been defined as a set of cognitive schemas involving negative expectations about the future, and has been measured by a 20-item true/false self-report inventory called the Hopelessness Scale (A. Beck, Weissman, Lester, & Trexler, 1974; Minkoff, Bergman, Beck, & Beck, 1973). Various studies have found a stronger link between intended and/or committed suicide and hopelessness than between suicide and depression (A. Beck, Brown, Berchick, Stewart, & Steer, 1990; A. Beck, Kovacs, & Weissman, 1975; Dyer & Kreitman, 1984). In these studies, depressed inpatients and outpatients with elevated hopelessness were at much higher risk for suicide than depressed patients with low hopelessness. These results indicate that understanding how individuals think about themselves and their future is an important aspect of suicidal ideation and behavior.

PSYCHOSOCIAL FUNCTIONING

As noted, depressive disorders and even presence of a few depressive symptoms have been associated with both immediate and long-term reductions in psychosocial functioning and well-being. No doubt the most comprehensive study on functioning and well-being associated with depression comes from the large scale Medical Outcomes Study (MOS). In this observational study, 1,790 primary care patients with depression, myocardial infarction, congestive heart failure, hypertension, and diabetes were followed for 2 years. Functional status and well-being were assessed with a 36-item short-form MOS Health Form which assessed bodily pain, limitations in role functioning due to physical and emotional health, limitations in physical functioning due to health, general health perceptions, restrictions in usual social activities due to health, and level of energy or fatigue (Tarlov et al., 1989; K. Wells et al., 1992). At baseline, patients with a depressive disorder had worse physical, social, and role functioning than individuals with depressive symptoms alone or patients with a general medical condition. Moreover, when patients with any depressive symptoms (those with or without a depressive disorder) were compared with the general medical patients, the depressed individuals still had significantly worse physical, social, and role functioning, spent more recent days in bed, had worse current health and reported more bodily pain than most of the nondepressed general medical patients (K. Wells et al., 1989). At 2-year follow-up, the functioning and well-being of the depressed patients had improved, although patients with major depression and dysthymia were still worse off than those with a general medical condition (Hays et al., 1995). Even those with subthreshold depressive symptoms had similar or worse levels of functioning and well-being at the 2-year follow-up than the medical patients.

Other studies have also reported significant reductions in outcome with depression. In a 1-year follow-up of 2,980 participants in the ECA Study, Broadhead and colleagues (1990) found that major depression and dysthymia were associated with the greatest risk of acquiring disability days and days lost at work, although minor depression was also associated with greater disability compared with asymptomatic individuals. Mintz et al. (1992) noted in their review that work impairment is a common feature of acute depressive episodes but concluded that treatment can lead to improvements in work functioning primarily by providing symptom relief. In the National Comorbidity Survey, individuals with an early-onset psychiatric disorder had significantly lower educational attainment leading the authors to estimate that 7.2 million Americans prematurely terminate their education due to early-onset psychiatric illness (Kessler et al., 1995). A number of other studies have documented that the greatest reductions in psychosocial functioning are found with major depression or dysthymia, and that more moderate but significant decrements are also apparent in subthreshold depressive states (e.g., Gotlib et al., 1995; J. Johnson et al., 1992; Lyness, Caine, Conwell, King, & Cox, 1993; Spitzer et al., 1994). Keitner and Miller (1990) in their review noted that there is considerable empirical evidence that the acute phase of major depression is associated with increased family difficulties in the form of problematic communication, impaired parenting, and poor problem-solving ability. Thus it should come as no surprise that the level of functional impairment associated with depression has resulted in a significant increase in health care utilization (J. Johnson et al., 1992; Spitzer et al., 1994) and significant economic burden (P. Greenberg et al., 1993; Simon, Ormel, VonKorff, & Barlow, 1995).

The negative impact of depression on psychosocial outcome is apparent even after symptomatic recovery from an acute episode. In a 5-year follow-up of 148 patients with bipolar illness and 240 with unipolar depression, depressed patients compared with nondepressed first-degree relatives were (a) found to have lower annual incomes, (b) less likely to have been employed over the previous year, (c) less likely to have improved their occupational status or increased their income, (d) less likely to have improved their educational attainment, (e) more likely to have experienced a separation or divorce, (f) more likely to rate their current marital relationship as poor, and (g) more likely to report deficits in other areas of functioning such as interpersonal relationships, involvement in recreational activities, and overall life satisfaction (Coryell et al., 1993). Interestingly, when the researchers separated out the 110 unipolar probands who had recovered and showed no episodes of major, minor, or chronic intermittent depression throughout the final two years of the follow-up period, their psychosocial impairment was almost as great as for the total unipolar sample. In a more recent 6-year follow-up study based on data from the NIMH Psychobiology of Depression Clinical Studies, Coryell et al. (1995) found sustained impairment in marital and interpersonal relationships, and in enjoyment of recreational activities but not work functioning in individuals with an untreated depression.

Coyne et al. (1998) recently investigated the perceived effects of depression in 60 depressed primary care patients, 82 nondistressed, nondepressed primary care patients, 40 distressed, nondepressed primary care individuals, and 48 depressed psychiatric outpatients. Based on a self-report questionnaire specifically constructed to assess perceived effects of depression, it was found that depressed patients identified as having recovered from their depressive episode scored significantly higher than the nondistressed groups on scales assessing lack of energy, perceived burden on others, need to work at not feeling depressed, need to work at maintaining relationships, imposition of limitations and sense of social stigma due to depression. Thus depression appears to have long-term repercussions on one's subjective sense of self and coping. These results indicate that depressive disorders and even depressive symptoms are associated with long-term impairment in social, occupational, and psychological functioning.

SUMMARY

This brief review of the outcome literature indicates that depressive disorders and even subclinical depressive symptoms are associated with significant short- and long-term impairment in psychosocial functioning and well-being. Depression can also be life-threatening in the form of increased risk for suicide. Moreover, the negative impact of a depressive disorder or symptoms may be compounded by the presence of another psychiatric disorder or a medical condition. Depressive disorders and symptoms are significantly more prevalent in patients with chronic medical conditions (e.g., K. Wells, Golding, & Burnam, 1988), and the presence of both a depressive condition and a medical illness can have a significant additive effect on reduced physical and social functioning (K. Wells et al., 1989). This leads us, then, to the sixth and final statement about depression that theories must take into account:

ISSUE 6: *Depressive symptoms and disorders can be life-threatening conditions that are associated with significant short- and long-term decrements in physical, psychological, social, and economic functioning.*

CONCLUSION

Depression is a complex, ubiquitous state that occurs with varying degrees of severity, can take a variable course, manifests itself in a variety of symptom forms and types, and is highly reactive to current life circumstances. Multiple social, psychological, and biological factors converge in an interactive fashion in the pathogenesis of depression. Because of space limitations and the focus of this book, we have not dealt with many psychosocial and biological factors that are important correlates and features of the depressive experience. These factors need to be acknowledged, and any theory of depression must account for the role they play in the depressive experience.

A prominent characteristic of depression that has been found in many studies is the gender difference in rates of depression with women approximately twice as likely to experience depression as men (Beaudet, 1996; Coryell, Endicott, & Keller, 1992; Kessler et al., 1994; Nolen-Hoeksema, 1987). Several explanations have been offered to account for these differential rates, and the conditions that are most likely associated with the higher risk for depression in women. A number of social factors are also associated with increased risk for depression such as severe adverse life events, lack of social support, and negative close interpersonal relationships (i.e., poor marital and family relations). Distal developmental antecedents to depression have also been reported such as childhood adversity (e.g., severe neglect, physical or sexual abuse, and to lesser extent, parental loss through death or divorce), previous depressive episodes in adolescence (Bifulco, Brown, Moran, Ball, & Campbell, 1998), history of parental depression (Hammen, Burge,

Burney, & Adrian, 1990; Warner, Weissman, Fendrich, Wickramaratne, & Moreau, 1992), and poor parenting styles involving rejection, lack of affection, excessive criticalness or overprotectiveness that can lead to difficult interpersonal relationships in childhood (Blatt & Zuroff, 1992). Personality factors such as neuroticism, harm avoidance, dependency (sociotropy), self-criticalness, autonomy, obsessionality, and perfectionism have been implicated as vulnerability factors to depression in a variety of studies (see review by Enns & Cox, 1997). And psychological variables such as low self-worth, negative attributional style, pessimism, and poor coping responses, to name but a few, have been implicated in depression. These latter processes are discussed more thoroughly in later chapters.

Age also appears to affect rates of depression, with the highest rates of major depression in young adults (aged 25 to 44 years) whereas rates for self-reported depressive symptoms show a curvilinear trend with the highest rates in the youngest (20s) and oldest (75+) age groups (Karel, 1997). Biological factors such as dysregulation in certain neurochemical pathways, particularly serotonin and possibly norepinephrine (McNeal & Cimbolic, 1986; Shelton, Hollon, Purdon, & Loosen, 1991), as well as reduced activity in particular regions of the brain, especially the prefrontal cortex (George et al., 1995), may be important in the pathogenesis of depression. Finally, considerable evidence now exists of a genetic vulnerability to unipolar depression that interacts with stressful life experiences to increase risk of onset in major depression (Kendler & Karkowski-Shuman, 1997; Kendler, Kessler, Neale, Heath, & Eaves, 1993; Kendler et al., 1995). The existence of these multiple, interactive etiological factors in depression requires the integration of biological, psychological, and social perspectives (Shelton et al., 1991). Almost 25 years ago, Akiskal and McKinney (1975) wrote their influential paper on the etiology of depression, arguing that psychological and biological events may be capable of setting in motion a final common biological pathway to depression. As shown in the chapters to come, the cognitive model of depression recognizes multiple determinants of depression and also postulates a "final common pathway" to depression, only this pathway is located within the meaning-making structures and processes of the information processing system.

In this introductory chapter, we have focused on aspects of depressive phenomena that are considered important in the diagnosis, assessment, and treatment of affective disorders and symptoms. A considerable amount of research has been devoted to each of these topics in the past few years so that any psychological theory of depression must take them into account if it is to offer a viable understanding of depressive phenomena.

The following six issues were discussed in this chapter:

1. Clinically significant depression is characterized by a sustained disturbance in mood involving behavioral inhibition, subjective negativity and, in more severe cases, disturbance in somatic functioning.
2. Depression consists of a heterogeneous group of disorders that vary in severity, chronicity, and clinical presentation.
3. Depressive states vary on a continuum of severity with milder, nonclinical affective symptoms at one end and the more severe clinical affective disorders at the other end.
4. Depressive symptoms and disorders show considerable covariation with other psychological conditions, especially anxiety and its disorders.
5. Depressive disorders are self-limiting conditions that often take a persistent and recurring course.
6. Depressive symptoms and disorders can be life-threatening conditions that are associated with significant short- and long-term decrements in physical, psychological, social, and economic functioning.

In subsequent chapters, our presentation of the cognitive model of depression focuses on how the model accounts for each of these important features of depression. The validity of any theoretical model is determined not only by its empirical support but also by its ability to address crucial aspects of the target construct. Thus the construct validity of the cognitive model of depression depends in part on its ability to incorporate into its theoretical account what is known about the salient features of depression. The six issues reviewed in this chapter represent fundamental aspects of depression and so must be addressed by the cognitive model. This is the focus of our discussion in Chapter 4, where we present the cognitive model of depression. Before describing the model, however, we want to lay the groundwork by tracing the historical roots of cognitive therapy in Chapter 2 and discuss the philosophical and theoretical assumptions of the model in Chapter 3.

CHAPTER 2

The Origins of Cognitive Theory and Therapy of Depression: A Historical Overview

THE PAST three decades have witnessed a significant growth in the status of cognitive theory (CT) and therapy of depression. Beginning as an alternative to the prevailing psychodynamic models of the 1960s, it has become a significant psychological theory and treatment of depression. Its impact on experimental clinical psychology is obvious when one considers the numerous studies that have investigated cognitive dysfunction in psychopathology derived in part from the cognitive model (for reviews, see D.A. Clark & Beck, 1989; Haaga et al., 1991). Furthermore the cognitive model and its treatment have been applied to a much wider range of disorders than anxiety and depression as exemplified by applications to eating disorders (Fairburn et al., 1991; G. Wilson & Fairburn, 1993), personality disorders (Beck, Freeman, et al., 1990), family and marital problems (N. Epstein, Schlesinger, & Dryden, 1988), and even schizophrenia (Perris, 1988).

To understand the growth of cognitive theory and therapy over the past 30 years, it is necessary to examine the historical context that gave rise to this perspective. In this chapter, we discuss the prevailing behavioral and psychodynamic theories and therapies of depression that characterized the 1960s and early 1970s. Major conceptual and methodological shortcomings led to an atmosphere of discontent and a call for change in how psychological disorders were understood and treated. It was within this period of transition from radical stimulus-response (S-R) behavioral theories to a cognitive, information processing perspective that Beck's cognitive therapy emerged as an alternative approach to theory and treatment.

Cognitive theory and therapy, however, were not merely the result of an emerging cognitive zeitgeist in the early 1970s (see December, 1974); the most influential factors in the development of the cognitive model and treatment came from Beck's own experimentation and clinical observations. In this chapter, we discuss Beck's early work as a psychoanalyst and the factors that led to his eventual dissatisfaction with this approach to depression. We examine the series of experimental studies that failed to consistently support his psychoanalytic concept of masochism but instead indicated the presence of negative cognitive patterns in depression. Weak experimental findings and observation of patient's verbalizations while undergoing classical psychoanalytic treatment led Beck to consider negative cognition rather than affect as the central psychological process that characterizes depression.

We conclude this chapter with a discussion of the pre-1970s version of cognitive theory of depression. Although cognitive theory and therapy have undergone considerable refinement and elaboration over the past two decades, nonetheless the basic concepts that underlie the cognitive theory of depression were developed during the 1960s. This basic model has proven to be very robust as evidenced by its application to a wide variety of psychological disorders in addition to depression.

A HISTORICAL CONTEXT FOR COGNITIVE THEORY

EARLY PSYCHOANALYTIC AND BEHAVIORAL THEORIES OF DEPRESSION

Psychoanalytic Theories

Psychoanalytic theory and therapy continued to dominate the psychological perspective on depression in the 1960s. Based on Freud's psychoanalytic formulation of depression published in *Mourning and Melancholia* (Freud, 1917), as well as Abraham's writings on the topic in 1911, the main tenet of 1960s psychoanalysis was that depression was characterized by anger turned inward as a result of an earlier object loss that had become part of the depressed person's ego (Bemporad, 1985). Together with the notion of a real or imagined "loss of a loved object," the concept of *retroflected anger* formed the cornerstone for the psychoanalytic understanding of depression. Psychoanalytic theorists viewed the symptoms of self-criticism and self-recrimination, which are so prominent in depression, as support for the concept of retroflected hostility.

In an attempt to understand this inward directed hostility, psychoanalytic theorists contrasted the intrapsychic processes involved in grief or mourning with those involved in melancholia or depression. Freud (1917) considered normal grief a reaction to loss of a real love object (i.e., death of a spouse), whereas depression was viewed as an identification with an imaginary or vaguely perceived object loss that is unconsciously identified with the ego or self (Mendelson, 1990). Because the object loss is now introjected as part of the ego and is accompanied by a regression to the oral phase of psychosexual development, anger becomes directed inwardly (oral introjection) rather than outwardly toward the real object (Bemporad, 1985; Mendelson, 1990). Later, Freud modified his position stating that the tendency to internalize loss objects is normal, and that depression is simply due to an excessively severe superego (Bemporad, 1985).

Among other early theorists who were influential in the development of a psychoanalytic model of depression, many emphasized the prominence of anal (obsessional) and oral (dependent) characteristics in the depressives' personality (Chodoff, 1972). In Rado's (1928) psychoanalytic theory, depressed individuals were considered very dependent on others and highly intolerant of "external narcissistic deprivations." Their self-esteem was based on the amount of love, acceptance, and approval they received from others (Mendelson, 1990). Because of their intolerance for deprivation, rather trivial amounts of disappointment could trigger a depression if highly dependent individuals could not win back the love they so needed from others (Mendelson, 1990).

Other theorists, such as Bibring, Jacobson, and Fenichel, also considered a loss of self-esteem, in which the ego finds itself in a hopeless and helpless state, the cardinal feature of depression (Bemporad, 1985). The lowered self-esteem occurs as a result of excessive narcissistic needs in which the depression-prone person fails to have these needs met in the external world. Thus these versions of the psychoanalytic model placed a greater emphasis on ego deficiencies rather than intrapsychic processes like retroflected depression. However, M. Klein (1934) turned to the quality of the mother-child relationship in the first year in an attempt to understand depression. If the child did not develop a loving and secure relationship with the mother, then he or she would not be able to overcome ambivalence toward love objects and so would become vulnerable for depression in adulthood (Gotlib & Hammen, 1992).

During the 1960s, then, psychoanalytic theories dominated clinical psychology and psychiatry. Depression was understood in terms of (a) inwardly directed anger, (b) introjection of love object loss, (c) severe superego demands, (d) excessive narcissistic, oral and/or anal personality needs, (e) loss of self-esteem, and (f) deprivation in the mother-child relationship during the first year. Many of these ideas continue to have a profound impact on contemporary theories of depression. We can see this influence in Beck's CT model of depression where the negative view of self, the importance of loss events in triggering depression, a hypersensitivity to loss of social resources, and the concept of the sociotropic personality (A. Beck, 1983) have been influenced by such psychoanalytic notions as loss of self-esteem, object loss, external narcissistic deprivation, and oral (dependent) personality, respectively.

Despite its continuing influence, there was considerable dissatisfaction with psychoanalytic theory and treatment. First, many of the central constructs of the model could not be operationally defined with sufficient precision to allow empirical investigation. Furthermore, when experimental research was attempted, predictions derived from the model were often not validated. In the area of depression, the concept of retroflected anger was not well supported by empirical studies (A. Beck, 1967). ⇐ Mendelson (1990) concluded his review of psychoanalytic theories of depression by stating: "A striking feature of the impressionistic pictures of depression painted by many writers is that they have the flavor of art rather than of science and may well represent profound personal intuitions as much as they depict the raw clinical data" (p. 31).

Second, there was a growing concern that the psychoanalytic emphasis on unconscious, intrapsychic processes and early childhood experiences was misguided thereby causing clinicians to overlook important aspects of depression such as the patient's conscious negative self-verbalizations (A. Beck, 1967), the effects of ongoing distressing and undesirable life circumstances (G.W. Brown & Harris, 1978), or neurophysiological variables (Mendelson, 1990). A third reason for the discontent was that psychoanalytic treatment of depression was costly, lengthy, and of questionable efficacy. Some behavioral researchers were particularly vocal about the relative ineffectiveness of psychodynamic therapies, not only for depression, but for other psychological disorders as well (H. Eysenck, 1952a, 1966; H. Eysenck & Rachman, 1965; Rachman, 1971). Even as recently as 1985, Bemporad commented that there were no large follow-up studies of the effectiveness of long-term psychoanalytic treatment for depression. Although Bergin and Lambert (1978) in their review of the psychotherapy outcome literature arrived at a more favorable conclusion about the efficacy of psychoanalytic psychotherapy for some types of "neurotic disorders," they concluded that psychoanalysis was not the treatment of choice given its length, expense, and lack of superior efficacy over the briefer forms of therapy. Thus, controversy over the effectiveness of psychodynamic psychotherapy as well as the increased demand for brief and effective treatments created a receptive environment in the 1970s for alternative approaches to depression.

Behavioral Theories

Behavioral models of depression in the 1960s and early 1970s were primarily based on the operant conditioning theory of learning. These theories viewed depression as an overgeneralized response (loss of interest and pleasure in a range of activities) triggered by a specific stimulus or event (Gotlib & Hammen, 1992). The early theories considered a reduction in the rate or effectiveness of positive reinforcement as the central problem in depression. Fester (1973) characterized depression as a reduction in the frequency of positively reinforced behavior, whereas Costello (1972) contended that depression resulted from a general loss of reinforcer effectiveness due to endogenous biochemical changes and/or disruption in a chain of behavior resulting from a loss, for example, of one of the reinforcers in the chain.

Lewinsohn (1974) formulated one of the most refined and elaborated behavioral models of depression of the day. Depressive symptoms of anhedonia, withdrawal, psychomotor retardation, and fatigue were considered central features of depression caused by a low rate of response-contingent positive reinforcement and/or a high rate of aversive experience (Hoberman & Lewinsohn, 1985; Lewinsohn, 1975). Three factors determined the amount of response-contingent positive reinforcement an individual received: (a) the availability of positive reinforcers and/or punishing experiences in the environment, (b) the instrumental behavior (social skills) of the individual needed to obtain positive reinforcement from the environment or to cope with aversive events, and (c) the number of potentially reinforcing or punishing events in the environment (Hoberman & Lewinsohn, 1985; Lewinsohn, 1974). Lewinsohn's initial model, then, emphasized a reduction in social reinforcement, the lack of effective social skills, and/or the increased presence of aversive experiences as psychological processes leading to the low rate of instrumental behavior, passivity, and dysphoria characteristic of depression (Gotlib & Hammen, 1992). In fact, Lewinsohn (1974) was explicit in stating that the cognitive features of depression, such as low self-esteem, pessimism, and guilt, which Beck considers central constructs in depression, are merely secondary to the feelings of dysphoria caused by a low rate of response-contingent positive reinforcement.

Despite their compatibility with the experimental method, the shortcomings in these early behavioral theories resulted in their questionable validity as models for clinical depression. Eastman (1976) offered a number of general criticisms of the behavioral models and their supporting research. These included (a) too little attention to fundamental research on depression, (b) inadequate treatment studies with overreliance on single case designs, (c) inadequate account of the affective symptoms of depression, (d) poor research methodology such as use of analog subjects, predominance of antidotal studies, and rarity of controlled experiments, and (e) imprecise terminology that makes the theories difficult to test empirically.

Blaney (1977) questioned the causal status of Lewinsohn's model. He noted that most of the supportive studies were merely correlational, showing that changes in level of reinforcing activities were associated with corresponding changes in mood state. However, these studies could not tease apart whether changes in reinforcing activities led to a change in depression level or vice versa. Thus, he concluded that Lewinsohn's theory would be more properly referred to as a characterization or description of depressed persons' interactions with their environment rather than a causal theory of depression. In fact, Blaney proceeded to review a number of experimental studies that failed to find reductions in depression following an increase in positive reinforcement activities. More recently, Lewinsohn and colleagues have proposed a new theoretical model of depression that includes cognitive variables such as heightened state of self-awareness, self-criticism, negative expectancies, and self-perceived social competence (Lewinsohn, Hoberman, Teri, & Hautzinger, 1985).

Learned Helplessness Model

Without question the most influential behavioral theory of depression during the 1970s was Martin Seligman's *learned helplessness theory*. Based on a series of laboratory experiments, Seligman and colleagues discovered that dogs given an inescapable shock while restrained in a Pavlovian hammock subsequently showed deficits in motivation (rarely tried to escape), learning (failed to learn new response-relief contingencies), and emotion (extreme passivity) in new situations (Seligman, 1975; Seligman & Maier, 1967; see also review by Peterson & Seligman, 1985). It was apparent that the helpless animals had learned that their response was independent of the outcome. Seligman (1975) concluded that this helpless state generalized to new situations because of an expectation of future uncontrollability. Furthermore, Seligman noted many parallels between laboratory-induced helplessness and depression, and so suggested that the model of learned helplessness may be an analog for clinical depression. In their review Peterson and Seligman (1985) noted that many parallels were found between learned helplessness and depression in terms of (a) symptoms (passivity, retarded response-relief learning, lower aggression, loss of appetite, feelings of helplessness, negative expectations, and catecholamine and indoleamine depletion), (b) causes (uncontrollable bad events), (c) treatment (exposure to contingencies, electroconvulsive shocks, and antidepressant drugs), and (d) prevention (early mastery training).

Throughout the 1970s, numerous experimental studies tested various hypotheses derived from the learned helplessness model on both humans and animals. Blaney (1977) noted that there were three kinds of empirical data generated to support Seligman's model: (a) studies that induced depression by exposure to uncontrollable aversive stimuli (often aversion was operationalized in terms of failure manipulation), (b) studies that reduced depression through a helpless-reduction procedure, and (c) correlational studies that found an association between learned helplessness states and depression. Positive results were frequently reported in terms of success at manipulating learned helplessness levels by exposure to uncontrollable negative stimuli or by exposure to success experiences. As well, other studies found that depressed individuals presented with many of the characteristics of learned helplessness (e.g., Hiroto & Seligman, 1975; D.C. Klein & Seligman, 1976; W. Miller & Seligman, 1975).

Despite these encouraging results, the intense empirical scrutiny finally revealed serious problems with the original learned helplessness model. These included (a) inconsistent findings, with many studies failing to find that subjects exposed to uncontrollable negative stimuli became depressed; (b) nonspecificity with learned helplessness not showing a unique relation to depressive states; (c) a possible confound with self-esteem in which helpless inductions could be construed as self-esteem manipulations rather than manipulations of perceived control; (d) failure of the model to account for the known heterogeneity of depressive disorders; (e) failure of learned helplessness to account for certain aspects of depression such as loss of self-esteem, self-blame, or suicide; and (f) inability of the helplessness model to explain the generality, persistence, or recurrence of depression (Blaney, 1977; Depue & Monroe, 1978b; Gotlib & Hammen, 1992; Peterson & Seligman, 1985). Depue and Monroe also questioned the relevance of the learned helplessness research for clinical depression because most of the studies had been conducted on nondepressed college students.

Given the problems inherent with the original model, Abramson, Seligman, and Teasdale (1978) introduced a cognitive version of the model by reformulating learned helplessness in terms of attributional processes. In this version of the theory, the mere presence of a negative event was not considered sufficient to produce a helpless or depressive state. Instead the event must be perceived as uncontrollable or noncontingent. Faced with such an experience, an individual tries to explain the cause for this upsetting event. To the extent that he or she makes an internal ("I caused the event"), global ("This negative experience is going to affect a number of situations"), and stable ("This will persist over time") causal attribution for the negative event, the person is more likely to expect that their actions cannot control desired outcomes now or in the future. Abramson et al. (1978) argued that the occurrence of this "depressogenic" attributional style can explain the onset of certain types of helplessness depressions as well as the generality, chronicity, and low self-esteem associated with depression. In later writings, however, the depressogenic attribution style was upgraded to the status of a predisposing vulnerability or risk factor for depression (Brewin, 1988; Peterson & Seligman, 1985). More recently, Abramson, Metalsky, and Alloy (1989) offered a further revision of the model calling it the *hopelessness theory of depression.* In this model, Abramson and her colleagues argue that in addition to inferences about the cause of negative life events (attributional style), one must also consider inferences about the consequences that may occur because of the event particularly in relation to the self (i.e., self-worth, personality, desirability). Together these proximal contributory causes will lead to the symptoms of a specific type of depression labeled hopelessness depression. The original learned helplessness model and its various revisions have had obvious heuristic value as psychological models for understanding depression. Today, the reformulated learned helplessness and hopelessness models continue to provide a fertile theoretical ground for clinical researchers interested in psychological processes in depression.

From Behavior to Cognition: A Paradigmatic Shift in Depression

As noted, behavioral and psychodynamic theories and treatment of depression came under intense criticism by the mid-1970s. Many of the prevailing behavioral theories, such as the learned helplessness model, had made significant changes to their theory by abandoning their sole reliance on behavioral concepts and adding cognitive constructs to explain depressive or anxious phenomena. It was during this era of discontent with the prevailing psychological models that Beck's view of depression as a cognitive disorder gained an interested and receptive hearing among behaviorally oriented clinicians and researchers. This emphasis on an information processing perspective represented a new and innovative approach to psychological disorders, offering an alternative to the limited stimulus-response nonmediational theories of the 1960s and early 1970s (see also Dobson & Block, 1988, for a review of the historical basis of cognitive-behavior therapy).

One cannot entirely attribute the intense interest in cognitive theory and therapy to the limitations of the prevailing behavioral and psychodynamic theories of the 1960s and 1970s. Another factor in the widespread acceptance of the cognitive model was the emergence of a paradigmatic shift in clinical psychology as a result of other influential behavioral theorists and clinicians advocating a more cognitive approach to the theory and treatment of psychological disorders.

Cognitive variables have long been recognized as important in psychopathology and psychotherapy. The philosophical underpinnings of cognitive therapy can be traced back to Greek Stoic philosophers such as Epictetus, Cicero, and Seneca (Ellis, 1989). Within psychoanalysis, a small group of analysts began to emphasize a more cognitive approach to treatment involving the correction of patients' misconceptions (Perris, 1988). Since the introduction of systematic desensitization by Wolpe (1958), behavior therapy had incorporated cognitive variables in its treatment approaches. Procedures like imaginal systematic desensitization, thought stopping, and guided imagery are examples of cognitive ingredients in early behavioral treatments. Moreover by the mid-1960s, some behaviorists attempted to apply the principles of conditioning to modify covert, private mental events in a treatment approach known as covert sensitization (Cautela, 1967). This early attempt by radical behaviorists to apply the principles of learning to the treatment of cognition ran into conceptual problems and lacked demonstrated empirical efficacy. Thus the covert conditioning movement rather than supporting the expansion of radical behaviorism to cognitive targets, ended up accentuating the need for a new theoretical approach to cognition (Dobson & Block, 1988; Mahoney & Arnkoff, 1978). The shift from behavior therapy to cognitive and cognitive-behavior therapy can be traced to three major developments within the clinical behavioral sciences.

One of the most important changes in clinical behavioral theory and therapy that paved the way for an emphasis on cognitive processes came with the publication of Albert Bandura's *Principles of Behavior Modification* (Bandura, 1969) and *Social Learning Theory* (Bandura, 1971). Based on his empirical work on vicarious or observational learning, Bandura's reconceptualization of learning in the form of social learning theory considered cognitive processes crucial in the acquisition and regulation of behavior (G. Wilson, 1978). Social learning theory rejected the strict S-R assumption of behaviorism with its emphasis on environmental determinism in favor of reciprocal determinism in which the person and environment were viewed as having a mutual influence on each other (Mahoney & Arnkoff, 1978). Bandura explained vicarious or observational learning by advocating such mediational symbolic processes as attention, retention, and motoric reproduction. Thus the introduction of social learning theory along with the cognitive reconceptualizations of other learning theorists (e.g., Abramson et al., 1978; Seligman & Johnston, 1973; see also December, 1974) led to a zeitgeist conducive to the emergence of cognitive theory and therapy (see also Dobson & Block, 1988; Mahoney, 1977; Mahoney & Arnkoff, 1978; G. Wilson, 1978).

A second major impetus to cognitive and cognitive-behavior theory and therapy came from clinical practice. Two therapeutic trends in the 1960s and early 1970s are noteworthy—the formation of more coherent forms of cognitive psychotherapy with the departure of Ellis and Beck from their psychoanalytic roots, and a more concerted emphasis on cognitive approaches by behaviorally trained psychologists like Mahoney, Meichenbaum, Davidson, and Goldfried (Perris, 1988). More recently, Hollon and Beck (1994) made a distinction between the cognitive therapies of Beck and Ellis that evolved out of a rejection of psychoanalysis, and the cognitive-behavioral therapies that grew out of behavior therapy and social learning theory. Both of these psychotherapy trends had a significant influence in the development of Beck's CT.

Rational-emotive therapy (RET) can be credited as the first contemporary systematic psychotherapy with a clearly defined cognitive orientation. This system of therapy originated with Albert Ellis who abandoned his psychoanalytic training and developed a treatment approach based on direct cognitive debate and behavioral homework assignments (Ellis, 1962). Ellis conducted his first outcome study of RET in 1957 followed by the publication of various books and articles on RET over the next 10 years (Ellis, 1989). Beck's own work on cognitive factors in depression began in the early 1960s and drew on some of the previous work reported by Ellis. Thus, the early cognitive and cognitive-behavioral theorists of the 1970s were indebted to the pioneering work of Albert Ellis (1962, 1977), who promoted the view that cognitive constructs such as irrational beliefs and negative thinking are the basis of psychological disturbance. RET advocated cognitive and behavioral intervention strategies as a means of promoting psychotherapeutic change. However, a central tenet of RET was the assumption that change could only be achieved if the core cognitive dysfunction (i.e., irrational beliefs) that underlie the disorder was modified (Ellis, 1962). RET had a significant impact on Beck's theory and practice during the early phase of its development. RET concepts like irrational beliefs or schemas and interventions such as logical persuasion were incorporated into the early versions of CT. However the influence of RET on Beck's cognitive theory and therapy has diminished greatly over the years. Today, Beck's cognitive theory and therapy bears little resemblance to RET.

As mentioned, the second major development in cognitive clinical theory and therapy during the 1970s was the introduction of cognitive-behavioral interventions such as stress inoculation training (Meichenbaum, 1977), problem-solving training (D'Zurilla & Goldfried, 1971; Spivak, Platt, & Shure, 1976), self-control therapy (Rehm, 1977), and self-control mastery (Thoresen & Mahoney, 1974). These approaches tended to view cognition in terms of covert behaviors and so adapted and expanded behavioral procedures that had been effective in modifying overt behavior to the problem of changing internal private events of the mind (Hollon & Beck, 1994). In the end, the behavioral and cognitive-behavioral approaches had their biggest impact on Beck's cognitive therapy rather than his theory. Many of the techniques such as setting a sessional agenda, goal setting, problem solving, homework assignments, self-monitoring, and pleasure and mastery tasks were directly borrowed from behavior therapy. However, it was his early training in psychoanalysis and the schools of cognitive and phenomenological psychology that had the greater influence on the development of Beck's cognitive theory.

A third trend that greatly influenced the development and acceptance of cognitive theory and therapy of depression was the call for a new, more cognitively based clinical theory by influential behaviorally trained clinical psychologists. One of the most influential books published at this time was Michael Mahoney's *Cognition and Behavior Modification* (1974). Mahoney questioned the validity and adequacy of a strict nonmediational behavioral theory that rejected the study of symbolic processes and constructs. He pleaded for an end to this "cognitive inquisition" and advocated a cognitive learning model with its emphasis on cognitive-symbolic processes as mediational constructs in human learning. Another important publication during this time was Donald Meichenbaum's *Cognitive Behavior Modification* (1977). In this book, Meichenbaum presents a systematic and empirically based form of treatment that targets cognitive variables with the use of both cognitive and behavioral strategies. In 1977, the journal *Cognitive Therapy and Research* was established as an outlet for research on cognitive processes in clinical disorders. These developments, together with an increasing emphasis in clinical research on cognitive processes at major behavioral conferences such as the *Association for the Advancement of Behavior Therapy* (AABT), the *British Association for Behavioural Psychotherapy* (BABP), and the various *World Congresses for Behavior Therapy* (and *Cognitive Therapy*) led to the phenomenal growth in cognitive and cognitive-behavioral theory and therapy. In a 1987 AABT membership survey, 69% of respondents identified themselves as having a cognitive-behavioral orientation (Craighead, 1990).

Whether the emergence of cognitive and cognitive behavior theories and therapies in the 1970s represented a paradigmatic shift from former radical behavioral approaches is a matter of debate for historians of psychology. G. Wilson (1978), for example, argued that the emergence of cognitive behavior therapy did not represent a paradigmatic shift but rather was an important extension and clinical application of reconceptualized behavioral models such as social learning theory. Mahoney (1977), on the other hand, considered the shift in clinical psychology to cognitive processes quite "revolutionary." Whatever the verdict, there is no doubt that major developments in both behavioral theory and practice led to a growth in cognitive behavior modification, a trend that had a significant impact on Beck's theory and therapy.

THE EMERGENCE OF COGNITIVE THEORY AND THERAPY

EARLY EXPERIMENTATION ON PSYCHOANALYTIC THEORY

It was within the zeitgeist of the 1960s and early 1970s that Beck developed his cognitive theory and therapy of anxiety and depression. The discontent with the traditional behavioral and psychodynamic therapies, and the convergence of thought between behavioral and disaffected psychoanalysts, along with increasing recognition of the importance of a cognitive approach to understanding and treating emotional disorders, provided considerable momentum for the propagation of cognitive theory and therapy. Despite the importance of these wider developments, there can be little doubt that the greatest influence on Beck's adoption of a cognitive approach can be attributed to his own experimentation and clinical observation.

Because of his training in psychoanalysis, Beck initially focused his experimental research on psychoanalytic constructs (A. Beck, 1988). One concept considered central to the psychoanalytic model of depression was the idea that inner directed or retroflected anger was a core psychological process that characterized depressive disorders. As a result, Beck embarked on a series of studies to demonstrate the existence of internalized anger in depression. Since psychoanalytic theory viewed dreams as products of the unconscious, he first investigated dream content in depressed patients but failed to find greater hostility or aggression in the dreams of depressed patients versus a nondepressed control group (for discussion, see A. Beck, 1988). However, he did find that the depressed patients had a greater number of dreams in which they were victims of some rejection, disappointment, or criticism (A. Beck & Hurvich, 1959). This led to an alternative hypothesis, that the core psychological process in depression may be a need to suffer or masochism.

To investigate the masochism hypothesis, Beck developed a coding scheme for scoring dreams for masochistic themes. In the first study (A. Beck & Hurvich, 1959), an independent blind rater scored the first 20 dreams of depressed and nondepressed patients ($n = 12$). A significant difference was found with the depressed patients having more masochistic dreams than the nondepressed. However, one problem became apparent. As yet, Beck and his colleagues did not have a reliable and valid method for making clinical diagnoses of depression or measuring the severity of depression (A. Beck, Ward, Mendelson, Mock, & Erbaugh,

1962). This resulted in a series of systematic studies involving clinical ratings of depressive symptoms that eventually resulted in the development of the Beck Depression Inventory (BDI), a self-report instrument for assessing the depth or severity of depression (A. Beck, 1967; A. Beck, Ward, Mendelson, Mock, & Erbaugh, 1961).

With the development of a reliable and valid measure of depression, Beck and colleagues were now ready to subject his theory of masochism to a large clinical study. However, Beck noted that there were strong parallels between the masochistic dream content of depressed patients and their attitudes and behavior during the waking state (A. Beck, 1961). Thus he initiated a number of studies to determine whether the "need to suffer" could be found not only in the depressed patient's dreams but also in other ideational phenomena such as early memories or storytelling, responses to verbal tests, and reactions to experimentally induced stress (A. Beck, 1967).

A larger study on manifest dream content was conducted on 218 psychiatric inpatients and outpatients categorized into nondepressed, moderate, or severe levels of depression based on the BDI (A. Beck & Ward, 1961). Analysis revealed that the depressed group had significantly more dreams of masochistic content than the nondepressed group. However no significant differences emerged between the mild and more severely depressed patients indicating that masochistic dream content was associated with the presence of depression rather than the intensity of the depressive state.

Additional studies were conducted on dream content, recall of earliest memories, responses to a structured projective test, and responses to personality test items to determine how pervasive the "need to suffer" was in depression (A. Beck, 1961). Analyses revealed significant group differences with the depressed patients relative to nondepressed patients recalling more masochistic early memories and offering more masochistic responses to the Focused Fantasy Test. As well, a correlation of .51 was found between the Depression Inventory (BDI) and a self-report Masochism Inventory. The author interpreted these results as indicating a significant relationship between masochism and depression. Beck concluded that other evidence suggested that masochism may be a relatively stable personality characteristic of depression-prone individuals rather than simply a result of the depressive state itself.

To determine whether the "need to suffer" represented a core psychodynamic motivational-affective process in depression, Beck and his colleagues conducted a number of experimental studies designed to manipulate specific variables that might elicit "masochistic behavior" (A. Beck, 1967). In one study, depressed and nondepressed male psychiatric patients ($n = 40$) were randomly assigned to a word completion task in which performance demands were manipulated so that one group achieved superior performance and the other group inferior performance. Analyses revealed that the superior performance group were significantly happier, more self-confident, and made more "happy judgments" in response to photographs of adults than the inferior performance group. Thus the experimental task succeeded in manipulating subjects' mood and social judgments. However, the predicted interaction between depression and the effects of inferior performance was not significant in self-rated affect, expressions of self-confidence as indicated by estimates of future performance on the word completion task, or judgments of facial expression in photographs. There was a nonsignificant trend for the depressed subjects to show a greater decrease in mood following the inferior performance. It is likely that the study lacked sufficient statistical power to obtain significant interaction effects given that the cell sizes ($n = 10$) were very small.

In a second study by Loeb, Beck, and Diggory (1971), performance of 20 depressed and 20 nondepressed patients was manipulated in a card sorting task to yield a "success" and a "failure" condition. Analyses revealed that the depressed patients were more affected by the success/failure manipulation than the low depressed patient group as indicated by lower estimates of future success on the task, a lower level of aspiration, and poorer self-evaluation of performance. The authors interpreted these results as indicating that the depressed patients were more pessimistic about their performance on the card-sorting task than nondepressed patients.

A. Beck (1967) concluded that together the studies on dream content and the experimental manipulation of verbal material were at best equivocal in their support of "the need to suffer" or masochism in depression. However, the studies did indicate that depressed patients were more negative and pessimistic about themselves and their performance than nondepressed subjects. In an effort to understand the implication of these findings, Beck began to question the need for a deep-seated motivational construct like "need to suffer" (see A. Beck, 1988). Instead, could the manifest dream content, negative expectations, and sensitivity to failure simply reflect how patients viewed themselves and their experiences? The results of these studies

> led to the conclusion that certain cognitive patterns could be responsible for the patients' tendency to make negatively biased judgments of themselves, their environment, and their future. The cognitive patterns, although less prominent in the nondepressed period, became activated during the depression. (A. Beck, 1967, p. 185)

Clinical Observations of Cognitive Phenomena

Concurrent with the anomalies that arose in his empirical research on psychoanalytic theory, Beck's clinical observations while treating depressed patients with psychoanalysis also were not consistent with psychoanalytic theory. In accordance with the standard psychoanalytic treatment protocol of the day, Beck requested that his patients free-associate during therapy sessions. During these sessions, he observed that patients were not reporting certain kinds of ideation that were important to understanding the nature of psychological disorders (A. Beck, 1976). Furthermore, patients failed to report this ideation not because of resistance or defensiveness but because they had not been trained to focus on such thoughts. To illustrate this point, A. Beck (1976, 1988) described a patient who expressed anger at him (manifest thought content) during a therapy session. While exploring with the patient his feelings, the patient spontaneously disclosed that while he was criticizing the therapist, he was aware of another stream of ideation involving self-critical thoughts about expressing his anger. A. Beck (1976) noted that this incident represented his first encounter with a second intermediate stream of thinking that patients are often not aware of initially. In arriving at a case formulation of this observation, he realized that these self-critical thoughts were a mediating variable between the patient's angry and guilty feelings (A. Beck, 1988).

Subsequent observations with other patients revealed that they too had streams of thoughts that previously had not been reported during sessions of free-association. Although these initial observations of a stream of automatic thoughts dealt with the transference (thoughts about the therapist), further inquiry revealed that individuals had automatic thoughts in their interactions with others. In fact, it became clear to Beck that patients were constantly communicating with themselves at this automatic level (A. Beck, 1976). As a result of explicitly instructing his patients to focus on their automatic thoughts and to record their presence, Beck was able to deduce a number of characteristics about the *negative automatic thoughts*. He (A. Beck, 1963, 1976) noted that negative automatic thoughts tend to (a) be very fleeting, (b) be specific and discrete, (c) be highly spontaneous, (d) be plausible to the patient, (e) have a consistent theme even though idiosyncratic to the individual, (f) precede emotional arousal, and (g) involve a distortion of reality. With the discovery of automatic thoughts from his clinical observations and the results from his empirical research demonstrating a general negativity toward the self and future (pessimism), Beck began to formulate his cognitive theory of depression.

AN EARLY VERSION OF THE COGNITIVE MODEL

A. Beck (1963, 1964) published his initial formulation of the cognitive nature of depression in two articles that appeared in the *Archives of General Psychiatry*. In these papers and his first book on the topic, *Depression: Causes and Treatment* published in 1967, Beck argued that the negative thinking that had long been recognized as a symptom feature of depression may in fact play a more central role in the characterization of the disorder than previously thought. Cognition rather than affect was considered the cardinal feature of depression.

The negative cognitive triad was an important construct in early cognitive theory (A. Beck, 1967). The first published study on the cognitive model (A. Beck, 1963) was based on interview data collected in the course of psychotherapy with 50 depressed psychiatric patients and 31 nondepressed patients. Results from this study provided many of the foundational concepts of the cognitive model. For example, the notion of cognitive content-specificity was postulated at this time. Beck noted that a specific ideational content characterized different psychological disorders such that depression is characterized by low self-esteem and self-blame, anxiety is characterized by personal danger, hypomania by self-enhancement, and paranoid states by accusations against others (see also A. Beck, 1971). Although not clearly stated at this time, one also sees in this paper the emergence of the *cognitive triad* (i.e., negative view of self, world, and future) as the characteristic thematic cognitive content in depression. A. Beck (1963) noted that cognitions involving low self-esteem, deprivation, self-criticism, and suicidal wishes were common in depression. Later he referred to this as a negative cognitive shift that occurs in depression when individuals come to view themselves, their world, and their future in a negative manner (A. Beck, 1991).

Another important cognitive concept introduced in the 1963 paper was the notion of *cognitive errors*. A. Beck (1963) found that depressed patients distorted reality in a systematic manner that resulted in a bias against themselves. He described a number of cognitive errors made in depression such as (a) arbitrary inference (drawing a specific conclusion in the absence of evidence or when the evidence is contrary to the conclusion), (b) selective abstraction (focusing on a detail out of context while ignoring other more salient features of the situation), (c) overgeneralization (drawing a conclusion on the basis of one or more isolated incidents), and (d) magnification/minimization (exaggerating or minimizing the significance or magnitude of an event). Later on, A. Beck et al. (1979) added minimization, personalization (a tendency to relate external events to oneself), and dichotomous thinking (tendency to place all experience in one of two categories) to the list of cognitive errors that are evident in depression. In this early paper, A. Beck (1963) clearly stated that any individual will be inaccurate or inconsistent in cognitive processing but that what characterizes the cognitive distortion in depression is the systematic negative bias against the self. This point has been lost by later critics of Beck's model who have misinterpreted his position as advocating accuracy in the cognitive processing of reality by nondepressed individuals (i.e., Coyne & Gotlib, 1983).

A. Beck (1967) postulated that the negative cognitive pattern leads to the other symptoms of depression, although he believed the relation between negative cognitive patterns and the physiological symptoms of depression was more tenuous. For example, depressed mood or sadness was considered the consequence of a negative view of self or world, whereas the loss of motivation was considered the result of the patient's hopelessness and pessimism (A. Beck, 1967). The cognitive model, then, represented a fundamental shift in conceptualizing depression in terms of "thought disorder" as opposed to affective disturbance.

Having delineated a cognitive characterization of depression, A. Beck (1964) turned his attention to possible cognitive variables that may act as predisposing vulnerability factors to depression. He proposed, "The vulnerability of the depression-prone person is attributable to the constellation of enduring negative attitudes about himself, about the world, and about his future" (A. Beck, 1967, p. 277).

These attitudes are repetitive stereotyped ways of construing across a variety of situations. As such, they may be regarded as manifestations of cognitive organizations or structures called schemas (A. Beck, 1964). Schemas were defined as cognitive structures "for screening, coding, and evaluating the stimuli that impinges on the organism" (A. Beck, 1967, p. 283). They enable individuals to make sense of their environment by breaking it down and organizing it into psychologically relevant facets. However, schemas also direct all cognitive activity whether it be ruminations and automatic thoughts or cognitive processing of external events (A. Beck, 1964). As structures, schemas can have qualities of flexibility-inflexibility, openness-closedness, permeability-impermeability, and concreteness-abstractness (A. Beck, 1967).

A. Beck (1967) hypothesized that in depression, idiosyncratic schemas involving themes of personal deficiency, self-blame, and negative expectations dominate the thinking processes. Both the content and form of depressive schemas are problematic. They tend to contain chronic misconceptions, distorted attitudes, invalid premises, and unrealistic goals in the form of inflexible, closed, and impermeable structures. A specific situation or stressor that would be expected to lower self-esteem might

activate the depressive schemas in vulnerable individuals. Once activated, the depressotypic schemas lead to the negative automatic thoughts
and cognitive errors previously noted.

Although Beck considered his cognitive theory applicable to other forms
of psychopathology such as anxiety, most of his clinical and research attention throughout the 1960s and 1970s was devoted to depression. It was not
until he published his treatment manual on cognitive therapy for depression (A. Beck et al., 1979) and a controlled clinical trial showing that cognitive therapy was more effective in treating depression than imipramine
(Rush, Beck, Kovacs, & Hollon, 1977) that Beck turned his attention to the
problem of anxiety. In 1985, Beck along with coauthors Gary Emery and
Ruth Greenberg published *Anxiety Disorders and Phobias: A Cognitive Perspective* documenting a systematic cognitive theory and treatment for anxiety disorders.

SUMMARY

In this chapter, we have traced the historical development of Beck's cognitive theory and therapy of depression. As we have seen, a paradigmatic
shift occurred in theory, research, and treatment during the 1960s and
early 1970s. Shortcomings were readily evident in the psychodynamic
and nonmediational S-R and R-R behavioral theories of depression.

It was within this emerging cognitive zeitgeist that Beck's cognitive
theory and therapy of depression was born. We have traced a number of
important influences on Beck's early theorizing and therapy including
(a) cognitive behavioral theories like Bandura's (1971) social learning theory, (b) cognitive-behavioral interventions such as stress inoculation
training, problem-solving training, and self-control therapy, (c) theories
of prominent behaviorally trained psychologists, such as Mahoney,
Meichenbaum, and A. A. Lazarus, who denounced nonmediational behavioral theory and treatment in favor of cognitive approaches, (d) Ellis's
rational-emotive therapy, and (e) theories of early experimental cognitive
psychologists like Bartlett, Kelley, and Arnold.

However, the greatest influences on theory development were the results of Beck's own experimentation and clinical observation. Because
crucial psychoanalytic hypotheses were not supported by laboratory
findings and were not true to the clinical phenomena observed in the
therapy session, Beck rejected his psychodynamic formulation of depression and embarked on a completely different approach to understanding
and treating depression. As discussed in Chapter 3, Beck's initial focus on
depression has spawned a perspective on the human condition that has
wide application to a host of psychological conditions and problems.

CHAPTER 3

The Philosophical and Theoretical Basis of Cognitive Theory

IN THIS chapter, we examine the philosophical and theoretical tenets of the cognitive model. Critics of the cognitive model have questioned whether it meets the criteria for a scientific theory. Blaney (1977) suggested that the cognitive model may not be a satisfactory scientific theory because of its ability to accommodate apparently contradictory experimental findings, thereby making it impossible to disconfirm. Coyne and Gotlib (1983) criticized that its key cognitive concepts were too imprecise and so required better operationalization. In their review, Beidel and Turner (1986) concluded that cognitive behavioral treatment strategies (which included Beck's cognitive therapy) do not have an adequate theoretical basis. Teasdale and Barnard (1993), on the other hand, argued that Beck's cognitive model of depression does not meet the criteria for a scientific theory but instead is a clinical theory whose primary purpose is to provide the clinician with a tool for understanding and treating depression.

Does the cognitive model meet criteria for a scientific theory? Does it have an adequate theoretical basis for conducting research and guiding treatment of depressive states? Most of this chapter will consider the philosophical and theoretical basis of cognitive theory. According to Popper (1959), a scientific theory must possess a set of assumptions that are both necessary and sufficient for defining the theoretical system. Thus in this chapter, we discuss the theoretical assumptions or statements that form the basis of the cognitive model. Each proposition describes a necessary characteristic of the model and, together with the remaining statements, defines the cognitive perspective. The theoretical statements refer to features of human nature that serve as assumptions for the cognitive model. The scientific status of the cognitive model, then, is in part dependent on a clear specification of its theoretical assumptions.

In the last section of the chapter, we examine Teasdale and Barnard's (1993) claim that Beck's cognitive model of depression constitutes a clinical rather than a scientific theory. We discuss whether this dichotomy between clinical and scientific theory is justified, and whether the cognitive model meets Teasdale and Barnard's criteria of an applied science model. From this discussion, we conclude that the cognitive model can be considered an applied science theory, and so can be evaluated in terms of its ability to account for relevant clinical phenomena and experimental findings.

PHILOSOPHICAL BASIS OF COGNITIVE THEORY

A central tenet of the cognitive model is that human information processing or meaning construction influences all emotional and behavioral experiences. This assumption of the centrality of cognition in human experience has a long history in philosophy, psychiatry, and psychology. The phenomenological approach to psychology, in which one's view of the self and personal world determines behavior, can be traced back to the Greek Stoic philosophy of Zeno of Cytium, Epictetus, Cicero, and Seneca (A. Beck & Weishaar, 1989; Ellis, 1989). Immanuel Kant proposed that mental disorders are the result of a failure to correct "private sense" with "common sense" (Raimy, 1975). Other 19th-century philosophers such as Heidegger and Husserl also emphasized the importance of conscious subjective experience. As noted by Raimy, the 19th-century hypnotists believed that "morbid ideas" were responsible for psychological disturbances. At the turn of the century, other noted medical researchers such as Dubois, Janet, and Breuer believed that pathogenic thoughts or ideas may be responsible for mental disorders (Raimy, 1975).

This emphasis on the importance of subjective consciousness in psychological problems was picked up by the neo-Freudians such as Alder, Sullivan, and Horney. Alder, for example, considered "mistaken opinions" the source of neurosis and emphasized the need for therapists to determine the conscious meaning that individuals attach to their experience (A. Beck & Rush, 1988; Raimy, 1975). Raimy interpreted Sullivan's notion of "parataxic distortions" in psychological disorders as synonymous with mistaken perceptions or conceptions, whereas Horney's concept of the "idealized self-image" can be understood in terms of a cluster of misconceptions about the self (Horney, 1945). In later years, the view that the source of psychological disturbance could be found in one's faculty constructions of reality is evident in the work of Rotter, George Kelly and, of course, Albert Ellis (Raimy, 1975).

The philosophical perspective that most closely captures the core assumptions of cognitive theory and therapy is that of existential phenomenology (A. Beck, 1985a; Moss, 1992; Pretzer & Beck, 1996). Cognitive theory holds that psychological or mentalistic phenomena have a "reality" along with material, spatial phenomena (A. Beck, 1985a). Although internal psychological phenomena are private to the individual experiencing them and are not directly accessible to another person, nevertheless these phenomena constitute one of a number of different perspectives that can be taken with respect to human function and adaptation (e.g., other perspectives are biological, behavioral, genetic, social).

Based on this philosophical perspective, the assumptions of cognitive therapy regarding human nature are for the most part consistent with "common sense." In the present context, common sense refers to a person's everyday experiences, with little formal theoretical explanation added. For example, a prominent role is given in cognitive theory to conscious and metacognitive processes in correcting psychological disorder. Such processes are obviously present within the ordinary experiences of people in their everyday lives. This may be contrasted to the core assumptions of other theories of psychopathology and psychotherapy that postulate constructs such as unconscious motivated drives (psychoanalysis) and classical and operant conditioning theories that postulate automatic associations generated without regard for—or uninfluenced by—the values, intentions, and meanings of events in a person's life. In the case of both psychoanalytic and behavioral theory, the processes that are said to control behavior are outside the awareness of—and therefore outside the control of—the person.

The philosophical assumptions of cognitive theory have a long history in philosophy, psychiatry, and psychology. A phenomenological perspective is assumed with its emphasis on conscious subjective experience, the centrality of the self, and the importance of meaning-making processes. Furthermore, cognitive theory does not subscribe to an epistemiology of *radical idealism* in which nothing exists outside subjective experience. Rather, the model assumes there is an existence that is external to the individual's own perceptions, but that this reality is not "objective" in the usual understanding of the term. Instead, reality is defined in terms of the circumstances that impinge on individuals. Although these "personal realities" will differ between individuals, we would also expect a significant degree of commonality given the consistency and regularity of exigencies that exist in the external world of all human beings. That is, our personal realities may differ, but we are all faced with the demands of survival, community, and productivity. Having explicated the broad philosophical orientation of cognitive theory, we now turn to consider the more specific theoretical assumptions that constitute the scaffolding of the model.

THEORETICAL ASSUMPTIONS OF THE COGNITIVE MODEL

Clinical cognitive theory is based on certain basic assumptions or premises. These implicit proposititons must be properly understood to follow the line of reasoning advanced in subsequent chapters, particularly Chapter 4.

A scientific theory must begin with a formal comprehensive statement that delineates all the assumptions that are both necessary and sufficient in defining the theoretical system (Popper, 1959). Further theoretical considerations may be derived logically from the core assumptions of the theory. However, these basic theoretical statements do not imply truth but rather serve to clarify and define a scientific theory.

The basic propositions of cognitive theory and therapy can be found more or less in a number of different sources (Alford & Beck, 1997; A. Beck, 1976, 1985a; A. Beck et al., 1979, 1985; Dobson & Block, 1988; Mahoney, 1977; Pretzer & Beck, 1996). In the following section, we discuss the propositions that are the basis of Beck's current cognitive model of psychopathology and emotion.

1. *The capacity to process information and form cognitive representations of the environment is central to human adaptation and survival.*

A fundamental premise of clinical cognitive theory is that information processing of the environment is essential for human adaptation and survival. To adapt to and survive in the world, humans have evolved systems of consciousness that include the ability to form conceptual representations of themselves as organisms in the world. In so doing, humans have also evolved the ability to both conceptualize time, and to transcend it. Human conceptual systems can include events taking place not only in the present, but also the past and anticipated future. In this way, we are presumably unlike the lower organisms that (for the most part) operate by means of unconscious, mechanistic, and relatively inflexible preprogrammed reflexes.

Broadly speaking, our information processing capability is represented in the cognitive functions of perceiving, assimilating, and elaborating the meaning of our experiences. As noted by Mahoney (1977), the occurrence of information processing means that humans respond primarily to cognitive representations of the environment rather than to the

environment itself. One consequence of this greater information processing capability and flexibility is the possibility of dysfunction associated
with its faulty operation. Cognitive theory of psychopathology articulates
the perceptual-interpretative variables implicated in psychopathology
and effective psychotherapy. The information processing (or meaning-
assigning) variables include all processes and structures necessary for the
person to make sense of—to make meaningful—the experiences of everyday life, including stressful and extreme environmental events. This
means that physiological variables, for example, are not part of clinical
cognitive theory, although such variables are obviously relevant to a complete understanding of psychopathological conditions like depression.

2. *Human information processing occurs at different levels of consciousness
as a means of promoting its efficiency and adaptability.*

Cognitive theory assumes that information processing occurs on a continuum of consciousness-unconsciousness that results in varying degrees
of awareness and accessibility to the processes and products of thought
(A. Beck, 1976). At one end of the continuum, we have the *preconscious,* unintentional, automatic level, whereas the other end is represented by
highly effortful, elaborative *conscious* processing (Alford & Beck, 1997).
Cognitive theory assumes that information processing functions interac-
tively, concurrently, and continuously while the human organism is
awake resulting in processes that vary in their level of consciousness. The
extent to which unconscious processes are involved at any point in time
will depend on the information processing demands imposed on the organism by the environment.
    The preconscious or unconscious level is primarily operative in those
situations or tasks that are either performed without the need for higher
level cognitive control, or that through practice have become automatized
by repetition. The use of mental heuristics would also fit this case. Information processing at the preconscious level will be highly efficient and
automatic but largely independent of direct control by intentional higher-
order processes. Information that is processed at this level will be primarily in response to environmental or contextual input, with the influence
of higher-order, schema-driven concerns playing a secondary role. Preconscious processing will be especially involved in information processing demands that are critical to the survival of the organism, that is,
when basic survival issues of preservation, safety, and reproduction are
implicated.
    Unlike the psychoanalytic theory of psychopathology, cognitive theory
characterizes cognition as accessible and knowable without the need to
circumvent a barrier of repressed drives or impulses. This means simply

that self-report of conscious experiences are taken as one source of valid data for therapist and patient to explore in treatment sessions. This is not to say, however, that everything the patient says or reports on questionnaires is valid; nor is it to imply that every relevant cognition of present and past events (e.g., traumatic or positive personal experiences) will be accessible to introspection. Cognitive theory recognizes the process of cognitive (and emotional) avoidance, but theorizes that there is no necessary mechanism that makes such processes in principle relegated to the inaccessible unconscious recesses of the mind. Moreover, this automatic cognitive processing is theorized to have some meaningful *content* that varies specifically from one disorder to the next. By content, we refer to the interpretation or meaning assigned to events. And it is this meaning that predicts emotional and behavioral responses.

The more conscious, readily accessible level of processing includes those experiences that are the focus of attentional resources and are conceptualized or observed through any of the sensory systems or by means of fantasy or imagery. By definition, human organisms are aware of and have access to conscious information processing. Although central higher-order control over conscious information processing increases the adaptability of human information processing, this occurs at the expense of speed and efficiency. Conscious information processing is particularly suited to the demands of learning, socialization, communication, and problem solving and so is primarily driven by higher-order central structures or schemas. Thus all human information processing is a balance between the speed and efficiency of the more basic preconscious level and the slower, deliberative, and more directive processing that occurs at the conscious level.

Cognitive psychotherapy functions at the conscious level to effect changes in the output or products of preconscious information processing by directing more attentional resources to the contents or data of automatic primal processing. If the therapy setting and therapist provide adequate safety and support, then it is possible for the patient to refocus (through the guidance of the cognitive therapist) on those experiences, memories, and fears that are operating prior to therapy at an involuntary level of experience. In this manner, the cognitive therapist makes the "unintended" products of automatic processing "intended," but not by any means in the same sense as in classical psychoanalysis. The differences include the following: (a) there is no assumption that the therapist will provide the correct interpretation; (b) there is no assumption that failure to acknowledge traumatic or other memories is due to motivated forgetting or repression; and (c) emotional reactions reported by the patient in session are interpreted in terms of the personal meaning the patient attributes to the event about which an emotional reaction is experienced, rather than in terms of castration fears, Electra, or other hypothetical causes that are not given in the personal experience of the patient. The latter point implies that emotional reactions and cognitive content that accompany such reactions are taken at face value. All this makes for a therapeutic approach that is in line with a patient's "common sense" experience rather than by theory-derived hypothetical constructs and processes.

3. *A basic function of information processing is the personal construction of reality.*

Humans actively participate in the construction of reality through the information processing system. Cognitive theory assumes that this process of organizing one's experiences in the world—including one's interpretation of self and other people—is not simply an act of representing, copying, or "coding" fixed objects but rather is a process that involves some degree of creativity. Put simply, the meanings derived from one's experiences are constructed according to characteristics of (a) the cognitive structures (schemas), (b) previous experiences that have been influential in providing the *content* of such structures, and (c) the characteristics or features of the present context.

The existence of these meaning structures or schemas represents an enduring characteristic of individuals resulting in specific tendencies or predispositions to interpret experiences in certain ways. Because our construction of meaning is only an approximate representation of reality (see Statement 6), these enduring meaning structures can constitute particular *cognitive vulnerabilities* or susceptibilities to reinterpret certain types of experiences in a faulty fashion. The notion of cognitive vulnerability is an important hypothesis in the cognitive model of depression.

More recently, an alternative perspective to the information-processing model has emerged among cognitive clinical theorists known as *constructivism* (see special issue of *Journal of Consulting and Clinical Psychology*—Mahoney, 1993). The main tenet of constructivism is that humans are "meaning-making" agents. Meichenbaum (1993) defines constructivism as "the idea that humans actively construct their personal realities and create their own representational models of the world" (p. 203). Similarly Neimeyer (1993) describes the core of constructivist theory to be "a view of human beings as active agents who, individually and collectively, co-construct the meaning of their experiential world" (p. 222). Likewise, as we can see by the present proposition, Beck's cognitive theory recognizes that individuals attach meaning to a situation in the form of cognitive representations, and that the way an event is uniquely structured (or constructed) by individuals influences how they feel and behave in particular situations (see A. Beck, 1985b; Beck et al., 1979). According to the model, the negativity that forms the core of the depressive disorders is in most cases generated by the dysfunctional cognitive processing biases of the person who suffers from depression. This bias is a function of the person's cognitive representation or private meaning of events, not characteristics of the world as such (the public meanings). Thus constructionistic cognitive approaches to treatment overlap with standard theory of cognitive therapy, although the radical constructionistic theory—which denies an objective reality—is inconsistent with the philosophical position of cognitive therapy.

Cognitive theory, then, assumes that human behavior is dependent on the person's ability to comprehend the social and physical environment within which the individual is situated. However, the cognitive model is often misunderstood as taking only a "realist" perspective (Mahoney, 1993). On the contrary, Beck's cognitive theory subscribes to a dual existence involving an objective reality and a personal, subjective phenomenological reality. In this manner, the cognitive perspective is consistent with that of contemporary conditioning theories that postulate both external physical stimulus characteristics and cognitive mediational constructs (Davey, 1992).

An important point was recently raised by Mahoney (1989), who expressed concern over dichotomizing constructivist theory:

> People do, indeed, co-create their realities, just as their realities co-create them. The future of heuristic theories in psychology must, however, liberate itself from the pendular swings of that dualism and somehow embrace the complexity of our position as both subjects and objects of construction. (p. 188)

Mahoney (1989) proceeded to differentiate between "critical constructivists" who do not deny the existence of the real world, and the "radical constructivists" who, as philosophical idealists, argue that there is no reality beyond our personal experience.

Cognitive theory is quite clear in its position on the "construction of reality." In social contexts where phenomenological realities intersect, there are multiple personal realities as well as an objective physical reality or context within which the subjective realities interact. These "realities" are equally valid in the sense that they are part of what exists. Cognitive theory and therapy, then, argues that knowing is an active process of devising theories or linguistic constructions about ourselves and the world around us. Because our linguistic constructions of life are our own personal theories that guide much of our emotional and behavioral responding, the cognitive therapist recognizes the importance of assuming the unique individuality of the client in therapy without abandoning the notion of a systematic, rule governed, and replicable psychotherapy approach (Held, 1996). Having said this, cognitive theory adopts a realist and modernist epistemology as opposed to an antirealist and postmodernist perspective. Cognitive theory and therapy acknowledges that there is an independent reality that does not originate in the knower (although it is the basis of the cognitive constructions that determine affect and behavior), and that general laws and meanings can be attained through reason, science, and technology (Held, 1995, 1996).

4. *Information processing serves as a guiding principle for the emotional, behavioral, and physiological components of human experience.*

An important assumption in cognitive theory is that information processing plays a primary role in subjective experience through its mediation and organization of thought, feeling, behavior, and sensation. Although our experience of, and response to, the environment involves cognitive, behavioral, affective, and physiological systems, it is our propensity for meaning-assignment or information processing that enables the complex interplay between the various psychological systems in our adaptation to the environment. The various meanings attached to events makes possible the activation of emotional, behavioral, motivational, affective, and physiological systems. Cognition is primary among the various psychological systems (i.e., emotion, behavior) in terms of providing an interpretation of the meaning of the activation of the other systems as a function of adaptation to changing circumstances. The ability of the information-processing system to organize the various psychological systems is a teleonomic process that facilitates adaptation of the person to the external environment. In the end, it is because of this primary organizing function of the information processing system that the cognitive model considers the modification of cognition a necessary ingredient in the therapeutic change process.

Cognitive theory derives from this proposition the *cognitive content-specificity hypothesis.* This hypothesis states that each affective state and psychological disorder has a specific cognitive profile. The cognitive content or meaning of an event determines the type of emotional experience or psychological disturbance an individual experiences (A. Beck, 1971, 1976; D.A. Clark & Beck, 1989). Thus (a) sadness involves appraisals of personal and significant loss or failure leading to a sense of deprivation, (b) happiness is associated with thoughts of personal gain or enhancement, (c) anxiety or fear results from evaluations of threat or danger to one's personal realm, and (d) anger the perception of an assault or transgression to one's personal domain (A. Beck, 1971, 1976).

5. *Cognitive functioning consists of a continuous interaction between lower-order, stimulus-driven processes and higher-order semantic processes.*

The cognitive model assumes that information processing is influenced both by "top-down" and "bottom-up" processes. This basic premise suggests that at any point in time human information processing is the product of, in varying degrees, the selection, abstraction, and elaboration of higher-order schemas (i.e., "top-down" processing) and the more basic processing of raw stimulus characteristics in the environment (i.e., "bottom-up" processing). Thus the cognitive model proposes two fundamental sources or orientations to information processing. The one can be referred to as a *contextualized* orientation in which data from the environment impact on the information processing without extensive higher-order schematic elaboration. The second orientation could be termed *inferential* because it involves the active selection, elaboration, and transformation of experience by higher-order cognitive structures.

The assumption of contextual and inferential orientations to information processing is important to understanding cognitive concomitants in psychopathology. The cognitive model posits that in psychopathological states, information relevant to a disorder is primarily processed inferentially or heuristically because dominant prepotent maladaptive schemas will select, abstract, and elaborate this information thereby determining individuals' interpretation of their experience. In nonclinical or normal states, interpretations will be more evenly balanced between information derived from the context and higher-order inferences. In nonclinical states individuals are both "constructivists" and "empiricists"; whereas in psychological disorders, individuals are driven primarily by their constructions or inferences of reality. Given this situation, cognitive therapy seeks to encourage the patient to adopt an empiricist approach, testing out inferences against the real-life context.

6. *Cognitive constructions are at best an approximate representation of experience.*

All human information processing is egocentric and so results in a biased or "filtered" representation of reality. This premise is logically related to our previous discussion concerning the constructive nature of meaning-assignment. Whenever humans process social or other experiential events, such events impinge on or interact with the human information processing system. However, that system itself is intrinsically limited in its structure and processing by the teleonomic purposes for which it originally evolved. Thus, there are assumed to be biases in information processing.

The concept "cognitive distortion" was coined to convey this intrinsic bias in processing, especially as it is implicated in psychopathological states and disorders of personality (A. Beck, 1963). However, cognitive theory and therapy has never claimed that information processing is inherently accurate or unbiased in normal conditions. Indeed, the notion of "accuracy" within clinical cognitive theory is far less relevant than the concept of "adaptation." The cognitive therapist is not primarily interested in whether a person may be entirely accurate in formulating his or her objective situation with respect to life problems. The more relevant question is whether the person is able to conceptualize the situation *in a manner that will facilitate mastery or coping.* Thus accuracy in perceiving or conceptualizing events is not assumed to vary as a function of normal versus psychopathological states. In fact, early in the development of cognitive theory, Beck noted:

> While some degree of inaccuracy and inconsistency would be expected in the cognitions of any individual, the distinguishing characteristic of the depressed patients was that they showed a *systematic error;* viz, a bias against themselves. (p. 328)

Cognitive theory, then, does not assert that information processing is distorted in psychological disturbance but is accurate or unbiased in non-clinical states. Instead, cognitive theory states that all information processing is at best a biased approximation of reality. What does distinguish information processing in clinical states is the extent to which systematic errors are present and the degree to which processing occurs inferentially as a result of prepotent dysfunctional schemas.

This assumption also challenges the belief that there is only one correct way to formulate a human understanding of the phenomena of interest. This view is obviously mistaken. Indeed, the inculcation of flexible thinking is one aim of cognitive therapy, and in so doing the cognitive therapist encourages the client to take multiple perspectives of events, situations, and people that the patient is typically viewing in a narrow, biased, unidimensional manner. This means that in explaining the onset, duration, and correction of a depressive episode, the application of cognitive theory will be only one of multiple potential theoretical positions that are possible for humans to construct. However, the empirical validity, parsimony, consistency, scope of explanatory power, and testability of the cognitive theory can be compared with that of the other "competing" theories to evaluate the scientific status of cognitive theory and therapy.

7. *Meaning-assignment structures (schemas) develop through repeated interactions between the environment and innate rudimentary schemas.*

The cognitive model postulates that meaning-making structures or schemas develop through the continuous interaction of the organism with the environment. In this way, the environment does have a profound influence in shaping the cognitive organization of individuals (A. Beck, 1970, 1985a).

Schematic development takes the form of increasing elaboration and connections with other schemas in the cognitive organization. Thus schemas that are activated frequently by external circumstances will become more elaborated thereby increasing their dominance within the cognitive organization. However, cognitive theory does not assume that meaning structures develop solely as a result of transactions with the environment. Instead, the model assumes that some genetic or biological propensity or prototype for meaning structures exists within the developing human organism. This rudimentary structure, then, constitutes the framework on which experience shapes the development of the cognitive organization. As can be seen in this proposition, the cognitive model readily acknowledges that the person-environment relationship can be described in terms of reciprocal determinism.

This reciprocal interaction between internal meaning-making structures or schemas and the characteristics or features of the environment can lead to maladaptive interpretations about the self, environment, and the future. The concept of the *negative cognitive triad*, then, is derived from this assumption. It states that in depression, an interaction between predisposing depressotypic schemas, or the propensity to make negative personal interpretations, and loss or deprivation experiences in the real world will result in the generation of negative interpretations or meanings about the self, world, and future.

8. *The organization of meaning representation is characterized by different levels of conceptualization, with broader more general concepts encompassing lower more specific units of structure.*

The cognitive model assumes a particular organizational pattern to the information processing system. Previously, the model proposed a hierarchical organization to information processing, with more basic organizational units like schemas feeding into broader levels of conceptualization such as modes and personality suborganizations (A. Beck, Freeman, & Associates, 1990). Derived from this notion, we now propose that cognitive organization is more accurately represented in terms of layers where general cognitive concepts encompass more specific conceptualizations.

At the most basic level of conceptualization, one finds the *schemas*. The schemas are the basic units of meaning representation and so are integral to other levels of cognitive conceptualization. At the next level, schemas cluster together to form *modes*. It is at the modal level that we find the cognitive representation of psychological disorders (Beck, 1996). An even broader level is apparent in personality which involves the interconnection of various modes and their schemas. We elaborate on this aspect of the cognitive model in more detail in Chapter 4. For now, it is enough to say that the architecture of information processing can be most accurately depicted in terms of layers of increasingly broader levels of representation, with the schemas assumed to be the building blocks of cognitive organization.

9. *Meaning-making structures of the information processing system are characterized by different levels of threshold activation.*

The cognitive model assumes that schemas and their conglomerates, modes, differ in their ease of activation by environmental stimuli. Activation of schemas occurs through the orienting process which matches the stimulus features of the environment with the relevant schemas so that the meaning of the situation can be construed. This matching of internal representations with external environmental demands is the fundamental *modus operandi* of the information processing system and enables the human organism to respond in a meaningful way.

Schemas and their modes differ in their resting levels of activation. Certain schemas have a low threshold of activation so that they may become hypervalent, thereby dominating the information processing system once activated. The frequency with which a schema is activated either by the environment or by other schemas determines its level of threshold activation. Frequent activation will lower threshold activation so that eventually the schema may become hypervalent. Hypervalent schemas and modes are characterized by (a) their facility to be triggered by a wide range of environmental stimuli, (b) their activation by even trivial matching stimuli, (c) their speed and efficiency of activation, (d) their ease of accessibility, (e) their dominance of the information processing system once activated, and (f) their resistance to deactivation.

The existence of hypervalent schemas and modes is readily apparent in psychopathological states. For example, in depression one finds prepotent, idiosyncratic dysfunctional hypervalent schemas of personal loss and failure, whereas in anxiety the hypervalent schemas of personal threat, danger, and vulnerability exist (A. Beck et al., 1979, 1985). It is likely that hypervalent schemas are also evident in other psychological conditions, such as in repetitive acts of behavior or emotional responding. An impulsive person, for example, may evidence hypervalent schemas involving immediate gratification, or an angry individual may have hypervalent schemas for offense and personal injustice.

Although hypervalent schemas and modes are difficult to deactivate, the threshold of activation that characterizes schemas and modes is modified by environmental exigencies. Different information from the environment may activate competing or compensatory schemas that will then deactivate or counter the dysfunctional hypervalent schemas. This is the fundamental process that underlies cognitive therapy. The cognitive therapist purposefully provides competing information and experiences that activate compensatory schemas, and this process deactivates hypervalent dysfunctional schemas.

10. *Two orientations are represented in the information processing system, the first aimed at the primary goals of the organism and the second aimed at secondary constructive goals.*

The cognitive model posits that two orientations are evident within the information processing system. The first orientation, the primitive or *primal level*, consists of schemas and modes involved in meeting the immediate and more basic requirements that are crucial to the survival of the organism (A. Beck, 1970, in press). In fact, cognitive organization at the primal level would be the most basic part of the information processing system, which evolved to ensure the survival of the organism. Thus the primal level is concerned with basic organismic needs and so has as its goals preservation, reproduction, dominance, and sociability (A. Beck, Freeman, & Associates, 1990).

The primal mode consists of basic cognitive, behavioral, affective, motivational, and physiological schemas concerned with the survival of the organism. Because of this rudimentary function, the primal mode evolved to maximize processing speed and efficiency. As a result, most primal processing occurs at the automatic or preconscious level, and when activated tends to dominate the information-processing system. As well, the primal schemas tend to be more rigid, inflexible, and relatively unelaborated. Primal mode activation, then, will take precedence over secondary processing requirements and so may interfere or conflict with personal goals or group norms (A. Beck, Freeman, & Associates, 1990). The cognitive basis of psychiatric and personality disorders can be found at the primal level where idiosyncratic and unrealistic concerns derived from the primitive schemas become hypervalent and dominate the information processing system.

The second orientation within the information processing system is concerned with productive activities that increase vital resources for the individual (A. Beck, 1996). Personal goals and aspirations are represented at this level, as well as the norms and guiding principles of society. This orientation is represented by positive modes and *constructive schemas* that are designed to maximize accuracy and adaptability. Consequently this processing tends to occur at the conscious level, and is more controlled and deliberate in nature. The schemas tend to be more elaborated, easier to access, and more flexible than schemas having a primal orientation. It is at this constructive level that we find the human capacity for analytical, rational thinking, problem-solving abilities, and creativity. In psychological disorders, the constructive schemas are less active because of the dominance of primal concerns (A. Beck, 1996).

Consistent with cognitive theory, Sjolander (1997) suggests that cognitive representations ". . . have been selected, not because they are more *true* than others, or *depict* reality, but since they allow us to *behave in an adaptive way—kill the antelope, make the spear,*" and so on (p. 596, emphasis in original). Regarding disordered (maladaptive) conditions such as depression, cognitive theory postulates a specific cognitive representation or *meaning* is linked to the systems that are responsible for actions that relate to survival (Alford & Beck, 1997). In the case of depression, the representation of self, world, and future is one of reduced possibilities for gain; the cognitive "loss" interpretation reduces perceived possibilities (strategies) for obtaining commodities necessary for survival and thriving. Thus, "negative cognitive bias" is a mental representation or construction of a specific context, a conceptualization, rather than an absolute quantity of something (i.e., "truth" or "accurate perception of the world"). Cognitive therapy, then, seeks to shift the information processing system from the primal (survival mode) to the secondary or constructive (gain) level of functioning.

11. *Psychological disturbance is characterized by excessive and/or deficient activation of the specific meaning-assignment structures of the information processing system.*

The cognitive model assumes that in negative psychological states a bias occurs in the information processing system in the form of excessive or deficient functioning of particular meaning structures or schemas.

What occurs in most psychopathological states is the excessive and inappropriate activation of specific idiosyncratic, primal schemas that introduce a selectivity and narrowing of information processing. At the same time, there is inadequate or deficient activation of other more adaptive schemas that would compensate for the selective and narrow focus of the dysfunctional primal schemas (A. Beck, 1987; A. Beck et al., 1985).

Psychological disorders will differ in the extent to which their cognitive dysfunction is the result of excessive activation of maladaptive schemas or deficient activation of more adaptive, compensatory schemas. Cognitive deficiencies are most apparent in disorders involving poor impulse control or aggressive acting out in which the individual acts without thinking or fails to process relevant information (Kendall, 1985). Other negative psychological states may involve excessive cognitive processing such as worry over failure in a difficult task performance, which can lead to the allocation of extra processing resources to reduce the negative effects of worry (M.W. Eysenck & Calvo, 1992). Depression, on the other hand, presents a complicated information-processing problem. The activation of dysfunctional depressotypic schema is associated with the excessive allocation of processing resources for schema-congruent negative self-referent information. However, deficiencies are also evident in the relative inactivity of the more functional positive schemas resulting in the failure to allocate sufficient processing resources to positive self-referent information (A. Beck, 1987).

As noted in Chapter 1, the cognitive model assumes a continuity between the milder, nonclinical states of depression and the more severe forms of disturbance such as major depressive disorder. The "psychological disturbance" assumption is a reaffirmation of the continuity perspective. The information-processing bias associated with psychological disorders is not considered qualitatively different from the cognitive errors and selective processing characteristics that have been found in normal nonclinical individuals (Markus, 1977; Markus & Wurf, 1987; Taylor & Brown, 1994). The difference is one of degree rather than kind. In negative psychological states, the bias in the information processing system (i.e., excesses and deficiencies) becomes significantly more exaggerated, especially when processing self-referent information.

The assumption of a biased information processing system in psychological disorders is a central proposition of the cognitive model. The existence of this bias is considered crucial to understanding much of the personal dysfunction and symptomatology associated with psychological disorders. It is within this context that the cognitive dysfunction that characterizes psychological disorders like depression is understood to play a primary role in the etiology, maintenance, and recovery process.

12. *Modification of meaning-assignment structures is central to the human change process.*

If dysfunctional or maladaptive information processing is considered central to the cognitive model of depression, then it should come as no surprise that modification of this processing system is considered crucial to the human change process. Cognitive therapy assumes that change in the maladaptive cognitions, processing strategies, and structures is critical to the symptomatic improvement that is evident during recovery from negative emotional disorders such as depression (A. Beck et al., 1979; Haaga et al., 1991; Robins & Hayes, 1993). A person who suffers from negative biases in the processing of personally relevant information (meaning) can potentially correct such biases through collaboration with a cognitive therapist. Consequently, cognitive therapy alleviates symptomatic distress by targeting for change the maladaptive structures and processes that characterize emotional disorders. The fact that a therapeutic relationship is necessary (but not sufficient) for clinical change in cognitive therapy implies that the responsibility is shared between therapist and patient. Thus, the concerns that cognitive therapy—by centering on the potential for personal cognitive control over emotions—"blames the victim" are mistaken (for a more complete discussion of this issue, see Gilbert, 1992, pp. 411–412).

A variety of intervention strategies (i.e., cognitive, behavioral, experiential, relational, or pharmacological) may be used to bring about change in the faulty information processing system (D.A. Clark, 1995). However the degree of symptomatic improvement brought about by these interventions will depend on the extent of change produced in the information processing system. Moreover, recovery will be more enduring and relapse reduced if the underlying maladaptive meaning-structures, and not just negative thinking, are targeted for change during treatment (A. Beck et al, 1979; Robins & Hayes, 1993).

SCIENTIFIC OR CLINICAL THEORY?

Given the previously described theoretical framework, does the cognitive model remain within the domain of scientific theory? Writers have questioned the scientific status of cognitive theory. Blaney (1977) criticized Beck's cognitive model as being too imprecise and too accommodating of contradictory findings on depression, thereby making it relatively immune to disconfirmation and so unsatisfactory as a scientific theory. Other writers have argued that key concepts, such as depressive schema, are incompletely specified and imprecise (Alloy, Hartlage, & Abramson,

1988; Coyne & Gotlib, 1983). In fact, Coyne and Gotlib (1986) charged that the key concepts in the cognitive model are "loosely metaphorical in nature" (p. 697). Beidel and Turner (1986) went even further, charging that cognitive behavior treatment strategies do not have an adequate theoretical basis and should instead be subsumed under the "established laws of learning" (p. 193–194). Williams, Watts, MacLeod, and Mathews (1997) also concluded that core concepts of the cognitive model such as "schema" are not clearly defined, that cognitive theory is less concerned with tacit cognitive processes (e.g., selective attention, encoding, and retrieval), and that the model was not designed to make experimentally testable predictions but rather to guide treatment.

Teasdale and Barnard (1993) argued that Beck's cognitive model of depression is a clinical rather than scientific theory, and so is inadequate as a guiding theory for experimentation on psychological disorders such as depression. These authors cite four problems with the cognitive model. First, like others, they claim that the concepts of Beck's model are too vague and imprecise to serve as a valid model for experimentation. Teasdale (1996) further commented that the imprecise, commonsense language of the cognitive model does not provide an adequate framework for integrating the findings and concepts of cognitive science with the therapeutic challenges that face the clinician. The second criticism of the cognitive model levied by Teasdale and Barnard is contained in their view that the theory was derived primarily from clinical observation and that:

> . . . the main purpose of the theory is to guide the clinician in understanding and treating patients, rather than to provide a detailed exposition articulated in precise theoretical terms. (Teasdale & Barnard, 1993, p. 7)

Third, Teasdale and Barnard claim that changes have been made to the theory over time in a rather unsystematic manner in response to difficulties encountered with earlier versions of the model. And finally, the theory fails to account for the results of experimental studies on the relation between mood and cognition. In particular, they claim that the cognitive model cannot account for differences between "intellectual" and "emotional" beliefs. As an alternative approach, Teasdale and Barnard recommend the *applied science approach,* which takes a "real-world" problem and utilizes existing experimental paradigms to develop in the laboratory the essential features of the problem. Theoretical accounts are then developed of experimentally demonstrated phenomena and refined through an iterative process by reference to the initial real-world problem and the laboratory findings.

Are these criticisms concerning the scientific basis of Beck's cognitive theory justified? A number of problems with these viewpoints must be addressed. First, how precise are the concepts of cognitive theory? Concepts like cognitive errors, schemas, and automatic thoughts have undergone considerable changes in the past 30 years and have resulted in greater precision and clarity in our terminology. However, the criteria for judging the precision of a theory is the degree to which it can generate testable, refutable hypotheses that can be subjected to experimental scrutiny. As will be shown in subsequent chapters of this book, Beck's cognitive theory has generated a considerable volume of empirical research, a point also acknowledged by Teasdale and Barnard (1993). If the theory was so imprecise, how was it able to generate such a body of research? Surely the precision of a theory must be judged in part by its heuristic value rather than subjective judgments on what seems too vague or imprecise to a particular reader. Naturally, cognitive theory like all theories must evolve and improve the precision and clarity of its constructs. But ultimately the test of the viability of a theory rests with the quality and quantity of research it generates on a particular "real-world" problem.

Teasdale and Barnard (1993) also stated that Beck's theory was derived from clinical observation and so is a clinical rather than scientific theory. We believe the authors have misrepresented the origins of cognitive theory. As discussed in Chapter 2, Beck's early formulation of cognitive theory was based on both his experimental studies on masochism and clinical observation. In fact, the continuing iterative process of laboratory experimentation and reference to a real-world problem (i.e., depression) through clinical observation fits very well with the applied science approach described by Teasdale and Barnard. Thus it is incorrect to characterize Beck's cognitive theory as a purely clinical theory derived solely from clinical observation. In the formative years of the model, key aspects of depression were operationalized in terms of laboratory paradigms (i.e., response to failure, performance expectations, memory recall, the effects of verbal reinforcement-punishment), and their findings had an important impact in shaping Beck's initial formulation of the cognitive model of depression. Contrary to Teasdale and Barnard, we suggest that this process fits very well with the development of a scientific theory of depression.

Third, Teasdale and Barnard (1993) claim that the changes made to cognitive theory were unsystematic in response to difficulties encountered with earlier versions of the model. We agree with Teasdale and Barnard that the cognitive model has evolved, but whether it has been done in an unsystematic fashion is open to interpretation. The model has been elaborated over the years as it has been applied to an increasing number of psychological disorders. When cognitive theory and therapy was applied to the treatment of anxiety and then personality disorders, this required revisions to the theory and therapy that could not be anticipated when it was only focused on depression. Thus the changes that occurred to cognitive theory and therapy were necessary as it was expanded to apply to an increasing number of "real-life" problems. A second impetus for change came from the findings of empirical research. Although one could rather cynically view this as an attempt to salvage the model in the face of contradictory evidence, is it not expected that a scientifically based theory would change in the face of disconfirming empirical findings? If data from the laboratory expose weaknesses or even contradictions to a theory, should the theory not be revised to account for these new findings? The alternative would be to hold on to psychological theories despite the results of empirical investigation. The changes that have been made to the cognitive model are evidence of its scientific orientation as it attempts to be responsive to the findings of laboratory research and the features of real-life problems.

And finally, the cognitive model has been criticized for failing to explain key findings in cognitive experimental studies of anxiety and depression. If this criticism is true, then it indicates that the theory, as with all scientific theories, can be refuted. We would also note that any scientific theory must not be so highly abstract that in the process it eliminates important characteristics of the phenomena of interest, in this case, subjective meaning assignment that serves adaptive functions. This, of course, is just the danger with cognitive theories that draw analogies between human information processing and nonhuman computational devices that manipulate and store symbols. The computer analogy breaks down because meaning is only present at the level of the operator who interprets the symbols in terms of the purposes of the operator.

We will, for the time being, suspend judgment on the empirical validity of cognitive theory and therapy because Chapters 5 through 10 provided comprehensive and detailed review of the relevant empirical research on depression. In the end, it is up to readers to judge for themselves the scientific viability of Beck's cognitive theory of depression in light of the empirical literature. In the meantime, we turn our attention to a detailed account of the cognitive model.

SUMMARY

In this chapter, we have presented the philosophical and theoretical foundations of cognitive theory and therapy. The cognitive model takes an existential phenomenological perspective that is consistent with a commonsense view of life. The origins of cognitive theory and therapy are rooted in the philosophy of the Greek Stoics and 19th-century phenomenologists like Kant and Husserl; certain structural elements of psychoanalysis; the cognitive psychology of Bartlett, Kelly, and Arnold; and the empiricism of behavior therapy (A. Beck & Weishaar, 1989; Pretzer & Beck, 1996). Subjective consciousness, the centrality of the self, and the proclivity for meaning construction are pivotal to the cognitive perspective.

Table 3.1 summarizes the theoretical assumptions of the cognitive model that are consistent with existential phenomenology. These implicit propositions state the fundamental assumptions that define the cognitive model. The concepts and hypotheses that comprise the cognitive model can be derived from these assumptions. The assumptions are not truths

Table 3.1

The Theoretical Assumptions of the Cognitive Theory of Depression

1. The capacity to process information and form cognitive representations of the environment is central to human adaptation and survival.

2. Human information processing occurs at different levels of consciousness as a means of promoting its efficiency and adaptability.

3. A basic function of information processing is the personal construction of reality.

4. Information processing serves as a guiding principle for the emotional, behavioral, and physiological components of human experience.

5. Cognitive functioning consists of a continuous interaction between lower-order, stimulus driven processes and higher-order semantic processes.

6. Cognitive constructions are at best an approximate representation of experience.

7. Meaning-assignment structures (schemas) develop through repeated interactions between the environment and innate rudimentary schemas.

8. The organization of meaning representation is characterized by different levels of conceptualization, with broader more general concepts encompassing lower more specific units of structure.

9. Meaning-making structures of the information processing system are characterized by different levels of threshold activation.

10. Two orientations are represented in the information processing system, the first aimed at the primary goals of the organism and the second aimed at secondary constructive goals.

11. Psychological disturbance is characterized by excessive and/or deficient activation of the specific meaning-assignment structures of the information processing system.

12. Modification of meaning-assignment structures is central to the human change process.

but rather statements that serve to clarify and define the cognitive model. Furthermore, they function to set the theoretical boundaries of cognitive theory and therapy (for discussion, see D.A. Clark, 1995). Whether a particular theoretical construct of depression or an intervention strategy is considered a variant of the cognitive model or not depends on whether it is consistent with the theoretical assumptions discussed in this chapter. Theoretical constructs and therapy approaches that subscribe to these assumptions can be integrated so that the cognitive model "provides a unifying theoretical framework within which the clinical techniques [and constructs] of other established, validated approaches may be properly incorporated" (Alford & Beck, 1997, p. 112). To the extent that theoretical constructs and therapy approaches diverge from these basic assumptions, they will be incompatible with Beck's cognitive theory.

Having described the philosophical and theoretical basis of cognitive theory, we then examined whether the model meets criteria as a scientific theory. We noted the arguments raised by Teasdale and Barnard (1993), Blaney (1977), and Coyne and Gotlib (1983) suggesting that the cognitive model may not be scientific. However, this conclusion may be premature because the scientific status of cognitive theory can only be judged in terms of its clinical utility and empirical validity. It is the purpose of the remaining chapters in this volume to consider the empirical status of the cognitive explanation for depression. Before proceeding with this evaluation, however, it is important to elaborate on cognitive theory based on the theoretical assumptions just presented. This is the topic of Chapter 4.

CHAPTER 4

The Cognitive Theory
of Depression

CHAPTER 3 focused on the theoretical assumptions that underlie the cognitive theory of depression. In this chapter, we expand on these precepts by providing a detailed description of the current version of the cognitive perspective on depression. As noted, the cognitive theory has undergone considerable elaboration since its inauguration more than 30 years ago. One aim of this chapter is to present within a single volume a complete and up-to-date description of the cognitive formulation of depression. Second, we will emphasize throughout this chapter precise definitions of each of the key concepts in the cognitive theory and explain how these concepts are functionally interrelated. And finally, this chapter provides the theoretical foundation from which we derive hypotheses at the descriptive and vulnerability levels. The empirical research relevant to these hypotheses is the focus of the remaining chapters in this book.

According to the cognitive formulation, **affect (or emotion)** *is a subjective state resulting from the appraisal or evaluation of internal or external stimuli* (A. Beck, 1976). Like other cognitive theories of affect or emotion, CT proposes that the manner in which an event or stimulus is appraised or evaluated determines the type, intensity, and persistence of the experienced emotion (see also S. Epstein, 1984; Frijda, 1987; Lazarus, 1977, 1989; Roseman, 1984; C. Smith & Ellsworth, 1985). Moreover, emotional experience occurs within the context of a dynamic interaction or transaction between the person and the environment (Lazarus, Kanner, & Folkman, 1980).

Cognitive theory focuses on four basic emotions that motivate or reinforce adaptive behavior involved in the attainment of basic human objectives such as survival, security, procreation, and sociability (A. Beck &

Clark, 1997; A. Beck, Freeman, & Associates, 1990). Moreover, there is a specificity between emotions and meaning assignment. *Sadness* is evoked by the perception of loss, deprivation, or defeat; whereas happiness or *elation* involves appraisals of gain. *Fear* and its emotional concomitant, anxiety, occur in response to evaluations of danger and personal vulnerability; whereas *anger* is elicited in response to perceptions of offense and injustice (A. Beck, 1991). The cognitive theory is applicable to the full range of emotion because it assumes a dimensional perspective on emotional experiences with affective disorders representing an exaggerated and persistent form of normal emotional functioning (A. Beck, 1991).

The cognitive theory also recognizes a close connection between personality, emotion, and psychological disorders. The cognitive-personality constructs of sociotropy and autonomy were introduced as an expansion of the cognitive theory of depression to account for the observed continuity between premorbid personality, an individual's cognitive structures, and the development of depression (A. Beck, 1983). This assumed link between emotion, personality, and psychological disorders has a long tradition in clinical and personality psychology (L.A. Clark et al., 1994; H.J. Eysenck, 1952b, 1997; Larsen & Diener, 1987; Watson & Tellegen, 1985).

The cognitive theory of depression adopts a schema-based information-processing paradigm of human functioning as evident from the theoretical assumptions discussed in Chapter 3. **Information processing** refers to *the structures, processes, and products involved in the representation and transformation of meaning based on sensory data derived from the external and internal environment.* Thus an information processing system with cognitive structures and processes that select, transform, encode, store, retrieve, and regenerate information in a meaningful way is at the heart of human adaptation and function (Ingram & Kendall, 1986). However, all cognitive operations within the information processing system are predicated on the existence of symbolic structures dedicated to the representation of meaning. It is this meaning-making capability that cognitive theory considers central to the human organism's adaptation to the environment. Although meaning representation is the core construct in the cognitive theory of emotion, these structures do not lead directly to subjective emotion. Rather meaning structures lead to cognitive, behavioral, and somatic phenomena that mediate between symbolic representation and the actual emotional response. Thus we concur with Lazarus and Smith's (1988) assertion that meaning representation (or knowledge) does not lead directly to emotion but rather to cognitions and evaluations of the personal significance of a situation or encounter for one's well-being. It is this cognitive phenomenal or "product" side of the theory involving

specific types of cognitions and evaluative patterns that, in part, constitute the emotional experience.

The chapter is organized around three main perspectives on cognition
as structure, process, and product. An overview of the cognitive theory of
depression is illustrated in Figure 4.1.

As can be seen in Figure 4.1, the structural level is represented by four
concepts that are integral to the cognitive theory; schemas, modes, and
personality, as well as the orienting schemas which are responsible for
the initial detection of stimuli. These structures, however, are not static
but are instead dynamic and operative. Cognition (i.e., structure, process,
and product) interacts with the environment or context within which the
person resides. As such the term "cognition" as used in cognitive theory
does not refer to a static set of "machinery" within the person, but rather
to the engagement of the person with the world at large. Cognition intrinsically is about some context. As defined in cognitive therapy, cognition
incorporates (i.e., represents) aspects of the world, thus providing a
person-environment synthesis. The cognitive theory considers *schemas,
modal activation, selective cognitive processing, states of consciousness,* and *attention* important aspects of a cognitive formulation of depression. Under
the products of the cognitive theory, we deal with the phenomenological
side of the cognitive organization—negative automatic thoughts, constructions, and perspectives. The chapter concludes with a brief consideration of self-representation within the cognitive theory of depression.

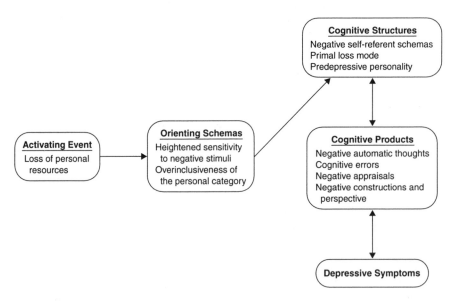

Figure 4.1 Cognitive Model of Depression.

COGNITIVE STRUCTURE:
THE REPRESENTATION OF MEANING

SCHEMAS

The concept of mental representation is a core assumption within mainstream cognitive science (Mahoney, 1991). For the cognitive theory, schemas are the basic elements or building blocks for the internal representation of meaning. **Schemas** are *relatively enduring internal structures of stored generic or prototypical features of stimuli, ideas, or experience that are used to organize new information in a meaningful way thereby determining how phenomena are perceived and conceptualized* (A. Beck, 1964, 1967; Williams et al., 1997). As hypothetical structures containing the stored representation of meaning, schemas are pivotal in guiding the selection, encoding, organization, storage, and retrieval of information within the cognitive apparatus. Furthermore, schemas have a consistent internal structure that is imposed on new information entering the cognitive system (Williams et al., 1997).

Schemas may be relatively simple so that they represent a single concept such as chair, or they may be more complex, involving the representation of a single, multifaceted concept such as one's level of interpersonal acceptance. The schemas that are prepotent in depression tend to be of the more complex variety. Two general features of schemas are important in cognitive theory—content and structure. Ingram and Kendall (1986) also recognized these features in their cognitive taxonomy, referring to cognitive structure as the way in which information is internally organized and cognitive propositions (e.g., beliefs) as the content or information that is actually stored within the information processing system. We turn first to consider the structural aspects of depressotypic schemas.

Schema Structure

As meaning structures of the information processing system, schemas can be described in terms of their structural characteristics as well as their content. Although the structural considerations of schemas have generally been ignored by cognitive-clinical theorists and researchers, their importance should not be overlooked in the generation of emotion. The cognitive theory recognizes that the availability/accessibility of schematic content as well as the way meaning is structured in memory influences the production of emotional states like depression, a point emphasized by Segal (1988).

One way that schemas may differ structurally from each other is in the *degree of interrelatedness* of the elements or ideas that comprise the schemas. We would expect that schemas characterized by tightly interrelated elements are more easily activated, that is are prepotent, and so may more readily dominate the information processing system once they are activated. This is because tightly knit schema may have a lower activation threshold, with activation of one element of the schema tending to spread readily to activation of all the elements (Segal, 1988).

Another important structural characteristic is the *degree of complexity* or number of ideas (elements) that comprise a schema. Complex schemas involving a relatively large number of interrelated ideas will have a greater influence on the information processing system because they are activated by a wider range of stimuli and experiences. For example, the belief "I am physically unattractive" will have a much greater impact on self-referent thinking and evaluations than the belief "My hair is thinning." The "physically unattractive" schema is more complex because it has many elements involving such possible beliefs as I am overweight, too short, have a big nose, or a double chin. A greater range of stimuli in our environment would potentially activate this schema because its consists of a larger array of elements. The more specific "thinning hair" schema would consist of beliefs related only to hair and so would be triggered by a narrower range of stimuli. This may be one reason why the schemas involved in self-representation, which tend to be more complex, play such a crucial role in emotional disorders like depression.

Other qualities may also be important in distinguishing the structural elements of schemas. Schemas may vary in *flexibility or rigidity, permeability or impermeability, concreteness or abstraction, valence and breadth* (A. Beck, 1967; A. Beck, Freeman, & Associates, 1990). The valence or the level of activation required to engage a schema and its breadth or range of activating stimuli are discussed later in this chapter. Schemas that are rigid (i.e., consist of specific absolutistic ideas or statements) and impermeable (i.e., not amenable to change by incongruent information) may be particularly difficult to modify and so remain unaltered despite the repeated presentation of disconfirming information. On the other hand, whether rigid and impermeable schemas are adaptive or maladaptive will depend on what the schemas represent. One would expect specific schema involving the representation of distinct objects, for example a "chair," to be fairly concrete and possibly rigid but highly adaptive because they represent features of the environment.

A higher level of abstraction is needed for the representation of the self. In depression, the negatively oriented schemas that represent the self tend to be more rigid, absolute, and impermeable (A. Beck, 1967; A. Beck, Freeman, & Associates, 1990). Depressed individuals would also be expected to have negative self-referent beliefs that are more tightly interrelated and complex than the negative self-constructs of nondepressed persons. Thus the cognitive theory recognizes that structural features as well as thematic content distinguish the schemas activated in depression from schemas dominant in the nondepressed state. Having considered structural characteristics that distinguish dysfunctional depressotypic schemas from more functional schemas, we turn now to consider differences in thematic content, which has been the major focus of cognitive theory and therapy of depression.

Schema Content

Schemas contain internal representations or beliefs that are abstracted from data or experiences received by the information-processing system and so provide the basis of one's interpretation of life experiences. Schematic content, then, may include attitudes and ideas about one's self and the world around us. This content is considered crucial to determining the type and intensity of our emotional response through its symbolic representation of situations or stimuli (see Chapter 3, Assumption 3). For this reason, cognitive theory and therapy has focused almost exclusively on the role of schema content or meaning in the generation of normal and especially abnormal emotional experiences (A. Beck, 1971). The cognitive theory of depression focuses on enduring dysfunctional or maladaptive concepts, beliefs, or attitudes about the self, personal world, and future that may lead to a greater vulnerability or risk for depression (A. Beck, 1967; A. Beck et al., 1979). Referred to as the *cognitive triad*, this negative view of self, personal world, and future, which has been identified as a prominent feature of the cognitive organization in depression, is apparent in the activated schematic content of the depressed person.

Cognitive theory also assumes that the activated internal structures most relevant to the depressive experience refer exclusively to the self and so are self-referent. The depressed person, then, may be perfectly capable of processing information about others in a reasonably realistic fashion, but shows a systematic bias to generate negative interpretations with self-referent information because of the dominance of negative self-referent schemas. A considerable amount of research has gone into the assessment of this negative schematic content either through the use of self-report measures like the Dysfunctional Attitudes Scale (A. Weissman & Beck, 1978) or experimental procedures like self-referent encoding, emotional Stroop color naming, or autobiographical memory recall (Segal, 1988; Williams, 1984).

Two aspects of negative self-referent schematic content are important in the cognitive theory of emotion. Schema content occurs at different levels of specificity and generality: some schemas deal with specific beliefs, others involve conditional assumptions, and still other schemas represent core issues for the individual. Second, different schemas correspond to various aspects of the biopsychosocial systems of personality or psychological functioning. We turn first to consider the differentiation of schematic content according to its level of abstraction and generality.

Levels of Generality.   The cognitive theory recognizes that depressotypic schemas have different levels of generality or applicability for individuals and their understanding of themselves and the world around them. At least three levels of schema abstraction or generalization have been identified in writings on the cognitive theory of depression.

First, at the most specific level of abstraction one can find *simple schemas* that deal with single objects or very specific ideas in our physical and social world. Examples would be the multitude of schemas we have for stimuli we encounter in our everyday lives such as shoes, lamps, telephone poles, and the like. Much of our fund of general beliefs involving shared or public meanings about ourselves and our environment would consist of simple schemas. These schemas play a limited role in producing depression because they have minimal relation to personal values or goals.

A second level of schema generality or abstraction is apparent in the existence of an *intermediary* class of beliefs, rules, and assumptions. These intermediate beliefs and attitudes often take the form of rules which people use to evaluate themselves, other people, and their experiences (A. Beck et al., 1985). Intermediate beliefs are less concrete, more personal, and generally applied to a broader range of experiences than the specific schemas. An important class of intermediary belief we find in depression are *conditional rules* that take the form of "If . . . then" statements (A. Beck, 1987; A. Beck, Freeman, & Associates, 1990). Some examples of common conditional schemas or assumptions in depression are "If I please my partner, then he or she will treat me well," "If I work hard, then I will succeed," and "If I am criticized, then it means that I have failed."

Two other classes of intermediary beliefs have also been identified by cognitive therapists. The first are *imperative beliefs* involving "should" or "must" (A. Beck, 1976; Ellis, 1962; Horney, 1945). Examples include "I should never make a mistake" or "I must have the love and acceptance of everyone I meet." Ellis (1962, 1977) documented the importance of such imperative statements in the emotional disorders, particularly depression. They are strongly linked to the personal goals and values that motivate individual responses and adaptation.

Another class of intermediary belief recently introduced by A. Beck (1996) is that of *compensatory beliefs*. These beliefs refer to various strategies that individuals utilize in response to their core and other intermediary beliefs. The compensatory beliefs and strategies are automatic and maladaptive, and so require no conscious cognitive effort to implement.

They are an important part of the primal modes and so are often active in psychopathological states. The compensatory strategies represented by these beliefs can be distinguished from more conscious, controlled coping responses that are adaptive or maladaptive depending on current environmental demands (see also discussion under "Differential Coping Hypothesis" in Chapter 9). As an example of compensatory beliefs, consider that in response to the core belief "I am unlovable" and the accompanying conditional belief "If I don't please others, they will hate me," the individual may develop the compensatory belief that "If I do whatever they desire, I can please others." The conditional rules, imperative statements, and compensatory beliefs arise from their link to prepotent core beliefs and our interactions with the world around us (J. S. Beck, 1995). Because of their highly personal nature, the intermediate schemas play a vital role in the cognitive basis of depression and so are a major focus in the cognitive treatment protocol for this disorder.

At the broadest level of generality, we find the core beliefs. Core schema are usually expressed in terms of absolute statements and generally refer to attributes about the self. Consequently, most of the core beliefs take the form of cognitive-conceptual schemas (see following discussion), forming an important component of the self-concept. For depression-prone individuals, core beliefs such as "I am a failure," "I am worthless," or "I am unlovable" may predominate (A. Beck, 1987). More recently, two broad categories of core belief that are an integral part of the self-concept have been identified—the belief that "I am helpless (effective)" and the belief that "I am (un)lovable" (A. Beck, in press). These beliefs refer to issues of survival (helpless) and attachment (unloved) that are basic aspects of human adaptation.

Because of the fundamental generic nature of core beliefs, they are usually more global, overgeneralized, and absolute than the intermediary beliefs (J. S. Beck, 1995). They also possess a positive/negative polarity that may be manifest in many different ways. Thus the bipolar core beliefs linked to survival involve the negative core beliefs of helplessness (e.g., self-descriptors such as passive, weak, inadequate, inferior, incompetent, trapped, defenseless, stupid, powerless) and the positive beliefs of effectiveness (e.g., assertive, strong, adequate, superior, free, protected, powerful, smart). The dualistic core beliefs of attachment involve negative beliefs of being unloved (e.g., unattractive, undesirable, rejected, alone, unwanted, uncared for, bad, dirty) and positive beliefs of being loved and accepted (e.g., loved, valued, accepted, attractive, good). The positive concepts of the core beliefs are acquired as a person matures and proves their efficacy and acceptance by others. Under normal circumstances, the positive concepts can neutralize the negative self-concepts, but when experiencing stress or an adverse life circumstance, the negative polarity of the core beliefs will emerge (A. Beck, in press). This is particularly apparent in depression where the negative core beliefs (helplessness and unlovability) become activated and dominate the cognitive organization so that they influence the individual's susceptibilities, reactions, and behavior. Particular aspects of the negative core beliefs that may be linked to specific life situations have been labeled *cognitive vulnerabilities*. They play a particularly important role in the cognitive formulation of the pathogenesis of depression and are discussed in greater detail later in this chapter.

The core beliefs of the self-concept usually develop at an early stage of development as a result of the child's interaction with significant others such as parents, siblings, teachers, and friends (A. Beck, 1987). Although core beliefs do give rise to the intermediary beliefs and assumptions, individuals are rarely cognizant of their existence or influence. However, we would expect that individuals with prepotent negative core beliefs would have a greater tendency to experience strong and frequent negative emotions such as dysphoria, whereas individuals with positive core beliefs would show a greater tendency for positive emotional responses such as euphoria or joy. Because negative core beliefs are considered critical factors in the pathogenesis of depression, an important goal in cognitive therapy is to bring the negative core beliefs to the patient's awareness.

Types of Schemas

More recently, different types of schemas have been proposed that correspond to different functions or aspects of the biopsychosocial systems of the organism (A. Beck, 1996; Beck, Freeman, & Associates, 1990). The first type of schemas, the *cognitive-conceptual schemas*, are integral to the selection, storage, retrieval, and interpretation of information (A. Beck, 1963). These schemas enable us to make inferences and interpretations that are central to our meaning assignment capabilities, although the personal constructions of reality that result are at best an approximation of actual phenomena (see Chapter 4, Assumptions 3 and 6). The intermediary and core beliefs, referred to previously, are represented by cognitive-conceptual schemas that relate to our self-identity, personal goals, and values. Because the internal representation of the self (i.e., self-concept) occurs at this cognitive-conceptual basis, one of the key functions of the cognitive-conceptual schemas is to evaluate stimuli in order to distinguish between concerns that are of a personal, self-referent nature, from concerns that have a more impersonal focus. Given our earlier contention that the faulty information processing in depression is primarily confined to the self-referent domain, this gives the cognitive-conceptual schemas a central role to the cognitive theory and therapy of depression.

The second type of schemas, *affective schemas,* are involved in the perception of feeling states and their various combinations. Affective schemas play a functional role within the psychobiological strategies concerned with the survival of the organism (A. Beck, 1996). Positive affect involving pleasure tends to reinforce adaptive behavior whereas negative affect tends to engage one's attention on a particular situation so that action can be taken to reduce potentially threatening or distressing circumstances. Affect, then, is functional, ensuring the long-term survival and adaptability of the human organism (A. Beck et al., 1985). The activation of these affective structures is integral to the experience of emotion.

Physiological schemas constitute a third type of cognitive structure representing somatic function and processes. The physiological schemas are involved in the processing of proprioceptive stimuli from the viscera and musculture of the body. These schemas are considered rudimentary but essential to the survival of the organism. They are vital to the representation of arousal and other basic physiological processes. The operation of the physiological schemas is particularly apparent in certain psychopathological conditions such as panic disorder and hypochrondriasis (A. Beck et al., 1985; D. M. Clark, 1986; McNally, 1994).

A fourth type of schema, the *behavioral schemas,* represent response disposition codes and action readiness programs that allow for the automatic and coordinated execution of the numerous motor responses involved in complex expressive behavior. The expressive action codes of the behavioral schemas vary in the extent to which they represent involuntary and innate action patterns, or voluntary, learned response dispositions. There are numerous behavioral response patterns that must be performed quickly, automatically, and effortlessly because they are crucial to our survival. These would include such expressive action patterns as (a) mobilization to escape or defend one's self against perceived danger, (b) the inhibition of risk-taking behavior, (c) the activation of avoidance behavior, and (d) the execution of behaviors focused on the conservation of resources when confronted with significant losses (A. Beck, 1995; A. Beck & Clark, 1997; A. Beck et al., 1985). In anxiety states, these schemas are activated during the immediate preparation stage (A. Beck & Clark, 1997).

We also recognize that other behavioral schemas represent more elaborated, learned response disposition patterns that involve a higher level of controlled information processing. These action programs are strongly linked to the cognitive-conceptual schemas and so are characterized by intentional, conscious processing. The activation of these intentional, learned behavioral response schemas has been labeled secondary elaboration in the cognitive theory of anxiety (A. Beck & Clark, 1997). Although the learned behavioral response schemas may operate more slowly than the innate, "primal" behavioral schemas, they are more flexible and so can be more efficiently applied to novel and difficult situations. As well, the learned behavioral response schemas can override the sometimes inappropriate activation of the innate primal behavioral schemas of survival.

The notion of behavioral schemas is particularly important in understanding the cognitive basis of anxiety and phobic disorders (A. Beck & Clark, 1997; A. Beck et al., 1985) because of the prominent role that avoidance and other threat-related behavioral responses (e.g., neutralizing rituals in obsessive compulsive disorder) play in the pathogenesis of anxiety. In depression, behavioral schemas representing conscious intentional strategies aimed at conserving one's energy and resources will be prominent (e.g., social withdrawal, lack of response initiation, isolation, passivity). An important task in cognitive therapy of depression involves the use of graded task assignment and mastery/pleasure exercises designed to counter the negative behavioral schemas active in episodic depression.

The *motivational schemas* are closely related to the behavioral domain. These schemas are relevant for varying levels of activity, directedness, and environmental responsiveness that exist in human beings (Pervin, 1994). Some of these schemas represent the automatic involuntary impulses and inhibitions associated with the primal behavioral strategies (A. Beck, 1996). These primal motivational schemas represent the biological goal-directedness involved in appetite, sexuality, pleasure, pain, reward, and punishment. Activation of these more rudimentary motivational schemas will be quite automatic and involuntary. The behavioral schemas associated with the biologically related motivational schemas will also be more primal in nature, with only minimal involvement of the cognitive-conceptual domain. For example, the automatic retraction or escape behavior executed in response to a painful stimulus involves the activation of primal motivational and behavioral schemas. There is a near universal basic motivation to avoid pain, and the quick retraction or escape when coming in contact with a pain-inducing stimulus is so stereotypic and, again, universal that the activation of primal behavioral schemas must be involved. In other words, we do not acquire a motive "not to touch hot stove burners" (and other burning objects) nor are we taught to pull our hand away should we come in contact with a hot burner.

Other motivational schemas are more elaborated, dealing with certain acquired motivations that are learned through our collective socialization process. These motivational schemas represent goal-directedness related to achievement, intimacy, interpersonal relatedness, and power. A third type of motivational schema focuses on more personalized, idiosyncratic goals, values, and expectancies. Motivational constructs proposed by other personality psychologists that would fall under this category include current concerns (Klinger, 1975), personal strivings (Emmons, 1986), and life tasks (Cantor, 1990) to name but a few. The motivational schemas representing acquired or personalized goals and values have a strong link with the cognitive-conceptual schema as well as the learned behavioral schemas. They also play an important role in the self-schema organization by representing goal striving related to issues of self-worth, productivity, and relatedness.

Dykman recently proposed a theoretical framework for understanding the contribution of motivational factors or goal striving to the manifestations of depression and depression proneness. This further elaboration is consistent with the current notion of maladaptive motivational schemas in depression. He argued that the goal striving most crucial in depression proneness "is the need to prove one's basic worth, competence and likeability" (Dykman, 1998, p. 141). Depression-prone individuals exhibit *validation seeking* characterized by personal strivings to prove their basic worth, competence, and likeability; whereas depression-resistant individuals are *growth seeking* such that their strivings are focused on learning, growth, self-improvement, and reaching their highest potential. Because depression-prone individuals are motivated to prove their self-worth, they will tend to appraise challenging and difficult situations as a test of their core worth, competence, or likeability. When the outcome from these situations is negative, validation seeking depression-prone persons will interpret this as an indication that they are lacking worth, competence, or acceptance by others. This evaluation would then lead to loss of self-esteem, disengagement from the task or situation, and depressed affect. Dykman reported results from five studies conducted on undergraduate samples that supported key predictions about validation seeking.

The importance of maladaptive motivational schemas in the cognitive basis of depression is evident in the prominence of motivation symptoms such as apathy, loss of interest, and anhedonia in the symptom profile of clinical depression (see Chapter 1). We postulate that in depression maladaptive motivation schemas are activated that represent limited and possibly restricted goal-directedness, reduced ability to derive pleasure from engaged activity, and a validation-seeking, self-worth orientation (Dykman, 1998). These schemas would lead to the sense of helplessness that often characterizes the depressed state. Having described the basic conceptual building blocks of the cognitive theory, the schemas, we consider next a more general level of conceptualization that has gained increasing attention in descriptions of the cognitive theory of depression.

MODES

The view that maladaptive idiosyncratic meaning structures or schemas form the basis of the cognitive dysfunction in emotional disorders has been the central premise of the cognitive theory for the past 30 years. However, A. Beck (1996) recently articulated several shortcomings with confining the conceptualization of emotion-related meaning structures to this single level of analysis. It was noted that simple schema theories cannot adequately account for (a) the high degree of symptom complexity seen in psychological disorders, (b) the broad systematic bias evident across many psychological domains suggesting a more global and complex schematic organization, (c) information processing involved in normal as well as abnormal emotional experiences, and (d) the cognitive basis of personality and its apparent continuity to psychopathology. A number of other cognitive theorists have concluded that a global or broader level of representation is needed to account for the cognitive basis of emotion (e.g., S. Epstein, 1994; Leventhal, 1985; Mandler, 1982; Mischel & Shoda, 1995; Oatley & Johnson-Laird, 1987; Teasdale & Barnard, 1993).

In the cognitive theory of depression the concept of mode represents a broader, more integrative, and organizing construct in the representation of meaning (A. Beck, 1996; see also Chapter 4, Assumption 8) than the more basic concept of schema. A **mode** is *a specific cluster of interrelated cognitive-conceptual, affective, physiological, behavioral, and motivational schemas organized to deal with particular demands placed on the organism.* Information processing at the modal level is characterized as more (a) complex, integrative, and global; (b) automatic, effortless, and less analytical; (c) hypervalent so that once activated it easily dominates the information processing system; and (d) "schema-driven." Thus appraisals or interpretations resulting from the activation of modal structures will primarily reflect characteristics of the mode itself rather than features of the situation. Because of this "top-down" or conceptually driven processing, meaning representation at the modal level is particularly relevant for understanding the cognitive basis of emotion and psychopathology. Distinct emotions and psychopathological states are the result of the activation of different modes. The cognitive theory proposes three major categories of mode.

Primal Modes

The first type of modal organization, the primal modes (see Chapter 3, Assumption 10), deals with immediate or basic issues related to the evolutionarily derived objectives of the organism (A. Beck, 1996). Self-preservation, procreation, safety, dominance, and sociability are so fundamental to the survival of the organism that they can only be met by a rapid, efficient, and automatic cognitive processing system. The primal modes meet these requirements and so have evolved to deal with the most basic needs of the organism. However, rapidity and efficiency are achieved at the cost of flexibility and amenability to conscious control. Consequently, primal mode processing may have a greater tendency to produce over- or underreaction to current environmental demands. Yet, it is important to recognize that primal processing is not always dysfunctional and may in fact be lifesaving in certain situations (A. Beck, 1996).

There are numerous primal modes each oriented toward implementing a particular goal-directed or compensatory strategy. The four basic emotions identified at the beginning of this chapter are each represented by a particular primal mode. The *threat mode,* for example, consists of (a) a perception of threat and insecurity derived from the cognitive-conceptual schemas, (b) feelings of anxiety or anger based on the affective schemas, (c) a perceived state of autonomic arousal contributed by the physiological schemas, (d) an intention to run or escape represented by the motivational schemas, and (e) a response action program aimed at dealing with the threat (i.e., fight or flight) derived from the behavioral schemas (A. Beck, 1996). The relevance of this mode for fear and anxiety disorders has been described elsewhere (A. Beck & Clark, 1997).

As illustrated in Figure 4.2, the *loss or deprivation mode* is characterized by (a) the perception of an actual or threatened loss of one's vital resources (cognitive-conceptual schemas); (b) a subjective state of dysphoria or sadness (affective schemas); (c) a perceived state of fatigue or

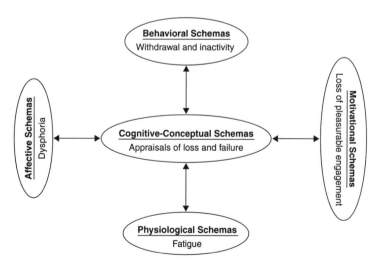

Figure 4.2 Primal Loss Mode Activation in Depression.

physiological deactivation (physiological schemas); (d) a state of helplessness, lack of goal-directedness, or loss of pleasurable engagement (motivational schemas); and (e) a response action plan characterized by withdrawal and inactivity (behavioral schemas). The *victim mode* involves (a) the perception of an injustice or offense against the self and self-interests (cognitive-conceptual schemas), (b) a subjective state of anger (affective schemas), (c) a perceived state of physiological activation (physiological schemas), (d) a perception that valued personal goals have been thwarted or blocked leading to frustration (motivational schemas), and (e) a response action plan characterized by verbal and/or physical attack directed at others (behavioral schemas). Each of these primal modes— threat, loss, and victim—evolved to deal with any situation that would threaten the survival of the organism.

Although positive affect or happiness may not be of the same valence as threat, loss, and anger, nevertheless, the emotion of happiness is integral to meeting the basic survival goals of the organism. There is considerable cross-cultural and psychophysiological evidence for the fundamental nature of happiness or enjoyment (Ekman, 1994; Ekman, Friesen, & Ellsworth, 1982; Izard, 1990, 1994; Lykken & Tellegen, 1996; J. Russell, 1991). Thus a *self-enhancement mode* is proposed characterized by (a) a perception of actual or anticipated personal gain (cognitive-conceptual schemas), (b) a subjective state of happiness (affective schemas), (c) perceived physiological activation (physiological schemas), (d) a state of pleasurable engagement (motivational schemas), and (e) an approach- or engagement-oriented response action plan (behavioral schemas). Activation of the gain primal mode would lead to the utilization of coping strategies that might maximize the survival and self-preservation of the organism. In extreme cases, it characterizes the underlying cognitive representation evident in mania.

If primal processing is involved, at least to some degree, in all emotional experiences, then how is the primal processing in psychological disorders different from primal processing associated with the normal range of emotions? There are at least two ways in which primal processing that leads to a clinical condition can be differentiated from primal processing in nonclinical individuals. First, a history of negative early childhood experiences may result in a primal mode that is unusually hypervalent and overgeneralized. For individuals with a cognitive vulnerability to depression, the primal loss mode will be prepotent and so more readily activated by a variety of situations that impinge on the individual. There also may be a genetic basis to modes so that depression-prone individuals inherit a predisposition to develop a hypervalent, overgeneralized primal loss mode. Whatever the genetic or developmental antecedents, activation of the loss mode in the vulnerable person tends to dominate the information processing system thereby preventing the activation of more adaptive compensatory modes of thinking. Second, certain situations or circumstances may be so chronically aversive or stressful that the primal mode is under a state of near constant stimulation. An example might be of an individual who experiences a very stressful work or family situation resulting in a *hypervalence* of the threat or victim mode. These situations could also be associated with a *hypovalence* of the self-enhancement mode resulting in a chronic negative emotional state characterized by anxiety, irritability, and unhappiness.

Constructive Modes

A second category of modes, the **constructive modes,** *are primarily acquired, or constructed through life experiences.* These modes promote productive activities aimed at increasing the vital resources of the individual (A. Beck, 1996). Our ability to relate effectively to others, to achieve and work productively, and to creatively meet the changing demands of our environment depends on information represented by the constructive modes. Constructive modes that might be necessary for healthy living include the capacity for intimacy or romance, effectiveness in interpersonal relations, achievement strivings, sense of personal mastery and effectiveness, creativity, independence, and other adaptive characteristics involving resilience, optimism, and rationality. Although the constructive modes are primarily strengthened and elaborated through learning experiences, it must be recognized that individuals may inherit a predisposition that facilitates the elaboration and refinement of the constructive modes. This can be seen in the traits of hardiness and resilience that are evident in some families.

The relation between the constructive modes and emotion is evident in two ways. First, the fulfillment of personal goals and expectations, as well as the expansion of vital resources, will be associated with positive emotions such as happiness, joy, and maybe even excitement. To the extent that constructive modes play a critical role in goal attainment, and productive and pleasurable activity, these modes will play a primary role in the cognitive basis of positive emotions. Second, intensely negative affective states such as depression may continue in part because of the inactivity or relative weakness of the constructive modes. Thus a shift from a negative to a euthymic mood state may not be possible until the constructive modes have been activated. The key to effective treatment of depression, then, involves a strengthening of constructive modes of thinking to maintain a shift in mood state from a negative to positive valence. In manic states, however, the constructive modes are as relatively inactive as in depressive states. In mania, it is the primal self-enhancement mode that becomes hypervalent and inappropriately dominates the information-processing system.

Minor Modes

The final category of modal thinking, the **minor modes,** represents *information related to prosaic activities in our everyday life such as reading, writing, conversing with others, driving a car, or engaging in athletic or recreational activities* (A. Beck, 1996). The minor modes have been acquired through our learning history and enable us to move and live adaptively in our immediate environment. These modes tend to focus narrowly on the immediate situation and are normally under flexible conscious control (A. Beck, 1996). They may also represent operations or procedural information that enables us to execute complex activities so that we can live and work adaptively in our environment. Conscious control over minor modal processing will be extensive, although still limited, because at times the information processing involved with activities like driving a car or reading a book can become quite automatic or effortless. Nevertheless, unlike the primal or constructive modes, there is considerable flexibility present in the minor modes so that we can easily switch from one mode of thinking to another. Although information processing at the theory level is an integral part of the cognitive basis of depression, the cognitive theory also recognizes another level of conceptualization that is equally important to understanding depression, that of the predepressive personality suborganization.

Personality

The cognitive theory defines **personality** *as a relatively stable organization of cognitive, affective, behavioral, motivational, and physiological schemas for representing adaptive or maladaptive responses to the normal demands and stresses of everyday life* (A. Beck, in press; A. Beck, Freeman, & Associates, 1990). The schematic structures of personality contain enduring orientations, rules, and behavioral inclinations that determine how we deal with the demands and opportunities of our environment and how we interact with others. Personality schemas represent our prevailing, enduring views and beliefs about ourselves as well as others with whom we come in contact (A. Beck, Freeman, & Associates, 1990). Consequently, they shape our perceptions, evaluations, and interpretations of our interpersonal relationships. Personality may also have a genetic basis in the form of inherited predispositions toward certain basic or "primeval" strategies for dealing with fundamental issues of survival and attachment (A. Beck, in press; Pretzer & Beck, 1996). However, it is also recognized that individual differences in patterns of interpretation and response are significantly influenced and modified by the experiences of life, especially early childhood experiences.

Because much of our adaptation and functioning occurs within an interpersonal context, personality and its dysfunctional variants, which we label personality disorders, are characterized not only by a set of interlocking schemas but also by particular behavioral inclinations or strategies that determine how we relate to others. These strategies of adjustment (or maladjustment) are represented within the personality schematic organization and deal with an individual's unique solution to reconciling the internal demands for survival and attachment with the external demands and exigencies of the environment (A. Beck, in press). In personality disorders, these interpersonal strategies or patterns of response tend to be overdeveloped or underdeveloped. For example, with the dependent personality disorder help seeking and clinging may be overdeveloped as enduring strategies for relating to others, whereas self-sufficiency and mobility are underdeveloped (A. Beck, Freeman, & Associates, 1990).

The concept of a schematic personality organization can be used to explain individual differences in vulnerability to depression. In 1983, the cognitive theory of depression was expanded to recognize that certain clusters of personality attributes or schemas may result in increased susceptibility to depression when these predisposed individuals experience a negative life stressor that matches their personality vulnerability (A. Beck, 1983). Two personality suborganizations were identified that may result in depressive vulnerability, sociotropy, and autonomy.

The sociotropic personality is oriented toward interpersonal relationships so that self-worth is based on receiving love and acceptance from others and maintaining close relations with others. The autonomous personality is oriented toward mastery and independence so that self-worth is based on productivity, achievement, and control. The prominent schemas for the sociotropic person represent one's self-evaluation in relation to others. Depressogenic sociotropic beliefs might be, for example, "They don't like me," "I am not wanted," "They just feel sorry for me," "I am unloved." Thus the sociotropic person fears abandonment and rejection by significant others. The schematic content of the autonomous person represents self-evaluation in relation to control, mastery, and achievement. "I have failed," "I am not in control of this situation," "I am helpless" are typical depressogenic autonomous beliefs. The autonomous person, then, fears being controlled, immobilized, or dependent on others. Each personality organization is also associated with a characteristic behavioral strategy. The sociotropic person will tend to rely on reassurance seeking, help, and appreciation from others and will avoid risk taking, uncertainty, or isolating one's self. On the other hand, the autonomous person will utilize strategies that involve task orientation, goal directedness, and problem solving and will avoid help seeking, reliance on others, and actions that constrain one's freedom of choice (A. Beck, 1983).

Two mechanisms are proposed for explaining how a sociotropic or autonomous personality orientation might lead to increased vulnerability to depression. First, the cognitive theory adopts a diathesis-stress perspective on the predisposition to depression. Thus the personality suborganization determines one's sensitivity and ability to cope with particular environmental stressors. The sociotropic person is more susceptible to perceived disruptions in social resources and so is at higher risk for depression after an event perceived as causing a loss of social acceptance or attachment. The autonomous person is more sensitive to circumstances that impede or thwart the attainment of valued goals and so is more vulnerable to depression after events perceived to involve a loss of independence, control, or accomplishment (A. Beck, 1987). Thus vulnerability to depression remains latent until activated by a matching life event.

Second, it must be recognized that some sociotropic or autonomous individuals are vulnerable to depression, whereas others may be relatively resistant to depression. This difference cannot be attributed solely to the presence or absence of matching life stressors. Rather, we propose that in addition to the occurrence of a congruent stressor, vulnerable individuals will exhibit strong connections between maladaptive personality schemas and the schemas of the primal loss mode. For nonvulnerable individuals, the schemas representing their sociotropic or autonomous concerns will not be as strongly connected with the primal loss mode but instead are more closely aligned with the schemas of the constructive modes. For example, a sociotropic person vulnerable to depression might have the belief "I must please others in order to be loved and accepted." This belief would also be apparent in the primal loss mode so that activation by a matching event (e.g., was unable to please spouse) would result in activation of this mode and the experience of a depressed mood. A nonvulnerable person might have the belief "I like to please others." This belief may be connected with the constructive modes so that the occurrence of a distressing event (e.g., was unable to please) results in adaptive coping.

The distinction between maladaptive and adaptive sociotropic and autonomous features has been recognized in empirical research on the Sociotropy-Autonomy Scale (SAS). As discussed in Chapter 8, certain aspects of autonomy such as fear of loss of control or solitude/insensitivity to others may be more closely related to psychopathology, whereas independence and self-determination may constitute adaptive features of autonomy (Bieling, Olshan, Brown, & Beck, 1998; D.A. Clark, Steer, Beck, & Ross, 1995). Although the distinction between maladaptive and adaptive features may not be as strong for sociotropy, there is some evidence that "excessive fear of other's appraisal (disapproval)" or "neediness" may be more pathologically oriented, and that "preference for affiliation" or "connectedness" may be less pathological or possibly even adaptive (Bieling & Olshan, 1998; Bieling et al., 1998; Rude & Burnham, 1995). A distinction must be made between adaptive and maladaptive sociotropic and autonomous beliefs, with a recognition that the strong interconnectedness between schemas of the personality and the primal loss mode provides the cognitive structural organization that can lead to the increased vulnerability of certain individuals to depression.

ORIENTING LEVEL

The final feature of cognitive representation is that of the orienting level of schematic organization. The **orienting schemas** are responsible for *a preliminary, rudimentary assignment of meaning based on a matching of environmental features with the various meaning-making organizations and structures of the information processing system.* These structures act as screeners; that is, a preattentive or preconscious stage of information registration. Mandler (1982) also recognized the need to postulate a set of cognitive-interpretative structures that provide an initial identification of the input so that meaning analysis can proceed. Information processing at this level will be quite rudimentary and undifferentiated, possibly limited to the recognition of stimulus valence and personal relevance (Mathews & MacLeod, 1994).

The orienting level of schematic representation plays a vital role in selectively activating the modes or schemas of the information-processing system. The orienting schemas act as "feature detectors," assigning a preliminary meaning to situations that impinge on the cognitive apparatus (A. Beck, 1996). By detecting certain relevant features of the situation, the orienting schemas then activate the meaning structures (modes or schemas) that represent the best match to the orienting classification. Thus the process of matching situation features via the orienting schemas provides the mechanism for schematic or modal activation in response to environmental input. Information processing at the orienting level is automatic in terms of being very rapid, involuntary, and outside conscious awareness (A. Beck & Clark, 1997).

The orienting schemas are firmly rooted in the biology and evolution-ary history of the organism. Although they can be modified by experi-ence, given the rudimentary nature of this level of processing, these schemas will remain quite elementary and undifferentiated throughout adult life. However, the orienting schemas may evidence certain biases, especially, for example, situations that threaten the vital resources and well-being of the individual. The emergence of threat or danger in our en-vironment usually results also in an instantaneous shift in attentional re-sources away from the activity we were engaged in toward the danger stimulus.

This adaptive function of the orienting schemas to assign attentional resources to stimuli that threaten the self is in part dependent on their dualistic nature. The orienting schemas rapidly allocate stimuli or events to "relevant to me" (i.e., personal) or "irrelevant to me" (i.e., impersonal) categories. The "not me" category includes events that do not fit with the significant concerns of the individual, that are neutral, or that are of little personal interest. However, the orienting schemas may be predisposed to give attentional priority to stimuli that are relevant to our personal concerns as opposed to stimuli that are more impersonal. In psy-chopathological conditions, the personal category becomes accentuated or hypervalent. As a result, the orienting schemas of the individual are overly inclusive so that irrelevant events become relevant, impersonal events become personal, and neutral events become negative or positively valenced. This is most evident in delusional paranoids who interpret to-tally irrelevant, innocuous, or remote events as personal. This also occurs to a lesser degree in depression where someone else's behavior is judged as personally relevant and negative even though it is not directed toward the individual. The cognitive dysfunction in depression is also evident even at this more rudimentary level of information processing.

SUMMARY

In this section, we provided a detailed account of the nature and function of the various structural components of the cognitive theory of depression. From our specification of the organization or interrelationships among the various structures within the theory (i.e., schemas, modes, personality, and orienting schemas), we have shown that meaning representation in depression is complex and multifaceted, requiring the operation of cogni-tive structures at varying levels of conceptualization. However, a cognitive explanation for depression cannot be adequately accounted for in terms of structure alone. The information processing system is a dynamic, fluid, and active system that is in a constant state of flux or change as it responds to the internal and external demands placed on it. For this reason, in the next section we discuss the operation or processing dynamics that characterize the information processing system.

COGNITIVE PROCESS: THE OPERATION OF THE INFORMATION PROCESSING SYSTEM

LEVELS OF ACTIVATION

A central tenet of the schema-based theory is that meaning-assigning structures (schemas) are subject to different levels or strengths of activation depending on the environmental demands (internal or external) placed on the organism (see Chapter 4, Assumption 9). The concept of activation is fundamental to the cognitive theory and can be traced to the very first description of the theory (A. Beck, 1964). It was proposed that depression involves hyperactive idiosyncratic depressogenic schemas that displace more appropriate schemas in the cognitive organization because of their greater strength of activation. By **activation** we mean *the process of matching situation or stimulus input features to schemas and modes thereby increasing their prominence within the information processing system.* Schemas and modes that are a good match to the stimulus input features will be primed or highly activated. Segal and Ingram (1994) have referred to this as *direct activation*, where the content of a situation or experience matches the information contained within a particular cognitive structure. A second type of activation called *indirect activation* occurs when stimulus content matches one element of a schema but because of the interrelated quality of other elements of schemas and modes, the entire structure becomes activated.

To illustrate this point, assume an individual has the dysfunctional belief "I am worthless unless I succeed at everything I do," which remains latent and inactive until a triggering event occurs. Direct activation might occur if the person experiences a very significant life stressor such as "being passed over for promotion" because this event would match the contents of the "must succeed at career" schema. Indirect activation of this schema might occur whenever the person is confronted with a much milder experience such as "hearing of the accomplishments of another person." In this case, the idea that others should be less successful than one's self is possibly an element of the "must succeed" schema that, if activated, serves to prime the entire schema or, at a more general level, the mode. The point is that activation or priming of schematic structures does not require a complete match between the stimulus input and the elements of the schema or mode. Activation can occur even if only part of the schematic elements are consistent with the characteristics of a stimulus.

en we refer to situational features that arouse modal activation, we are not simply referring to external events or stimulation. The human information-processing system is capable of reflecting on itself and so input can originate internally in the form of (a) monitoring and evaluating one's own thoughts and feelings; (b) recall of past experiences and memories; (c) selective focus on different aspects of the self such as one's strengths, abilities, and conflicts; (d) daydreaming, fantasies, and other types of reflection on one's goals and values; and (e) imagined rehearsal or planning of possible response action strategies (Mischel & Shoda, 1995).

Activated schemas or modes will tend to dominate the information processing system, thereby making it difficult for other meaning structures to operate within the system. Furthermore, once activated, schematic structures tend to be self-perpetuating by causing individuals to selectively attend to information that conforms to the schema (Lundh, 1988). In depression, for example, this can lead to the type of vicious cycle described by Teasdale (1983). Activated modes will cause information processing to proceed in a conceptually driven manner so that attention is directed toward schema- or mode-congruent information (Williams et al., 1997). One of the tasks in cognitive therapy is to help the depressed patient process novel and schema-incongruent aspects of situations so that alternative constructive modes of thinking are primed and the depressogenic primal loss mode is deactivated.

The cognitive theory proposes that individuals predisposed to clinical disorders, such as anxiety or depression, may have latent hypervalent primal threat or loss modes that remain in a chronic subthreshold state of activation so that a relatively minor stressful event can result in their activation (A. Beck, 1996). The idea that certain cognitive modes remain in a state of subthreshold activation is particularly relevant to depression where the disorder often takes a chronic recurring course. Individuals will differ in the activation thresholds for various modes or schemas because of individual differences in developmental and learning history. Repeated activation of primal loss mode schemas by an increasingly wider range of stimuli will lower the activation thresholds for these schemas resulting in increased susceptibility to relapse and recurrence of depression.

Previously, we noted that schemas and their modes possess the quality of *valence* or a resting level of activation. Certain modes will be hypervalent; that is, their threshold for activation may be quite low (A. Beck, Freeman, & Associates, 1990). Modes with a low activation threshold, as well as the orienting schemas can be triggered by relatively mild or even innocuous stimuli. Prepotent modes (and orienting schemas) also may be triggered by a wider range of stimuli than modes with a higher activation threshold. Modes that deal with critical survival issues of the organism and/or basic aspects of self-definition or identity will tend to have a lower activation threshold. In addition, modes that have been repeatedly activated because of a succession of life experiences can become hyperactive (A. Beck, 1996). Even these prepotent modes, though, remain latent until activated by an internal or external stimulus.

A distinction must be made between activation and accessibility (see Segal, 1988). Riskind and Rholes (1984) defined **accessibility** as *"the ease or speed with which a concept, schema, or bit of information can be retrieved from long-term memory and placed in short-term memory"* (p. 4), or as Segal (1988) noted, the ease with which certain types of information come to mind. The more frequently a construct is activated, the more accessible it becomes and this in turn increases the likelihood that it will be activated in future instances of the construct (Segal, 1988). Thus one effect of modes with low activation thresholds is that they may become highly accessible (as well as hypervalent and prepotent), thereby exerting a dominant influence on one's thinking, feelings, and behavior. In depression, once the schemas of the primal loss mode are activated, they may remain in this heightened state for months. This will result in greater accessibility to depressotypic beliefs and interpretations while processing relevant stimuli.

ATTENTION AND CONSCIOUSNESS

Any viable cognitive theory must consider the role of attention within the information processing system. A. Wells and Matthews (1994) defined **attention** as *"the selection or prioritization for processing of certain categories of information"* (p. 10). The two broad functions of attention, then, are to select and intensively process information. In the present theory, the activation of schemas via the feature-matching process (orienting schemas) constitutes the fundamental process in attention.

An important issue in any discussion of attentional processing concerns the distinction between automatic and controlled or effortful levels of cognitive processing. Considerable research has demonstrated that both automatic and controlled processes are involved in the processing of emotion-relevant information (Hartlage, Alloy, Vazquez, & Dykman, 1993; Lazarus, 1991; Mathews & MacLeod, 1994; McNally, 1995; A. Wells & Matthews, 1994; Williams, Watts, MacLeod, & Mathews, 1988). Automatic processing (a) is effortless, involuntary, or unintentional; (b) is generally outside conscious awareness though some automatic processes may become accessible to consciousness; (c) is relatively fast and difficult to stop or regulate; (d) consumes minimal attentional or processing capacity; (e) relies on a parallel type of processing; (f) is stereotypic involving familiar and highly practiced tasks; and (g) utilizes low levels of cognitive processing with minimal analysis (A. Beck & Clark, 1997; Logan, 1988; McNally, 1995; Sternberg, 1996; A. Wells & Matthews, 1994). A. Wells and Matthews considered "independence from attentional resources" and "insensitivity to voluntary control" the key criteria for automaticity.

Controlled or strategic processes are considered qualitatively different from automatic processing. Controlled processing (a) is intentional, voluntary, or effortful; (b) is fully conscious; (c) is relatively slow and so more amenable to regulation; (d) consumes considerable attentional or processing resources; (e) relies on serial processing where information is processed one step at a time; (f) can deal with novel, difficult, and unpracticed tasks with many variable features; and (g) utilizes higher levels of cognitive processing involving semantic analysis and synthesis (A. Beck & Clark, 1997; McNally, 1995; Sternberg, 1996). The current theory, then, recognizes that the attentional processing of information will involve both automatic and controlled processes. The extent of automatic and controlled processing involved in the activation of any particular mode will depend on the particular mode in question and the situational context.

We would expect, for example, that activation of the primal loss mode in depression will be relatively automatic given its importance for survival (A. Beck & Clark, 1997). The primal loss mode or depression may represent a genetically determined adaptation that evolved to limit depletion of one's resources during times of perceived defeat or deprivation involving either an actual or symbolic loss (A. Beck, 1995, in press). On the other hand, activation of the constructive modes will primarily involve controlled, effortful processing at a more conscious level. However, activation of the meaning structures involved in depression is never entirely automatic or controlled. Rather the dynamic interplay and constantly changing nature of the cognitive apparatus ensures the simultaneous operation of automatic and controlled or strategic attentional processes at any moment in time. Furthermore, it would be erroneous to conclude that preconscious automatic processing is always primitive because abstract and symbolic processes can also occur automatically at certain times (Lazarus, 1991). Nevertheless, the difference might be in the relative contribution of automatic and controlled processing, with the primal modes showing relatively more automatic processing because of their survival value and the constructive modes showing relatively more controlled processing because of their more reflective nature.

No discussion of cognitive processing and attention would be complete without a consideration of consciousness. **Consciousness** refers to *the state of attending to, or being aware of cognitive processes and products of the information processing system.* Sternberg (1996) noted that conscious attention serves to (a) monitor our interactions with the environment so that we can determine how well we are adapting, (b) links our past (memories) and present (sensations) thus providing a sense of continuity of experience, and (c) assists in controlling and planning for future actions.

From the foregoing discussion, it is evident that the cognitive theory does not assert that all cognitive processing, or schema activation, is under conscious voluntary control. On the contrary, schema activation may be automatic, outside awareness and so nonconscious. However the distinction between conscious and nonconscious processing is a matter of degree rather than kind. Thus differences in the level of awareness in one's cognitive processes will vary along a continuum from complete conscious awareness to an absolute nonconscious process (i.e., subliminal registration of information). Furthermore level of awareness of one's cognitive processing is not a stable characteristic but rather will vary across time and situations depending on the information processing demands placed on the individual.

SUMMARY

In this section, we have discussed the dynamic, changing nature of the information processing system. Information impinging on the cognitive apparatus involves an everchanging activation and deactivaton of schemas and their clusters, the modes. The demands of the situational context and the matrix of activation thresholds that characterize the meaning-making structures of each individual will determine the cognitive, behavioral, and physiological output that constitutes emotional states like depression. We now turn to consider the various "products" or the output side, of the cognitive theory that describe the consequences of the faulty information processing system in depression.

COGNITIVE PHENOMENA AND THE PRODUCTS OF DEPRESSION-RELATED COGNITIVE STRUCTURES

One of the basic assumptions of the cognitive theory is that the activation of meaning-assigning structures (i.e., schemas, modes, and personality characteristics) in large part determines how one thinks, feels, and behaves. These thoughts, feelings, and behavior represent the output side, the products of the information processing system. The phenomena described in this "output" side of the theory have a bidirectional or reciprocal relationship with our meaning-making structures. This is particularly evident in clinical disorders like depression where maladaptive meaning structures lead to pervasive and negativistic self-referent thinking. However, it is readily apparent that frequent negative self-referent thoughts or cognitions serve to reinforce and strengthen the depressogenic mode in a self-perpetuating vicious cycle. The more frequently an individual engages in negativistic self-referent thinking, the more convinced one becomes of the veracity and applicability of the underlying depressogenic self-referent beliefs and attitudes. Consequently, the cognitive therapist uses the very cognitive products derived from these structures to effect change in the underlying negative meaning structures or schemas. This cognitive phenomenon represents the "output" or response side of the information processing system and so constitutes the felt emotional experience. In episodic depression, one is subjectively aware of the negative automatic thoughts and negativistic interpretations but usually not the depressogenic schemas that underlie the depressed state. Thus our discussion at this point shifts from the cognitive structures and processes responsible for depression, to a description of the cognitive phenomena that characterize depression.

NEGATIVE AUTOMATIC THOUGHTS

As noted in Chapter 2, the origins of the cognitive theory of depression can be traced to the clinical observation that depressed individuals engage in negative automatic thinking that appears to run parallel to their more controlled, conscious thought processes. Termed *negative automatic thoughts*, this observation became the wellspring from which the more elaborated cognitive theory of depression developed (see A. Beck, 1967, 1976). Thus at its earliest stage of development, the cognitive theory very much emphasized the influence of cognitive output (i.e., negative automatic thoughts and cognitive bias) in normal and abnormal emotional states. Although this focus has given way in more recent years to an increased emphasis on the underlying meaning-making structures that may give rise to our emotional experiences, the importance of the cognitive products of the information processing system for affect and behavior should not be overlooked.

The cognitive phenomena that led to the formulation of the cognitive theory of depression was based on introspective reports by depressed patients experiencing within the therapeutic session a type of negative thinking that was quite unintended and that ran parallel to their more reflective thoughts (A. Beck, 1976). As a result of further clinical observation and experimentation, a number of characteristics were deduced about these negative automatic thoughts such as their tendency to be (a) transient, (b) highly specific and discrete, (c) spontaneous and involuntary, (d) plausible, (e) consistent with the individual's current affective state or personality disposition, and (f) a biased representation of reality including the self (A. Beck, 1967, 1970, 1976). In depression, the content of the negative automatic thoughts revolves around themes of personal loss and failure (e. g., "I am a failure," "Nobody loves me," "I'm a social outcast") resulting from activation of the primal loss mode. The cognitive theory asserts that a distinct cognitive profile is evident in the automatic thought content associated with different affects and psychological disorders (A. Beck, 1971; see Chapter 5 for discussion of the content specificity hypothesis). Thus in depression, self-referent thought content focuses on personal defeat and deprivation, whereas in anxiety automatic thoughts center on physical or psychological threat, danger, and vulnerability.

If automatic thoughts and images can dominate consciousness thereby creating the subjective experience of a mental set or mood state, how do individuals shift from one mental set to another? Change is possible because of the shifting situational features that impinge on us as well as our ability to engage in reflective thinking derived from the constructive modes. We can monitor, evaluate, and reconsider our own thoughts and inclinations, thereby activating alternative, more constructive modes of thinking. In the treatment of depression, the cognitive therapist uses various strategies to teach individuals how to engage in more functional reflective modes of thinking, which then challenge and modify the negative automatic thoughts that emanate from the primal loss mode (A. Beck, 1970).

COGNITIVE ERRORS

The cognitive theory asserts that because of our meaning-making propensity, we are constantly evaluating, interpreting, or appraising both internally and externally derived information; that is, we are involved in a fairly continuous state of cognitive processing. Lazarus and Folkman (1984) defined **cognitive appraisal** as *"the process of categorizing an encounter, and its various facets, with respect to its significance for well-being"* (p. 31). These appraisals or interpretations are highly evaluative in their attempt to impose some degree of meaning or understanding on the context in which people find themselves. Cognitive processing involves some degree of inaccuracy and inconsistency because our cognitive constructions are at best an approximate representation of experience (A. Beck, 1963; see Chapter 3, Assumption 6). However in states of high or intense emotion, or in clinical emotional states like anxiety or depression, the biases (i.e., errors) in our cognitive processes may become even more pronounced and systematic because of the activation of hypervalent meaning structures.

A number of cognitive appraisal biases have been described in past writings on the cognitive theory of depression. These include arbitrary inference, selective abstraction, overgeneralization, minimization, personalization, and dichotomous thinking (see Chapter 2, for definition of each error). In addition, the depressed person perceives negative situations as caused by the self and assigns blame to the self ("It is all my fault"). Seligman and colleagues have written extensive about the role of negative attributional style in the pathogenesis of depression (Abramson et al., 1978; Peterson & Seligman, 1984). The result of these cognitive processing errors is that in depression there is a selective elaboration of the negative features of life circumstances, which leads to the overly negative and pessimistic interpretations, evaluations, and appraisals of one's self and current context. Although information processing studies have provided some evidence of bias in the judgments and manipulation of information by individuals in a depressed state (Haaga et al., 1991), the results across different studies are by no means consistent (see Chapter 7 for discussion). Moreover, recent studies have indicated that nondepressed individuals may have a positivity bias as evidenced by interpretation and memory recall that favor positively valenced material (Matt, Vazquez, & Campbell, 1992; Taylor & Brown, 1994). It is apparent, then, that making sense of ourselves and the world around us is not a rational, objective process. Rather our interpretations and appraisals are very much a product of the modes and schemas that dominant our information processing system.

COGNITIVE CONSTRUCTIONS AND PERSPECTIVES

Based on the cognitive processing strategies previously described, individuals form opinions or constructions of specific situations or entities. A **construction** is *a conceptualization of an event, person, or experience that provides meaning or understanding to the individual.* For example, a parent relating to a child on a daily basis forms a theory, idea, or construction about that child's personality. This construction then influences how the parent interprets future actions of the child, the emotional response the parent may have toward the child, and the type of parenting behavior directed toward the child. The construction, then, would be the final product of a history of processing information derived from interactions with the child. A person's construction of another individual or entity can be discerned from the types of appraisals and automatic thoughts that are triggered by the target stimulus.

A final cognitive product that is linked to our underlying meaning-making structures is that of a perspective. **Perspective** refers to *the broad view that individuals take of a particular domain or of their own personal world at a given time.* A perspective is a broad term referring to a certain theme or orientation that is evident in the thoughts, appraisals, and constructions that individuals generate. For example, an individual may have a depressive perspective in which the self is viewed as defective or worthless and others are seen in a judgmental or an uncaring light. A person with a paranoid perspective would tend to see others as manipulative, deceitful, or malicious. Thus an individual's perspective is evident as a more generalized and durable orientation to life that results from the frequent and sustained activation of specific meaning-making structures. Understanding the perspective of another, especially those with whom we have close relationships, is vital to the development of satisfying and healthy relationships.

SELF-SCHEMA ORGANIZATION IN THE COGNITIVE THEORY

Theory and research on the self has a long and venerable tradition in psychology dating back to the seminal work of William James (1890/1948). A large and diverse literature on the self now exists within personality, social, and, more recently, social cognitive psychology. Given the breadth of this discourse, it is beyond the scope of this work to provide a comprehensive account of the psychological theory and research on the self. However, the self plays a central role in understanding depression because of the self-referent orientation of the faulty information processing that characterizes depression. Thus in this concluding section of the chapter, we discuss the self as understood within the current theoretical framework. We will confine our discussion to the structures and processes of the self that are involved in emotion, especially depression. Two fundamental questions will guide this discussion—how is the self represented or structured in the cognitive theory, and what function does the self play in emotional states like depression?

Self-Schemas and the Cognitive Theory

A fundamental assumption of the cognitive theory is that self-knowledge or the internal representation of the self within the information processing system is the basis of all the self-referent processes and functions that may be implicated in the experience of emotion (see also Markus, 1990; C. Smith, 1991; Strauman & Higgins, 1993). The self-representational structure that has received the most attention in cognitive theories of the self is that of the self-schema. Markus (1977) defined **self-schemas** as *"cognitive generalizations about the self, derived from past experience, that organize and guide the processing of self-related information contained in the individual's social experience"* (p. 64). Within this framework, self-concept is viewed as a mosaic of the individual's self-representations within life domains such as family, work, social relations, and leisure (Markus & Wurf, 1987).

The representation of the self as a cognitive structure suggests that the schemas comprising the self-system or self-concept are highly interrelated (Segal, 1988). Moreover, the cognitive theory does not assume that self-knowledge or concept can be located in a single unitary cognitive structure. One would expect instead to find self-schemas within the behavioral, motivational, physiological, and affective domains because some degree of self-other differentiation is necessary within each of these subsystems. Having said this, it is apparent that most of the self-schemas will be cognitive-conceptual in nature given the importance of self-evaluation in social information processing.

A number of structural and content features of self-representation have been identified that alone or in combination will influence the type of emotional and behavioral patterns that individuals exhibit (Markus & Wurf, 1987; Roberts & Monroe, 1994; Strauman & Higgins, 1993).

- Self-schemas may differ in terms of their importance or centrality. Core self-representations will be more elaborated and tend to have a greater effect on behavior and emotion than more peripheral self-schemas. In depression, negative self-schemas of helplessness and/or unlovability may be central to self-representation.
- Some self-schemas may represent actual views of the self whereas others may refer to possible, idealized, or hoped-for views of the self.
- Self-representations may differ in their temporal orientation in terms of past, present, or future views of the self.
- Cognitive theory in the past has recognized the importance of valence, distinguishing positive from negative views of the self (A. Beck, 1976).
- Differences may be apparent in the degree of efficiency and certainty that is associated with one's self-view. For example, lack of self-certainty and poor schema consolidation may be a vulnerability marker for depression (Kuiper & Olinger, 1986).
- Some self-schemas may be rigidly based on a few primarily external sources of information, whereas healthier self-schemas would be based on more varied and flexible internal sources of information.

- Self-schemas may differ in accessibility, with individuals being more sensitive to information that is consistent with highly accessible self-schemas (Swallow & Kuiper, 1988).

- Self-schemas may vary in their complexity. Linville (1985) has argued that variability in affect and self-appraisal may be related to the degree of complexity evident in the self-representations.

- There is probably a strong interpersonal orientation to self-schemas that encodes information about the "self-in-relation-to-others" (see Safran & Segal, 1990). This is particularly evident in the self-schemas relevant to depression where disruption and loss within the interpersonal realm play such prominent roles.

Researchers are divided over whether the content of the self-structures is the primary determinant of psychological functioning, or whether the relationship between the various self-structures is more critical to social information processing. In the self-discrepancy theory proposed by Higgins (1987), it is the relationship between self-beliefs or structures rather than the content of these structures per se that influences different emotional and motivational states (Strauman & Higgins, 1993). Higgins (1987) proposed three domains to the self—the *actual self* (representations of attributes you believe you actually possess), the *ideal self* (representations of attributes you would like to possess), and the *ought self* (representations of attributes you believe you should possess). These latter two self-domains constitute guides or standards for behavior (Higgins, Strauman, & Klein, 1986; Strauman, 1992). In their theory, it is the discrepancy or incompatibility between the actual versus the ideal or ought selves that is associated with emotional consequences. Thus actual:ideal discrepancy is associated with dysphoric or dejection-related moods, whereas actual:ought discrepancy is associated with anxiety or agitation-related emotions. A number of studies have found that a different pattern of self-guide discrepancies is associated with different clinical and nonclinical emotional states (see Higgins, 1987; Higgins, Klein, & Strauman, 1985; Higgins et al., 1986; Strauman, 1992). Thus the structure, content, and interrelationship or discrepancy between different parts of the self-schema organization all contribute to our understanding of the role of the self in depression.

THE SELF IN DEPRESSION

Self-schemas influence all aspects of the processing of self-relevant information including the selection, encoding, organization, and retrieval of personally meaningful stimuli. This is evident by findings that (a) individuals show a heightened sensitivity or even bias for self-relevant information (e.g., Dworkin & Goldfinger, 1985), (b) they process self-congruent information more efficiently and are more resistant to information that is inconsistent with the self-structures (e.g., Dance & Kuiper, 1987; MacDonald & Kuiper, 1985; Markus, 1977; Segal & Vella, 1990), and (c) individuals show enhanced recall and recognition of self-relevant stimuli (Markus & Wurf, 1987; Strauman & Higgins, 1993). Thus there is considerable experimental evidence that self-representational structures exert a strong influence on the processing of personally meaningful information. The self system operates to interpret the stimuli or events that have been allocated to the personal category by the orienting schemas. In normal reactions, the appropriate functional, adaptive, and adjustive beliefs are imposed on incoming data and then elicit an appropriate affective/motivational/behavioral response. In psychopathological conditions, the self system is represented in the activation of more dysfunctional primal modes. Thus the activation of the primal loss mode means that the self-schemas that are prepotent in depression have a negative and pessimistic orientation resulting in the negative self-referent thoughts and interpretations described earlier.

The current theory proposes a second function of the self-schemas; that of monitoring and evaluating aspects of personal performance (A. Beck, 1976). The self-schemas contain self-evaluative information to generate self-judgments and provide for the maintenance of self-esteem or self-worth (Harter, 1990; Roberts & Monroe, 1994). Kuiper and Olinger (1986) developed a self-worth contingency theory to explain the cognitive basis of depression. The theory proposes that the content and degree of schema integration or consolidation will determine an individual's perceptions of self-worth. In particular when individuals maintain dysfunctional contingencies of self-worth ("If . . . then" beliefs) as represented in some items of the Dysfunctional Attitudes Scale (A. Weissman & Beck, 1978), they are more likely to experience a negative mood state. As long as one's self-worth contingencies are being met, mood state will remain normal (Dance & Kuiper, 1987). When an individual perceives repeated failure in meeting self-worth contingency beliefs, then a decrease in self-esteem will occur along with a decline in mood state.

Dance and Kuiper (1987) also indicated that individuals may evaluate their role performance on the basis of these self-worth contingencies. When role loss or strain is perceived in relation to the self-worth contingencies, the individual will experience a decline in self-esteem and mood state. Empirical support for the self-worth contingency theory was reported in a study by Kuiper, Olinger, and Swallow (1987) where individuals holding dysfunctional self-worth contingency beliefs had more assertion and social skills difficulties and lower perceived satisfaction in social relationships than individuals who did not hold dysfunctional self-worth contingency beliefs.

Swallow and Kuiper (1988) suggested that self-schemas may be evaluated and modified through interpersonal interactions in the form of social comparisons. People are motivated to compare themselves with others as a basis of self-evaluation and self-enhancement. Swallow and Kuiper note that we engage in this social comparison process (a) to reduce uncertainty about the self, (b) to obtain information needed to make ability-relevant decisions, (c) to cope with stress or anxiety, and (d) to enhance one's self relative to others. The outcome of a social comparison process will depend on structural aspects of the self-schema (i.e., self-schema complexity, accessibility, consolidation) as well as the target of the comparison process. Thus a positive self-evaluation and enhanced self-esteem may occur when people compare themselves with disadvantaged others, whereas lower self-worth occurs when individuals compare themselves with advantaged others and fail to discount the confounding factors that make such a comparison inappropriate. The explication of a social comparison process as an important factor in determining self-worth contingency or evaluation provides a valuable social cognitive basis to the structure and function of the self.

Finally Beck, Freeman, & Associates (1990) argued that an important function of the self-schema is self-regulation or inner-directed control over cognition, affect, and behavior. For this reason, self-schemas were viewed in terms of an internal control system responsible for monitoring, evaluating, and directing all aspects of one's psychological functioning. Other researchers on the self have also recognized that self-referent processes play an important role in the regulation of affect, motivation, and cognition (Markus & Wurf, 1987; Strauman & Higgins, 1993). Taken together, it is apparent that structural and functional aspects of self-representation play a vital role in affect (see also Markus, 1990; Safran, Segal, Hill, & Whiffen, 1990). Research on the cognitive basis of depression must recognize the importance of self structures and processes if it is to offer a clear exposition of the mechanisms underlying the pervasive negativity toward the self that is a core symptom feature of this disorder.

CONCLUSION

In this chapter, we presented a schema-based cognitive theory of depression which is an elaboration of the original theory described elsewhere (A. Beck, 1967, 1976). As an information processing theory, the cognitive theory can be understood in terms of the structures, processes, and products involved in the representation and transformation of information. However, the theory also recognizes the importance of the environment in the cognitive-emotive relationship because operation of the information processing apparatus will be greatly influenced by the context and informational features that provide input to the system.

According to the cognitive theory, the structures, processes, and products of faulty or biased information processing are core aspects of the depressive experience. Because the information processing system is responsible for meaning-making capability, it is fundamental to human adaptation and functioning. Emotional responses to the situations and circumstances of everyday life will depend on how these experiences are processed or understood by the cognitive apparatus. Our cognitive organization imposes meaning on our life circumstances and so shapes our emotional response. However the generation, transformation, and application of meaning and the accompaniment emotional states, like depression, are complex and multifaceted in nature requiring an understanding of the information processing system at structural, operational, and phenomenological levels of conceptualization. The schema-based information processing theory of depression presented here recognizes these three levels of conceptualization.

At the structural level, we proposed that the information processing apparatus in depression is characterized by the dominance of beliefs or schemas about the self, world, and future that are overly negative and pessimistic. As the basic structures in the representation of meaning, the negative schemas activated in depression tend to be more complex, tightly interrelated, rigid, and impermeable than the negative schemas in the nondepressed state. Furthermore, the negative self-referent orientation of the depression-related schemas provides the conditional rules, imperatives, and compensatory beliefs that guide the processing of self-referent information. Two core beliefs involving helplessness and unlovability may be fundamental to self-representation in depression. We also noted that information processing in depression can be understood in terms of the interaction of various types of cognitive-conceptual, affective, physiological, behavioral, and motivational schemas that represent the different functions of the human organism.

The interconnectedness of the schemas relevant to depression reflects the fact that meaning representation most critical to the pathogenesis of depression occurs at a broader, more integrative level—the mode. Depression is viewed in terms of the activation of a cluster of interlocking schemas dealing with primal concerns of loss or deprivation. This primal loss mode is characterized by (a) cognitive-conceptual schemas leading to the perception of an actual or threatened loss of one's vital resources;

(b) affective schemas representing the subjective state of dysphoria or sadness; (c) physiological schemas involving a perceived state of fatigue or physiological deactivation; (d) motivational schemas associated with a state of helplessness, lack of goal-directedness, or loss of pleasurable engagement; and (e) behavioral schemas representing a response action plan characterized by withdrawal and inactivity. The cognitive organization of the depressed, then, is characterized by the dominance of this primal loss mode and the relative inactivity of more adaptive, reflective constructive modes of thinking. Because of the automatic, involuntary nature of primal processing, the depressed individual is not readily able to recognize this bias or imbalance in the self-referent information processing system.

At the structural level, the cognitive theory also recognizes the importance of personality schematic suborganizations, particularly in relation to predisposing factors to depression. Two personality orientations, the sociotropic and the autonomous, are proposed as having specific relevance to the pathogenesis of depression. Sociotropic or autonomous individuals, who endorse negative beliefs, are thought to have greater susceptibility to depression because their personality suborganization may be associated with greater sensitivity to negative life stressors that match their personality orientation (a diathesis-stress perspective) and because their personality schemas may be more closely interlocked with the primal loss mode. Thus a distinction is made between depression-prone individuals with maladaptive sociotropic or autonomous schemas, and depression-resistant individuals who may possess more adaptive sociotropic or autonomous beliefs. Finally, in depression, cognitive structures responsible for the initial registration of stimuli—the orienting schemas—may show an attentional bias for negative self-referent information.

Having explicated the cognitive structures involved in depression, we next described a second level of conceptualization involving the operation of the cognitive apparatus in terms of levels of activation, attention, and consciousness. The cognitive theory postulates that in depression negative self-referent schemas of the primal loss mode become highly activated as a result of negative life stressors. Once activated, these prepotent cognitive structures dominate the information processing system leading to the negativistic interpretations and thinking that characterize the depressed state. Furthermore, the theory proposes that these depressogenic cognitive structures remain in a latent or subthreshold state of activation in the nondepressed state until primed by a congruent stressful event.

The activation of depression-related cognitive structures leads to the production of the negativistic cognitive phenomena that are so characteristic of the depressed state. It is this third level of conceptualization, the cognitive phenomena associated with a biased information processing system, that was first recognized in the cognitive theory of depression. Negative automatic thoughts, cognitive processing errors that result in biased negativistic evaluations and interpretations, and a generally negative and pessimistic perspective on life are prominent features of the depressive thinking style. In the final section of this chapter, we discussed the structural and functional properties of self-representation and its role in understanding the cognitive basis of depression. Because the biased or faulty information processing evident in depression is primarily evident in the processing of self-referent material, the self-system plays a central role in the cognitive basis of depression.

As noted in Chapter 3, the adequacy of a scientific theory is judged by how well it explains the phenomena under consideration and its heuristic value as a catalyst for empirical research. In the final chapter of this book, we evaluate how well the cognitive theory accounts for depression in terms of the issues outlined in Chapter 1. The cognitive theory of depression presented in this chapter has led to the formulation of hypotheses that deal with variables that are descriptive of the depressive state as well as variables that contribute to the pathogenesis of depression. The next six chapters discuss in detail research relevant to these hypotheses and thus provide an overview of the empirical status of the cognitive theory of depression.

CHAPTER 5

Descriptive Hypotheses:
Negative Cognition in Depression

In Chapter 4, we posed the central issue addressed in this book—what is the scientific status of the cognitive model of depression? As noted in that chapter, researchers have questioned whether CT is indeed a scientific theory (Beidel & Turner, 1986; Blaney, 1977; Coyne, 1989; Coyne & Gotlib, 1983; Rachman, 1997; Teasdale & Barnard, 1993). One of their main criticisms is that the cognitive model, though highly plausible, cannot account for key findings in the experimental studies of the cognitive basis of depression.

Over the years, numerous reviews have been published in journals, edited volumes and books evaluating the empirical research on the cognitive basis of depression (i.e., Ackermann-Engel & DeRubeis, 1993; A. Beck, 1991; D.A. Clark & Beck, 1989, 1997; D.A. Clark & Steer, 1996; Coyne & Gotlib, 1983; Gotlib & Hammen, 1992; Haaga et al., 1991; Hammen, 1988a; Segal, 1988; Segal & Ingram, 1994; Segal & Shaw, 1986a). Some of these reviews have a specific focus on earlier versions of the cognitive model, whereas others take a broader perspective on the general role of cognition in depression. At present, Haaga et al. (1991) can be considered the most comprehensive review of the empirical status of CT of depression. Nevertheless, another comprehensive review of the empirical literature is justified despite the articles previously cited. Many of these reviews are highly selective and focus only on specific aspects of the cognitive model. As such, they provide an inadequate basis for an overall evaluation of its empirical status. Also, most reviews refer to earlier writings on the cognitive model and so may have less relevance for the formulation described here. The empirical research on the cognitive basis of depression is voluminous and continuing to grow at an exponential rate. Thus any review is bound to become dated within a short time resulting in the need for periodic updates.

In the following six chapters we present a detailed and comprehensive review of the voluminous research on the cognitive basis of depression. We cannot guarantee that all relevant empirical research on the cognitive model has been included in our review, despite our best efforts to present a broad coverage of the literature. We tried to review a sufficient number of studies so that some conclusions could be reached about the empirical status of the CT hypotheses. Also, studies that were more methodologically rigorous, or that provided a more direct test of the CT model, were given greater emphasis.

The nine descriptive hypotheses of the cognitive model of depression are presented in Table 5.1 Because these hypotheses have received so much research attention, we have divided the review over three chapters. They all focus on aspects of cognitive functioning at the descriptive level of depression. These hypotheses refer to the organization and function of the structures, processes, and products that constitute the cognitive basis of depression, as well as their relationship to other depressive phenomena. Studies that address the descriptive hypotheses of CT focus only on cognitive functioning during the depressive episode. Their sole purpose is to investigate the cognitive dysfunction that characterizes depression. There is no attempt to draw inferences of causality at the descriptive level. The possible causal status of certain cognitive constructs will be discussed in Chapters 8 through 10.

Coyne and Gotlib (1986) argued that research on cognitive functioning at the descriptive level is uninteresting because it is devoid of any implication of causality. Research findings at this level of analysis may simply indicate that negative cognition is a consequence of depression or, even worse, a tautology that reflects the most obvious observation about depression—that depressed individuals tend to complain about themselves and their situation. Segal and Shaw (1986b), however, noted that investigations at the descriptive level are important because they inform us of the interdependent processes of depression and how changes in information processing might be associated with other concurrent changes in mood, behavior, and even biochemistry. Also, research at the descriptive level ties one into the more observable signs and symptoms of depression (i.e., phenomenology), and so avoids more remote inferences of causality and the precipitants of depression. We would add that research on the descriptive correlates of depression can inform us of processes that may warrant further investigation as causal factors or potential change agents in depression. Thus research on the descriptive hypotheses is crucial to gaining a better understanding of the cognitive basis of depression.

Table 5.1
The Descriptive Hypotheses of the Cognitive Model of Depression

Hypotheses	Statement
Negativity	Depression is characterized by the presence of absolute and pervasive negative self-referent thinking about the self, world, and future.
Exclusivity	Depression is characterized by the exclusion of positive self-referent thinking.
Content-Specificity	Each psychological disorder has a distinct cognitive profile that is evident in the content and orientation of the negative cognitions and processing bias associated with the disorder.
Primacy	Negative cognition and biased information processing will critically influence the behavioral, affective, somatic, and motivational symptoms of depression.
Universality	Heightened negative cognition, reduced positive thinking, and self-referent negativity processing bias are evident in all subtypes of depression.
Severity/Persistence	Extent of negative self-referent cognition, reduced positive thinking, and negativity processing bias are linearly related to depression severity and persistence.
Selective Processing	Depression is characterized by a selective processing bias for mood-congruent negative self-referent information that is linked to one's current life concerns.
Schema Activation	Negative affective states like depression are characterized by an increased accessibility to the negative self-referent schematic structures of the loss mode.
Primal Processing	The negative self-referent thinking, cognitive appraisals and perspectives in depression are the product of primal mode processing that is involuntary, unintended, rapid, and less amenable to conscious awareness.

In this chapter, we review the empirical status of the negativity, exclusivity, and content-specificity descriptive hypotheses. These three hypotheses deal with negative cognition at the most basic level of conceptualization. Together they assert that depressive states are characterized by a preponderance of negative self-referent thinking and a relative reduction in positive self-referent cognitions. Moreover, depression can be distinguished from other types of psychological disorders by a distinct cognitive content involving themes of personal loss, failure, and deprivation. These first three descriptive hypotheses, then, contend that negative cognitive phenomena constitute core-specific features of the depression experience. The first descriptive hypothesis of the cognitive model is the negativity hypothesis.

NEGATIVITY HYPOTHESIS

Depression is characterized by the presence of absolute and pervasive negative self-referent thinking about the self, world, and future.

According to CT, negative cognitive content concerning the self, world, and future (referred to as the negative cognitive triad) is a core integral feature of depressive symptomatology (A. Beck, 1967, 1987). Negative cognition is considered as much a part of the depressive experience as other defining phenomena of the disorder such as sad affect, loss of interest and pleasure, behavioral inhibition, and somatic disturbance. Furthermore, this hypothesis asserts that negative self-referent thinking will only be present during depressive and dysphoric mood states. With remission of a depressive disorder or the reinstatement of a more positive, or even neutral mood state, the negative cognitive triad will no longer be evident (A. Beck, 1964, 1987). In Chapter 4, we described cognitive phenomena, such as automatic and voluntary thoughts, constructions, and perspectives, that are products of an activated primal loss mode and so would be characterized by negativity. Reviewers have concluded that the negativity hypothesis has been consistently supported in numerous empirical studies (Ackermann-Engel & DeRubeis, 1993; A. Beck, 1991; D.A. Clark & Steer, 1996; Gotlib & Hammen, 1992; Haaga et al., 1991).

HEIGHTENED NEGATIVITY IN DEPRESSED STATES

The negativity hypothesis was first derived from interview data collected on 50 depressed and 31 nondepressed patients undergoing psychotherapy (A. Beck, 1967). It was discovered that the depressed sample differed from the nondepressed group by the preponderance of negative cognitions dealing with low self-evaluation, sense of personal deprivation, self-criticism, and hopelessness. These observations led to the proposal of a primary cognitive triad in which depression is characterized by a negative view of self, world, and future.

A number of retrospective self-report questionnaires have been developed that specifically assess depressotypic negative cognitive content. Some examples include the Cognitions Checklist (A. Beck et al., 1987), Hopelessness Scale (A. Beck et al., 1974), Automatic Thoughts Questionnaire (Hollon & Kendall, 1980), and Crandell Cognitions Inventory (Crandell & Chambless, 1986). The Cognitions Checklist, for example, consists of a 14-item depression subscale reflecting negative thoughts about one's self, past experiences, and future expectations, whereas the 12-item anxiety subscale represents thoughts about physical and personal danger (A. Beck et al., 1987; Steer, Beck, Clark, & Beck, 1994). The Automatic Thoughts Questionnaire (Hollon & Kendall, 1980) consists of 30 negatively valenced thought statements in which respondents indicate how frequently each thought occurred to them over the preceding week.

With all these measures, individuals are given a predetermined list of negative self-referent thought statements (e.g., "Life isn't worth living," "I'm worthless," "I will never overcome my problems," "There's no one left to help me") and are asked to indicate on Likert-type scales how often each thought occurs to them. Numerous studies have shown that both clinically depressed and nonclinical dysphoric groups score significantly higher on these inventories than nondepressed controls (Blackburn, Jones, & Lewin, 1986; Crandell & Chambless, 1986; Dobson & Shaw, 1986; Dohr, Rush, & Bernstein, 1989; Harrell & Ryon, 1983; Hedlund & Rude, 1995; Hollon & Kendall, 1980; Hollon, Kendall, & Lumry, 1986; Ingram, Kendall, Smith, Donnell, & Ronan, 1987; Lam, Brewin, Woods, & Bebbington, 1987; Ross, Gottfredson, Christensen, & Weaver, 1986; Whisman, Diaz, & Luboski, 1993).

D.A. Clark et al. (1998) administered the Hopelessness Scale (HS), which assesses negative expectations about the future, and the Cognitions Checklist (CCL), a measure of the frequency of anxious and depressive self-statements, to 52 depressed psychiatric inpatients, 21 clinically depressed medical patients with a chronic physical illness, 54 nondepressed medical patients, and 25 normal controls. All depressed patients, whether from the psychiatric or medical sample, met *DSM-III-R* diagnostic criteria for major depression or dysthymia. After controlling for level of symptom severity, hopelessness and frequency of depressive self-statements significantly differentiated the depressed psychiatric inpatients but not the depressed medical patients from the nondepressed medical and normal controls.

These results, then, support the negativity hypothesis but suggest that, in some cases, specialized measures of negative cognition may provide a more comprehensive assessment of the thought content of depressed individuals from special populations such as the chronic medically ill. Most of the items on the HS and CCL deal with issues commonly seen in psychiatric populations and so may miss some concerns that may be unique to individuals struggling with a chronic medical illness. We should add, though, that a number of studies have reported that negative cognition items of standard psychiatrically based measures like the BDI can distinguish depression in medically ill patients (A. Beck, Guth, Steer, & Ball,

1997; D.C. Clark, Cavanaugh, & Gibbons, 1983; Rapp, Parisi, Walsh, & Wallace, 1988). Nevertheless, the failure of a negative cognition measure to distinguish depression in a sample may result from low content validity for that particular population. The questionnaire might fail to contain enough items that are sensitive to the cognitive themes that characterize the population under consideration. It must be remembered that negative self-referent thinking in depression can be quite idiosyncratic. Thus a cognitive measure that adequately captures the negative thought content in one population of depressed individuals may not be perfectly applicable to a different population of depressed persons.

There is considerable evidence that the elevated scores on negative cognition inventories during depressive episodes fall to within the normal nondepressed range once the depression remits (Blackburn et al., 1986; Dobson & Shaw, 1986; Dohr et al., 1989; Hamilton & Abramson, 1983; Hedlund & Rude, 1995; Hollon et al., 1986). This finding is consistent with the predictions of the negativity hypothesis which states that negative self-referent thinking is a characteristic or symptom of episodic depression.

THE NEGATIVE COGNITIVE TRIAD

The negativity hypothesis states that negative thoughts about the self, world and future characterize the depressed state. Only a few studies have directly investigated the negative cognitive triad in depression. Beckham, Leber, Watkins, Boyer, and Cook (1986) developed the Cognitive Triad Inventory to specifically assess the negative cognitive triad. Three subscales composed of 10 items each assess either a negative view of the self, the world, or the future. A mixture of positive and negative valenced thought statements are included in each subscale and respondents indicate how much they agree with the item right now. The strongest convergent validity was found for the View of Self and View of Future subscales.

In another study, Blackburn et al. (1986) found that depressed patients made significantly more negative interpretations concerning the self, world, and future than nondepressed controls. Based on thoughts recorded in the Daily Record of Dysfunctional Thoughts, Blackburn and Eunson (1989) found that depressed patients treated with cognitive therapy recorded more thoughts with self and world than future concepts. Other studies have found support for the negative cognitive triad in depression using measures of low self-esteem, self-criticalness, pessimism, and hopelessness (for review, see Haaga et al., 1991).

Haaga et al. (1991), however, questioned the conceptual distinctiveness of the three components of the triad and suggested that it might be clearer to reduce the cognitive triad to a single dimension of negative view of self. The negative view of future and world, they argue, is understood in reference to the self and so can be considered subcomponents of a more global negative self-view. Alternatively, we suggest that one can retain the three distinct elements of the cognitive triad but instead restrict the negative view of self to intrapersonal evaluation, the negative view of world to an evaluation of the "self-in-relation-to-others" (an interpersonal orientation), and the negative view of future to pessimistic expectations about one's future (this latter orientation is already evident in the Hopelessness Scale). This might require the development of new instruments that more precisely assess the self and world. In fact, the Beck Self-Concept Test (A. Beck, Steer, Epstein, & Brown, 1990) was developed to assess the negative view of self. Depressed patients had significantly lower Beck Self-Concept Total Scores than individuals with other psychiatric conditions or nondepressed controls. The results indicated that a negative view of self was characteristic of depression.

NEGATIVITY AND TAUTOLOGY

Critics of the cognitive model have argued that research showing elevated levels of negative cognition in currently depressed patients is meaningless at best and tautological at worst. Coyne and Gotlib (1983) stated that the demonstration of elevated negative cognition on paper-and-pencil tests is tautological because researchers often select depressed groups on the basis of symptom measures, like the Beck Depression Inventory (BDI), which contain negative cognition items. Thus the significant correlations between cognition and symptom measures might be due to item overlap. At worst, they argue that this research is meaningless because it merely states the obvious—that depressed individuals are negative about themselves and their situation (Coyne, 1989; Coyne & Gotlib, 1986).

There are a number of problems with this criticism of the cognitive negativity research. First, many of the methodologically stronger clinical studies categorized patients into depressed and nondepressed groups based on Research Diagnostic Criteria (RDC) or *DSM* criteria for major depression (Blackburn et al., 1986; Dobson & Shaw, 1986; Dohr et al., 1989; Hedlund & Rude, 1995; Hollon et al., 1986). Consequently item overlap between procedures used to establish diagnosis and the negative cognition measures was kept to a minimum. As noted in Chapter 1, negative cognition symptoms play a very minor role in *DSM-IV* diagnostic criteria for major depression.

Second, Coyne and Gotlib present a simplified understanding of circularity. Lazarus and Folkman (1986) argued that circularity may be not only an inevitable part of any exploratory research but it can also advance our knowledge and understanding of phenomena. They noted, "circularity occurs when there is total redundancy among the variables being correlated [or contrasted]" (Lazarus & Folkman, 1986, p. 64). As evidenced by the diagnostic criteria and procedures used in the negativity studies, this type of circularity is not present. In fact, the charge of tautology could be levied against any cross-sectional descriptive symptom study. This criticism is less relevant for negative cognition than other types of symptom studies, such as research into low positive affect and reduced motivation (e.g., L.A. Clark & Watson, 1991b), because these latter symptoms are more directly part of the diagnostic criteria used to select for depression than are the negative cognition symptoms.

Third, Haaga (1992) has argued that judgments of the distinguishability of constructs should not be framed in terms of binary, all-or-nothing decisions—that two measures are either redundant or distinct. Rather he advocates the use of a continuous variable approach to judge whether two measures more or less overlap (i.e., are confounded) or are distinguishable. In reference to a study by Sullivan and D'Eon (1990) in which the authors concluded that catastrophizing may not be distinct from depressive symptoms because it overlapped with the cognitive component of depression and failed to correlate with the somatic items of the BDI, Haaga noted that this finding could also be interpreted substantively; that catastrophizing is a correlate of depression, especially the cognitive component of depression. Haaga's arguments can be applied more generally to the "cries of tautology" that arise from the critics of the cognitive model. These critics appear to view tautology from a dichotomous or all-or-nothing perspective rather than judging cognition and symptom measures in terms of degrees of distinctiveness or commonality. Moreover, like Sullivan and D'Eon, these critics often interpret a close association between a cognition and symptom measure as a sign of confounding constructs or overlapping items rather than the more substantive interpretation—that a putative cognitive construct may be a correlate of depression.

Negativity and Production Methods of Assessment

A more serious concern is raised by Coyne (1989) who questions whether item endorsements on retrospective self-report inventories can be assumed to represent the rate of occurrence of negative cognitions. Glass and Arnkoff (1983) suggest that item endorsement on cognition inventories might reflect (a) the impact or importance of the thought, (b) a "translation process" whereby the person matches his or her idiosyncratic or fragmented actual thought to the thought statement on the inventory, (c) one's self-concept, or (d) an affective experience. Although it is difficult to validate self-report cognition inventories because of the private inferential nature of cognition, nevertheless considerable psychometric data now exist supporting the construct validity of some of the more widely used cognition questionnaires (for reviews, see D.A. Clark, 1988; Glass & Arnkoff, 1997).

The empirical evidence for the negativity hypothesis is not entirely dependent on retrospective questionnaires. Other methodologies have also been used to assess cognitive content in depression, though admittedly these alternative assessment procedures have been utilized less frequently than structured questionnaires. As previously mentioned, Blackburn and Eunson (1989) used a thought-sampling procedure in which depressed patients recorded their negative thoughts on the Daily Record of Dysfunctional Thoughts. They found that thoughts of self-deprecation and a hostile world were linked to increases in feelings of anxiety and depression. Other studies using thought production methods such as the thought-listing technique (Cacioppo & Petty, 1981), thought sampling (Hurlburt, 1979), experience sampling (Csikszentmihalyi & Larson, 1987), and think aloud (Genest & Turk, 1981) have generally supported the association between frequency of negative cognitions and an increase in depressed mood (for reviews, see Cacioppo, von Hippel, & Ernst, 1997; Davison, Vogel, & Coffman, 1997; Hurlburt, 1997). Kammer, Behrmann, Siemer, and Feld (1986), used a think-aloud method to compare the verbalizations of depressed and nondepressed psychiatric patients on a 5-minute experimental failure task. The depressed group generated significantly more task-interference thoughts, particularly thoughts that focused on their negative feelings, and fewer task-facilitating thoughts during the failure experience. They also spontaneously generated more internal failure attributions during the failure task than the nondepressed controls. Despite these encouraging results, few studies have utilized thought production methods with clinically depressed patients (D.A. Clark, 1988). More clinical research is needed with these assessment approaches to broaden the empirical basis of the negativity hypothesis beyond its current overreliance on structured questionnaires.

EXCLUSIVITY HYPOTHESIS

Depression is characterized by the exclusion of positive self-referent thinking.

As originally stated, the exclusivity hypothesis refers to the "automatic exclusion of positive self-evaluations" (A. Beck, 1987, p. 8). As noted in Chapter 4, this results from domination in the cognitive organization of the primal loss mode and the relatively weak activation of the constructive modes. Furthermore, the hypothesis was derived from clinical observation that negative thinking is so pervasive and plausible in depression that positive thoughts are often ignored or discounted. The hypothesis does not state that depressed individuals have no positive thoughts just as the negativity hypothesis does not assert that nondepressed people never have at least some negative thinking. Such an extreme position was never intended because it does not fit with clinical observation of the depressed (or nondepressed) state. Cognitive theory argues that in depression a significant decline in positive thinking is present relative to the nondepressed state. Exclusivity refers not to an absolute or literal absence of positive cognitions, but rather to the depressed person's tendency to automatically discount or reject (i.e., exclude from further consideration) positive thinking about themselves and their world because of the absolute, pervasive, and veracious nature of the negative automatic thoughts.

Haaga et al. (1991) have argued that if exclusivity is understood as a relative decline in positive thinking, then it adds nothing beyond the negativity hypothesis and should be deleted from future revisions of CT. We disagree with this assertion. A "relative decline" interpretation of exclusivity deals with aspects of depression not covered by the negativity hypothesis. First, it asserts that the problem in depression cannot be restricted to excessive negative thinking, but also involves a reduction in positive thoughts. Thus researchers interested in measuring depression and therapists desiring to treat the disorder must consider the depressed individual's tendency to exclude or discount positive cognitions. Second, it asserts that the relative absence of positive thinking may be as integral to the depressive experience as the relative presence of negative thinking. And third, it indicates that depression depends not only on the activation of the loss mode leading to negative thinking, but also to the relatively weak activation of the more constructive, compensatory modes that are responsible for positive cognitions. Thus the exclusivity hypothesis does refer to depressive phenomena that are distinct from the referents of the negativity hypothesis. In a confirmatory factor analysis of the Automatic Thoughts Questionnaire Negative (ATQ-N) and Positive (ATQ-P) subscales, Bryant and Baxter (1997) found that a hierarchical model with correlated second-order factors of Positive and Negative Automatic Cognitions provided a significantly better fit to the data than a single latent factor with positive and negative cognition as opposite ends of a unitary automatic thoughts dimension. This indicates that positive and negative cognitions are better conceptualized as correlated but distinct dimensions, a finding that supports our contention that a separate exclusivity hypothesis is needed to account for the relative decline in positive thinking in depression.

The empirical support for the exclusivity hypothesis is not as strong as for the negativity hypothesis, in part because researchers have tended not to measure the presence of positive cognitions in their depression studies. Furthermore, if the exclusivity hypothesis is misrepresented to mean the complete absence of positive thinking, then this position is not supported by studies indicating that depressed individuals do experience positive cognitions (Haaga et al., 1991). In fact, Segal and Muran (1993) noted that 70% of the personal self-descriptive adjectives chosen by depressed patients in their studies were positively valenced. Significant differences between depressed and nondepressed groups were attributable to a very low endorsement rate (5%) for negative trait adjectives by the nondepressed participants. Other self-referent encoding studies have found that depressed individuals have equivalent endorsement rates for positive and negative trait adjectives (see Haaga et al., 1991).

EMPIRICAL SUPPORT FOR THE EXCLUSIVITY HYPOTHESIS

Although a few depression cognition measures include positive thought statements along with the usual negative items (e.g., Crandell Cognitions Inventory, Cognitive Triad Inventory for Children; see Laurent & Stark, 1993), the most widely used measure of positive cognitions is a revision to the Automatic Thoughts Questionnaire (ATQ) made by Ingram and Wisnicki (1988). They developed 30 positive self-statement items (labeled ATQ-P) that were designed to complement the original 30 negative items of the ATQ (ATQ-N). Since then, the ATQ-P has been used in studies to investigate the frequency of positive self-statements in clinical and nonclinical populations.

Consistent with the prediction of the exclusivity hypothesis, a number of studies have found that diagnostic or psychometrically defined depressed samples (adults and children) report a significantly lower frequency of positive cognitions on self-report instruments like the ATQ-P than nondepressed groups (Ingram, 1989; Ingram, Atkinson, Slater, Saccuzzo, & Garfin, 1990; Ingram, Kendall, Siegle, Guarino, & McLaughlin, 1995; Ingram, Slater, Atkinson, & Scott, 1990; Ingram & Wisnicki, 1988; Kendall, Howard, & Hays, 1989; Laurent & Stark, 1993). Furthermore, as one would expect, the ATQ-P has a moderate negative correlation with measures of depression, anxiety, and general distress, but a positive correlation with measures of positive affect, life adjustment, and well-being (Burgess & Haaga, 1994; Crewdsen & Clark, 1997; Ingram & Wisnicki, 1988). Ingram, Kendall, et al. (1995) found that nondysphoric students receiving a positive mood induction reported significantly more positive thoughts (i.e., higher ATQ-P scores) than control participants. In their

their confirmatory factor analysis, Bryant and Baxter (1997) found that ATQ-N and ATQ-P both had equivalent relations with a second-order Happiness factor. However, frequency of positive cognitions has a weaker association with depression symptom measures than does frequency of negative thoughts, prompting some to question whether presence of negative thinking may not be more characteristic of dysfunction than an absence of, or reduction in, the frequency of positive thinking (Kendall, 1992; Kendall & Hollon, 1981). Even in studies where reduced levels of positive cognitions have accounted for unique variance in depression measures, the actual amount of variance explained by positive cognitions is substantially less than the variance explained by negative cognition measures (Kendall et al., 1989; Lightsey, 1994).

Two studies examined whether frequency of positive cognitions might moderate the relationship between life events and dysphoria. Lightsey (1994) found that negative life events were significantly less predictive of dysphoria (BDI scores) in students with higher levels of positive cognition (ATQ-P scores). This finding was replicated in another study involving a student sample (Bruch, 1997). These findings suggest that frequency of positive cognitions may be less directly related to depression and instead function primarily as a coping mechanism or buffer against the impact of negative life stressors (Ingram & Wisnicki, 1988; Ingram, Atkinson, et al., 1990; Lightsey, 1994). Thus it may be that frequency of positive cognitions should be conceptualized as a coping mechanism that is highly relevant for depressive states. Ingram and Wisnicki (1988) also questioned whether decreases in positive cognition might reflect severity of a depression.

Based on their tripartite model of anxiety and depression, L.A. Clark and Watson (1991b) argue that measures that assess the frequency of positive cognitions should differentiate depression from other psychological states, such as anxiety, because low positive affect (PA) is considered a specific defining feature of depression. Watson and Kendall (1989) commented, "Depression measures should more strongly assess the lack of positive emotional experiences (a critical, differentiating feature)" (p. 504). Empirical support for this assertion is mixed. Crandell and Chambless (1986) found that only one-third of the positive items on their questionnaire were endorsed significantly less often by the depressed group compared with the nondepressed psychiatric or normal control groups. Ingram and Wisnicki (1988) found that the ATQ-P had low correlations with both anxiety and depression measures, whereas Ingram (1989) found that psychometrically defined depressed and socially anxious groups did not differ in reporting a low level of position cognitions. Laurent and Stark (1993) did find that a low frequency of positive cognitions differentiated children with depression (pure and mixed cases) from those with an anxiety disorder. Burgess and Haaga (1994) found that the ATQ-P was significantly correlated with the BDI after controlling for anxiety, but not with the Beck Anxiety Inventory (BAI) after partialing out the effects of depression. Thus the research is unclear at this time on whether frequency of positive cognitions affords greater discrimination of depression over the differentiation that is already achieved by measures that focus exclusively on the assessment of negative self-referent cognitions (e.g., the Cognitions Checklist, ATQ).

According to the exclusivity hypothesis, a relatively low frequency of positive self-referent thoughts characterizes the depressed state because of an automatic exclusion of positive self-evaluations (A. Beck, 1987). In a study by Crowson and Cromwell (1995), nondepressed individuals were significantly more oriented toward an audiotape containing the ATQ-P positive cognition items, whereas depressed individuals were equally drawn to audiotaped positive and negative thought statements. Also, as previously discussed, depressed individuals do report positive self-referent thoughts, though at a lower frequency than nondepressed persons (see Haaga at al., 1991). This raises the question of whether it is the absolute or raw number of positive cognitions that is related to dysfunction, or whether it is the balance, the ratio of positive to negative cognitions, that is most predictive of psychological adjustment and well-being.

STATES OF MIND (SOM) MODEL

The States of Mind (SOM) Model asserts that it is the balance or ratio of positive and negative cognitions rather than the absolute number of each thought valence that is most closely related to functional and dysfunctional states (R. Schwartz, 1986, 1997; R. Schwartz & Garamoni, 1986, 1989). The view is that cognitive balance is associated with optimal functioning and well-being, whereas excessive polarity or imbalance (too many negative or positive thoughts) is associated with dysfunction (R. Schwartz, 1986; R. Schwartz & Garamoni, 1989).

Five distinct states of mind are defined around a cognitive-affective set point conceptualized in terms of a balance or imbalance based on the ratio of positive thoughts to the sum of positive and negative cognitions $(P/(P + N))$, or the ratio of negative thoughts to the sum of positive and negative cognitions $(N/(N + P))$. Optimal health and adjustment are associated with a positive dialogue in which the ratio of positive thoughts to the sum of positive plus negative is defined around a set point of .62 (±.06). Moderately anxious or depressed individuals are characterized by a negative dialogue defined as a ratio of negative thoughts to the sum of negative plus positive cognitions of .38 (±.06). Mild levels of anxiety and depression are associated with an internal dialogue of conflict defined as .50 (±.05).

Empirical support has been found for the SOM model, with healthy, nonpathological groups characterized by a positive dialogue that approximated the set point value of .62, mildly anxious/depressed individuals reported an internal dialogue of conflict, and individuals with moderate depression or anxiety a negative dialogue (R. Schwartz, 1997; R. Schwartz & Garamoni, 1986). McDermut and Haaga (1994) found that SOM ratios based on depression-related cognitions were specifically related to depression symptom measures, though SOM ratios derived from an anxious cognition measure were not uniquely related to the Beck Anxiety Inventory. These results suggest that cognitive balance should be defined not only in terms of positive and negative valence, but should also take into account the content of the thought; such as whether the thought deals with loss and failure or harm and danger.

One issue that has not been adequately addressed is whether SOM ratios add anything to the prediction of depression over what can be achieved by simply measuring the raw frequency of positive or negative cognitions. Is dysfunction best characterized in terms of a balance or ratio of negative to positive thoughts, or is the actual number of negative or positive thoughts that occupies the stream of consciousness a better characterization of dysfunction? Very few studies have directly examined this question. Bruch (1997) found that frequency of negative thoughts was as good a predictor of dysphoria in undergraduates as the more elaborate SOM ratios.

Another issue concerns whether SOM ratios are robust or are highly sensitive to measurement effects. In a study of SOM in social phobia, Heimberg, Bruch, Hope, and Dombeck (1990) found differences in SOM classification depending on whether analysis was based on a self-report questionnaire or thought-listing technique. Finally, several studies have not supported the model's assertion that positive monologue (predominance of positive self-statements thought to characterize mania) is associated with psychopathology. McDermut and Haaga (1994) found that students having a positive monologue SOM were not dysfunctional. In fact, a moderate level of positive monologue may be adaptive, leading some to question whether a positive dialogue is the optimal SOM level. In light of these considerations R. Schwartz (1997) recently offered a reformulated *balanced states of mind model* in which different psychological states of mind are defined in terms of deviations from optimal ratios of positive to negative thoughts depending on the particular mood state of the individual. Healthy individuals in a positive or cheerful mood state have an optimal dialogue of .81, whereas the superoptimal SOM of .87 is evident in healthy individuals who have a pervasive feeling of well-being resulting from success in some important life task. Whether the balanced states-of-mind approach satisfactorily addresses some of the weaknesses noted with SOM must await the results of empirical investigation.

SUMMARY

There is now moderate empirical support for the view that in depression positive self-referent thinking is reduced, at least more so than in nondepressed states. However, the reduction of positive self-referent thoughts is relative and not absolute. Depressed individuals do have positive cognitions but at a significantly lower frequency than nondepressed individuals, although this latter statement has not necessarily been supported by all studies, as seen in Segal and Muran's (1993) self-descriptive trait findings. Also, research using the SOM model suggests that the ratio of negative to positive thoughts is a useful analysis of the thought activity in the depressive state. Whether it is the absolute number of positive thoughts or the ratio of negative to positive cognitions that is most predictive of depression, one can at least conclude from this body of research that a diminished capacity to engage in positive self-referent thinking is probably a noteworthy feature of depression.

Many issues remain unresolved. It is likely that "nonpositive thinking" is less critical to depression than the presence of "negative thinking" (Kendall, 1992). Whether the reformulated balanced states of mind model provides a more powerful analytic approach for understanding cognitive-affective relationships awaits empirical investigation. Finally, it is likely that research into positive and negative thinking in depression would benefit from taking into account the specific content of the cognitive measures (McDermut & Haaga, 1994), which would bring together the idea of cognitive specificity and exclusivity. Whatever the case, a comprehensive cognitive assessment in depression should include an evaluation of the frequency of both positive and negative self-referent thinking.

CONTENT-SPECIFICITY HYPOTHESIS

Each psychological disorder has a distinct cognitive profile that is evident in the content and orientation of the negative cognitions and processing bias associated with the disorder.

The content-specificity hypothesis states that psychological disorders or states can be distinguished by the form and content of their associated dysfunctional cognitions, beliefs, attitudes, and processes. Thus in depression, the predominant cognitive theme is about personal loss or deprivation, whereas in anxiety the primary concern is about physical or psychological threat or danger (A. Beck, 1967, 1971, 1987; D.A. Clark & Steer, 1996). This distinctive cognitive content is evident in other psychological states such as mania (an exaggerated positive view of self, world, and future), obsessive-compulsive disorder (unrealistic appraisals of the harmfulness of one's thoughts and the importance of mental control), and paranoia (attribution of negative bias to others). These distinct cognitive profiles, then, allow us to differentiate among emotional states or disorders. As noted in Chapter 4, the distinctive content evident in such cognitive products as negative automatic thoughts and perspectives results from the activation of different primal modes of the information processing system.

The distinctive cognitive profile of depression is evident in the content and orientation of the structures, processes, and products of the information processing system. Thus at the modal or schematic level, depression is characterized by attitudes and beliefs reflecting a negative view of self, world, and future as well as an overwhelming sense of loss and failure. At the cognitive processing level, depression is distinguished by an enhanced processing of negative self-referent information and minimization of positive self-referent material. At the cognitive product or automatic thoughts level, we find negative cognitions that take the form of pervasive, absolute statements about past personal losses and failures. This latter can be distinguished from the automatic thinking in anxiety that is more situational, future-oriented, and probabilistic (A. Beck & Clark, 1988; D.A. Clark & Beck, 1989). In sum, then, dysfunctional thinking in depression reflects activation of the loss mode, whereas cognitive functioning in anxiety is characterized by threat mode activation.

EMPIRICAL SUPPORT FOR THE CONTENT-SPECIFICITY HYPOTHESIS

Most of the research on cognitive content-specificity has compared cognitive functioning in depression and anxiety. In fact, it is difficult to find studies that have examined whether the cognitive profile of depression is distinguishable from the profile found in other psychological states such as anger, paranoia, mania, and the like. Because of this, our primary focus is on studies that have directly compared cognitive measures in anxiety and depression.

Group Comparison

A number of studies have compared clinically diagnostic or subclinical groups of depressed and anxious individuals on a variety of cognitive content measures. Most have found that the depressed or dysphoric individuals report a significantly higher frequency of personal loss and failure cognitions as well as negative beliefs and evaluations about the self than individuals with a variety of anxiety states including panic, generalized anxiety, social phobia, or test anxiety (A. Beck, Freeman, & Associates, 1990; A. Beck, Steer, & Epstein, 1992; A. Beck et al., 1987; Blackburn et al., 1986; D.A. Clark et al., 1990; Hollon & Kendall, 1980; Ingram, 1984a, 1989; Ingram, Kendall, et al., 1987; Sanz & Avia, 1994; Steer et al., 1994).

Only a few studies have found that anxious individuals report significantly more threat and danger cognitions, or are more inclined to interpret stimuli as threatening, than depressed persons (A. Beck et al., 1987; D.A. Clark et al., 1990; Ingram, Kendall, et al., 1987; Sanz & Avia, 1994), leading to the suggestion that cognitive specificity may be less evident with threat and danger cognitions than loss and failure thinking. In fact some researchers have found equivalent levels of threat and danger cognitive content and processing in anxiety and depression (G. Bulter & Mathews, 1983; M. Greenberg & Beck, 1989), or no group differences in either loss and failure or harm and danger thinking in depression and anxiety (Whisman et al., 1993). Laurent and Stark (1993) compared diagnosed depressed, anxious, and control youngsters from grades 4 through 7 on a number of self-report instruments of anxious and depressive cognitions. The most consistent finding was no significant difference between the depressed and anxious groups in the content of their negative cognitions, prompting one to question whether content-specificity may be less evident in children and adolescents than adults (see also Garber, Weiss, & Shanley, 1993).

Although most of the studies on content-specificity have utilized retrospective self-report measures to compare the frequency or endorsement rates for loss and failure versus threat and danger cognitions and beliefs in anxious and depressed groups, a few studies have compared the groups on measures of cognitive errors. There is some evidence that patients with major depression show more cognitive errors such as dichotomous thinking and overgeneralization, especially to negative events, than anxious patients (Macpherson, 1989), although failure to find differences between the two diagnostic groups in cognitive processing errors have also been reported (G. Bulter & Mathews, 1983; Fennell & Campbell, 1984; Mitchell & Campbell, 1988).

Self-representational differences have also been found between anxiety and depression. Based on Higgins' self-discrepancy theory (Higgins, 1987), studies have found that depression in clinical and nonclinical samples is characterized by a discrepancy between the actual self-concept and ideal self-evaluative standards, whereas anxiety is characterized by a discrepancy between the actual self-concept and ought self-evaluative standards (Strauman, 1989, 1992).

Content-specificity has also been investigated from an information processing perspective. Using a self-referent encoding task (SRET) to assess selective encoding in depressed and anxious outpatients and normal controls, M. Greenberg and Beck (1989) found that the depressed group consistently endorsed as self-descriptive and recalled significantly more negative depression-relevant trait adjectives than anxious and normal controls, though there were no significant group differences for the positive depression-relevant words. However, the anxious group did not consistently show selective endorsement patterns and trait recall differences for the anxious-relevant stimuli, suggesting that the processing of anxious trait adjectives was similar in depressed and anxious individuals. In a review of two SRET studies conducted on dysphoric, anxious and nondysphoric-nonanxious undergraduates using positive, negative, and neutral depression-relevant and anxiety-relevant trait adjectives, M. Greenberg, Vazquez, and Alloy (1988) found that the dysphoric group had an even-handed and nonspecific processing of positive and negative self-referent depression- and anxiety-relevant material, whereas the anxious students showed weak content-specificity in the form of enhanced self-descriptive ratings and recall of anxiety-relevant trait adjectives. In another article on this same data set, M. Greenberg and Alloy (1989) concluded from reaction time and trait adjective endorsement patterns that the balanced or even-handed processing of positive and negative personally relevant (both depression and anxiety-related) trait adjectives was specific to mild depression or dysphoria and not anxiety.

Ingram, Kendall, et al. (1987) reported that "purely" dysphoric students recalled significantly more depression-relevant trait adjectives, whereas the purely test-anxious subjects recalled significantly more anxious content trait adjectives. Sanz (1996) obtained different SRET results with psychometrically derived dysphoric students showing equivalent recall of positive and negative self-referent trait adjectives and the psychometrically defined social phobic group recalling more positive than negative trait words. Clifford and Hemsley (1987) found no significant differences in trait adjective recall of depressed and schizophrenic patients. Strauman (1992) found that a differential autobiographical memory retrieval bias was only apparent when individuals were provided with self-guide cues. In that condition alone, the highly anxious students recalled significantly more memories with anxious content, whereas the dysphoric students recalled significantly more depressive content memories. P. Watkins, Mathews, Williamson, and Fuller (1992) reported that depressed patients recalled significantly more depression-related words than controls on a cued-recall task, whereas the controls recalled significantly more of the physical threat-related words than the depressed group. Using a visual probe detection task, Westra and Kuiper (1997) found that dysphoric students had significantly enhanced detection latencies when the probe followed hopelessness and loss words, whereas anxious students had significantly better performance for probe discriminations following threat adjectives. Overall, however, content-specificity was stronger in depression than anxiety as seen in the significant congruent self-referent endorsement patterns and a trend toward enhanced recognition memory for congruent stimuli (i.e., hopelessness and loss adjectives) in the former group alone. Support for content-specificity can be found in a number of information processing experimental studies indicating that evidence for the hypothesis is not simply an artifact of response bias or item overlap on retrospective endorsement measures (i.e., ATQ, CCL, HS).

As previously mentioned, very little research has focused on the differentiation of cognitive content in depression from other diagnostic groups. Hollon et al. (1986) found that clinically depressed individuals scored significantly higher than nondepressed substance abuse and schizophrenic patients on the ATQ but not on the Dysfunctional Attitudes Scale (DAS), though Ross et al. (1986) found that the ATQ scores of depressed psychiatric inpatients differed significantly only from nondepressed substance abuse patients and not a sample diagnosed with schizophrenia. Westra and Kuiper (1997) did obtain distinct content-specificity processing effects for dysphoric students in comparison with anxious, bulimic, and Type A individuals. At this time, too few studies have compared the cognitive content of depression with other diagnostic categories to conclude whether loss and failure cognitions can reliably and accurately distinguish depression from other affective and psychological states.

Correlated Measures

A large number of studies have examined the correlational patterns associated with self-report measures of anxious and depressive cognitions. Most studies have found some evidence of convergent and discriminant validity, with measures of loss and failure beliefs and cognitions more highly correlated with measures of depressive symptoms than with anxious symptoms in both clinical and nonclinical samples (D.A. Clark, 1992; Garber et al., 1993; Harrell, Chambless, & Calhoun, 1981; Steer et al., 1994; G. Thorpe, Barnes, Hunter, & Hines, 1983), though failure to support discriminant validity has also been reported (LaPointe & Harrell, 1978; Zurawski & Smith, 1987). In addition, some studies have found no evidence of specificity for anxious thoughts or symptoms, with either thoughts of harm and danger correlating with both anxiety and depression, or anxiety correlating with both depressive and anxious thinking (D.A. Clark, 1992; Garber et al., 1993; Harrell et al., 1981; G. Thorpe et al., 1983).

Many studies have utilized partial correlations and multiple regression analysis to control for the high correlation between anxiety and depression symptom measures. Findings from these studies have generally supported the content-specificity hypothesis with negative cognition measures of loss, failure, and hopelessness showing a significant relationship with depressive symptoms even when anxiety and/or threat cognitions are partialed out of the equation (Alford, Lester, Patel, Buchanan, & Giunta, 1995; Ambrose & Rholes, 1993; A. Beck, Riskind, Brown, & Steer, 1988; R. Beck, Perkins, & Wilson, 1993; D.A. Clark, 1986; D.A. Clark, Beck, & Brown, 1989; D.A. Clark, Steer, Beck, & Snow, 1996; Jolly & Dykman, 1994; Jolly & Kramer, 1994; Jolly et al., 1994; McDermut & Haaga, 1994; Rholes, Riskind, & Neville, 1985), though again there is less evidence for the specificity of threat and danger cognitions (Jolly & Kramer, 1994; Jolly et al., 1994; McDermut & Haaga, 1994). Jolly and Kramer (1994) concluded from their hierarchical regression and principal components analyses of the CCL and symptom measures in adult psychiatric outpatients that a general nonspecific cognition factor accounted for more variance in symptom measures than the specific or unique components.

In a clinical study, Waikar and Craske (1997) found that depression was characterized by higher negative outcome expectancy (i.e., hopelessness) and a greater sense of helplessness in one's ability to control the likelihood of positive and negative future life experiences. These results, then, only partially confirmed Alloy et al.'s (1990) view that anxiety is characterized by helplessness in controlling important future outcomes, whereas depression is characterized by hopelessness or a high perceived probability of future negative outcomes. Wickless and Kirsch (1988) found that anxiety was uniquely associated with threat cognitions but sadness was associated with both threat and loss cognitions in a group of nonclinical students. However, negative results have also been achieved, particularly in nonclinical samples (LaPointe & Harrell, 1978), leading D.A. Clark and Steer (1996) to conclude that cognitive content-specificity may not be as apparent in less distressed nonclinical samples.

Issues in Cognitive Content-Specificity

There are three issues pertinent to our discussion of cognitive content-specificity in depression. First, does specificity depend on which aspect of the cognitive triad is under investigation? Is specificity more evident in negative self and future than in negative world cognitions (Haaga et al., 1991, p. 219)? Blackburn et al. (1986) found that negative thinking about the world but not about the self or future was higher in depressed relative to anxious patients. However, M. Greenberg and Beck (1989) did find consistent evidence of content-specificity in depression for endorsement of negative trait adjectives about the self, world, and future. Hopelessness or negative view of the future rather than loss cognitions may be the best predictor of future depression but not anxiety (Alford et al., 1995; Rholes et al., 1985). Most studies have not disentangled the specificity of the components of the cognitive triad. Given the inconsistent results obtained by the few studies that have attempted this differentiation, we can only conclude that to date there is no reason to believe that one component of the negative cognitive triad is more specific to depression than the other components, though further research is needed on this issue.

Second, is content-specificity of depression more evident as a reduction in positive cognitions or as an increase in negative cognitions? L.A. Clark and Watson (1991a, 1991b) proposed in their tripartite model of anxiety and depression that a low frequency of positive cognitions is a unique feature of depression, whereas a high frequency of negative thoughts about personal loss and failure is a common feature of both anxiety and depression. This argument is based on their view that negative cognitions characterize states of negative affect (NA), with high NA a common symptom feature of both anxiety and depression. However, symptoms such as loss of interest, low motivation, and anhedonia, which characterize a state of low positive affect (PA), are considered unique to depression.

If one interprets a decline in positive cognitions as reflecting a state of low PA, then L.A. Clark and Watson (1991a) would expect a low rate of positive thinking to be more specific to depression than a high rate of negative cognitions. Bryant and Baxter (1997) did find that ATQ-N was related to both anxiety and happiness, whereas ATQ-P was more strongly related to happiness than anxiety. Burgess and Haaga (1994) also found that a low rate of positive cognitions was specifically associated with depressive but not anxious symptoms. Similar results were reported by Jolly and Wiesner (1996), who found that the ATQ-P had a significantly stronger relationship with depression than anxiety in an adolescent inpatient sample. There is no evidence, however, that a low rate of positive thinking is *more specific* to depression than a high rate of negative cognitions (see review by D.A. Clark & Steer, 1996). In fact, Ingram (1989) found that dysphoric subjects reported significantly more negative automatic thoughts than socially anxious individuals but the two groups did not differ significantly in reporting fewer positive thoughts relative to normal controls. Ingram, Kendall, et al. (1995) concluded that it is still unclear whether the ATQ-P is specifically related to different kinds of psychological distress.

It may be that the cognitive content-specificity hypothesis and tripartite model of L.A. Clark and Watson (1991b) should be considered complementary rather than contradictory views of the relationship between anxiety and depression. Factor analysis of depression and anxiety symptom and cognition measures have indicated that these measures possess both common and unique dimensions (D.A. Clark et al., 1989). Furthermore, in two recent studies, we found that a large common second-order factor that corresponded to NA or general distress was hierarchically related to two lower first-order factors that distinguished anxiety and depression (D.A. Clark, Steer, et al., 1994; Steer et al., 1995). The cognitive items of the BAI and BDI had strong loadings on their respective first-order factors supporting the specificity of cognitive symptoms. However, the presence of a large common general factor in the anxiety and depression measures was consistent with the tripartite view of general distress common across affective states. Jolly and Kramer (1994) also found evidence of specific and nonspecific dimensions in anxiety and depression cognition measures and concluded that a general cognition dimension may be evident in NA which comprises more discrete depression and anxiety elements. Even though the general cognition factor accounted for more variance in the depression and anxiety symptom measures, the authors suggested that the specific dimensions would offer better discrimination among cognitive states. In another study, Jolly et al. (1994) found that NA and anxious cognitions accounted for significant variance in anxiety symptom measures, whereas NA, low PA, and depressive cognitions significantly predicted depressive symptoms. Thus both common and specific elements must be considered when investigating the cognitive and noncognitive symptom features of anxiety, depression, and other psychological disturbances (see also discussion by Mineka et al., 1998).

A third issue concerns whether cognitive content-specificity is equally apparent across various levels of disturbance. Ambrose and Rholes (1993) first raised the possibility that specificity may vary depending on the frequency level of negative cognitions. In a large sample of community children and adolescents, they found a linear relationship between depressive cognitions and symptoms, but a curvilinear relationship between anxious cognitions and symptoms. At low frequency levels, threat cognitions had a stronger association with anxious than depressive symptoms but as the frequency of threat cognitions increased, the relationship with anxious symptoms decreased and the association with depressive symptoms strengthened. Loss cognitions showed a uniform association with depressive symptoms throughout the entire frequency range, though at lower levels loss cognitions showed greater nonspecificity than at more extreme frequency levels. Ambrose and Rholes concluded that the content-specificity hypothesis may need to be modified to take into account the differing relations with anxiety and depression that occur at different frequency levels of negative thinking.

In a recent study, we failed to confirm the results of Ambrose and Rholes (1993), instead generally finding a strong linear component in most of the regression analyses of anxious and depressive cognition and symptom measures with the quadratic and cubic components accounting for only a trivial amount of additional variance at best (D.A. Clark et al., 1996). However, we did find that cognitive-symptom specificity may be less evident in individuals with lower levels of symptom distress such as normal controls or medically ill individuals, though the lack of specificity in the medical sample may be due to the lower content validity of the negative cognition measures for this sample. At the very least, these findings indicate that cognitive content-specificity may depend on the level of disturbance evident in the sample under investigation.

CONTENT-SPECIFICITY, COMORBIDITY, AND MEASUREMENT

Research on the cognitive profile of depression is complicated by the high comorbidity between anxiety and depression (Alloy et al., 1990; Brady & Kendall, 1992; T. Brown & Barlow, 1992; L.A. Clark, 1989; L.A. Clark et al., 1995; Flint, 1994; Mineka et al., 1998; Regier et al., 1990) as well as the high correlation between anxiety and depression measures of cognitions and symptoms (L.A. Clark & Watson, 1991b; Dobson, 1985; Feldman, 1993; Gotlib, 1984; Gotlib & Cane, 1989; Ollendick & Yule, 1990). Thus in any study, the failure to find cognitive-symptom specificity may be due to a high rate of secondary anxiety or depression in patients with a principal diagnosis of depression or an anxiety disorder (Haaga et al., 1991). Alternatively, certain instruments such as the State-Trait Anxiety Inventory are known to be poor measures of symptom specificity because they contain a high proportion of items that tap symptoms common to anxiety and depression, or even symptoms of the unintended construct (Gotlib & Cane, 1989). This state of low discriminant validity is further complicated because even with optimal measures, the natural co-occurrence of anxiety and depression may approximate a correlation coefficient of .45 (L.A. Clark & Watson, 1991b). Obviously, it will be difficult, if not impossible, to demonstrate content-specificity if cognition and symptom measures of low discriminant validity are utilized.

There is some evidence that the differential diagnosis and measurement of depression can be improved if one assesses the distinct cognitive content of depression. In a study of symptom differences in outpatients with a principal *DSM-III* diagnosis of major depression, dysthymia, panic disorder, or generalized anxiety disorder, we found that items assessing a negative view of self, anhedonia, and dysphoria distinguished major depression and dysthymia, whereas panic symptoms, threat cognitions and anxiousness differentiated panic disorder and generalized anxiety (D.A. Clark, Beck, et al., 1994). Riskind et al. (1991) also found that hopelessness and thoughts of loss and failure differentiated dysthymia from generalized anxiety, whereas in a more recent study we found that negative cognition, hopelessness, and the subjective items of the BDI distinguished depressed psychiatric inpatients from depressed and nondepressed medical and control groups even after controlling for common or nonspecific symptoms (D.A. Clark et al., 1998). Using a receiver operating characteristic analysis comparing the differentiation of "pure" major depression and "pure" panic disorder, Somoza, Steer, Beck, and Clark (1994) found that depression scales (i.e., BDI, CCL-D and Hamilton Rating Scale of Depression) were better discriminators of the two diagnostic groups than the anxiety scales (i.e., BAI, CCL-A and Hamilton Rating Scale of Anxiety). These results suggest that cognitive content variables such as hopelessness, loss, and failure may be helpful in making a differential diagnosis of depression from anxiety (for reviews, see Di Nardo & Barlow, 1990; Watson & Kendall, 1989). Meanwhile, studies have found that measures with a significant number of cognitive items assess distinct depression and anxiety symptoms, again indicating that more precise measurement of depression may be obtained by including items that assess negative cognitive content of loss and failure (D.A. Clark, Steer, et al., 1994; Cox et al., 1993; Endler, Cox, Parker, & Bagby, 1992; Lovibond & Lovibond, 1995; Steer et al., 1995).

Summary

In past reviews of the cognitive theory of depression, authors have been divided with some claiming relatively strong empirical support for the content-specificity hypothesis (Ackermann-Engel & DeRubeis, 1993; Haaga et al., 1991; Segal & Shaw, 1986a), and others arguing that support is relatively weak or inconsistent (Coyne & Gotlib, 1983; Gotlib & Hammen, 1992; Gotlib, Kurtzman & Blehar, 1997). Our own review of the literature suggests there is strong empirical support for the specificity of negative cognitive content in depressive states. However, several issues and questions remain for future investigation.

First, the specificity of threat and danger cognitions may be less apparent with a number of studies showing that this thought content may be linked to both anxiety and depression. Ambrose and Rholes (1993) suggest that the specificity of anxious thinking may diminish as the individual experiences an elevated frequency of this type of thinking.

Second, certain sampling characteristics may influence the strength and direction of the cognitive-symptom relationship. Specificity may not be as evident in child, and possibly adolescent, samples as it is in the adult population. In addition, we found evidence of a tendency toward non-specificity in less distressed medical and normal control groups.

Third, most of the research has focused on specificity at the cognition level. Those studies that have investigated types of cognitive errors or belief content have produced more equivocal results. In fact, there is very little evidence for the content-specificity of dysfunctional beliefs or attitudes. However, the DAS was never intended to have high specificity for depression. The instrument was derived through clinical observation rather than driven by theoretical considerations. The DAS items assess both positive and negative beliefs that were thought to attenuate and accentuate, respectively, in depressed patients. Although it was assumed that these beliefs are activated during depression, it was also realized that these same beliefs would be evident in other psychological disorders such as anxiety. Thus the instrument was labeled the "Dysfunctional Attitudes Scale" and not the "Depressotypic or Depressogenic Attitudes Scale."

Fourth, empirical support for cognitive content-specificity of depression is not limited to retrospective self-report measures. Instead, the few studies that have investigated this issue using information processing experiments have produced supportive results. As well, there is some indication that the cognitive profile of depression is distinct from various types of psychological disorders other than anxiety, though additional research is needed on this topic.

Fifth, the specificity of loss and failure content in depression is apparent both as an increase in negative thinking and as a reduction in positive cognitions. Moreover, content-specificity seems equally evident in all three elements of the negative cognitive triad, though once again, too few studies have examined this issue to assert this finding with confidence.

Sixth, research on content-specificity does have diagnostic, assessment, and conceptual implications. We found evidence that the differential diagnosis of depression may be improved if one adequately assesses the negative cognitive symptoms of depression. In addition, measures that contain a higher proportion of depression-specific cognitive items appear to possess better discriminant validity than measures with few cognition items.

And finally, studies that examined both the common and specific symptoms of depression and anxiety suggest that the more distinct negative cognition dimensions of anxiety and depression may be linked to a higher order negative affect or general negative cognition dimension (Bryant & Baxter, 1997; Jolly & Kramer, 1994). This hierarchical conceptualization of negative thinking may provide the most accurate understanding of the relationship between the common and specific cognitive elements of anxiety and depression (see also Mineka et al., 1998). Alternatively, Joiner and his colleagues have argued that the general symptom structure of anxiety and depression is basically nonhierarchical consisting of three distinct first-order dimensions of low positive affect (depression), physiological hyperarousal (anxiety), and negative affect (general distress). Confirmatory and exploratory factor analyses based on anxiety and depression self-report symptom measures supported this nonhierarchical version of the tripartite model in child and adolescent patients, as well as a nonclinical university student sample (Joiner, 1996; Joiner et al., 1996). Thus the exact structure of the symptom relationship between anxiety and depression is still a matter of much debate and research interest.

CONCLUSION

In the past, reviewers have concluded that there is modest to strong empirical support for most of the descriptive hypotheses of the cognitive model (Ackermann-Engel & DeRubeis, 1993; Gotlib & Hammen, 1992; Gotlib & McCabe, 1992), although Haaga et al. (1991) appeared more guarded in their conclusion. A look at these reviews suggests that this rather optimistic opinion is based largely on the strong empirical support evident for the three hypotheses reviewed in this chapter—negativity, exclusivity, and content-specificity. It is readily apparent that depression is characterized by a preponderance of negative self-referent thinking and, possibly to a lesser extent, a reduction in positive cognitions. This shift in the cognitive balance of one's thinking argues for a prominent role for cognition in depressive mood disorders.

Numerous studies have shown that clinically depressed and even nonclinical, dysphoric individuals have a significantly higher frequency of negative self-referent thoughts and beliefs than nondepressed controls. There is strong empirical support, then, for the *negativity hypothesis*. However, the negative cognitive content of depression is a characteristic of episodic depression that remits when sufficient symptomatic recovery from depression is attained. Further research and instrumentation development are needed to determine whether negativity is equally apparent in the depressed patient's views of the self, personal world, and future. Also research into the negativity hypothesis has relied almost exclusively on retrospective cognition and symptom questionnaires that in some cases contain too many overlapping items, thereby inflating the correlation between the cognitions and symptoms. More research utilizing thought production methods of cognitive assessment is needed to address this criticism.

Haaga et al. (1991) suggested removal of the *exclusivity hypothesis* from cognitive theory because research has shown that positive thinking is not completely excluded in depression. We argued for a reinterpretation of the exclusivity hypothesis so that it now refers to a relative decline in positive thinking in depression rather than an absolute denial or absence of positive thought patterns. Furthermore, we cited evidence that positive and negative cognitions are related but distinct phenomena so that decline in positive thinking can not be assumed under the negativity hypothesis.

The empirical support for the exclusivity hypothesis is more modest than it is for the negativity hypothesis, in part because fewer studies have investigated the frequency of positive cognitions in depressed samples. Yet most of this research has found that depressed and dysphoric individuals report significantly fewer positive self-referent cognitions, though the presence of negative cognitions still emerges as the most salient cognitive symptom of depression. In fact, positive self-referent thinking may be less directly related to depression and instead more indicative of an adaptive coping mechanism or a healthy adjustment to life. Another research direction under the States-of-Mind Model of Schwartz and colleagues (R. Schwartz, 1997; R. Schwartz & Garamoni, 1986) suggests that it is the balance or ratio of positive to negative thoughts that is critical for optimal functioning or dysfunction. Future investigations are needed that assess all types of self-referent and other-referent thinking so that the relationship between frequency of positive and negative thoughts, and symptoms of depression as well as psychological health and well-being can be determined. Until then, we can only conclude that a somewhat diminished capacity to engage in positive self-referent thinking appears to be a noteworthy feature of depression.

Group comparison, correlational, and multiple regression studies involving both clinical and nonclinical samples have provided considerable empirical support for the *content-specificity hypothesis;* that is, that a distinctive cognitive profile involving a loss and failure perspective characterizes depressed and dysphoric states. Moreover, experimental information processing studies on encoding and retrieval of self-referent material have confirmed that depression and, to a lesser extent, dysphoric states have a distinct cognitive profile of loss and failure. The cognitive content-specificity of depression is evident in reductions in positive thinking as well as increases in negative cognitions, and appears to assist in the differential diagnosis and measurement of depression and anxiety. However, descriptive symptom research indicates that both common and specific symptoms are evident to varying degrees in all psychological disorders including anxiety and depression, and so research on cognitive content-specificity must take this into account (Mineka et al., 1998). As an example, cognitive content-specificity of depression may be less apparent in nondistressed samples or children and adolescents where general distress may account for a greater proportion of the variance in emotional disorder. In the end, virtually all the content-specificity research has contrasted depression with anxiety so we have very little evidence on whether the cognitive profile of depression is distinguishable from the cognitive content evident in other psychological disorders or states. Further research is needed that contrasts depression with disorders other than anxiety. In addition, greater emphasis should be placed on linking cognitive content-specificity to other symptom models of depression and anxiety such as L.A. Clark and Watson's (1991b) tripartite model, Barlow's three-factor model (Barlow, Chorpita, & Turovsky, 1996), or the integrative hierarchical model offered by Mineka et al. (1998).

Most of the research on the negativity, exclusivity, and content-specificity hypotheses has relied on retrospective self-report questionnaires. Although critics of the cognitive model contend that these measures are tautological and confounded with imprecise and overlapping items, our review of the literature leads to a different conclusion. Many of these measures have shown moderate to strong convergent, discriminant and predictive validity. Moreover in Chapter 11, we explain that many of these same measures of cognition have proven clinical utility as clinical assessment and treatment outcome measures. As researchers advocating a scientist-practitioner perspective, a dismissive attitude toward cognitive questionnaire research is unacceptable. As evident from Chapter 6, many of these measures have been helpful in elucidating the functional status or role that negative cognition plays in depressive disorders.

CHAPTER 6

Descriptive Hypotheses: The Role of Negative Cognition in Depression

THE NEXT three descriptive hypotheses of the cognitive model of depression—primacy, universality, and severity/persistence—refer to the role of negative cognition and biased information processing in depressive disorders. In Chapter 5, we presented evidence that a negative self-referent cognitive perspective is a salient feature of the depressive state. This body of research suggests that depression cannot be adequately understood without taking into account the themes of personal loss, failure, and deprivation that dominate the cognitive perspective of the depressed individual.

In this chapter, we examine the impact this pervasive negative self-referent cognitive perspective may have on the pathognomonic course of depression. If the negative cognitive structures, processes, and products of the information processing organization play a central role in depression, then this negative cognitive orientation should have a significant impact on the behavioral, affective, and motivational symptoms of depression (A. Beck, 1987). Furthermore, this negativity bias should be apparent in all types of depression regardless of the finer distinctions that might be made at some other level of diagnostic conceptualization. We would also expect the severity and persistence of depressive states to continue unabated as long as negativity dominates the information processing system. If cognitive factors are crucial to understanding and treating depression, then these structures, processes, and products should play a prominent role in shaping the depressive experience.

PRIMACY HYPOTHESIS

Negative cognition and biased information processing will critically influence the behavioral, affective, somatic, and motivational symptoms of depression.

Haaga et al. (1991) noted that there has been considerable confusion over the cognitive model's understanding of cognitive primacy. What is meant by this hypothesis is that negative cognition and processing bias are such core, integral or primary components of the depressive experience that a change in cognition will lead to an increase or decrease in the intensity of other depressive symptoms (A. Beck, 1987; D.A. Clark & Steer, 1996). CT does not assert a temporal or causal primacy to cognition; that is, that negative cognition causes depression. Critics often mistakenly assume that in the cognitive model negative cognition has a fundamental causal priority over affect and other symptoms of depression (Coyne & Gotlib, 1983; Teasdale & Barnard, 1993). It has been stated very clearly and explicitly in other writings—*Negative cognition does not cause depression* (A. Beck, 1987). Moreover, Segal and Shaw (1986a) noted that cognitive primacy merely asserts that negative cognition and processing are an integral part of depression that allows access "to the system of integrated dysfunctions which characterize the disorder and which are observable at both a molecular (biochemical changes) and a molar (cognitive changes) level of analysis" (p. 672).

At the same time, primacy is an empirically testable hypothesis (A. Beck, 1991) and should not be relegated to a merely "interpretative" status, a convenient strategy for helping clinicians organize their patients' problems (Haaga et al., 1991). Rather the primacy hypothesis assigns a central role to cognition in the moderation of other depressive symptoms. Negative cognition is a moderator rather than a mediator of depressive symptoms. As primary moderating variables, negative cognition and biased processing will have a major impact on the severity and duration of other depressive symptoms. The term "primary," then, refers to the primary role or influence that negative cognition has on the clinical presentation of depression. However, the influence of negative cognition and information processing on the persistence and severity of the affective, behavioral, somatic, and motivational symptoms of depression does not imply that negative cognitive functioning is the sole contributor to the occurrence of these depressive symptoms.

The primacy hypothesis is as important to testing the cognitive theory of depression as the other descriptive hypotheses discussed in this section. It is consistent with the fourth assumption of the cognitive model described in Chapter 3, that "information processing serves as a guiding principle for the emotional, behavioral and physiological components of human experience." The conceptual basis of the primacy hypothesis is evident in the central role played by the cognitive-conceptual schemas in the information processing system (see Chapter 4). Because of the primacy hypothesis, cognitive theory asserts that change in negative cognition and processing is integral to achieving change in the noncognitive symptoms of depression.

The empirical basis of the primacy hypothesis revolves around three sources of information. First, we will review a series of mood induction studies that use the production of negative self-referent thoughts to create depressivelike mood shifts. Here the question becomes whether the production of negative self-referent thinking can lead to depressivelike states. A second line of research examines whether negative cognition and imagery is associated with the same type of psychophysiological and facial expressive changes that one sees in depression and dysphoria. If so, then this research would suggest that negative thinking can lead to depressive mood-congruent changes even at the physiological level. A final set of studies examines whether a reduction in negative thinking is associated with a corresponding reduction in depressive symptoms or mood state. By seeking to determine the influence that negative self-referent thinking has on mood state and other aspects of depression, these studies test the empirical basis of the primacy hypothesis.

PRODUCTION OF NEGATIVE COGNITION AND DYSPHORIA

One of the most widely used procedures for inducing happy or sad mood states is a cognitive manipulation introduced by Velten (1968). In the Velten Induction Procedure (VIP), subjects are asked to read a series of self-referent mood statements and to "try to feel the mood suggested by the statements" (Velten, 1968, p. 474). The depression induction statements tend to fall into two categories involving self-devaluation such as "I've doubted that I am a worthwhile person" and "I'm discouraged and unhappy about myself," or suggestions about physical sensations associated with depression such as "I feel rather sluggish now" and "I'm getting tired" (Frost, Graf, & Becker, 1979). In addition to the self-statements of Velten, several other procedures that have been used to induce mood shifts such as listening to mood-related music, autobiographical memory recall, films, solitary recollection, facial expressions, social feedback, and hypnotic suggestions (Martin, 1990). However, it is the self-statement mood induction that is most relevant for testing whether the production of negative self-referent thoughts is associated with a negative or depressive mood state.

Over the past 20 years, many studies have been conducted using the VIP to induce depressed mood (for extensive reviews, see D.M. Clark, 1983; Martin, 1990). From this literature, two general findings emerge. First, most, but not all individuals, who read negative self-referent statements experience a depressed or dysphoric mood state as evidenced by a significant change from a preinduction neutral mood to a postinduction depressed mood state. D.M. Clark (1983) noted that 30% to 50% of subjects fail to respond to the VIP. Albersnagel (1988), for example, found that only 33% of his subjects evidenced substantial mood change in the expected direction, with 17% actually showing a significant mood shift in the opposite direction.

One cannot interpret the failure of the depressive VIP statements to induce dysphoria as an indication that negative self-referent cognition does not affect depressed mood in these individuals. The criterion used to indicate a change in mood state can vary from study to study, though most use a shift of at least 10 points on a mood visual analogue scale to indicate a successful change in mood state (Martin, 1990). Albersnagel (1988) used a criterion based on statistical significance that may have been more stringent than the raw change scores used in other studies. Also the failure to respond to the depression statements of the VIP could reflect subjects' inability to generate or focus on the negative self-referent thoughts suggested by the statements rather than on the failure of negative self-referent thinking per se to elicit depressed mood. In fact, the variable success rate with the VIP could be taken as evidence that the mere exposure to negative self-referent statements is insufficient to cause dysphoria. Rather, it may be that individuals must succeed in actually processing or generating the type of negative self-referent thoughts represented by the statements to obtain a depressed mood state.

The VIP can only be considered of relevance for testing the primacy hypothesis if the transient mood state induced by the self-referent statements is similar, if only temporarily, to naturally occurring depressive states. D.M. Clark (1983) in his review has argued that the negative mood state induced by the VIP produces "a good analogue of mild, naturally occurring retarded depression" (p. 27). He noted that a number of depressivelike symptoms have been found in the brief dysphoria induced by negative self-referent VIP statements. These include psychomotor retardation, loss of pleasure and incentive, indecisiveness, facial EMG, reduced social responsiveness, and differential accessibility of positive and negative cognitions and memories. Martin (1990) concluded that all six mood induction procedures that she reviewed, including the VIP, produce levels of dysphoria equivalent to an intermediate or moderate clinical level. Although generally similar to naturally occurring depressive states, it must be remembered that VIP dysphoria is transient and so obviously differs significantly in terms of persistence and duration from "natural" depression (D.M. Clark, 1983). Chartier and Ranieri (1989) found that although undergraduate students assigned to a Velten mood induction condition produced significantly greater negative mood change than an analogue failure task, the Velten-induced dysphoria did not persist beyond 6 to 12 minutes into the postinduction period.

Martin (1990) concluded that studies are divided over the specificity of VIP. Thus in some studies the VIP depression statements led to an increase in depression alone (Frost et al., 1979; Polivy & Doyle, 1980; Slyker & McNally, 1991; Sutherland, Newman, & Rachman, 1982; Teasdale & Russell, 1983); whereas in other studies significant increases were seen in both depression and anxiety, that is, in multiple rather than single discrete emotions (Brewer, Doughtie, & Lubin, 1980; Polivy, 1981; Strickland, Hale, & Anderson, 1975; A. Wilson & Krane, 1980). However, more studies have found specific depression effects with the negative VIP statements and so the lack of specificity in other studies could be due to the use of highly correlated measures of anxiety and depression such as the Multiple Affect Adjective Checklist (e.g., Polivy, 1981, Experiment 2). Also a few studies have found that women produce significantly stronger mood induction effects than men (Albersnagel, 1988; Gouaux & Gouaux, 1971; Rholes, Riskind, & Lane, 1987), though D.M. Clark (1983) concluded in his review that other studies have failed to find gender differences, so there is mixed support for the contention that mood induction is more effective in women than men. Whatever the case, the possibility of gender differences in mood induction effectiveness is consistent with studies showing greater mood-congruent encoding and retrieval for women as well as epidemiological studies that report a higher rate of depressive disorders in women.

We have interpreted the success of the VIP as support for the primacy hypothesis because the production of negative self-referent statements is associated with various features or symptoms of depressed mood. However, an alternative interpretation is that the effects of the VIP are entirely the result of demand characteristics with subjects not showing genuine mood shifts but rather reporting effects to comply with the demands of the study (Buchwald, Strack, & Coyne, 1981). After all, individuals are explicitly instructed to "try to get into the mood suggested by the statements" while reading the negative self-referent statements. Polivy and Doyle (1980) found that subjects given explicit instructions to act as if they were elated or depressed did show a significant shift in mood in

the expected direction. However like Coleman's (1975) demand characteristic condition, Polivy and Doyle (1980) found that some individuals
told to role-play an emotion actually shift into the suggested mood state.
The researchers concluded that the induction effects of the Velten technique, although contaminated by demand characteristics, still seems to
produce some real emotional arousal in subjects. Recently, Slyker and
McNally (1991) found that subjects simply given instructions to get into
an anxious or depressed mood produced as much mood shift in the expected direction as a group who received the traditional VIP. However,
the authors concluded that there was no evidence that the mood changes
produced by the VIP or instructions-only conditions were due to demand
characteristics because of the differential pattern of findings obtained on
their various dependent variables.

Martin (1990) also concluded that there is no evidence that the VIP is
simply a matter of subject compliance or demand characteristics. She
noted: (a) the negative statements of the VIP have produced depression-
like changes on measures that cannot easily be simulated such as psychophysiological and behavioral variables, (b) changes have been noted in
VIP-induced dysphoric states even when subjects did not know they were
being observed, and (c) mood induction has been associated with the predicted differential mood-congruence effects on the autobiographical
memory task (i.e., time taken to retrieve pleasant and unpleasant memories), an effect that would be difficult for subjects to "second-guess." Finally, Alloy, Abramson, and Viscusi (1981) found that subjects instructed
to simulate depression produced highly exaggerated scores on the Multiple Affect Adjective Checklist (MAACL) scales and failed to show the
typical mood effects on judgments of control relative to individuals given
the standard VIP depressive statements. These latter findings, then, indicate that the response changes noted with the VIP cannot be dismissed
simply as the effects of demand characteristics.

A second issue concerns the type of statements that are most effective
in producing the mood changes seen with the VIP. Frost et al. (1979) divided the VIP depression statements into those that suggest the somatic
or physical symptoms of depression and those involving negative self-
evaluation. Contrary to predictions of the primacy hypothesis, the somatic
statements were more effective in producing a depressed mood than the
self-devaluation statements. However, Riskind, Rholes, and Eggers (1982)
failed to confirm this finding. Instead, they found that self-devaluation
and somatic VIP statements produced similar induction effects. More importantly, only the self-devaluation VIP group showed a significant difference from the elation condition in recall times for positive versus negative

memories. The authors concluded that the VIP self-devaluation state-ments may have a direct cognitive priming effect on the availability of memories. These same results were replicated in a second study by Rholes et al. (1987). They concluded from their analyses that self-evaluative cognitions can affect memory retrieval even in the absence of significant mood effects, whereas somatic VIP statements can only affect memory retrieval for negative versus positive events if they generate a strong mood effect. Thus the self-devaluation statements of the VIP may directly prime cognitive phenomena, such as enhanced accessibility of negative memories, that are known to be evident in depressive states. Also, other studies have found that the VIP depression statements are associated with a significant reduction in self-esteem (Coleman, 1975; A. Wilson & Krane, 1980). These results are consistent with the primacy hypothesis, which would predict that the generation of self-devaluation cognitions should lead to cognitive, affective, motivational, and behav-ioral concomitants of depression because of the activation of the loss mode.

It could be argued that the Velten mood induction procedure is rather artificial because individuals are requested to intentionally generate neg-ative thoughts to standard verbal statements in an experimental context. However, evidence from two research areas corroborates the findings of the VIP studies. One of these was recently introduced by Kuyken and Brewin (1994). They found that depressed women with reported histories of child abuse had frequent and persistent intrusive memories related to the abuse. In a subsequent study, Brewin, Hunter, Carroll, and Tata (1996) suggested that the occurrence of spontaneous intrusive memories (and thoughts) of past or immediate life events might be a result of schema ac-tivation. Iintrusive thoughts, images, and impulses are unwanted, unac-ceptable, and repetitive cognitive events that interrupt ongoing activity, have an internal origin, and are difficult to control (Rachman, 1981). Brewin et al. (1996) assessed life events, intrusive memories as indicated by the intrusion and avoidance subscales of the Impact of Event Scale (IES); (Horowitz, Wilner, & Alvarez, 1979), and depressive symptom severity in 31 outpatients with major depression. Abnormally high levels of spontaneous intrusive memories, especially of events involving illness and death, were common in depressed men and women. Sadness, anger, helplessness, and guilt were the most common emotions associated with these intrusions, though depression severity was not significantly corre-lated with number of intrusive memories except for child abuse memo-ries. Lepore (1997) also used the IES to find that frequency of intrusive thoughts prior to a major examination was associated with increases in self-reported depressive symptoms, although analysis of a written expression manipulation that allowed for emotional expression of the exam-related intrusions suggests that the impact of an intrusion rather than its frequency may have a greater influence on emotions. Further research on intrusive thoughts in depression would benefit from the use of other methods of cognitive assessment such as thought listing or daily diary measures in addition to the current reliance on retrospective questionnaires like the IES. Nevertheless, whether frequency or appraised impact is the most critical variable, this emerging research on intrusive thoughts and memories in depression supports the contention of the primacy hypothesis that what we think, however unintended or spontaneous it may be, will have a significant influence on how we feel.

A second related area of research, referred to as thought suppression, explores the impact that intentional suppression of particular thoughts may have on mood. Roemer and Borkovec (1994), for example, found that the occurrence of thoughts related to a significant past loss, whether in a thought expression or suppression condition, was associated with a significant increase in MAACL-R Depression scores after the experiment, whereas anxious and neutral target thoughts did not produce this effect. M. Reynolds and Salkovskis (1992) also found that subjects asked to monitor negative intrusive thoughts during a monotonous experimental task had significantly higher postexperimental depression ratings than a positive intrusive thought monitoring group. Other studies have found that dysphoric individuals will experience more negative thought intrusions than nondysphoric subjects even when they are trying to suppress or control these unwanted thoughts (Conway, Howell, & Giannopoulos, 1991; Howell & Conway, 1992). Such findings highlight the reciprocal spiraling effects that have often been noted between negative mood and cognition. These studies indicate that the more spontaneous, naturally occurring negative thoughts that have been recorded by subjects in the laboratory can also lead to a significant increase in depressed affect.

The findings from experimenter-initiated mood induction studies as well as research that involves the monitoring of "subject-initiated cognition" (i.e., intrusive thoughts and memories) indicate that the occurrence of negative thoughts can influence the course of transient depressive mood state. This can be taken as support for the primacy hypothesis which asserts that the production of negative cognition can directly influence or affect the various symptomatic features that comprise depressive affective states. Moreover, the cognitive priming hypothesis of Riskind (1989) is entirely consistent with the cognitive model's view that the primacy of cognition can be traced to activation of the primal loss mode, which is the basis of depressotypic cognition.

REDUCTION OF NEGATIVE COGNITION AND DEPRESSED AFFECT

If negative cognition and biased information processing can influence the symptoms of depression, then direct reduction of negative thinking should lead to a corresponding decrease in depressed affect. Although only a few studies have examined this aspect of the primacy hypothesis, the results are generally consistent with the cognitive model. Teasdale and Rezin (1978a, Experiment 1) found in a single case study involving two depressed patients that reduction in negative thought frequency during an experimental session in which subjects processed externally presented information (a distraction manipulation) led to a decrease in depressed mood. In a second experiment involving 13 depressed patients, however, Teasdale and Rezin (1978a, Experiment 2) did not find the predicted effect of reducing negative thought frequency on depressed mood. This rather discouraging result may have been due to an inadequate reduction in negative thought frequency during the experimental session. Only 7 of the 13 patients achieved significant reductions in negative thoughts when attempting to distract themselves from negative rumination by processing external information. Thus the experiment did not provide an adequate test of the primacy hypothesis because a sufficient degree of thought reduction must be obtained before one can test its effects on mood.

In a later study, Fennell and Teasdale (1984) found that a brief standardized distraction manipulation, which involved describing slides of outdoor scenes, resulted in a significant reduction in negative thought frequency relative to a control condition only in low endogenous depressed patients. For these patients, reduction in negative thinking was associated with lower depressed mood, reduced counting time, and increased writing speed after the experiment relative to the control condition. The authors concluded that the results, at least with the low-endogenous patients, indicate that reduction in naturally occurring depressive thoughts will alter depressive affect.

A number of clinical treatment studies have examined the effects of decreasing negative thought frequency or intensity and its corresponding effects on mood within a session of cognitive therapy. Persons and Burns (1985) investigated the relationship between thought and mood change in 17 patients with anxious and depressive symptoms who were treated with cognitive therapy in a private practice setting. Within-session mood changes and belief ratings in negative automatic thoughts and rational responses were collected from the Daily Record of Dysfunctional Thoughts (DRDT) used during a single cognitive therapy session for each patient. Analysis revealed that 14 of the 17 patients evidenced significant within-session decreases in negative mood and belief in their negative automatic thoughts. Furthermore, change in automatic thought belief ratings correlated significantly ($r = .64$) with change in mood state. The authors concluded that change in degree of belief in automatic thoughts as well as a good relationship with the therapist were significant contributors to improvement in mood during the therapy session.

Teasdale and Fennell (1982) compared the effects of 30 minutes of cognitive restructuring with a thought exploration control condition and measured their effects on reducing depressive thought frequency, belief ratings, depressed mood, and speech rate in five depressed patients receiving cognitive therapy. Cognitive restructuring produced more change in depressive thought belief ratings and self-rated depressed mood than the thought exploration manipulation. The fact that a decrease in belief in a targeted depressive thought was associated with a corresponding decrease in self-rated dysphoria suggests that a reduction in the salience of negative thinking is associated with a reduction in depressed mood.

These clinical studies, although methodologically weaker for showing direct cognition-mood effects than the experimental manipulations of Teasdale and colleagues, indicate that reductions in the frequency or intensity (i.e., degree of belief) of negative depressotypic thinking may be responsible for an immediate decrease in depressive affect. Again this is entirely consistent with the predictions of the primary hypothesis. If negative cognitions and biased information processing have direct effects on depressive symptoms, then a reduction in one should lead to a corresponding reduction in the other.

PHYSIOLOGICAL CONCOMITANTS OF NEGATIVE COGNITION

One of the most compelling sources of evidence for the cognitive primacy hypothesis comes from psychophysiological and cortical brain activity research on emotion and cognition. If negative cognition and biased information processing have a significant effect on emotional states like depression, then one would expect a link between cognition and the physical or biological basis of emotion. Thus evidence that the production of conscious affectively valenced thoughts or images is associated with a particular peripheral or central physiological response pattern can be taken as strong evidence for the direct influence of cognition on emotion. This is because psychophysiological assessment is considered a more objective, concurrent, and independent measure of cognitive processing and emotion than self-report approaches (Kendall & Hollon, 1981), although G. Miller (1996) has warned that "we should not treat biological data as immune from the interesting confounds that self-report data fall victim to" (p. 623). Problems such as demand characteristics, expectancy effects, social desirability, and response bias, which can introduce confound into self-report measures, may be present, though to a much lesser degree, in psychophysiological responses. The critical question is whether one observes peripheral physiological and central cortical changes when individuals generate negative thoughts or images and report a negative subjective mood state.

Over the past several years, various studies have reported significant changes in autonomic nervous system responses (heart rate, skin conductance latency, and amplitude) when individuals think or imagine positive or negative emotionally valenced stimuli. In some studies, production of negative thoughts or images has been associated with significantly elevated heart rate (Jones & Johnson, 1978; Schuele & Wiesenfeld, 1983; G. Schwartz, Weinberger, & Singer, 1981; Vrana, 1993), though cognition and imagery associated with high arousal emotions such as fear may produce greater heart rate increases than imagery associated with low-arousal emotions such as sadness (Ekman, Levenson, & Friesen, 1983; Levenson, 1992; Witvliet & Vrana, 1995). Moreover, other studies have failed to find a significant difference in cardiac responsiveness to negative (or irrational) compared with positive (or rational) or neutral cognitive stimuli (Master & Gershman, 1983; Matheny & Blue, 1977; Orton, Beiman, LaPointe, & Lankford, 1983; Rogers & Craighead, 1977).

D.A. Clark (1984) found significant elevations in heart rate and respiration in response to personally relevant unpleasant (anxious or depressive) thoughts compared with personally relevant pleasant cognition especially among students who reported a high frequency of depressive and anxious thoughts on a self-report cognitions questionnaire. There was no significant difference when cardiac and respiration associated with the unpleasant thoughts were compared with responses generated to a standard neutral thought condition. Other studies have also found elevated respiration rate when individuals produce negative or distressing thoughts as opposed to positive or neutral cognitions (May & Johnson, 1973; Rimm & Litvak, 1969; Schuele & Wiesenfeld, 1983), though again failure to find differential effects on respiration rate have also been reported (Jones & Johnson, 1978; Master & Gershman, 1983; P. Russell & Brandsma, 1974). These mixed findings for both cardiac and respiration rate suggest that cardiovascular and respiratory responses may not be a clear and unequivocal physiological indicator of the affective valence of cognition. Cardiac, and possibly respiratory, responsiveness may be more relevant for anxious and phobic images, which have a more prominent autonomic arousal component and a higher activity level (Jones & Johnson, 1978, 1980). Because there is a close coupling between the respiratory and cardiovascular systems (Turpin & Sartory, 1980), it is not surprising that these response systems may be equally poor physiological measures of depressive cognition.

The evidence for a link between negative emotional cognition or imagery and skin conductance is also very mixed. Most studies suggest there is no relationship between skin conductance and the emotional valence of thoughts or images (Jones & Johnson, 1978; Matheny & Blue, 1977; Schuele & Wiesenfeld, 1983; Vrana, 1993; Witvliet & Vrana, 1995). However, other studies have obtained significant skin conductance responses to startle probes during high-arousal imagery (i.e., fear) indicating that this physiological variable is modulated more by arousal than the evaluative and affective valence of stimuli (Rogers & Craighead, 1977).

The startle reflex is another physiological response pattern that has been shown to be sensitive to attentional demands and the affective valence of external and internal or imaginal stimuli (Lang, Bradley, & Cuthbert, 1990; Vrana, Spence, & Lang, 1988). The startle reflex is a diffuse skeletomuscular response to an intense stimulus involving eyeblink, "... forward and downward head movements, raising and drawing forward of the shoulders, contraction of the abdomen and abduction of upper limbs and flexion of lower limbs toward the trunk" (E. Cook, Hawk, Davis, & Stevenson, 1991, p. 5).

In psychophysiological experiments, startle potentiation has been measured with electrodes placed for bilateral measurement of eyeblink startle. At irregular intervals while processing externally presented emotional stimuli or generating emotional images, participants are given loud bursts of white noise (i.e., probes) to elicit a startle response. Vrana et al. (1988) found that eyeblink startle response magnitude was significantly greater when individuals viewed negative or unpleasant slides (mainly fear stimuli) as opposed to pleasant or neutral material. Cook et al. (1991) found that eyeblink startle magnitude was significantly greater when participants generated sad, fearful, or anger images of standard affective situations compared with when they generated pleasant or joyful images. A breakdown of this difference indicated that only the high-fear subjects showed greater startle potentiation for negative versus positive emotional imagery. No difference in valence effects was found for the low-fear subjects indicating that affect modulation of the startle probe response may be related to individual differences. In a later study, Witvliet and Vrana (1995) found that eyeblink magnitude was greater and latency shorter during negatively as opposed to positively valenced imagery. At this point, there is some debate over whether eyeblink startle magnitude is indicative of stimulus valence and eyeblink latency of stimulus arousal properties, or whether eyeblinks are larger and faster during high-arousal than during low-arousal imagery, or whether affective valence and arousal affect both startle blink magnitude and latency (Witvliet & Vrana, 1995). Overall, these results are consistent with cognitive primacy by indicating that negative cognition and imagery can influence the response pattern of another physiological variable, the startle probe reflex.

There is now considerable evidence that a specific pattern of facial muscle activity is a component of emotion or specific "affect programs" that elicit biologically prewired facial expressions (Dimberg, 1990). Facial electromyographic (EMG) studies indicate that positive emotions are associated with an increase in zygomatic muscular activity, whereas negative emotions such as sadness, depression, anger, and disgust are associated with increased corrugator activity (Dimberg, 1982, 1990; G. Schwartz, Ahern, & Brown, 1979; Vrana, 1993; Witvliet & Vrana, 1995). Clinically depressed patients also show elevated levels of corrugator EMG and changes in corrugator EMG can differentiate patients who improve with treatment compared to those who do not improve (Carney, Hong, O'Connell, & Amado, 1981; G. Schwartz et al., 1978). Of relevance to the present discussion, significant elevations in corrugator activity have also been found when clinically depressed and nonclinical individuals generate sad or depressing thoughts and images compared with when they produce pleasant or positive emotional mental stimuli (G. Schwartz, Fair, Salt, Mandel, & Klerman, 1976; Teasdale & Bancroft, 1977; Teasdale & Rezin, 1978b; Witvliet & Vrana, 1995). D.A. Clark (1984) found that corrugator EMG response was significantly greater when individuals generated negative thoughts as opposed to pleasant or even neutral cognitions. Furthermore, intratrial analyses revealed that the increase in corrugator activity was significantly greater when subjects were actually thinking the unpleasant thoughts as opposed to when they were receiving instructions to generate the thought. G. Schwartz et al. (1976), however, found that the primary difference in the facial muscle activity of depressed and nondepressed individuals occurred in response to generating positive imagery without any instructions to actually feel an emotion previously associated with the imagined happy or sad past situation. These results mirror findings often reported in the information processing studies. Differences between depressed and nondepressed may be even more evident in response to positive than negative stimuli. Overall, though, there is fairly strong evidence that the production of negative thoughts or images is associated with an increase in corrugator EMG facial muscle activity.

A growing number of neuroscience studies have focused on the brain function and structure associated with cognition, emotion, and psychopathology. Several cortical features have been examined such as cerebral lateralization, electroencephalographic (EEG) asymmetries in various brain regions, event-related brain potentials (ERPs) and cerebral blood flow. In each case, measurement of brain activity in a particular region has been shown to vary with performance on a cognitive or affective task indicating that a particular region of the brain may be specialized for a certain type of cognitive or affective processing (Heller & Nitschke, 1997). Relative increases in activity in a particular brain region during a cognitive or emotive task suggest enhanced performance, whereas an information or emotional processing deficit would be evident if the brain region was not adequately activated during performance (Heller & Nitschke, 1997).

In a review of neuropsychological aspects of cognition in depression, Heller and Nitschke (1997) concluded from studies of EEG asymmetries and positron emission tomography (PET) cerebral blood flow that depression is associated with reduced activity in the left anterior and right posterior regions of the brain. In addition, these authors noted that studies on emotion have found less left than right anterior activity for unpleasant affect and sad mood states. In their review of neuropsychological studies that examine the cognitive functions associated with the brain regions implicated in depression, however, Heller and Nitschke noted that evidence for the asymmetric lateralization of emotion depends on whether anterior or posterior regions are considered. They suggest that considerable evidence exists that depression and sad mood states are associated with reduced levels of right posterior brain activity. In a study of perceptual asymmetry using the chimeric faces task, Heller, Etienne, and Miller (1995) found that highly depressed students had significantly smaller left hemispatial biases, which is consistent with findings of reduced brain activity over the right parietotemporal regions in depressed patients. However, studies of anterior brain function are inconclusive on whether depressed and unpleasant affect are associated with reductions in left or right anterior hemisphere functioning, or both. Davidson (1992, 1993) has proposed that hemispheric asymmetry is important in understanding the experience of emotion, with positive approach-related emotion (i.e., happiness) associated with more left anterior (frontal and anterior temporal) activation, and more right anterior activation during negative withdrawal-related emotion (i.e., disgust). Although most of the studies on hemispheric asymmetry and emotion have used external emotion-relevant stimuli (e.g., slides, facial expressions), it would be interesting to know whether differences in hemispheric activation are evident to internally or cognitively elicited emotion.

EEG and PET scan studies provide a more direct measure of the regional brain activity associated with depression and sad affect than neuropsychological studies of brain function. Unfortunately, very few of these studies have directly investigated whether the production of negative cognitions or biased self-referent processing is associated with corresponding changes in brain activity. ERP research can be used to identify different patterns of cerebral response to varying levels of stimulus expectancy. It is assumed that the more unexpected a stimulus, the greater the amplitude of various endogenous components of ERPs (Blackburn, Roxborough, Muir, Glabus, & Blackwood, 1990). Blackburn et al. found that clinically depressed patients but not normals or recovered depressed individuals had a significantly smaller P300 amplitude of the ERP when presented with negative compared with positive or neutral self-referent words. The authors noted that studies have shown that depressed individuals have a negative bias and so the smaller P300 amplitude is consistent with the view that depressed patients were more expectant of negative stimuli in their environment than nondepressed individuals.

G. Miller (1996) reported on two ERP studies of cognitive biases in depressed inpatients versus nondepressed controls. In the first study, the N400 amplitude was examined in response to pleasant and unpleasant words. The magnitude of the N400 component of ERP appears to be sensitive to automatic semantic expectancy (Chung et al., 1996). The depressive patients showed no negative N400 deflection to the pleasant words which is consistent with the view that in depression there is relatively little response to pleasant stimuli. In another study, depressed patients showed a deficit in N200 production, and to a lesser extent P300, relative to nondepressed normals in response to the presentation of happy, sad, or neutral photographs of human facial expressions and emotional word stimuli. In a study by Chung et al., students were induced into a pessimistic or optimistic mood state and then read brief daily life event stories with a positive or negative ending. Subjects in the pessimistic mood had an expectancy bias for negative story outcomes as evidenced by a N400/P300 effect over the posterior brain region, whereas subjects in an optimistic mood showed ERP differentiation for good and bad outcomes over the medial frontal region. These studies suggest that naturally occurring or induced depressed and nondepressed individuals may show differences in ERP topography when they process emotionally valenced material. Negative cognition and the processing of negative stimuli appear to be associated with distinctive changes in brain activity as indicated by analysis of endogenous components of ERPs, though differences emerge across studies in the exact form that ERP response patterns take to the cognitive processing of emotional stimuli.

Finally, a study by George et al. (1995) provides an example of how PET technology can be used to assess the cortical concomitants of emotion. Eleven healthy women underwent happy, sad, and neutral mood induction by having each woman recall specific events in her life that would make her feel sad, happy, or neutral. At the same time, subjects were shown three affect-appropriate human faces. Analysis of $H_2^{15}O$ PET images revealed that transient sadness was associated with significant increases in cerebral blood flow throughout the limbic, paralimbic, and brainstem structures (i.e., right medial frontal gyrus, left dorsolateral prefrontal cortex, bilateral cingulate gyrus, caudate, putamen, thalamus, fornix, left insula and left midline cerebellum), whereas transient happiness was associated with a widespread decrease in cerebral blood flow in the bilateral temporal-parietal and right prefrontal cortex. In an earlier study, Pardo, Pardo, and Raichle (1993) measured regional cerebral blood flow in 7 healthy individuals under a resting control condition and while imagining past situations that made them feel sad. Self-induced dysphoria was associated with increased bilateral blood flow activity in the inferior and orbitofrontal cortex, a finding somewhat at variance to George et al. (1995). More recently S.C. Baker, Frith, and Dolan (1997) measured cerebral blood flow in 9 nonclinical volunteers while performing either a verbal fluency or word repetition task. Individuals were assessed while in elated, neutral, and depressed moods, which were induced by a combination of procedures that included presentation of the Velten mood induction statements. Both elated and depressed mood induction were associated with significant bilateral cerebral blood flow increases in the lateral orbitofrontal cortex. The depressed mood was also associated with decreased blood flow in the rostral medial prefrontal cortex which is consistent with previous research that decreased blood flow is evident in the prefrontal cortex of patients with a clinical depressive disorder. S. C Baker et al. concluded that the findings of Pardo et al. and their study suggest that the lateral orbitofrontal cortex is involved in affective states more generally, and that differentiation of emotional states may be represented by distinct patterns of neural discharge within this region of the brain. They also argued that the discrepant findings reported by George et al. may be due to the use of autobiographical memory and visual inspection of mood congruent facial expressions to induce distinct mood states. This task could introduce a confound between changes in neural activity associated with recalling a past memory and neural changes associated with mood induction. George et al., however, suggested that their findings may indicate that transient sadness also involves increased activity in many limbic structures and that the prefrontal activation found in their study was more medial than that found by Pardo et al.

It has been reported that at least a subset of depressed patients have metabolic reduction in the left anterolateral prefrontal cortex (Baxter et al., 1985, 1989). George et al. (1995) concluded from these and other PET studies that primary depression is associated with prefrontal lobe hypoactivity (see also S.C. Baker et al., 1997 for similar conclusion). George et al. speculated that the medial prefrontal and limbic hyperactivity they found with transient sadness might evolve into a compensatory pattern of medial prefrontal hypometabolism in individuals susceptible to depression, although the findings of S.C. Baker et al. and Pardo et al. (1993) are more consistent with decreased prefrontal blood flow in depression. R.G. Robinson (1995), in his commentary on the George et al. study noted that research on blood flow changes in emotion indicates that sadness and happiness are both bilaterally mediated and that it is the anterior limbic and paralimbic structures that have been found most consistently to mediate emotion. However, he reiterates a caution raised by George et al. Regional blood flow changes may be an epiphenomenon and not causally related to emotional states. Also although cerebral blood flow is assumed to reflect metabolic activity, the relationship between blood flow changes and focal neuronal or receptor activity is not well understood. Whatever the link between brain metabolism, neuronal activity, and both normal and abnormal negative emotional states, the implication of these findings for the cognitive primacy hypothesis is clear-cut. Individuals requested to concentrate on sad, depressing memories show significant changes in regional brain activity. Thus negative cognitive emotional processing is associated with cortical changes, highlighting the influence that thought can have on regional brain function and structure.

SUMMARY

In this section we have emphasized that negative cognition and processing bias are an integral feature of depression. The primacy hypothesis reflects the importance we place on cognition by stating that negative cognition and the biased information processing of negative self-referent information can directly influence other behavioral, motivational, affective, and somatic symptoms of depression. Our position on the primacy of cognition, though not to be misconstrued as a statement of causal priority, may be a unique feature of the cognitive model. Other depression researchers have taken a different perspective and argued for the primary importance of other symptoms of depression. Sobin and Sackeim (1997), for example, contend that psychomotor symptoms may have a unique significance in terms of diagnosis, prognosis, and possibly the pathophysiological concomitants of depression. Low energy level has been suggested as a specific, distinguishing feature of depression (Buchwald & Rudick-Davis, 1993; Christensen & Duncan, 1995). L.A. Clark and Watson (1991b) considered anhedonia and low positive affect of central importance in defining depression, a view consistent with other researchers who argue for the primary importance of deficits in motivation or the pursuit of valued personal goals (Lecci, Karoly, Briggs, & Kuhn, 1994). Thus the primacy of negative cognition in depression should not be regarded as self-evident but instead must be subjected to empirical scrutiny to determine its validity.

To date, the mood induction studies provide the most direct empirical test of the primacy hypothesis. Individuals who are instructed to think negative self-referent thoughts as represented in the depressive statements contained in the VIP report a significant increase in subjective ratings of dysphoria, as well as changes on other measures of behavioral, motivational, and psychophysiological variables that are associated with depression. D.M. Clark (1983) concluded that the VIP can induce a transient state of depression that is comparable to a naturally occurring mild retarded depression. Moreover, the induction effects of the VIP cannot be entirely explained away as an artifact of demand characteristics, and it is apparent that the self-devaluation statements of the VIP may have a priming effect by making negative depressotypic constructs more accessible. Thus results from the VIP studies indicate that the production of negative self-referent thinking is associated with increases in many of the features of transient depressed mood that also characterize the symptom presentation of mild to moderate clinical depression.

Despite the generally encouraging results of the VIP, a number of issues pertaining to the primacy hypothesis remain unanswered. First, few studies have investigated why some individuals do not show the criterion shifts in mood with the VIP. Although personality and demographic variables have been investigated, it would be important to know whether failed induction is due to individuals not engaging in the negative self-referent thinking suggested by the VIP depression statements. Second, more research is needed on mood induction in clinically depressed individuals to determine whether the production of negative self-referent thinking leads to an increase in other depressive symptoms. Finally, induction studies which use dependent measures that clearly assess the core diagnostic symptoms of depression (i.e., loss of interest and pleasure, fatigue, loss of energy, excessive guilt and worthlessness) will provide a stronger test of the primacy hypothesis.

Only a few studies have examined the immediate effects of reducing negative thinking on the symptoms of depression. The studies we reviewed by Teasdale and colleagues support the primacy hypothesis in that patients who showed a reduction in negative thoughts also evidenced corresponding reductions in depressed mood. However, the sample sizes are often small, and too few studies have been conducted with sufficient methodological rigor for one to confidently assert that a direct link between reductions in negative thinking and decreases in other depressive symptoms has been empirically demonstrated.

Considerable evidence now exists that the production of negative thoughts and images or memories is associated with peripheral physiological and central cortical changes. In particular, negative cognition has been differentially associated with corrugator facial muscle increases, startle reflex potentiation, and cortical changes as indicated by various endogenous components of ERPs and regional cerebral blood flow studies. This research, then, indicates that negative thinking is associated with changes at the physiological level. Cerebral blood flow studies indicate that the generation of negative self-statements is associated with increased activity in the lateral orbitofrontal region and decreased activity in the rostral medial prefrontal cortex. Thus the production of negative thoughts and images, and possibly even biased information processing, may provide an important link to understanding the physiological concomitants of depression and other negative emotional states.

UNIVERSALITY HYPOTHESIS

Heightened negative cognition, reduced positive thinking, and self-referent negativity processing bias are evident in all subtypes of depression.

The universality hypothesis asserts that the negative self-referent cognitive organization that is represented in the descriptive hypotheses of the cognitive model is applicable to all subtypes of depression, whether unipolar, bipolar, major, minor, endogenous, or nonendogenous in nature. Furthermore, the negative cognitive triad will also be apparent in nonclinical states of dysphoria and subclinical depressive conditions. However, as will be discussed in Chapter 7, the selective processing bias in these milder depressive states may be primarily characterized as a reduction in positivity bias and an evenhanded processing of both positive and negative self-referent information.

In their review of the empirical status of the universality hypothesis, Haaga et al. (1991) concluded that negative cognitions have been found to be a prominent characteristic of most depressive subtypes. A. Beck (1991) in his review also stated that negative depressotypic phenomena have been found across all subtypes of depression such as unipolar and bipolar, reactive and endogenous categories. Although most of the research on the cognitive model has focused on unipolar major depression and, to a lesser extent, dysthymia, there is some evidence that the model is applicable to a wider range of depressive phenomena.

Only a few studies were found that assessed cognitive content and biased information processing in depressed bipolar patients. In an early study on mood state-dependent learning, Weingartner, Miller, and Murphy (1977) had 8 bipolar patients in varying states of mania and depression generate (i.e., encode) and then subsequently recall 20 word associations to common nouns on successive occasions over periods of 8 to 20 weeks. Analysis revealed that recall was better when mood state at retrieval matched mood state when word associations were encoded than when there was a mismatch between the encoding and retrieval mood states. Blaney (1986), however, noted that this effect could reflect mood-congruent memory rather than mood-dependent memory.

As an extension and replication of Weingartner et al. (1977), Eich, Macaulay, and Lam (1997) tested 10 patients with rapid-cycling bipolar I or bipolar II disorder on letter association retention, inkblot recognition, auto-biographical event generation and autobiographical event recall on four separate occasions in varying mood states. Contrary to Weingartner et al., no differences between mood states were found on the letter-association task so that neither mood memory dependence or congruence was evident. On inkblot recognition and autobiographical event recall, retrieval was significantly better during matched than mismatched moods, thereby demonstrating mood-dependent memory recall and recognition. However, analysis of the autobiographical events generated at the encoding sessions revealed evidence of a significant bias to retrieve positive memories during hypo(manic) mood, but an evenhandedness to retrieve both positive and negative memories during the depressed mood states. Thus consistent with the cognitive model, biased information processing has been found during the depressed (and manic) states associated with bipolar depression, though at this time it is unknown whether reduced positivity and/or enhanced negativity bias best characterizes the dysfunctional information processing in bipolar depression. Moreover, the findings of Eich et al. indicate that both mood memory-dependent and congruent effects may be operating when individuals with bipolar disorder encode and retrieve material.

A number of studies have investigated the presence of negative cognitive content in various subtypes of depressive disorders and conditions. Generally, the results have been positive for the universality hypothesis, with significant elevations in negative self-referent cognitions and beliefs evident in bipolar (Hollon et al., 1986; Rose, Abramson, Hodulik, Halber-stadt, & Leff, 1994), endogenous and nonendogenous (Eaves & Rush, 1984; Norman, Miller, & Dow, 1988; Zimmerman & Coryell, 1986), psychotic and nonpsychotic (Zimmerman, Coryell, Caryn, & Wilson, 1986), and dysthymic (D.A. Clark, Beck, et al., 1994) depressions, although Rose et al. found that individuals with chronic/dysthymic depressions without personality disorders did not have higher scores on the Dysfunctional Attitudes Scale (DAS) and a more negative attributional style when compared with other depression subtypes. Moreover, depression secondary to medical illness has also been associated with elevations in negative self-referent thinking and cognitive errors (D.C. Clark et al., 1983; Lefebvre, 1981; Plumb & Holland, 1977), though measures that assess negative cognition in psychiatric samples may not measure the full range of negative self-referent thinking that characterizes the depression associated with a chronic medical illness. D.A. Clark et al. (1998), for example, found that depressed medically ill patients did not score significantly higher on the CCL-D than nondepressed medical and healthy control groups. Finally, we have noted throughout the present review that numerous studies have found significant elevations in negative self-referent thinking and a differentiated pattern of information processing in mild subclinical depressive and even experimentally induced dysphoric states in otherwise healthy individuals, indicating that the negative cognitive organization posited by the cognitive model is evident in secondary depressive states as well as the less severe but nonetheless dysfunctional subclinical minor depressions described in Chapter 1.

These findings provide considerable support for the universality hypothesis. The cognitive organization posited for unipolar major depression appears to be applicable to a broad range of depressive phenomena and diagnostic subtypes with varying levels of depressive severity. Having said this, we must remind the reader of one caveat. Under the selective encoding hypothesis, we will see that a clear bias for processing negative self-referent material may only be evident in severely depressive states, though the empirical support for this assertion is by no means clear-cut. If this assertion is upheld in the research literature, then a qualifier must be added to the universality hypothesis. That is, negative self-referent cognition resulting from activation of the loss mode may characterize all depressive states, but the compensatory adaptive modes may be more readily accessible in milder depressive states. This might account for the tendency for mild depression to manifest an evenhandedness in the processing of positive and negative information. Thus universality may be seen in the activation of the depressotypic loss mode, but differences may be apparent across levels of depression severity in the ability to activate compensatory positive or adaptive modes of thinking and processing.

NEGATIVE COGNITION AND HOPELESSNESS DEPRESSION

Although the research previously discussed indicates that the negative cognitive organization is evident across different diagnostic subtypes of depression, some researchers have suggested that within particular diagnoses, such as unipolar major depression, only a subset of individuals will show the negative cognitive content and processes proposed in the cognitive model. Abramson, Alloy, and Metalsky (1988) argue that depression is really a heterogeneous group of disorders and that the negative cognitive characteristics of depression described by the cognitive model really constitutes a subtype of depression which they call *negative triad depression*. This negative triad depression resembles but is not identical to the *hopelessness* depression subtype proposed by Abramson et al. (1989). Abramson et al. (1988) suggest the term *negative cognition depression* to refer to a "subtype of depression defined by the intersection of hopelessness depression and negative triad depression" (p. 12). Thus these authors challenge the view that the cognitive organization proposed by cognitive theory is universally applicable to all individuals who suffer with depression. Instead, they argue that the model will be valid for only a subset of depressive experiences that fall into the negative cognitive triad or hopelessness depressive subtypes.

Negative cognition or hopelessness depression is proposed as a theory-based construct that does not completely map onto any of the current descriptive psychiatric categories but instead cuts across a number of nosological depression classifications (Abramson, Alloy, & Hogan, 1997; Abramson et al., 1989). Hopelessness depression is characterized by a number of symptoms such as retarded initiation of voluntary responses, sad affect, suicide, lack of energy, apathy, psychomotor retardation, sleep disturbance, brooding, difficulty in concentration, and mood-related negative cognitions (Abramson et al., 1989). Lower self-esteem and dependency will sometimes accompany the other symptoms of hopelessness depression. The core symptom of this type of depression, hopelessness, is viewed as a proximal sufficient causal agent for triggering and maintaining the other symptoms of hopelessness depression (Abramson et al., 1989; Alloy, Abramson, Metalsky, & Hartlage, 1988).

If the cognitive organization proposed by the cognitive model is not universally applicable but instead relevant only to those depressed individuals who present with negative cognition or hopelessness depression, then two crucial questions must be addressed. First, is there any evidence that only a subset of clinically depressed individuals show the negative self-referent thinking as posited by the cognitive model? Hamilton and Abramson (1983) had 20 depressed and 20 nondepressed psychiatric inpatients and 20 normal community adults complete the DAS, BDI, Hopelessness Scale and Attributional Style Questionnaire (ASQ) at time of admission and then again at discharge from hospital. As expected, at admission the depressed patients scored significantly higher than nondepressed psychiatric and community controls on all the measures. By discharge, however, the depressed patients showed significant reductions on all the cognition measures. Further analysis revealed considerable heterogeneity among depressed group on the DAS total score. Hamilton and Abramson (1983) decided to explore this heterogeneity by dividing the depressed group into a high DAS ($n = 10$) and low DAS group. The high-scoring group consisted of all depressed patients who scored greater than the highest DAS score for the community control group on either testing occasion (DAS Total Score = 144). The high-scoring DAS depressed group exhibited more negative attributional style than the low-scoring DAS group who in turn did not differ from the nondepressed normal group. Also, the high-scoring DAS group did not differ significantly in depression severity (BDI Total Score) from the low-scoring DAS group. The authors concluded that some depressed patients may not exhibit a negative cognitive style (elevated dysfunctional beliefs), and this absence of negative cognition is not due to presence of a less severe depressive state.

Norman, Miller, and Klee (1983) divided a sample of clinically depressed patients into a high and low cognitive distortion group based on their scores on the Cognitive Bias Questionnaire. The high cognitive distortion depressed group was significantly more depressed as indicated by the BDI Total Score and had more cognitive symptoms of depression than the low cognitive distortion depressed group. I. Miller and Norman (1986) also subdivided the participants in their two studies into high and low cognitive distorters on the basis of their response to the Cognitive Bias Questionnaire (CBQ). In the first study, 27% ($n = 8/30$) of the depressed inpatients at admission fell into the high distortion group, whereas in the second study 65% ($n = 13/20$) of the depressed inpatients were categorized as high cognitive distorters. Analysis revealed no differences in depression severity between high and low depressed cognitive distorters, though the high distorters showed more persistent cognitive distortion after clinical improvement than the depressed low-scoring group. In a later study, Norman et al. (1988) divided a depressed inpatient sample into high cognitive dysfunction ($n = 24/72$, 33%) and low dysfunction on the basis of their scores on the DAS and CBQ. To be considered in the high cognitive dysfunction group, patients had to score at least one standard deviation above the mean of nondepressed normals on both measures. The high cognitive dysfunction depressed group were more severely depressed, more hopeless, had more frequent negative automatic thoughts, less perceived social support, and overall poorer social adjustment than the depressed low cognitive dysfunction group. The authors conclude that only 40% to 50% of episodic depressed patients will exhibit the elevated levels of cognitive dysfunction posited by the cognitive model. However, findings from these studies are inconsistent on whether depressed patients who score low on negative cognition measures do so simply because they are less severely depressed.

Even if one accepts these findings that only a subset of depressed patients show the negative cognitive organization, then a second question that must be addressed is whether there is any evidence for a specific negative cognition or hopelessness subtype of depression. Can this subtype of depression be reliably identified in clinically depressed samples? Although Abramson et al. (1989) maintain that hopelessness depression is not defined solely on the basis of symptom clusters or profile, nonetheless as a first step toward validating the theory we would expect to find that the postulated core symptom features of hopelessness depression should co-occur in the experience of a subset of depressed individuals.

In a sample of 80 depressed inpatients, Whisman, Miller, Norman, and Keitner (1995) identified a high hopelessness group ($n = 32$; 40%) and a low hopelessness group ($n = 24$; 30%) on the basis of their scores on the Hopelessness Scale (A. Beck et al., 1974). Group comparisons on depressive symptomatology as assessed by the BDI and Modified Hamilton Rating Scale of Depression revealed that the high hopelessness depressed group scored significantly higher than the low hopelessness group on symptoms of retarded initiation of voluntary responses, sad affect, and suicide but did not differ significantly on the secondary hopelessness symptoms of lack of energy, psychomotor retardation, and sleep disturbance. Moreover, group differences were apparent on other symptoms not hypothesized as part of the hopelessness symptom profile such as body image change, sense of failure, and self-dislike, which suggests that hopelessness depression is associated with a negative view of the self. Finally, inspection of pooled within-group correlations between the hypothesized symptoms of the hopelessness profile suggested a lack of internal consistency. The authors also found that high hopelessness was associated with greater social dysfunction, elevated cognitive dysfunction (i.e., more frequent negative automatic thoughts, dysfunctional attitudes, and cognitive bias) and poorer response to pharmacological and cognitive-behavioral treatment. This study provided only partial support for the existence of a symptom profile of hopelessness depression as described by Abramson et al. (1989).

Other studies have also not been able to completely identify a hopelessness subtype of depression as described in the hopelessness theory of depression. Haslam and Beck (1994) used taxometric statistical procedures to explore the covariational patterns among symptom indicators. Analysis was based on the BDI item responses of 531 outpatients with major depression assessed at the Center for Cognitive Therapy in Philadelphia. None of the analyses that were conducted found evidence of internal coherence among the symptoms hypothesized by the hopelessness model. In a second study on 400 major depressed outpatients,

Haslam and Beck (1993) again failed to find a hopelessness depression subtype using a clustering algorithm developed for artificial intelligence applications. Whisman and Pinto (1997) used a taxometric analytic procedure to examine the latent structure of hopelessness and the symptoms of hopelessness depression in 120 depressed adolescent inpatients. Hopelessness was measured with the Hopelessness Scale for Children (HSC), whereas depressive symptoms were assessed with the BDI. Hopelessness was significantly correlated with five of the six hypothesized symptoms of hopelessness depression as indicated by specific BDI items, and the HSC total score had significantly greater association with a hopelessness symptom composite scale based on the sum of these five BDI hopelessness symptom items than with other BDI symptom items not predicted to be associated with hopelessness. However, the taxometric analysis on the HSC and hopelessness depression symptom composite failed to find a latent structure indicating that hopelessness may be dimensional rather than a distinct category or subtype as suggested by the hopelessness theory of depression.

Spangler, Simons, Monroe, and Thase (1993) found that depressed adult outpatients who met hopelessness depression criteria by exhibiting a depressive attributional style and a negative life stressor differed from other patients on some of the hypothesized hopelessness depression symptoms but not others. Alloy, Just, and Panzarella (1997) used a daily diary of life events and symptoms to determine whether attributionally vulnerable nondepressed students either alone or in combination with daily negative events exhibited higher within-day and across-day levels of hopelessness depression symptoms but not nonhopelessness symptoms. Analysis revealed that the attributionally vulnerable group had significantly higher average levels and greater within-day and across-day variability of hopelessness depression symptoms but not nonhopelessness symptoms compared with nonattributionally vulnerable persons. Moreover, the mean correlation between pairs of hopelessness depression symptoms was significantly higher ($r = .77$) than the mean correlation between hopelessness and nonhopelessness symptom pairs ($r = .69$). The authors conclude that their results provide substantial support for the predictions of a hopelessness subtype of depression, at least in a nondepressed student sample.

Finally, Metalsky and Joiner (1997) developed a 32-item self-report inventory, called the Hopelessness Depression Symptom Questionnaire (HDSQ), to specifically measure eight hypothesized symptoms of the hopelessness depression subtype—motivational deficit, interpersonal dependency, psychomotor retardation, anergia, apathy/anhedonia, insomnia, difficulty in concentrating, and suicidality. Exploratory and confirmatory factor analysis based on 435 students indicated that at the first-order level the HDSQ comprises the eight subscales hypothesized by the hopelessness model, and that at a second-order level these eight distinct symptom dimensions are associated with one latent variable called symptoms of hopelessness depression. A diathesis-stress analysis with a subset of the sample revealed that subjects with a depressive attributional style and negative life events showed a significant increase in HDSQ scores from Time 1 to Time 2 but not in BDI residual scores. Thus both the psychometric analyses and the results of the diathesis-stress regressions support the existence of a hopelessness subtype of depression symptoms.

SUMMARY

Haaga et al. (1991) concluded that there is empirical support for the universality hypothesis in that elevated levels of negative cognitions have been found across the traditional nosological categories of depression. We would concur with Haaga et al.'s conclusion based on our own review of the literature. However, we would also note that too few studies have investigated negative cognitive content, and especially negative information processing, in other *DSM-IV* depressive subtypes such as dysthymia, bipolar depression, or major depression with melancholic or endogenous features. To date, the vast majority of studies have focused exclusively on unipolar nonpsychotic major depression and the few studies that have compared different depression diagnostic subtypes have relied entirely on retrospective self-report cognition questionnaires. Thus more research is needed to draw firm conclusions on whether the negative cognitive organization that has been so evident in major depression and subclinical forms of depression is equally apparent in other diagnostic subtypes of depression.

One cannot uncritically accept the findings from some studies that claim that only 40% to 50% of episodically depressed individuals show the negative self-referent thoughts and beliefs predicted by the cognitive model. All these findings are based entirely on self-report measures of cognition. Thus we do not know whether the failure of some depressed patients to score highly on these measures is because they do not experience negative self-referent thinking, or whether it is because of psychometric limitations of the instruments themselves (i.e., low sensitivity). Also in some studies, the low negative cognition depressed patients were not as severely depressed as the high cognition group suggesting that low scores on negative cognition measures might reflect a very mild depressive state in at least some depressed patients.

Few investigators have actually examined why some depressed individuals score low on negative cognition measures. Is it possible that a certain response bias, self-presentational style, or defensiveness may be present so that these individuals refuse to answer in a socially undesirable or pathological direction? Also, it is well known among cognitive therapists that some depressed patients seem to be unaware of their thinking and so need to be trained in becoming more aware of their cognitions. It is also well known that there are individual differences in self-consciousness or awareness of one's internal mental contents. It is premature to conclude that depressed patients who score low on negative cognition measures do not have negative automatic thoughts or biased information processing. Further research is needed to understand the source of these low cognitive depression scores.

If one accepts the view that all depressed patients do not necessarily exhibit negative cognition, then the possibility of a negative cognition subtype of depression needs to be explored. We have reviewed several studies that have searched for such a theory-based subtype in the form of hopelessness depression. The evidence for a distinct hopelessness depression symptom subtype is mixed at this time. Prospective studies based on non-depressed samples have found evidence for a hopelessness depression subtype, whereas studies of depressed clinical samples have found only partial support for the model. At this time, it is unclear whether the construct of hopelessness and hopelessness symptoms are better conceptualized as dimensional variables than as a distinct subtype of depression. As well, revisions may be needed to the hopelessness symptom profile. Low self-esteem has been found to have a strong association with hopelessness and so should be included as an important feature of hopelessness depression (Whisman & Pinto, 1997). Spangler et al. (1993) argued that cognitive symptoms may be characteristic of hopelessness rather than depression and so should be put back into the symptom profile of the hopelessness subtype. Interestingly, Abramson et al. (1989) excluded cognitive symptoms from their original formulation of hopelessness depression because of their findings on depressive realism. More recently, negative cognitive symptoms have made it back into the core symptom list of hopelessness depression in the form of mood-exacerbated negative cognitions (Abramson, Alloy, & Hogan, 1997). Metalsky and Joiner (1997) argued that anhedonia should also be included in the symptom profile of hopelessness. Too few studies have directly investigated the hopelessness depression subtype to draw firm conclusions about its validity. However, the existence of this proposed theory-based subtype represents a challenge to the universality hypothesis of the cognitive model. Which of these two views will prevail must await a more thorough evaluation by the research community.

SEVERITY/PERSISTENCE HYPOTHESIS

Extent of negative self-referent cognition, reduced positive thinking, and negativity processing bias are linearly related to depression severity and persistence.

According to this hypothesis, the negative cognitive content and processing bias that characterizes depression is closely associated with the severity and persistence or duration of the depressive episode. Thus the more severe the depressive state, the more frequent and pervasive the negative self-referent automatic thoughts and the more prominent the negativity processing bias. We would also expect the negative cognitive organization to predict the duration or persistence of the depression. Negative cognition should be particularly apparent in persistent depressive states like dysthymia.

Two implications follow from this hypothesis. First, the presence of negative cognition and processing bias may be barely present, or at least inconsistent, in very mild and/or transient dysphoric mood states. As the depression deepens, the negative cognitive organization becomes more prominent and stable. This suggests that the descriptive hypotheses of CT may not be as well supported in mild depressive states as in more severe full-blown clinical depression. As well, the extent of negative cognition and processing bias may provide the clinician with an indicator of the severity of the depressive state.

A second implication of this hypothesis concerns the relationship between negative cognition and the other symptoms of depression. We predict that a linear relationship exists between depression severity and the frequency of negative cognition. Thus increases in depressive symptomatology will be associated with a corresponding increase in negative cognition at each level of depression severity. This is to be contrasted with a nonlinear relationship in which negative cognition may not be apparent until a certain threshold of depression severity is reached.

SEVERITY OF DEPRESSION AND NEGATIVE COGNITION

M. Johnson and Magaro (1987) reviewed the research literature on cognitive processing deficits and content-related investigations in affective disorders. They concluded that the deficits in short-term memory, encoding operations, and psychomotor speed are severity-related so that the more severe the symptomatology the more disrupted the memory processes. These memory deficits are limited to the duration of the depressive illness. M. Johnson and Magaro also commented that reduced effort and adoption of a conservative response bias may modulate depressed patients' performance on memory tasks. Regarding research on memory content, they stated that the selectivity for negative self-referent content that has been found across a number of memory studies is not related to diagnostic status but rather is dependent on mood state. M. Johnson and Magaro contend that mood state appears to activate self-schema content in depression so that whether one is suffering a diagnosable affective disorder or is nondepressed but experiencing a transient dysphoria, a negative mood state will elicit similar negative memory content in both individuals. However, the authors also concluded that memory content in depression will be affected by both mood state and severity of psychopathology. They suggest that mood state provides contextual cues and schema activation so that negatively toned material is selectively encoded and recalled, whereas severity of clinical depression leads to low effort and a conservative response bias. The cognitive model, on the other hand, envisions a different sequence to the relationship of negative mood and cognition. External stimuli activate negative self-schema, the outcome of which is the depressive experience including a dysphoric mood state. In this context, then, negative mood state is not considered a prime for negative self-schema activation, although an existing negative mood state would certainly strengthen any negative schemas that have been activated by external circumstances.

Many studies have found moderate to high correlations between measures of negative cognition and memory and both self- report and clinician rating scales of depressive symptoms (e.g., A. Beck et al., 1987; D.A. Clark et al., 1990, 1996; Dobson & Shaw, 1986; Garber et al., 1993; Hollon et al., 1986; G. Lloyd & Lishman, 1975; Steer et al., 1994), although a positive correlation between negative cognition and depression severity measures has not always been found (Hamilton & Abramson, 1983; Williams, Healy, Teasdale, White, & Paykel, 1990). Moreover, regression analyses have demonstrated that negative cognition measures have a unique and specific relationship with depression severity even after controlling for other relevant diagnostic and symptom predictor variables (D.A. Clark et al., 1989; Rose et al., 1994). Support for the severity hypothesis is also apparent from the regression studies showing a stronger relationship between congruent negative cognitions and symptoms than between incongruent cognitive content and symptoms (see Chapter 5 for discussion of content-specificity hypothesis). Despite a few contrary findings, the majority of studies have found a strong positive relationship between negative cognitions and heightened depression severity.

The relationship between negative cognition and depression severity appears to hold even when depression is assessed by diagnostic interviews or clinician rating scales, such as the Hamilton Rating Scale of

Depression, that place greater emphasis on the motivational, behavioral, and somatic symptoms than on the more cognitive and subjective symptoms of depression (A. Beck et al., 1987; D.A. Clark et al., 1989; Dobson & Shaw, 1986). In a longitudinal study based on samples generated by the NIMH Collaborative Study of the Psychobiology of Depression, hopelessness as measured by the Beck Hopelessness Scale was closely related to depression severity as indicated by the Longitudinal Interval Follow-Up Evaluation, an interview based on the RDC (M. Young et al., 1996). Other studies have purposefully excluded cognitive items from their symptom measures and still found a significant correlation between negative cognition and severity of depression as indicated by the noncognitive symptom items (Jolly & Dykman, 1994; Rose et al., 1994). Thus the strong positive relationship between negative cognition and depressive symptom severity cannot be discounted as a mere tautology resulting from the correlation between measures with overlapping item content as suggested by Coyne (1989, 1994a; Coyne & Gotlib, 1983; see discussion by Haaga et al., 1991).

Previously in our review of the empirical literature on the content-specificity hypothesis, we discussed the results of a study by Ambrose and Rholes (1993) who stated that the relationship between negative cognitions and symptoms varies as a function of severity. Their findings suggested a curvilinear relationship between threat cognitions and anxiety symptoms but a linear relationship between loss cognitions and depressive symptoms. In their study, low frequency of threat and loss cognitions was more closely associated with anxious than depressive symptoms, but as the frequency of negative thinking increased, both threat and loss cognitions became more closely associated with depressive than anxious symptoms. In a related study, D.A. Clark et al. (1996) found that the degree of specificity between cognitive and symptom measures varied with level of symptom severity. These studies indicate that severity may also play a critical role in the type of relationship one finds between cognition and symptoms. The more severe the level of disturbance, the more likely one will find a close relationship between negative cognition and the other symptoms of depression.

Persistence of Depression and Negative Cognition

The severity/persistence hypothesis predicts that negative cognition and biased information processing will persist as long as the other symptoms of depression are present. Once depressed, individuals with elevated levels of negative self-referent thinking and biased information processing will also present with more intense or severe and persistent episodes of depression. Two predictions derive from this aspect of the hypothesis. First, we would expect elevated levels of negative cognition throughout the depressive episode, but once the depression remits, negative cognition and biased information processing should be less apparent. And second, acutely depressed individuals with higher levels of negative thinking should show poorer recovery and therefore more persistent depression than similarly depressed individuals with lower levels of negative cognition and processing. A large literature now confirms the first prediction of this hypothesis. Negative cognition and biased memory remain elevated in episodic depression but shift to within normal levels once the depression remits (e.g., Bradley & Mathews, 1988; Dobson & Shaw, 1987; Dohr et al., 1989; Fogarty & Hemsley, 1983; Hollon et al., 1986; Lewinsohn, Steinmetz, Larson, & Franklin, 1981; Myers, Lynch, & Bakal, 1989; Teasdale, Taylor, Cooper, Hayhurst, & Paykel, 1995).

The second prediction of this hypothesis—that the greater the negative thinking pattern and biased information processing in symptomatically depressed individuals, the more persistent the depressive episode—has also received considerable empirical support. Dent and Teasdale (1988) found that number of global negative traits endorsed as self-descriptive but not frequency of negative self-statements was a significant predictor of level of depression 5 months later. Lewinsohn et al. (1981) also found that failure to improve by 8-month follow-up was predicted by elevated scores on negative cognition measures even after controlling for initial depression level. In a more recent study, Williams et al. (1990) reported that clinically depressed patients with high scores on Burns' Dysfunctional Attitudes Questionnaire at admission were more likely to remain depressed after 6 weeks of treatment than were the low DAQ depressed patients. Brittlebank, Scott, Williams, and Ferrier (1993) found that although DAS was a poor predictor of depressive symptom severity at 3 or 7 months, a tendency to produce overgeneral autobiographical memories in response to positive word cues was highly correlated with Hamilton Rating Scale of Depression scores at both follow-up intervals.

Eaves and Rush (1984) found a relationship between increased negative cognition and longer duration or persistence of a clinical depressive episode, though A. Beck et al. (1988) did not find a relationship between duration of episode in major depression and level of hopelessness. However, Beck, Steer, et al. (1990) did find that patients with recurrent-episode major depression and dysthymia but not single-episode major depression had significantly less positive self-concepts than did panic disorder patients. Hammen, Miklowitz, and Dyck (1986) failed to find that recall scores for depressed-content self-referent adjectives predicted 1-week or 1-month BDI depression scores in college students. Edelman, Ahrens, and Haaga (1994) found that dysphoric students who overgeneralized from specific negative events were more dysphoric 3 weeks later than were dysphoric students who did not overgeneralize. Contrary to predictions, students who made positive inferences about themselves also tended to be more dysphoric at 3-weeks' follow-up. The interaction between presence of positive life events and tendency to make stable, global attributions for positive events proved to be a weak ($p < .07$) predictor of recovery from dysphoria.

Overall, the findings from these studies suggest a positive relationship between persistence of depression and at least some cognitive variables. Teasdale's (1988) differential activation hypothesis also directly addresses the relationship between negative cognition and persistence of depression. The hypothesis predicts:

> For a given level of depression, those demonstrating certain patterns of negative thinking are more likely to remain depressed than equally depressed subjects with less of such negative thinking. (p. 263)

Our review of the literature on persistence (see also review by Teasdale, 1988) provides strong evidence for a relationship between persistence of depression and presence of negative cognitive content and processing. As noted by Teasdale, negative cognition appears to affect the course that a depressive episode may take with elevated levels of negative cognition associated with greater persistence of, and poorer recovery from, depressive symptoms. However, more research is needed to disentangle which components of the negative cognitive organization is most predictive of the persistence of episodic depression.

CONCLUSION

Our review in this chapter of the relevant empirical literature confirms that a negative cognitive organization plays an important role in shaping the depressive experience. Evidence was found to support the primacy, universality, and severity/persistence hypotheses to varying degrees. The themes of personal loss, failure, and deprivation that dominate the information processing apparatus of the depressed person has a significant impact on the behavioral, affective, motivational, and somatic symptoms of depression, is linked to heightened severity and persistence of the depressive states, and has been reported across various subtypes of depressive experiences. We conclude this chapter by highlighting some of the major findings and unresolved questions about the role of negative cognition in depression.

In considering empirical support for the *primacy hypothesis*, we focused on evidence that negative cognition and biased information processing are associated with behavioral, motivational, and physiological variables that characterize the depressive state. Production of negative cognitions, as found in the Velten mood induction procedure, has been shown to produce brief dysphoric mood states with subjective, behavioral, motivational, and physiological concomitants that are very similar to the symptom presentation seen in mild to moderate clinical depression. Moreover, there is convincing evidence that these effects are not entirely the result of demand characteristics and that the production of negative self-evaluative cognitions may directly prime or access the negative constructs associated with depression. In addition, other studies have reported that naturally occurring negative thoughts experienced during thought suppression experiments are associated with an increase in depressive mood. Recent work on intrusive memories in depression again confirms the impact that negative cognition can have on perpetuating depressive feelings and symptoms. These findings, combined with a few studies that have shown an immediate decrease in depressed mood with reduction in the frequency of negative cognitions, suggests a primary or influential role for negative self-referent cognition in the depressive experience. However, studies are needed that more directly test the primacy hypothesis by examining the impact that the actual production of negative self-referent thoughts might have on the frequency and severity of specific motivational, behavioral, somatic, and affective symptoms of depression. If clinically depressed individuals are instructed to produce negative cognitions, would we see a greater decline in their level of interest, motivation, energy, behavioral initiation, and the like compared with that of nondepressed persons?

Studies on the physiological concomitants of cognition and emotion indicate that the production of negative, sad thoughts or images is associated with an autonomic arousal and facial muscle pattern that is very similar to the physiological profile evident in depression. Moreover, individuals exhibiting this depressed physiological response pattern to negative thoughts and images also report a negative subjective mood state. Studies of brain region activity based on EEG, ERP, and cerebral blood flow analysis have found significant differences in regional brain activity when individuals experience sad or happy mood states induced by the production of positive or negative thoughts and memories. Although the specific cortical response pattern associated with negative cognitive emotional processing may vary somewhat across studies, this research is consistent in showing significant changes in brain activity when individuals process emotionally valenced cognitive stimuli. We conclude from this that negative self-referent thinking can have a primary or influential affect on the subjective, motivational, behavioral and even peripheral physiological and central cortical concomitants of depression and negative emotion.

A review of the empirical literature relevant for the *universality hypothesis* indicates that the negative cognitive organization posited by the cognitive model has been found in most diagnostic subtypes of depression as well as in secondary depression, subclinical minor depression, and experimentally induced dysphoric mood states. Although a number of studies have suggested that negative cognition may be applicable to only a subgroup of depressed patients, such as those presenting with hopelessness depression, most of this research is based on scoring distributions on negative cognition questionnaires. It is not at all clear whether low scores on cognition questionnaires reflect the absence of negative thinking or a response bias (i.e., unwillingness to admit to negative thinking). In addition, evidence for a distinct hopelessness subtype of depression is not consistent. In fact, hopelessness may be more appropriately conceptualized on a dimensional rather than categorical basis. Whatever the case, more research is needed on individuals who meet diagnostic criteria for depression but nonetheless endorse few items on negative cognition questionnaires. If "noncognitive depression" emerges as a valid distinction, then it would be important to understand whether these are atypical depressions that may have important etiologic, prognostic, and treatment implications.

The final descriptive hypothesis of the cognitive model examined was the *severity/persistence hypothesis*. We found relatively consistent evidence for a close relationship between depression severity and negative cognition, even after controlling for item overlap and highly correlated measures. Higher levels of episodic depression severity are associated with a greater intensity of negative self-referent cognitive content. However, not only is cognitive dysfunction, as described in the cognitive model, associated with increased depression severity, but a number of studies have also reported a connection with persistence. Elevations in negative cognitive content and processing during depression are predictive of poorer recovery suggesting that the more extensive the activation of the negative cognitive organization during depression, the more persistent the depressive condition. What remains to be seen is further refinement on exactly which components of the negative cognitive organization are most strongly connected with greater persistence of depressive symptomatology. Having examined the nature and role of negative cognition in depression, we now consider research on the structures and processes of the depressotypic information processing system.

CHAPTER 7

Descriptive Hypotheses: Selective Information Processing in Depression

IN CHAPTERS 5 and 6, the focus has been on descriptive hypotheses that deal with the nature and function of negative cognitive content in depression. We now shift to the structures and processes involved in the depressotypic information processing system. The remaining three descriptive hypotheses of the cognitive model—selective bias, schema activation, and primal processing—all deal with the postulated depressotypic structures and processes that characterize the information processing system of the depressed individual. If a pervasive negativity dominates the information processing system in depression, then the effects of this processing bias should be evident in attention, encoding, retrieval, comprehension, and interpretation of material.

It will become immediately apparent to the reader that the research relevant to these three hypotheses has drawn heavily, both conceptually and methodologically, from experimental cognitive psychology, social cognition, and cognitive neuropsychology (Gotlib et al., 1997). Thus information processing tasks have been employed to study attention, encoding, recall, and judgment biases in depression. This propensity for borrowing from the experimental paradigms of mainstream cognitive psychology can be traced back to advocates like Ingram and Kendall (1986), who argued that the cognitive basis of depression can best be understood by adopting the concepts and methods of experimental information processing. Even more recently, Williams et al. (1997) argued that the main contribution of the experimental cognitive-processing perspective will be in understanding emotional disorders rather than in offering new approaches to treatment. Ingram and Kendall stated that the information processing perspective views the person as

> an information processing system and focuses largely upon the structures and operations within the system and how they function in the selection, transformation, encoding, storage, retrieval and generation of information and behavior. (Ingram & Kendall, 1986, p. 5)

A large number of studies have investigated information processing in depression and so have relevance for the selective bias, schema activation, and primal processing hypotheses. Research on bias at the earlier perceptual stages of information processing, such as studies of selective attention, relied on more experimental methodologies to explicate the distinctive processing features associated with depression. Investigations that focus on the latter, more elaborative or strategic and conceptual phases of information processing, such as causal attributions, expectancies, and inferential judgments, have tended to rely on self-report measures. Each of these methodological approaches, whether it be an experimental information processing task or conscious, deliberative responses to a predetermined set of stimuli, can provide valuable insights into the cognitive basis of depression, provided the methodology is suited to the research question under investigation.

In the following discussion, we focus on studies that have direct implication for the selectivity, activation, and primal processing hypotheses. Some of these studies were designed as a direct test of the cognitive model, whereas others were conducted to test other cognitive theories of depression. As well as examining the actual findings generated by these studies, we will also discuss conceptual and methodological issues that arise from this research. As we review the pertinent empirical literature, four questions are of particular importance to the cognitive model:

1. Is the negativity bias in depression a pervasive generalized phenomenon, or is it evident only when processing highly specific emotional material?
2. What structures and processes of the information processing system are involved in the depressotypic cognitive bias? Is negativity evident at the earliest stages of perceptual encoding, or is the bias only apparent at the later more strategic stage involving the retrieval and interpretation of conceptual material?
3. Is the selective processing bias in depression characterized by enhanced processing of negatively valenced stimuli, an evenhanded

processing of both positive and negative information, or reduced processing of positive material?

4. To what extent does the processing bias in depression involve automatic, preconscious versus strategic, effortful processing of material?

The research literature pertaining to selective information processing in depression is vast, and so our discussion must be rather circumscribed and the studies included in our review selective. Our focus is on research with a direct bearing on the validity of the selectivity, activation, and primal processing hypotheses. Excellent review articles and books are available to the reader interested in a deeper and more comprehensive treatment of the information processing research on emotional disorders (Blaney, 1986; Brewin, 1988; Dalgleish & Watts, 1990; Gotlib et al., 1997; Ingram & Reed, 1986; Mathews, 1997; Mathews & MacLeod, 1994; Matt et al., 1992; Mineka & Sutton, 1992; Segal, 1988; Teasdale & Barnard, 1993; A. Wells & Matthews, 1994; Williams, Mathews, & MacLeod, 1996; Williams et al., 1997).

SELECTIVE PROCESSING HYPOTHESIS

Depression is characterized by a selective processing bias for mood-congruent negative self-referent information that is linked to one's current life concerns.

The selective processing hypothesis states that depressed individuals show a bias for sampling the negative aspects of their self-referent experiences. This bias is rooted in an automatic tendency to selectively focus on the negative features of one's personal experience and to exclude or overlook the positive elements of the situation (A. Beck, 1987). Because the information processing system has limited capacity, there will be competition for resources and therefore selective processing of information (Williams et al., 1997). From the vast array of stimulus material that bombards the individual, certain aspects of this informational matrix will selectively capture attentional resources and be further encoded for more elaborated processing within the cognitive organization. In depression, we find a mood-congruent bias for encoding negative material that is characterized by a heightened sensitivity for self-referent information involving themes of loss, failure, and deprivation. This type of selective processing, then, leads to further negativity in the form of biased interpretations and elaboration of the mood-congruent material.

This biased processing is highly specific because it will only be evident when processing personal, self-referent information. The systematic negativity bias in depression is not pervasive and so we would not expect biased processing of impersonal or general information. In fact, CT has never predicted that perceptions and interpretations of depressed individuals are always biased (Segal & Shaw, 1986a). The degree of negativity bias will depend on the severity of the depression, the perception of loss or threatened loss of valued resources, and the information processing of personally relevant information (Segal & Shaw, 1986a). Also the selective processing bias is more likely to occur when cues are ambiguous (A. Beck, 1967) because under these circumstances evaluations and judgments will be more dependent on "schema-based processing" than "stimulus-based processing."

In the past, CT has identified a number of systematic errors of interpretation and elaboration, such as selective abstraction, arbitrary inference, overgeneralization, dichotomous thinking, personalization, and magnification and minimization (A. Beck, 1963, 1976; A. Beck et al., 1979), which are derived from the negativity bias. An entire sequence or progression, then, is apparent in the form of faulty or biased information processing, which begins with self-referent attentional negativity bias and can end with the systematic errors of interpretation and elaboration. The proposed existence of a selective bias for negative self-referent information in depression results from the hypervalent primal loss mode described in Chapter 4. It is also consistent with our basic assumption that all information processing is an approximate representation of experience (see Assumption 6, Chapter 3).

Two issues must be clarified before considering the empirical evidence for the selective processing hypothesis. First, Haaga et al. (1991) noted that CT has been unclear in distinguishing between cognitive bias and distortion. Alloy and Abramson (1988) state: "an 'erroneous' or 'distorted' inference would consist of a judgment or conclusion that disagrees or is inconsistent with some commonly accepted measure of objective reality," whereas an inferential bias refers to "a tendency to make judgments in a systematic and consistent manner across specific times and situations" (pp. 226, 227).

Although the phrase "distortion of reality" has been used in past writings in reference to the faulty information processing in depression, it does not refer to a deviation from some standard of "objective reality" but rather to a tendency for showing a systematic negativity bias. A. Beck (1963) states:

> While some degree of inaccuracy and inconsistency would be expected in the cognitions of any individual, the distinguishing characteristic of the depressed patients was that they showed a *systematic error* (original italics);

viz., a bias against themselves. Systematic errors were also noted in the idiosyncratic ideation of the other nosological groups. (p. 328)

Thus CT is clear on this issue, though the terminology used in past writings may have been imprecise. The faulty information processing in depression is characterized by a systematic negativity bias when processing self-referent information and not a distortion of "objective reality."

In a related vein, CT now conceptualizes the systematic negativity bias in terms of a cognitive shift (A. Beck, 1991; D.A. Clark & Beck, 1989). Thus the model accepts that in neutral or positive mood states, a self-referent positivity bias may be present. As the mood state shifts toward mild depression, however, the positivity bias is neutralized by the emergence of processing for negative features leading to a more "balanced" elaboration of both positive and negative features. As the depression becomes more severe, the faulty information processing shifts toward a decidedly negative orientation (see also Ruehlman, West, & Pasahow, 1985). Thus the faulty information processing in depression is viewed in terms of a cognitive shift from a systematic emphasis on the positive to a bias for the negative.

The selectivity hypothesis indicates that in depression a negativity bias will be apparent in a number of cognitive processes involving the selection, encoding, organization, interpretation, storage, and recall of self-referent information. Because selective processing can be investigated at many different stages of information processing, many experimental and questionnaire studies are relevant for testing this hypothesis. Furthermore, there is considerable overlap in studies relevant for the selective processing hypothesis and those that are relevant for the schema activation hypothesis. To avoid redundancy, our review of the information processing literature is divided in the following manner. In this section, we discuss studies that primarily have their focus on the earlier stages of information processing involving the selective attention, encoding, and elaboration or interpretation of information that is presented to the individual. This research investigates how the cognitive apparatus processes incoming stimulus arrays or information. Thus we review research on (a) mood-congruent attentional or perceptual processing, (b) self-focused attention, (c) encoding and recognition/recall, (d) judgment or interpretation of social and other performance-based information, (e) causal attributions, and (f) the biased elaboration of complex social information presented in the hypothetical scenarios found in self-report measures of cognitive errors. When discussing mood-congruent memory studies, we focus on explicit memory tasks; that is, tasks involving a conscious, effortful reflection of previous experience (Graf & Schacter, 1985). Studies that primarily assess the latter stages of information processing such as the structure, contents, and accessibility of memory storage or meaning representation (i.e., the modified Stroop studies), and the retrieval or recall of information from long-term memory (i.e., autobiographical memory studies) are reviewed under the schema activation hypothesis.

One final point must be raised before reviewing the empirical basis for selective processing in depression. Although the occurrence of a selective processing bias in depression is consistent with the activation of an underlying negative schematic structure, support for selective processing does not depend on demonstrating the existence of depressogenic schemas. Because the negative selective processing bias in depression is proposed at the descriptive or phenomenological level, it merely asserts that a mood-congruency effect will be evident in the selective attention, encoding, retrieval, and elaboration of self-referent information. Research that investigates whether negative self-referent schema are present in depression is discussed under the schema activation hypothesis.

ATTENTIONAL BIAS STUDIES

This first series of studies focuses on the earlier stages of information processing to determine whether an attentional bias may be evident in the encoding of information. Williams et al. (1997) stated that attentional bias occurs, "when there is a discrete change in the direction in which a person's attention is focused so that he/she becomes aware of a particular part or aspect of his/her stimulus environment" (p. 73).

These authors further explain that selective attention can occur in any sensory modality, that it is often passive and involuntary although it can involve voluntary aspects of processing, and that it occurs in response to a discrete change in the internal or external environment. They note that research into selective attention can be studied in terms of *facilitated task performance* (attention to mood-congruent stimuli improves performance), or as *debilitated task performance* (attention to mood-congruent stimuli draws attention away from task performance).

Facilitated Performance: Stimulus Identification Tasks

A series of studies have investigated attentional bias in depression by examining which stimuli are processed at the most rudimentary perceptual level of information processing. Selective attention can be measured in terms of facilitated performance in which a perceptual encoding bias would be evident by an increased speed or improved accuracy in recognizing particular stimuli (Williams et al., 1988). In a study that investigated attentional bias in terms of lowered visual threshold, Powell and Hemsley (1984) found that depressed inpatients showed a trend ($p < .078$)

toward better tachistoscopic recognition of unpleasant words than normal controls. In another study involving rapid presentation of stimuli (33 ms) followed by a perceptual mask, depressed students were more accurate than nondepressed controls in identifying negative words that were previously rated as highly self-descriptive (von Hippel, Hawkins, & Narayan, 1994). Matthews and Antes (1992) compared the eye fixations of dysphoric and nondysphoric students to 16 pictures with clearly demarcated happy and sad regions. Analysis revealed that the dysphoric subjects fixated on the sad regions of the pictures more than the nondysphoric but all subjects looked significantly more often, longer, and sooner at the happy compared with the sad regions of the pictures. Findings from this study suggest that both dysphoric and nondysphoric subjects may have a positive attentional bias, though relative to nondysphoric individuals, the attention of the dysphoric students was also drawn to the sad stimuli. The authors interpreted these results as indicating a type of "perceptual defense" which in nondepressed states divert attention away from depressive stimuli, though in dysphoric states this cognitive avoidance of the negative may be attenuated.

In an early study, Dixon and Lear (1962) found that depressed inpatients but not normals had a differential perceptual response to emotional and nonemotional words. Only the depressed patients showed an increase in visual thresholds to neutral stimuli presented in the left eye when depressive but not nondepressive words were presented to the right eye at a subliminal level of brightness. Gerrig and Bower (1982), however, did not find evidence of lower recognition thresholds for mood-congruent words with students given a happy or angry mood induction. Blackburn et al. (1990) found that depressed inpatients but not normal controls had a significantly smaller P300 amplitude in response to supraliminal presentation of negatively toned sociotropic and autonomous trait adjectives than positively toned words. The amplitude of the P300 event-related potential is assumed to measure strength of internal processing of stimuli. Prior research has shown that P300 amplitude measures expectancy of stimulus presentation such that smaller amplitudes are associated with a higher expectancy level. Thus Blackburn et al.'s results indicated that depressed inpatients had significantly higher expectancy for negatively toned words as indicated by their smaller P300 amplitude. Findings from these studies indicate that depressed individuals may show some selective or enhanced perceptual encoding of negative self-relevant stimuli, and/or reduction in attentional bias for positive material.

Facilitated Performance: Lexical Decision Tasks

Stimulus identification studies do not provide unequivocal support for an attentional bias in depression because differences in the identification of emotional stimuli could be due to variations in subjects' willingness to report stimuli (Mathews, 1997), though this criticism is less relevant for the eye fixation study of Matthews and Antes (1992). The lexical decision task, in which subjects are presented with strings of letters and then simply asked to decide whether the letter string is a word or not, circumvents this problem because it requires a more neutral response. Studies using the standard lexical decision task have generally not found a decision bias for negative words in depression (D.M. Clark, Teasdale, Broadbent, & Martin, 1983; C. MacLeod, Tata, & Mathews, 1987). However, a more sophisticated priming version of lexical decision, provided evidence for depression-congruent priming effects in a subliminal (below threshold of conscious awareness) and, in clinical depressed patients, both subliminal and supraliminal (above threshold of conscious awareness) conditions (Bradley, Mogg, & Williams, 1994, 1995). Although we would interpret these findings as consistent with an attentional bias in depression, the lexical decision priming task is more appropriately considered a test of the integrative processes associated with implicit memory. Thus these findings have greater relevance for demonstrating an automatic memory bias in depression.

Debilitated Performance: The Stroop Interference Effect

In other studies, the Stroop task has been used to investigate attentional bias in depression. Here attentional bias is reflected in a decrement in performance, which for the Stroop involves interference in time taken to name the color in which various types of words are printed. Thus a selective attentional bias in depression is evident as a longer latency to name the color of negative, depression-related words than neutral words because some of the attentional resources needed to encode color is siphoned off for unintended processing of the word itself (Williams et al., 1988). A number of studies have found emotional Stroop interference effects across a range of clinical conditions including depression (Gotlib & McCann, 1984; Klieger & Cordner, 1990; Williams & Nulty, 1986; for review, see Williams et al., 1996; Williams et al., 1997) although, admittedly, some studies have reported negative results (Doost, Taghavi, Moradi, Yule, & Dalgleish, 1997; Hedlund & Rude, 1995; Hill & Knowles, 1991). Overall, though, most studies have found that depressed individuals show significantly greater color-naming interference to depression-related words than to nondepressed words.

Various design modifications have been introduced to the traditional Stroop color-naming task, including the use of a word priming manipulation. Here target words that are to be color named are paired with related or unrelated word primes. Generally, these Stroop priming studies have also found that depression is associated with greater interference effects with negative prime-target word pairs (Gotlib & Cane, 1987; Segal, Gemar, Truchon, Guirguis, & Horowitz, 1995). However, an attentional bias in depression was not found with the use of a modified subliminal version of the Stroop (Mogg, Bradley, Williams, & Mathews, 1993).

Overall, findings with the emotional Stroop task are consistent with a negative attentional bias in depression, although once again, these results cannot be taken as unequivocal support. Group differences in latency to color name could be due to a response bias or a tendency to "output" certain emotional words rather than to an attentional or encoding bias for the emotional stimuli (Dalgleish & Watts, 1990; Williams et al., 1988). Also more recent research on the Stroop interference effect indicates that attentional bias is evident for any personally relevant concerns (Williams et al., 1997). In a related vein, S. Thorpe and Salkovskis (1997) found no correlation between color naming latencies to neutral, spider, and non-spider emotional words and level of anxiety in spider phobics and controls, indicating that the amount of interference in the Stroop task may not be related to anxiety per se but instead to preoccupation of spider-phobic individuals with spider-related information. In support of this finding, Riemann and McNally (1995) reported that significant Stroop interference effects were obtained around the positive as well as negative current concerns of normal subjects. These findings lead one to question whether Stroop interference can be taken as a measure of mood-related attentional bias. Indeed, S. Thorpe and Salkovskis (1997) suggested that Stroop interference may reflect a more strategic (i.e., response-related) deployment of attentional resources for threat in anxiety rather than the presence of a preattentive automatic threat-processing bias. However, Williams et al. (1996) concluded in their review that there is a disproportionate color-naming interference for negative stimuli in emotional disorders that is greater than the attentional bias toward stimuli of current concern. They suggested that emotional breakdown may occur when individuals can no longer expend the extra effort that is needed to override the tendency of current concern-related stimuli to capture attention. Whatever the exact mechanisms that underlie emotional Stroop color-naming interference, these studies indicate that in depression there is a selective attentional bias for negative self-referent material, although the Stroop interference effects in depression cannot be taken as evidence for a perceptually derived preconscious attentional bias for negative stimuli.

Facilitated/Debilitated Performance in Multistimulus Detection Tasks

A third type of study, the visual dot probe task, is thought to be a superior experimental paradigm because it can detect attentional bias to stimuli independent of a possible response bias (Williams et al., 1988). Also the visual dot probe is a multiple stimulus attentional task that makes different cognitive processing demands from single stimulus tasks such as the Stroop. Individuals are shown emotion and neutral word pairs followed by presentation of a dot that replaces one of the two words. Detection latency for the probe is a sensitive measure of visual attention because participants take longer to respond to the probe if their attention has been drawn to another stimulus (Williams et al., 1988).

In one of the first studies using this task on a clinical sample, C. MacLeod, Mathews, and Tata (1986) found that anxious but not depressed patients had longer probe detection latencies for threat words, though processing of depression-related words was not assessed. However, the clinical groups were poorly matched and the greater age and chronicity of the depressed group may have resulted in poorer concentration and motivation, which may have affected their performance on the attentional deployment task (Mathews, Ridgeway, & Williamson, 1996). In a more recent study, Mogg, Bradley, and Williams (1995) modified the task so that half of the word pairs were presented subliminally (14 ms) and the other half supraliminally (1 s). In addition, anxiety-relevant, depression-relevant, or positive words were matched with a neutral word. Analysis revealed that depressed participants had significantly longer probe detection latencies to both anxious and depressive words in the supraliminal but not the subliminal condition. The authors concluded that the attentional or encoding bias in depression may involve both automatic and controlled processes, whereas the positive subliminal results for anxiety suggests automatic preconscious attentional bias in anxiety only.

In a similar experiment involving the visual probe detection task, Mathews et al. (1996) found that clinically depressed but not anxious patients had a significant attentional bias or vigilance for social threat words, whereas the latter group showed greater vigilance for physically threatening words. Although Mathews et al. argue that the attentional bias for social threat in depression was apparent only with a longer stimulus exposure length, this conclusion is not statistically defensible because they did not obtain a significant interaction with exposure duration in their ANOVAs. Hill and Dutton (1989), however, did not find that dysphoric students had a selective attentional bias for self-esteem threatening words in a dot probe detection task, though there was a nonsignificant trend for dysphoric women, in particular, to recall more self-esteem threatening words than nondysphoric women.

Bradley, Mogg, Millar, et al. (1997) employed a pictorial version of the probe detection task in which photographs of happy or threatening facial expressions were paired with a neutral facial expression. There was no evidence of a selective attentional bias for threatening facial expressions by dysphoric college students. The nondysphoric students showed a significant tendency to shift their attention away from the threatening faces and to be more vigilant for the happy faces, although this latter effect did not attain statistical significance. The negative results for attentional bias in depression may be due to the use of more mildly depressed individuals, or to the use of pictorial rather than verbal stimuli.

More supportive findings for attentional bias in depression were obtained by Bradley, Mogg, and Lee (1997). They conducted two studies using the visual dot probe detection task in which depressive, anxious, and neutral words were presented at short (14 ms), medium (500 ms) and long (1,000 ms) exposure intervals. In the first study, students who scored less than 10 on the BDI were randomly assigned to a sad or neutral musical mood induction condition. Individuals in the sad mood condition showed significantly more vigilance for depression but not anxiety words in the medium, and to a lesser extent, longer exposure conditions. There were no significant group differences under brief stimulus exposure. A positive correlation ($r = .36$) was found between bias for depression words in the 500 ms exposure condition and the POMS Depression Scale. In the second study, dysphoric and nondysphoric students failed to show a significant difference on the dot probe detection task in any of the exposure conditions. However, reclassification of participants into high- and low-trait anxiety revealed significantly greater vigilance for negative words (combination of anxiety and depression words) in the brief exposure condition for the high-trait individuals. Partial correlations indicated that bias for negative words in the brief exposure was significantly correlated with trait anxiety, whereas negative word bias was positively associated with depression measures in the long exposure condition. The authors concluded from these findings that an attentional bias for negative material is apparent in depressed mood, but that this bias is not evident at an early preconscious level of processing. They further suggest that the attentional bias in anxiety involves an automatic orienting to negative stimuli (early stage of encoding), whereas in depression the attentional bias is characterized by difficulty in disengaging one's attention from negative material that has come into the focus of attention (later stage of encoding).

Gotlib, McLachlan, and Katz (1988) employed a variant of the visual probe detection task, called the deployment-of-attention-task, to assess attentional bias in students identified as depressed on the BDI. Instead of using a dot probe, the word pairs were replaced by two color bars, and participants indicated which color bar they thought occurred first. This would indicate which of the two words had been the focus of one's attention. Analysis indicated that the dysphoric students attended to manic-content words less often and depression-content words more often than nondys-phoric students. However, further analysis revealed that these group differences were due to the nondepressed students exhibiting an attentional bias for positive or manic words, whereas the depressed students failed to show a selective bias for any of the word types. In a replication study, Mogg et al. (1991) also found that attentional bias was due to normal or nonanxious participants attending to manic words more and depression words less than the mildly anxious students. They also found that the color perception positivity bias in nonclinical individuals was due to low state anxiety rather than low depression and concluded that the effects produced by the deployment-of-attention-task were fragile.

McCabe and Gotlib (1995) extended the deployment-of-attention-task to clinically depressed and nondepressed women. Analysis revealed that the clinically depressed women attended equally to negative-, neutral- and positive-content trait adjectives, whereas the nondepressed showed an effect in the form of less attention toward the negative-content stimuli. Furthermore, partial correlations revealed that the attentional data were related to trait anxiety and depression more than to state anxiety. Thus in three published reports of the deployment-of-attention-task, there was no evidence of an selective negative attentional bias associated with depression (or anxiety), though in two studies the nondepressed, nonanxious showed an attentional positivity bias and in the third study a "protective" attentional bias against negative material.

Multistimulus detection tasks have not always produced uniform results. Nevertheless, the most consistent finding has been of an association between increased vigilance for negative material and depressed mood, or reduced vigilance for positive material. Bradley, Mogg, and Lee (1997) offered the most plausible explanation for these findings. They suggest that in depression there is an attentional bias for depression-related stimuli, but it occurs later with processes involved in sustaining attention. Anxiety, on the other hand, may involve bias with earlier, preconscious attentional processes that deal with the initial orientation toward stimuli. It is also likely that the demonstrated selective vigilance for particular stimuli is fragile and depends on conditions such as (a) duration of exposure intervals, (b) severity and/or co-occurrence of multiple emotional states, and (c) accuracy of match between stimulus content and the current concerns of the subject group (Mathews et al., 1996).

Debilitated Performance: Dichotic Listening Tasks

Selective attentional processing has also been investigated using a dichotic listening task in which subjects repeat or "shadow" stimuli presented in one ear while attempting to ignore the stimuli presented simultaneously in the "unattended" ear. McCabe and Gotlib (1993) presented clinically depressed and nondepressed students with positive, negative, and neutral word pairs with one word presented simultaneously to each ear. Within-subject but not between-subject differences were found in reaction-time latencies for the depressed but not the nondepressed subjects across different word content indicating that the depressed group was more distracted by negative than positive or neutral content words presented in the unattended ear. Ingram, Bernet, and McLaughlin (1994) had formerly depressed and never depressed subjects repeat an affectively neutral story presented in one ear while depressive, positive, and neutral adjectives were presented to the unattended ear at 10-second intervals. With induction of a sad mood state, formerly depressed subjects had significantly more tracking errors in both the negative and positive distracter conditions whereas the never depressed subjects had fewer tracking errors. These results suggest an attentional encoding bias for emotional stimuli in vulnerable individuals experiencing a sad mood state. Dichotic listening studies, however, have been criticized as a poor test of preconscious attentional processing because attentional switching may occur between the attended and unattended channels so that subjects may have momentary awareness of stimuli presented in the unattended channel (see Williams et al., 1997, for further discussion). Although the results of dichotic listening may not provide unequivocal evidence of preconscious attentional processing, these studies can be used to investigate unintended or involuntary selective encoding bias in depressed relative to nondepressed individuals.

Summary of Attentional Bias

Many different information processing tasks have been used to study attentional bias in depression. Although findings have not always replicated completely across different studies, nonetheless one overall finding can be drawn from this research—there is evidence of a selective attentional encoding of negative material in depression. On the basis of earlier attentional studies on anxiety and depression, several cognitive experimental researchers had concluded that vigilant or biased attentional processing for threat material was specific to anxiety whereas depression was associated with a more conscious, ruminative, or elaborative processing mode (Mathews & MacLeod, 1994; Mineka & Sutton, 1992; Williams et al., 1988). With later, more refined attentional processing studies, however, this conclusion is no longer tenable. We do see evidence of attentional bias or vigilance for negative emotion-congruent information in depression, but this attentional bias in depression is not identical in form (and certainly not in content) to the bias we see in anxiety. From our review, we offer a number of conclusions about the attentional bias in depression.

First, the encoding bias in anxiety and depression may occur in different aspects of attentional processing. Bradley, Mogg, and Lee (1997) argue that bias in depression for negative material may occur later in the information processing system with processes that are involved in sustaining attention. Anxiety, on the other hand, may involve bias with earlier, preconscious attentional processes that deal with the initial orientation toward stimuli. Mathews et al. (1996) also observed that attentional vigilance for negative material in depression may be stronger with longer exposure intervals that are above the threshold of awareness, indicating that more elaborative, conscious processes are involved in the attentional bias in depression. As discussed further under the primal processing hypothesis, Bradley, Mogg, and Lee (1997) also concluded that depression is associated with bias in both the automatic and strategic aspects of memory, as well as in sustained attention to negative information, whereas bias in anxiety is primarily associated with automatic, preconscious shifts in attention to threat-related stimuli.

Second, attentional bias in depression can operate on at least two levels. In some studies, depressed patients showed significantly greater vigilance, or interference effects, for negative information. In other studies, however, the attentional difference was due to the nondepressed who showed a positive attentional bias and possibly an attentive "avoidance" of negative stimuli. Thus the effects of depression on attention may be twofold. It may involve an upset in the "normal" encoding imbalance or asymmetry for positive information by increasing attention toward negative material. This would be evident as evenhanded attention to positive and negative information in depression. In other conditions, the attentional bias in depression is evident as increased vigilance for negative self-referent material.

This brings us to a final consideration. Evidence for a negative attentional bias or evenhanded attentional processing in depression may depend on numerous experimental and information processing variables. Encoding differences between depressed and nondepressed individuals may be more apparent when subjects must choose among several possible targets because there is a critical competition for processing resources (Mathews, 1997). Also the different results found with the visual dot probe task of Macleod and Mathews and the deployment-of-attention-task of Gotlib and colleagues may reside with the type of response required in each task. The visual probe task essentially involves a signal detection response, whereas the deployment-of-attention-task requires a decision (McCabe & Gotlib, 1995). Finally, Mathews et al. (1996) noted that level of depression severity and type of stimulus used in an attentional processing task may influence whether processing differences are found. We can conclude that selective attentional processing of negative material has been found in depression and this may be connected to the negativity that has been demonstrated at the later more strategic, elaborative, and conceptually driven stages of information processing.

SELECTIVE INTERPRETATION

A second research perspective on selective encoding examines the types of judgments, inferences, or interpretation of meaning that individuals generate when confronted with complex or ambiguous information. When a variety of meanings can be accessed, which one becomes dominant or accessible and which ones are suppressed can be taken as an indictor of an encoding bias (Mathews, 1997). A selective negativity bias in depression should be evident not only in attentional processes, but also in the later more elaborative, interpretative, and integrative processes of information encoding such as the generation of judgments of contingency, causal attributions, future expectancies, perceptions of feedback, self-evaluative judgments, and self-referent encoding.

Stimulus Interpretation

In a test of responses to ambiguous stimuli, Hedlund and Rude (1995) presented subjects with 40 scrambled sentences that could be answered with a positive or negative solution. The clinically depressed patients generated significantly more negative solutions to the scrambled sentences than nondepressed participants.

Other studies have investigated encoding bias in depression by examining responses to stimuli of greater personal and emotional salience. Crowson and Cromwell (1995) allowed subjects to freely choose to listen to a positive or negative tape-recorded message that consisted of items taken from the ATQ-N and ATQ-P. Nondepressed college students listened to the positive messages significantly more and rated them as having better tonal quality, whereas the depressed students showed no preference for the negative or positive messages. Moretti et al. (1996) administered dysphoric and nondysphoric students tachistoscopic presentations of happy and sad facial expressions each paired with a neutral facial expression. The stimulus pairs were presented for 300 ms, and participants were asked either to judge which facial expression was more informative about one's self (self-referent) or another person (other-referent). Analysis revealed that the dysphoric students rated the positive and negative expressions as equally informative and with comparable speed in the self-referent condition. In the other-referent condition, the dysphoric individuals performed as the nondysphoric participants did in the self-referent condition showing a preference for, and greater processing speed of, the positive expressions. Interestingly, the nondysphoric group found positive and negative expressions equally informative in the other-referent condition. These findings were replicated with a group of clinically depressed patients. These results suggest that in depression an evenhandedness may be evident for the encoding of positive and negative stimuli for the self, whereas nondepressed individuals appear to show a positivity encoding bias in reference to the self and an evenhandedness when processing information directed toward others.

Research on conscious effortful interpretations of discrete stimuli presented in a laboratory setting suggests that depression can influence how information is encoded or processed but not in terms of a negativity bias. Instead, depressed individuals showed a tendency toward processing both positive and negative stimuli, whereas it was the nondepressed who evidenced a selective bias for encoding positive self-referent information. However, these studies relied on the presentation of standard, discrete stimuli that may have lacked sufficient personal relevance to elicit the negativity bias that has been found in other cognitive-clinical studies of depression.

Judgment of Contingency

In the original studies, judgment of response contingency and control were investigated to test hypotheses derived from the learned helplessness model of depression. In these studies, subjects performed a task, such as pressing or not pressing a button, when a certain colored light was switched on. Although individuals were led to believe their response (button press) caused a particular outcome (illuminated light), in reality the outcome was controlled by the experimenter. Thus the experimenter controls the frequency and valence of the outcome thereby varying the amount of contingency between the subject's response and the outcome. It was hypothesized that depressed individuals would show a negative or pessimistic bias in their interpretations, perceiving less response-outcome contingency (greater sense of uncontrollability) than nondepressed individuals. However, numerous studies have found that mildly depressed individuals are more accurate in judging the degree of control they have over the outcome in both contingent and noncontingent (totally random) response-outcome conditions. In fact, it is the nondepressed who showed a biased misinterpretation or "illusion of control" by overestimating the amount of control they had over the outcome (for reviews, see Ackermann & DeRubeis, 1991; Alloy & Abramson, 1979, 1988; Dobson & Franche, 1989; Ruehlman et al., 1985). Such a finding is not only at variance with cognitive theory, but it challenges one of the basic tenets of the reformulated learned helplessness model—that depressed individuals are more likely to perceive that their responses cannot lead to decreases in the likelihood of aversive outcomes or in the increased likelihood of desired outcomes.

These studies, however, are not very informative about the encoding bias in depression because most are based on student analogue samples and very few have been conducted with clinically depressed patients. An exception to this is a study by Dobson and Pusch (1995) in which clinically depressed, remitted depressed, and never depressed individuals were all overly optimistic in their estimates of control in a noncontingency judgment task. Nevertheless, these studies have low ecological validity because it is unlikely that the highly structured discrimination responses produced in a tightly controlled experimental setting has much resemblance to the complex cognitive and behavioral response patterns produced by depressed individuals confronted with highly complex but ambiguous life problems. Also, the experimental manipulation may itself be biased by aligning itself more closely with the depressed person's expectation of low response-outcome contingency so that their tendency to produce more negative judgments accurately describes the contingencies of the experiment. In sum, judgment of contingency studies provide a weak experimental analogue for studying negative encoding bias in depression.

Causal Attributions

A more relevant body of research for the selective processing hypothesis can be found in the numerous studies that have investigated causal attributions in depression. When people are confronted with what they perceive as uncontrollable bad or undesirable events, or they perceive that highly desirable outcomes are improbable, they search for explanations as to why the undesirable events occurred and why desirable events did not occur (Abramson et al., 1978; Peterson & Seligman, 1984). Brewin (1988) defined causal attributions as "the process whereby people decide what causal factors have produced a given event or outcome" (p. 93). The reformulated learned helplessness theory of depression proposed by Abramson et al. (1978) states that one's reaction to undesirable events depends on whether the event is perceived as uncontrollable (i.e., that undesirable outcomes are perceived as not contingent on any personal response), and the type of causal explanation generated for the event. If the cause of the undesirable event is attributed to something about the person (internal explanation), is thought to persist across time (stable explanation), and is perceived to affect a variety of outcomes (global explanation), then a state of helplessness depression will develop (Abramson et al., 1978; Peterson &

Seligman, 1984, 1985). The model further proposed that people may show some degree of consistency in their attributional or explanatory style. Thus individuals who exhibit a depressive explanatory style, that is they tend to make internal, stable and global causal attributions when bad events happen to them, are at higher risk for depression when they encounter negative events (Peterson & Seligman, 1984). As well, one's explanatory style will affect the depressive experience itself. The generality and chronicity of a depressive state will depend on the extent to which global and stable helplessness attributions are generated. Low self-esteem is derived from making internal attributions of helplessness, and the intensity of depressive symptoms depends on the certainty of the expectation of uncontrollability for important or highly valued outcomes (Abramson et al., 1978).

In the hopelessness theory of depression, Alloy, Abramson, et al. (1988) noted that the expectation that highly desired outcomes are unlikely to occur, or that highly aversive outcomes are likely, and the belief that one does not possess within his or her repertoire a response that will change the likely occurrence of these outcomes are proximal sufficient causes of one subtype of depression labeled *hopelessness depression*. The authors contend that negative life events can lead to expectation of hopelessness (an immediate precursor to the symptoms of hopelessness depression) when individuals explain negative event occurrence in terms of stable and global causes. If an internal causal attribution is also made, then hopelessness will be accompanied by lowered self-esteem. Alloy, Abramson, et al. (1988) noted that the reformulated learned helplessness model and its more recent protégé, hopelessness theory, postulate that depressogenic attributional style, or the generalized tendency to make global, stable, and internal attributions to negative events, will lead to increased vulnerability to depression when a negative event occurs that matches the content areas of a person's negative attributional style. Thus in the presence of positive life events or in the absence of negative stressors, individuals with the depressogenic attributional style will be no more likely to develop hopelessness depression than nonvulnerable individuals. Thus a diathesis-stress perspective is proposed for explaining how depressogenic attributional style might lead to depression, in particular hopelessness depression.

Research on causal attributions in depression is relevant to the selective processing hypothesis because attributional judgments represent a type of inference derived from selected processing of particular informational elements of personal experience. To arrive at a biased stable, global, and internal explanation for the occurrence of negative life stressors, some features of life experiences may have been overemphasized and other features practically ignored. For example, people who blame themselves for the breakup of a relationship (internal attribution) and who conclude that all their valued relationships will end up in conflict and separation (global attribution) with no hope of reconciliation (stable attribution), will have selectively processed negative aspects of the breakup to arrive at this very pessimistic causal inference. Because of the selective encoding that must be involved in the production of excessively pessimistic attributions to negative experiences, research on causal attributions in depression has direct relevance for the selective processing hypothesis of the cognitive model. Haack, Metalsky, Dykman, and Abramson (1996) provided dysphoric and nondysphoric students with bogus success or failure feedback about their scores on tests of social sensitivity and social intelligence. Analysis revealed that all students used relevant current situational information (i.e., the bogus success or failure feedback) to make causal inferences.

It is beyond the scope of this book to review the very large research base that has developed over the past two decades on depressive explanatory style and the reformulated learned helplessness or hopelessness models of depression. Excellent reviews of this literature have been published (Brewin, 1985; Gotlib & Hammen, 1992; Joiner & Wagner, 1995; D. Miller & Moretti, 1988; Peterson & Seligman, 1984; Robins, 1988; Sweeney, Anderson, & Bailey, 1986). Based on these critical reviews as well as findings from selected studies, we focus on conclusions that can be reached about the status of the depressogenic attributional style. We also highlight a few conceptual and methodological issues that have still not been resolved by empirical investigation.

Across many studies conducted on both nonclinical and clinical samples of children, adolescents and adults, it has generally been found that current level of depression is associated with a tendency to make stable, global, and internal attributions for negative events. This is not to suggest that studies consistently find evidence for pessimistic or depressive attributional style. More than one reviewer has commented on the considerable variability in level of support across studies and questioned whether much of this may be due to insufficient statistical power (Robins, 1988).

Most studies have found that a negative attributional style tends to return to normal levels once the depression remits. Furthermore, Sweeney et al. (1986) concluded from their meta-analysis that there is some evidence that a positive or enhanced attributional style (internal, stable, and global attributions for positive events) is related to decreases in depression, though the effect sizes were smaller than for the relationship between negative attributional style and depression. Two studies have shown that clinically depressed patients and dysphoric college students who showed an enhanced attributional style for positive events had significantly greater reductions in hopelessness and depressive symptoms (J.G. Johnson, Han, Douglas, Johannet, & Russell, 1998; Needles & Abramson, 1990). In the Johnson et al. study involving recovery in clinically depressed patients, enhanced attribution for actual recent positive events mediated the relationship between generalized attributional style for hypothetical positive events and decreases in hopelessness. Reductions in hopelessness in turn mediated the relationship between enhanced attributions for recent positive events and decreases in depressive symptoms. These findings not only support the hopelessness model of depression, but suggest that stable, global, and internal attributions for positive events may be a salient process in recovery from depression.

The question of whether pessimistic attributional style is a specific feature of depression has been the subject of considerable investigation. Schlenker and Britt (1996) found that dysphoric students made relatively evenhanded or nonoptimistic attributions for hypothetical events that happened to them, but made clearly optimistic attributions for causes of hypothetical events that happened to their best friend. These results suggest that dysphoric students are not generally pessimistic about events that happen to other people. Rather they are only less optimistic or more pessimistic about events that happen to themselves. Haaga et al. (1995) found that individuals who thought more about the causes of events had stronger relations between attributional style and depression than individuals who thought less about event causality.

In studies of the specificity of the depressive attributional style in relation to other psychological disorders, the evidence for specificity is weak at best. Heimberg, Vermilyea, Dodge, Becker, and Barlow (1987) found that dysthymic patients differed significantly from nondepressed anxious patients and normals in showing the hypothesized negative attributional style for hypothetical negative events but no group differences were evident for causal ratings of the positive events. In a later study, Heimberg et al. (1989) failed to find specificity, with dysthymic, socially phobic, and agoraphobic patients all exhibiting the depressive attributional style. Luten, Ralph, and Mineka (1997) found that pessimistic attributional style for hypothetical loss and failure events was not specific to depressed mood but was related to high levels of negative affect and to anxious mood. The relationship between anxious mood and pessimistic attributional style was independent of its relationship with depression. Brewin (1988) noted that negative causal attributions have been shown to predict health behavior and adjustment in response to the onset of physical illness. Most of the research to date suggests that negative attributional style is not a unique and specific characteristic of depression.

The question of whether a pessimistic attributional style for negative events may constitute a vulnerability factor for depression has been investigated in a number of studies. This literature is discussed more fully in Chapter 8, but suffice it to say at this point there is some evidence that a general negative attributional style, as indicated by responses to hypothetical negative life events, is a causal factor for self-reported depressive symptoms in the presence of a matching negative life stressor. This diathesis-stress research is by no means consistent on the causal status of negative attributional style, and at least some reviewers have concluded that the evidence for the vulnerability perspective on negative attributional style is very weak (Brewin, 1988). However, many of the methodologically stronger prospective studies of Metalsky and colleagues, which have produced more positive findings in favor of attributional diathesis-stress model (e.g., Metalsky, Halberstadt, & Abramson, 1987; Metalsky & Joiner, 1992; Metalsky, Joiner, Hardin, & Abramson, 1993), were published after Brewin's review. Contrary to the attributional vulnerability hypothesis, Parry and Brewin (1988) failed to find evidence that negative attributional style interacted with negative life experiences in a large community sample of working-class women. Overall, though, we conclude that there is some evidence that a negative attributional style may be associated with higher risk for depression.

Most of the research on negative attributions in depression has utilized the Attributional Style Questionnaire (ASQ) or some variant of this instrument (Peterson et al., 1982). Individuals are presented with six positive and six negative hypothetical events and asked to write down one major cause for each event. They then rate the cause along the three attributional dimensions of stability, globality, and internality. The ratings for each of these dimensions tends to have very low internal reliability so researchers are advised to create composite attributional scores by summing across ratings within the positive and negative events. However, Gotlib and Hammen (1992) noted that the interpretation of this composite score is not clear. There is some evidence that the three attributional dimensions do not have equivalent status. Stability and globality attributions may have a more direct relationship with depression than internality (Abramson et al., 1989; Robins, 1988). Thus it may be that internality should not be included in the attributional composite score. Second, it is assumed that individuals' ratings on the ASQ hypothetical events will generalize to their casual attributions for real life events. There is some evidence that this assumption is not warranted and that more equivocal results are obtained when causal ratings are made for actual stressors (Gotlib & Hammen, 1992; D. Miller & Moretti, 1988; Peterson, Raps, & Villanova, 1985). Finally, in the standard ASQ, causal ratings are summed over different types of negative or positive life events. However, research on the diathesis-stress model of attributional vulnerability suggests that the content of the negative event may play an important role in the pathogenesis of depressive symptoms. Metalsky et al. (1987) found that ASQ attributional ratings for negative hypothetical achievement events predicted students' depressive mood to receiving low midterm grades, but causal attributions for negative hypothetical interpersonal events were not predictive of depressed mood. A number of assessment and measurement issues, then, remain unresolved in the research on attributional style in depression.

Given the impressive amount of research attention devoted to explicating the role of causal attributions in depression, one would assume that inferences of causality must be the most important interpretative process for determining the depressogenic potential of negative stressors. Although attributional style was emphasized as a core critical cognitive process in the reformulated learned helplessness model, the supremacy of causal attributions in the pathogenesis of depression has recently been challenged. Hammen (1988a) argued that the appraisals or meaning that individuals attach to life stressors, such as their perceived impact, personal significance, and future consequences, will have a salient influence on the life event-depression relationship. Abramson et al. (1989) recognized that three types of inference will determine whether hopelessness depression occurs in response to a negative life event: (a) causal attributions for why the event occurred, (b) inferences about the consequences that will result from the occurrence of a negative life event, and (c) inferences about the self in terms of self-worth, abilities, personality, and desirability as a result of the stressor. Brewin (1988) suggested that the emphasis on causal attributions for events may be misguided, and that moral self-evaluations in relation to the occurrence of negative life events (i.e., evaluations of whether one's response to a life event has been adequate or not) may be more important in determining whether a depressed mood state. Finally negative expectancies for future events has been shown to mediate the relationship between negative and positive attributional style, and self-reported depression, although negative attributional style also had a direct relation with depression (Hull & Mendolia, 1991; Tripp, Catano, & Sullivan, 1997). Byrne and MacLeod (1997) found that attributional differences for mood-disturbed (mixed anxious and depressed) students were only apparent for reasons given for why negative events would occur and positive events would not occur. This suggests that accessibility to explanations for events will have an impact on attributional style. There is considerable evidence that in depression a negative causal attributional style is present. To this extent, this research is evidence that a selective processing bias is apparent in depression. However, other inferential and interpretative processes must be studied to determine the extent that depression-biased negative encoding occurs at the later more elaborative and effortful stages of information processing.

Future Expectancy Judgments

If the negative encoding bias in depression is reflected in the inferences, judgments, and interpretations one generates to self-referent material, then it is hypothesized that depressed individuals should have more negative expectancies for future success or failure than nondepressed individuals. In fact, the hopelessness theory of depression postulates that a core proximal sufficient cause of hopelessness depression is the expectation that desirable events are highly unlikely whereas undesirable events are highly likely to occur. Another core feature of the hopelessness theory is the expectation that one is helpless to change the likelihood of the occurrence of these events (Abramson et al., 1989).

A. MacLeod and Cropley (1995) found that dysphoric subjects had significantly higher subjective probability estimates for a list of standard future negative events than nondysphoric controls, though the two groups did not differ in the probability judgments for the future positive event statements. Partial correlations revealed that level of depression as assessed by the BDI was uniquely related to probability estimates for future negative events and being able to quickly think of specific examples of negative events, whereas level of hopelessness was specifically related to lower probability estimates for future positive events and longer latency to think of specific examples of positive events. In a second study, A. MacLeod and Byrne (1996) had students formed into anxious, mixed anxious/depressed, and control groups write down positive and then negative future events they expected to experience within the next week, the next year, and the next five years. The anxious and mixed groups expected significantly more negative future experiences than the controls, but only the mixed anxious/depressed group generated fewer positive future experiences than controls. These results seem to suggest that anxiety is associated only with an increase in negative future thinking, whereas depression is associated with both an increase in negative and decrease in positive future thinking. Expectancies for future negative events may be related to some general factor common to both anxiety and depression, such as negative affect, and decreases in future positive thinking may be related to a more specific feature of depression such as low positive affect. A. MacLeod, Pankhania, Lee, and Mitchell (1997) found that parasuicide patients anticipated significantly fewer positive future events but not more negative future events than normal controls. Thus it may be that the specific relation between depression and reduced positive future thinking in the MacLeod and Byrne (1996) study is due to the presence of greater hopelessness in the mixed anxious/depressed group.

Pietromonaco and Markus (1983) found that dysphoric individuals had significantly higher probability estimates for the occurrence of hypothetical self-referent future sad but not happy events, and they were more likely to endorse negative inferences for these events than nondysphoric students (for similar results, see Alloy & Ahrens, 1987; G. Butler & Mathews, 1983). Andersen (1990) found that negative outcome certainty (estimates that future negative events were extremely likely to happen) and, to a lesser extent, lack of positive outcome certainty were associated with dysphoria in college students. As noted, structural equation modeling studies have shown that a generalized outcome expectancy not only has a direct influence on dysphoria but can also play a mediational role between attributional styles and depression such that the more positive a person's expectancies, the less likely he or she will be depressed (Hull & Mendolia, 1991; Tripp et al., 1997). Dunning and Story (1991) reported that dysphoric undergraduates were less realistic in their predictions of the types of future events that might occur to them over the next semester than nondysphoric participants. Furthermore, not only were the dysphoric students more likely to predict the occurrence of future aversive events, but they were also more likely to actually experience negative events than nondysphoric students. The authors conclude that these results do not support the depressive realism hypothesis that depressed individuals are more accurate in their evaluations of themselves and their social world than nondepressed individuals.

Finally, a few studies have found negative expectancy bias when investigating subjects' performance on chance-determined laboratory tasks that appear to be controllable, or their performance on aptitude or achievement tests. The most common finding in these studies is either no differences in expectancy between dysphoric and nondysphoric groups, or that dysphoric subjects are more accurate about their chances of success than the nondysphoric subjects who overestimate their expectancies of success (Craighead, Hickey, & DeMonbreun, 1979; Morris, 1996; for review, see Ackermann & DeRubeis, 1991; Alloy & Abramson, 1988; Ruehlman et al., 1985). Thus a selective negativity bias is less apparent when subjects generate predictions about their performance in standard, less personally engaging laboratory tasks.

A negativity bias has been found in the expectancies of depressed and dysphoric individuals when predictions are made about personally relevant and meaningful future experiences. Individuals who are depressed or dysphoric exhibit a bias for expecting more negative future experiences and fewer positive future events. This latter interpretative bias may be a unique feature of depression and due to the elevated levels of hopelessness present in depressive states. The strong evidence for selective future expectancy thinking in depression supports the view of the cognitive model that a selective negativity bias is present in how depressed individuals interpret not only past experiences, but also anticipated future events.

Perception and Recall of Feedback

Another area of interpretative research involves comparisons of depressed and nondepressed groups on immediate perception and subsequent recall of experimenter-provided evaluative feedback about subjects' task performance or their interpersonal behavior in a simulated social interaction. Because individuals are required to process and evaluate information provided to them by the experimenter, these studies allow one to determine whether depression is associated with a negative encoding bias when individuals are given feedback on their performance in evaluative or interpersonal tasks.

Numerous studies have investigated immediate perception and recall of task-performance evaluative feedback within experimental contexts. In many of these studies, depressed or dysphoric individuals were found to evaluate their own performance on experimental tasks, or tests, more negatively and to focus more on the negative and less on the positive aspects of evaluative feedback than nondepressed controls (Dykman, Abramson, Alloy, & Hartlage, 1989; Loeb et al., 1971; Roth & Rehm, 1980; Vestre & Caulfield, 1986; Weary & Williams, 1990). However, discrepancies have frequently been reported from this general finding. Several studies have found that the only difference between groups is with the perception of positive and not negative feedback. In these studies, the nondepressed tended to overestimate and the depressed underestimate positive feedback (DeMonbreun & Craighead, 1977; Dennard & Hokanson, 1986; Whitman & Leitenberg, 1990).

Other studies have found that the main difference between depressed and nondepressed individuals is in the recall rather than the initial perception of evaluative feedback. However, differences in selective recall of feedback may depend on whether one receives a low or high rate of positive or negative feedback, and whether the feedback is presented in an ambiguous or unambiguous fashion (Buchwald, 1977; DeMonbreun & Craighead, 1977; Dennard & Hokanson, 1986; Finkel, Glass, & Merluzzi, 1982; Nelson & Craighead, 1977). Rude, Krantz, and Rosenhan (1988) found no difference between clinically depressed and nondepressed women in their response to "flattering" and "unflattering" feedback received on a previously completed bogus personality test. Both groups rated the flattering feedback as more accurate than the unflattering or negative feedback. Ingram (1984a) found that students in a negative mood induction recalled significantly more unfavorable feedback about their performance on a personality inventory and had longer latencies to a concurrent reaction time task than positive mood and control subjects who received the same unfavorable feedback. However, other studies have failed to find significant differences between depressed and nondepressed individuals in their immediate perception and recall of neutral task performance feedback (Craighead et al., 1979; DeMonbreun & Craighead, 1977). Morris (1996) found that dysphoric students did not differ from their nondysphoric counterparts in the degree of positive self-enhancing bias evident in their ratings of the validity of contrived feedback they received about their performance on an aptitude test.

In a well-designed study of task performance evaluation, Dykman et al. (1989) found that only dysphoric students who had negative schema content showed a negative encoding bias in an ambiguous feedback condition. Also in some studies, the depressed subjects were more accurate, or at least less extreme, in their interpretation and/or recall of performance evaluative feedback than the nondepressed individuals, who tended to overestimate positive feedback (Dykman et al., 1989; Finkel et al., 1982; Nelson & Craighead, 1977). This finding appears supportive of depressive realism (Alloy & Abramson, 1988).

Another series of studies investigated encoding bias in terms of evaluations and recall of interpersonal behavior in simulated laboratory-based social interactions. In these studies, depressed or dysphoric and nondepressed groups are videotaped while conversing with a confederate or unfamiliar peer. Typically, subjects evaluate their social performance in the simulated conversation and are provided a mixture of positive and negative bogus feedback about their social competence. As well, confederates frequently evaluate the subject's performance, and external raters may be used to "objectively" evaluate participants' interpersonal behavior. Thus multiple measures of actual and perceived interpersonal behavior are often available in each study.

Numerous studies found that depressed or dysphoric subjects evaluated their social interactions more negatively than nondepressed individuals (Dow & Craighead, 1987; Dykman, Horowitz, Abramson, & Usher, 1991; Gotlib & Meltzer, 1987; Hoehn-Hyde, Schlottmann, & Rush, 1982; Lunghi, 1977; Roth & Rehm, 1980). Contrary results were reported in a few studies in which no significant group differences were found, or differences emerged in an opposite direction with the nondepressed showing more negativity than the depressed (Doerfler & Aron, 1995; Ducharme & Bachelor, 1993; Loewenstein & Hokanson, 1986). Hoehn-Hyde et al. (1982) found that depressed patients rated standard videotaped negative social interactions as more socially undesirable than nondepressed controls in the self-referent but not the other-referent condition. These evaluative differences were not apparent when individuals rated the neutral or positive social interactions. Ducharme and Bachelor (1993) found that dysphoric individuals had negative expectations about their social competency, but they did not evaluate their actual social behavior more negatively than nondysphoric controls. In addition, Gotlib (1983) found that depressed subjects perceived standard feedback of their interpersonal behavior more negatively and recalled more of the negative aspects of this evaluation than nondepressed individuals. In some studies, external judges and/or confederates rated the social functioning of depressed subjects more negatively than the nondepressed (Dykman et al., 1991), whereas others failed to find such differences between groups (Doerfler & Aron, 1995; Dow & Craighead, 1987; Gotlib & Meltzer, 1987). Finally, several studies have found that the self-evaluations of the depressed subjects are closer to the evaluations of subjects' social behavior offered by external judges than is the self-evaluation of the nondepressed group (Ducharme & Bachelor, 1993).

The findings from these studies suggest that depressed and dysphoric individuals do not process the positive elements of interpersonal and task performance feedback to the same degree as nondepressed subjects. The evidence is less consistent that depressed individuals selectively encode negative feedback, although findings from the interpersonal and task performance studies suggest that a negative encoding bias in depression is more apparent if the evaluation is on a global level, is self-referent rather than other-referent, and deals with the more interpretative rather than perceptual aspects of selective encoding. Also, certain experimental conditions may be necessary to detect an encoding bias; these include (a) a sufficiently high rate of positive or negative bogus feedback must be given to individuals performing an evaluative or interpersonal laboratory task, (b) the feedback must have a self-referent orientation, (c) measures of cognitive functioning should target the more elaborative and strategic aspects of inferential processing, and (d) severely depressed individuals should be used rather than mildly dysphoric college students (see also Gotlib & Hammen, 1992).

On the other hand, Alloy and Abramson (1988) concluded from their review of this literature that the bias may be evident in the nondepressed, with the depressed showing a more realistic or accurate appraisal of the feedback they received. And yet, a number of studies have not found that depressed or dysphoric subjects are more accurate in their perception or recall of performance feedback than nondepressed individuals (Doerfler & Aron, 1995; Koenig, Ragin, & Harrow, 1995), calling into question the basic assertion of the depressive realism hypothesis. What we can conclude from this literature is that depression does affect the encoding, and especially the retrieval, of evaluative and interpersonal performance feedback. Whether depressed people selectively process the negative aspects of feedback information or show a reduced processing of the positive features of performance feedback will depend on the context and characteristics of the information available to individuals. More research is needed to elucidate the conditions that facilitate or inhibit a negative encoding bias of performance information in depressed individuals.

Self-Evaluative Encoding

There is considerable empirical evidence that depressed and dysphoric individuals evaluate themselves more negatively on personality characteristics than nondepressed individuals. Vestre and Caulfield (1986) found that dysphoric students interpreted neutral personality descriptive statements provided to them by the experimenter as less positive than the nondysphoric group. However, further analysis revealed that the dysphoric individuals were more accurate in their interpretations than the nondysphoric. Wenzlaff and Grozier (1988) provided dysphoric and nondysphoric students success or failure feedback on a test of social perceptiveness. The dysphoric group judged social perceptiveness to be more important after receiving failure feedback, whereas the nondysphoric subjects rated social perceptiveness more important after receiving success feedback. Furthermore, the dysphoric but not nondysphoric students generated lower estimates of their general proficiency after receiving negative feedback on the social perceptiveness test. Finally, Dykman (1996) had dysphoric and nondysphoric students imagine themselves in a series of hypothetical positive and negative events and then complete self-ratings on 49 bipolar trait adjectives after each scenario. In response to the negative hypothetical events, dysphoric students rated themselves more negatively, especially on global personality traits, than the nondysphoric group. These studies suggest depressed mood is associated with a negative encoding bias that affects self-evaluative judgments though this may be more apparent when individuals are exposed to a prior negative experience.

Self-Referent Encoding

Numerous studies have investigated selective encoding by examining recall bias for positive, negative, and neutral stimuli that were previously presented to the individual. The best example of this approach is the *self-referent encoding task* (SRET) which involves the incidental (free recall of trait adjectives without prior warning) or intentional (free recall of trait adjectives with prior warning) recall of a previously presented list of positive, negative, and neutral trait adjectives. Although this task is unable to disentangle whether recall bias is due to selective encoding or selective retrieval of trait adjectives, nevertheless it can be taken as indirect evidence for an encoding bias. This is particularly true because the majority of the studies calculate the recall bias on trait words that were previously rated as self-descriptive. The selective encoding hypothesis would predict a *mood-congruency* effect in the recall of self-referent trait adjectives. It is predicted that in a sad or depressed state, individuals will show enhanced encoding of negative trait words, which would be reflected as a negative recall bias; whereas in an elevated or happy mood state, an enhanced encoding and recall bias will be evident for the positive trait words.

Davis (1979) was one of the first to apply the incidental recall paradigm to study schematic processing in clinically depressed and nondepressed individuals. Although he did not vary the hedonic tone of his stimulus materials, he did find that the depressed group recalled significantly fewer adjectives than the nondepressed subjects only in the self-referent and not in the structural or semantic conditions. Since then, many studies have used positive and negative trait adjectives and found evidence of mood congruency effects in individuals' judgments of the self-descriptiveness of trait adjectives as well as in their incidental or intentional recognition and recall of the trait words. Thus individuals in a naturally occurring or experimentally induced sad or depressed mood state will endorse and subsequently recall significantly more negative than positive trait adjectives, whereas nondepressed individuals or those given an elated mood induction show enhanced judgment and recall of positive trait adjectives (Bradley & Mathews, 1983, 1988; Dennard & Hokanson, 1986; Derry & Kuiper, 1981; Dunbar & Lishman, 1984; Ingram, Kendall, et al., 1987; Ingram, Partridge, Scott, & Bernet, 1994; Kuiper & Derry, 1982; Nasby, 1994, 1996; Ruiz-Caballero & González, 1994).

The robustness of the negative biased recall in depression, however, should not be overstated. D.M. Clark and Teasdale (1985) found gender differences with women but not men showing the predicted differential recall of unpleasant adjectives in an induced sad mood and enhanced recall of pleasant adjectives in a happy mood. Ingram, Partridge, et al. (1994) found that the more severe the level of depression, the greater the tendency to recall trait depressive information. M. Greenberg and Beck (1989) reported a content-specificity endorsement and recall effect, with clinically depressed outpatients showing enhanced encoding of negative self, world, and future-oriented trait adjectives compared with a nondepressed but anxious psychiatric control group. Other studies have failed to find any recognition or recall differences between the depressed or dysphoric and nondysphoric (Clifford & Hemsley, 1987; Dobson & Shaw, 1987; Hasher, Rose, Zacks, Sanft, & Doren, 1985; Pietromonaco & Markus,

1983; Roth & Rehm, 1980). In still other studies, the main difference is in the enhanced judgment and recall of positive trait adjectives by the nondepressed individuals and/or an evenhandedness in the recall of the dysphoric or depressed subjects (Gilboa, Roberts, & Gotlib, 1997; Kuiper & Derry, 1982; Kuiper, Olinger, MacDonald, & Shaw, 1985; Myers et al., 1989; Rude et al., 1988; Sanz, 1996). Hammen, Miklowitz, et al. (1986) found that nondysphoric students had a significant recall bias for positive trait adjectives, whereas the mildly dysphoric showed an evenhanded recall pattern and the moderately dysphoric a confused or inefficient schema-based recall. The authors concluded that their findings support the view of Kuiper and colleagues that an evenhanded or clear negativity recall bias may be a function of depression severity. However, in a study of 21 depressed inpatients and nondepressed controls, Breslow, Kocsis, and Belkin (1981) also found that the only intentional recall difference of a previously presented story was that the depressed individuals recalled fewer positive story elements than the nondepressed. Myers et al. (1989) also found that an intentional recall difference between clinically depressed and normal controls was a function of the recall bias for hypomanic trait words by the control group. Thus it is still unclear whether a clear encoding and retrieval bias for negative material will only be evident in the more severely depressed, with mild depressive states associated with a mixed or evenhanded processing of positive and negative material.

Several methodological variables may influence whether a negative mood congruency effect is detected in these recall studies. One issue is whether recognition or recall is a better indicator of memory bias. Ferguson, Rule, and Carlson (1983) argued that recognition is a better index of memory strength than recall, whereas Martin and D.M. Clark (1986a) suggested that recall may be less affected by response bias than recognition memory. Across SRET studies, similar results have been obtained whether recognition or recall indices have been used. However, less encouraging results have been obtained when using response latency or time taken to decide whether an adjective is self-descriptive or not as an indicator of processing bias (Bradley & Mathews, 1983; Derry & Kuiper, 1981). It is likely that decision time is indicative of a different cognitive process than judgment or recall data. A third variable to consider is whether the stimulus information used in encoding experiments will influence the results. Positive and negative trait adjectives tend to show stronger mood-congruous retrieval effects, whereas positive and negative abstract nouns produce weaker effects (Teasdale & Barnard, 1993). Finally, negative judgment and recall bias in depressed mood are specific to self-referent encoding and are not evident when encoding the trait adjectives according to other criteria such as the word's semantic or structural characteristics, or whether the adjectives are descriptive of another person (Bradley & Mathews, 1983, 1988; Davis, 1979; Nasby, 1994, 1996).

Two main criticisms have been levied against the SRET studies. First, many of the studies used a mixture of mood state and personality trait words in their stimulus list (Segal & Muran, 1993). In these studies, the congruency between mood state and words recalled would be confounded if the stimulus words merely described the current mood state experienced by the subject. Ingram, Partridge, et al. (1994) investigated the state and trait adjective distinction by presenting subclinically depressed and nondepressed students with state-depressive, trait-depressive, and nondepressive adjectives in an incidental or intentional recall condition. Dysphoric subjects showed enhanced recall of state-depressive adjectives in both the incidental and intentional conditions, whereas enhanced recall for the trait-depressive adjectives was only apparent in the intentional (i.e., effortful) recall condition. The authors concluded that in more automatic incidental recall, dysphoric individuals do not show selective elaboration of trait depressive information. In a replication study comparing clinically depressed inpatients and nondepressed controls, Ingram, Fidaleo, Friedberg, Shenk, and Bernet (1995) found very different results. The clinically depressed did not show specific processing of trait-depressive information in intentional or incidental recall but rather a more diffuse processing of any depressive information whether it had a state or trait orientation. The nondepressed group, on the other hand, showed a greater tendency to recall nondepressed information in both the intentional and, to a lesser extent, incidental recall conditions. Ingram, Fidaleo et al. (1995) concluded from their studies that a specific statelike negative processing bias is more evident than traitlike negative bias in subclinical depression; whereas in severe clinical depression, a diffuse processing pattern is evident so that both negative trait and more situational or state self-descriptors are processed.

A second criticism of the SRET is that incidental or intentional recall may be more indicative of a response bias rather than the selective encoding of material. Zuroff, Colussy, and Wielgus (1983, 1986) suggested that the selective recall bias in depression may primarily reflect a motivation or willingness on the part of depressed individuals to report negative self-referent material. To test this response bias hypothesis, Zuroff et al. (1983) presented dysphoric, previously dysphoric, and nondysphoric students with a list of 20 positive and 20 negative adjectives and the groups were subsequently tested for their recall and recognition memory of the self-descriptive adjectives. Dysphoric students recalled more negative words than the nondysphoric group. However, signal detection analysis of the recognition test revealed that the dysphoric subjects used less stringent criteria for recognizing the negative adjectives indicating that a primary factor in the selective recognition and recall of negative information by the dysphoric group may be a greater willingness of these subjects to report negative self-relevant stimuli rather than to an enhanced encoding and retrieval of this material. Dunbar and Lishman (1984) also found differences between depressed and nondepressed subjects in their signal detection analysis of recognition data. Unlike Zuroff et al. (1983), however, their results suggested that depressed individuals had a response bias against reporting pleasant words, rather than a response bias for reporting negative stimuli. Martin and Clark (1986a, 1986b) raised a number of methodological and conceptual problems with Zuroff et al.'s (1983, 1986) suggestion that negative selective self-referent processing in depression primarily reflects a response rather than memory bias. They conclude that the signal detection analyses of Zuroff et al. (1983) and Dunbar and Lishman (1984) have not established a role for response bias in explaining the enhanced negative recall bias in SRET studies.

The SRET has been one of the most widely used experimental methods for investigating selective encoding bias in depression. Generally, the results have been supportive of the selective encoding hypothesis. Depressed and dysphoric individuals have been shown to have enhanced self-referent processing of negative adjectives and attenuated processing of positive information. However, the results are by no means consistent and many factors may influence the extent of the self-referent processing bias. Furthermore, the SRET results are primarily indicative of mood congruency rather than a reflection of an underlying negative schema accessibility as evidenced by the inconsistent results obtained by Ingram and colleagues when comparison was made of state and trait adjectives. The issue of response bias has not been satisfactorily resolved, and Haaga et al. (1991) suggested that differences in recall bias were weaker when depressed groups were compared with similarly distressed psychiatric controls. This, however, may be due to an elevated level of neuroticism in psychiatric control groups. Studies have found that elevated neuroticism is associated with a recall bias for negative information (Martin, Ward, & Clark, 1983; G. Young & Martin, 1981).

Finally, SRET is not the optimal task for studying encoding bias in depression. Because the enhanced recall of negative information may be due to the effects of depression at both the encoding and retrieval stages, recognition and recall bias are at best an indirect measure of the effects of depression on encoding. Nevertheless, given the extensive research that has been done with the SRET, one cannot completely discount the relevance of these findings for the selective processing hypothesis. Overall, the results indicate that depression affects how self-referent information is processed, as evidenced by enhanced encoding and recall of negative self-referent material and/or a reduced processing of positive information.

Self-Focused Attention

Self-focused attention has been defined "as an awareness of self-referent, internally generated information that stands in contrast to an awareness of externally generated information derived from sensory receptors" (Ingram, 1990b, p. 156). Pyszczynski and Greenberg (1987) indicated that individuals can adopt a *depressive self-focusing style* in which one focuses on the self when negative outcomes are salient but avoids self-focus when exposed to positive outcomes. This depressive self-focusing style is thought to maintain and even exacerbate depressive symptoms by minimizing the positive emotional effects of success and maximizing the negative psychological effects of failure (Pyszczynski & Greenberg, 1987). In this conceptualization, self-focused attention refers to a specific encoding orientation or style whose predictions are consistent with the selective processing hypothesis of the cognitive model.

Self-focused attention has been assessed by self-report measures like structured questionnaires and sentence completion tests as well as by experimental manipulation, such as completing a task in front of a large mirror, which supposedly heightens one's self-focus or self-consciousness. Across a number of studies, depressed or dysphoric individuals show significant elevations in dispositional and state self-focused attention when compared with nondepressed controls (e.g., Ingram, Lumry, Cruet, & Sieber, 1987; for reviews, see Ingram, 1990b; Pyszczynski & Greenberg, 1987), although heightened self-focused attention also characterizes other clinical disorders like anxiety and alcohol abuse. In his review Ingram (1990b) concluded that "it appears difficult to find a psychological disorder that is not characterized by a heightened degree of self-focused attention" (p. 165).

Although elevated self-focused attention does not differentiate depression from anxiety (e.g., Sanz & Avia, 1994), greater specificity may be evident in the content of the self-focused attention so that what characterizes depression is maladaptive self-focused attention or self-absorption on negative self-referent content as reflected in one's thoughts, cognitive processes, and schematic functioning (Borden, Lister, Powers, Logsdon, & Turner, 1993; Haaga et al., 1991; Ingram, 1990a, 1990b). There is considerable evidence that depressed or dysphoric individuals exhibit a tendency to self-focus that is consistent with a selective self-referent encoding bias. Increases in negative self-focused attention can intensify the negative affect in depression (Pyszczynski & Greenberg, 1987), whereas inducing an external focus in dysphoric individuals can reduce levels of depressed mood (Nix, Watson, Pyszczynski, & Greenberg, 1995). Whether this depressive self-focusing style is primarily characterized by an enhanced self-focus attention to negative self-referent thought content, as predicted by cognitive theory, or a decrease in an exaggerated self-focus on positive thought content, as predicted by the depressive realism hypothesis, has not been settled by the research to date.

Cognitive Encoding Errors

A number of self-report questionnaires have been developed to assess the errors of interpretation proposed by the cognitive model (A. Beck, 1963, 1967, pp. 234–35). These measures typically present hypothetical vignettes of interpersonal and achievement-related situations involving typical life experiences. One of the earliest self-report measures is the Cognitive Bias Questionnaire (CBQ) developed by Krantz and Hammen (1979). Subjects are presented with somewhat vague and ambiguous vignettes of potentially problematic situations that individuals often encounter in their daily lives. Each vignette is followed by four questions with four response options reflecting a depressed-distorted, depressed-nondistorted, nondepressed-distorted, or nondepressed-nondistorted option. Subjects choose the response option that best represents how they would respond to the situation if it actually happened to them. The depressed-distorted response options incorporate cognitive errors such as arbitrary inference, selective abstraction, overgeneralization, and maximization/minimization. In studies using either the original CBQ, or a revised version that substitutes positive, negative, and neutral vignettes for the original ambiguous story outcomes, depressed and dysphoric individuals report significantly more depressed-distorted responses than nondepressed individuals, though this effect may be most apparent when negative story information is provided (Krantz & Gallagher-Thompson, 1990; Krantz & Hammen, 1979; Krantz & Liu, 1987; I. Miller & Norman, 1986).

Another measure, the Cognitive Response Test (CRT), consists of 50 open-ended situations representing common types of social interaction (J. Watkins & Rush, 1983). Individuals write down the first thought that comes to them after reading the situation statement. Responses are then coded as irrational (involves demandingness, absolutism, attribution to luck or exaggeration) versus rational (no cognitive errors present) and a depressed (cognition involves negative view of self, world, or future) versus other orientation. Analysis revealed that clinically depressed patients produced significantly more irrational-depressed and fewer rational responses than nondepressed psychiatric and normal controls. Dobson and Shaw (1986) also found that clinically depressed patients scored significantly higher on the CRT irrational-depressed scale than nondepressed psychiatric and normal controls, and that the scale correlated with other measures of depressive symptoms and cognition.

Although other self-report measures of cognitive errors have been reported in the literature, such as the Interpretations Inventory (Dobson & Breiter, 1983) and Burns' Cognitive Distortion Questionnaire (Burns, Shaw, & Croker, 1987), they have not been used extensively and evidence for their validity is lacking. Burns et al. (1987) did not find a significant difference between depressed and nondepressed groups on the total distortion score of their measure, and Dobson and Breiter (1983) found that the Interpretations Inventory had a low correlation ($r = .26$) with depression severity as measured by the BDI. However, Lefebvre (1981) found that depressed low back pain patients had significantly higher scores on the total score, catastrophizing, overgeneralization, and selective abstraction (but not personalization) subscales of the Cognitive Error Questionnaire than nondepressed pain patients. Others have used more general measures with subscales relevant for only one or two cognitive errors. Sullivan and D'Eon (1990) found that catastrophizing was correlated with depression in a sample of chronic pain patients (although this relationship was apparently due to overlapping item content), whereas others have found that overgeneralization is associated specifically with depression (Edelman et al., 1994; Ganellen, 1988).

Wenzlaff and Grozier (1988) found that dysphoric students magnified failure significantly more than nondysphoric individuals as evidenced by their tendency to judge the trait of social perceptiveness as personally more important after they received failure feedback on a test of this personality trait. Blackburn and Eunson (1989) did a content analysis of the Daily Record of Dysfunctional Thoughts of 50 depressed patients undergoing cognitive therapy and found that cognitive errors were present in much of the thinking recorded by patients. The most common errors were arbitrary inference (44%), magnification (25%), overgeneralization (19%), selective abstraction (8%), and personalization (4%). Selective abstraction was most often associated with a depressed mood state.

Using the Articulated Thoughts During Simulated Situations method of cognitive assessment, White, Davison, Haaga, and White (1992) found that clinically depressed patients produced more cognitive biases in their think-aloud responses to three simulated situations than nondepressed psychiatric controls. However, there were no significant group differences on specific cognitive errors such as selective abstraction, overgeneralization, magnification, personalization, and dichotomous thinking.

M. Cook and Peterson (1986) found that diagnostically depressed female students compared with nondepressed controls gave more irrational justifications or reasons for why they believed that a particular cause led to the occurrence of an undesirable event within the past year. Irrational justifications were defined in terms of cognitive errors such as arbitrary inference, selective abstraction, overgeneralization, and magnification/minimization. McDermut, Haaga, and Bilek (1997) compared clinically depressed and nondepressed students on the causes generated to positive and negative personal events that occurred to them during the last year. Responses were coded by independent raters as an irrational justification (contains errors like arbitrary inference, selective abstraction, and overgeneralization) or a logical justification. Analysis revealed that the depressed subjects produced more biased or illogical justifications in explaining negative events but were less biased in their justifications for positive events.

Generally, studies using questionnaire measures of cognitive bias have shown that depressed and dysphoric individuals are more biased when processing negative self-referent situations. This bias is specific to negative, personally relevant information and does not represent a biased processing of all information. However, studies that have attempted to compare groups at the more specific level of the individual cognitive errors described in the cognitive model have met with more limited success. One of the main reasons for these inconsistent results at the more specific level is the substantial overlap between the different types of cognitive errors so that raters have not been able to reliably distinguish one type of cognitive error from the other (Krantz & Hammen, 1979; J. Watkins & Rush, 1983). If possible, a more detailed coding scheme is needed that can pick up on the nuances that distinguish between specific types of cognitive errors. However, critics of the cognitive model have expressed reservations about the use of retrospective questionnaires for the assessment of cognitive processes such as encoding bias and errors of inference or reasoning (Coyne, 1989; Coyne & Gotlib, 1983). This view may be overly harsh because the biased negativity in depression that is frequently found in questionnaire studies has also been reported in laboratory-based research using information processing tasks borrowed from experimental and social cognitive psychology like the emotional Stroop, the visual dot probe, the performance feedback, and the self-referent encoding tasks.

DEPRESSIVE REALISM

No doubt the most serious challenge to the selective processing hypothesis comes from the depressive realism perspective. If this view merely asserted that nondepressed individuals are also biased in showing a selective processing for positive or self-enhancing information, then this could be easily accommodated within the selective processing hypothesis of the cognitive model. However, depressive realism goes one step further by asserting that the perceptions and inferences of depressed individuals about self-referent events are actually more accurate and realistic, whereas it is the processing of the nondepressed or normals that is biased and unrealistic in the direction of an overly positive or optimistic perception and judgment of self-referent experiences (Abramson & Alloy, 1981; Ackermann & DeRubeis, 1991; Alloy & Abramson, 1979, 1988). This "sadder but wiser" perspective is clearly at odds with the selective processing hypothesis, which asserts that the perceptions and interpretations evident in depression are not more accurate but instead show a systematic bias for negative self-referent information.

As is evident from the studies previously reviewed in this section, an evenhandedness is often found in the perceptions and interpretations of depressed individuals for positive and negative information, whereas the significant group differences can be attributed to the enhanced processing of positive material by the nondepressed subjects. This pattern of finding is considered strong evidence for the depressive realism hypothesis because it suggests that it is the nondepressed who are "distorted" by showing unbridled optimism or positivity, whereas the depressed exhibit more realistic processing of both positive and negative information (for review, see Alloy & Abramson, 1988). However, there are many problems with this hypothesis, which have been discussed in three reviews of the topic (Ackermann & DeRubeis, 1991; Dobson & Franche, 1989; Haaga & Beck, 1995).

It must be acknowledged that only studies that contrast the perceptions and judgments of depressed individuals against a relatively objective standard of judgment provide a clear and direct test of depressive realism (Ackermann & DeRubeis, 1991; Dobson & Franche, 1989). Many of the studies that may appear to support depressive realism can not be taken as support for the hypothesis because they simply contrast the responses of depressed and nondepressed individuals. Studies of differences between depressed and nondepressed in expectancies, attributions, and self-referent encoding, as well as the perception of task or interpersonal performance feedback and self-evaluation, cannot shed light on depressive realism because they do not include an independent verifiable standard to determine a correct response or, if they do include an objective standard, the interpretation of what constitutes a correct response is unclear (Ackermann & DeRubeis, 1991).

The judgment of contingency studies is considered "strong" evidence for depressive realism (Alloy & Abramson, 1988). In the vast majority of these studies, the dysphoric subjects are more accurate in judging contingency than nondysphoric individuals, although in the two studies involving clinically depressed individuals, depressive realism was not found.

That is, the depressed group was not more accurate in their judgments of contingency than the nondepressed, but instead either all groups perceived control accurately or they were all overly optimistic in their judgments of control (Dobson & Pusch, 1995; Lennox, Bedell, Abramson, & Foley, 1990). Thus the results of judgment of contingency studies are problematic because results clearly supporting depressive realism have only been found in nonclinical, dysphoric subjects. Also these studies suffer from low ecological validity. It is doubtful that one can generalize from responses to these tightly controlled standardized laboratory judgment tasks (i.e., judging contingency between button press and onset of a green light) to individuals' reactions to the more complex and ambiguous real life response-contingency situations encountered in everyday life (Dobson & Franche, 1989).

In studies involving perception and recall of task performance feedback, Dobson and Franche (1989) concluded that, of the studies demonstrating distortion, almost twice as many found that the depressed or dysphoric subjects were negatively biased compared with the number of studies that reported a positive distortion in the nondepressed. Also there is some evidence that negative bias in depression is more likely under high but not low rates of success feedback. This suggests that findings may vary depending on the type of task used as well as whether the feedback contingencies might inadvertently conform to the negative bias of the depressed thereby creating a situation where negative processing emerges as the more accurate response. For example, low rates of success feedback would more likely conform to the depressed person's relatively negative expectations of the amount of success feedback they would receive and so no distortion would be evident. High rates of success feedback create a situation that is contrary to the depressed individual's expectation, and so we expect to find a negative processing bias operating in this situation (Dobson & Franche, 1989). If one accepts the schematic processing hypothesis in which the depressed have a negative processing bias because of underlying depressogenic schemas and the nondepressed a self-enhancing processing bias because of optimistic, positive self schemas, then we would expect depressed individuals to show more accurate processing in experimental paradigms involving a negative situation (i.e., noncontrol) because this would conform to their schematic processing or preconceptions (Ackermann & DeRubeis, 1991; Haaga & Beck, 1995). Thus the experimental conditions used in some studies may have unwittingly provided feedback so that the negative expectancies and judgments of the depressed provide a better match with the experimental conditions than the more positive orientation of the nondepressed.

Finally, Dobson and Franche (1989) noted that, in the studies of perception and recall of interpersonal feedback, mixed results have been obtained, with some studies finding evidence of negative distortion by the dysphoric group, others finding evidence of positive distortion by the nondysphoric subjects, and still others finding no significant difference. The majority of these studies, though, would at first appearance support depressive realism as evidenced by no significant differences between the ratings of the depressed and some external criterion. However, a major problem with these studies is that the "objective" criterion used is the ratings of subjects' interpersonal behavior by external observers. There is evidence that trained raters may be more negative or critical in their interpersonal evaluations than, for example, peers who interacted with the depressed subject. This, then, calls into question whether external raters can be considered a measure of objective accuracy or reality (Ackermann & DeRubeis, 1991; Ducharme & Bachelor, 1993; Gotlib & Meltzer, 1987).

In our review of the research on selective encoding, we found many studies where the depressed or dysphoric group did not make more accurate perceptions or judgments than the nondepressed individuals (e.g., Doerfler & Aron, 1995; Dunning & Story, 1991; Koenig et al., 1995; Morris, 1996). Other problems have been noted with the depressive realism literature. Most of the research is based on subclinical dysphoric samples. As Haaga and Beck (1995) argued, these samples may differ in important characteristics from diagnostic clinically depressed groups. In subclinical or dysphoric depression, there may be more overlap between depression and anxiety, as well as differences in cognitive balance. That is, an even-handedness in the processing of positive and negative information may be present in mild dysphoric states, whereas only in the severely depressed do we see a systematic negative processing bias (A. Beck, 1991; A. Beck & Clark, 1988; Ruehlman et al., 1985). If this is the case, then use of subclinical dysphoric samples does not provide an adequate test of processing features in depression. Another problem that can be raised concerns whether the judgments obtained in the laboratory procedures used in these studies are generalizable to the types of judgments individuals would make in the naturalistic environment. Not only is the type of task used in the laboratory rather artificial, but certain characteristics of information delivery, such as the rigidity and fixedness of the experimental trials, may not reflect the vague and ever-changing conditions we find in naturalistic social settings (Haaga & Beck, 1995).

Haaga and Beck (1995) concluded that the depressive realism studies may be too limiting to offer a valid means of studying the cognitive theory of depression. They suggest that in designing experiments that offer a truly objective criterion for evaluating the accuracy of subjects' judgments, researchers may be forced to exclude a high proportion of clinically relevant cognitions. From our review, we would conclude that the evidence for the strong version of depressive realism is not compelling.

Whether depressed, or even dysphoric, individuals are more accurate than nondepressed individuals in their perceptions and judgments probably depends largely on the exigencies of the laboratory task. But even in the laboratory, the robustness of the depressive realism phenomena is questionable. We have also noted particular difficulties in generalizing from these laboratory paradigms to the type of judgments one would find in the naturalistic social environment. There is little evidence that depressed individuals make more accurate and realistic judgments in their everyday lives than nondepressed individuals. To this extent, depressive realism does not represent a credible challenge to the selective processing hypothesis of the cognitive model.

Summary

Contrary to the conclusions reached by other reviewers (Ackermann-Engel & DeRubeis, 1993; Gotlib & Hammen, 1992; Haaga et al., 1991), there is empirical support for the selective processing hypothesis. Mathews (1997), in his review, concluded that the most obvious generalization across these studies is that selective encoding of information is occurring in emotionally disordered individuals. However, given the large number of studies that have investigated the perceptions, evaluations, and judgments of depressed or dysphoric individuals, we are now in a position to offer some refinements to the original processing hypothesis, which emphasized the negative processing bias in depression.

First, it is evident that encoding bias is not specific to depression but is probably germane to the human condition. Thus nondepressed as well as depressed individuals show processing biases. It would be incorrect to assume that only the depressed are biased and the nondepressed unbiased or accurate in their perceptions. The literature demonstrates that nondepressed individuals are also biased in their information processing, although in a positive, overly optimistic self-enhancing direction.

Second, the selective processing hypothesis of depression must be revised to include not only the enhanced processing of negative information, but the biased exclusion of positive material as well. The type of encoding bias present will depend on a combination of factors including the individual's level of depression, the material that is being processed, and contextual cues present during the encoding exercise. However, the most important factor may be the type of information processes targeted by a cognitive task. We concluded from the attentional processing studies that depression is characterized by distinctive attentional processing that may take the form of attentional vigilance for negative emotionally congruence self-referent information and/or an evenhanded attention to positive and negative self-referent material. This selective attentional processing may serve as the basis for the enhanced processing of negative material, which has been found more consistently in studies involving conceptually based cognitive tasks such as expectancies, self-evaluations, judgments, and inferences. Gilboa et al. (1997), however, noted that the evenhanded processing often seen in depressed or dysphoric individuals, which can be considered a decline in the positive processing bias of the nondepressed, cannot be solely explained by the effects of negative mood state on information processing. In their study, nondysphoric participants under an experimentally induced sad mood continued to show a positive recall bias, whereas only the naturally occurring dysphoric group evidenced the evenhanded recall pattern. Thus factors in addition to presence of negative mood state may be affecting the differential processing seen in dysphoric individuals.

Previously, we suggested that these differential patterns of selective encoding may depend on depression severity (and perhaps persistence) such that a clear negativity bias may only be present in more severe depressions, whereas an evenhanded processing of positive and negative self-referent information will be seen in milder, naturally occurring depressive states. Others have also posited a similar dissociation between processing bias and levels of depression (Gotlib & McCabe, 1992; Mathews et al., 1996; Ruehlman et al., 1985; see similar conclusion reached for mood-congruent recall by Matt et al., 1992). Kuiper and colleagues (Dance & Kuiper, 1987; Kuiper & Olinger, 1986) proposed a self-worth contingency model of depression based on the SRET studies in which the self-schemas of nondepressed are viewed as positive and well consolidated, the clinically depressed also have well consolidated but negative content self-schemas, and the mildly depressed have poorly consolidated self-schemas containing both positive and negative content. The data, however, have not provided consistent support for this assertion because evenhanded processing has also been found in studies involving clinically depressed as well as the mildly dysphoric groups. Nevertheless, evidence for attentional bias for negative material has been found most consistently in studies of clinically depressed patients, indicating that severity may be operating as a confounding variable in many studies.

Third, information processing strategies are very much influenced by contextual cues and situational demands. Thus whether a negative or positive bias, or evenhandedness, is evident in the encoding strategies of depressed or nondepressed individuals depends on the type of information processed as well as the situational demands. In his study of the interpretation and recall of feedback received from performance on an aptitude test, Morris (1996) found that dysphoric and nondysphoric students used a similar self-enhancing processing bias (i.e., higher validity judgments with more favorable feedback) when encoding performance feedback, but a schematic processing strategy when subjects recalled their feedback. This suggests that different information processing demands will lead to different encoding strategies and therefore different results. This is also consistent with the view that one must match the experimental context with negative schematic processing to elucidate the selective negative encoding bias in depression (Ackermann & DeRubeis, 1991). This may explain why there is such apparent discrepancy across the different experimental paradigms used to study selective encoding. Researchers will need to pay closer attention to the cognitive tasks used in their studies and the type of processing strategies elicited by these tasks.

Fourth, there is considerable evidence that the encoding bias in depression is highly specific or self-referent in nature. It is not that depressed individuals always select the most negative interpretation (or attend to both positive and negative material equally), but rather they tend to be more negatively oriented or evenhanded when presented with highly significant self-referent information. In fact, a strong negativity bias may only be apparent with self-referent information that is particularly significant to the current concerns of the individual. Most of the experimental studies in this area focus on the processing of standard somewhat abstract or general information that may not tap into the personal, vital concerns of the individual. Brewin (1988) also noted that often the tasks used to assess bias have not been sensitive enough or even relevant to the subjects' actual concerns. Thus what is gained in precision and experimental control may be lost in ecological validity so that the scales are tipped against the selective encoding hypothesis.

And finally, it is apparent across all the studies we reviewed that the encoding negativity bias in depression is more robust with the integrative and elaborative processes involved in conceptually based cognitive tasks than with perceptually driven attentional processing studies. In our review of the more recent attentional processing studies, we concluded that there is evidence of an attentional bias for negative self-referent material in depression. Unlike anxiety, however, this attentional bias occurs at the later, more elaborative stages of information processing and so may function to sustain attention onto negative information (Bradley, Mogg, et al., 1997). Furthermore, our extensive review of the research on selective interpretation of negative material again indicates that there is considerable support for an enhanced encoding of negative, especially conceptually based, information in depression. This negativity bias was evident in conceptual processes such as causal attributions, future expectancies, recall

of interpersonal and evaluative performance feedback, self-eva...
judgments, self-referent trait adjective recall, and systematic errors of inference. From the question of biased encoding in depression, we turn now
to consider the basis of this selective processing—the activation of negative self-schema.

SCHEMA ACTIVATION HYPOTHESIS

Negative affective states like depression are characterized by an increased
accessibility to the negative self-referent schematic structures of the loss
mode.

One of the fundamental assumptions of the cognitive model is that the
cognitive content and processing that characterizes depression results
from the activation of underlying dysfunctional meaning-making structures called schemas, and their clusters, the modes (A. Beck, 1967, 1996;
see also Chapter 3, Assumptions 1 and 3). In depression, the selective processing of negative self-referent material is the product of activated
schemas involving loss, failure, and deprivation (see Chapter 4 for further
discussion). Thus research that is focused on explicating the content and
structure of the hypothesized negative self-schemas of depression is an
integral test of the cognitive model.

Before discussing the empirical basis of the schematic model of depression, it is important to clarify the role of schema at the descriptive level of
the model. The concept of schema was first proposed to explain the mechanism responsible for the biased thought processes involved in depression (A. Beck, 1964). Because it was proposed that schemas take a primary
role in directing the dysfunctional information processing that characterizes depression, other writers assumed that the cognitive model asserts
that the activation of maladaptive schemas causes depression. However,
cognitive theory is quite clear in stating that a combination of factors may
cause depression including biological, genetic, stress, and personality
variables (A. Beck, 1967). Thus the theory restricts the conceptualization
of schema activation to that of a hypothetical explanation for the development of depression (A. Beck, 1991). From this perspective, then, negative
self-referent schemas constitute a hypothesized feature of depression
that can be tested at the descriptive level without invoking any notion of
causality. Critics of the cognitive model have considered the empirical evidence for dysfunctional schemas weak because they have focused exclusively on causal aspects of the concept (Coyne, 1989; Coyne & Gotlib,
1986; Gotlib & McCabe, 1992). However, it is first necessary to determine

whether negative self-referent schemas are an integral feature of depression as postulated by the model. This would be evident as a mood-congruency effect involving the schematic processing of self-referent information. Although it is proposed that mood congruent schematic-driven processing is evident at all phases of information processing, it would be particularly evident in the formation and retrieval of memories. This is because the stored contents of memory constitute the internal representations of meaning. Naturalistic and experimental procedures that assess memory content and structure, then, provide an important test of the schema activation hypothesis.

There are three aspects to the concept of schema that must be clarified before discussing the relevant empirical literature. First, it is important to make a distinction between accessibility or activation and availability. Segal (1988) described *availability* in terms of "differences in the content of stored personal constructs between depressed and nondepressed people" (p. 151). Thus it could be postulated that depressed individuals have available only negative maladaptive self-referent schemas whereas the nondepressed have different schemas available to them (i.e., more positive, adaptive self-schemas). However, the empirical evidence does not support the availability hypothesis since depressed and nondepressed individuals can evidence both negative and positive self-schematic processing depending on their current mood state and the cognitive task at hand.

The second hypothesis, *accessibility*, refers to the speed or ease with which a schema or bit of information can be retrieved from long-term memory (Riskind & Rholes, 1984). Here the schematic differences between depressed and nondepressed becomes the ease with which certain types of concepts are accessed. Depressed mood, then, increases access to negative schematic views about the self, world, and future; whereas in a nondepressed mood state, the negative schematic content is no longer accessible (Segal, 1988). In fact, Riskind and Rholes (1984) argued that in nondysphoric individuals one may have to cognitively prime negative schemas to gain access to them. The cognitive model adopts an accessibility rather than availability perspective on schematic processing in depression. The view that in depression there is increased accessibility or activation of constructs, representations, and interpretations of negative stimuli and experiences is consistent with the differential activation hypothesis proposed by Teasdale (1983, 1988). The empirical literature on mood-congruent memory is most consistent with an activation or accessibility view of depressotypic schemas. (We consider the terms *accessibility* and *activation* interchangeable. As noted by Segal, 1988, the more frequently a schema is activated, the more accessible it becomes. Thus highly activated or hypervalent schemas will be much more accessible to the individual.)

Finally, Segal (1988) has noted that it is important to consider both schema content and structure. The accessibility of schemas refers primarily to their stored contents, which in depression is negative and self-depreciating. Various questionnaires and experimental tasks have been developed to assess negative schematic content in depression. However, Segal argued that heightened accessibility to negative schema content does not demonstrate the existence of negative self-schema as cognitive structures. To demonstrate differences at the structural level, one must show that depressed and nondepressed individuals have differences in the interconnectedness of the personal constructs or elements that make up the schema. Segal noted that self-representation as a cognitive structure consists of individual elements or constructs that are interrelated to varying degrees. As a result of this interrelatedness, activation of one construct should lead to activation of neighboring constructs. If depression is characterized by the existence of negative self-schematic structures, then negative stimuli should have a strong priming effect on other negative stimuli. For nondepressed individuals who do not possess a negative self-schema structure, presentation of negative stimuli should not have a priming effect for other negative stimuli. Before we examine the evidence for schematic structural differences in depression, we first discuss the evidence for differences in schema content.

NEGATIVE SCHEMA CONTENT

Dysfunctional Attitudes Scale

One of the first attempts to study the negative schematic content of depression involved the development of self-report measures to assess the dysfunctional beliefs and attitudes that were thought to characterize depression. The most widely accepted paper-and-pencil test of the maladaptive beliefs or schema content proposed by the cognitive model is the Dysfunctional Attitudes Scale (DAS) developed by A. Weissman and Beck (1978). This 100-item instrument (40-item versions of the DAS were also developed) was designed to "reflect the relative presence or absence of the appropriate distorted, idiosyncratic beliefs that characterize depressed patients" (A. Weissman & Beck, 1978, p. 9). Numerous studies have shown that the DAS correlates moderately with other cognition and symptom measures of depression, and that depressed patients score significantly higher on the DAS than nondepressed individuals (Blackburn et al., 1986; D.A. Clark et al., 1989; Crandell & Chambless, 1986; Dobson & Breiter, 1983; Dobson & Shaw, 1986; Dohr et al., 1989; Eaves & Rush, 1984; Garber et al., 1993; Hamilton & Abramson, 1983; Oliver & Baumgart, 1985; A. Weissman & Beck, 1978). However, elevated DAS scores have been found in other psychological disorders (Zimmerman, Coryell, Corenthal, & Wilson, 1986) and so the DAS may be sensitive to a broader psychological state than depression, such as general distress, neuroticism, or negative affectivity (D.A. Clark et al., 1989; Hollon et al., 1986). As noted previously, the DAS was never intended to apply only to depression because it was expected that dysfunctional beliefs would be found in other emotional disorders like anxiety. However, the exact nature of the relationship between dysfunctional attitudes and broader mood constructs remains unresolved. McDermut et al. (1997), for example, found that clinically depressed patients scored significantly higher than nondepressed individuals on the Beliefs Scale, a 20-item measure of irrational beliefs developed by Malouff and Schutte (1986), even after controlling for negative affect.

The use of questionnaires to study schema content has recently come under intense criticism. Segal (1988) argued that the DAS cannot provide evidence of negative cognitive "structure" because endorsement patterns for clusters of beliefs reflect the interrelation of attitudes at a descriptive level rather than the functional connection between elements, which reflects self-schema at a structural level. Although some have also questioned the relevance of the DAS for depression given its low specificity (Segal, 1988; Segal & Muran, 1993; Segal & Shaw, 1986a), high specificity is not necessary for phenomena to be core features of a disorder (Garber & Hollon, 1991). Gotlib and McCabe (1992) further reasoned that if schemas represent automatically activated structures, then questionnaires cannot assess schema content because they require individuals to make conscious and deliberate responses to a predetermined set of items. Segal and Swallow (1994) noted that responses on questionnaires may be more reflective of self-presentational biases than purely cognitive factors. Because of these perceived limitations with questionnaire measures, cognitive-clinical researchers have searched for alternative methodologies to assess schema content.

Self-Scenario Assessment

Muran and Segal (1993) developed an idiographic self-scenario procedure to assess negative schema content in depression. They argue that this approach is superior to questionnaire measures because the patient has considerable influence in determining the assessment stimuli, and so a broader range of schematic content can be assessed and measured on a number of different dimensions (Segal & Muran, 1993).

The procedure involves collaborating with the patient in the development of a set of scenarios that include a relevant stimulus situation, as well as typical affective, motoric and cognitive responses. After establishing the reliability and clinical relevance of the various components of the self-scenarios by randomly presenting the components of each scenario to the patient, the therapist, and a third-party observer, the five scenarios are reconstructed into their original form and the patient is asked to rate each scenario on eight parameters: frequency, preoccupation, accessibility, alternatives, self-efficacy, self-view, interpersonal view, and chronicity (Segal & Muran, 1993). Although still in a pilot phase, Segal and Muran presented the results of self-scenario assessment on four depressed patients undergoing cognitive-interpersonal therapy. Despite demonstrating adequate interrater reliability, the self-scenario ratings showed only slight changes across treatment. Muran, Segal, and Samstag (1994) reported single-subject analyses on 8 depressed or anxious patients who were offered 20 weeks of cognitive therapy (results of 4 cases were previously reported in Segal and Muran, 1993). Analyses of the self-scenerio dimensions again confirmed its interrater reliability and also some discriminant and predictive validity in terms of sensitivity to treatment change. Obviously, it is too early to determine whether self-scenario assessment is a viable approach to the measurement of negative schema content. However, the potential of this highly innovative approach should not be overlooked by researchers interested in exploring schema content in depression.

Trait Adjective Ratings

As previously discussed under the selective processing hypothesis, SRET studies assume that ratings of the self-relevance or descriptiveness of personality trait adjectives are indicators of self-schema content. The most consistent findings from these studies is that depressed and dysphoric individuals endorse significantly more negative trait adjectives than nondepressed persons. However, there are serious limitations with trait adjective endorsement as an indicator of self-schema content. First, many of the trait adjectives describe sad mood rather than personality traits. Thus the enhanced endorsement of negative words could be due solely to the influence of mood state (Segal, 1988; Segal & Muran, 1993). In fact, Ingram, Fidaleo, et al. (1995) found that inpatients with major depression had better intentional recall of state but not trait depressive information, whereas in their earlier analogue study they found that dysphoric students recalled significantly more state and, to a lesser extent, trait negative adjectives than nondysphoric controls (Ingram, Partridge, et al., 1994). These results support Segal's contention that trait adjectives may not be an accurate indicator of schema content.

A second problem with ratings on trait adjectives is that depressed individuals still rate more positive than negative trait words as self-descriptive, though the depressed individuals are significantly different from the nondepressed groups by their endorsement of relatively more negative trait words (Bargh & Tota, 1988; Segal, Hood, Shaw, & Higgins, 1988; Segal & Vella, 1990). This causes one to question whether trait adjectives can adequately represent the core internal representation of the self in depression.

A third problem with ratings of trait adjectives is that they assess negative thinking or schema content at the very specific propositional level of single words. Given the complexities of the situations and personality factors that may activate cognitive representations or schemas in depression, it is doubtful that standard single word adjectives can provide a valid sampling of personally relevant mood-dependent schematic content. As evident in a study by Teasdale, Taylor, et al. (1995), depressive thinking is better understood at a generic level than in terms of changes in specific constructs. This raises serious questions about the validity of trait adjective ratings (and recall) as markers of negative schematic content in depression.

Sentence Stem Completion

Another approach to the assessment of schema content is a sentence completion task recently introduced by Teasdale, Taylor, et al. (1995). The purpose of the study was to test differential predictions derived from a construct accessibility versus schematic mental model theory of negative thinking in depression. According to Teasdale, Taylor, et al. construct accessibility theories, such as the schema activation hypothesis of the cognitive model, hold that negative cognitions and processing occur in depression because the depressed state lowers the threshold of activation for specific constructs such as "failure," "loss," and "hopeless." On the other hand, schematic mental model theories, such as the Interacting Cognitive Subsystems (ICS) theory (Teasdale & Barnard, 1993), propose that the depressed state causes activation of mental models that encode interrelationships between generic features of experience. Moreover, the schematic mental models approach suggests that the schemas activated in depression involve more globally negative views of the self, particularly the self-in-relationship-to-world. Teasdale, Taylor, et al. (1995) argue that differential predictions from the schema (construct) accessibility and schematic mental models approach can be derived by setting up tasks in which the two levels of abstraction are contrasted (specific construct activation versus activation of interrelated generic features).

Teasdale, Taylor, and colleagues (1995) developed 12 sentence stems from selected DAS items that represented anticipated outcomes of social approval or success. Participants were asked to complete each sentence stem with the first word that entered their mind. The 12 sentence stems

were purposively selected so that a positive answer would reflect gre
dysfunctional thinking. For example, the sentence stem "If I could alwa
be right then others would _____ me" would require a positive answer,
such as the word "like," to reflect dysfunctional thinking. Teasdale, Taylor, et al. stated that schema accessibility would predict that depressed
individuals would respond with a functionally related negative completion word (e.g., resent) because it assumes the activation of specific constructs in depression. On the other hand, the ICS schematic mental model
approach would predict that depressed individuals would respond with a
dysfunctional positive completion (e.g., like) because it assumes changes
in higher-order interrelationships between patterns of constructs.

Two groups were compared, 41 clinically depressed patients and 40
nondepressed normals, at Time 1 and then three months later at Time 2.
Analysis revealed that the depressed patients gave significantly more
positive word completions to the DAS sentence stems than the nondepressed control group. Furthermore, significant improvement in depressed mood over 3 months was associated with a reduction in positive
sentence stem completion, whereas the unimproved depressed group
showed an increase in positive completions. The authors interpreted
these results as consistent with the ICS view that mood-congruent depressive thinking derives from changes at a more generic level in which
cognitive representation reflects interrelationships between constructs.
The results would be considered inconsistent with the schema activation
hypothesis, which they argued proposes that depressive thinking is
derived from the activation of specific negative constructs. However,
D. Brown and Johnson (1998) were unable to replicate Teasdale, Taylor,
et al.'s (1995) findings in a sample of 293 undergraduates. Students exposed to a self-referent sad mood induction condition did not produce
significantly more DAS positive stem completions, although participants
with high DAS scores assigned to the sad condition produced significantly more positive stem completions than the low DAS students. This
finding raises questions about the mood-congruent nature of positive
stem completions and is more consistent with the cognitive model's view
that conditional dysfunctional beliefs or imperatives (i.e., "If, . . . then"
statements) represent an important feature of cognitive vulnerability to
depression.

We have devoted a considerable amount of space to describing the Teasdale, Taylor, et al. (1995) study because of its importance for the schema
activation hypothesis. At first glance, it appears that the hypothesis is not
supported by the findings of this study. However, the pivotal assumption
behind this study is that the schema activation hypothesis predicts that
depressed persons would respond to the DAS sentence stems at a more

evel with a negative sentence completion that is hedon-
ith negative mood state. We disagree with Teasdale,
point and argue that the schema activation hypothe-
uepressed persons would respond with positive word
.ns to the DAS sentence stems. Our differential predictions arise
in our opposing views of how the cognitive model conceptualizes
schema.

Teasdale, Taylor, et al. (1995) characterize Beck's concept of schema as
referring to specific, propositional, negative meanings that are directly related to depressed mood. From this perspective, then, schema accessibility
would predict that depressed individuals respond with semantically or
linguistically consistent (i.e., functionally related) negative sentence completions. However, we contend that Teasdale and colleagues have erected
a "straw argument" because they have misrepresented the nature of
schematic content and structure as described in Beck's cognitive theory of
depression. First, the concept of schema is more generic than reflected in
Teasdale, Taylor, et al.'s description. The original definition of schemas
was formulated as follows:

> The focus (of schemas) is broad and has been applied both to small pat-
> terns and to large, global patterns. . . . the focus (here) is on the broader,
> more complex schemas such as the self-concepts. . . . (A. Beck, 1967,
> pp. 282–283).

Also as noted in Chapter 4, schemas are not specific, static constructs but
rather "an array of interrelated concepts" with propositions referring to
meaning that underlie the logical relationships between concepts. Thus
the concept of schema proposed in cognitive theory is much more generic
or broadly based and relational than depicted in Teasdale, Taylor et al.'s
characterization. The constructs or schema activated in depression are
not represented as specific, isolated words or concepts.

Second, the present cognitive model asserts that modes or clusters of
interrelated schemas constitute the cognitive structures activated in depression. Representation at the modal level recognizes interconnections
between cognitive, behavioral, motivation, and affective schemas. Thus
mood-congruent negative thinking in depression is traced to the activation
of the loss mode representing a broad higher-order level of activation involving patterns of interrelationships between different types of schema.

Finally Teasdale, Taylor, et al. (1995) contend that automatic thoughts
are represented at more specific levels than are "schematic mental models." However, again this represents a misconception of how cognitive theory understands *negative automatic thoughts*. An automatic thought is not

independent of context, as suggested by Teasdale, Taylor, et al., but rather is an overgeneralized reaction derived from the interaction of a given context (stimulus) and preexisting schema (Alford & Beck, 1997; A. Beck, 1967). More importantly, what makes a negative automatic thought *negative* is not the semantics of independent words, but rather the meaning of the automatic thought as a whole.

If one accepts the current cognitive conceptualization of schemas and modes as generic, higher-order representations of interrelated constructs, then the empirical finding of Teasdale, Taylor, et al. (1995) that depressed patients gave more "positive" completions (e.g., "like") to DAS sentence stems is entirely consistent with the schema activation hypothesis. Although we disagree with Teasdale and colleagues' interpretation of their findings, the sentence stem completion task may be a useful method for tapping into the generic, interrelated schematic and modal content activated in depression. As evident from the D. Brown and Johnson (1998) study, it is unclear whether positive stem completion reflects mood-congruent phenomena or is an indicator of cognitive vulnerability to depression.

Autobiographical Memory Recall

The final approach to schema content takes a decidedly more experimental approach. If depression involves greater access or activation of mood-congruent negative self-referent schemas, then this should be evident as selective encoding, interpretation, and recall of stimulus material. In particular, we would expect the personal memories and experiences retrieved during depression to reflect the activation of negative schematic content. Thus the schema activation hypothesis predicts *mood-congruence retrieval*, which is enhanced recall of material that is congruent in affective tone with a person's mood state at the time of retrieval (Teasdale & Barnard, 1993).

In our previous discussion of the empirical literature on selective encoding, self-evaluation, judgment, and recall of self-referent stimuli, we found evidence that depressed mood is associated with a selective mood-congruent encoding of negative self-referent material. Although these results are consistent with the schema activation hypothesis, they provide at best an indirect test of the hypothesis. This is because encoding studies examine the biasing effects of mood on immediately learned or processed material rather than directly assessing the stored contents of memory that more closely represents enduring self-schema content. For this reason, recall studies provide a more direct test of schema content than encoding studies. Two types of recall study have dominated cognitive research on depression—the SRET and autobiographical memory recall.

As noted, the most consistent finding across the SRET studies has been either mood-congruent recall (and encoding) for negative trait adjectives or an evenhanded recall of positive and negative material in depression. Although these results are generally consistent with the schema activation hypothesis, the SRET provides a poor test of schema content. This is because the task cannot disentangle the prior effects of selective encoding from the biased retrieval of negative information. Also recall in SRET is open to the same shortcomings noted for trait adjective ratings in general.

Autobiographical memory recall provides a more direct assessment of enduring negative self-schema content in depression. In the typical experiment, participants are presented with a set of neutral or valenced cue words and asked to report the first memory that comes to mind in response to the cue. Autobiographical memory consists of discrete experiences that involve an individual's participation in particular acts or situations. The experimental procedure of cued memory recall has a long history that can be dated back to Galton (J.A. Robinson, 1976).

Two advantages of this approach are that it can assess recall without depending on recent encoding of material, although a problem with interpreting recall differences in autobiographical memory is that group differences could be due to the types of life events people have experienced rather than to the effects of mood on memory (Teasdale & Barnard, 1993; Williams et al., 1988). However, a second advantage of autobiographical memory is that it assesses more general, personal memories and experiences that are likely to have greater ecological validity than the standard single word descriptors found in the SRET. Reiser, Black, and Abelson (1985) proposed that recall of autobiographical memories involves accessing the knowledge structures (i.e., schemas) used to encode an event, then using this information to predict features of the to-be-retrieved event, thereby directing memory search to paths that are likely to lead to the stored event. Williams (1996) argued that cued autobiographical memory recall can access memories for events that may precede an emotional disturbance. These considerations suggest that the autobiographical memory retrieval may provide a valid sampling of the negative self-schema content that is integral to the depressive experience.

In numerous studies, depressed and dysphoric individuals have shown enhanced mood-congruent retrieval of negative or unpleasant personal memories, and diminished retrieval of positive memories compared with nondepressed controls. This effect has been found with the use of either neutral or valenced cue words (Fogarty & Hemsley, 1983; G. Lloyd & Lishman, 1975), and whether retrieval is measured in terms of speed of recall (G. Lloyd & Lishman, 1975; Teasdale & Taylor, 1981) or probability of recalling more negative than positive memories (Fogarty & Hemsley, 1983; Teasdale & Taylor, 1981).

The demonstration of a negative mood-congruent recall effect cannot be attributed to depressed patients having more genuinely negative or unpleasant life experiences because increased accessibility of negative memories has been found even in normal individuals placed under an experimental sad mood induction (Teasdale & Taylor, 1981). Teasdale and Fogarty (1979), however, found that an experimentally induced sad mood in normals significantly increased the latency to retrieve pleasant memories (i.e., reduced accessibility) with no significant effect on retrieval latency for unpleasant memories (for similar results, see Riskind et al., 1982). In a replication study, Teasdale, Taylor, and Fogarty (1980) found that an induced elated mood significantly increased the probability and reduced the latency of recall for happy memories, whereas the sad mood induction was associated with a weaker, nonsignificant trend to increase accessibility to unhappy memories. Parrott (1991) found that the recalled memories of induced happy subjects contained significantly more positive and less negative affect than the memories of sad induced subjects according to affective ratings of the memories made by independent judges. Generally, then, studies of induced mood and dysphoria within the nonclinical population seem to indicate that the primary recall difference is in accessibility to positive rather than negative memories. That is, nondysphoric and happy individuals show greater accessibility to positive memories than dysphoric or unhappy individuals (Fitzgerald, Slade, & Lawrence, 1988). The mild depressions in nonclinical samples may be characterized by decreased accessibility to positive memories, whereas it is only in the more severe clinical depression that we find consistent evidence of enhanced accessibility to negative memories.

In a particularly important study on autobiographical memory in 12 patients with diurnal mood variation, D.M. Clark and Teasdale (1982) found that the probability of recalling unhappy memories was greater during the time of day when patients were most depressed, whereas happy experiences were more likely to be recalled while patients were in a less depressed mood state. No within-group differences, however, were found in latency to retrieve happy and unhappy experiences. These findings indicate that the increased retrieval or accessibility of unpleasant memories is very much a mood state congruency effect rather than the product of the depressive syndrome or an enduring characteristic of vulnerability to depression. Strauman (1992) found that only when dysphoric students were presented with word cues involving actual:ideal self-guides was there enhanced recall of negative affect childhood memories. The author concluded that vulnerability to depression may not be detected simply by the occurrence of a distressed mood state, but depends on the activation of self-evaluative knowledge structures as evidenced by the distinctive effects of self-guides on childhood memory recall.

Positive correlations have also been reported between recall of negative memories (and/or reduction in the accessibility to positive memories) and the intensity of the depressive state (Fogarty & Hemsley, 1983; G. Lloyd & Lishman, 1975; Teasdale & Taylor, 1981), although negative results have also been reported (Teasdale & Fogarty, 1979). As well, reduction in depression severity is associated with a tendency to recall more positive and fewer negative memories (Fogarty & Hemsley, 1983). Williams et al. (1988) concluded that the biasing effect of mood on personal memory retrieval is robust across different methods of cueing and whether the mood state is induced or naturally occurring. Teasdale and Barnard (1993) also concluded that mood congruence recall of autobiographical memories and retrieval of other verbal material presented under laboratory conditions is an established empirical phenomenon. This is particularly well illustrated in a mood-congruence recall study by Teasdale and Russell (1983) in which students in an elated mood induction recalled significantly more positive personality trait words from a previously presented word list; whereas students in the sad mood induction recalled significantly more negative trait words.

Despite the robustness of mood-congruent recall, important issues have arisen from this research paradigm. First, it is not clear whether mood-congruent retrieval of negative self-referent material is specific to depression because other constructs, such as neuroticism (Lloyd & Lishman, 1975; Mayo, 1983; see review by Martin, 1985), are also associated with a negative recall effect. Because neuroticism and depression are highly related constructs, evidence that negative retrieval bias is related to neuroticism does not detract from the relevance of enhanced negative recall in depression. Williams and Broadbent (1986) also found that patients who recently attempted suicide were significantly slower at retrieving positive memories than normal controls, although there were no significant group differences in the retrieval of negative memories. Moreover, the overdose group differed significantly from the normal controls on several mood dimensions, which suggests that the recall differences may be due to a mixed rather than specific mood disturbance (see discussion by Williams et al., 1988).

A second issue in autobiographical memory research is the possibility that a confound is introduced by having subjects themselves rate the hedonic tone of their memories. Thus the mood-congruent recall could simply reflect a tendency of depressed individuals to rate rather neutral experiences more negatively (see discussion by Williams et al., 1988). D.M. Clark and Teasdale (1982) found that depressed mood had two separate effects—it influenced the type of memories recalled but it also affected subjects' hedonic rating of the memories. However, the latter effect was insufficient by itself to explain the memory bias results. Also other studies have found mood-congruent recall even when subjects rated their retrieved memories while in a neutral mood state (Teasdale et al., 1980) or when independent raters evaluated the affective quality of the memories (Parrott, 1991). These findings indicate that mood-congruent recall cannot be explained as an artifact of differential mood effects on memory evaluation.

A third issue discussed by Williams (1996, 1997) is the finding that depressed compared with nondepressed individuals tend to retrieve overly broad or general personal memories rather than more specific concrete examples of past experiences. Thus in response to memory cues, the depressed individual gives generic statements that summarize events whereas nondepressed persons are more likely to recall specific personalized experiences. Williams (1997) labeled this phenomenon mnemonic interlock because depressed individuals seem unable to use descriptive information stored in the upper layers of memory containing general memory information to aid in their memory search for retrieval of more specific events that are stored in the lower layer of the memory database. This tendency to retrieve overgeneralized memories is not unlike the cognitive error of overgeneralization that cognitive theory asserts is a characteristic tendency found in depressed individuals when they process self-relevant information. Williams (1997) suggested that this generic encoding and retrieval of memories will inhibit adaptive reinterpretation and understanding of past events, frustrate the depressed person's efforts to engage in effective problem-solving, and retard progress in therapy because it affects the way in which individuals recall events about themselves.

In support of this contention, studies have found that depressed and dysphoric individuals as well as individuals recovering from a suicide attempt recall a significantly greater number of summary or generalized memories, whereas the nondepressed recall a greater number of single-event or specific memories, though this effect appears to be more pronounced for the recall of positive than negative memories (Brittlebank et al., 1993; Halbach-Mofitt, Singer, Nelligan, Carlson, & Vyse, 1994; Moore, Watts, & Williams, 1988; Williams & Broadbent, 1986; Williams & Dritschel, 1988). Kuyken and Brewin (1995) found that clinically depressed women who reported memories of childhood sexual abuse retrieved significantly more over-generalized personal memories to both positive and negative cues than depressed women with no history of childhood physical or sexual abuse. As well increased avoidance of childhood physical or sexual abuse memories was correlated ($r's$ ranged .30 to .33) with over-generalized memory retrieval. To understand the findings, the authors suggest that high levels of adversity may increase the importance of positive and negative events so that more information processing resources are focused on these events. This increased processing, in turn, will facilitate the development of schematic representations of positive and negative events which increases the likelihood that general rather than specific events are retrieved. Another possible explanation for the connection between early sexual abuse in depressed women and retrieval of over-general memories is that the attempt to avoid instances of distressing intrusive memories may interfere in one's ability to retrieve specific memories in response to autobiographical cues. Whatever the exact cognitive mechanism, it is evident that early traumatic experiences can influence the organization and retrieval of long-term memory. Thus the breakdown in retrieval that is reflected in the increased recall of over-generalized personal memories cannot be attributed exclusively to the presence of depression. Instead over-generalized memory retrieval also appears to depend on the type and extent of past traumatic experiences encoded in long-term memory.

Evidence that experiences are remembered in an over-generalized fashion is consistent with clinical experience. In cognitive therapy, practitioners often use Socratic questioning to elicit from depressed patients more detail about their troubling past experiences before introducing cognitive restructuring techniques to challenge the validity of their negative interpretations of past events.

A final issue that has emerged from the autobiographical recall literature is the occurrence of mood-incongruent retrieval in which sad mood causes a significant increase in the retrieval of happy memories. Such findings present a direct challenge to the schema activation hypothesis. Parrott and Sabini (1990) assessed autobiographical memory recall in five different mood conditions (two were naturalistic, being conducted outside the laboratory and three were more artificial using musical mood manipulation in a laboratory setting). They found mood-incongruent recall in four of the mood and memory experiments (more positive memories in sad mood, more negative memories in happy mood state). Only in the third experiment, in which subjects were informed that the study involved the effects of mood on cognitive efficiency and were asked to try to change their mood to fit with the tone of the music, was the usual mood-congruent recall effect obtained.

Teasdale and Barnard (1993) argue that these results indicate that one must access information stored within the Implicational-Propositional cycle to achieve mood-congruent retrieval. Mood states produced by more direct, external sensory input, as in Parrott and Sabini's (1990) more naturalistic mood conditions, or moods that for other reasons fail to elicit the internally regenerating Implicational-Propositional cycles of emotional memory store, will not produce mood-congruent recall.

Parrott and Sabini (1990), however, offer a different explanation for mood-incongruent recall. They suggest that the effect reflects mood regulation in which happy as well as sad individuals try to regulate or balance their mood state by recalling mood-incongruent past events. Based on their findings in the third experiment, Parrot and Sabini suggested that the mood-congruent recall found in other studies may be attributed to subjects' inhibiting their natural mood regulation tendencies to comply with the experimenter's mood induction instructions to maintain a happy or sad mood state. However, this subject compliance explanation for mood-congruent recall was not supported in a later study (Parrott, 1991). Yet a more parsimonious explanation of mood-incongruent recall may be in terms of mood regulation or repair effects (i.e., response strategies) on memory. Also, mood-incongruent recall may not be a robust finding. Parrott and Sabini were able to obtain this effect with only the first of three personal memories subjects were requested to recall. As well, the autobiographical memory task used in their experiments differed from the norm in that stimulus words were not used to cue memory recall. It may be that cue words provide an important associative function in personal memory recall (see J.A. Robinson, 1976) that affects the mood-memory relationship. Whatever the case, mood-incongruent encoding and retrieval do not pose a direct challenge to the schema activation hypothesis, but rather indicate that researchers should be aware of subjects' automatic efforts to control their mood state. It may be that steps should be taken to ensure that participants do not undermine mood induction effects by engaging in mood regulation strategies, such as the recalling of mood-incongruent memories. This may be less problematic with clinically depressed subjects in which the ability to alter a dysphoric mood state is severely impaired.

Summary

Generally, there is fairly strong support for the increased accessibility of negative self-referent schema content in depression. However, the robustness of this support must be qualified by methodological limitations inherent in much of the research relevant for this hypothesis (see Blaney, 1986, for extended discussion). As we have seen, questionnaires as well as experiments involving the presentation of standard single-word personality trait descriptors are probably at best weak indicators of the more complex, idiosyncratic self-referent evaluations and experiences that comprise the negative schematic content involved in depression. Other methodologies, such as sentence completion stems or idiographic self-scenario scripts, have not been used sufficiently to gauge their validity and reliability.

The mood-congruent recall studies, especially those involving autobiographical memory, offer the strongest evidence for enhanced accessibility to negative schema content in depression. Evidence from these studies, however, suggests that in mild depression or dysphoria the main difference may be in reduced accessibility to positive memories (Blaney, 1986), whereas the enhanced access to negative material may only be seen in the more severe depressive states. In their meta-analysis of mood-congruent recall studies, Matt et al. (1992) also concluded that nondepressed individuals show a differential recall for positively valenced material, the subclinically depressed or dysphoric show no differential recall patterns for positive or negative stimuli, and the clinically depressed show a biased recall for negatively valenced information. Furthermore, certain cautions may be in order when relying on the findings from autobiographical memory. Dalgleish and Watts (1990) noted that autobiographical memory may not be a valid index of memory disturbance in depression because clinically depressed patients often report that their problem is not that negative memories in general are easy to recall but rather they are troubled by the frequent, spontaneous intrusion of a few highly charged negative emotional memories. Also researchers must pay greater attention to the possibility that individuals will engage in mood-regulating strategies to repair a discrepant mood state. Nevertheless, until newer methods with greater ecological validity are developed, autobiographical memory will continue to provide one of the best methods for assessing schematic content in depression.

Interconnectedness and the Structure of Negative Schemas

As a cognitive structure, schemas or schematic models are internal structures of generic information consisting of highly interrelated elements or concepts (Segal, 1988; Teasdale, 1996; Williams et al., 1988). As noted earlier, self-schema structure can be defined in terms of the degree of interrelatedness between various elements or constructs. If depression is characterized by activation of negative self-schema, then negative self-referent constructs should be more highly interconnected compared with nondepressed individuals who do not possess activated negative self-schemas. The best experimental paradigm for investigating the structural characteristics (i.e., interrelatedness of constructs) of schemas would involve the presentation of priming stimuli (e.g., trait adjectives). If negative constructs are more highly organized in depression, then priming effects for negative material should be stronger for depressed compared with nondepressed individuals. Segal has argued that priming methodologies that test the organization of traits assumed to be related to a construct against traits not expected to be related to the construct can assess schema structure independent of mood effects. We review three experimental priming methods that assess negative schematic structure in depression—the primed Stroop task, the emotional priming paradigm, and the primed lexical decision task.

In the primed Stroop task, participants color-name positive and negative self-referent target trait adjectives that are paired with semantically related or unrelated words. If negative cognitive structures are activated in depression, then a negative target word paired with a negative word prime should lead to greater interference (i.e., longer color-naming latencies) than unrelated prime-target word pairs (Segal, 1988). For example, in depression the target word "loser" should cause greater color-naming interference when paired (i.e., primed) with the word "disliked" than when paired with an unrelated or neutral prime word like "chair." For nondepressed individuals, we would not expect to get differential priming effects (i.e., more or less color-naming interference) for related versus unrelated trait word pairings. Lack of differences in color-naming latencies between related and unrelated prime-target pairs suggests no particular structural relationship among the self-referent constructs represented by the trait words.

Segal et al. (1988) tested the primed Stroop task with 14 patients with unipolar major depression, 9 with anxiety disorder, and 14 normal controls who color-named self-descriptive target trait words primed with a self-descriptive or neutral (nonself-descriptive) trait adjective. Color-naming latencies were significantly longer for the related prime-target pairs than the unrelated pairs. Depressed patients evidenced the schematic prime-target interference effects (longer color-naming latencies) for both positive and negative prime-target pairs even though they had significantly higher self-description ratings for negative trait adjectives than nondepressed subjects. The nondepressed controls did not show greater relatedness for the schematic (positive and negative self-referent) prime-target word pairs.

In a second study, Segal and Vella (1990) found that subjects had longer response latencies for schematic (highly self-descriptive) adjectives and for related prime-target word pairs than for target stimuli paired with neutral or personally nonrelevant adjectives. Once again, the depressed patients, but this time also the nondepressed controls, showed a relatedness effect for schematic prime-target word pairings (both positive and negative) that were previously rated as highly self-descriptive. In addition, Segal and Vella found that the relatedness effects extended to extremely nondescriptive prime-target adjectives indicating that both highly self-descriptive and nondescriptive trait adjectives may be interconnected in the self-schema. Segal et al. (1995) found that depressed patients had significantly longer color-naming latencies only for negative self-descriptive prime-target word pairs, whereas non-self-referent negative as well as positive prime-target adjectives did not show a relatedness effect.

Segal and Gemar (1997) found that posttreatment Hamilton Rating Scale of Depression scores were significantly associated with color-naming interference for negative self-descriptive prime-target traits only such that patients with less depression after treatment showed less negative self-relevant interference effects than patients who remained depressed following cognitive therapy. Because this effect was not evident for positive or nonrelevant prime-target pairs, the authors concluded that treatment had a specific effect on the negative self-schema structure. These findings, then, suggest that the self-schema in depression is characterized by a higher degree of interconnectedness for negative constructs, but there is also some evidence for the interrelatedness of positive constructs as well. In addition, self-schemas in depression may also be defined in terms of highly nondescriptive constructs. Possibly, self-definition in depression depends as much on who we think we are not, as it does on who we think we are (Blatt & Bers, 1993).

Another experimental paradigm relevant to the study of cognitive structure is the primed lexical decision task. Individuals are presented with a target letter string that can be either a word or nonword, and they must decide whether the letter string is a word or not by pressing buttons indicating either a "word" or "nonword" on a response box. The dependent variable is latency to decide whether the stimulus was a word or nonword. In the primed lexical decision task, a prime word is presented on some of the trials followed by a mask and then the target word requiring a lexical decision. In the studies by Bradley and colleagues, the prime and target were the same word. The time interval between presentation of the prime and target word also can be varied to investigate the effects of exposure intervals on lexical decision. The prediction is that the presentation of primes that are related or identical to the target letter strings should enhance the lexical decision times, and for depressed individuals this effect should be greatest for depressed words.

Matthews and Southall (1991) compared clinically depressed and nondepressed controls on a primed lexical decision task involving positive, negative, and neutral target letter strings paired with an associated (semantically related, e.g., DESPERATE-DESIRABLE) or noninformative (the standard word "BLANK") word prime. On some trials, stimulus onset asynchrony (SOA) or the time interval between the prime and target string was short and on other trials longer to test for automatic and controlled information processing. Depressed patients showed significantly slower lexical decision times to neutral strings than to the positive or negative strings in the unprimed short SOA trials but not in the long SOA trials. Priming did not have any influence on lexical decision times for the normal group but for the depressed individuals short-SOA priming did have a strong effect on decision times for neutral strings. The authors interpreted these results as indicating that depressed patients have higher resting activation thresholds for positive and negative than neutral concepts. In fact, the depressed patients were actually slower in responding to the emotional words than controls thus failing to show enhanced priming effects for depressive words. Bradley et al. (1994) were critical of Matthews and Southall's use of semantically related or associative priming because such a task involves both integrative and elaborative processing. To address this problem, Bradley and colleagues presented the same word as prime and target but varied the prime-target exposure interval. Priming effects are reflected in faster lexical decision times because of previous exposure to the words.

Bradley et al. (1994) compared high and low negative affect students on primed and unprimed lexical decision using words with varying affective content. The high negative affect group showed selective priming for depression and positive words in a subliminal condition only (i.e., short SOA), and this effect was more strongly correlated with depression than anxiety scores. In a later study, Bradley et al. (1995) found that clinically depressed patients had greater priming of lexical decisions for depression-related words in both subliminal and supraliminal conditions. The significant priming effects of depression-related material supports the view that negative schematic structures are activated in depression leading to a mood-congruent memory bias.

Finally, Power and Brewin (1990) introduced another variation on priming methodology in which subjects are presented with hypothetical positive and negative life events that act as primes for the endorsement of positive and negative trait adjective targets. Primes are presented at short or long SOAs, and the dependent variable is the time taken to determine whether a trait adjective is self-descriptive or not. In a study of normal individuals, Power and Brewin (1990) found that esteem-threatening primes led to slower endorsement of negative trait adjectives and survival-threatening primes led to faster rejection of the negative adjectives. In addition, both types of primes were associated with lower endorsement rates for negative trait targets, but the effects were evident only in the longer SOA trials. In a second study, Power, Brewin, Stuessy, and Mahony (1991) used four basic emotion terms as primes—happiness, sadness, anger, and fear. Once again, normals evidenced slower endorsement times to negative trait words primed by fear, sadness, or anger emotion words presented at longer SOA intervals. The results of these studies suggest that when presented with negative emotional stimuli, normal individuals engage in a general affect-repair process that involves inhibited response to negative material.

In a replication study involving clinically anxious patients and normal controls, Dalgleish, Cameron, Power, and Bond (1995) also found that normals were significantly slower to endorse negatively primed negative adjectives at the long SOA. Unlike previous studies, however, this inhibitory effect was also present following positive primes and in the neutral (no-prime) condition. For the anxious patients with a diagnosis of GAD, the inhibitory effect was not present but instead a trend toward facilitation; that is, faster endorsement times for negative adjectives that were primed by negative life event terms. One could interpret these findings as indicating that nondepressed or normal individuals do not possess a negative schematic structure involving highly interrelated negative elements, whereas the priming or facilitation effect seen in the anxious may reflect the greater influence of interrelated negative schematic elements. Nevertheless, the general trend from these studies is to find slower endorsement for trait words primed by a negative life phrase suggesting that nondepressed individuals may engage in mood repair and defensiveness when presented with negative stimuli.

Summary

Based on our review of the empirical literature, we have concluded that there is fairly strong support for the schema activation hypothesis in terms of increased access to negative self-referent schema content. The most compelling evidence for increased access to negative schema content in depression comes from the mood-congruent encoding and retrieval studies. As indicated by numerous reviewers, mood-congruent encoding and retrieval are now considered robust and well-established empirical phenomena (Blaney, 1986; Dalgleish & Watts, 1990; Teasdale & Barnard, 1993; Williams et al., 1988). However, at least two qualifications must be raised within this context.

First, some studies have found evidence of mood-congruent asymmetry (Blaney, 1986). That is, rather than finding a strong selectivity for recalling negative memories in depression, mood seems to have a greater effect on the recall of pleasant than unpleasant memories. The typical finding in these studies is that nondepressed or elation-induced subjects have significantly enhanced recall of pleasant memories compared with the dysphoric or depressed group. Blaney (1986) also pointed out that the actual level of "unpleasantness" ratings for memories recalled in the sad mood induction condition suggests that these memories may be more neutral or balanced than actually unpleasant. Overall, normal or nondepressed individuals have a bias for encoding and retrieving positive material. Whether mood congruence in depression involves a "drift away from positivity toward neutrality" (Blaney, 1986, p. 238) or increased access to negative self-referent material may depend on the severity of the depression and the information processing demands placed on the individual (see also Matt et al., 1992). Whatever the case, both reduced access to positive schematic content and increased access to negative material provide consistent support for the schema activation hypothesis.

A second issue concerns our interpretation of the mood congruence and priming effects. In our review of the empirical literature on schema structure, we concluded that the demonstration of significant priming effects with negative self-descriptive concepts supports the schema activation hypothesis as reflecting the effects of negative schematic structures during depressed mood. This conclusion is based on Segal's (1988) contention that the selective priming effects evident with the modified Stroop color-naming task, primed lexical decision making, and the emotional priming task demonstrate the existence of highly interrelated negative elements or concepts indicative of a negative self-referent schematic structure.

An alternative explanation for mood-congruent recall and selective priming is that these findings represent the effects of different motivated states or strategies. Power and Brewin (1990) explain their emotional priming results in terms of a general process of affect-regulation. That is, the slower endorsement of negative adjectives when primed with negative life event terms suggests a tendency to inhibit the processing of negative self-related material possibly in an effort to repair a momentary state of negative affect. The negative priming effects in depression could also be seen as a breakdown in the normal inhibitory processing of negative self-referent information that is integral to negative mood regulation in nondepressed individuals. Blaney (1986) raised a number of alternative explanations for mood-congruent recall such as subjects' motivation to improve self-esteem, to overcome their own weaknesses, to engage in a self-verification process, or to comply with the experimenter's instructions. Although this latter possibility was not supported in the study by Parrott (1991), Blaney's (1986) other considerations indicate that differences in personality, self-concept, or motivational states could account for some of the differences seen in mood-congruent recall studies. We have seen in our review that neuroticism, for example, is associated with mood-congruent recall of negative self-referent material. Mathews and MacLeod (1994) concluded that there is evidence that both state and trait variables influence emotion-linked selective processing in an interactive fashion. The existence of other variables, however, does not necessarily negate the effects of mood on encoding and retrieval processes.

In conclusion, we would assert that the evidence for mood-congruent encoding and retrieval as well as selective priming is consistent with the schema activation hypothesis. However, we recognize that the findings from these studies are by no means unambiguous, and that other variables may be influencing the information processing differences in depressed and nondepressed individuals. On the other hand, the results can also be interpreted as consistent with the view that enhanced accessibility and activation of negative self-referent schematic structures and reduced access to positive self-related schema are salient features of the cognitive basis of depression.

PRIMAL PROCESSING HYPOTHESIS

The negative self-referent thinking, cognitive appraisals, and perspectives in depression are the product of primal mode processing that is involuntary, unintended, rapid, and less amenable to conscious awareness.

In Chapter 3, we noted that one of the basic assumptions of the cognitive model is that information processing occurs at varying levels of consciousness (see Assumption 2). The higher-order information processing involved in learning, problem-solving, socializing, and communicating will be more effortful, deliberate, and conscious than cognitive tasks involving lower-order processes. Higher-order processing is thus more amenable to self-conscious monitoring, interpretation, and evaluation.

We also acknowledged another type of information processing that is more automatic, rapid, involuntary, and less accessible to awareness. In Chapter 4, we described information processing of the primal modes as more automatic, rapid, and efficient. Because the cognitive model asserts that in depression the primal loss mode is hypervalent or has a lower activation threshold (see Chapter 4), it is hypothesized that the enhanced processing of negative self-referent in depression primarily reflects automatic rather than effortful processes. We have stated this prediction as the primal processing hypothesis. On the other hand, the positive thoughts and appraisals involved in more constructive thinking will primarily involve effortful or strategic processing because these schemas have a higher activation resting level during depression. Thus in depression we would expect to find enhanced automatic processing of negative self-referent information in support of the primal processing hypothesis but a decrease or interference in the more effortful processing of positive stimuli. Brewin (1988) also reviewed evidence for the existence of two cognitive systems, the one conscious and effortful and the other unconscious and involuntary, which together influence individuals' thinking and behavior.

In an extensive and detailed review of the literature on automatic and effortful processing in depression, Hartlage et al. (1993) provided considerable support for predictions that are consistent with the primal processing hypothesis of the cognitive model. First, they concluded that depression interferes with the effortful processing of neutrally valenced material as evidenced by studies showing significant detrimental effects of depression on general intelligence, problem-solving, general learning, recall of semantically encoded words, reading comprehension (more effortful) but not on more automatic processes like word recognition, motor performance, and cognitive speed. The authors indicate that the cause for this interference in effortful processing may be the narrowing of attention onto depression-relevant thoughts, though there is also evidence that the interference effect may be due to a reduction in the attentional capacity available in depression. This pattern of interference in effortful processing, with automatic processing remaining intact, seems to be a specific characteristic of depression.

Hartlage et al. (1993) concluded from their review of the research on automatic and effortful processing that negative self-referent content is processed automatically in depression. This automatic negative self-referent processing is evident in the form of significantly biased encoding and retrieval of negative material relative to nondepressed controls. Furthermore, the authors state that the phenomena of negative automatic thoughts and negative attributional inferences also meet most of the criteria for automatic processing. Hartlage and colleagues proposed that depression-prone individuals may have a tendency to automatically process negative content. With the occurrence of stress, attentional focus narrows (or attentional capacity is reduced) so that negative content is all that is processed because it requires minimal attentional resources given its basis in automatic processing. More positive information that would counter negative thoughts and appraisal is not as readily processed because it requires effortful processing which itself has been decreased by stress. The end result, then, is the occurrence of a depressive episode. This formulation, based on their review of the relevant literature, is very consistent with the primal processing hypothesis of the cognitive model.

Before reviewing the empirical literature on automatic or primal processing in depression, it is important to clarify what is meant by automatic processing. In Chapter 4, we noted that automatic processing (a) is effort-less, involuntary, or unintentional, (b) is generally outside conscious awareness though some automatic processes may become accessible to consciousness, (c) is relatively fast and difficult to stop or regulate, (d) consumes minimal attentional or processing capacity, (e) relies on a par-allel type of processing, (f) is stereotypic involving familiar and highly practiced tasks, and (g) utilizes low levels of cognitive processing with minimal analysis (A. Beck & Clark, 1997; Hartlage et al., 1993; Logan, 1988; McNally, 1995; Sternberg, 1996; A. Wells & Matthews, 1994). This is to be contrasted with effortful or strategic processing which is inten-tional, voluntary, fully conscious, and relatively slow. Despite interest in the role of automatic and strategic information processing in depression, considerable confusion has arisen in the literature over the use of these terms. There are a number of reasons for this state of affairs.

First, as noted by Hartlage et al. (1993), researchers often fail to distin-guish between automatic processing and the cognitive products derived from this processing. Earlier we stated that the processing associated with primal mode activation is more automatic than strategic or effortful in nature. In keeping with the recommendation of Hartlage et al., we sug-gest that it is the activation of the primal mode which is automatic rather than the negative thoughts, appraisals, constructions, and perspectives which are the cognitive products of this automatic modal processing. Having said this, we would contend that the thoughts, appraisals, and constructions resulting from primal mode activation will bear some of the characteristics of automatic processing because of their origins in primal mode activation.

A second source of confusion is the tendency to think categorically of cognitive tasks in terms of their capacity to assess either automatic or ef-fortful processes. McNally (1995) noted that most cognitive tasks involve both automatic and strategic processes so that it may be very difficult, if not impossible, to develop pure-process experimental tasks that involve solely automatic or strategic processing. One alternative that has been suggested is to view automaticity as lying on a continuum with effortful processing, such that we proceed from inherited automatic processes at one end, to learned automatic and then veiled effortful processes in the middle and finally to highly accessible effortful processes at the other end (Hartlage et al., 1993).

A third source of confusion resides with the multifaceted nature of the term "automatic processing." McNally (1995) noted that a unitary con-cept of automatic processing is no longer tenable—that there are varieties of automaticity depending on which of the defining characteristics of the concept is emphasized. In a recent paper on the cognitive model of anxi-ety, we suggested that it may be better to consider cognitive processes and products in terms of the defining characteristics of automatic and strategic processing rather than consider some cognitive tasks as involving "purely" automatic processes, whereas others involve purely effortful or strategic processing (A. Beck & Clark, 1997).

Two aspects of the primal processing hypothesis that must be emphasized are the automaticity of self-referent processing itself and then the dysfunctional consequences or effects of automatic primal processing. Moretti and Shaw (1989) provide an excellent discussion of each of these points. They note that although automatic information processing rarely impairs performance, it is more likely to have detrimental effects if (a) criteria for detecting dysfunctional processing are ambiguous and performance feedback is not readily available, (b) processing involves performance of complex stimulus-response sequences, (c) information processing occurs within a state of heightened affective arousal and limited attentional resources, and (d) heightened or chronic accessibility of certain constructs is evident. Based on these considerations, Moretti and Shaw (1989) note that dysfunctional automatic processing is most likely to occur when processing social and self-referent information, especially because of the chronic accessibility of self-referent constructs. Dysfunctional automatic processing occurs in depression because of the hypervalent state of negative self-constructs as well as the presence of the previously noted criteria or risk factors that lead to dysfunctional automatic processing. The negative self-referent processing in depression is considered dysfunctional because it produces cognitions that perpetuate negative affect and inhibit adaptive functioning.

In light of these considerations, we now review the empirical evidence for automatic processing, or more specifically dysfunctional automatic processing of self-referent information in depression. We accept the view that automatic and strategic processing occur on a continuum so that cognitive tasks differ in the relative degree of automatic or strategic processing that is required. For this reason, we discuss cognitive tasks as involving relatively more or less automatic processing. Since automaticity is not a unitary concept, we organize our review around the critical defining features of automatic information processing. Throughout, the critical question we seek to address is whether there is empirical support for the primal processing hypothesis—that negative self-referent information is processed automatically in depression.

UNINTENDED PROCESSING OF NEGATIVE INFORMATION

Earlier we noted that A. Wells and Matthews (1994) considered "insensitivity to control" one of the key criteria of automaticity. McNally (1995) concluded that unintended or involuntary processing of threat-related material was a feature of automaticity that has been found rather consistently in the attentional processing studies of anxiety. If automatic or primal processing occurs in depression, then it must be shown that negative self-referent processing occurs involuntarily, or in an unintended fashion. That is negative self-referent processing must be shown to occur outside the conscious, intentional control of the depressed person. In this section, we examine five types of experiments that indicate that negative self-referent information processing in depression or dysphoria is unintended or involuntary. Because many of these studies have been discussed more extensively in sections on the selective processing and schema activation hypotheses, we will restrict the focus of our present discussion to the relevance of these studies for unintended processing.

First, studies of attentional encoding involving stimulus identification, modified Stroop interference, multiple stimulus detection, and dichotic listening present positive, negative, and neurtal self-referent stimuli outside the voluntary control or intention of the subject. Generally, these studies have found that depressed individuals show either a processing bias for negative self-referent stimuli, or an evenhanded encoding of positive and negative material. A study of event-related potentials by Blackburn et al. (1990) provides particularly strong evidence of unintended negative self-referent information processing in depression. They found that the P300 amplitudes to negatively toned trait adjectives were significantly smaller in depressed inpatients than normal controls. Because attentional encoding studies typically assess performance in terms of interference or facilitation effects produced by unintended or involuntary stimulus presentation, evidence of these effects can be taken as providing empirical support for the unintended encoding of negative self-referent information in depression.

Second, the demonstration of mood-congruent recall in the incidential recall version of the SRET also provides evidence of unintended negative self-referent processing in depression. With incidential SRET, subjects first complete self-descriptive ratings on a list of positive, negative, and neutral personality trait adjectives but are not told that they will be asked subsequently to recall the list of adjectives. Thus the mood-congruent bias on the incidental recall task can be taken to represent unintended encoding and retrieval of trait adjective stimuli. In these studies, the general pattern of findings has been enhanced recall of negative or depressive-content trait adjectives for clinically depressed patients, whereas mildly depressed or dysphoric individuals show equivalent recall of positive and negative trait words and the nondepressed enhanced recall of positive self-referent information (e.g.,

Derry & Kuiper, 1981; M. Greenberg & Beck, 1989; Ingram, Fidaleo, et al., 1995; Ingram, Partridge, et al., 1994; Kuiper & Derry, 1982). Thus mood-congruent recall bias for negative material in depressive disorder provides indirect evidence for unintended information processing in depression (see also Hartlage et al., 1993; Moretti & Shaw, 1989).

A third set of studies that demonstrates unintended processing of negative self-referent information are the priming studies discussed under the schema activation hypothesis. The differential effects of positive and negative stimulus primes on color-naming interference or endorsement of positive, negative, and neutral target stimuli provide examples of unintended information processing. As discussed previously, Segal and colleagues (1995) found in their primed Stroop color-naming task that self-descriptive negative trait adjectives primed by self-descriptive negative phrases caused significantly more color-naming interference than any other prime-target pairing. These results again point to unintended processing of negative stimuli in depression.

Fourth, the unintended nature of negative information processing in depression can be assessed in terms of degree of mental control. There is considerable evidence from the thought suppression literature that people do show at least some ability to control their thoughts, though mental control is far from complete (Wegner, Schneider, Carter, & White, 1987). More often than not, attempts to control one's thoughts can lead to a subsequent paradoxical increase or resurgence of the unwanted thought (see Wegner, 1994, for further discussion). Given this ironic or counterintentional aspect to mental control, one would expect that depressed individuals might have less mental control over their negative cognitions than nondepressed subjects if, in fact, negative self-referent thinking occurs more automatically or without intention. Also, we would expect poorer mental control of thoughts if there is interference in effortful processing in depression (Hartlage et al., 1993).

Wenzlaff, Wegner, and Roper (1988, Experiment 1) found that dysphoric students instructed to suppress thoughts about a negative life-event vignette they had previously read had a greater resurgence of negative description thought intrusions compared with dysphoric subjects not instructed to suppress, or the nondysphoric controls who showed a steady decrease in negative thought intrusions over time. This resurgence in thought intrusions was not evident for dysphoric or nondysphoric subjects who were instructed to suppress thoughts of a positive life-event vignette. Moreover, the dysphoric subjects tended to use other negative thoughts to distract themselves from the unwanted negative descriptive intrusions, whereas nondepressed individuals used positive thought distracters.

In Experiment 2 (Wenzlaff et al., 1988), it was shown that the dysphoric subjects knew that positive thoughts were more effective distracters than negative thoughts, and in Experiment 3 the dysphoric subjects were less capable of using positive distracters that were provided to them by the experimenter than nondysphoric individuals. These findings indicate that the dysphoric individual's use of negative distracters is not due to a strategic, effortful coping strategy but rather a result of unintended processes. Wenzlaff et al. (1988) concluded that the resurgence in negative but not positive thought intrusions in dysphoric subjects who tried to suppress or control their negative thoughts, and their tendency to use negative thought distracters in their mental control efforts, reflects automatic or unintended processing of negative thoughts due to an increased accessibility of this material during depression. Other studies have also found that depressed and dysphoric states are associated with reduced ability to control one's thoughts, especially negative self-referent cognitions (Conway et al., 1991; Howell & Conway, 1992; M. Reynolds & Salkovskis, 1992; Sutherland et al., 1982).

In a later study, Wenzlaff, Wegner, and Klein (1991) found a strong association between suppressed thoughts and mood state. In the first experiment, normal subjects who experienced either a positive or negative mood state during suppression of a neutral target thought experienced a significantly greater rebound of the target thought during a subsequent thought expression period that involved reinstatement of the suppression mood state than subjects exposed to a discordant suppression-expression mood state. In a second experiment, subjects who expressed a target thought after suppression showed a tendency to reinstate the mood state that occurred during the previous suppression period. The authors conclude that attempts to control or suppress unwanted thoughts, particularly during a negative mood state, may cause a strong bond to form between the "to-be-suppressed" thoughts and mood state so that one tends to prompt the other.

In another experiment, Wegner, Erber, and Zanakos (1993, Experiment 2) found that under cognitive load subjects instructed to suppress thoughts about personal success or failure showed more Stroop color-naming interference to success or failure words than individuals instructed to think about success and failure. Again, these results are interpreted as showing that efforts to mentally control one's thoughts can lead to heightened accessibility, especially under the conditions of reduced cognitive capacity that occurs with cognitive load manipulations. There is considerable evidence, then, that depressed and dysphoric individuals are less able to control their negative self-referent thinking as shown by a resurgence in negative thought intrusions after efforts to suppress the unwanted negative thoughts. Moreover, this reduction in mental control may be due to the increased accessibility of negative self-referent thoughts, a strong coupling between negative thoughts and dysphoria, and the detrimental effects of reduced cognitive capacity on effortful control processes (Hartlage et al., 1993). In the end, these studies provide considerable evidence for unintended and involuntary negative self-referent thinking in depression.

A final set of studies we will consider in our review of the empirical basis of unintended thought in depression deals with the phenomenon of *implicit memory*. Implicit memory is a form of retention without awareness that involves "memory for information that was acquired during a specific episode and that is expressed on tests in which subjects are not required, and are frequently unable, to deliberately or consciously recollect the previously studied information or episode itself" (Schacter, 1990, p. 338; see also Roediger, 1990). Implicit memory has been studied using a variety of cognitive tasks that involve some degree of priming or transfer so that the extent of implicit memory is reflected in better recall performance on a memory task for subjects who have had a prior relevant experience than for individuals who did not have this prior experience (Roediger & McDermott, 1992). As can be seen from this definition, implicit memory can provide a powerful test of unintended processing in depression. If negative information is processed without intention, we would expect depressed and dysphoric individuals to show superior recall of negative self-referent information on implicit memory tasks relative to nondepressed controls.

Many studies have investigated implicit memory in depression using either homophone spelling, lexical decision, word-fragment, or word-stem completion. In homophone spelling, subjects are presented with a list of homophones (a word that can be spelled in two different ways, depending on its meaning (e.g., *fair, fare*). Usually the least common spelling of the word is presented during the "study" period. In the recall phase, subjects are read a list of words containing the previously presented homophones as well as nonhomophone distracters. If subjects show a tendency to spell the homophones in the less common way, then this is taken to reflect implicit memory recall, that is, the effects of prior exposure to the list of homophones during the study period. In the word-stem completion and word-fragment tasks, subjects are exposed to a list of positive, negative, and/or neutral words and then subsequently given either word stems (first three letters of a word) or word fragments (a scattering of letters that comprise the word) and asked to complete the partial words with the first word that comes to mind. If subjects complete the word fragments or word stems with the previously presented words, then this indicates the effects of prior encoding of the word list. In lexical decision making, implicit memory is indicated if subjects show quicker lexical decisions to previously presented words compared with new or unprimed words. To date, most of the research on implicit memory in depression has relied on word-stem, word-fragment, or lexical decision tasks.

The most consistent finding from these studies is that depressed or dysphoric individuals do not show a significant mood-congruent implicit memory bias or priming effect for negative self-referent material, although depressed subjects were found to recall more depression words on the explicit memory (free or cued recall) tasks (Bazin, Perruchet, De Bonis, & Féline, 1994; Denny & Hunt, 1992; P. Watkins et al., 1992). However, Elliott and Greene (1992) found that depressed patients had impaired performance on both implicit and explicit memory tasks for nonvalenced words, whereas Hertel and Hardin (1990) failed to find that dysphoria was associated with impaired performance on implicit memory. Ruiz-Caballero and González (1994) found that dysphoric subjects had a mood-congruent priming effect for negative word stem completion (implicit memory). In a later study, Ruiz-Caballero and González (1997) replicated their previous study by finding a mood-congruent bias for negative trait adjectives in dysphoric students on both implicit (word-stem completion) and explicit (free recall) memory tasks. Significant mood-congruent priming effects for depressive adjectives have also been found in primed lexical decision tasks for high negative affect and clinically depressed patients (Bradley et al., 1994, 1995).

At first glance, the mixed findings for mood-congruent bias in implicit memory may cast doubt on the view that negative self-referent information is processed automatically in depression. However, Roediger (1990) noted that most implicit memory tests are data-driven and so rely on perceptual processing, whereas explicit memory tests rely on variations in meaning and so are more conceptually based (see also Roediger & McDermott, 1992). As noted earlier when discussing selective encoding, evidence for mood-congruent bias in depression has been stronger with conceptually than perceptually oriented tasks. Also Ruiz-Caballero and González (1997) found that priming effects for word-stem completion was significantly greater when initial exposure involved semantic processing of trait words (i.e., subjects rated the pleasantness of each word). Thus the mixed findings with implicit memory may reflect the information processes assessed rather than the level of automaticity apparent in mood-congruent processing bias.

P. Watkins, Vache, Verney, Mathews, and Muller (1996) employed a word association implicit memory task to investigate conceptually driven automatic mood-congruent memory bias in depression. In this task, diagnostically depressed and nondepressed students were presented a list of positive, negative, and neutral words in a "study" phase of the experiment. Individuals were instructed to imagine a scene that involved themselves and the word presented to them. After a 30-second distracter task, subjects participated in the "test" phase in which they were exposed to another set of words that were either associates of the previously studied target words that had been presented in the study phase (primed), or were new words that had not been previously studied (unprimed). They were asked to generate as many one-word associations as possible to the word cues. P. Watkins et al. (1996) found that depressed college students had significantly higher priming scores for negative target words (i.e., produced more previously studied negative words when generating word associations during the test phase), whereas the nondepressed had significantly higher priming scores for positive target words. This indicates that an automatic or unintended negative mood-congruent bias may be more evident in conceptually driven than perceptually driven processes in depression. Although replication of this finding is needed, these results suggest that a mood-congruent bias in implicit memory is evident in depression when the critical mode of information processing (i.e., conceptual processing) is assessed.

We suggest there is rather compelling evidence for the unintended processing of negative self-referent information in depression. The strongest support for this assertion comes from evidence of Stroop interference effects from depressive-related words, the reduced mental control of negative thoughts, and the evidence of mood-congruent bias especially in conceptually based implicit memory tasks. The following section focuses on another feature of automaticity, the rapid processing of information.

RAPID PROCESSING OF NEGATIVE INFORMATION

If negative self-referent information is processed automatically in depression, then we would expect more efficient or rapid processing of negatively valenced information. This would be evident as faster reaction times or shorter response latencies for encoding, recall, or self-evaluative judgments of negative self-referent material.

In general, the most consistent finding from the SRET studies is that depressed or dysphoric individuals do not differ significantly from nondepressed subjects in the time taken to judge the self-relevance of negative trait adjectives (Bradley & Mathews, 1983; Derry & Kuiper, 1981). Others have found that depressed or dysphoric subjects show equivalent reaction times to the endorsement of positive and negative self-referent trait adjectives, whereas nondepressed individuals have differentially faster decision times to positive self-referent trait adjectives (Gilboa et al., 1997; M. Greenberg & Alloy, 1989). Ferguson et al. (1983) found that non-depressed subjects had significantly shorter decision times when making self-referent judgments to positive than negative trait adjectives. However, contrary to prediction, still other researchers have found that depressed individuals actually take longer to make self-judgments to depressive than nondepressive trait adjectives (Bargh & Tota, 1988; MacDonald & Kuiper, 1985; Myers et al., 1989).

This same pattern of result is evident with mood-congruent recall times, in which most studies show no significant difference between depressed or dysphoric and nondepressed in latencies to recall negative trait adjectives or personal memories (D.M. Clark & Teasdale, 1982; Fitzgerald et al., 1988; Teasdale & Fogarty, 1979; Teasdale & Taylor, 1981; Teasdale et al., 1980), although a few positive exceptions also appear in the literature (G. Lloyd & Lishman, 1975). Moreover, numerous studies did find significant differences on recall of positive traits or memories, with nondysphoric subjects showing quicker retrieval of positive traits or memories than depressed and dysphoric individuals (Fitzgerald et al., 1988; Teasdale & Fogarty, 1979; Teasdale et al., 1980). Lishman (1974) also found that nondepressed normals had quicker recall of pleasant than unpleasant personal memories, whereas Strauman (1992) obtained significantly faster times for retrieval of childhood memories in response to self-guide cues. In each case, quicker reaction time was taken to indicate heightened accessibility and more efficient processing of information. Dalgleish et al. (1995), however, found that patients with generalized anxiety disorder, a disorder that is closely related to depression, had shorter reaction times to the endorsement of negative trait adjectives that were associated with negative primes than the neutral, no-prime adjectives.

These results provide at best mixed and inconclusive evidence that negative self-referent information is processed more rapidly in depressed than nondepressed individuals. In fact, it may be that the nondepressed show more rapid processing of positive self-referent material. However, Bargh and Tota (1988) have argued that self-judgment response latencies are not an appropriate measure of processing efficiency or automaticity because one cannot determine how much of the decision latency is due to automatic construct activation, and how much of it is due to attentional factors like decision and response selection that are influenced by self-presentational factors. For this reason, the authors advocate the use of concurrent memory load to assess automaticity or efficiency of processing.

MINIMAL CAPACITY PROCESSING OF NEGATIVE INFORMATION

The minimal capacity criteria state that automatic processes can occur in parallel without interfering with other cognitive operations (Hartlage et al., 1993). This can be tested by introducing a memory load manipulation in which individuals have to remember neutral material, such as digits, while simultaneously processing personally relevant information. If the depressed person processes negative material more automatically than nondepressed information, then the memory load should cause less interference while processing negative compared with positive stimuli. For example, Bargh and Tota (1988) had dysphoric and nondysphoric college students participate in an SRET in which they were asked to make yes-no decisions to 30 depressed-content and 30 nondepressed-content trait adjectives on either a structural, semantic, other-descriptive, or self-descriptive basis. Half of the subjects from each group were required to hold a series of six digits in memory while making the adjective judgments (memory load condition), whereas the remainder made their trait adjective judgments without memory load. Following this, all subjects completed an incidental free recall of the adjectives. The memory load had significantly less effect on the self-judgment latencies of the dysphoric subjects for depressed-content than nondepressed-content adjectives, whereas the reverse pattern was evident for the nondysphoric group. For the other-referent judgments, memory load had less effect on latencies for nondepressed-content adjectives for both dysphoric and nondysphoric subjects.

Employing a modified version of the Bargh and Tota (1988) experiment, Andersen, Spielman, and Bargh (1992) asked nondepressed, mildly depressed, and moderately depressed university students to make quick judgments about the likelihood that standard future positive and negative events would occur to themselves or an average student under cognitive load (hold 6 digits in memory) and no load conditions. For the moderately depressed, the introduction of a cognitive load did not increase response judgment latency for either positive or negative self- or other-targeted future events. However, the cognitive load did significantly increase the future event judgments of the nondepressed and mildly depressed groups. The minimal impact of the cognitive load on the future event judgments of the moderately depressed suggests that these evaluative judgments are made more automatically by depressed than nondepressed individuals.

MacDonald and Kuiper (1985) presented clinically depressed, nondepressed psychiatric, and normal subjects a list of depression-related and nondepression-related personal adjectives and measured time to decide whether the adjective was self-descriptive or not. Half of the subjects in each group participated in a memory load manipulation concurrent with the self-reference rating task. Clinically depressed subjects took significantly longer to make "no" decisions to depressed-related adjectives than did nondepressed psychiatric and normal controls. The authors interpreted this result and other comparisons as indicating that clinically depressed and nondepressed psychiatric controls processed self-schema congruent content faster and more efficiently than incongruent content. However, they failed to find any interaction between the concurrent memory load and decision times. Although MacDonald and Kuiper concluded that the absence of memory load effects indicates that schema-congruent self-referent decisions were processed automatically or with minimal attentional demands, Bargh and Tota (1988) note that the null interaction only means that all self-referent judgments involve automatic processing or that all self-referent judgments are equally nonautomatic and attentional. The evidence for minimal attentional capacity, they argue, cannot be made on the basis of supporting the null hypothesis.

Hartlage (1990) conducted a study to determine whether depressed and depression-prone (attributionally vulnerable) students automatically make internal attributions for negative life events and external attributions for positive life events compared with nondepressed and nondepression-prone students. Subjects were presented with a phrase denoting a positive or negative life event (e.g., "get poor evaluation"). This was followed within 360 ms by a target word (e.g., "unmotivated"); individuals judged whether the target represented an internal (person-oriented) or external (circumstance-oriented) cause for the event. The dependent variable was time taken to make the causal attributional judgment. One half of the subjects in each group held six digits in working memory while making their attributional judgments. Analysis revealed that people in general do not make attributions automatically but that nondepressed individuals automatically make *external* attributions for negative events (i.e., as evidenced by quicker judgments or facilitation when negative prime event and external target matched), and that attributionally vulnerable (i.e., depression-prone) students automatically make attributions in general, and especially *external* attributions for positive events. Moreover

> . . . memory load did not interfere with apparent facilitation/inhibition effects associated with attribution match/mismatch when depressive attributional type primes were presented to depression-prone subjects. (p. 100)

These results, then, provide some evidence that attributions may be made automatically and require minimal processing capacity.

Wegner et al. (1993, Experiment 2) found that subjects instructed to suppress thoughts about personal success or failure had significantly more Stroop color-naming interference to words related to success or failure events when under a concurrent memory load condition, whereas high memory load subjects instructed to think about (i.e., express) success or failure thoughts showed significantly less interference to event related words. The ironic effects of mental control on Stroop color naming was not evident with the low-load subjects. The authors interpret these results as indicating that efforts to exert mental control increase the accessibility of the to-be-suppressed thought. These results also indicate that mental control is an effortful process requiring considerable cognitive capacity. When less cognitive processing capacity is available because attention is diverted to another task, the ironic effects of thought suppression become even more pronounced (see also Wegner & Erber, 1992, for similar results).

In a similar vein, Ingram (1984b) has argued that processing of negative self-referent information in depression should require more attentional or cognitive processing capacity and not less. He states that "deeper" and more elaborated information processing will require greater cognitive processing capacity. Because depression involves the activation of a depression node, processing of self-referent depression-related material will be deeper and more elaborated, thereby requiring more cognitive processing capacity. In support of this position, Ingram (1984a) found that subjects in an induced negative mood state had significantly longer latencies in a simple reaction time task when they concurrently received negative performance feedback than the positive mood group who also received negative feedback. Also the negative mood group had significantly longer latencies when receiving negative feedback as opposed to positive feedback. These results, then, indicate that encoding of negative feedback required greater cognitive processing capacity in the negative mood group so that less capacity was available for processing than was needed to respond efficiently to the reaction time task.

There is some evidence that the processing of negative self-referent information is automatic in terms of requiring a minimal amount of attentional or cognitive processing capacity. The strongest support comes from the studies by Bargh and Tota (1988) and Andersen et al. (1992), although Bargh and Tota indicate that the type of automaticity they have demonstrated is postconscious and context-dependent; that is, it occurs in the context of controlled thought. Ingram (1984b), however, argues that negative self-referent information processing in depression may require more rather than less cognitive processing capacity, and the results of Wegner et al. (1993) indicate that efforts to control mood or mood-related thoughts will require considerable cognitive processing capacity. Thus the ironic effects of mental control become particularly pronounced when cognitive processing capacity is reduced.

The literature, then, presents two seemingly contradictory predictions. According to the primal processing hypothesis, the processing of negative self-referent information in depression should require minimal cognitive capacity, whereas the depth-of-processing model of Ingram (1984b) predicts the opposite effect with more elaborated, high attentional capacity processing of negative self-referent material occurring in depression. It may be that whether negative information processing in depression requires minimal or maximum processing capacity depends on the mode of information processing required. In Ingram's (1984a) study, subjects had to read and comprehend written performance feedback. This task taps into highly effortful, strategic processing, whereas the self-judgment task of Bargh and Tota (1988) is more unintended. Thus it may be that when cognitive tasks are used that primarily involve effortful, strategic, intended, and elaborated processes, negative self-referent information in depression will require significantly more attentional processing capacity than positive information. For cognitive tasks involving less elaborated, more unintended processing, however, depression will be associated with automaticity and so require minimal processing resources to handle negative self-referent material. More research is needed to determine the context in which negative self-referent information in depression will require minimal or maximal cognitive processing capacity.

Preconscious Processing of Negative Information

A final aspect of automaticity that has been examined is whether negative self-referent information processing in depression occurs preconsciously (outside conscious awareness). Studies that present positive, negative, and neutral stimuli subliminally or below the threshold of awareness are able to test this aspect of the primal processing hypothesis. Generally, findings from these studies are mixed. Thus there is evidence of selective processing of negative self-referent stimuli presented below awareness in the stimulus identification studies (Dixon & Lear, 1962; Powell & Hemsley, 1984; von Hippel, Hawkins, & Narayan, 1994). However, it is not certain whether these results reflect a preconscious processing of negative stimuli in depression or a response bias. It may be that depressed or dysphoric subjects are perceiving partial cues to the word and are more or less willing to guess at the negative stimuli (Mathews, 1997).

In their primed lexical decision task Bradley et al. (1994) found that high negative affect subjects showed greater subliminal priming of depression-relevant than neutral words, and in a later study using clinically depressed patients, depression-congruent priming occurred in both subliminal and supraliminal conditions. Bradley et al. (1995) noted that they have found evidence of depression-congruent preconscious or subliminal priming effects in four separate clinical and nonclinical studies. The authors interpreted these subliminal priming effects as reflecting preconscious or automatic integrative processing of negative self-referent material in depression. However, the finding of supraliminal priming effects indicates that more strategic, elaborative processing of mood-congruent material also occurs in depression. In addition, Matthews and Southall (1991) failed to find a depression-congruent bias in clinical depression to very short stimulus presentations (240 ms) in a lexical decision task with associate priming and Mathews et al. (1996) noted that vigilance for social threat words by depressed patients was more evident with long exposure than with short exposure intervals. Mogg et al. (1993) also did not find evidence of a preconscious attentional bias in depression for negative self-referent material in a subliminal version of the emotional Stroop color-naming task, nor in a later study did they (Mogg et al., 1995) find evidence that depressed individuals had preconscious attentional processing of negative stimuli in a subliminal condition of the visual probe detection task.

In a series of social cognition experiments on the automatic activation of evaluative responses to attitude objects, Bargh, Chaiken, Govender, and Pratto (1992) subliminally presented attitude object primes (e.g., landlord) and their associated adjective targets (e.g., horrible) at a stimulus onset asynchrony of 300 ms. Participants were required to make an evaluative judgment of whether the adjective was "good" or "bad" in meaning. Analyses revealed that when the valence of the attitude object prime matched the valence of the adjective target, this facilitated the evaluative response latencies, whereas there was a relative inhibition of evaluative latencies when there was a mismatch between the prime and target valence. These results indicate that a stored evaluative response to attitude objects can be activated in an automatic, unintended, and preconscious fashion by the mere subliminal presence of the attitude object. In other words for objects or stimuli with an associated evaluation stored in memory, the mere presence of this object will elicit an automatic preconscious evaluative response in the form of "good" or "bad" judgments.

In a later experiment Chartrand and Bargh (Bargh, personal communication, October, 1998) found that subliminal presentations of positive and negative prime-target pairs affected subsequent mood state, with greater sadness associated with the strongly negative attitude object-adjective presentations and the happiest mood with the strongly positive presentation condition. Further analysis revealed correlations in the range of .30 to .40 between subsequent BDI scores and the size of the prior automatic positive and negative evaluation effects. Together these findings indicate that stimuli (i.e., attitude objects) can be automatically and preconsciously evaluated as "good" or "bad," and that subsequent depressed mood is related to this prior automatic evaluative response. These results are entirely consistent with the proposed operation of the orienting schemas (see Chapter 4) which provide quick, automatic evaluations of incoming stimuli for further processing by the cognitive organization.

Taken together, there is evidence of preconscious processing of negative material in depression. However, results seem to vary across studies depending on the type of cognitive tasks used to assess preconscious processing. Preconscious processing in depression may be less apparent with tasks that primarily involve perceptual processing, such as the visual probe detection experiment, whereas preconscious processing may be more robust with cognitive tasks that tap into the more integrative and conceptual processes such as found in the priming experiments. Whatever the case, the preceding studies indicate that preconscious processing of negative material can be found in depression.

SUMMARY

Most researchers who have reviewed studies on information processing in depression and anxiety have concluded that there is little evidence of a preconscious attentional bias in depression (Mathews & MacLeod, 1994; Mineka & Sutton, 1992; Williams et al., 1988). As seen from this review, however, there is considerable empirical support for the primal processing hypothesis, with depressed and possibly dysphoric individuals showing more automatic and efficient processing of negative, particularly, self-referent material (Ackermann-Engel & DeRubeis, 1993; Gotlib & Hammen, 1992; Haaga et al., 1991).

Two factors must be considered when discussing automatic information processing in depression—the type of automaticity and the mode of operation. In our review, we found strong and consistent evidence for unintended processing of negative self-referent material. Thus depressed and even dysphoric individuals showed an unintended and involuntary processing of negative self-referent information. This is entirely consistent with the primal processing hypothesis and the activation of the loss mode that leads to the involuntary processing of negative information. In fact, Hartlage et al. (1993) and Moretti and Shaw (1989) note that the unintended nature of negative information processing is consistent with the notion of automatic dysfunctional processing and negative automatic thoughts in depression.

Evidence that negative self-referent information is processed more rapidly and occupies less cognitive processing capacity (indicators of greater cognitive efficiency) has been more mixed. Measures of response latency have not been particularly supportive of rapid processing of negative material, and too few studies have investigated cognitive processing capacity to draw a firm conclusion of the effects of depression on this aspect of information processing. There is, however, evidence that at least some aspects of negative information processing occur outside conscious awareness.

A second consideration when discussing automaticity is the mode of cognitive operation. Automaticity in depression may occur primarily with conceptual and integrative processes rather than with perceptually driven tasks. In this regard, Williams et al. (1988) stated that preattentive, automatic processing can occur in operations such as sensory registration, semantic labeling, associative spread, and disambiguation of a stimulus. They noted that there are passive and automatic processing elements to long-term memory retrieval. In their second edition of *Cognitive Psychology and Emotional Disorders,* Williams et al. (1997) continue to maintain that depression is primarily characterized by bias in the more elaborative, strategic, and conceptually based memorial processing of negative self-referent material, whereas anxiety is characterized by selective perceptual encoding of threat stimuli.

Although anxiety and depression may affect different aspects of information processing, there is considerable evidence for an automatic biased processing in depression that occurs not only in memory retrieval, but also in encoding and elaborative processing of negative self-referent material. Bradley, Mogg, et al. (1997) concluded that there is an automatic attentional processing in depression that may be characterized by a difficulty in disengaging one's attention from negative material that has come into the focus of attention. Furthermore, automatic processing in depression may occur only when integrative, evaluative judgments, and certain stimulus interpretation operations are involved such as semantic labeling and associative spread. Whatever the case, we can conclude that there is considerable empirical evidence that at least certain cognitive operations involve the automatic processing of negative self-referent material. This can be taken as support for the primal processing hypothesis of the cognitive model.

CONCLUSION

At the beginning of this chpater, we posed four questions that focused on the distinctive features of the structures and processes of the depressed individual's cognitive organization. As shown in this chapter, many studies have investigated cognitive processes in an attempt to understand the cognitive basis of depression. Overall, the support for the selectivity, activation, and primal processing hypotheses has been strong given the tremendous diversity in methodology across studies. The bias in depression is not generalized, however, but instead appears highly specific to material of personal relevance to the individual. Not all structures and processes within the information processing system are equally affected by depression. Instead the latter more integrative and elaborative processes involved in memory, inferences, evaluation, and judgments may be more affected by depression than the earlier, perceptually based processes. It is also clear the depression does not simply, or always, lead to enhanced processing of negative material but instead may equally reduce a naturally occurring tendency to selectively process positive self-referent information. Thus at times an evenhanded processing of positive and negative material may be associated with depressed states in certain contexts. We also believe there is considerable evidence that in depression negative self-schematic structures become activated leading to involuntary and automatic processing of schema-congruent information. In this section, we briefly summarize some of the conclusions we can draw about each of the hypotheses.

Evaluation of the *selective processing hypothesis* indicates there is now substantial empirical evidence that depressed and dysphoric individuals differ from nondepressed individuals in the processing of information about themselves. The nature of this difference—whether it primarily involves a reduction in naturally occurring positivity bias or presence of a negativity bias—is a matter of considerable debate and mixed evidence in the literature. Overall, we must conclude that empirical support for selective encoding is strong, though it requires considerable explanation and qualification. The processing difference cannot be described unequivocally as an enhanced selectivity bias for negative material. Rather the precise nature of the emotional processing difference in depression seems to depend on the type of stimuli, the information processing requirements of a task, and related contextual or situational cues. For this reason, we are summarizing evidence for mood-congruent selective processing in depression by considering the different levels or types of cognitive processing.

It is apparent from studies on attentional processes that depression affects the unintended, involuntary encoding of self-referent material.

However, evidence of an automatic, preconscious attentional bias for negative information in depression has been inconsistent (a similar conclusion was reached in reviews by Mathews & MacLeod, 1994; Mineka & Sutton, 1992; Mineka et al., 1998). Instead, the most consistent finding for depression is either an attentional vigilance for negative self-referent material or an evenhanded perception of positive and negative information because of an increased attention for, but not *selective* attention to, negative stimuli. This latter finding represents a shift away from the selective attentional bias for positive material found with nondepressed individuals and, possibly, their attendant tendency to ignore negative information. Thus the attentional studies reviewed in this chapter support the selective encoding hypothesis but suggest a twofold aspect of the attentional bias in depression involving both attentional vigilance for negative and reduced selective attentional processing bias for positive material. In some cases, then, depending on the cognitive task, an evenhanded attentional processing of positive and negative information may be apparent.

Evidence for a selective negative encoding bias in depression is more robust with studies involving evaluation, judgments and inferences of emotion-relevant material. Across a wide range of studies involving perception and recall of interpersonal and task performance feedback, self-evaluation, causal attributions, and expectancy of future success or failure, there was more empirical support for a selective encoding or processing bias for negative information in depression, though once again many studies reported that the most prominent finding was of a positive processing bias in the nondepressed and an evenhanded encoding of positive and negative information in depression. Detection of a negative processing bias in depression may be more evident in studies that use moderately to severely depressed individuals and that provide highly credible, self-evaluative feedback to tasks that are perceived to have a significant impact on one's self-worth. With the SRET studies, once again mixed results have been obtained, although more consistent evidence has emerged in favor of a negative self-reference encoding bias in depression.

Together with the questionnaire-based studies on self-focused attention and cognitive processing errors, we can conclude that a selective encoding bias for negative self-referent information is more apparent in depression when one assesses the integrative, elaborative, and strategic processes involved in making inferences, evaluations and judgments of emotionally relevant and conceptually driven information. When attentional processes are involved, depression may affect the later stages of attentional processing by interfering with the ability to shift one's focus away from negative material. In our review of depressive realism as an alternative explanation for the selective encoding differences between depressed and nondepressed states, we found little empirical support for the contention that depression actually enhances the accuracy of self-referent encoding. Instead, the empirical findings suggest that depression is associated with information processing of self-referent material that is quite distinct, but not more accurate, than the processing evident in the nondepressed. Our review of studies of early attentive bias and later more elaborative information processing indicates that depression is associated with a reduction in positivity bias and, in many instances, enhanced processing of negative self-referent information.

Under the *schema activation hypothesis*, the cognitive model adopts an accessibility or activation rather than availability perspective on schematic processing in depression. Thus the model predicts mood-congruency effects or increased accessibility to negative self-referent schematic content and structures during depression. Strong support for the hypothesis can be found across a variety of studies showing that depressed individuals have increased accessibility to negative self-referent schema content. This has been evident in the form of biased mood-congruent recall of negative autobiographical memories and endorsement of negative belief statements and trait adjectives as well as in responses to idiographic scenarios and completion of belief sentence stems. However, activation of negative schematic content may also be affected by variables such as (a) level of symptom severity so that increased accessibility to negative content may be present only in more severe depression, (b) presence of mood repair strategies which may counter efforts to elicit negative schematic content, and (c) memory-processing features that may influence whether specific or more general schema content is retrieved.

Consistent with Segal's (1988) view of schema structure in terms of the interrelation among functional elements or constructs, we reviewed experimental studies that contrasted positive, negative, and neutral prime-target word pairs to investigate encoding and retrieval differences between depressed and nondepressed individuals. Findings from studies using modified Stroop priming, primed lexical decision or, to a lesser extent, the emotional priming task of Power and colleagues, indicate that negative self-descriptive material does tend to have significantly greater priming or relatedness effects with depressed than nondepressed individuals. This increased associative effect of negative self-referent prime-target pairs is consistent with the activation of negative schematic structures in depression. These results, then, are supportive of the schema activation hypothesis, though given the complexity and inconsistency of these findings, considerably more research is needed in this area.

According to the cognitive model, activation of the loss mode during depression is associated with the automatic processing of negative schema-congruent information. We referred to this as the *primal processing hypothesis.* In our review of the relevant literature, we examined features of automaticity to determine whether there was any evidence that negative self-referent information is processed more automatically in depression. Findings from attentional processing, mood-congruent incidental recall, schematic priming, the ironic effects of intentional thought suppression, and conceptually based implicit memory studies provide strong support for the assertion that the negative self-referent processing bias in depression occurs unintentionally or involuntarily. However, the picture for more rapid processing of negative self-referent information in depression is doubtful given the contradictory and inconclusive findings when comparing the decision times of depressed and nondepressed individuals for trait adjective endorsement or recall.

Evidence that in depression negative self-referent information requires minimal processing capacity is also limited. This aspect of automaticity has not received sufficient attention in the cognitive experimental depression literature to warrant a firm conclusion. Ingram (1984a) has argued that the processing of negative self-referent material may require more rather than less processing resources. Too few studies have contrasted these two positions to determine under what conditions information processing in depression requires maximal or minimal processing resources. A final feature of automaticity, the processing of negative information outside conscious awareness, was evident in some selective attention and priming studies. We conclude with Bradley et al. (1995) that there appears to be preconscious integrative processing of negative self-referent material in depression. Empirical support for automaticity or the primal processing hypothesis is strongest for unintended or involuntary and then preconscious processing of negative self-referent material. There is less evidence that negative processing in depression is more rapid and efficient, and requires less processing resources than the processing of negative self-referent material by the nondepressed.

This concludes our review of the empirical research on the cognitive basis of depression. Having established that depressive mood, symptoms, and disorders can have a fairly profound impact on the content, direction, and function of our information processing system, we next consider (in Chapters 8–10) how cognitive factors may contribute to the onset, course, and recovery from depression. Research from this perspective is interested in determining whether there might be a cognitive vulnerability to depression.

CHAPTER 8

Cognitive Vulnerability: Empirical Status of the Stability Hypothesis

IN CHAPTER 1, we noted that depressive disorders often take a persistent and recurring course even though individual depressive episodes may be self-limiting. With lifetime risk for depression at approximately 12% for men and 21% for women (Kessler et al., 1994), it is evident that a significant minority of the general population are prone to depressive disorders. A large body of research has now established an important link between the occurrence of stressful major life events (e.g., death, divorce, loss of job, bankruptcy, accidents, onset of serious physical illness) or chronic life adversities (e.g., long-term medical illness, living with alcoholic partner, marital conflict), especially events that represent a loss or exit from social resources, and the onset of depressive disorders (for reviews, see G.W. Brown & Harris, 1989; Monroe & Simons, 1991; Paykel & Cooper, 1992).

It is apparent from community and clinical studies that stressors play an important role in both the onset of depressive symptoms and the course of the disorder (Gotlib & Hammen, 1992). However, the magnitude of the relation between depression onset and negative life events may be quite modest (Hammen, Mayol, deMayol, & Marks, 1986), and most individuals do not develop a depressive disorder when faced with difficult and stressful life experiences (Coyne & Whiffen, 1995). Hammen (1991) concluded from her finding that women with unipolar depression had significantly more negative interpersonal stress and conflicts than women with a chronic medical illness or normal women, and that the relationship beliefs and behaviors of depressed women may contribute to the increased occurrence of these negative interpersonal stressors.

Most life event researchers recognize that cognitive factors play an important mediating role in the life event-depression relationship. That is, the meaning individuals attach to a stressful event will determine its impact on the individual (Hammen, 1985). In addition, a considerable research effort has been directed toward explicating possible predisposing factors or diatheses that might interact with the occurrence of life events to explain individual differences in susceptibility to depression. In fact, any model of depression must explain why some individuals seem so prone to developing a depressive disorder whereas other individuals seem resilient even in the face of comparable life adversity. The occurrence of severe life events in and of itself, then, does not provide a sufficient explanation for the onset or reoccurrence of depression.

A COGNITIVE THEORY OF VULNERABILITY TO DEPRESSION

In Chapters 5 through 7, we discussed the empirical support for the descriptive hypotheses of the cognitive model. These hypotheses focus on the cognitive products, structures, and processes that characterize the depressive episode. The cognitive model, however, also postulates a second level of conceptualization, that of cognitive structures as predisposing or vulnerability factors to depression. As noted in Chapter 4, the cognitive theory of depression proposes that enduring schema content in the form of maladaptive attitudes, beliefs, and assumptions about the self, personal world, and future may be associated with increased vulnerability to depression (A. Beck, 1967; A. Beck et al., 1979). This notion, that idiosyncratic maladaptive beliefs may contribute to increased susceptibility to depression, has resulted in considerable misunderstanding in the literature over the term "cognitive vulnerability." In a review of 30 years of theory and research on cognitive therapy, A. Beck (1991) asserted that cognitive theory does not claim that depression is *caused* by negative cognitions. Cognitive theory recognizes that depression is caused by a combination of factors within the biological, genetic, familial, developmental, personality, and social domains. Thus CT considers the activation of maladaptive schemas an integral mechanism for the development of depression. In the current theory presented in Chapter 4, the activation of prepotent idiosyncratic schemas of the primal loss mode will play an important contributory role in the onset of depression when other predisposing factors are also present. Over the years, CT has emphasized two main facets to cognitive vulnerability or predisposition to depression.

In the 1960s and 1970s, cognitive vulnerability to depression was viewed in terms of idiosyncratic, prepotent schematic content involving beliefs, attitudes, and assumptions individuals hold about themselves and their world around them (A. Beck, 1964, 1967). These schemas, which are relatively dormant or inactive during nondepressed states, can acquire increased potency during depression to the point that they dominate the information processing system leading to the negative automatic thoughts and negative or "nonpositive" processing biases that characterize depression.

Kovacs and Beck (1978) discussed features of the maladaptive schemas that may account for their vulnerability characteristic. First, predisposing schemas remain latent or inaccessible until reactivated by certain internal or external stimuli. Once reactivated, the maladaptive schemas are hypervalent and so override more constructive modes of processing information leading to the biased negativity that characterizes depression. Second, the content of the maladaptive schemas represent salient idiosyncratic themes of self-evaluation and relationships with others. Because the self-assessment and relational content of these depressotypic schemas was considered a critical defining aspect of their vulnerability property, self-report measures of adaptive and maladaptive belief content, such as the Dysfunctional Attitudes Scale (DAS), were thought to be important measures of cognitive vulnerability to psychological disorders like depression.

Third, because the maladaptive schemas in depression are inflexible, rigid, and absolutistic, they lead to erroneous conclusions about the individual and his or her circumstances. Fourth, continued reactivation by a wider range of conditions may lower the activation threshold so that the maladaptive schemas are more easily triggered by stimuli. Fifth, the development of depressotypic schemas may stem from certain childhood experiences such as the loss of a parent, rejection, imitation of a parent who holds views of personal inadequacy, and exposure to critical or rigid parenting (see also Leahy & Beck, 1988). Once a certain maladaptive belief is learned, such as "I am unlovable," interpretations consistent with this assumption will reinforce this maladaptive self-schema. Finally, in adulthood the depressotypic schemas become stable and enduring latent features of one's self-view (Kovacs & Beck, 1979). The attempt to document the existence of enduring, maladaptive schematic beliefs, assumptions, and attitudes as a significant contributory factor in depression became an important topic of cognitive-clinical research throughout the late 1970s and early 1980s.

By the mid-1980s, the cognitive view of vulnerability to depression shifted from an emphasis on specific idiosyncratic negative schemas or assumptions to more general superordinate personality constellations or modes. Two personality constructs were introduced as possible vulnerability factors in depression and other emotional disorders, *sociotropy* and *autonomy* (A. Beck, 1983). The sociotropic or socially dependent personality places a high value on close interpersonal relationships. Self-worth depends on attaining the love and approval of others, maintaining close interpersonal relationships, and avoiding the rejection or displeasure of other people. Autonomy, on the other hand, is a personality orientation that places high value on personal independence, achievement, or mastery, and freedom of choice and control from others. The autonomous person derives a sense of self-worth from being able to assert independence, control, and mastery or accomplishment over personal challenges and situations. As dimensions of personality, sociotropy and autonomy will be evident, to a certain degree, in everyone. As discussed in Chapter 4, a distinction must be made between the maladaptive sociotropic and autonomous beliefs that characterize the depression-prone individual, and the more adaptive sociotropic and autonomous beliefs found in those who are resistant to depression.

Highly sociotropic individuals are more sensitive to situations that are perceived as a disruption of their social resources, whereas autonomous individuals are more sensitive to circumstances that are perceived to impede or thwart goal-seeking behavior (A. Beck, 1983). Thus the highly sociotropic person is more likely to become depressed after an event that is perceived as involving a threatened or actual loss of social acceptance or personal attractiveness. The highly autonomous individual will be more susceptible to depression after an event perceived as a loss or threatened loss of independence, control, or accomplishment (A. Beck, 1987; D.A. Clark & Beck, 1989). Sociotropy and autonomy, in themselves, are not predisposing contributors to depression. It is only when a precipitating stressor impinges on a maladaptive aspect of the personality for which it is congruent—a failure event triggers helplessness beliefs in the autonomous and relationship loss activates unlovability beliefs in the sociotropic person—that there is increased vulnerability to depression. Thus the personality dimensions in themselves are informative about vulnerability only insofar as they tell us something about the interaction between the self and the environment.

Blatt and Zuroff (1992) have noted that the CT concepts of sociotropy and autonomy share many similarities with other theories of depression that also emphasize relatedness and self-definition as core predisposing personality orientations in depression. Blatt and Maroudas (1992) also compared and contrasted the cognitive concepts of sociotropy and autonomy with three contemporary psychoanalytic theories of depression and noted that all four models proposed two major types of depressed patients based on personality: those dependent on interpersonal relationships, and those preoccupied with achievement, self-definition, and self-worth.

The introduction of the concepts of sociotropy and autonomy in understanding vulnerability to depression is not a complete departure from the earlier emphasis on maladaptive idiosyncratic beliefs and assumptions. A. Beck (1987) notes that the prepotent maladaptive schemas, described in earlier writings on cognitive theory, represent the cognitive schematic basis of the predepressive personality organization. However, the theory now stipulates that an individual's vulnerability to depression will depend, to a considerable degree, on their specific personality constellation. This cognitive-personality association has led to two streams of research on sociotropy and autonomy. The first has taken a broader personality orientation and used a self-report personality questionnaire called the Sociotropy-Autonomy Scale (SAS). The second research strategy has employed "Approval by Others" and "Performance Evaluation" subscales of the DAS to assess the specific schema or belief content that underlies sociotropy and autonomy.

How do the concepts of predisposing maladaptive schemas and the personality dimensions of sociotropy and autonomy fit with the cognitive model presented in Chapter 4? Sociotropy and autonomy are suborganizations of personality involving clusters of schemas. For the depression-prone individual, the personality constellation will include strong links to the primal loss mode. Experiences that activate the sociotropic or autonomous personality in the depression-prone individual will also tend to activate the primal loss mode. Because of this strong connection, vulnerable individuals are more likely to experience a depressive state. For nonvulnerable individuals, the sociotropic and autonomous personality are more likely to be associated with constructive modes so that activation of personality suborganization will lead to a more balanced nondepressive emotional state. We propose that **cognitive vulnerability to depression** is characterized by *latent core maladaptive schemas, especially involving issues of helplessness and unlovability, that form the cognitive basis of personality suborganizations with strong connections to the primal loss mode. A range of internal or external stimuli may activate these latent schemas of the dominant personality constellation and, by association, the primal loss mode leading to the development of depressive symptoms.*

COGNITIVE VULNERABILITY AND CAUSALITY

The most persistent criticism of the cognitive model of depression has been directed toward the proposal of latent, predisposing cognitive structures for depression. Ingram, Miranda, and Segal (1998) note that to be considered a vulnerability marker of depression, a cognitive construct must meet the minimum criteria of *sensitivity* (i.e., is present in depressed individuals), *specificity* (i.e., is more frequent in depression than in controls), and *stability* (i.e., is always present in vulnerable individuals even when depressive symptoms are absent). Reviewers have concluded that the cognitive variables proposed as vulnerability factors do not meet all three minimum criteria (especially the stability criteria) and so believe there is scant empirical support for the existence of enduring, predisposing cognitive structures that play a significant role in the etiology of depression (Ackermann-Engel & DeRubeis, 1993; Barnett & Gotlib, 1988c; Coyne & Gotlib, 1983; Coyne & Whiffen, 1995; Gotlib & Hammen, 1992; Haaga et al., 1991; Teasdale & Barnard, 1993). In their second edition of *Cognitive Psychology and Emotional Disorders*, Williams et al. (1997) draw the following conclusion about the CT view of cognitive vulnerability:

> One of the major ambiguities in Beck's theory has been whether particular emotion-related schemata come into operation only when a person is in the relevant emotional state or whether they are present beforehand and contribute to the development of the emotional condition. In fact, the evidence for dysfunctional schemata being present *before* (original italics) someone becomes anxious or depressed is not at all good. (p. 11)

This conclusion about the conceptual and empirical status of the contributory or vulnerability hypotheses of CT is based almost exclusively on studies that found that DAS scores decreased significantly, and sometimes to within the normal nondepressed range, with the remission of depressive symptoms or the lack of consistent findings with the cognitive diathesis-stress studies. For several reasons, however, we believe this conclusion may be premature.

First, many of the studies on cognitive vulnerability have significant methodological shortcomings that lead one to question whether they provide an adequate or fair test of cognitive vulnerability (for discussion, see Coyne & Whiffen, 1995; Haaga et al., 1991). As we review the empirical research on each of the vulnerability hypotheses, we will discuss these methodological problems.

Second, the question of vulnerability as it pertains to the cognitive model of depression has often been a source of misunderstanding. A. Beck (1991) stated that cognitions do not cause depression:

> I have argued elsewhere that it seems far-fetched to assign a causal role to cognitions because the negative automatic thoughts constitute an *integral* (italics original) part of depression, just like the motivational, affective,

and behavioral symptoms. To conclude that cognitions cause depression is analogous to asserting that delusions cause schizophrenia. (p. 371)

If negative automatic thoughts and selective cognitive processing are not causes of depression, what role does the activation of latent dysfunctional schemas play? Once again, cognitive theory asserts that the activation of latent maladaptive schemas is not the sole cause of depression but rather is the cognitive mechanism by which depression develops (A. Beck, 1991; Kovacs & Beck, 1978). Any combination of genetic, biological, personality, and environmental factors may be necessary to activate the depressotypic information processing system characterized by negativity.

If we adopt the terminology suggested by Abramson et al. (1988), latent maladaptive schemas or modes are proximal contributory factors to the development of depression. Abramson et al. define contributory cause in the following way:

A contributory cause of some set of symptoms is an etiological factor that increase the likelihood of the occurrence of the symptoms, but that is neither necessary or sufficient for their occurrence. (p. 6)

According to this definition, then, latent maladaptive schemas and modes increase the likelihood or risk for depression, but their existence is neither necessary nor sufficient on their own to cause the development of depressive symptoms. However once the latent maladaptive schemas and their connections with the primal loss mode are activated, the probability that depressive symptoms will occur is greatly increased. We suggest that studies on cognitive vulnerability view maladaptive schemas in terms of contributory factors to depression rather than as necessary and sufficient causal agents of depression (also see discussion by Garber & Hollon, 1991).

Third, the cognitive model does not assume that sociotropy and autonomy, or other maladaptive schemas or schema clusters, are the only contributors to the development of depression. Other vulnerability factors have been implicated in depression such as dependency and self-criticism (Blatt, 1974; Blatt & Zuroff, 1992), perfectionism (Hewitt & Flett, 1993), negative attributional style (Peterson & Seligman, 1984), low self-esteem (Roberts & Monroe, 1994), pessimistic explanatory style (Seligman, 1990), hopelessness (Abramson et al., 1989), and neuroticism (Martin, 1985), to name but a few possible etiologic constructs. These constructs, alone or in combination, may interact with the maladaptive schemas and predepressive personality proposed in CT to contribute to the development of depression. Most of the depression vulnerability research has been tied to a single theoretical perspective so that the interactive effects of different contributory factors proposed by "competing" depression models have not been adequately investigated. The Consensus Development Conference on Cognitive Models of Depression convened in Baniff, Canada, also recommended that more research is needed that integrates and contrasts different models of depression (Segal & Dobson, 1992).

Finally, recent studies that have addressed some of the methodological criticisms of the early cognitive vulnerability research have provided support for the influence of predisposing, contributory cognitive factors in the onset and maintenance of depression (Gotlib et al., 1997). This emerging literature, along with our previous points, suggests that cognitive vulnerability to depression should be considered a possible contributory factor in the development of depression.

The vulnerability formulation is an important part of the cognitive theory of depression. Although several hypotheses have been identified that are applicable to cognitive vulnerability, we begin our discussion with the stability hypothesis since it was the first cognitive vulnerability hypothesis to be subjected to empirical scrutiny. Table 8.1 presents all the cognitive vulnerability hypotheses that are discussed in Chapters 8, 9, and 10.

The stability, depression onset, and relapse/recurrence hypotheses (the latter two hypotheses are discussed in Chapter 9) deal with the central contributory relationship that cognitive constructs and processes are postulated to play in the predisposition and maintenance of depression. Most of the research on the vulnerability aspects of the cognitive model has concentrated on these three hypotheses, as well. In Chapter 10, we discuss the empirical status of the remaining six cognitive vulnerability hypotheses that deal with related aspects of the cognitive basis of the pathogenesis of depression. In keeping with the shift in emphasis within the cognitive model, we categorize the empirical literature relevant to the different hypotheses into studies that focus on maladaptive beliefs, attitudes, and schemas, and then the studies that deal with the specific cognitive-personality constructs of sociotropy and autonomy.

STABILITY HYPOTHESIS

The latent cognitive structures and content that contribute to susceptibility to depression are relatively stable across time, situations, and mood states, although they will remain inaccessible unless activated by a priming stimulus.

The cognitive theory asserts that the negative latent self-schemas and maladaptive personality, such as excessive sociotropy or extreme autonomy,

Table 8.1

The Vulnerability Hypotheses of the Cognitive Model of Depression

Hypotheses	Statement
Stability	The latent cognitive structures and content that contribute to susceptibility to depression are relatively stable across time, situations, and mood states, although they will remain inaccessible unless activated by a priming stimulus.
Depression Onset	A negative event that matches the content of the prepotent self-schemas and maladaptive personality constellation associated with the primal loss mode will lead to a heightened risk of depression onset in persons with no previous diagnosable depression.
Depression Recurrence	A negative event that matches the content of the self-referent schemas and maladaptive personality constellation associated with the primal loss mode will lead to a heightened risk of recurrence of depression in previously depressed patients.
Self-Evaluation	The cognitive structures and content that contribute to susceptibility to depression will guide self-perceptions, self-evaluations, and self-appraisals especially when elicited by schema-congruent situations.
Congruent Processing	When activated, the cognitive structures and content that predispose for depression will selectively bias information processing for stimuli congruent with the cognitive vulnerability organization.
Relationship	Cognitive structures and content that predispose for depression are associated with a characteristic interpersonal style that affects the quality and nature of social relations with significant others.
Differential Coping	Maladaptive coping responses and compensatory strategies will play a more significant role in depression when personality-event congruence is present than when personality-event incongruence is present.
Symptom Specificity	The predepressive personality suborganization associated with the primal loss mode will influence depressive symptom presentation such that sociotropy is associated with symptoms of deprivation and autonomy with symptoms of defeat and self-depreciation.
Differential Treatment	The predepressive personality suborganization of the primal loss mode will influence attitudes and response to treatment such that sociotropic individuals are more responsive to interpersonally and emotionally engaging interventions, whereas autonomous persons are more responsive to less personal and more problem-focused interventions.

that play a contributory role in the development of depression are enduring, traitlike characteristics that are present across time, situations, and mood states (Kovacs & Beck, 1978), although whether they are active or latent will depend on a triggering stimulus. The stable, enduring feature of these latent cognitive structures suggests that they exist before, during, and after a depressive episode (Haaga et al., 1991). That is, the negative self-schemas and maladaptive personality constellation, as predisposing contributory factors in depression, are viewed not simply as symptoms that are concomitant, statelike features of the depressive episode but rather as latent enduring or persistent vulnerability factors in depression. Coyne and Whiffen (1995) also commented that if variables are hypothesized to play a contributory causal role in depression, then they should show persistence or endurance beyond the depressive episode itself. Stiles and Gotestam (1988b) noted that endurance is an important characteristic of the notion of cognitive vulnerability or depressotypic schemas. Segal and Swallow (1994) argued that measures of depressive cognition must demonstrate that they are not merely alternative measures of mood or the cognitive expressions of affect. One way to demonstrate this distinctiveness, then, is to show that some form of depressotypic cognition persists beyond the depressive state.

From the very beginning, CT has argued that these predisposing cognitive structures, though enduring and stable, nonetheless remain relatively latent, dormant, or inaccessible during the nondepressed state (A. Beck, 1964, 1967). The view of latent and inaccessible cognitive variables that predispose and contribute to the development of depression has been criticized as an untenable, nonfalsifiable concept that cannot be tested empirically (Beidel & Turner, 1986; Coyne, 1989; Coyne & Gotlib, 1983). Admittedly, measurement of these latent structures is difficult because nondepressed individuals do not necessarily have direct access to their content. Nevertheless, if prepotent latent cognitive structures are valid causal entities, then researchers must find ways to access this material in the nondepressive state (Haaga et al., 1991). Cognitive researchers have developed indirect experimental methods for assessing latent cognitive structures or priming methodologies for activating the dormant content (Segal & Dobson, 1992).

In our review of evidence for the stability hypothesis of CT, we begin first with studies that have investigated the stability of individuals' scores on the DAS before and after recovery from depression. We then examine evidence for stability in the personality constructs of sociotropy and autonomy. Finally, we conclude by discussing the empirical support for three explanations proposed for the generally negative findings on stability of cognitive variables—lack of measurement sensitivity, failure to use priming procedures, and the mood-state hypothesis of Persons and Miranda (1992).

DYSFUNCTIONAL ATTITUDES

The Dysfunctional Attitudes Scale (DAS) is a clinically derived self-report instrument originally developed to measure the extent to which individuals hold maladaptive beliefs and assumptions that predispose to depression and other forms of psychopathology (A. Weissman & Beck, 1978). Individuals are presented with a series of statements that reflect faulty or maladaptive beliefs about one's self and personal world, and are asked to rate their level of agreement on a 7-point bipolar scale from +3 ("totally agree") to −3 ("totally disagree"). As noted in Chapter 7 under the schema activation hypothesis, the construct validity of the DAS has been supported in numerous studies showing that the measure is sensitive to depression. Furthermore, even though they may not be specific to depression, this does not mean that high DAS scores can't be predictive of susceptibility to depression. A variable can be nonspecific but still play a contributory role if it is one of several interacting causal factors in the disorder (Garber & Hollon, 1991). Also, as noted previously, the DAS was not intended to be a specific measure of depression. It was expected that many of the maladaptive belief statements contained in the DAS would probably have relevance for other psychological states such as anxiety.

If the DAS assesses maladaptive schema content that predisposes to depression, then based on the stability hypothesis one might erroneously think that high scores on this instrument should persist beyond the depressive episode. A number of studies have investigated this and found that the elevated scores on the DAS evident during the depressive episode tend to return to normal, or near normal levels, once the depressive symptoms remit (see reviews by Barnett & Gotlib, 1988c; Haaga et al., 1991; Ingram et al., 1998; Miranda & Gross, 1997; Stiles & Gotestman, 1988b). Thus in most studies, DAS scores decrease significantly with remission of depressive symptoms to the point that asymptomatic formerly depressed individuals usually do not differ significantly in their DAS scores from nondepressed normal controls (Blackburn et al., 1986; Blackburn & Smyth, 1985; Dohr et al., 1989; Hamilton & Abramson, 1983; Hollon et al., 1986; Reda, Carpiniello, Secchiaroli, & Blanco, 1985; Schrader, Gibbs, & Harcourt, 1986; Scott, Harrington, House, & Ferrier, 1996; Silverman, Silverman, & Eardley, 1984). Ingram et al. (1998) concluded from their review of the literature on the stability of the DAS and other measures of cognition that most studies have found that depressive cognition is state dependent.

Contrary results that on first glance appear to support the persistence of the DAS Total Score have also been reported in the literature. Dobson and Shaw (1986) found that the DAS scores of remitted depressed patients did not decrease significantly with recovery from depression but a reanalysis of these data by Barnett and Gotlib (1988c) showed that the remitted depressed group did not differ significantly in their DAS scores from a nondepressed normal control group. In two other studies, DAS scores remained elevated in remitted depressed patients (Eaves & Rush, 1984), although in the study by Peselow, Robins, Block, Barouche, and Fieve (1990), there was a significant decrease in posttreatment DAS scores in the treatment responder group. Further analysis revealed that only the partial treatment responders continued to evidence elevated posttreatment DAS scores, whereas those showing complete treatment response did not differ from the normal controls in their DAS scores at retest. These findings, then, suggest that elevated DAS scores at posttreatment may be due to the presence of residual depressive symptoms rather than reflecting an underlying vulnerability for depression.

Although most of the research on the stability and consistency of dysfunctional attitudes has compared individuals who are symptomatic and asymptomatic for depression, a few studies have taken other approaches to the question of the persistence of maladaptive beliefs. In a large prospective community study, Lewinsohn et al. (1981) found that individuals who were not depressed at an initial assessment but developed a depressive episode when reassessed at Time 2 did not endorse significantly more dysfunctional beliefs at Time 1 on a beliefs inventory that was comparable to the DAS. However, Fresco (1991) compared the DAS scores of subsyndromal cyclothymic, hypomanic, dysthymic, and normal college students across three different mood states. The subclinical cyclothymic and dysthymic students scored significantly higher on the DAS than hypomanic and normal controls and their DAS scores did not change significantly across the three mood states.

Randolph and Dykman (1998) assessed perceptions of parenting, dysfunctional attitudes (i.e., the DAS), and depressive symptoms (i.e., BDI and Depression-Proneness Rating Scale) in 247 undergraduates. Based on a path analysis, Randolph and Dykman found that perfectionistic and critical parenting were causally linked to dysfunctional attitudes which was in turn related to proneness for depression even after controlling for current level of depression. Although research on the DAS Total Score and other belief inventories has not supported the persistence of dysfunctional attitudes beyond the depressive episode, the Randolph and Dykman study showing a link between negative parenting, dysfunctional attitudes, and the development of depressive symptoms suggests that it may be premature to conclude that the DAS Total Score is merely another cognitive measure of depressive symptoms.

It is also possible that the DAS Total Score does not provide a sufficiently fine-grained analysis of the maladaptive belief content in depression. Several factor analytic studies indicate that the DAS is a multidimensional measure, and that specific subscales such as "Need for Approval," "Need to Please Others," "Disapproval-Dependence," and "Success-Perfectionism" may provide a more sensitive and stable measure of the vulnerability constructs proposed by the cognitive model (A. Beck, Brown, Steer, & Weissman, 1991; see also Cane, Olinger, Gotlib, & Kuiper, 1986; Dyck, 1992). Calhoon (1996), however, failed to replicate the DAS factor structure of A. Beck et al. (1991) in a nonclinical student sample, suggesting that maladaptive beliefs may be less specific in nonclinical than clinical samples. In support of Beck et al.'s contention that DAS subscales may be more sensitive, J.O. Goldberg, Segal, Vella, and Shaw (1989) found that the DAS Approval by Others and Performance Evaluation subscales correlated with the Millon Clinical Multiaxial Inventory Dependency and Negativism subscales, respectively, in a sample of depressed outpatients.

The DAS subscales have been used to support the diathesis-stress hypothesis in relapsed depression. In a reanalysis of data from the NIMH Treatment of Depression Collaborative Research Program, Blatt and colleagues (Blatt, Quinlan, Pilkonis, & Shea, 1995) found that the DAS Perfectionism (i.e., Performance Evaluation) but not the Need for Approval subscale was a significant predictor of poor treatment outcome for depression. If the DAS subscales map onto the postulated vulnerability markers proposed by the cognitive theory better than the total score, they may evidence greater stability and predictive value than the total score.

In general, the research on the DAS Total Score as a marker of cognitive vulnerability for depression has not been supported when investigated in unprimed studies. Most studies have failed to find the persistence of elevated scores on the DAS beyond the depressive episode, suggesting that the endorsement of negative belief statements may reflect a symptom rather than a vulnerability factor in depression. However, it is premature to conclude that the DAS is merely another symptom measure of depression.

The persistence of cognitive vulnerability beyond the depressed state can only be tested by priming the latent maladaptive schemas. The cognitive theory holds that the cognitive structures are stable but their activation level varies depending on the current context. We have also seen that the DAS subscales may provide a finer-grain analysis of the dependency (i.e., sociotropic) and individualism (i.e., autonomous) constructs postulated by the cognitive model, and so it may be that certain DAS subscales will show more or less temporal stability than the Total Score, although more research is needed at the subscale level of analysis.

It is also possible that specific DAS items reflecting idiosyncratic core personal beliefs will show greater stability as vulnerability markers in depression-prone individuals. Reda et al. (1985) found that a subset of DAS belief items persisted beyond the depressive episode, although Haaga et al. (1991) raised several inconsistencies with this study. Nevertheless, research using idiographic assessment approaches are needed to determine whether vulnerable individuals may hold specific core personal beliefs that show the persistence expected of vulnerability constructs. Finally, more research is needed to investigate the stability or consistency of belief endorsement across time, situations, and different mood states. To date, the consistency of the DAS has been tested almost exclusively on episodic versus remitted depression using the DAS Total Score. However, CT predicts that item endorsements on the DAS will fluctuate because dysfunctional beliefs are latent during the nondepressed state. The theory proposes that personality traits like sociotropy and autonomy will show greater stability than dysfunctional attitudes (Blackburn, 1996), and so we turn now to research that has focused on this aspect of the cognitive model.

SOCIOTROPY AND AUTONOMY

To assess the cognitive-personality constructs of sociotropy and autonomy, a 60-item questionnaire was developed consisting of 30 sociotropic items and 30 autonomous items (A. Beck, Epstein, Harrison, & Emery, 1983). Initial item development and factor analysis conducted on 378 outpatients at the Center for Cognitive Therapy in Philadelphia revealed that the sociotropy items consisted of three dimensions, "Concern about Disapproval," "Attachment/Concern about Separation" and "Pleasing Others," whereas the autonomy items factored into "Individualistic Achievement," "Mobility/Freedom from Control by Others" and "Preference for Solitude." However, subsequent empirical research noted limitations with the SAS Autonomy Total Score and so a revision of the SAS was undertaken (D.A. Clark & Beck, 1991) that resulted in a 59-item revised version of the instrument (D.A. Clark et al., 1995). At the same time, Clive Robins and his colleagues (Robins et al., 1994) developed an alternative self-report measure of sociotropy and autonomy, called the Personal Style Inventory (PSI), which again attempted to rectify some of the psychometric problems found with the original SAS autonomy items.

A number of studies have been conducted on the concurrent and discriminant validity of the original 60-item SAS. The SAS Sociotropy Total Score correlates more highly with other construct-related measures of interpersonal dependency, as well as with measures of predictive constructs like anxiety, depression, depression-proneness, low self-esteem, neuroticism, and negative affectivity, than with measures of unrelated constructs like social desirability, positive affectivity, the Eysenck Personality Inventory subscales of Psychoticism and Extraversion, and the DAS Perfectionism subscale (Barnett & Gotlib, 1988b; Blaney & Kutcher, 1991; Cappeliez, 1993; D.A. Clark & Beck, 1991; Gilbert & Reynolds, 1990; Jolly, Dyck, Kramer, & Wherry, 1996; Moore & Blackburn, 1994; Nietzel & Harris, 1990; Pilon, 1989; Robins, 1985; Rude & Burnham, 1995; Sahin, Ulusoy, & Sahin, 1992; Talbot, 1994). Jolly et al. (1996), however, concluded from their analyses that sociotropy overlaps with the concept of negative affectivity (Watson & Clark, 1984), and so questions have been raised about the distinctiveness of sociotropy from other more general vulnerability constructs like neuroticism or negative affectivity. In a cluster analysis of the SAS based on 2,067 psychiatric outpatients (D.A. Clark, Steer, Haslam, Beck, & Brown, 1997), a sociotropic dependent cluster of patients had more extensive psychopathology, a severe generalized symptom presentation, and higher levels of negative self-referent thinking, a finding consistent with sociotropy as a nonspecific vulnerability factor for general distress.

Bieling et al. (1998) conducted separate exploratory factor analyses on the 30 sociotropy and 30 autonomy items of the SAS based on 2,067 outpatients of the Center for Cognitive Therapy in Philadelphia. Two sociotropy factors, "Excessive Fear of Other's Appraisal (Disapproval)" and "Preference for Affiliation," and two autonomy factors, "Independent Goal Attainment" and "Desire for Control/Fear of Losing Control," emerged from the two exploratory factor analyses conducted on 1,034 outpatients, and were supported by the findings from confirmatory factor analyses conducted on the other half of the sample ($n = 1,033$). Correlations with depressive symptom measures revealed that excessive fear of the disapproval of others was significantly more correlated with depression as measured by the BDI ($r = .39$), Hopelessness Scale ($r = .39$) and Hamilton Rating Scale of Depression ($r = .30$) than was preference for affiliation (r's ranged .20 to .22). For SAS Autonomy, desire for control/fear of losing control correlated positively with depression measures (r's ranged .19 to .10), whereas the independent goal attainment factor showed a negative correlation with the BDI, Hopelessness Scale, and Hamilton Rating Scale of Depression. Two conclusions can be drawn from this study. First, the sociotropy subscales had a closer relationship with depression than the autonomy subscales. And second, it is evident that there are both pathological and nonpathological elements to sociotropy and especially autonomy, as measured by the SAS. For sociotropy, excessive fear of disapproval was more pathological than preference for affiliation, whereas for autonomy the difference is even clearer with independent goal attainment showing a negative relationship with depression and desire for control/fear of losing control exhibiting a slight positive relationship with depression measures.

Another study on the construct validity of the SAS was reported by K.D. Baker, Nenneyer, and Barris (1997), in which they administered the SAS, DEQ, and Implications Grid, based on Kelly's (1955) personal construct theory, to 63 inpatients with *DSM-III-R* major depression or dysthymia. They found very little convergence between the SAS and DEQ. Not only did the DEQ Dependency and SAS Sociotropy ($r = -.05$), and Self-Criticism and Autonomy ($r = -.02$) subscales not correlate, but classification of depressed patients into personality subtypes based on the two questionnaires revealed that very few patients would be mutually classified by the two instruments. Analysis of responses to the Implicational Grid revealed that depressed patients classified as autonomous showed greater response to hypothetical shifts in self-construal only on the achievement issues, whereas the depressed sociotropic patients responded equally to self-construal shifts on dependency and achievement issues. The authors concluded that the DEQ and SAS assess distinct features of depression and that SAS Sociotropy may assess a general vulnerability factor, whereas SAS Autonomy may show greater vulnerability specificity with a more exclusive focus on achievement issues.

Although K.D. Baker et al. (1997) suggest that autonomy may have greater specificity than sociotropy, support for the construct validity of the SAS Autonomy Total Scale has been mixed. The Autonomy Total Score appears to have low correlations with a number of construct-related measures of autonomy, independence, self-criticalness, and conscientiousness. As well, SAS Autonomy did not correlate with symptom measures of depression or anxiety, or with self-esteem questionnaires. Moore and Blackburn (1994) administered a battery of self-report measures to clinically depressed patients and found that SAS Sociotropy correlated specifically with depression, but not anxiety, as well as with the DAS Total Score. SAS Autonomy, on the other hand, was not significantly correlated with BDI depression or the DAS. Thus researchers have questioned the construct validity of SAS Autonomy, concluding that the scale may produce inconsistent and nonsignificant results because of item heterogeneity. Some of the autonomy items deal with themes of solitude and insensitivity to others that appear more dysfunctional in nature, whereas other items represent achievement and independence issues that seem to assess rather healthy aspects of functioning (Barnett & Gotlib, 1998b; Bieling et al., 1998; Blaney & Kutcher, 1991; Pilon, 1989; Robins et al., 1994; Rude & Burnham, 1993). In fact, Robins and Block (1988) concluded from their study on the SAS and life events that autonomy may serve as "an event-buffer" against the development of depression. These findings, then, support our contention that there are maladaptive and adaptive aspects to sociotropy and autonomy, in particular (see Chapter 4).

Two new self-report measures were developed to address the limitations of SAS autonomy. Robins and colleagues developed a 48-item Revised Personal Style Inventory (PSI) to assess sociotropy and autonomy (Robins et al., 1994). The 24 sociotropy items deal with concern about what others think, dependency, and pleasing others, whereas the 24 autonomy items assess perfectionism/self-criticalness, need for control, and defensive separation. Findings from various studies indicate that PSI sociotropy and autonomy show good convergent and discriminant correlations with measures of related personality and vulnerability constructs (Flett, Hewitt, Garshowitz, & Martin, 1997; Robins et al., 1994; Zuroff, 1994). Furthermore as evidenced in the following sections, the PSI scales have been shown to be differentially associated with the expected types of life events and symptom composites in depression.

Robins et al. (1994) claimed that the PSI is an improvement over the SAS because PSI Autonomy is correlated with depression measures. However, D.A. Clark et al. (1995) found that the PSI Autonomy Scale had a higher correlation with the Revised SAS Sociotropy Scale ($r = .27$) than with the Revised SAS Independence ($r = .20$) subscale. Zuroff (1994) also reported a moderate correlation between PSI Sociotropy and Autonomy ($r = .35$ for men; $r = .30$ for women), which is probably due to the inclusion of self-criticism items in PSI Autonomy. Self-criticism is a more general construct that is associated with both achievement and interpersonal concerns (D.A. Clark et al., 1995), and self-criticism as a vulnerability factor overlaps with self-criticism as a symptom of depression. This overlap is problematic because predictors (i.e., self-criticism) should be distinct from the phenomena they intend to predict (i.e., depressive symptoms) if researchers are to avoid tautology. Also the higher correlation between PSI Sociotropy and Autonomy is undesirable if one wishes to study specific vulnerability factors in depression (Barnett & Gotlib, 1988c; Coyne & Whiffen, 1995). Finally, it should be noted that many of the items on PSI Sociotropy were drawn from the SAS, and so the high correlation between the sociotropy scales of the two instruments is to be expected ($r = .76$; D.A. Clark et al., 1995). In many recent studies, researchers have assumed that the PSI is a better measure of sociotropy and autonomy than the SAS.

Our review of the psychometric studies suggests that it remains unclear whether the PSI represents a significant improvement over the SAS, particularly the Revised SAS.

A second attempt to improve on the measurement of sociotropy and autonomy was undertaken in our own laboratory. Thirty-three new autonomy items were written to assess characteristics of the autonomous personality that were not covered extensively in the original SAS (i.e., holding excessively high standards of achievement, action-orientation to work, insensitivity to the social effects of one's actions, primary focus on positive outcomes, less reflective mode of thinking, rigid and dogmatic stance on issues, and excessive striving for individualistic expression). Psychometric analyses (D.A. Clark & Beck, 1991; D.A. Clark et al., 1995) carried out on successive samples of college students resulted in a 59-item SAS consisting of one Sociotropy scale (29 items), and two autonomy subscales, Solitude/insensitivity toward others (13 items) and Independence (17 items). Only two of the 29 Sociotropy items were from the new item pool indicating that the Revised SAS Sociotropy is practically identical to the original 30-item SAS Sociotropy Scale. On the other hand, the two new autonomy subscales, Solitude and Independence, are quite different from the original SAS Autonomy because they contain many items from the new item pool. Initial studies with the Revised SAS look promising. One of the autonomy subscales, SAS Solitude, showed the predicted relationships with depression and other construct-related measures (D.A. Clark et al., 1995). SAS Independence was not correlated with depression but was associated with measures of positive functioning and adjustment, a finding consistent with the negative correlation between the SAS Independent Goal Attainment subscale of autonomy and depressive symptoms reported by Bieling et al. (1998).

In the only other published study to date on the Revised SAS, Dunkley, Blankstein, and Flett (1997) administered a 74-item version of the SAS-R (a precursor to the more recent 59-item SAS-R), the NEO-PI-R, DEQ, and CES-D to 233 undergraduates. The authors report data only on the SAS Sociotropy and Solitude subscales. Zero-order and semipartial correlations revealed that SAS Sociotropy and DEQ Dependency were predicted by NEO-PI-R high agreeableness (compassionate, supportive toward others) and neuroticism, whereas SAS Solitude and DEQ Self-Criticalness were uniquely predicted by high neuroticism and low agreeableness. Hierarchical regression analysis revealed that much of the relationship between SAS Sociotropy and Solitude, on the one hand, and depression on the other, is through shared variance with neuroticism. In men, however, Sociotropy and Solitude accounted for a small but significant amount of unique variance in CES-D scores beyond neuroticism, whereas for women only Solitude emerged as a significant unique predict of depression scores after partialing out neuroticism. The authors, however, concluded that although SAS Sociotropy and Solitude have strong relations with neuroticism, they are also clearly distinguishable constructs in terms of their interpersonal content and, to a lesser extent, their small but unique relation to depression.

These initial results, then, support our contention that solitude/insensitivity to others might constitute the vulnerability feature of autonomy, whereas independence is more likely an adaptive personality orientation (see also Bieling & Olshan, 1998; Bieling et al., 1998). However, too few studies have used the Revised SAS and the measure has not been employed with a clinically depressed sample so it is unknown whether the revised measure is a significant improvement over the original SAS autonomy scales.

The cognitive theory predicts that personality traits are more stable than depressotypic beliefs (Blackburn, 1996). However, some people will show a predominantly sociotropic or autonomous personality orientation, whereas others may have a fairly evenhanded mixture of both personality orientations (A. Beck, 1983). As well, individuals can shift from one personality suborganization to the other depending on the context and other factors. Because of this, sociotropy and autonomy are considered to be largely orthogonal or uncorrelated factors. As superordinate schemas or central value systems, sociotropy and autonomy will show greater stability than more specific beliefs (though not necessarily the core beliefs of the self-schemas), but given the strong situational and behavioral influences on personality, one should not expect an exceptionally high level of stability, especially across situations (A. Beck & Epstein, 1982; for discussion, see also Blatt & Maroudas, 1992, p. 161).

Only a few studies have examined the stability of SAS Sociotropy and Autonomy in remitted depression. Moore and Blackburn (1996) investigated the stability of the SAS in 119 patients with primary unipolar depression after 16 weeks of either cognitive therapy or medication. The test-retest correlation for SAS Sociotropy and Autonomy was .77 and .72, respectively, and there was no significant change on either scale between testing sessions, although patients who were asymptomatic after 16 weeks showed a significant decline on SAS Sociotropy but not on SAS Autonomy. These results suggest that SAS Sociotropy and Autonomy have some degree of stability with moderate changes in mood but sociotropy may be sensitive to large changes in mood. In a more recent study, Scott et al. (1996) followed 20 patients given medication treatment for depression over a 3- and 6-month follow-up period. Over 6 months, the DAS Total Score decreased significantly from pretreatment levels, whereas the SAS Sociotropy and Autonomy scores did not change significantly. Sociotropy but not autonomy correlated with the DAS Total Score, whereas higher SAS Autonomy scores predicted recovery from depression at six months. SAS Sociotropy showed no relation to outcome at 3 or 6 months.

In a study involving 20 currently depressed, 20 remitted depressed patients, and 20 normal controls, Franche and Dobson (1992) found that both the currently and remitted depressed groups had significantly higher social dependency scores on the Depressive Experiences Questionnaire and the Interpersonal Dependency Inventory than normal controls. Given the moderately high correlation between the DEQ Dependency subscale and the SAS Sociotropy Scale (D.A. Clark et al., 1995; Robins, 1985), this finding supports the consistency of sociotropy or dependency as a stable vulnerability factor related to one's personal schema rather than as a mood-congruent marker of episodic depression (Franche & Dobson, 1992). Fairbrother and Moretti (1998) administered the Personal Style Inventory, BDI, BAI, and Selves Questionnaire, a measure of actual-ideal and actual-ought self-discrepancy, to 28 clinically depressed, 20 remitted depressed, and 20 nondepressed individuals. Analysis revealed that PSI Sociotropy and Autonomy correlated significantly with both indices of self-discrepancy, and that both personality dimensions and actual-ideal discrepancy accounted for significant variance in the BDI. Pairwise comparisons between groups revealed that the currently depressed tended to score higher on PSI Sociotropy than the remitted depressed group ($p < .06$) but the two subsamples showed no significant difference on PSI Autonomy. In turn, the remitted depressives scored significantly higher than controls on PSI Sociotropy and tended to score higher on PSI Autonomy ($p < .07$). These findings, then, support the consistency of elevated sociotropy and autonomy across currently and remitted depressed samples.

In an analysis involving 715 outpatients of the Center for Cognitive Therapy, Philadelphia, factor analysis of the SAS produced two sociotropic dimensions, "Approval/Acceptance" and " Closeness to Others," and one dimension of autonomy consisting mainly of items involving individualistic achievement and mobility or freedom of control from others. Test-retest correlations on 108 patients who received 12 weeks of cognitive therapy revealed moderately high temporal stability on all three scales (Approval/Acceptance $r = .57$, Closeness to Others $r = .79$, Autonomy $r = .63$), although significant reductions were evident on the two sociotropic factor scales but not on the autonomy scale. Comparison of relatively pure anxious and depressed groups revealed that the depressed patients scored significantly higher on Approval/Acceptance and the anxious had a nonsignificant trend ($p = .08$) to score higher on Closeness to Others, whereas there were no diagnostic group differences on the SAS autonomy scale.

These findings, though tentative, suggest that sociotropy and autonomy may be more stable than the beliefs assessed by the DAS (Blackburn, 1996). Furthermore, the significant correlations between SAS Sociotropy and the DAS Total Score, as well as the differential scores evident with diagnostic groups, support our earlier view that sociotropy may be more pathologically oriented with a saturation of items relevant to neuroticism or vulnerability to general distress (see also Bieling & Olshan, 1998 for similar conclusion). On the other hand, SAS Autonomy has emerged as one of the most stable of the depression personality constructs, but its overall relation to depression, especially the independence factor, remains uncertain. Nevertheless, these initial findings suggest that sociotropy and possibly some aspects of autonomy may represent enduring personality traits with relevance to depression.

Stability of Information Processing Bias

The failure to find negative schemas in nondepressed vulnerable individuals may be due to the use of self-report measures. If these vulnerability schemas are latent in nondepressed individuals who are predisposed to depression, then one cannot expect depression-prone individuals to have conscious access to the contents of these schemas and therefore endorse dysfunctional belief statements. Gotlib and McCabe (1992) argued that questionnaires that rely on conscious and deliberate responses cannot represent latent automatically activated structures and so provide a poor test of cognitive vulnerability. If this argument holds, then one should find greater temporal stability and a more consistent performance of episodic and recovered depressives on information processing tasks that do not rely on conscious self-report.

Some studies have failed to find persistence of negative processing bias or increased accessibility to negative cognitive constructs with recovery from depression. Segal and Gemar (1997) found a significant reduction in negative interference scores for self-relevant adjectives on the primed emotional Stroop color-naming task in depressed patients who improved following cognitive therapy for depression. No relationship was found between change in depression and positive interference scores. McCabe and Gotlib (1993) found that individuals who had recovered from their depression no longer exhibited a selective attentional interference effect from negative content adjectives in a focused-attention dichotic listening task. Gotlib and Cane (1987) also found that recovered depressed patients no longer showed color-naming interference to depressed-content words in an emotional Stroop task. Herbert, Nelson-Gray, and Herbert (1989) failed to find differences between remitted depressed individuals and a never-depressed group in their response to tachistoscopic presentation of rational and irrational statements. Teasdale, Taylor, et al. (1995) also found in their DAS sentence completion study that improvement in depression was associated with a significant reduction in dysfunctional positive stem completions.

Studies employing SRET have again failed to find persistence of a bias to rate negative trait adjectives as more self-descriptive or to show a selective recall bias for negative self-referent trait adjectives in remitted depression (Bradley & Mathews, 1988; Dobson & Shaw, 1987), though Teasdale and Dent (1987) did find that in a neutral mood state recovered depressed women endorsed more negative trait adjectives and recalled fewer positive (but not negative) words than never depressed women. Hammen, Miklowitz, & Dyck (1986) also found that dysphoric students who showed an enhanced recall for negative self-reference words at Time 1 did not show this effect at Time 2 if they were no longer depressed. Lewinsohn and Rosenbaum (1987) found that currently depressed individuals recalled their parents more negatively, whereas the remitted depressed group did not differ from the never depressed in their recall of parental behavior. Moretti et al. (1996) reported that their remitted depressed group was more similar to nondyphoric participants than a currently depressed group in perceiving that positive facial expressions were more interpersonally informative for making self-evaluative judgments than were negative facial expressions. Finally, Blackburn et al. (1990) failed to find any significant differences in the P300 evoked potential amplitude of recovery depressed or normal groups when processing positive or negative trait words.

Not all the studies have failed to find stability of negative information processing bias. Hedlund and Rude (1995) found that formerly depressed patients responded in a significantly more negative direction than never depressed individuals on two information processing tasks—scrambled sentences and incidental recall tasks but not on a Stroop color-naming exercise. The researchers concluded that negative cognitive processing is not only concomitant to depression but that it can be demonstrated in depression-prone individuals.

Gilboa and Gotlib (1997) randomly assigned previously dysphoric and never dysphoric participants to a positive or negative autobiographical mood induction condition. Although the previously dysphoric group showed more persistent dysphoria to the negative mood induction than the never-dysphoric group, the two groups did not differ significantly in their performance on an emotional Stroop color-naming task following negative mood induction. Both groups showed greater interference for negative words following the negative mood induction versus the positive mood manipulation. In a second experiment, Gilboa and Gotlib (1997) again found that the previously dysphoric had more persistent dysphoria in response to the negative mood induction but again failed to differ from the never depressed in their Stroop color-naming performance. However, the previously dysphoric did recall more negative words than did the never-dysphoric group, but this difference was independent of current mood state. The authors concluded from their findings that negatively biased memory recall may be a persistent vulnerability marker for depression or dysphoria, whereas attentional and judgmental biases may not be markers of cognitive vulnerability to depression. Moreover, the previously dysphoric group's greater persistence of dysphoric mood following the negative mood induction suggests that affect regulation style (i.e., tendency to experience longer dysphoric mood) may play a role in elevating one's vulnerability to depression or dysphoria.

The empirical research is equivocal on whether information processing studies provide a better measure of enduring cognitive vulnerability to depression than self-report instruments. The tacit cognitive processes of selective attention, encoding, and retrieval assessed by these studies appear to be concomitants of depression, although the findings of Rohde, Lewinsohn, and Seeley (1990) remind us that most psychosocial variables associated with depression are state dependent. Also, Gilboa and Gotlib's (1997) findings indicate that memory recall may be a better marker of persistent vulnerability to depression than the presence of negative attentional or possibly even judgmental bias. However, one would have to be cautious in concluding that experimental information processing is better suited for assessing cognitive vulnerability than self-report measures. The two approaches are complementary but provide only an indirect measure of latent schemas because they rely on processes that are the by-products of schema activation. It is unlikely, then, that the lack of stability of measures like the DAS can be attributed to the use of self-report questionnaire methodology. The following section presents another explanation that is far more plausible in accounting for the difficulties in demonstrating negative cognitive endurance beyond episodic depression.

PRIMING AND THE MOOD-STATE DEPENDENT HYPOTHESIS

One of the main challenges for research on cognitive vulnerability is the necessity to take into account the CT view that the cognitive structures and contents or schemas that are hypothesized as the predisposing cognitive basis of depression are latent or inaccessible during the nondepressed state (A. Beck, 1964, 1967; Kovacs & Beck, 1978). CT argues that a variety of stimuli or contextual cues may prime or activate maladaptive depression-related schemas. Furthermore, the maladaptive schemas may come to be evoked more easily by a wider range of stimuli and more completely dominate the cognitive organization with successive reactivation (Kovacs & Beck, 1978). Thus the notion of priming or activation of latent dysfunctional schemas is a core feature of the cognitive model. *The inconsistent findings reviewed previously for unprimed schematic measures in remitted depressives is entirely predicted by the cognitive model.* It is therefore incumbent upon researchers interested in causal factors in depression to first determine whether latent dysfunctional cognitive structures can be primed in vulnerable nondepressed individuals, the range of effective priming stimuli, and the effect of primed maladaptive schemas on cognitive and emotional functioning (Haaga et al., 1991; Segal & Dobson, 1992). Segal and Ingram (1994) define priming as:

> a collection of procedures or techniques for the activation of a hypothetical mental structure, often without the subject's conscious recollection that such activation has occurred. (p. 667)

In the past, only a few studies actually ensured that negative self-referent cognitive structures had been activated or primed in nondepressed states (Haaga et al., 1991; Segal & Ingram, 1994). This is particularly true of earlier studies on the stability of the DAS in remitted depression. Researchers, however, have begun to recognize the necessity of priming negative schemas in nondepressed and remitted depressed individuals. Three main priming methodologies have been identified in the cognitive-clinical literature; schema-congruent stressors, negative mood state induction, and presentation of words or phrases that have conceptual or associative links with negative self-referent cognitive content (Segal & Ingram, 1994). Schema activation via event priming is discussed under the onset and relapse hypotheses. For now, we are focusing on empirical research that has used mood or cognitive (conceptual) priming methodologies.

Emotional Priming

Persons and Miranda (1992) proposed a mood-state dependent hypothesis to explain the apparent lack of persistence in dysfunctional attitudes as evidenced by the failure of remitted depressives to show elevated scores on the DAS. They begin with the CT view that dysfunctional attitudes are latent in depression-prone individuals (i.e., remitted depressed patients) but add that individuals' ability to consciously report on these beliefs depends on their current mood state. The more negative the mood state, the more likely it is that vulnerable persons can report the content of their dysfunctional schemas.

Persons and Miranda (1992) contend that negative mood state may prime or activate latent dysfunctional schemas because mood is encoded in an associative memory network along with the dysfunctional belief. If dysfunctional beliefs in vulnerable individuals are tightly linked to negative mood, then access to these beliefs may be difficult unless a negative mood state is reinstated (Miranda & Gross, 1997). Three predictions are derived from this hypothesis. First, scores on self-report measures of dysfunctional schematic content and processes will not be elevated in remitted depressive and other vulnerable individuals who are not in a negative mood state because the dysfunctional beliefs are deactivated, latent, or inaccessible. Second, reinstatement of negative mood will lead to elevated scores on measures of dysfunctional beliefs in vulnerable (i.e., remitted depressives) but negative mood will not affect the scores of nonvulnerable individuals because they have never learned the dysfunctional beliefs and so they are not encoded in the associative network. The third prediction is that dysfunctional thinking or vulnerability will predict subsequent depressive symptoms in recovered depressives who are in a negative mood but vulnerability will not predict depressive symptoms in recovered patients in a positive mood state (Miranda & Gross, 1997; Persons & Miranda, 1992).

Miranda and Gross (1997) in their review of the empirical evidence for the mood-state dependent hypothesis noted that there was both indirect and direct evidence for the hypothesis. Indirect evidence is provided by studies showing that individuals with a prior history of depression or dysphoria (i.e., vulnerable) had significantly more negative self-referent thinking, encoding, and recall bias than individuals without a prior history of depression (i. e., nonvulnerable) only when a negative mood state is induced. Hedlund and Rude (1995) found that previously depressed individuals recalled a greater number of negative words and had more negatively biased interpretations on two out of three information processing tasks after a self-focused manipulation. However, the authors state that the self-focus manipulation was not intended to induce a depressed mood and analysis of the BDI and Multiple Affect Adjective Checklist subscales failed to reveal any significant differences between the formerly depressed and never depressed groups. Thus findings from this study could be viewed as contradictory to the mood-state dependent hypothesis because negative information processing was demonstrated in remitted depressives despite no significant elevation in dysphoric mood.

Teasdale and Dent (1987) found that, in normal mood state, recovered depressed women endorsed significantly more global negative trait adjectives as self-descriptive than never-depressed women. Although showing poorer recall of positive trait words, there were no group differences on recall of negative trait adjectives. During a sad mood manipulation, the recovered and never-depressed groups did not differ in the number of negative words rated as self-descriptive but the recovered depressed group *recalled* significantly more negative words endorsed as self-descriptive and significantly fewer positive trait words than the never-depressed group. Using a dichotic listening task, Ingram et al. (1994b) found that formerly depressed participants made more tracking errors to a neutral story when presented with a series of positive or negative distracter words in the unattended ear than never depressed individuals but only if exposed to a sad musical mood induction. Moreover, the vulnerable (i.e., remitted depressed) individuals showed enhanced attentional allocation to both positive and negative stimuli. As noted previously, Gilboa and Gotlib (1997) failed to find differences between previously dysphoric and never-dysphoric groups on color-naming interference or incidental recall of negative words as a function of negative mood induction.

Miranda (1992) found that dysfunctional thinking was predicted by the occurrence of negative life events in individuals with a prior history of depression but not in a group of never-depressed individuals. This interaction, though, occurred independent of current level of depression suggesting that presence of negative mood was not necessary for the activation of dysfunctional thinking by stressors. The indirect evidence for the mood-state dependent hypothesis is equivocal because it is not at all clear whether induction of a negative mood state in vulnerable individuals is associated with the type of negative information processing biases that reflects activation of depressotypic schemas.

More direct support for the mood-state dependent hypothesis has been tested in a few studies that investigated whether presence of a negative mood state is associated with an increase in the endorsement of dysfunctional attitudes in vulnerable but not in nonvulnerable persons. Miranda and Persons (1988) found that nondepressed women with a history of episodes of depressive states reported significantly higher DAS scores than nondepressed women without past depression only if they completed the DAS while in a negative mood induction state. Negative mood induction did not have this priming effect in women without a history of depression. Similar results have been obtained in other studies (Miranda, Persons, & Byers, 1990), and in a study by Miranda, Gross, Persons, and Hahn (cited in Miranda & Gross, 1997), an increase in negative mood resulting from viewing a sad film led to an increase in dysfunctional attitudes in formerly depressed but not never-depressed individuals.

Roberts and Kassel (1996) found support for the mood-state dependent hypothesis in a study of undergraduates classified as "remitted dysphorics" or "never dysphoric" on the basis of a self-report depression diagnostic measure. The remitted dysphoric group, who also had significantly heightened current depressive symptoms, showed significant correlations between negative affect (but not low positive affect), positive and negative cognitions, dysfunctional attitudes, and self-esteem; whereas there was no significant correlation between negative affect and cognitive measures for the never-dysphoric group. The authors interpret these findings as evidence that automatic thoughts, dysfunctional attitudes, and low self-esteem are mood-state dependent phenomena in depression-prone persons.

Findings less supportive of the mood-state dependent hypothesis have also been reported. Blackburn and Smyth (1985) did not find that recovered depressives exposed to a sad mood induction scored higher on the DAS than never-depressed controls. This negative finding, however, could be due to the failure of the mood manipulation procedure. Also, vulnerable nondepressed individuals as determined by elevated levels of negative automatic thoughts or endorsement of dysfunctional attitudes may be more sensitive to sad mood manipulations than nonvulnerable individuals (Stiles & Gotestam, 1989; Stiles, Schroder, & Johansen, 1993). This suggests that dysfunctional thinking can also prime negative mood states versus negative mood priming dysfunctional cognition, as emphasized by the mood-state dependent hypothesis.

Dykman (1997) randomly assigned never-depressed and recovered-depressed college students to a positive, negative, or no induction mood manipulation. All participants completed the DAS while in the induced mood state, and in a second session one week later, they imagined themselves in positive and negative situations and rated how depressed or happy they would feel in each situation. Contrary to the mood-state dependent hypothesis, correlations between the DAS and resting mood state was similar in the recovered and never-depressed groups. Furthermore, the recovered depressives did not show a differential increase in their endorsement of dysfunctional attitudes with a negative mood induction compared with the never-depressed group, nor was there any association between depressed mood reactions at Time 2 and differential priming of dysfunctional attitudes in recovered and never-depressed individuals at Time 1. In fact, as predicted by the cognitive theory, dysfunctional attitudes were predictive of future depressive reactions regardless of the presence or absence of a previous history of depression. The findings from this study, then, are not supportive of the mood-state dependent hypothesis.

Before leaving the topic of emotional priming, two caveats are worth noting. First, although we acknowledge that negative mood and latent dysfunctional schemas in vulnerable individuals may be more closely coupled than in nonvulnerable persons, we do not agree with Persons and Miranda (1992) as to the mechanisms responsible for this "emotional priming" effect. Instead, we agree with Riskind (1989) and interpret the effects of negative mood-induction manipulations on accessibility to dysfunctional schemas as a result of *cognitive priming*. This is apparent with the Velten procedure in which participants are given self-evaluative statements to read. However, even the musical mood-induction requests that subjects try to get into the mood suggested by the music, leaving open the possibility that subjects may use cognitive processes such as negative personal memories to instill a dysphoric mood.

Based on the cognitive theory, Riskind (1989) argued that mood should be conceptualized as a cognitive state in which mood induction cognitively primes self-referent schemas thereby leading to increased recall of schema-congruent self-referent material. Thus studies on the mood-state dependent hypothesis cannot rule out a competing explanation—that the increased accessibility to dysfunctional beliefs among vulnerable individuals may be the result of *cognitive priming* facilitated by the mood-induction procedure as opposed to the activation of an emotion associative network that then elicits the dysfunctional belief. In fact, the diathesis-stress component of the cognitive theory (discussed under the depression onset hypothesis) postulates that an external event activates negative self-schemas so that the occurrence of the negative mood state is one aspect of the depression. If one assumes that mood state primes cognition, then what processes account for the mood state? The cognitive model argues that cognitive structures and processes are involved in the induction of a negative mood state as part of the depressive experience.

On a related vein, we can't accept Persons and Miranda's (1992) contention that cognitive vulnerabilities will only be apparent during negative mood states. Rather, the activation of dysfunctional attitudes will predict depressive symptoms whether or not the current mood state is negative, and whether or not the individual has a past history of depression. Thus differential predictions can be derived from the two models with the mood-state dependent hypothesis predicting significant interactions between current mood and dysfunctional attitudes only with recovered depressives, whereas the cognitive model predicts direct relations between dysfunctional attitudes and depressive symptoms in all persons for whom these attitudes have been activated.

Miranda and Gross (1997) have proposed a revision of the mood-state dependent hypothesis that brings it more in line with the cognitive model. They suggest that there may be multiple points of potential difference between vulnerable and nonvulnerable individuals in how negative emotion might lead to dysfunctional thinking and depression. In particular, they suggest an early evaluation phase in which vulnerable individuals may be more likely to engage in biased negative evaluation of external or internal stimuli leading to more negative feelings that then precipitate brief episodes of dysfunctional thinking. This reformulation of the mood-state dependent hypothesis more closely resembles the CT interpretation of mood and dysfunctional attitudes in vulnerable individuals as reflecting the effects of cognitive priming on latent maladaptive schemas.

Cognitive Priming

Most of the studies that have employed priming methodologies to activate latent maladaptive cognitive structures have relied on the use of negative mood induction procedures with vulnerable (i.e., formerly depressed) individuals. Segal and Ingram (1994), however, noted that cognitive or conceptual priming can also be used in which subjects are presented with primes (e.g., words, phrases) that are semantically linked with the hypothesized latent depressotypic construct or schema. According to cognitive theory, presentation of negative prime stimuli lead to negative information processing bias in vulnerable individuals but not in nonvulnerable persons because the negative word primes activate or trigger latent depressotypic schemas in the vulnerable individuals.

Only a very few studies have utilized semantic primes to test for information processing differences in formerly depressed and never-depressed individuals. Gotlib and Cane (1987) used a semantic priming manipulation with their modified Stroop color-naming procedure but failed to find increased interference effects for negatively valenced target words after depressed patients were discharged from the hospital. Segal and Gemar (1997) found a reduction in negative interference scores on a primed emotional Stroop color-naming task with patients who were less depressed following treatment with cognitive therapy. Although too few studies have investigated the effects of cognitive priming methodologies in recovered depressives, the preliminary results are not as supportive for the persistence of depressotypic schemas in remitted depression as evident for studies using an emotional priming manipulation. This very much contrasts with our conclusion in Chapter 7 that the introduction of semantic priming manipulations provided more consistent support of the increased accessibility of negative self-constructs in episodic depression. Priming procedures may have to be more robust and direct with recovered asymptomatic depressives. For example, more meaningful, personally significant phrases depicting stressful events as opposed to single negative trait words might be a more effective prime for activating the latent maladaptive schemas in remitted depression. More exploratory research is needed to determine whether a certain type of semantic stimuli can be used to prime dysfunctional schemas in depression-prone individuals. In our discussion of the relapse hypothesis, we describe studies which show that negative life events and situations can trigger the latent negative constructs in depression.

CONCLUSION

As noted, for a variable to be a vulnerability marker of depression it must be sensitive, specific, and stable (Ingram et al., 1998; Segal & Ingram, 1994). As shown in this review, studies that have not included a priming manipulation have found that most depression cognitive measures are state dependent, with levels of negative thinking and endorsement of dysfunctional attitudes returning to within the normal range once the depression remits. However, these studies are based on a misunderstanding of the cognitive theory of depression and so do not provide a relevant test of cognitive vulnerability. The results are entirely consistent with the predictions of cognitive theory that depressotypic schemas remain latent and inaccessible in asymptomatic depression-prone individuals unless reactivated by a priming stimulus. Furthermore, Segal and Ingram noted that most of the studies showing a lack of persistence of dysfunctional attitudes in remitted depression (a) failed to take into account the effects of treatment on cognitive measures, (b) used a variety of depressive cognition measures, (c) adopted inconsistent criteria for determining remission, and (d) failed to ensure that negative modes of thinking were indeed accessible prior to assessment (see also Ingram et al., 1998).

In keeping with cognitive theory, research on the stability of the DAS Total Score in asymptomatic formerly depressed individuals suggests that activation of maladaptive depressotypic schemas does not persist beyond the depressive episode. If elevated DAS scores had been present, then cognitive theory predicts that these individuals would still be depressed. Most of these studies, however, failed to ensure that vulnerable nondepressed individuals actually had access to latent negative cognitive structures. Studies that included a priming manipulation, such as a mood induction, provided positive evidence for the persistence of dysfunctional beliefs in a latent form beyond the depressive episode. The DAS Total Score may not be the most stable measure of cognitive vulnerability because it provides a more global aggregated score across a variety of dysfunctional attitudes. Research is needed to determine whether specific DAS subscales provide a more sensitive and stable finer-grained assessment of cognitive vulnerability. It may be that the most stable and persistent indicator of cognitive vulnerability will be found with idiographic indicators of dysfunctional beliefs or individual item endorsements. For example, an individual who holds the core belief "I am unlovable" may show temporal stability only on DAS items that directly assess this core belief. Muran et al. (1994) reported only slight changes in negative self-schema appraisals across cognitive therapy sessions for eight outpatients using an idiographic self-scenario assessment process. These results may indicate that a greater level of persistence and sensitivity will be achieved with measures that focus on specific individualized core self-schema content rather than with the more generalized nomothetic retrospective self-report questionnaires of schema content.

As predicted by the cognitive model, greater persistence was evident with measures of predepressive personality, especially the SAS Autonomy Total Score, than with measures of dysfunctional beliefs. Although only a few studies have compared currently depressed and formerly depressed groups on the SAS, these initial studies found some evidence that cognitive-personality vulnerability is not merely a concomitant of depression. However, studies employing information processing paradigms to assess for the presence of negativity in the tacit cognitive processes associated with depression, such as attentional allocation, encoding, and retrieval, have not fared as well. Most studies have failed to find evidence of negative biased information processing in recovered depressives, suggesting that biased information processing is symptomatic of the depressive state. Gilboa and Gotlib (1997), however, suggested that negative memory recall bias may be a better marker of cognitive vulnerability to depression than negative attentional bias. This suggests that not all cognitive processes may be sensitive indicators of vulnerability so that research into the cognitive predisposition to depression may have to be more cognizant of whether particular information processing tasks are real markers of vulnerability.

In their extensive review of the priming studies, Ingram et al. (1998) concluded that there is considerable empirical support that priming prior to the introduction of cognitive assessment allows one to detect depressotypic cognition in asymptomatic depression-prone individuals. They further state that these priming effects have been demonstrated with measures of dysfunctional cognition and beliefs as well as studies on information encoding, retrieval, and attentional bias. Most of these studies, however, have relied on emotional priming procedures, especially mood induction, to elicit negative cognitive content in individuals with a prior history of depression, and so the robustness of these priming effects is unclear. Alternative priming procedures are needed that more clearly distinguish between cognitive and affective priming processes than the Velten mood induction procedure used in most previous studies.

To account for the findings with emotional priming, Persons and Miranda (1992) proposed a mood-state dependent hypothesis which asserts that a negative mood state must be created in vulnerable individuals before they have access to their latent negative cognitive constructs. They suggested that activation of an emotional associative network is the mechanism responsible for this mood-state dependent phenomena. We discussed several problems with the mood-state dependent hypothesis, not the least of which is the failure of some recent studies to support specific predictions of the hypothesis. We also believe the mechanism underlying the mood-state dependent effect is better explained in terms of cognitive priming than in activation of an emotion node in an associative network. The cognitive model does not agree with Persons and Miranda's (1992) contention that a negative mood state must be created to access negative cognitive content in vulnerable individuals. Rather, the necessary criterion is that the latent dysfunctional cognitive structures must be activated for depression-prone individuals to have access to their depressotypic cognitive content. This may or may not be achieved with the aid of mood induction manipulations, which in essence amount to a cognitive manipulation since participants are instructed to generate negative self-statements or distressing memories to elicit a sad mood state.

The lack of evidence for the persistence of cognitive dysfunction beyond the depressive episode is consistent with the cognitive theory of latent schemas. To demonstrate their latency, specialized strategies are necessary. The shift toward the inclusion of priming manipulations and measures or information processing tasks (i.e., incidental recall) indicative of more specific negative schematic content promises to provide a more direct test of the CT view of the persistence of latent dysfunctional schemas in depression-prone individuals. In Chapter 9, we consider two other primary hypotheses of cognitive vulnerability that deal with the diathesis-stress component of cognitive theory.

CHAPTER 9

Cognitive Vulnerability: Empirical Status of the Diathesis-Stress Hypotheses

THE DIATHESIS-STRESS component of the cognitive model of depression has without question received the most intense scrutiny by depression researchers of all of the cognitive vulnerability hypotheses. In Chapter 8, we emphasized that cognitive theory takes a diathesis-stress perspective on predisposition to depressive states, symptoms, and disorders. Cognitive vulnerability in the form of dysfunctional schemas and maladpative personality are diatheses that remain latent in the nondepressed state until primed or activated by an eliciting event or stimulus. The prime most actively researched as a trigger for maladaptive schemas is proximal negative life stressors and daily hassles.

Two aspects to the cognitive diathesis-stress hypothesis can be identified. In the early formulation of the cognitive model, it was proposed that maladaptive predisposing schemas remain latent in the depression-prone individual until activated by life stresses that may match traumatic situations from childhood or adolescence that led to the negative attitudes in the first place (A. Beck, 1967). Kovacs and Beck (1978) noted that eventually the range of circumstances that can trigger maladaptive schemas may expand so that situations only marginally similar to the original conditions under which the schemas developed can precipitate depression. Thus, situations that lower self-esteem, thwart important personal goals, or signal physical deterioration or death—or even nonspecific stressors that are perceived as overwhelming—can elicit psychological disturbance (A. Beck, 1967).

In a later refinement of the cognitive model, it was proposed that certain personality constellations, especially sociotropy and autonomy, may predispose individuals to be particularly responsive to situations that match the specific issues or sensibilities represented within their personality suborganization (A. Beck, 1983). Thus a congruence or match between the occurrence of certain types of external events and the existence of a specific personality constellation is more likely to produce a susceptibility to depression or other psychopathology than with external events that do not impinge on this vulnerability (A. Beck, 1991). An autonomous individual with maladaptive personality features (i.e., fear of losing control, solitude/insensitivity to others) is at greater risk of a depressive state than a more sociotropic person to situations perceived to constrain, frustrate, interfere, or represent a loss of self-determination, goal-oriented behavior, personal independence, and control. The highly sociotropic person with maladaptive personality features (i.e., fear of disapproval from others) is more susceptible to depression than the person invested in autonomy in response to events perceived as a loss of social resources, nurturance, and acceptance from others (A. Beck, 1983, 1987, 1991). Thus, whether a person overreacts to a particular set of circumstances depends on whether the events pierce his or her "Achilles heel," as reflected in the person's preponderance of maladaptive personality characteristics.

Four characteristics of the diathesis-stress hypothesis of the cognitive model must be recognized. First, the hypothesis emphasizes that it is not the mere occurrence of a congruent life event that triggers depression in vulnerable individuals, but rather it is the perception that an event impinges on personal issues or concerns that are central to the individual's self-view that can elicit a depressive response. Thus how individuals appraise or evaluate events is a critical mediating factor in the depressotypic property of the stressor. For example, a highly sociotropic individual may not become depressed in response to the breakup of a romantic relationship if the relationship is no longer of high personal value or importance to the individual. The diathesis-stress hypothesis, then, recognizes that the appraisal or meaning that the event has for the individual is an important determinant of a stressor's depression-eliciting potential. Events that are meaningful in their relevance to an individual's current definition and evaluation of self-worth will have a greater emotional impact on the individual than would less relevant events (Hammen, 1985; Hammen, Ellicott, Gitlin, & Jamison, 1989).

A second consideration is that the diathesis-stress hypothesis of the cognitive model is not applicable to all highly sociotropic or autonomous individuals. As noted, there are adaptive as well as maladaptive characteristics associated with each personality dimension. Thus susceptibility to depression in the face of negative social stressors will only be evident in sociotropic individuals who have a preponderance of maladaptive sociotropic schemas, whereas persons with more adaptive sociotropic schemas will show resistance to depression even when experiencing a negative interpersonal situation. The same differential outcome is predicted for autonomous individuals with a concentration of maladaptive versus adaptive autonomous schemas in response to a negative achievement event. Thus researchers must ensure that the maladaptive aspects of sociotropy and autonomy are adequately represented in any diathesis or personality measures used in cognitive diathesis-stress studies.

Third, it must be recognized that the cognitive model does not assert that the only pathway to depression is through the interaction of a congruent eliciting event and underlying cognitive vulnerability. Instead, cognitive theory has consistently recognized that there are multiple causal factors in depression involving any combination of biological, genetic, stress, or personality factors (A. Beck, 1967, 1987, 1991). In a letter to the *Archives of General Psychiatry*, Riskind and Steer (1984) stated this position succinctly:

> Actually, the model proposes that a confluence of factors contribute multiple causes of depression, and these factors include the following predisposing and precipitating conditions: (1) stress or loss, (2) deficiencies in problem-solving or social skills, (3) disequilibrium of the brain-blood chemistry, and (4) cognitive phenomena such as dysfunctional attitudes. (p. 1111)

The cognitive diathesis-stress hypothesis, then, is considered one possible pathway in the etiology of depression for some individuals. However, we would expect that a substantial number of people may develop a depression in the absence of the postulated match between predisposing cognitive diathesis and a congruent triggering life event. This would be particularly true for individuals who possess a high general vulnerability factor (e.g., are emotionally very fragile) or individuals who face overwhelming stress in their life.

And finally, the cognitive model considers cognitive vulnerability or diathesis a moderator variable in the relationship between negative life events and depression. Baron and Kenny (1986) define a moderator as a

> ... qualitative (e.g., sex, race, class) or quantitative (e.g., level of reward) variable that affects the direction and/or strength of the relation between an independent or predictor variable and a dependent or criterion variable. (p. 1174)

A moderator affects the causal relation between two variables and so is tested by the interaction term in multiple regression analyses when both the moderator and the independent variable are continuous. Mediators, on the other hand, account for the relationship between a predictor and the criterion variable and are generated by an independent or predictor variable. Kwon and Oei (1992) tested a model in which dysfunctional attitudes act as a *moderator* between negative life events and depression, whereas negative automatic thoughts act as a *mediator.* As a moderator, dysfunctional attitudes interact with negative life events to affect the occurrence of depressive symptoms, and negative automatic thoughts "mediate or transmit the impact of negative life events to affect the occurrence of depressive symptoms" (p. 311). The distinction Kwon and Oei have made between cognitive moderators and mediates is entirely consistent with our understanding of the role of dysfunctional attitudes and negative automatic thoughts in the negative life event-depression relationship.

DEPRESSION ONSET HYPOTHESIS

A negative event that matches the content of the prepotent self-schemas and maladaptive personality constellation associated with the primal loss mode will lead to a heightened risk of depression onset in persons with no previous diagnoseable depression.

In this section, we discuss the relevant empirical literature that has tested the depression onset hypothesis. Our review is restricted to studies that have used nonclinical individuals because this research is most applicable for identifying vulnerability markers for depressive states. Research on remitted depressives will be considered under the next hypothesis on relapse. Our reason for splitting the research literature between these two hypotheses is that studies testing cognitive diathesis-stress in remitted depression address a very different question than studies that test for vulnerability markers of depression in nondepressed, nonclinical samples. As noted in Chapter 1, there is a very high relapse and recurrence rate in depression. However, the cognitive variables and mechanisms involved in the onset of an initial episode may differ in important ways from the contribution these variables make in the recurrence of depressive symptoms. A strong version of the "scar hypothesis" suggests that the maladaptive information processing in depression is a scar or permanent residual deficit that is created by having experienced a depressive episode (Lewinsohn et al., 1981; Rohde et al., 1990). Although Ingram et al. (1998) concluded that there is no empirical evidence to support this strong version of the scar hypothesis, it may be that a weaker version of the hypothesis is more tenable. That is, episodic depression could lead to some changes in self-schematic structures such that negative self-schemas and cognitive processes are more readily activated (i.e., easily accessible) in the person who has experienced a serious depressive episode, as proposed by Teasdale's (1988) differential activation hypothesis. Whatever the ultimate finding on the scar hypothesis, it seems prudent at this point to provide separate reviews of the empirical studies using never-depressed and remitted-depressed samples.

We will include both cross-sectional and prospective research designs in this review. Cross-sectional studies provide only a weak test of cognitive diathesis-stress because they do not allow one to examine temporal causal connections between cognitive diathesis, stress, and the onset of depressive symptoms. Garber and Hollon (1991), however, noted that cross-sectional studies can make an important contribution by first identifying potentially causal variables that can be explored by the more powerful prospective research designs. Ingram et al. (1998) noted that cross-sectional research designs are an invaluable tool of descriptive psychopathology because they enable one to identify cognitive factors that may be specific to depression. Because of their correlational nature, however, cross-sectional designs cannot determine whether a cognitive variable is a cause or consequence of depression. Furthermore, cognitive theory considers cognitive constructs at the descriptive level (see Chapters 5–7), such as the cognitive triad, as neither cause nor consequence but rather an intrinsic part of the depression. These constructs are appropriately studied with cross-sectional designs. The schemas or beliefs and predepressive personality variables play a more contributory role in the pathogenesis of depression, and so prospective research designs offer a more powerful test of these constructs. Because prospective research designs can test for the temporal antecedence and causal status of the diathesis, greater weight will be placed on prospective or longitudinal studies of cognitive diathesis-stress (Barnett & Gotlib, 1988c; Haaga et al., 1991; Ingram et al., 1998).

Finally, as in our review of the empirical support for previous hypotheses, we will consider the research on the DAS, SAS, and other measures or indices of cognitive diathesis separately. Haaga et al. (1991) noted in their review of research relevant to the depression onset hypothesis that no published studies had investigated cognitive diathesis-stress as a predisposing factor in the onset of *syndromal* depression. Because of this, they suggested that diathesis-stress studies that examine whether cognitive vulnerability can lead to increased risk of depressive *symptoms* provide relevant supportive findings for the depression onset hypothesis. The studies reviewed in this section deal almost exclusively with cognitive diathesis-stress predictors of depressive symptom severity (i.e., elevations in BDI scores) because researchers have continued to focus most of their attention on the precipitants of depressive symptoms rather than diagnoseable depressive episodes. However, these studies are highly relevant for the onset hypothesis given the evidence for a continuity between milder depressive states and the more severe diagnoseable depressive episodes (see Chapter 1).

THE DAS AND DEPRESSION SYMPTOM ONSET

Cross-Sectional Research Design

Some of the earliest studies on cognitive diathesis-stress employed a cross-sectional research design, with the DAS Total Score as a measure of cognitive vulnerability (or the diathesis), and examined its interaction with life event measures in the prediction of depressive symptom severity, as assessed by the Beck Depression Inventory. According to the depression onset hypothesis, the interaction between the DAS and life events should be a significant predictor of BDI scores with high DAS scores in the presence of significant negative life events associated with an increase in depression.

Persons and Rao (1985) used a 21-item measure of dysfunctional beliefs to examine cognitive diathesis-stress in predicting depression severity in a sample of diagnostically mixed psychiatric inpatients. (We consider this a cross-sectional study because the authors used a stacked data set in which data collected at three different points of time were collapsed together in the same analysis.) The interaction between dysfunctional beliefs and negative life stressors was not significant, although maladaptive beliefs did have a direct relationship with BDI scores. The authors concluded that the failure of dysfunctional beliefs to interact with negative life events suggests that they are not involved in the development of depression.

Wise and Barnes (1986) reported a significant interaction between the DAS and frequency of self-reported negative life events in predicting BDI depression in a sample of nonclinical students but not in a sample of clinical students. However, the DAS and negative life events showed significant direct relationship with depression severity in the student clinical sample. Olinger, Kuiper, and Shaw (1987, Study 1) developed a self-report measure of life events that they thought might directly impinge on dysfunctional attitudes. The measure, called the Dysfunctional Attitudes

Scale—Contractual Conditions, was constructed by rewording DAS items so they referred to belief-specific events. Regression analysis with a student sample revealed a significant interaction between the DAS and the DAS-CC life event measure in predicting BDI depression. As well, high DAS scores were associated with elevated appraisal ratings on the importance and emotional impact of life events and with increased frequency of ruminative thoughts about one's negative life stressors. In a second nonclinical study (Olinger et al., 1987, Study 2), the interaction between DAS and life events was again confirmed using different measures of perceived stress and frequency of negative life experiences. In a later study, Kuiper, Olinger, and Martin (1988, Study 1) found a significant interaction between the DAS and frequency of daily hassles in predicting BDI scores in nonclinical students. In their second study (Kuiper et al., 1988, Study 2), high as opposed to low sores on the DAS in nonclinical students was associated with elevated levels of physiological arousal and self-reported anxiety when participants were required to perform a moderately stressful experimental task.

In a study based on a nonclinical African-American student sample, Schroeder (1994) found that the DAS and negative life events and daily hassles were significant direct predictors of BDI depression, but the interaction term failed to reach statistical significance. In their cross-sectional study, Kwon and Oei (1992, Study 1) used regression analysis and structural equation modeling with data collected on nonclinical students. They found that the interaction of dysfunctional attitudes and negative life events had both direct and indirect effects on BDI depression. As a direct effect, high DAS scores interacted with increased incidence of negative life events to predict elevated BDI, whereas in an indirect effect the interaction was mediated by the presence of negative automatic thoughts. These results, then, support Kwon and Oei's view of dysfunctional attitudes as a moderator and negative automatic thoughts as a mediator of the life event-depression relationship.

Somewhat different results were reported by Robins and his colleagues in two studies that compared the interaction and mediation hypotheses of dysfunctional attitudes, frequency of negative life events, and event perceptions. The former hypothesis proposes that depression is related to an interaction of event perceptions with event frequency, and that event perceptions, in turn, are a result of the interaction of dysfunctional attitudes and negative life event frequency (Robins, Block, & Peselow, 1990a). In contrast, the mediation hypothesis proposes that dysfunctional attitudes and life event frequency are related to depression through individuals' perceptions of life events. In two studies, one based on a student sample (Robins & Block, 1989, Study 2) and the other based on a comparison of clinically depressed and schizophrenic patients (Robins et al., 1990a), support was found for the mediation hypothesis in which dysfunctional attitudes and stressful life events were related to depression through life event perceptions. The interaction of dysfunctional attitudes and frequency of negative life events was not significantly related to BDI depression or diagnosis in either study, nor was there a significant interaction between frequency of negative events (or the event frequency × DAS interaction term) and event perceptions.

Miranda (1992) found that individuals with a history of depression endorsed more maladaptive beliefs, as assessed by the Cognitive Events Schedule, and reported higher subjective probabilities for negative views of the self, world, and future following stressful life events whereas these relationships were not evident in persons without a history of depression. However, Garber and Robinson (1997) did not find that children of mothers with a history of nonbipolar mood disorders, who could be considered at high risk for depression, had significantly higher DAS scores than low-risk children whose mothers had no history of depression. Nevertheless, Ingram et al. (1998) concluded from their review of high-risk research on children of depressed parents that there is some evidence that depressed mothers may indeed pass on negative cognitive characteristics to their children which then form the basis of the child's negative self-schema that can be activated by negative life events. This is based on research showing that depressed mothers and their children report more negative self-attributions than nondepressed mothers and their children. Also in a study by Taylor and Ingram (cited in Ingram et al., 1998), children of depressed mothers who participated in a negative mood induction showed lower endorsement of positive self-descriptive trait adjectives and enhanced recall of negative trait words in a self-referent encoding task; whereas children of nondepressed mothers evidenced no differences in recall. These differential findings held even after controlling for current levels of depression in the children.

A few studies have examined the relationship between life events and DAS subscales. Mongrain and Zuroff (1989) constructed anaclitic (i.e., social approval) and introjective (i.e., performance evaluation) subscales of the DAS and tested their relationship with undergraduate women's appraisal of the stressfulness of hypothetical anaclitic and introjective life events. There was a tendency for anaclitic and introjective attitudes to be related to increased stress appraisal ratings for their concordant hypothetical life event, although the relationships were weak and the prediction of anaclitic life events was qualified by a significant interaction between the DAS anaclitic and introjective subscales. In a cross-sectional study involving 329 undergraduates, Rude and Burnham (1993) failed to find a significant interaction between the DAS Approval by Others or Performance Evaluation subscales and negative interpersonal and achievement events, respectively.

Simons, Angell, Monroe, and Thase (1993) investigated the relationship between achievement and interpersonal subscales of the DAS and scores on a self-report (Psychiatric Epidemiology Life Events Research Interview; PERI) and an interviewer-based (Bedford College Life Events and Difficulties Schedule; LEDS) measure of life events. A large discrepancy was found between the self-report and interviewer-based life event measures, with the former yielding more life events and higher severity ratings than the latter. There was also evidence that dysfunctional attitudes influence the number of self-reported life events reported and perceived severity ratings for events occurring in a particular content domain. The DAS Achievement subscale was significantly associated with the frequency and severity ratings for PERI (but not LEDS) achievement events, although there was no significant relationship between self-reported interpersonal life events and the DAS Interpersonal subscale. Interestingly, the Attributional Style Questionnaire (ASQ) but not the DAS scores were associated with frequency of LEDS-defined dependent (but not independent) events in patients with no previous history of depression. The authors suggest that cognitive factors may be associated with the generation of stressful events prior to the onset of depression. These findings indicate that achievement-related dysfunctional attitudes can influence the number of events reported and how one rates their severity.

The cross-sectional studies suggest that high scores on the DAS and a greater number of stressful life events may increase one's level of depression. This interactive relationship has not been a consistent finding, however, and it may be stronger in nonclinical than clinical samples. Also it may be that the DAS shows stronger direct relations with depressive symptom severity in clinical groups. The results of Simons et al. (1993) also suggest that dysfunctional attitudes can influence individuals' reporting and appraisal ratings of life stressors. However, questions about the causal status of dysfunctional attitudes and life events can only be addressed with prospective research designs.

Prospective Research Designs

Barnett and Gotlib (1988a) administered the BDI, General Health Questionnaire, DAS, Life Experiences Survey, and a measure of social support to 57 female undergraduates on two occasions separated by a 3-month interval. The main effect of Time 1 DAS scores was not a significant predictor of BDI change scores at Time 2, nor did T1 DAS interact significantly with number of negative life events at Time 2. Although the three-way interaction of T1 DAS × T2 life events × T2 social support was not significant, the two-way interaction of T1 DAS × T2 social support was a significant predictor. University women with elevated dysfunctional attitudes and low perceived social support showed significantly greater increases in mild depression at T2.

Because of the small sample size and exclusive focus on women, Barnett and Gotlib (1990) sought to replicate their earlier study. Once again, measures of dysfunctional attitudes, life events, social support, and self-reported depressive symptoms were taken in 199 female and 69 male college students on two occasions separated by 3 months. Hierarchical regression analyses controlling for T1 BDI depression revealed that for women neither the main effects or interaction between the DAS Total Score (or the DAS Approval by Others or Performance Evaluation subscales) and negative life events predicted T2 BDI scores. However, there was a significant interaction between DAS and social support indicating that women with high DAS and low social support had an increase in depressive symptoms at T2. For men, neither the DAS Total Score nor subscales showed any direct relationships or interactions with life events in the prediction of T2 BDI scores. In both prospective studies, then, Barnett and Gotlib failed to find evidence that dysfunctional attitudes interacted with negative life events to predict mild depression or dysphoria.

Kwon and Oei (1992, Study 2) found that the interaction of negative life events and DAS scores did account for a small but significant variance in BDI scores at a 3-month reassessment in nonclinical students. Furthermore, results from structural equation modeling generally confirmed the moderating role of dysfunctional attitudes and the mediating role of negative automatic thoughts, though the integrated model had to be modified suggesting that some causal paths to the prediction of depression may be unstable. Wong and Whitaker (1994) did not find that the DAS or scores on the College Student Life Event Schedule contributed significantly to the prediction of BDI or CESD depression in a small sample of students retested at a 3-month follow-up, though both dysfunctional attitudes and life events were significantly associated with concurrent depression level. The interaction between dysfunctional attitudes and life events was not reported in their analyses.

In a recent prospective study involving university undergraduates, Dykman and Johll (1998) reported that neither the DAS nor its interaction with negative life events was a significant predictor of BDI depression at a 14-week reassessment when all participants were included in the analysis. However, the researchers argued that cognitive theory is best conceptualized as an *acute-onset model.* Following from the recommendation of Depue and Monroe (1986) that heterogeneity among high-scoring respondents should be limited when testing acute-onset models so that chronic

conditions are excluded, they reanalyzed their data by eliminating participants who were initially symptomatic for depressive symptoms (i.e., BDI
score greater than 9 at T1). Regression analyses revealed a significant
main effect for the DAS and the DAS × Stress interaction for the initially
asymptomatic but not the symptomatic students. For the students with
T1 BDI scores below 10, high stress and elevated levels of dysfunctional
attitudes predicted BDI scores at T2. Analysis for asymptomatic men and
women revealed the predicted DAS × Stress interaction for women but
not for men. Thus cognitive diathesis-stress conformed to an acute-onset
model with the DAS × Stress interaction evident only in participants who
were asymptomatic for depressive symptoms at T1. The researchers also
found that cognitive-event vulnerability was only evident in women and
not men. These findings suggest not only that gender differences may
exist in cognitive diathesis-stress vulnerability to depression but that
researchers should utilize an acute-onset model when testing cognitive
diathesis-stress hypotheses.

The preceding studies tested cognitive diathesis-stress vulnerability by
examining the relationship between the DAS and aggregrate scores on
life event checklists. A different methodological approach is to determine
whether elevated scores on the DAS predicts depressive symptoms in
participants undergoing a single common stressor. Stiles and Gotestam
(1988a) found that elevated scores on the DAS at the time of induction
into the Norwegian army predicted BDI scores 3 months later while the
recruits were posted in northern Norway and separated from their families. G.P. Brown, Hammen, Craske, and Wickens (1995) administered the
DAS and BDI to a group of undergraduates 3 or 4 days before a midterm
examination and then again 2 to 6 days after students received their examination grades. The stressor was examination performance measured
as the difference between students' expected and actual performance on
the exam. Hierarchical regression analysis with post-exam BDI as the dependent variable revealed significant interactions between the DAS Total
Score or its subscales (with the exception of the Vulnerability subscale),
and performance discrepancy on the midterm exam. The DAS Perfectionistic Achievement subscale showed the strongest interaction with the congruent stressor, poorer than expected exam performance, in predicting
elevated post-exam BDI scores. Students with higher scores on the DAS
administered before the exam and poorer than expected exam performance showed the highest levels of postexam self-reported depression.
These results not only support the cognitive diathesis-stress model, but
suggest that specific DAS subscales may confer particular vulnerability
when matched with a congruent stressful event.

Finally, the interaction of life events and dysfunctional attitudes has
also been investigated using measures other than the DAS. Lewinsohn

and colleagues conducted a large community study in which individuals completed a battery of measures on cognition, depression, life events, relationships, and self-esteem on two occasions separated by one year. Diagnosis at T2 was based on a semistructured interview using the Schedule for Affective Disorders and Schizophrenia, and dysfunctional attitudes were assessed with five items selected from the Personal Beliefs Inventory. In the first published report Lewinsohn et al. (1981) found that individuals who were not depressed at T1 but later became depressed during the one-year time period of the study (i.e., new cases) did not differ significantly on any of the T1 cognitive variables from the control group who were nondepressed on both assessment occasions. In a second set of analyses on this data set, Lewinsohn et al. (1988) found that T1 dysfunctional beliefs and other cognitive variables did not interact with an elevation in major life events in the prediction of depression symptom onset. However, the cognitive variables, including the Personal Beliefs Inventory, were better predictors of T2 depression level when assessed by the CES-D. This led Lewinsohn and colleagues to suggest that negative cognitive style is not directly an antecedent for developing a depressive episode but rather has indirect effects through its links with the development of negative affect, which itself may confer greater risk for depression. Thus dysfunctional attitudes are considered at best an indirect precipitant of depression and at worst a concomitant of the depressive episode. Furthermore, these data did not support the onset hypothesis as indicated by the failed interaction between dysfunctional attitudes and life events in predicting new cases of depression at T2. However, one can question whether the researchers adequately assessed cognitive vulnerability given their reliance on participants' responses to only five belief statements.

Summary

Our review of the relevant empirical research on dysfunctional attitudes and the depression onset hypothesis indicates inconsistency across studies on whether high scores on dysfunctional attitudes self-report measures represents a cognitive vulnerability that moderates the relationship between negative life events and increased risk for depression. Evidence for and against cognitive diathesis-stress can be found in both cross-sectional and prospective nonclinical studies. However, one can discern several trends from these studies. First, enough studies have reported findings consistent with the depression onset hypothesis to suggest some merit in further research with the DAS as a measure of cognitive diathesis for depressive symptoms and disorders.

Second, more favorable results may be obtained with asymptomatic nonclinical samples because this allows for a better test of cognitive vulnerability within an acute onset model (Dykman & Johll, 1998).

Third, the DAS may tap into the vulnerability aspect of dysfunctional attitudes better than other self-report retrospective belief measures reported in the literature. In fact the findings of G.P. Brown et al. (1995) suggest that DAS subscales may be a better test of cognitive diathesis than the Total Score by providing a tighter fit between underlying diathesis and congruent stressor. Barnett and Gotlib (1990), however, did not find a significant life event congruence effect with the DAS subscales in the prediction of depressive symptom severity, though our review of the relapse literature shows that significant interactions have been found between the DAS Social Approval and Performance Evaluation subscales and their matching life events in predicting relapse in recovered depressives.

Fourth, many of these studies provide evidence that dysfunctional attitudes influence how individuals appraise their negative life experiences. Simons et al. (1993) found that elevated levels of dysfunctional attitudes can even affect the number of life events endorsed and severity ratings on self-report life event checklists. Although this finding is entirely consistent with the cognitive model, it highlights a particular difficulty researchers will have in separating out the effects of the diathesis from those of the stressor in predicting depressive states. At the very least, this suggests that researchers will have to pay closer attention to appraisal processes in their studies on cognitive diathesis-stress (see Haaga et al., 1991 for a similar argument). And finally, gender differences may be apparent with women more inclined to show evidence of dysfunctional attitudes interacting with negative life stressors in depression than men. This possible gender difference is not well understood but it suggests that researchers may not be justified in basing their analyses on total samples. Next we consider the sociotropy and autonomy scales as another major area of research on cognitive-event congruence in depression.

The Sociotropy-Autonomy Scale and Depression Symptom Onset

Numerous studies have tested whether the personality constructs of sociotropy and autonomy moderate or interact with congruent negative life events in the onset or exacerbation of self-reported depressive symptoms in nonclinical samples. In most of these studies, the original SAS developed by A. Beck et al. (1983) was used to assess personality vulnerability, and self-report life event checklists assessed negative life experiences. Selected items from these life event inventories were typically categorized by independent evaluators as negative interpersonal or achievement events so that congruence between personality and life events could be examined. Depressive symptom severity served as the dependent variable and was most often assessed with the BDI. Separate hierarchical regression analyses tested for significant interactions with the predicted congruent personality-life event interactions (i.e., sociotropy/negative interpersonal events and autonomy/negative achievement events) as well as the incongruent effects (i.e., sociotropy/negative achievement events and autonomy/negative interpersonal events). We begin with a review of the cross-sectional studies followed by a consideration of the prospective research designs.

Cross-Sectional Studies

The most common finding of the cross-sectional studies is that SAS Sociotropy shows a significant interaction with negative interpersonal events in its association with BDI depression severity, whereas the SAS Autonomy Total Score fails to evidence a significant interaction with negative achievement events (Bartelstone & Trull, 1995; D.A. Clark, Beck, & Brown, 1992; Robins & Block, 1988; Rude & Burnham, 1993; for review, see Nietzel & Harris, 1990). Robins (1990, Study 1) dichotomized SAS scores into high and low sociotropy and autonomy groups (a practice highly criticized by Coyne and Whiffen, 1995, which we discuss more fully in the final section of this chapter) in a sample of depressed outpatients and a comparison group meeting Research Diagnostic Criteria for schizophrenia. A significant interaction between the high sociotropy—low autonomy group and negative interpersonal events was found for the depressed but not the schizophrenic sample. No other interactions were significant. In the second study, Robins (1990) compared dysphoric and nondysphoric college students. There was a trend for the highly sociotropic and highly autonomous individuals in the dysphoric group to report greater frequency and impact ratings for negative interpersonal and achievement events, respectively, though these differences did not attain statistical significance.

In some studies sociotropy evidenced high specificity by not interacting with the incongruent negative achievement life events (Bartelstone & Trull, 1995; D.A. Clark et al., 1992; Rude & Burnham, 1993), whereas in other studies it had a significant interaction with both negative interpersonal and achievement events (Robins & Block, 1988). D.A. Clark and Oates (1995)[1] failed to find a significant interaction between the Revised SAS Sociotropy Scale and negative interpersonal life events or daily hassles. However, the Revised SAS has two subscales for autonomy, Solitude and Independence. Regression analysis revealed a specific and significant interaction between SAS Solitude and negative achievement life

---

[1] This study was supported by a research grant (no. 410-92-0427) from the Social Sciences and Humanities Research Council of Canada awarded to David A. Clark.

events (i.e., failures) but not daily hassles. The SAS Independence scale failed to interact with either negative achievement life events or daily hassles. Burgess, Dorn, Haaga, and Chrousos (1996) investigated personality-event congruence among 26 patients suffering from Cushing syndrome, an endocrine disorder in which depression is a complication, and 12 healthy controls. Analysis of the Life Experience Survey or Hassles Scale failed to reveal any evidence of personality-event congruence for SAS Sociotropy or Autonomy among patients with Cushing syndrome. Within-group correlations indicated that autonomy was not associated with any of the life event or hassles scales, whereas sociotropy correlated with both interpersonal and achievement hassles. The researchers concluded from their findings that sociotropy may be a consequence of depression because of its high correlation with depression severity in Cushing syndrome, a disorder in which depression is assumed to be caused by biological dysfunction rather than by the interaction of personality vulnerabilities with congruent environmental stressors.

Three studies have examined personality-event congruence in response to hypothetical personality-specific life experiences. Lightbody and McCabe (1997) had students, classified as sociotropic, or autonomous on the basis of the Personal Styles Inventory, imagine neutral, sociotropic, or autonomous threat scenarios. The students classified as sociotropic showed a significant increase in negative affect and a significant decrease in positive affect after imagining both types of threatening scenarios, whereas the hypothetical threatening experiences had no specific mood effects on the autonomous students. In an earlier study of this type, Robins (1986) had undergraduate students listen to social rejection or achievement failure tapes and imagine that the events were happening to them. The only significant effect found was that elevated scores on the Attachment/Separation subscale of SAS Sociotropy predicted depressed mood in response to hypothetical social rejection. SAS Autonomy failed to interact with either type of tape, nor did the achievement failure tapes vary with level of sociotropy.

In a study by Allen, Horne, and Trinder (1996), 100 undergraduates completed the PSI and were subsequently exposed to six standardized imagery scenarios involving two neutral scenes, two social rejection scenes, and two achievement failure scenes. Self-ratings of mood and physiological arousal were obtained in response to each of the scenarios. Analysis revealed that the social rejection and achievement failure imagery scripts elicited significant elevations in corrugator supercilii muscle activity but not heart rate, and produced significantly greater self-ratings of distress than the neutral scripts. Hierarchical regression analysis indicated that elevated scores on PSI Sociotropy predicted greater subjective distress to the social rejection condition, and to a lesser extent, the achievement failure scripts. Furthermore, elevated PSI Sociotropy was also a significant predictor of increased corrugator EMG response to the social rejection but not the achievement failure scenes. PSI Autonomy was not a significant predictor of self-ratings of mood or EMG response to any of the imagery scripts.

Finally, Thompson and Genest (1995) compared the convergent validity of the SAS and PSI in a sample of 144 undergraduates. They found a strong correlation between the PSI and SAS Sociotropy scales ($r = .81$) but a more moderate correlation between the two autonomy scales ($r = .42$). Correlations with ratings on the perceived degree of upset associated with self-reported negative life experiences revealed low to moderate correlations with the PSI Sociotropy but not the Autonomy scale. These findings provide support for congruence between sociotropy and negative interpersonal events but not between autonomy and negative achievement events. We now turn, however, to the prospective studies that provide a more stringent test of the onset hypothesis.

Prospective Studies

Alford and Gerrity (1995) administered the SAS, BDI, and BAI to 112 undergraduates in a 4-week prospective research design. Hierarchical regression analysis controlling for T1 symptoms and concurrent symptom measures revealed that SAS Sociotropy was uniquely predictive of T2 anxiety but not depression, whereas SAS Autonomy failed to predict any T2 symptoms. The researchers did not include a life event measure so personality-event congruence was not tested. Pilon (1989) screened 1,282 undergraduates and, based on the Schedule for Affective Disorders and Schizophrenia, selected three groups: never depressed ($n = 25$), formerly depressed ($n = 29$), and relapsed depressed ($n = 25$). All three groups were then administered the SAS, DAS, and Hamilton Rating Scale of Depression in a 2-week prospective study. At T2, participants completed a stress battery in which they identified the most stressful event that had occurred over the previous two weeks. They then rated their degree of endorsement for three statements that reflected interpersonal concerns related to their most stressful life event and three statements indicative of achievement-related concerns. Hierarchical regression analysis conducted separately on each of the three groups failed to find a significant main effect or interaction between sociotropy and interpersonal stress-related concerns in the prediction of T2 scores on the Hamilton Rating Scale of Depression. However, SAS Autonomy was predictive of Hamilton depression in the never-depressed and formerly depressed groups, and the interaction between autonomy and achievement stress-related concerns was a significant predictor of T2 depression in the formerly depressed group alone.

It is difficult to interpret these results for personality-event congruence because frequency of negative interpersonal or achievement-related events was not measured in this study. Pilon (1989) examined the extent to which personality interacted with individuals' ratings of the degree to which they perceived that interpersonal- or achievement-related stakes were involved in their most stressful experience of the last two weeks. This study is interesting because it is one of the few to use strict diagnostic procedures in a nonclinical population and then find more supportive evidence for personality-event congruence for SAS Autonomy than for SAS Sociotropy.

Three prospective studies examined personality-event congruence in nonclinical student samples. Robins, Hayes, Block, Kramer, and Villena (1995) administered the SAS, BDI, and Life Experiences Survey to 164 undergraduates who scored 14 or more on the BDI at a prior screening session. Participants were administered the battery of measures on two occasions separated by one month. A series of hierarchical regression analyses controlling for T1 BDI, gender, and the main effects of personality and life events revealed that both sociotropy and autonomy interacted significantly with negative interpersonal and achievement events in the prediction of T2 BDI. These results can be considered only partial support for the cognitive diathesis-stress hypothesis because although personality-life event interaction predicted future depressive symptom levels, the interactions proved to be nonspecific which is contrary to the onset depression hypothesis' proposal of a domain-specific interaction between vulnerability and life events.

Freeman and Genest (1995) administered the PSI, BDI, and Life Experiences Survey to 128 students on two occasions separated by a 14-week interval. Hierarchical regression analysis failed to reveal a significant interaction between sociotropy and negative interpersonal events in the prediction of T2 BDI, although a significant three-way interaction between PSI Autonomy, negative achievement events, and gender was significant. For women, high autonomy in the presence of negative achievement events resulted in large increases in T2 BDI, whereas for men high autonomy and negative achievement stressors resulted in only slight increases in T2 depressive symptom severity.

The third prospective study (D.A. Clark, Purdon, & Beck, 1997) was carried out in our own laboratory in which 179 students completed an extended version of the SAS (D.A. Clark & Beck, 1991)[2], the Negative Life

---

[2] This study was supported by a research grant (no.410-92-0427) from the Social Sciences and Humanities Research Council of Canada awarded to David A. Clark.

Experiences Inventory-Student Version which was a retrospective life event measure we specifically designed for use with student populations, and the BDI. Participants were tested over a 3-month interval. Hierarchical regression analysis controlling for T1 BDI, main effects of personality, and life events were performed with the two-way congruent and incongruent interactions entered on the final step. Sociotropy had a significant interaction with negative interpersonal but not negative achievement events in the prediction of BDI residual scores. Solitude, a subscale of autonomy, had a significant interaction with negative achievement events only, whereas Independence, the other autonomy subscale of the Expanded SAS, failed to show a significant interaction with either life event scale. Descriptive analyses performed on the Sociotropy × Interpersonal Event interaction confirmed predictions of the cognitive model. The only participants to show a significant increase in their T2 BDI depression level were those who scored high on SAS Sociotropy and reported a greater number of negative interpersonal life events. On the other hand, the Solitude × Negative Achievement Event interaction was caused by individuals with high Solitude and few negative achievement events showing the greatest decline in BDI scores over the 3-month retest interval.

The prospective studies we have examined are fairly evenly split over whether personality-event congruence is evident in sociotropy or autonomy. In two studies (Freeman & Genest, 1995; Pilon, 1989), more favorable results were found for autonomy than for sociotropy. On the other hand, in our own prospective study (D.A. Clark et al., 1997) there was more evidence for personality-event congruence in sociotropy than in autonomy. Robins et al. (1995) provided some evidence for cognitive diathesis-stress but the failure to find domain-specific interactions between personality vulnerabilities and their congruent type of life event can only be taken as weak support for cognitive diathesis-stress.

Summary of Sociotropy-Autonomy Research on Depression Onset

As discussed, a strong version of the depressive onset hypothesis states that a specific match or congruence will be found between personality vulnerability and type of stressor. As evident from this review of the empirical literature, consistent support for cognitive personality-event congruence has eluded researchers to date. We might be tempted to conclude that evidence is stronger for a specific congruence between sociotropy and negative interpersonal events than between autonomy and negative achievement events. However, studies have found that elevated scores on the SAS or PSI Sociotropy scales confer increased vulnerability to depressive symptoms in the face of both interpersonal- and achievement-related stressors. This nonspecificity as well as the moderate correlation between sociotropy and measures of depressive symptoms has led to the suggestion that elevated sociotropy scores may be, in part, a consequence rather than cause of depression (Burgess et al., 1996), although Coyne and Whiffen (1995) in their review concluded that sociotropy and dependency measures are less affected by depression than other vulnerability constructs such as self-criticism. It would also be premature to completely write off the hypothesized relationship between autonomy and negative achievement events. A sufficient number of studies have found significant interaction effects to warrant further investigation. It is apparent, though, that personality-event congruence in the prediction of depressive symptoms is a fragile effect that may depend on a number of intervening variables as well as the properties of cognitive diathesis and stress measures. Next, we consider the findings from cognitive diathesis-stress studies that have relied on vulnerability measures other than the DAS or SAS.

VULNERABILITY STUDIES OF RELATED CONSTRUCTS

One of the earliest studies to investigate whether depressotypic self-schemas interacted with schema-congruent life events to predict depressive symptoms was conducted by Hammen, Marks, Mayol, and deMayo (1985). They followed 94 undergraduates over a 4-month period, with monthly checkups in which participants completed a special 120-item Life Experiences Survey and telephone interviews involving diagnostic evaluations for depression and interview-based life events assessments. Prior to the follow-up assessments of stressful life events and depression, students were asked to recall examples of life experiences that made them feel bad, good, helpless, or critical. Based on a categorization of these behavioral examples or life experiences into interpersonal, achievement or other content by independent raters, 46 students were classified as having a dependent-oriented self-schema and 32 students were categorized as having a self-critical or achievement-related self-schema orientation.

Correlational analysis revealed that the dependent schematic students had significantly higher correlations between negative interpersonal events and depression than between negative achievement events and depression on the interview-elicited life events and, to a lesser extent, on the Life Experiences Survey. The dependent group also produced a significantly stronger association between negative interpersonal events and depression than the self-critical schematic students. The latter group, however, showed a trend toward evidencing a specific association between negative achievement events and depression, though most of the within-group and between-group comparisons were not significant. Further analysis indicated that the dependent and self-critical schematic groups tended not to differ significantly in the frequency of negative interpersonal or achievement events reported, their subjective appraisal of threat associated with the events, recall accuracy of the events, or patterns of event causation.

Overall, then, one of the first studies on cognitive-event vulnerability provided evidence that individuals who have a dependent self-schematic orientation are more susceptible to depressive symptoms and a diagnosable depressive episode when they experience negative interpersonal events than when they experience negative achievement events. The evidence for a domain-specific interaction between self-critical schemas (i.e., autonomy) and negative achievement events in predicting depression was rather weak.

Numerous studies have investigated whether vulnerability constructs other than maladaptive schemas or sociotropy and autonomy interact with specific types of life events to increase susceptibility to depression. Studies employing the Depressive Experiences Questionnaire (DEQ) have found evidence for personality-event congruency between Blatt's (1974) vulnerability factor of dependency and negative interpersonal or social rejection events, although self-criticism appears to be associated with both negative interpersonal and achievement events (Lakey & Ross, 1994; Zuroff & Mongrain, 1987). Other studies have failed to find any evidence of specific personality-event congruence for DEQ Dependency or Self-Criticalness (Zuroff, Igreja, & Mongrain, 1990).

Perfectionism is another personality construct that has shown some evidence of diathesis-stress effects in predicting depressive symptoms. Hewitt and Flett (1991) proposed a multidimensional model in which *self-oriented perfectionism* refers to an achievement-based need to attain high self-standards, and two dimensions based on an interpersonal orientation: *other-oriented perfectionism*, which involves the need for others to be perfect, and *socially prescribed perfectionism*, in which one believes other people expect perfection from one's self. In several studies, self-oriented perfectionism has shown a specific interaction with negative achievement events in predicting depressive symptoms, though less consistent evidence of specific congruency effects have been found for socially prescribed perfectionism and negative interpersonal events (Hewitt & Flett, 1993; Hewitt, Flett, & Ediger, 1996). Other-oriented perfectionism is uncorrelated with depression because it has an external focus on the limitations of others rather than an internal focus on one's own deficiencies (Hewitt & Flett, 1993).

Negative attributional style is another depression vulnerability construct that has received considerable attention from diathesis-stress researchers. In various studies, a generalized tendency to attribute negative life events to stable, global causes as indicated by responses on the Attributional Style Questionnaire (ASQ), as well as expectations of future negative consequences and negative impact on the self resulting from a major life event, have all shown significant interactions with the occurrence of negative stressors to predict the onset and maintenance of depressive symptoms, especially the persistence of depressive symptoms (Metalsky et al., 1987; Metalsky & Joiner, 1992; Metalsky et al., 1993).

In a study of 57 depressed outpatients, individuals with a match between their tendency to make depressotypic attributions for negative interpersonal or achievement events and the occurrence of such an event 3 months prior to their depressive episode were more likely to evidence many of the symptoms of hopelessness depression than patients with a mismatch between attributional diathesis and stressor (Spangler et al., 1993). Metalsky et al. (1987) also found that attributional diathesis for depression may be content-specific to particular types of stressor as indicated by their finding that only attributions to negative achievement events interacted with the experience of obtaining a low grade on an exam to predict dysphoria. J.D. Brown and Siegel (1988) found that attributions for negative events involving uncontrollable but not controllable causes were significantly related to increases in depressive symptoms.

The attributional vulnerability model of depression may not be as applicable to the prediction of depression in children or adolescents. Hammen, Adrian, and Hiroto (1988) followed 79 children (8–16 years of age) over a 6-month period with an initial assessment involving a diagnostic interview, and completion of the Children's Depression Inventory and the Children's Attributional Style Questionnaire. At the 6-month evaluation, the diagnostic interview was again administered as well as an interview measure of stressful events. Nearly one-third of the children had either a new onset of depression or a continuation of a previous depressive episode at follow-up (many of these children were at high risk for depression because their mothers had a history of depressive disorder). Neither the main effect of attributional style nor its interaction with stressful life events, however, predicted depression diagnostic status at follow-up, although the main effect of stress threat ratings was a significant predictor. These negative results may indicate that the attributional vulnerability model is less applicable to depression in children, or it could be that the negative findings are because Hammen et al. failed to test for domain-specific effects (i.e., match between negative attributions for interpersonal events and frequency of negative interpersonal experiences).

Needles and Abramson (1990) found that global, stable attributions for positive events interacted with the occurrence of positive life events to predict reductions in hopelessness and remission of depressive symptoms in dysphoric college students. This finding was replicated in a follow-up study of 52 depressed psychiatric inpatients treated with antidepressant medication (J.G. Johnson et al., 1998). Not only did attributional style for positive events predict decreases in hopelessness depression but decreased hopelessness mediated the relationship between attributions for recent positive events and decreased depressive symptoms.

There is evidence that the dysfunctional attitudes proposed by Beck's cognitive theory and negative attributional style as described in the hopelessness model (Abramson et al., 1989) may constitute distinct pathways to depression. Confirmatory factor analysis of the interpersonal and achievement subscale scores on the DAS and the Attributional Style Questionnaire (ASQ) for 59 outpatients with major depressive disorder revealed that the DAS and ASQ form distinct but correlated dimensions (Spangler, Simons, Thase, & Monroe, 1997). In addition, when patients were categorized in terms of whether or not they showed a match between their domain-specific scoring on the DAS or ASQ and a congruent life stressor, there was very little overlap in the diathesis-stress matching. Depressed patients who showed a match between their elevated scoring on the interpersonal or achievement subscales of the DAS and negative interpersonal or achievement stressors generally did not also show a match between their ASQ subscale scoring and life events. This indicates that clinically depressed patients who evidence increased vulnerability because of a diathesis-stress match according to Beck's cognitive model cannot be assumed to show elevated cognitive vulnerability as described by other models such as the hopelessness model of depression.

Most of the diathesis-stress studies have found support for the attributional vulnerability hypothesis, which suggests that the tendency to attribute global, stable causes to certain negative (and possibly positive) life events may be a significant diathesis that affects the onset, course, persistence, and even recovery from depressive symptoms. However, whether this hypothesis is generalizable to the depressions experienced in children and adolescents may be questionable, and it is evident that negative attributional vulnerability to depression cannot be assumed to also confer increased vulnerability for dysfunctional attitudes. This later conclusion, however, is only tentative because it is based on one cross-sectional study. Further research is needed on the relationship between attributional diathesis-stress and the diathesis-stress constructs of the cognitive model.

Chronic self-focused attention has also been proposed as a vulnerability factor for depression. Pyszczynski, Holt, and Greenberg (1987) found that a heightened self-focused attention partially mediated the more pessimistic judgments about future life events made by students identified as dysphoric based on elevated scores on the BDI. However, T.W. Smith, Ingram, and Roth (1985) failed to find a significant interaction between dispositional self-focused attention and self-report of negative life events in the prediction of BDI scores in a cross-sectional student study. In a later article describing two studies, Ingram, Johnson, Bernet, Dombeck, and Rowe (1992) found some evidence that chronically self-focused individuals may be more cognitively and emotionally reactive. These data, then suggest that self-focused attention should be investigated as a possible moderator of the relationship between vulnerability and stress as predictors of depression. However, it is not clear whether heightened self-focused attention predisposes to depression, is an intrinsic symptom of depression, or is a consequence of the depressive experience (see review by Ingram, 1990b). Next, we consider high-risk behavioral studies, which provide a particularly powerful test of cognitive vulnerability.

HIGH-RISK BEHAVIORAL STUDIES

Studies that employ a high-risk behavioral paradigm provide a particularly powerful test of cognitive vulnerability by selecting individuals who are thought to be vulnerable to depression because they possess a particular theoretically defined risk factor (Ingram et al., 1998). One of the most comprehensive and ambitious studies on cognitive vulnerability is the Temple-Wisconsin Cognitive Vulnerability to Depression Project under the direction of Lauren Alloy, Lyn Abramson, and their colleagues (Alloy & Abramson, 1996). In this 5-year longitudinal study, the etiologic aspects of the hopelessness model and Beck's cognitive theory of depression were tested using a prospective high-risk behavioral research design. In the first phase, 5,378 first-year students at the University of Wisconsin-Madison and Temple University were administered the Cognitive Style Questionnaire (CSQ) to assess attributional style, consequences, and characteristics about the self for positive and negative hypothetical life events, and the 40-item DAS as a measure of depressotypic beliefs and attitudes.

Alloy and Abramson (1996) revised the 40-item DAS by adding 24 items that assessed dysfunctional beliefs specific to the interpersonal and achievement domains. Participants who were currently nondepressed but who scored in the highest quartile on both the CSQ composite score for negative events and the DAS Total Score comprised a potential High Risk (HR) for depression group, whereas students who scored in the lowest quartile on both measures were eligible as a Low Risk (LR) group. A random subset of students who met selection criteria for the HR or LR groups were invited to participate in the second phase of screening. At Phase II, 313 eligible HR and 236 eligible LR students were given diagnostic interviews to assess for current depressive disorder or any other psychiatric disturbance that would meet *DSM-III-R* diagnostic criteria. This second screening resulted in a final sample of 173 HR and 176 LR participants who did not meet criteria for any current psychiatric disorder and who agreed to participate in the 5-year study. Within one month of the final screening, the sample was administered a comprehensive Time 1 assessment battery that included measures of cognitive diathesis (DAS, CSQ, Sociotropy-Autonomy Scale, Self-Referent Encoding Task), negative life events (both questionnaire and structured interview), appraisals of life events, hopelessness (Hopelessness Scale), coping style, social support, and presence of Axis II personality disorders and dimensions. Thereafter, participants were assessed every 6 weeks for two years and then every 16 weeks for three years with a battery of measures again dealing with life events, cognitions (Automatic Thoughts Questionnaire), symptoms (Beck Depression Inventory, Halberstadt Mania Inventory, 90-item Symptom Checklist), and diagnosable episodes of depression. In addition, participants were assessed at the end of each calendar year for a 5-year period after the Time 1 assessment.

At the time of writing, Alloy, Abramson, and colleagues are still collecting follow-up data and analyzing this rich data set. Nevertheless, some initial findings have been reported indicating that cognitively vulnerable high-risk individuals may show characteristics that are consistent with a proneness to depression. Abramson, Alloy, et al. (1997) reported that the DAS Approval by Others and Performance Evaluation subscales correlated with negative attributions for both interpersonal and achievement events. Furthermore, the HR group scored significantly higher on SAS Sociotropy, the Depressive Experiences Questionnaire (DEQ) Dependency subscale and the DEQ Self-Criticalness subscale, but tended to score lower on SAS Autonomy, than the LR group. These findings suggest some overlap between cognitive vulnerability to hopelessness depression as indicated by negative inferential patterns on the CSQ and other constructs of personality vulnerability to depression.

Alloy, Abramson, Murray, Whitehouse, and Hogan (1997) compared the HR and LR groups on a Self-Referent Encoding Task at the Time 1 assessment that yielded five cognitive variables: self-descriptive trait ratings, response latency for self-descriptive ratings, provision of past behaviors that exemplify trait words judged to be self-descriptive, ratings of probability that they would engage in hypothetical behaviors typical for different trait domains, and incidental free recall of trait words after a 2-hour time period. The HR group judged as self-descriptive significantly more negative depression-relevant and fewer positive depression-relevant trait adjectives than the LR group. Also the HR group was significantly slower in endorsing positive depression-relevant words as self-descriptive and in rating negative depression-relevant traits as not self-descriptive than the LR participants. As well, the HR group gave significantly higher probability ratings to negative and lower ratings for positive traits than the controls, though there was only a trend toward group differences on the number of past behavioral examples given for self-descriptive trait words. For the incidental recall data, the HR group recalled significantly fewer positive depressive adjectives, though the HR and LR groups did not differ significantly in their recall of negative trait adjectives and the Risk (HR vs. LR) × Content × Valence interaction only approached statistical significance ($p < .06$). The authors concluded that negatively biased self-referent processing is evident in nondepressed but vulnerable individuals.

Preliminary findings have been reported at conference proceedings on the prospective incidence of Axis I disorders on a subset of 75 HR and 113 LR participants over the first 2½ years of follow-up data (Abramson, Alloy, Hogan, & Whitehouse, 1997; Alloy & Abramson, 1997).[3] Students in the HR group had no lifetime history of any depressive disorder. Analysis revealed significantly higher incidence of *DSM-III-R* and/or RDC major depression (17% vs. 1%), RDC minor depression (39% vs. 6%), any episodic depression (41% vs. 7%), hopelessness depression (41% vs. 5%) or any anxiety disorder (7% vs. 3%) in the HR versus the LR group. These preliminary findings provide strong evidence that cognitive vulnerability predisposes individuals to clinically significant full-blown depressive disorders. We place the highest weight on this study because of its prospective nature, the use of a standardized diagnostic interview to establish the presence of depression, and the exclusion of individuals with a prior history of depression. Thus the increased vulnerability to depression in the high-risk group cannot be attributed to the residual effects of prior depression but instead reflects the effects of a negative attributional style and dysfunctional belief system. However, these results are only preliminary, and we must await the final analyses based on the complete sample followed over the full 5-year time period before we can accept these findings with confidence.

In an earlier retrospective high-risk behavioral study, Alloy, Lipman, and Abramson (1992) found that 39 students who scored in the nondepressed range on the BDI but whose score for negative outcomes on the ASQ was in the highest quartile had a significantly higher rate of *DSM-III-R* depressive episodes and hopelessness depression in the previous 2 years than nondepressed students who scored in the lowest quartile on the ASQ. In another high-risk behavioral study Alloy et al. (1997) selected high- and low-risk groups based on students' scores on the ASQ (this was not part of the CDV project). The HR group ($n = 54$) scored in

---

[3] We are grateful to Lauren Alloy for providing us a copy of these papers reporting on their preliminary findings.

the top quartile indicating stable, global, and internal attributions for both good and bad events, whereas the LR group ($n = 54$) showed an extreme positive self-serving attributional style by indicating internal, stable, and global attributions for positive events and external unstable and specific attributions for negative events. All participants scored below 16 on the BDI and completed daily diary ratings of life events and symptoms of depression versus mania over a 28-day time period.

Analysis revealed that the HR group had higher average levels and greater within-day and across-day variability in hopelessness depression symptoms than the LR group. In addition, only when the number of daily life events was low did the HR group evidence significantly greater across-day variability in hopelessness depression symptoms than the LR group. Findings from the high-risk behavioral studies provide strong support for cognitive vulnerability and the depression onset hypothesis of the cognitive model. A negative attributional style and dysfunctional schemas (i.e., beliefs), then, act as vulnerability factors that confer increased etiological risk for the onset of both clinical and subclinical depressive disorders and symptoms.

SUMMARY OF THE DEPRESSION ONSET HYPOTHESIS

The cognitive model posits that in some individuals a preexisting cognitive vulnerability exists in the form of negative self-referent schemas or an excessively dependent or autonomous personality suborganization that can lead to an increase in depressive symptoms and states in the presence of a negative life event that matches this predisposing vulnerability. In nonclinical individuals, this cognitive diathesis-stress formulation is expressed in the form of the depression onset hypothesis. Haaga et al. (1991) concluded from their review that the depression onset hypothesis is difficult to test, and that partial tests of the hypothesis have yielded mixed, mainly negative findings. We conclude from our more recent review of a greater number of studies that although support for this hypothesis continues to be somewhat mixed, a stronger case can be made for cognitive predisposition to depression in light of the findings from the high-risk behavioral studies. Furthermore, several factors may determine whether cognitive diathesis-stress is in fact found in any particular study.

Some of the earliest research on cognitive diathesis-stress investigated the relationship between the DAS Total Score and negative life events. The cross-sectional studies suggest that elevated DAS scores and negative life events may have a stronger association with depressive symptom severity in nonclinical than in clinical samples. The prospective studies have not consistently found a significant interaction between the DAS

Total Score and negative life events in the prediction of future depressive symptoms, though the attitude/life event interaction may be more predictive in women and with individuals who initially score in the low range on the BDI. Also, the DAS Approval from Others and Performance Evaluation subscales may provide a more specific test of life event congruence, although the research findings appear to be divided on this issue.

Cross-sectional studies have found fairly consistent support for an association between depressive symptom severity and the interaction of SAS Sociotropy with negative interpersonal events. Fewer studies have supported the specific interaction of SAS Autonomy and negative achievement life experiences. However, SAS Sociotropy has also shown a significant interaction with negative achievement events leading some to question whether an elevation in sociotropy is a consequence of depression or a nonspecific construct related to general states such as negative affectivity or subjective distress. The prospective studies have been more supportive of a specific congruence between autonomy and negative achievement events in the prediction of depressive symptoms, although the evidence from this research for sociotropy and negative interpersonal experiences is evenly split between studies finding personality-event congruence; others finding incongruence; and still others, congruence with both interpersonal and achievement events.

Studies have also investigated other vulnerability constructs that may interact with negative life experiences to predict depression. There is some evidence that DEQ Dependency interacts with negative interpersonal events, although DEQ Self-Criticalness appears to be more nonspecific in its relation to both negative interpersonal and achievement stressors. Self-oriented perfectionism may show a specific congruence with negative achievement events, and a negative attributional style for specific types of life experiences may interact with the occurrence of these particular events to predict elevations in depression, especially hopelessness depression symptoms. It is evident, then, that factors other than sociotropy, automony, or dysfunctional attitudes may act as a predisposing diathesis in depression for at least some individuals.

The empirical status of the depression onset hypothesis appears stronger than in the earlier review by Haaga et al. (1991). A sufficient number of studies have reported a significant interaction between the cognitive vulnerability constructs proposed by the cognitive model and specific matching life stressors to provide at least partial support for the hypothesis. However, the hypothesis may be qualified by factors such as gender differences, the initial level of depression in the sample, and the manner in which life events are assessed. Moreover, as noted in our review, the strongest support for cognitive diathesis-stress can be found in the high-risk behavioral studies. Findings from the Temple-Wisconsin

Cognitive Vulnerability to Depression Project suggest that negative attributional style and dysfunctional attitudes confer increased vulnerability to depressive symptoms and episodes. The conceptual and methodological shortcomings of the cognitive diathesis-stress research, (to be discussed) may be why many of these studies have not provided a fair or even adequate test of the depression onset hypothesis. Before we discuss these limitations, however, we must consider studies that have examined cognitive diathesis-stress in recovered depressed samples.

DEPRESSION RELAPSE/ RECURRENCE HYPOTHESIS

A negative event that matches the content of the self-referent schemas and maladaptive personality constellation associated with the primal loss mode will lead to a heightened risk of recurrence of depression in previously depressed patients.

As discussed in Chapter 1, most individuals with a diagnosable depressive disorder will experience a recurrence of their depression even after complete remission of the initial depressive episode. Recurrence refers to the onset of a new episode of depression after a prolonged interval in which an individual has remitted from the initial depressive episode, whereas relapse is the return of clinically significant symptoms within a relatively short time period following remission (Abramson et al., 1988). A recurrent episodic pattern is one of the most important features of major depressive disorders that requires further understanding and consideration in treatment regimens. Piccinelli and Wilkinson (1994), in their review of follow-up studies of major depression, concluded that although 90% of patients may recover from a depressive episode within a 5-year period, 26% will have a recurrence of at least one depressive episode within one year of recovery and 75% will have a recurrence within a 10-year follow-up period. According to the cognitive model, individuals who possess an underlying cognitive vulnerability in the form of dysfunctional schemas or an excessively sociotropic or autonomous personality suborganization may be particularly susceptible to relapse and recurrence of depression, especially when a matching negative life stressor occurs.

Previously depressed individuals may be more cognitively vulnerable than never-depressed individuals and so may have an increased sensitivity to certain types of negative life stressors that can trigger a recurrence of depressive symptoms. This could occur because one consequence of having experienced an episode of clinically significant depression is that it produces certain changes in the cognitive structures of the primal loss mode so that subsequent depressions are more easily triggered. Teasdale (1988) proposed the *differential activation hypothesis* to suggest that in previously depressed individuals past episodes of depression result in an increased accessibility of negative schemas and depressotypic processing during even mild states of dysphoria. The negative self-referent constructs and representations of a person who has already experienced at least one episode of major depression will be more readily accessible in response to environmental triggers than individuals who have never had a diagnosable depressive episode because these negative constructs have been associated with previous experiences of depression. This prior association between negative cognition and past episodic depression leaves remitted depressed individuals with an increased risk that they will slip into another depressive episode when they experience mild dysphoric states because these negative mood states are more likely to activate negative self-referent constructs, leading to an interpretation of experiences as highly aversive and uncontrollable. On the other hand, negative thinking in never-depressed individuals is less likely to result in biased global, negative interpretations during mild dysphoria because it has not been associated with a previous depressive state. Thus the differential activation hypothesis attributes the high rates of recurrence in major depression to an increased accessibility of negative self-referent structures and processes during mild dysphoric states in those who recovered from depression.

Segal, Williams, Teasdale, and Gemar (1996) proposed a further refinement and elaboration of the differential activation hypothesis. They operationally define risk of recurrence as:

> The ease with which these structures [knowledge structures with dense interconnections to depressed mood and memory] can be re-activated in the presence of mild dysphoric states and the corresponding difficulty of calling to mind information associated with euthymic states. (p. 372)

The authors invoke the concepts of kindling and sensitization to further explain the heightened susceptibility to recurrence of previously depressed individuals during mild dysphoric mood states. Because negative self-referent semantic structures have been associated with previous depressive episodes, this will strengthen the associative links between negative depressotypic constructs so that a wider range of stimuli can elicit an array of densely interconnected depression-related constructs. This is similar to the process of *kindling* in that eventually, with continued reactivation of negative memory structures, only minimal cues will be needed to activate the array of depressive constructs because their dense interconnections means that activation of one element in the array is likely to activate the entire structure. A second process, *sensitization*, refers to the lowering of the activation threshold for depressotypic constructs because of the repeated activation of these structures during previous depressive experiences. Thus the stronger interconnections and lower activation threshold for negative self-referent constructs in the remitted depressed caused by chronic activation during previous experiences of depression means that depressotypic information processing is more likely to occur in these individuals to increasingly minimal cues and even milder dysphoric states. The tendency of the activated negative self-referent structures to lead to biased information biasing and negative automatic thoughts sets up a vicious cycle whereby the dysphoric mood state can escalate into a more severe depressive episode in the person with remitted depression.

Based on the Interacting Cognitive Subsystems model, Teasdale, Segal, and Williams (1995) state that risk for recurrence and relapse of depression depends on the ease with which depressive interlock configurations resulting from an initial depressive episode are reinstated during mild negative affect. The authors describe depressive interlock in terms of depressotypic schematic models that produce negative specific meanings that lead to the synthesis of further negative schematic models, which in turn produce a continuation of negative specific meanings and establish a self-perpetuating depressive interlock configuration. The Interacting Cognitive Subsystems model suggests:

> The risk of depressive interlock becoming (re-) established is particularly high for "globally negative" models of the self or future; such models can be reinstated by a wide range of negative specific meanings and so are particularly likely to be regenerated by their own negative outputs. (Teasdale, Segal, et al., 1995, p. 30)

The differential activation hypothesis, and its more recent reformulation in terms of depressive interlock or the kindling and sensitization of depressotypic cognitive structures, has some support from research on the mood-state dependency hypothesis (see discussion under the stability hypothesis) showing that recovered depressives have increased accessibility to dysfunctional attitudes only during negative mood states, whereas individuals without a history of depression showed no differential increase in dysfunctional attitudes during dysphoria. Furthermore, Segal, Gemar, and Williams (1998) compared the cognitive reactivity to musical mood induction of 15 patients who recovered from a major depressive episode after receiving cognitive behavior therapy with 17 recovered depressed patients treated with pharmacotherapy. Analysis revealed that the remitted pharmacotherapy group showed a significant increase in their endorsement of dysfunctional attitudes as measured by the DAS as a result of the induction of a dysphoric mood, whereas the cognitive behavior therapy group evidenced no significant increase in their DAS scores between pre- and postinduction. In a follow-up approximately 2½ years after treatment, Segal et al. used hierarchical regression analysis to determine whether post-induction DAS scores predicted recurrence of a depressive episode after controlling for preinduction DAS, number of previous depressive episodes, and time since original testing. Analysis revealed that postinduction but not preinduction DAS scores were a significant predictor of recurrence rates indicating that individuals who showed increased accessibility to dysfunctional attitudes during a dysphoric mood state had a greater risk of relapse or recurrence. Two implications can be drawn from this study. First, cognitive behavior therapy may produce more substantive changes in cognitive vulnerability structures than pharmacotherapy by reducing the accessibility of depressotypic cognitive representations during mild dysphoric moods. As evident by the follow-up analyses, this may also reduce relapse and recurrence rates in the previously depressed. Second, the findings provide support for the differential activation and mood-state dependency hypotheses that relapse and recurrence of depression in recovered depressives may be related to heightened accessibility to cognitive vulnerability structures during dysphoria. This research suggests that the elevated risk for recurrence and relapse of depressive symptoms in remitted depression may be due to an increase in the accessibility of the negative self-referent structures brought about by the experience of having a clinically significant depressive episode. This would lead to a heightened cognitive vulnerability or risk for future episodes of depression in those with remitted depression, and this increased cognitive vulnerability may be particularly evident during mild dysphoric mood states.

Although cognitive-clinical researchers have focused on possible changes in cognitive processes and structures resulting from an initial episode of depression, researchers have posited other changes that may occur. Coyne and Calarco (1995) conducted focused groups and a survey on the personal experiences of individuals who recovered from depression. Compared with never-depressed women, previously depressed women indicated that (a) they were afraid of becoming depressed again, (b) they had a greater sense of needing to keep balance in their life, (c) they had to fight harder to maintain a positive attitude, (d) fatigue was more common and they had to hide their symptoms, (e) they reduced their self-expectations and avoided long-term plans, (f) they perceived they were a greater burden on others and avoided social commitments, and (g) they felt a sense of stigma for having been depressed. There is also evidence that depression can lead to changes in certain personality traits such as decreased sociability, increased interpersonal dependency, lack of social self-confidence, less dominance and activity, increased sensitivity to others, and low self-esteem (Cofer & Wittenborn, 1980; Hirschfeld, Klerman, Clayton, & Keller, 1983), although analysis of the large-scale prospective study of Lewinsohn and colleagues suggests that there are relatively few residual psychosocial effects resulting from a depressive episode (Lewinsohn et al., 1981; Rohde et al., 1990).

The view that a clinically significant depressive episode may alter the structure and accessibility of the depression-prone individual's cognitive representations of the self and future is entirely consistent with the cognitive model of depression put forth in this book. There are, however, differences among writers on what triggers or primes the increased cognitive vulnerability in remitted depression. Teasdale, Segal, and others have argued that mild dysphoric mood states will trigger the depressotypic cognitive representations of the recovered depression-prone person. Our view, on the other hand, is that negative life experiences or stressors serve to reactivate negative dysfunctional schemas and maladaptive personality suborganizations, and so the increased vulnerability in recovered depression is due to a heightened sensitivity to negative life experiences that match one's underlying cognitive vulnerability. Whereas Teasdale, Segal, and associates emphasize heightened accessibility and reactivation of depressotypic structures during negative mood states, the cognitive model focuses on the greater cognitive reactivity of the remitted depressed person to an increased range of negative life stressors.

The depression relapse and recurrence hypothesis states that increased risk for depression among recovered depressives results from an initial episode of depression that causes a lowering of the activation threshold for dysfunctional self-referent schemas and personality suborganization of the primal loss mode so that a wider range of less intense matching negative life stressors can activate the depressotypic cognitive structures and subsequent biased information processing. Empirical support for this cognitive diathesis-stress perspective would be evident if relapse and recurrence rates in recovered depressed samples were predicted by the significant interaction of cognitive diathesis (i.e., dysfunctional attitudes or personality) and the occurrence of matching negative life stressors. We now examine support for the depression relapse hypothesis.

DAS AND RELAPSE/RECURRENCE OF DEPRESSION

A few studies have examined whether elevated DAS scores alone are predictive of relapse and recurrence rates in major depression without taking into account the presence or absence of negative life stressors. Rush, Weissenburger, and Eaves (1986) assessed 15 female depressed outpatients at pretreatment, posttreatment, and a 6-month follow-up. All patients were remitted at posttreatment, but 6 had relapsed by a 6-month follow-up. Partial correlations and stepwise regression analysis controlling for current depression level revealed that elevated posttreatment DAS scores were predictive of increased levels of depressive symptoms at follow-up as measured by the BDI and Hamilton Rating Scale of Depression. This finding was replicated in two other studies in which high posttreatment DAS scores were associated with increased risk for relapse of depressive symptoms during the follow-up period (Simons, Murphy, Levine, & Wetzel, 1986; Thase et al., 1992). In the Temple-Wisconsin Cognitive Vulnerability to Depression Project, the high-risk group with a prior history of depression had significantly higher recurrence rates of depressive episodes over the 2½ year follow-up period than the low risk group with a past history of depression (Abramson, Alloy, Hogan, & Whitehouse, 1997). Thus presence of dysfunctional attitudes does appear to confer increased vulnerability for relapse and recurrence of depression.

The relapse vulnerability potential of dysfunctional attitudes may only be evident when patients are tested in an asymptomatic state, such as after successful response to treatment. Williams et al. (1990) retested 31 patients with major depressive disorder 6 months after they received active treatment. Pretreatment scores on Burns' DAS predicted recovery from depression with elevated scores linked to increased likelihood of the persistence of depression at 6 months. However, pretreatment DAS scores did not predict relapse rates, indicating that presence of dysfunctional attitudes is predictive of relapse only if assessed when the patient is asymptomatic. In a more recent study, Ilardi, Craighead, and Evans (1997) used survival analysis to determine whether DAS predicted recurrence rates in 50 depressed inpatients treated with antidepressant medication and followed over approximately 4 years posttreatment. Neither pretreatment nor follow-up DAS scores predicted whether patients experienced a *DSM* depressive episode during follow-up. However, DAS scores were not obtained at posttreatment when most patients were asymptomatic. Thus the absence of support for dysfunctional attitudes as a relapse vulnerability factor may be due to a failure to ensure that dysfunctional attitudes were assessed when patients were asymptomatic. Overall, then, there is evidence that the continued presence of dysfunctional attitudes after remission of depressive symptoms (i.e., high posttreatment DAS scores) acts as a relapse vulnerability factor, with high DAS scores conferring an elevated risk of relapse and recurrence of depression.

Segal and his colleagues employed a diathesis-stress research design to determine whether dysfunctional attitudes interact with the occurrence of congruent or matching negative life events to predict relapse in patients who had recovered from a major depressive episode within the past three months. The researchers published two articles on this data set. In the first published report 46 remitted depressed patients were recruited from the community and followed over a six-month period during which they completed three assessment packages every two months (Segal, Shaw, & Vella, 1989). Past history of depression and relapse rates for depressive episodes during the follow-up were established by interview using the Schedule for Affective Disorders and Schizophrenia-Lifetime Version (SADS-L). Based on a median split on the Approval by Others and Performance Evaluation subscales of the 40-item DAS, 16 patients were identified as high in self-criticalness and 10 were classified as high in dependency. Life events were assessed by the Psychiatric Epidemiology Research Inventory (PERI) and independent raters categorized 33 of the life event items as representing self-critical concerns and another 33 as indicative of dependency issues. Correlational analysis revealed that the dependent group showed significant associations between number of negative interpersonal life events endorsed on the PERI, appraisals of the stressfulness of interpersonal events, and increased scores on the BDI. In addition, there was a marginally significant point-biserial correlation between number of interpersonal events and relapse rate for the dependent subtype. For the self-critical group, there was no evidence of a specific association between number of negative achievement events and depression symptom severity or relapse rates. Manova and hierarchical regression analysis revealed higher relapse rates for the dependent group after the experience of an interpersonal rather than after an achievement event. No such congruency effect was found for the self-critical subtype.

Two major problems are apparent in the study by Segal et al. (1989). The classification of depressive vulnerability on the basis of cutoff scores has been severely criticized because of its arbitrariness and consequent loss of participants who score in the middle range on personality measures (Coyne & Whiffen, 1995). Also, the sample sizes were very small, so it is likely that the study had reduced statistical power for detecting personality-event congruency effects. The second published article on this data set rectified both problems. A larger sample size was utilized ($n = 59$) with 30 individuals relapsing over the one-year follow-up period. In addition, personality vulnerability was treated as a continuous variable and hierarchical regression used to test for personality-event congruency effects. As well, the authors used a stringent test of vulnerability-event congruence by first partialing out the effects of number of prior episodes of depression, a variable known to be a strong predictor of relapse. Regression analysis predicting relapse rates revealed a significant interaction between DAS Performance Evaluation and number of negative achievement events endorsed on the PERI as well as ratings of the stressfulness of these events. In a parallel set of regression analyses, DAS Approval by Others showed no significant interaction with number or stressfulness ratings on negative interpersonal events. When Segal, Shaw, Vella, and Katz (1992), however, examined congruency for proximal events that occurred within 2 months of relapse, the Performance Evaluation and achievement event interaction was no longer a significant predictor of relapse, whereas the DAS Approval by Others and stressfulness ratings on negative interpersonal events was a significant predictor of relapse.

The two studies by Segal and his colleagues do not provide convincing evidence that the DAS subscales interact with congruent life events to predict depressive relapse. The findings proved to be highly unstable with the earlier study (Segal et al., 1989) finding evidence for congruence only for DAS Approval by Others and negative interpersonal events, whereas the second study (Segal et al., 1992) found contrary results with personality-event congruence primarily for DAS Performance Evaluation and negative achievement events. Moreover, this interaction was not reliable, with analyses over the last two months failing to find the Performance Evaluation by negative achievement event interaction. Also, Segal et al. (1992) did not depict the interaction by computing predicted relapse rates to ensure that the interaction conformed to the prediction that higher relapse rates would be found for individuals reporting elevated scores on DAS Performance Evaluation and an increased rate of negative achievement events. It is possible that the significant interaction may have been caused by a deviation in an unexpected direction (e.g., low risk of relapse associated with low DAS Performance Evaluation scores and absence of negative achievement stressors).

The strongest evidence to date is that elevated scores on the DAS Total Score present at posttreatment when the patient is asymptomatic for depression may constitute a vulnerability marker for relapse. This suggests that individuals who continue to evidence a negative self-referent schematic content after remission may have the highest susceptibility to the occurrence of future depressive episodes. As noted previously, Segal et al. (1998) found that this cognitive vulnerability to relapse may only be detectable when activated by a priming condition like a mood induction manipulation. These studies, then, provide at least partial support for the relapse hypothesis and suggest that an increased accessibility to negative schemas that persists after a depressive episode (though it may only be detected with a priming challenge) may lead to a heightened risk for relapse and recurrence of episodic major depression. However, the DAS diathesis-stress studies testing for congruency between negative schema content (i.e., DAS subscales) and life event content provide only tentative and rather inconsistent support for the depression relapse/recurrence hypothesis posed for this section. Although the diathesis-stress studies of Segal and colleagues cannot be taken as support for a cognitive-event relapse vulnerability, the few significant interactions that were found suggest that future research on this issue is warranted. However, a better prediction of depression relapse and recurrence rates may be provided by more stable traitlike personality measures. The following studies have investigated the relapse/recurrence potential of sociotropy and autonomy.

SAS and Depressive Relapse/Recurrence

Hammen and her colleagues published three articles based on a sample of unipolar and bipolar patients admitted to the UCLA Affective Disorders Clinic. All were initially administered the SAS and then followed over the next 2 years with an interview-based assessment of stressful life events every 3 months. An independent judge blind to individuals' SAS scores classified events as reflecting predominantly interpersonal or achievement content. The onset or exacerbation of depressive and manic symptoms was evaluated during visits to the treating psychiatrist who completed detailed symptom checklists.

In the first published report of this research, Hammen, Ellicott, Gitlin, and Jamison (1989) collected data on 22 unipolar and 25 bipolar patients who were followed over a 6-month period. Patients were classified as having a primarily sociotropic personality orientation if their SAS Sociotropy score exceeded their Autonomy score by more than three points and the reverse if SAS Autonomy exceeded their Sociotropy score. This classification yielded 8 sociotropic and 12 autonomous unipolar patients and 8 sociotropic and 15 autonomous bipolar participants. Five of the unipolar patients had life events and symptom exacerbation over the 6-month follow-up. Inspection of the life event/symptom relationship for these individuals revealed that the sociotropic patients were more likely to have experienced a negative interpersonal event and the autonomous unipolar patients were more likely to have had a negative achievement stressor. The bipolar group showed no such personality/event congruence with the onset or worsening of symptoms. Further analysis of total symptom scores revealed that autonomous patients who experienced achievement events had significantly more depressive symptoms than autonomous patients with interpersonal events, whereas the sociotropic patients with interpersonal events did not differ significantly in depressive symptoms from sociotropic participants with negative achievement events. Once again, these differences were not apparent in the bipolar sample. The researchers concluded that their findings supported the diathesis-stress hypothesis of the cognitive model by showing that depressive symptom relapse and recurrence was more likely after unipolar depressed individuals experienced a negative life stressor that was congruent with their predominant cognitive-personality suborganization.

In their second article based on this data set, Hammen, Ellicott, and Gitlin (1989) reported on a 2-year follow-up of 27 unipolar depressed patients. This time personality-event congruence was investigated using hierarchical regression analysis so that personality was treated as a continuous variable. This avoided the problems inherent in personality classification procedures that are at best based on arbitrary cutoff scores and result in the exclusion of a significant proportion of the sample who exhibit a mixed personality orientation. Also, only patients who showed a true onset of depressive symptoms over the follow-up period ($n = 18$) were included in the regression analyses. Analysis revealed that only the SAS Autonomy and negative achievement event interaction was a significant predictor of the severity of depressive symptoms during follow-up. SAS Sociotropy and negative interpersonal events failed to emerge as a significant predictor of depressive symptoms either alone or in combination. Thus relapse vulnerability was again evident for congruence between autonomy and negative achievement events but not for sociotropy and negative interpersonal stressors.

In a final report based on a larger sample of 49 bipolar patients, Hammen, Ellicott, and Gitlin (1992) examined symptom onset and severity for patients' worst period within an 18-month time interval. Classification of participants into predominantly sociotropic or autonomous personality types based on either a 13-point discrepancy or a z-score transformation failed to yield significant personality-event congruence on symptom exacerbation. Hierarchical regression in which personality was treated as a continuous variable did produce a significant SAS Sociotropy × interpersonal event interaction. When this interaction was broken down, however, it did not conform to the predicted relationship between sociotropy and negative interpersonal events. Instead, the interaction was caused by bipolar patients with low sociotropy scores having relatively few symptoms at low levels of interpersonal stress, whereas high sociotropy patients had elevated symptoms at both high and low levels of interpersonal stress and low sociotropy patients had greater symptom severity only with a greater number of interpersonal stressors. Thus once again, we find that the prediction of the cognitive theory of personality-event congruence as a relapse vulnerability factor was not found in bipolar patients.

Experimental Schema Studies of Relapse Vulnerability

A few studies have used an experimental information processing approach to determine whether the existence of latent negative self-referent schemas is a vulnerability factor for depressive relapse and recurrence.

Teasdale and Dent (1987) found that, compared with never-depressed women, recovered depressed women had mildly elevated levels of depression, had higher neuroticism scores, endorsed more negative trait adjectives as self-descriptive when in a neutral mood state, and recalled more negative and fewer positive trait words following a sad mood induction. Although these results support an underlying negative schematic vulnerability to depression in the recovered depressed sample, Teasdale and Dent did not report any follow-up data to determine whether this negative recall bias was predictive of depressive relapse and recurrence rates.

Moretti et al. (1996) used an experimental task in which participants were simultaneously presented a neutral and positive or negative facial expression for 750 ms. Individuals were asked to make a forced-choice judgment on which of the two facial expressions reflected the strongest emotional reaction to how this hypothetical person would feel about you (self-referent condition) or would feel about someone else (other-referent condition). Individuals who remitted from an episode of clinical depression showed a tendency to consider positive facial expressions as more informative than the negative stimuli for judging both their own interpersonal receptiveness and that of others. The authors noted that this pervasive positivity bias, which was directed toward the processing of interpersonal information relating to both the self and others, was even greater than evident in the nondysphoric never depressed control group. Moretti et al. (1996) speculated that an overly positive bias may make individuals with remitted depression more vulnerable to recurrence because overwhelming stressful events could siphon off attention resources that would be needed to maintain such a heightened state of positivity bias. However, no follow-up was reported on the remitted depressed sample, so we cannot determine whether an excessive positivity bias is a marker of relapse/recurrence vulnerability.

The final study in this section was already discussed under the stability hypothesis. Gilboa and Gotlib (1997) compared attentional and memory processing of undergraduate students who met diagnostic criteria for a previous episode of major depression, based on the Inventory to Diagnosis Depression-Lifetime Version, with never-depressed or dysphoric students while undergoing a positive and negative mood induction. Although the negative mood induction had a more persistent impact on the previously dysphoric than the never-dysphoric group, they did not differ significantly on the emotional Stroop task. These findings were replicated in a second study, although a test of incidental recall revealed that the previously depressed had significantly better recall of negative trait words presented in the Stroop task than the never-dysphoric group. The authors concluded that a negative bias in memory functioning and a maladaptive affect regulation style (as evidenced by the protracted sadness in the negative mood induction) may constitute vulnerability to recurrent dysphoria. Once again, though, this hypothesis could not be evaluated because a follow-up period was not included so that relapse and recurrence rates could be determined.

Numerous information processing biases have been suggested as possible vulnerability risk factors for a recurrence of depression and dysphoria in those with a history of depressive disorder. However, the critical follow-up studies have not been conducted and so the question of whether an excessively positive processing bias, negative memory functioning, or negative affect regulation are markers of cognitive vulnerability for depressive relapse and recurrence remains unanswered. Consistent with our previous discussions, we conclude from these studies that any future research on cognitive vulnerability to depressive relapse must ensure that the depressotypic cognitive constructs have been primed or activated and that individuals are followed over a sufficient time interval to detect relapse and recurrence rates of depression.

Summary

Haaga et al. (1991) concluded that there was some evidence that the continued presence of dysfunctional beliefs was associated with an elevated risk for depressive symptoms among individuals who recovered from an initial episode of depression. However, they felt that the empirical evidence for personality-event congruence as a predictor of depressive relapse and recurrence was ambiguous. In a later review, Coyne and Whiffen (1995) also concluded that the evidence from longitudinal studies that cognitive/ personality diathesis-stress is a causal factor in depressive relapse/ recurrence is at best ambiguous. Ingram et al. (1998), however, argue that Coyne and Whiffen's appraisal of the literature is too pessimistic, and that there is clear empirical evidence that a match between personality and life stress confers greater risk for depressive relapse or recurrence than mismatches between personality and type of life stressor.

Our own review of the empirical literature would place us somewhere midway between the conclusions reached by Coyne and Whiffen (1995) and those of Ingram et al. (1998). Empirical support for the relapse/ recurrence hypothesis posed for this section must be considered somewhat mixed. There is some emerging evidence to support the view that individuals with remitted depression may have heightened accessibility to negative self-referent schemas or meaning representations, that these structures may be more highly interrelated, and that depressotypic schemas may be more easily triggered by a priming mood induction or stressor because of a lower activation threshold. In addition, studies on the DAS Total Score indicate that the continued presence of dysfunctional attitudes at posttreatment is predictive of higher relapse rates, although pretreatment and follow-up DAS scores are not predictive of relapse. Presumably, the presence of dysfunctional attitudes during an asymptomatic state is the critical condition associated with relapse vulnerability.

The prospective studies on personality-event congruence using either the DAS or SAS subscales have produced rather fragile interactions between personality and life events. We agree with Ingram et al. (1998) that the occurrence of life events that match one's predisposing personality seems to confer greater vulnerability to relapse of depressive symptoms, but the findings are quite ambiguous at the present time. The few studies that have assessed schemas using experimental information processing tasks have not included follow-up periods for examining prediction of relapse. At this time, we can only conclude that there is sufficient empirical support to warrant continued research on the relapse/recurrence hypothesis of the cognitive model. However, the methodological and conceptual weaknesses and limitations of this research are so substantial that one can question whether the depression onset and relapse hypotheses of the cognitive model have been fairly and adequately tested, with the possible exception of the more recent high-risk behavioral studies.

CRITIQUE OF COGNITIVE DIATHESIS-STRESS

In Chapter 8, we noted that most depression researchers recognize that meaning assignment plays a critical mediating role between life events and the onset of depressive symptoms and disorders. It is not the mere occurrence of stressful events that leads to depression; instead, the depressotypic potential of life events resides in whether an event is interpreted as representing significant actual or anticipated personal loss. The core argument at the contributory level of the cognitive model is that some individuals possess latent prepotent dysfunctional schemas and a vulnerable personality suborganization that play a critical role in the onset and maintenance of depressive symptoms and disorder when activated by a congruent life stressor. These dysfunctional schemas have strong links to the primal loss mode and so when activated lead to the development of depressive symptoms. However, this cognitive vulnerability to depression will not be evident unless primed by an activating stimulus.

As discussed in the opening section of Chapter 8, many reviewers have concluded that there is little empirical support for the etiologic aspect of the cognitive model (Ackermann-Engel & DeRubeis, 1993; Barnett & Gotlib, 1988c; Coyne & Gotlib, 1983; Coyne & Whiffen, 1995; Gotlib & Hammen, 1992; Haaga et al., 1991; Teasdale & Barnard, 1993). They argue that most studies have failed to find evidence of latent predisposing dysfunctional schemas and personality vulnerabilities that are present prior to the depressive episode. Instead, the weight of the empirical evidence points to biased cognitive processes and dysfunctional structures as concomitants of the depressive experience.

In Chapters 8 and 9, we presented the empirical evidence for three core hypotheses of the cognitive model at the contributory level. We did not arrive at the same conclusion of previous reviewers (see similar conclusion by Gotlib et al., 1997). In terms of the stability of depressotypic cognitive structures and predisposing personality, evidence has been found for the existence of these cognitive vulnerability constructs in nondepressed individuals who are theoretically at risk for depression. However, support for the stability of depressotypic cognitive structures beyond the depressive state is not evident unless either an activating stressful event is present or a dysphoric mood state is induced that ensures access to these latent structures. For the depression onset and relapse/recurrence hypotheses discussed in this chapter, the level of empirical support for diathesis-stress varied considerably from study to study. At this point, we are not able to assert that cognitive or personality diathesis-stress has garnered strong and consistent empirical support as a vulnerability model of depression. There have been a sufficient number of positive findings to suggest that these hypotheses are worth further investigation. However, the diathesis-stress research conducted to date on the contributory hypotheses have produced inconsistent results because most studies suffer from significant methodological shortcomings that preclude one from drawing any firm conclusions about the validity of the cognitive vulnerability hypotheses.

It is beyond the scope of this chapter to offer a full and detailed discussion of the methodological and conceptual limitations that have plagued cognitive diathesis-stress studies. The reader is referred to extensive reviews (Barnett & Gotlib, 1988c; Blatt & Zuroff, 1992; Coyne & Whiffen, 1995; Haaga et al., 1991; Ingram et al., 1998; Monroe & Simons, 1991; Nietzel & Harris, 1990; Segal & Dobson, 1992). In the following subsections, we summarize the main criticisms of the cognitive diathesis-stress studies and suggest recommendations for improving research in this area.

Reliance on Unprimed Experimental Designs

A major criticism of many studies on cognitive vulnerability is their failure to ensure that high-risk nondepressed individuals actually have access to the latent depressotypic cognitive structures and processes that are thought to act as a predisposition to depression. Some reviewers have concluded that unprimed studies do not provide a fair or adequate test of the stability or persistence of depressotypic cognitive structures beyond the depressive experience (Haaga et al., 1991; Ingram et al., 1998; Segal & Ingram, 1994). In fact, the cognitive model is emphatic that individuals predisposed to depression, such as those with a history of depression, will not show any cognitive differences from nonvulnerable, nondepressed individuals because the meaning structures of the primal loss mode remain latent or inaccessible during the nondepressed state. Activation of these structures by the occurrence of a congruent stressor, the introduction of a semantic prime, or the induction of a dysphoric mood state is necessary before one can investigate the effects of these underlying vulnerability structures. Because many studies that purport to test the vulnerability hypotheses of the cognitive model do not include a priming manipulation, we can conclude that their negative results are not a threat to the model. In fact, their results are entirely consistent with the predictions of the cognitive model. Consequently, our first recommendation is that research on cognitive vulnerability in nondepressed, high-risk samples must ensure that a priming or activating manipulation is introduced to ensure access to the hypothesized predisposing cognitive structures.

SAMPLING BIAS

Many reviews on the empirical status of cognitive vulnerability fail to differentiate between studies conducted on never-depressed and recovered depressed samples. This distinction is important and so we have proposed two separate hypotheses, one dealing with onset that must be tested in nonclinical samples and one dealing with relapse/recurrence that must be investigated with remitted depressed samples. The cognitive structures and processes involved in an initial onset of depression may differ from those involved in recurrence. Although Ingram et al. (1998) concluded that there is no strong empirical evidence for the "cognitive scar hypothesis," they also admitted that this hypothesis has not been adequately tested. Hirschfeld et al. (1989) found that the experience of depression left an adverse effect on the personality of recovered depressed patients. Thus there is enough suggestive evidence, particularly when considering the differential activation and kindling/sensitizing theories of Teasdale, Segal, and colleagues (Segal et al., 1996; Teasdale, 1988; Teasdale, Segal, et al., 1995), to argue for separating the nonclinical studies from the remitted depression studies when evaluating the empirical support for cognitive vulnerability.

Another issue involving sample characteristics concerns the level of depression or dysphoria that should or should not be present in a sample to provide a valid test of etiology. As discussed, it has been argued that acute-onset models of depression should be tested only on individuals who are initially asymptomatic and then become symptomatic after experiencing a stressful event (i.e., Monroe, Bromet, Connell, & Steiner, 1986). When individuals with depressive symptoms are included in the initial sample, this can compromise a longitudinal test of the acute-onset model by introducing the possibility of reverse causative associations (i.e., presence of disorder brings on life stress). The cognitive theory adopts an acute-onset perspective as is evident from the onset hypothesis. However, very few studies testing the onset or the relapse/recurrence hypotheses have ensured that all participants in their study at Time 1 were asymptomatic for depressive symptoms. Robins et al. (1995), for example, purposefully selected individuals who scored 14 or above on the BDI, whereas Dykman and Johll (1998) conducted separate analyses on initially asymptomatic (BDI less than 10) and combined samples. Robins et al. (1995) failed to find specific congruence effects with SAS Sociotropy and Autonomy, with both personality factors showing a significant interaction with both negative interpersonal and achievement events. Dykman and Johll (1998), on the other hand, found that the DAS interacted with level of stress only for the initially asymptomatic sample. In other studies, high scores on the DAS did not predict subsequent relapse rates unless the recovered depressed sample was initially asymptomatic such as at post-treatment (Ilardi et al., 1997; Williams et al., 1990). Thus the relatively poor findings for cognitive/personality event congruence and cognitive relapse vulnerability studies may be due to a failure to exclude participants with depressive symptoms at Time 1.

Another sample characteristic that deserves greater attention in the cognitive vulnerability studies is gender differences. Most studies run their analyses on total samples without any consideration of whether cognitive and life event variables may play a different causal role in the onset or recurrence of depression in women and men. This difference is entirely possible given the difference in depression rates as well as the social and cognitive processes that may be unique to the pathogenesis of depression in women (G.W. Brown & Harris, 1989; Nolen-Hoeksema, 1987). In some studies, life events or related variables such as social support have interacted with cognitive variables in women but not in men (e.g., Barnett & Gotlib, 1990; Dykman & Johll, 1998). Because of limited sample sizes, some researchers have treated gender as extraneous variance that is partialed out of regression analyses. This is not a satisfactory solution because it assumes that gender differences are extraneous variance that only detracts from diathesis-stress relationships. Cognitive vulnerability may interact in a different way or with different types of life experiences in men and women, and so we suggest that researchers conduct separate analyses on men and women. Important relationships and interactions may be obscured by running analyses on combined samples.

The inconsistent findings across the onset and recurrence studies may be due to the limited sample size used in many prospective studies of cognitive vulnerability. Given the moderate-to-weak effect sizes expected for personality-event interactions in the prediction of depression severity, large samples are needed to ensure adequate statistical power (Green, 1991). With small samples and inadequate statistical power, findings will be difficult, if not impossible, to replicate across studies. Researchers, then, must ensure that their sample sizes are sufficient to provide a fair statistical test of cognitive diathesis-stress.

Sample size is particularly crucial given that the cognitive model assumes that only some individuals who get depressed will be cognitively vulnerable and that others may develop depression in ways not specified by the model. Abramson et al. (1988) noted that cognitive diathesis-stress theories are *sufficiency* and not necessity models of depression. Furthermore, they argue that because depression is a heterogeneous disorder with different etiological pathways, an adequate test of cognitive diathesis-stress must ensure that a sufficient number of the high-risk group actually possess the postulated cognitive diathesis. Abramson et al. make the further point that cognitively vulnerable individuals are predisposed to a specific subtype of depressive experience, negative cognition depression, and so the researcher must ensure that this type of depression is adequately represented in their sample. We do not agree with Abramson and her colleagues that cognitive diathesis is relevant to such a circumscribed subtype of depression. However, we think they have a valid point about the need to ensure that one's sample includes a sufficient number of cognitively vulnerable individuals to test the model. This condition can be met by collecting data on larger samples to increase the likelihood that at least some of the participants will possess the cognitive diathesis, or by using high-risk behavioral studies that specifically identify vulnerable individuals for further investigation.

ASSESSMENT OF THE COGNITIVE/PERSONALITY DIATHESIS

One of the major difficulties in comparing findings across studies is that researchers often investigate different constructs under the rubric of cognitive diathesis or employ different measures of the same construct. Two questions can be raised in this regard. First, what is the relationship between different cognitive diatheses such as dysfunctional attitudes, sociotropy, autonomy, self-criticalness, dependency, negative attributional style, and hopelessness vulnerability? Is there sufficient overlap between these different constructs to justify drawing general conclusions across studies? A second major issue is whether the cognitive diathesis should be treated as a dimensional construct, or whether a typological approach is more appropriate.

In the Temple-Wisconsin Cognitive Vulnerability to Depression Project, Abramson, Alloy, and Hogan (1997) reported that a significantly greater proportion of the cognitively vulnerable group (defined as upper quartile scores on the Cognitive Style Questionnaire and DAS) had elevated scores on SAS Sociotropy (but not SAS Autonomy), DEQ Dependency, and DEQ Self-Criticalness than the cognitively nonvulnerable group. These researchers concluded that vulnerability to hopelessness depression overlaps with other constructs of psychological diathesis such as sociotropy, dependency, and self-criticalness. In a similar way, Coyne and Whiffen (1995) assumed that measures of diatheses derived from different models, such as SAS Sociotropy and DEQ Dependency or SAS Autonomy and DEQ Self-Criticalness, assess highly related and overlapping constructs; and so they drew broad conclusions that were applied equally to different psychological models of depression. This attempt to integrate findings across studies can lead to inaccurate and false conclusions because correlations between measures of similar constructs tend to fall in the low-to-moderate range indicating that the measures do not assess equivalent constructs (Barnett & Gotlib, 1988b; Blaney & Kutcher, 1991; D.A. Clark et al., 1995; Robins, 1985). Although an evaluation of the empirical support for cognitive diathesis-stress will be complicated by considering each diathesis scale separately, it is unwarranted to integrate findings across studies using different measures given their modest level of convergent validity.

A second issue that has been hotly debated in the depression literature on cognitive diathesis-stress is whether personality diathesis should be treated as discrete types or as continuous personality dimensions. Coyne and Whiffen (1995) are critical of typological approaches to personality, especially the use of cutoff scores to define extreme scoring groups (see also Haaga et al., 1991 for similar view). We agree with Coyne and Whiffen's arguments against the use of cutoff scores to define high-scoring groups. As they note, there have been inconsistencies across studies on whether to define personality groups in terms of median splits, upper and lower quartiles, or positive and negative z score values on competing scales. This still leaves the researcher with the problem of excluding large numbers of individuals because they show a mixed low or high scoring pattern on competing constructs such as sociotropy and autonomy. To accommodate these limitations, the dimensional nature of personality constructs should be retained under most circumstances.

There are exceptions to this general recommendation for a dimensional approach to personality research. First, a statistical approach to typological research, such as cluster analysis, avoids many of the pitfalls Coyne and Whiffen (1995) raise against categorization based on cutoff scores because all individuals are included in the analysis. Moreover, cluster analysis, which seeks to find naturally occurring distinct types in a data set, is not necessarily incompatible with dimensional analysis. It can be used to summarize naturally occurring co-variations of personality that are distinct groupings in terms of being differentiable on various personal and clinical features. In this case, it is not necessary to adopt a strong form of cluster analysis in which clusters are assumed to reflect categorical discrete latent entities (Haslam, personal communication, September 1995).

To date, it is not clear whether cluster analysis will yield new information on personality diathesis in depression. In a study conducted on the patients from the Center for Cognitive Therapy, cluster analysis based on the six subscales of the SAS revealed that SAS Autonomy may be heterogeneous with at least two relatively distinct types of individuals; the one being highly independent and presenting with a more severe symptom presentation and the other highly individualistic and achievement-oriented with less severe disturbance (D.A. Clark, Steer, et al., 1997). On the other hand, Robins and colleagues did not find that cluster analysis added any new information beyond more traditional dimensional analyses when investigating the relationship between PSI Sociotropy and Autonomy, and self-reported symptom patterns (Robins, Bagby, Rector, Lynch, & Kennedy, 1997). So it is not clear at this time whether cluster analytic procedures will provide new insights into personality vulnerability in depression. No doubt, the more expedient approach would be to maintain the dimensional integrity of these personality constructs. We also need to recognize that researchers using more complicated, time-consuming, and costly experimental designs, such as certain information processing studies, may want to select extreme scoring groups because only a limited number of participants can be included in a study. In this case, though, caution must be exercised in generalizing from the findings because of the highly selective sample.

Coyne and Whiffen (1995) argue that the language used in the cognitive model and other theories that advocate personality diathesis-stress designs indicates that the theorists assume that personality constructs like sociotropy and autonomy are typological rather than dimensional in nature. This is a misunderstanding of the cognitive model. Sociotropy and autonomy are personality dimensions not types. Although the terms "types," "modes," and "clusters" appear in the first description of the these personality constructs (A. Beck, 1983), the same source makes clear that sociotropy and autonomy were not envisioned as categorically distinct latent personality types. Rather, the conceptualization of sociotropy and autonomy as uncorrelated, situationally sensitive, and fluctuating constructs clearly fits with a dimensional rather than typological approach to personality.

A final issue raised by Coyne and Whiffen (1995) concerns the distinction between vulnerability to depression and the symptoms of depression. They noted that an ideal measure of depression vulnerability should have low or even nonsignificant correlations with measures of depression or distress in nonclinical samples because strong correlations would weaken the predictive validity of the diathesis by introducing a confound between the causal and expressive aspects of depression. In nonclinical studies, SAS Sociotropy has a low correlation ($r = .20$ to $.26$) with the BDI, whereas SAS Autonomy has an even lower or nonexistent association with self-reported dysphoria (D.A. Clark et al., 1995; Robins, 1985). In some but not all nonclinical studies, somewhat higher correlations have been reported between PSI Sociotropy and Autonomy, and measures of dysphoria or distress (Flett, Hewitt, et al., 1997; Robins et al., 1994; Zuroff, 1994), suggesting that the PSI scales may have a slightly closer relationship with manifest depression than the SAS. For the PSI Autonomy scale, this may be due to a higher proportion of self-criticism items. It is unclear from the empirical studies whether self-criticism meets the criteria necessary to constitute a vulnerability factor or whether it is more accurate to conceptualize it as part of the depressive symptom state (Coyne & Whiffen, 1995). Whatever the case, sociotropy and autonomy appear to be quite distinct from the depressive experience and so in this regard they meet the criteria for vulnerability.

Inadequate Assessment of Stress

Stress is a complex construct that has been defined in different ways and assessed with varied measurement instruments and procedures. Volumes have been written on the conceptual and methodological challenges involved in researching the relationship between life stress and illness onset (e.g., G.W. Brown & Harris, 1989; Gotlib & Hammen, 1992; Lazarus & Folkman, 1984), and excellent critical reviews and commentaries on life event research in depression have been published (see Alloy, Hartlage, et al., 1988; Coyne & Whiffen, 1995; Ingram et al., 1998; Monroe & Simons, 1991; Paykel & Cooper, 1992). Despite controversies in the life event research, studies have consistently demonstrated an association between major and, to a lesser extent, minor negative life events and depression, with several prospective designs indicating that major stressors, especially those involving significant personal loss, are causally linked to depression (Finlay-Jones & Brown, 1981; Gotlib & Hammen, 1992; Paykel, 1979). Ingram et al. noted that stress disrupts mechanisms that maintain a person's physiological, emotional, and cognitive stability. In this context, stress is viewed as factors operating external to the individual, although recent studies indicate that vulnerable individuals play a role in creating their own stressful lives (Hammen, 1991; Monroe & Simons, 1991). Another avenue in which diathesis or personality vulnerability can influence stress is through its impact on event appraisals. As noted previously, how an event is appraised—the meaning of the event for the individual—will influence whether an event becomes a precipitating factor in depression (G.W. Brown, 1989). Ingram et al. argue that although personality diathesis may influence life events via the capacity for stress generation and event appraisal, it is still viable to consider stress and vulnerability as distinct constructs in the pathogenesis of psychological disorders. Having said this, the diathesis-stress component of the cognitive model has often not been adequately tested in studies because of the use of weak and possibly invalid measures of stress. Three methodological problems confront research on cognitive diathesis-stress.

The first issue concerns the reliability and validity of retrospective self-report checklists of stress. Although most of the studies that have tested the onset and relapse hypotheses of the cognitive model relied on self-report life event checklists, the validity of these measures has been questioned by researchers (G.W. Brown, 1989; Coyne & Whiffen, 1995; Monroe & Simons, 1991; Simons et al., 1993). Two problems emerge with self-report life event questionnaires. First, individuals are not very accurate in their recall of stressors and so those vulnerable to psychological distress may overreport or exaggerate difficult events in their life (Alloy, Hartlage, et al., 1988; Paykel & Cooper, 1992). Simons et al. found that depressed patients self-reported far more events on the PERI life event checklist than met criteria for a life stressor on the LEDS structured life event interview. In an earlier study, Monroe (1982) found that even nonclinical individuals may underreport as much as 60% of the life events that occurred within the past 4 months. Second, Monroe and Simons argued that self-report checklists confound the occurrence of external life stressors with the individual's own perception of the event, with the latter influenced by personality diathesis. Thus to ensure a clean and accurate assessment of life events, most depression researchers recommend the use of structured life event interviews with trained external judges to evaluate the severity and impact of the event. Although it is difficult to argue against these recommendations, structured life event measures have not produced more or less consistent support for the onset or relapse hypotheses than self-report life event checklists. The general pattern of relationship between personality and events may be what has most importance in predicting depression, and not the precise count of the actual number of certain types of life events (e.g., whether a person experienced three or five separate and distinct negative interpersonal events in the last 6 months). Alloy, Hartlage, et al. (1988) suggest that a self-report scale followed by a brief follow-up interview might prove a reasonable compromise between the rigors of life event interviews and the efficiency of questionnaire methodology.

A second problem is whether stress should be assessed by an aggregated score that represents a summation over endorsed checklist items, or whether single highly distressing events may be more important in the stress-illness relationship. Although most cognitive diathesis-stress studies represent the stress component as an aggregated score, Coyne and Whiffen (1995) argue that the occurrence of single severe life events may confer the greatest risk for the onset of depressive disorders. More research on the depression onset and relapse hypotheses is needed that focuses specifically on the fateful single life events that may be associated with the highest risks for depression (Shrout et al., 1989).

A related problem in many prospective cognitive diathesis-stress studies is the failure to ensure that an adequate base rate of significant negative life events has occurred between the initial assessment at Time 1 and the follow-up testing at Time 2. Abramson, Alloy, and Hogan (1997) point out that findings from diathesis-stress studies will depend on levels of stress in the population under investigation. Because of the interactive nature of diathesis-stress formulations, no differences in levels of depression will be evident between vulnerable and nonvulnerable individuals at very low or very high levels of stress. At very low levels of stress, no one will become depressed, whereas at very high levels of stress most individuals will succumb to depression. It is only at a moderate range of stress where the highly vulnerable group will be relatively more susceptible to depression than the nonvulnerable group. Thus in nonclinical studies in which life events are assessed over a relatively short period (e.g., 4–8 weeks), significant stressors may occur at a very low rate, or most of the events that occur may be relatively mild and innocuous. In these studies, few of the highly vulnerable individuals can be expected to become depressed and so the study may lack the necessary predictive power to test the onset and relapse hypotheses. It is incumbent on researchers to ensure that a sufficient number of participants in a prospective study have been exposed to a moderate level of stress in the follow-up period so that diathesis-stress formulations can be properly investigated. It may be necessary to target segments of the population who have recently experienced severe and significant major life events such as death, separation, divorce, unemployment, or medical illness, to ensure that a sufficient level of stress is apparent for a fair investigation of diathesis-stress.

The onset and relapse hypotheses posit a specific interaction between cognitive diathesis and type of stressor in depression. Highly sociotropic individuals, for example, are thought to be more susceptible to depression after experiencing a negative interpersonal stressor, whereas the highly autonomous person is considered at higher risk for depression after a negative achievement event. The ability to test this hypothesis depends on the accuracy of categorizing life events into interpersonal and achievement categories. In most studies, external raters have been able to categorize life event questionnaire items into interpersonal and achievement concerns with a high degree of reliability. Abramson, Alloy, and Hogan (1997), however, have questioned whether this interpersonal/achievement taxonomy of events can lead to an adequate test of the specific diathesis-stress hypothesis. They argue that vulnerability does not fall as neatly as one would like into interpersonal and achievement event domains because individuals may respond to different aspects of a stressful event. For example, a job demotion might be categorized as a negative achievement event and most likely to precipitate depression in an autonomous individual who is highly sensitive to issues of mastery, control, and achievement. However, a job demotion could also trigger a depressive response in a highly sociotropic job because it could result in a change in work environment and loss of contact with valued work colleagues. It is doubtful that life events fall into clearly distinguishable discrete categories of sociotropic and autonomous concerns, which means that content-based taxonomies may be arbitrary and so weaken the possibility of finding differential personality × event interactions.

A possible response to this problem might be to abandon any pretense of an objective a priori event classification scheme and instead focus on whether there are personality differences in the response to different features of stressful events. Pilon (1989) had participants rate the extent to which three sociotropic stakes ("losing the affection of someone important to you," "losing the approval or respect of someone important to you," and "appearing to be an uncaring person") and three autonomous stakes ("not achieving an important goal at your job or in your work," "losing your self-respect," and "harm to your own health, safety, or physical well-being") were evident in the most stressful life event that had happened within the past 2 weeks. Summing over these stakes, Pilon found a main effect for sociotropic stress in predicting

Hamilton Depression level, and a significant interaction between SAS Autonomy and autonomous stakes in formerly depressed students. These results may have been stronger if a longer follow-up period had been used. Future research on cognitive diathesis-stress may want to consider an event taxonomy that is based on the needs, motives, and perspectives of the individual.

NEGLECT OF EVENT APPRAISALS

According to cognitive theory, the mere occurrence of a negative life event is not sufficient to trigger the latent dysfunctional self-schemas or personality vulnerability that predispose to depression. For life stressors to activate an underlying vulnerability to depression, the event must be perceived by the individual as representing a threatened loss of personally valued resources. Thus how an event is appraised is a critical mediating factor in whether the event has the potential to activate depressotypic cognitive structures and processes.

In empirical studies, individuals' appraisals of life experiences have shown significant associations with depression. Appraisal dimensions that have been implicated include degree of perceived upset associated with an event, outcome expectations, uncertainty, threat, uncontrollability, change associated with the event, centrality or importance of the event, amount of social support and negative attributional style (J.D. Brown & Siegel, 1988; Gong-Guy & Hammen, 1980; Gruen, Folkman, & Lazarus, 1988; Hammen & Cochrane, 1981; Peacock & Wong, 1990; Robins & Block, 1989, Study 2; Robins, Block, & Peselow, 1990b). In two studies conducted by Robins and colleagues, negative life event perceptions were significant unique predictors of depression diagnosis or symptom severity in clinical and nonclinical samples even after controlling for frequency of life events (Robins & Block, 1989; Robins et al., 1990a). In addition, the mediation hypothesis was supported in each study, indicating that the occurrence of stressful life events and presence of dysfunctional attitudes may lead to maladaptive event perceptions that are in turn linked to depression. In one of our own studies (D.A. Clark et al., 1992), we found that ratings of the perceived loss associated with negative events significantly distinguished dysphoric from nondysphoric students after accounting for the main effects of SAS personality and frequency of negative interpersonal or achievement events. However, the perceived loss ratings did not interact significantly with personality to predict dysphoric mood state. Robins et al. (1990b) introduced an alternative viewpoint on event appraisals. They found that nonendogenous depressed patients reported significantly more dysfunctional attitudes and negative life events than endogenous patients, although both groups did not differ significantly in their appraisals of their most upsetting life event. The authors concluded that biased perceptions of life events may be a concomitant of depression, whereas dysfunctional attitudes may be an etiologic factor in nonendogenous depressions.

If we accept the prevailing view that event appraisals are a crucial component of cognitive diathesis-stress, then why is it that so few studies on cognitive vulnerability actually included event appraisal ratings in their research design? Haaga et al. (1991) concluded in their review that research at that time had not yet directly tested the hypothesis that personality diathesis will influence how a stressful event is evaluated. Alloy, Hartlage, et al. (1988) also recommended that life events be rated along appraisal dimensions. Fisher (1989) proposed that ratings of life event occurrence be replaced with a more general assessment of reported life problems that would take into account the personal meanings that individuals attached to their life circumstances. There are at least three reasons why cognitive-clinical researchers have neglected to include event appraisal variables in their diathesis-stress designs.

First, it is unclear which appraisal dimensions are most relevant to cognitive vulnerability. Is it perceived loss to valued personal resources, degree of upset or severity, uncontrollability, or some other variable that is most crucial in the appraisal process? Is a specific appraisal dimension more critical to one particular personality-event interaction than another (i.e., interpersonal events for sociotropic persons and achievement events for the autonomous individuals), or do general nonspecific appraisal processes determine the particular impact of the event on personality? Second, the introduction of yet another set of variables greatly adds to the complexity of diathesis-stress research designs. If appraisal variables are included, then the critical experimental hypotheses would now be tested in three-way interactions that are much more difficult to interpret.

And finally, critics have argued that one must disentangle the person-centered diathesis from the environmentally oriented stressor to assess diathesis-stress formulations (Coyne & Whiffen, 1995; Monroe & Simons, 1991). Obviously, the introduction of respondent-based event appraisals blurs the distinction between diathesis and stress. However, Haaga et al. (1991) argued that an attempt to create pure and uncontaminated measures of event and person characteristics is not consistent with cognitive theory, which advocates a more integrative approach to the assessment of person-environmental causes of depression. Despite the increased complexity involved with event appraisal variables, research on the diathesis-stress aspect of cognitive vulnerability to depression must begin to consider event valuation to provide a full and accurate test of cognitive theory.

Inadequate Investigation of the Full Cognitive Vulnerability Model

In their review of the empirical basis of the cognitive vulnerability model, Haaga et al. (1991) concluded that no study at that time had incorporated all the conditions necessary to test the model adequately. That conclusion is as apt today as it was 10 years ago. As this critique shows, serious shortcomings can be found in sample selection, measurement of the diathesis and stress, neglect of personal meaning and appraisal variables, and limited use of more powerful prospective research designs. In addition the diathesis-stress relationship is probably not linear, as assumed in most studies, but instead is probably characterized by *threshold effects* where stress can trigger a depressive episode only when exceeding an above-threshold value of the diathesis (Monroe & Simons, 1991).

A further complication is that the diathesis or predisposition to depression may be relatively common in the general population but the frequency of stressors capable of eliciting depression may be relatively low (Monroe & Simons, 1991). Coyne and Whiffen (1995) also argued that diathesis-stress hypotheses will be difficult to test in an unselected nonclinical sample because of the relatively low base rate of depressive disorders in the general population (see also Coyne, 1994b). The "base rate problem" poses a significant challenge for researchers to design studies that are powerful enough to detect diathesis-stress interactions.

A final consideration is that multiple diatheses are likely to operate in the pathogenesis of depressive disorders. Not only may other types of personality vulnerabilities impact on the depressotypic potential of any specific diathesis, but factors like coping resources, social support, and possibly biological constitution may mediate or interact with the proposed diathesis-stress relationship. Given all the shortcomings and complexities in cognitive diathesis-stress research, it is noteworthy that so many studies provided support for the core hypotheses of cognitive vulnerability to depression. The inconsistencies across studies are understandable in light of the methodological and conceptual challenges discussed. In Chapter 10, we examine additional vulnerability hypotheses that deal with auxiliary processes that may moderate cognitive diathesis-stress vulnerability to depression.

CHAPTER 10

Cognitive Vulnerability: Empirical Status of the Secondary Hypotheses

CHAPTER 9 focused on the three primary hypotheses of cognitive vulnerability—stability, onset, and relapse. These three hypotheses deal with the core tenets of the cognitive theory of vulnerability to depression (A. Beck, 1967, 1987, 1991). The validity of the etiologic features of the cognitive model rests primarily on the empirical status of these hypotheses. However, other constructs and processes that are involved in the cognitive formulation play a secondary, albeit significant, role in the cognitive predisposition to depression.

In this chapter, we discuss empirical support for six other hypotheses that are important to the cognitive formulation of a predisposition to nonendogenous, reactive depression (Table 10.1). The first four hypotheses—self-evaluation, congruent processing, relationship, and coping—are relatively new derivations from the cognitive model. Although not explicitly stated in previous writings, these hypotheses deal with processes that are entirely consistent with earlier formulations of the cognitive model. The last two hypotheses—symptom specificity and differential treatment—were described in A. Beck (1983) and deal with the specific effects of personality vulnerability on depressive symptom presentation and response to treatment.

Because these hypotheses deal with processes and mechanisms that are less central to cognitive vulnerability of depression, they have not been as well refined and elaborated in previous writings. As well these hypotheses have not received extensive attention from researchers. Thus

Table 10.1
The Secondary Vulnerability Hypotheses of the
Cognitive Theory of Depression

Hypotheses	Statement
Self-Evaluation	The cognitive structures and content that contribute to susceptibility to depression will guide self-perceptions, self-evaluations, and self-appraisals especially when elicited by schema-congruent situations.
Congruent Processing	When activated, the cognitive structures and content that predispose for depression will selectively bias information processing for stimuli congruent with the cognitive vulnerability organization.
Relationship	Cognitive structures and content that predispose for depression are associated with a characteristic interpersonal style that affects the quality and nature of social relations with significant others.
Differential Coping	Maladaptive coping responses and compensatory strategies will play a more significant role in depression when personality-event congruence is present than when personality-event incongruence is present.
Symptom Specificity	The predepressive personality suborganization associated with the primal loss mode will influence depressive symptom presentation such that sociotropy is associated with symptoms of deprivation and autonomy with symptoms of defeat and self-depreciation.
Differential Treatment	The predepressive personality suborganization of the primal loss mode will influence attitudes and response to treatment such that sociotropic individuals are more responsive to interpersonally and emotionally engaging interventions, whereas autonomous persons are more responsive to less personal and more problem-focused interventions.

our review of the relevant literature is relatively brief, and any conclusions that can be drawn from this literature should be considered tentative. An extensive critique of the research would also be premature, and so we conclude with a few comments on the direction that future research might take in this area.

SELF-EVALUATION HYPOTHESIS

The cognitive structures and content that contribute to susceptibility to depression will guide self-perceptions, self-evaluations, and self-appraisals especially when elicited by schema-congruent situations.

As discussed in Chapter 4, the cognitive model proposes that the maladaptive schemas and personality suborganization that characterize cognitive vulnerability to depression have a self-referent orientation. These self-oriented cognitive structures or schemas comprise an internal representation of the self, or self-concept, that organize and guide the processing of self-referent information (Markus, 1977). That is, self-schemas exert a dominant influence on the selection, encoding, organization, and retrieval of personally meaningful stimuli. In addition, self-schemas are involved in monitoring and evaluating personal performance and so contain self-evaluative information and judgments of personal worth that reflect one's level of self-esteem.

The cognitive model has consistently emphasized the importance of negative self-schema structures and processes in understanding cognitive vulnerability for depression:

> The vulnerability of the depression-prone person is attributable to the constellation of enduring negative attitudes about himself, about the world and about his future. Even though these attitudes (or concepts) may not be prominent or even discernible at a given time, they persist in a latent state like an explosive charge ready to be detonated by an appropriate set of conditions. Once activated, these concepts dominate the person's thinking and lead to the typical depressive symptomatology. (A. Beck, 1967, p. 277)

To be pathogenic, these negative attitudes or schemas about the self must be associated with negative value judgments, self-blame, and negative expectations about the future (A. Beck, 1967). For depression-prone individuals, activation of their latent negative self-schemas will lead to excessively negative or pessimistic self-perceptions and self-evaluations. These self-appraisals, involving observations about the self, and self-evaluations (value judgments about the self in terms of good-bad, worthy-worthless, lovable-unlovable), are derived from self-schemas activated by stimuli or experiences that impinge on the person's personal domain (A. Beck, 1976; A. Beck, Freeman, et al., 1990).

The importance of negative self-evaluations in depression has been well recognized in the research literature (e.g., A. Beck, Steer, et al., 1990; Strauman, 1989). For example, Dykman (1996) had dysphoric and nondysphoric students imagine 16 positive or negative hypothetical life experiences and rate their self-evaluation of themselves after each scenario on 49 trait adjectives. The dysphoric individuals endorsed more extreme, global negative self-evaluations, whereas the nondysphoric individuals tended to make more circumscribed self-evaluations. Stiles and Gotestam (1989) found that students who reported a high frequency of negative automatic thoughts toward the self and future experienced a significantly greater increase in sad mood following a mood induction procedure than students low in negative automatic thoughts. These findings suggest a close coupling between negative self-evaluation and depressed mood.

In their self-worth contingency model, Kuiper and Olinger (1986) proposed that negative self-evaluation is a marker of episodic depression. In vulnerable nondepressed individuals a positive self-evaluation will be evident because individuals are meeting "the self-worth contingencies of their dysfunctional attitudes" (Swallow & Kuiper, 1987, p. 158), whereas in episodic depression a negative self-evaluation is evident because one's self-worth contingencies are not being met. Self-worth contingencies are dysfunctional attitudes characterized by a contractual basis for self-worth (e.g., "My value as a person depends on what others think of me") (Swallow & Kuiper, 1987). According to this model, vulnerability for depression consists of a poorly consolidated view of the self because the individual relies on dysfunctional attitudes to determine self-worth (Dance & Kuiper, 1987). Once again, priming is necessary (i.e., failure to meet self-worth contingencies) before the association between dysfunctional beliefs and negative self-evaluations is apparent.

Other studies, however, suggest that negative self-evaluation itself may be a direct predictor of depression. Hammen (1988b) found that low self-concept contributed significantly to the prediction of depressive diagnoses over a 6-month period in children of depressed mothers. Garber and Robinson (1997) reported that children of mothers with a history of depression (vulnerable individuals) had lower perceived self-worth, more negative attributional style, greater self-criticalness, lower perceived academic and behavioral competence, and more frequent negative automatic thoughts than children at low risk of depression even after controlling for current levels of depression. Thus the research is not consistent on whether negative self-evaluation has to be primed to be apparent in vulnerable individuals or whether it is a trait variable present at all times in the depression-prone individual.

Fennell (1997) proposed a cognitive conceptualization of low self-esteem based on an elaboration of the cognitive model (A. Beck, 1976). She defined self-esteem in terms of schema, or a generic cognitive representation of the self as a whole person. In her model, low self-esteem consists of a core belief in which an individual reaches a fundamental negative conclusion about the self (e.g., "I am incompetent") as a result of an interaction between temperament and certain negative experiences during childhood. From this core negative self-referent belief, dysfunctional assumptions in the form of conditional statements (e.g., "If I can please everyone, then they will like me") develop to guide one's behavior. As long as the standards and expectations dictated by these assumptions are met, the person with low self-esteem will function normally. However, when a critical incident occurs in which the standards of the dysfunctional assumptions are not met (e.g., one tries to please a significant other, but does not receive the expected love and acceptance from this person), then the core negative self-referent belief is primed or activated and sets in motion a vicious cycle that involves negative predictions, physiological arousal (anxiety), dysfunctional behavior, biased interpretations of situations as confirmation of the central negative view of the self, self-critical thinking, and finally depression. According to this cognitive model of low self-esteem, negative self-schema or self-evaluation plays a central role in the pathogenesis of depression. Furthermore, like Swallow and Kuiper (1987), Fennell (1997) argues that the depressotypic effects of low self-esteem will not be apparent until a critical incident occurs in which certain expectations for the self are not met. Thus the negative self-schemas, though persistent and enduring across time and situations, must be activated or primed by certain critical experiences.

Another theoretical model of self-esteem, proposed by Roberts and Monroe (1994), also considers vulnerable self-esteem (i.e., characteristics of self-esteem that increase risk for future depression) a critical factor in the etiology and maintenance of depression. They describe three major features of this inner core of vulnerable self-esteem. Vulnerable self-esteem consists of *structural inadequacies* such as the existence of relatively few important external sources of positive self-worth, a greater preponderance of negative possible selves or core negativity about the self, and large discrepancies between positive and negative domains of the self or the actual and ideal selves. In addition, certain *self-esteem deflating processes* are evident such as negative overgeneralization and narcissistic intolerance (i.e., inability to tolerate discrepancies between the real and ideal self). Finally, *poor consolidation* is also apparent in terms of uncertainty, inconsistency, and slower or less efficient processing within self-evaluative knowledge structures. This inner core of self-esteem vulnerability will lead to heightened reactivity in the form of poor resilience to negative primes and temporal instability of one's self-esteem. Because of an inner self-esteem vulnerability, the depression-prone individual's self-esteem is more reactive to daily stressors and other negative experiences and so will appear temporally unstable. These outward manifestations or reactivity of self-esteem would affect other psychosocial factors in depression such as maladaptive coping resources, self-generation of stress, poor affect regulation, and interpersonal conflict. Like Fennell (1997), Roberts and Monroe viewed self-schemas as providing the structural foundation or self-evaluative knowledge on which self-esteem is based. This is seen in their characterization of vulnerable self-esteem in terms of poor consolidation of self-evaluative knowledge structures.

Roberts and Monroe's (1994) integrated model of self-esteem does not argue that an enduring state of low self-esteem leads to vulnerability to depression. Rather, the inner core of self-esteem vulnerability confers greater risk for depression through heightened reactivity of self-esteem caused by a lack of resilience to negative primes. Thus it is the temporal instability of self-esteem (or a labile self-esteem), not trait low self-esteem, that characterizes the self-esteem vulnerability to depression. The model also adopts a diathesis-stress perspective on depression vulnerability. A labile or temporally unstable self-esteem will only be apparent in response to daily stressors and life events. Thus the model predicts that high labile self-esteem will interact with negative stressors to predict depressive symptoms. Roberts and Monroe note that the inner core of self-esteem vulnerability, though relatively inaccessible to conscious awareness, will be experienced by individuals as vacillations in their feelings of self-worth and self-regard in response to daily events and experiences.

Several prospective studies have been conducted to determine whether the main effects of self-esteem stability and its interaction with negative life experiences are significant predictors of depressive symptoms. In one of the first studies to address this question, Roberts and Monroe (1992) assessed trait self-esteem, self-esteem stability (i.e., multiple assessments of self-esteem before and after midterm exams), and self-report depressive symptoms in 192 undergraduates 3 weeks before midterm examinations and then 1 week after grades were received. Analysis revealed that highly unstable self-esteem but not trait self-esteem interacted with academic stress to predict depression primarily in students who initially scored in the nondepressed range on the BDI prior to the examination period. Thus an unstable self-esteem acted as a diathesis, predicting increases in depressive symptoms only after academic failure in the initially asymptomatic students.

A. Butler, Hokanson, and Flynn (1994) reported additional results that support Roberts and Monroe's (1992) finding that self-esteem lability may be a better predictor of vulnerability to depression than low trait self-esteem. Self-esteem lability refers to an "excessive reactivity of state self-worth to daily threats and boosts" (Butler et al., 1994, p. 166). As self-esteem lability increases, less life stress is needed to trigger a depressive state so that high lability represents a marked risk for the onset of major depression when the individual is confronted with a significant and meaningful loss. In their study, three groups of undergraduates were selected as currently depressed, previously depressed (nondepressed vulnerable), or never depressed based on whether they met criteria on three self-report depression measures. Participants then completed daily measures of self-esteem and experiences over a 30-day period. Analysis revealed that the previously depressed had significantly greater state self-esteem fluctuations in response to both positive and negative daily events than the never-depressed group, whereas the two groups did not differ significantly on the Self-Attitude Inventory, a measure of trait self-esteem. In a second part of this study, 73 participants were available for a 5-month follow-up. Twelve of these individuals became new cases of depression defined as nondepressed at Time 1 but who met criteria for depression at follow-up. Analysis at Time 1 revealed that the new cases had significantly higher self-esteem lability scores than nondepressed controls, whereas the two groups did not differ in their Time 1 trait self-esteem. In hierarchical regression analyses based on the full sample, Time 2 depression scores were predicted by a combination of elevated levels of recent life stress and high self-esteem lability to both positive and negative events. These findings, then, suggest that state self-esteem lability may be a vulnerability factor in depression rather than trait low self-esteem. In other studies, however, low trait self-esteem has been shown to predict future self-reported depressive symptoms (BDI scores) in individuals with relatively stable self-esteem and in persons with unstable self-esteem (Roberts, Kassel, & Gotlib, 1995).

Roberts and Kassel (1997) also found that labile self-esteem acted as a diathesis for depressive symptoms in persons with initial low levels of depression or in persons prone to depression as indicated by relatively severe previous episodes of self-reported depressive symptoms. However labile self-esteem only acted as a vulnerability to depressive symptoms when associated with the occurrence and perception of life stress. Thus the relation of self-esteem instability to depression must be understood within a diathesis-stress perspective because it appears to be associated with adverse reactions to life stress, and so will have little direct impact on depression when stresses are not present. In addition, Roberts and Kassel found that the effects of labile self-esteem were not due to a depletion in self-esteem resources, which led the authors to suggest that possibly a sense of hopelessness, or difficulty maintaining optimism following negative experiences, may be the mechanism by which labile self-esteem impacts on depression. Whatever the exact processes involved, temporal instability and fluctuations in self-esteem may be an important diathesis for vulnerability to depression. Roberts and Gotlib (1997) found that temporal variability in global self-esteem, and even in more specific self-evaluations, predicted the development of depressive symptoms following stressful life events. However, Gable and Nezlek (1998) found that temporal instability across a number of constructs related to psychological well-being in general predicted risk of depressive symptoms. They suggest that vulnerability to depression may be represented by day-to-day instability of psychological states more generally than to fluctuations in self-esteem more specifically.

These studies indicate that temporal instability or highly reactive fluctuations in self-esteem acts as a vulnerability diathesis for depressive symptoms, especially in individuals with a history of depressive episodes. Thus, a highly unstable or labile self-esteem may also confer increased vulnerability to depressive relapse and recurrence. At this point, many issues still remain unresolved, but at the very least this research highlights the importance of self-esteem or its variability in the pathogenesis of depression.

As noted, CT views cognitive vulnerability to depression in terms of maladaptive schemas and predepressive personality constructs like sociotropy and autonomy. Kovacs and Beck (1978) stated that the maladaptive schemas that predispose to depression deal with aspects of one's experience that concern self-evaluation and interpersonal relationships. As a result, negative self-evaluations and low self-esteem should be apparent when maladaptive attitudes and beliefs are activated in nondepressed vulnerable individuals. A strong relationship is predicted between elevated scores on the DAS or other measures of negative schematic content, and indices of negative self-evaluation and self-concept.

Likewise, elevations in sociotropy and autonomy would be associated with negative self-appraisal and self-judgments on issues congruent with the predepressive personality constellation. Thus the highly sociotropic person is more likely to generate negative self-appraisals when confronted with negative self-referent information or experiences within the interpersonal domain, whereas the highly autonomous person is more likely to make negative self-evaluations when experiencing difficulties with issues of independence and productivity. This hypothesis states that negative self-evaluations will only be evident when primed by schema (or personality) congruent experiences. Thus a positive correlation between cognitive vulnerability and negative self-evaluation measures may not be detectable unless the latent dysfunctional schemas are primed by a triggering event. Finally, the findings from research on temporal instability of self-esteem and risk of depression suggest that individuals with dysfunctional attitudes or a predepressive personality constellation may also exhibit high levels of self-esteem instability and reactivity to stressful life events. Thus self-esteem variability could act as a moderator for the cognitive vulnerability-life event relationship to depression.

EMPIRICAL SUPPORT FOR THE SELF-EVALUATION HYPOTHESIS

The most direct empirical test of the self-evaluation hypothesis would involve the use of a priming manipulation, either through mood induction or exposure to a distressing situation, with vulnerable (e.g., recovered depressives) and nonvulnerable individuals, followed by an assessment to determine whether there was a stronger relationship between negative self-evaluation and measures of cognitive vulnerability (i.e., DAS or SAS scores) in the vulnerable group. To our knowledge, no published studies have conducted this critical test of the self-evaluation hypothesis. Less direct, though relevant, support is provided by unprimed studies of the relationship between cognitive vulnerability and negative self-evaluation in nondepressed vulnerable groups such as recovered depressives. Studies that examine the relationship between cognitive vulnerability and self-evaluation in currently depressed or nondepressed normal samples provide only suggestive evidence of whether further research on these constructs with nondepressed vulnerable groups is warranted. This brief discussion begins with the few studies that have investigated the relationship between self-evaluation and cognitive vulnerability in the currently depressed and nondepressed samples.

If there is a connection between negative self-evaluation and vulnerability to depression, then at the very least we should find a significant correlation between these two constructs in currently depressed individuals in which the hypothesized negative self-schemas have been activated. As expected, a positive correlation has been found between DAS scores and measures of negative self-perception or self-evaluation in clinically depressed individuals (Blackburn et al., 1986). However, other studies have found only a low to modest relationship between maladaptive beliefs and negative self-evaluation in episodic depression. Gara et al. (1993) used a free response format to assess perceptions of self and others in 31 clinically depressed and 27 nondepressed controls. Although the depressed group produced significantly more negative perceptions of the self and important others (i.e., parents, significant other, friends) and fewer positive perceptions of self and other than the control group, the DAS correlated only −.23 with positive self-evaluation and .32 with negative self-evaluation. A. Beck, Steer, et al. (1990) also found that the DAS correlated only −.21 with the Beck Self-Concept Test in 550 depressed and/or anxious outpatients.

The relationship between the DAS and negative self-evaluation has also been investigated in nondepressed samples. In a study of dysphoric and nondysphoric college students, Oliver, Maier, Ross, and Wiener (1990) found that the DAS and Selves Questionnaire (Higgins et al., 1985) were not significantly related after controlling for current level of depression.

Consistent with predictions of the self-worth contingency model that negative self-evaluation will be evident in vulnerable persons only when self-worth contingencies are not being met, Kuiper et al. (1985) found that students classified as depressed-vulnerable (high BDI and high DAS scores) endorsed as self-descriptive and recalled significantly more depression-content self-referent adjectives, whereas the nondepressed vulnerable group (low BDI and high DAS scores) did not show any evidence of negative self-schema processing. In another study (Kuiper et al., 1987, Experiment 1), regression analysis revealed that high DAS scores were predictive of higher endorsement rates of depressive content adjectives. However, further analysis involving classification of participants into depressed and nondepressed vulnerable and nonvulnerable groups indicated that the nondepressed vulnerable group endorsed more positive than negative adjectives, whereas the depressed subjects, regardless of their DAS scores, endorsed more depression-content adjectives. Finally, Swallow and Kuiper (1987) found that high scores on the DAS were associated with a significant decrease in ratings of perceived similarity of self to others which in turn appears related to an increasingly negative self-view. Generally, studies on currently depressed or nondepressed samples have not found a strong relationship between elevated scores on the DAS and negative self-evaluation.

Very few studies have investigated the relationship between negative self-evaluation and cognitive vulnerability in vulnerable nondepressed samples. Although Blackburn et al. (1986) did not report the correlation between the DAS and their measure of negative self-evaluation in the recovered depressed group, the fact that the recovered depressed group scored similar to the current depressed group on the negative self-evaluation measure but similar to the nondepressed group on the DAS suggests a lack of relationship between these two measures in the asymptomatic depressed subjects. Garber and Robinson (1997) found that after controlling for current level of depression, children of mothers with a history of depression did not have significantly higher scores on the DAS than low-risk children despite significant differences in perceived self-worth.

In an analysis of data from the Temple-Wisconsin Cognitive Vulnerability to Depression Project, Alloy, Abramson, et al. (1997) compared nondepressed high and low cognitively vulnerable students. As discussed in Chapter 9, analysis revealed that compared with the low-risk group, the high-risk group (a) endorsed significantly more negative self-referent trait adjectives, (b) was slower at endorsing positive trait words and somewhat faster at endorsing negative words, (c) provided more past behavioral descriptions for why negative words were self-descriptive and fewer examples for why positive adjectives were self-descriptive, (d) gave more negative judgments of future expectations, and (e) recalled significantly fewer positive depressive adjectives (but did not differ from the low-risk group in recall of negative trait adjectives). The authors interpreted these findings as suggesting that negative self-referent encoding and retrieval bias may not simply be concomitants of episodic depression but an indictor of cognitive vulnerability to depression.

The findings of Alloy, Abramson, et al. (1997) can be viewed as support for the self-evaluation hypothesis. Individuals identified as vulnerable in part by their elevated scores on dysfunctional attitudes were shown to have a negativity bias on information processing tasks indicative of negative self-evaluation. The one inconsistent finding was the failure of the high-risk group to recall significantly more negative depression-relevant trait adjectives. This result, then, failed to support Gilboa and Gotlib's (1997) contention that memory recall bias may be a better marker of cognitive vulnerability than attentional, judgmental, or encoding processes. We can conclude that an enhanced relationship between elevated DAS scores and negative self-evaluation as an indicator of cognitive vulnerability has not been clearly established, although the results of Alloy, Abramson, et al. suggest that more research in this area is definitely warranted. The critical research on the self-evaluation hypothesis and DAS has not yet been carried out. Studies are needed that compare nondepressed vulnerable (high DAS scorers) and nonvulnerable (low DAS scores) groups exposed to a relevant stressor versus no stressor condition to ensure that dysfunctional schemas are activated. The dependent measure would be indices of negative self-evaluation. According to the self-evaluation hypothesis, only the vulnerable group in the stress condition would show elevated levels of negative self-evaluation.

Very little research has been conducted on the relationship between the SAS and negative self-evaluation. We are not aware of any published studies on the relationship between SAS Sociotropy or Autonomy and negative self-evaluation in currently depressed or recovered depressed samples. However, a few studies have reported on the correlation between the SAS and self-esteem measures in nondepressed college student samples. Barnett and Gotlib (1988b) found that SAS Sociotropy correlated −.48 and −.47, respectively, with the Jackson Personality Inventory Self-Esteem and Rosenberg Self-Esteem scales, whereas SAS Autonomy correlated .23 and .10, respectively, with these self-esteem measures. Dozois, Dobson, and Tait (1995) investigated the relationship between self-complexity and personality in 120 female undergraduates classified as nondysphoric, mildly dysphoric, or moderately dysphoric. They failed to find any relationship between self-complexity for positive or negative self-evaluation in achievement or social domains and SAS Sociotropy or Autonomy.

We have conducted a series of studies in our own laboratory on the relationship between the SAS and measures of self-evaluation in nondepressed college student samples.[1] In one study, an extended version of the Rosenberg Self-Esteem Questionnaire developed by Metalsky et al. (1993) and the Revised SAS were given to 184 students. The Extended Self-Esteem Questionnaire (ESEQ) assesses participants' level of agreement to 10 self-referent statements each concerning one's perceived success within school and social relationships. Partial correlations between the SAS scales and ESEQ scales were calculated controlling for the high correlation (.80) between the two ESEQ subscales. SAS Sociotropy showed evidence of domain-specific negative self-evaluation with a −.30 correlation with self-esteem scores in social relationships but a −.08 correlation with self-esteem in the academic sphere. SAS Solitude, which we have argued may be the vulnerability component of autonomy, correlated −.23 with ESEQ social and .06 with ESEQ academic. The SAS Independence scale failed to correlate with either self-esteem scale.

A second study investigated discrepancy between the actual, ideal, and ought self by having 185 students rate 10 positive sociotropic and 10 positive autonomous trait adjectives for degree of personal relevance in each of the three selfhood domains. The trait adjectives were taken from a list of sociotropic and autonomous trait words developed by Ivy Blackburn (for description see Blackburn et al., 1990). Revised SAS Sociotropy correlated .29 and .37, respectively, with an ideal-actual self-discrepancy in both sociotropic and autonomous trait adjectives, and a ought-actual self-discrepancy ($r = .30$) with the autonomous words. SAS Solitude failed to correlate with any of the self-discrepancy measures, whereas SAS Independence correlated −.40 with an ideal-actual discrepancy with the autonomous trait adjectives. Discrepancies between ideal-actual and ought-actual selves have been linked with negative self-evaluation. Thus the results of this study support a connection between sociotropy and selfhood discrepancies, whereas the results for autonomy are less consistent.

In a final study, we examined the relationship between Emmons' (1986, 1991) personal strivings and the Revised SAS in 50 undergraduates. Personal strivings are unique to each individual, representing what individuals are characteristically trying to do in their everyday life. We used the Personal Striving List (Emmons, 1992) to assess personal motives of achievement, affiliation, intimacy, and power, which are related to individuals'

───────────────

[1] These studies were supported by a research grant (no. 410-92-0427) from the Social Sciences and Humanities Research Council of Canada awarded to David A. Clark.

self-representational organization. SAS Sociotropy correlated slightly with affiliation ($r = .25$) and intimacy ($r = -.26$) strivings. The negative correlation with intimacy is to be expected because intimacy on the Personal Strivings List refers to positive commitment to another, loyalty, friendship, and responsibility; whereas SAS Sociotropy refers to a much more maladaptive and self-serving dependence on others. SAS Solitude also correlated negatively with Personal Striving Intimacy ($r = -.44$), whereas SAS Independence correlated positively ($r = .33$) with Personal Strivings Achievement. These results, then, provide some evidence of a link between SAS sociotropy and autonomy and self-representation in domains congruent with one's personality suborganization.

SUMMARY

In this section, we have examined the relationship between cognitive vulnerability and negative self-evaluation. At this time, we can only conclude that the empirical evidence for the self-evaluation hypothesis is tentative at best. In part, this must be attributed to the lack of research that exists between cognitive vulnerability measures like the DAS, SAS, or information processing indices, and self-evaluation and self-perception measures. Moreover, the critical studies comparing the self-evaluative processes in nondepressed vulnerable and nonvulnerable groups after priming with a congruent, meaningful activating event have not been done.

We can draw only a few tentative remarks from the research to date. It may be that the DAS Total Score does not have a strong relationship with negative self-evaluation even when negative schemas have been activated as in currently depressed individuals. Whether a closer relationship would be evident with the DAS subscales or particular items that reflect idiosyncratic core beliefs has not been investigated. There does seem to be some evidence of a relationship between SAS sociotropy and negative self-evaluation. However, the extent of this negative self-evaluation remains to be seen. In some studies, we found evidence that the negative evaluation may be quite global, whereas other studies indicated that it may be confined to social or interpersonal concerns. Also the initial attempt by Dozois et al. (1995) to investigate possible structural or organizational differences in self-representation between high and low SAS scorers met with limited success. However, such differences may not be apparent until dysfunctional schemas are activated by a distressing event. The research of Kuiper and colleagues suggests that the self-evaluative processing of nondepressed vulnerable individuals will be positive under normal conditions, and that negativity may become apparent only when self-worth contingencies are threatened. Thus it may not be possible to adequately test the self-evaluation hypothesis in nondepressed vulnerable individuals without a priming manipulation. Finally, the positive research findings on self-esteem instability and depression suggest it would be interesting to determine whether cognitively vulnerable individuals evidence greater self-esteem instability and lability than nonvulnerable individuals.

CONGRUENT PROCESSING HYPOTHESIS

When activated, the cognitive structures and content that predispose for depression will selectively bias information processing for stimuli congruent with the cognitive vulnerability organization.

According to the cognitive model, activation of the maladaptive schemas and cognitive-personality suborganization that predisposes for depression will lead to a bias in selective attention, encoding, and retrieval of information. In Chapter 7 under the selective processing hypothesis, we reviewed a substantial body of evidence that depression is characterized by enhanced encoding, memory, and judgments of negatively valenced self-referent material and reduced processing of positive information. The congruent processing hypothesis, however, takes this one step further. Although biased valence processing may be a cognitive characteristic of depression, the congruent processing hypothesis refers to domain-specific processing. The cognitive model asserts that cognitive structures and content that predispose for depression can bias the cognitive apparatus so that information congruent with the maladaptive schemas and personality suborganization will be selectively processed and elaborated over information less relevant or congruent with cognitive vulnerability. It is because of this heightened processing sensitivity to information congruent with vulnerability schemas that individuals will show different emotional reactions to negative life experiences.

The following case illustrates this hypothesis. Mary was a very bright medical student who excelled in just about everything she put her hand to. In her final year, she was ranked within the top five students in the entire medical school and was on full scholarship. She had a number of job offers, and her future looked promising indeed. However, Mary was severely depressed, meeting *DSM-IV* diagnostic criteria for major depression, and she had a pretreatment BDI score of 28. The event that triggered this depressive episode was the breakup of a 3-month romantic relationship one year earlier. Since that time, Mary had been in an emotional crisis convinced that she would never be happy and fulfilled in her life unless she got back with her boyfriend. She re-interpreted her entire academic experience and relationships with others negatively because of this relationship breakup. Thus she now believed that she would never be a successful physician and that people really did not like her. She could easily provide examples and convincing arguments about why her future looked bleak and why she would never enter into a mutually fulfilling relationship. Even though there was considerable evidence that the man who broke up with her had personal issues that thwarted their relationship, she interpreted the loss as entirely her fault, the consequences of which would be a life full of misery and broken dreams.

Why would loss of a 3-month dating relationship trigger a major depression in Mary when dating relationship breakups are common among young adults and rarely lead to clinical depression? According to the congruent processing hypothesis, we suggest that Mary had a predisposition for depression that influenced how she processed experiences congruent with her underlying cognitive vulnerability. In fact, on interview, it was apparent that she was a highly sociotropic, perfectionistic, and achievement-driven individual with a chronic state of low self-esteem. This was confirmed by her scoring profile on the Revised SAS. She obtained a Sociotropy score of 99 which is extremely high, whereas her two autonomy scores, Solitude and Independence, were within the normal range. Being a highly sociotropic individual, Mary selectively attended to, encoded, recalled, and elaborated information that signaled a loss of social resources. Thus her information processing system was biased toward processing interpersonally oriented material because of her sociotropic personality suborganization. For sociotropic individuals, negative social experiences will be more elaborately processed leading to depression, whereas positive interpersonal experiences may also be more selectively valued and therefore sought after in the nondepressed state. In this regard, Mary described the 3 months she was dating her boyfriend as the best period in her life. Her entire self-referent information processing system appeared oriented toward the selective processing of negative interpersonal rejection and social disapproval material in her everyday life, an orientation that was congruent with her sociotropic personality organization and maladaptive interpersonal schemas.

A number of predictions can be made about the relationship between cognitive vulnerability and information processing. Highly sociotropic individuals may show a processing bias for interpersonal material, whereas autonomous individuals would have a processing bias for mastery and achievement-related information. At the level of maladaptive schemas and beliefs, information that is congruent with a particular dysfunctional belief may be processed more readily than schema-incongruent information. Thus individuals who believe they should never make a mistake would tend to be hypersensitive to performance evaluative information. However, the selective information processing effects of personality and schema vulnerability may only be evident when maladaptive schemas and personality are activated or primed in the nondepressed vulnerable individual. The congruent processing hypothesis deals with an aspect of the cognitive model which Haaga et al. (1991) referred to as the "subjective valuation" hypothesis.

EMPIRICAL SUPPORT FOR THE CONGRUENT PROCESSING HYPOTHESIS

Kuiper and colleagues have shown in their research using the Self-Referent Encoding Task with nondepressed vulnerable (high DAS, low BDI scores), depressed vulnerable (high DAS, high BDI scores) and nondepressed nonvulnerable individuals (low DAS, low BDI scores) that enhanced encoding and retrieval of negative self-referent trait adjectives is only seen in the vulnerable dysphoric group (Kuiper et al., 1985). Based on a trait adjective self-rating exercise, MacDonald, Kuiper, and Olinger (1985) found that nondepressed vulnerable individuals may be more like mildly dysphoric individuals in having a lower degree of self-schema consolidation than nondepressed nonvulnerable controls. As previously reported, Alloy, Abramson, et al. (1997) found that vulnerable nondepressed students defined in terms of high scores on the DAS and Cognitive Style Questionnaire (attributional style measure) recalled significantly fewer positive depression-relevant words than a nonvulnerable group, although the groups did not differ in their recall of negative trait words.

Whittal and Dobson (1991) conducted a study comparing emotional reactions and memory recall in nondepressed vulnerable and nonvulnerable groups that involved a priming manipulation. Students who scored high or low on the DAS social approval subscale were given an opportunity to interact with a peer stranger for 5 minutes. On completion of the interaction, subjects rated their partners on personality dimensions and were given false feedback indicating that their partner had rated them poorly on the same personality dimensions. After receiving the social disapproval feedback, subjects completed the MAACL and were given the personality ratings a third time and asked to recall how they had been rated by their partner. No differences were evident between the two groups with all subjects showing accurate recall of the evaluation given to them a few minutes earlier. Although this study used a priming manipulation to investigate information processing in nondepressed vulnerable individuals, it has several design limitations. Memory recall was assessed by recognition rather than recall. As noted in Chapter 7, memory bias is more difficult to detect on recognition memory tasks. Also the time between encoding (subjects given false feedback) and recall was only a few minutes and so did not allow enough opportunity for memory decay. Because of this, the authors encountered a ceiling effect with all subjects accurately recalling the false feedback. Finally, provision of only negative feedback may not be the optimal context for demonstrating encoding and retrieval biases. More ambiguous tasks, containing both positive and negative evaluation, may create a better context for selective memory bias. Despite these shortcomings, this study offers an interesting experimental paradigm for studying information processing differences in cognitively vulnerable groups

Some initial research has also examined differences in information processing and the SAS. Moore and Blackburn (1993) found that sociotropy scores correlated significantly with faster latency to recall negative sociotropic but not negative autonomous autobiographical memories in 20 clinically depressed patients. The correlations between SAS autonomy and speed of recall for negative sociotropic or autonomous memories were not significant. The relationship between sociotropy and biased recall of negative sociotropic memories held even when the effects of depression severity were partialed out of the association. But in a study involving 24 depressed patients and 24 nondepressed matched controls, Nunn, Mathews, and Trower (1997) failed to find evidence for a personality-congruent information processing bias. Consistent with predictions of the selective processing hypothesis (see Chapter 7), the depressed patients (but not controls) were significantly slower to color-name negative (both sociotropic and autonomous) trait words than positive words, and endorsed primarily negative and fewer positive interpretations to ambiguous scenarios. Thus there was clear evidence of a negative interference effect and interpretative bias in depression. In stepwise regression analyses, SAS Sociotropy and Autonomy failed to predict Stroop interference effects for sociotropic or autonomous words, nor was there any evidence of a congruence effect between personality and differential endorsement of sociotropic or autonomous interpretations. The results of this study suggest that neither the sociotropic or autonomous personality suborganization is associated with selective processing of information that matches the current concerns or personality of the depressed individual.

In another study, Roxborough, Blackburn, and Glabus (1996) used the P300 evoked potential as a psychophysiological indicator of encoding processing bias. A small P300 amplitude is associated with "expected" stimuli and larger amplitudes are associated with "unexpected" stimuli. It was hypothesized that depressed sociotropic patients would have significantly smaller P300 amplitudes (i.e., an expectancy bias) when presented with negative sociotropic trait adjectives, whereas the depressed autonomous individuals would have smaller amplitudes when presented with negative autonomous trait words. Subjects were 15 clinically depressed, 15 asymptomatic recovered depressives, and 15 normal controls. Contrary to the findings of an earlier study (Blackburn et al., 1990), depressed and recovered depressed participants produced significantly larger P300 amplitude responses to negative than neutral words suggesting that the negative words were perceived as unexpected stimuli. However, because P300 amplitude is sensitive to both the objective and subjective probability of events, the use of fewer emotive and many more neutral words in the Roxborough et al. (1996) study may have resulted in the larger P300 amplitudes being generated by the less frequently occurring emotive words.

Of relevance to the congruent-processing hypothesis, the researchers found information processing differences with personality orientation. Subjects were defined as sociotropic or nonsociotropic and autonomous or nonautonomous based on cutoff scores found in Nietzel and Harris (1990). Sociotropic individuals in the control and recovered depressed groups showed a significant positive bias for sociotropic words (i.e., smaller P300 amplitudes to positive sociotropic words), whereas the depressed sociotropic patients showed an evenhanded processing of positive and negative sociotropic trait words. Nonsociotropic individuals did not show processing differences for positive and negative sociotropic words presumably because the words were not personally relevant for them. Even stronger findings were obtained for autonomy. The autonomous control subjects showed a positive bias for autonomous words, the depressed autonomous had smaller P300 amplitudes or an expectancy bias for negative autonomous words, and the recovered autonomous group showed little difference in their processing of positive or negative autonomous words. Furthermore, no significant differences were found in the processing of positive or negative autonomous words by the nonautonomous depressed and, to a lesser extent, control subjects. However contrary to predictions, the recovered nonautonomous subjects did have significantly smaller P300 amplitudes to negative autonomous words. The results of this study provide preliminary evidence that congruence between cognitive-personality vulnerabilities and type of self-referent information (i.e., sociotropic vs. autonomous material) may determine whether information processing bias is present. However, these results must be taken cautiously. The sample sizes were very small, numerous between-group comparisons were made without correction for Type I error and the personal meaning of the stimuli were not assessed so it was difficult to reconcile unexpected and contradictory findings. Also, the researchers failed to report critical within-group comparisons of P300 amplitudes to autonomous and sociotropic trait words to determine whether sociotropic and autonomous individuals showed a differential pattern of content-specific information processing bias.

Lightbody and McCabe (1997) classified 61 undergraduates as sociotropic or autonomous based on their scores on the PSI Sociotropy and Autonomy Total Scales. Participants were randomly assigned to either a neutral, sociotropic threat, or autonomous threat imagery condition. After the imagery condition, which served as a priming manipulation, participants were presented with a list of positive and negative sociotropic, autonomous, and neutral trait adjectives. Incidental recall of the trait words revealed that sociotropic individuals recalled significantly more positive sociotropic words after the neutral imagery induction, and significantly fewer positive sociotropic words after both the sociotropic and autonomous threat conditions. No differences emerged in the recall of negative sociotropic words, nor did the autonomous subjects show any recall bias for positive or negative autonomous words. Thus in this study, there was some evidence of recall bias for positive sociotropic words among the sociotropic group, although the authors did not report whether the sociotropic group recalled more sociotropic than autonomous trait adjectives. There was no evidence of a recall bias for autonomous words among the autonomous subjects even though a priming manipulation (sociotropic or autonomous imaginal threat) was introduced. The authors, however, note that the generally negative findings may be due to the words not being encoded self-referentially.

Finally, two studies were completed in our laboratory by Rama Gupta-Rogers (1998) involving the use of the SRET and modified Stroop color-naming task to investigate personality-congruent information processing in sociotropic and autonomous individuals.[2] In the first study based on undergraduate women, the Revised SAS was used to select 39 high sociotropic, 36 high independent (autonomous), and 39 control (low sociotropy, low independent) groups. Participants made self-descriptive ratings of Blackburn's (1993) list of 72 positive and negative autonomous, sociotropic, and neutral trait adjectives and completed an incidental recall of the trait words that immediately followed the self-descriptive rating task. Analyses revealed that the sociotropic group rated the positive sociotropic words as significantly more self-descriptive than positive autonomous words, although their ratings were not significantly higher

[2] These studies were part of a doctoral dissertation under the supervision of David A. Clark. Funding for this research was provided by a research grant (no. 410-92-0427) from the Social Sciences and Humanities Research Council of Canada awarded to the thesis supervisor.

than the independent or control groups. The independent participants rated positive autonomous words as significantly more self-descriptive than the sociotropic ($p < .06$) and control ($p < .05$) groups, but within-group comparisons indicated that the independent subjects did not rate the positive autonomous trait words as more self-descriptive than the positive sociotropic words. Also as BDI depression level increased, significantly more negative than positive trait words were endorsed. Analysis of the incidental recall data revealed that the sociotropic group recalled significantly more positive sociotropic than positive autonomous trait words, and their recall for the positive sociotropic material was significantly better than that of the independent and control groups. BDI level did not influence recall of positive or negative sociotropic words for the sociotropic group. However, a content-specific recall bias was not evident with the independent or control groups. Thus the high sociotropic participants showed selective encoding and retrieval of personality congruent trait adjectives, whereas there was no evidence of selective information processing in the independent (i.e., autonomous) group.

A second study (Gupta-Rogers, 1998) investigated conscious and non-conscious attentional bias in sociotropic, independent, and control groups using a modified Stroop color-naming task described by C. MacLeod and Rutherford (1991). Eighty-five undergraduate women (most participated in the previous study as well) were randomly assigned to either a depressed or neutral musical mood induction, followed by presentation of the 48 most relevant (based on the first study ratings of self-relevance) positive and negative sociotropic, autonomous, and neutral trait adjective words from Blackburn's list. Half of the trait words were presented for a brief exposure (the stimuli were supposed to be presented for 20 ms but later checks revealed that the actual exposure time was 50 ms) with a backward masking procedure to prevent conscious awareness of the stimuli, whereas the remaining trait words had longer exposure times. Analysis failed to reveal any selective attentional bias (i.e., increased color naming latencies) for personality congruent words at either exposure interval for the sociotropic or independent groups. No consistent differences on color-naming latencies were found with mood even though participants given the depressed mood induction showed a significant increase in dysphoria.

A number of subjects in each experimental group showed attrition when retested with the Revised SAS. Thus reanalysis was conducted with the 62 participants who continued to evidence high scores on the SAS Sociotropic or Independence scales. A significant three-way interaction of Group (Sociotropic, Independent, Controls) × Mood (sad vs. neutral induction) × Specificity (sociotropic vs. autonomous trait words) emerged in this analysis. A breakdown of this interaction indicated that in the neutral mood condition personality-incongruent trait words caused significantly greater interference in color naming, whereas color naming of personality-congruent words was much faster. This suggests that the processing of personality-congruent stimuli in sociotropic and independent individuals leads to facilitation effects so that any attributes associated with the matching stimuli, such as color of the stimuli, are processed faster and more efficiently. This facilitation effect was not found in the control group. Furthermore, the processing of personality-incongruent words showed inhibition effects as indicated by the large color-naming interference effects found for the sociotropic and, to a lesser extent, the independent group for nonmatching stimuli. The introduction of a sad mood, however, completely reversed the processing bias of the sociotropic and independent groups. For the dysphoric sociotropic students, personality-congruent (sociotropic) trait words showed a reduced facilitation effect, with personality-incongruent (autonomous) words now causing faster color naming (i.e., facilitation effect) rather than an interference effect. The findings were even more dramatic for the dysphoric independent group. For this group, the sad mood induction caused a complete reversal so that personality congruent (autonomous) words, and to a lesser extent, personality incongruent (sociotropic) traits now caused significant interference in color naming. Although one must be cautious when interpreting these complicated findings because of the unreplicated and post hoc nature of the analyses, nevertheless, they suggest that personality and mood may have qualitatively different effects on attentional processing. Personality dimensions, such as sociotropy and autonomy, may be associated with increased efficiency or facilitation effects when processing matching or congruent self-referent stimuli, whereas negative mood state causes a significant reduction in the facilitated processing of congruent stimuli, or even an interference (inhibitory effect with congruent self-referent information). In the future, researchers may want to utilize information processing tasks that focus on facilitated performance and elaborative processing because these tasks may be more sensitive to the effects of personality on the cognitive apparatus than experimental paradigms that rely on interference effects to index processing bias.

Summary

Only a few studies have examined the effects of dysfunctional attitudes and personality on information processing and the role this might play in cognitive vulnerability to depression. Thus only tentative conclusions can be drawn about the empirical support for the congruent processing hypothesis. There is some evidence that dysfunctional schemas and the cognitive-personality constructs of sociotropy and, to a lesser extent, autonomy may be associated with selective attention, encoding, and retrieval of content-specific information that is congruent with one's dominant vulnerability orientation, although Nunn et al. (1997) failed to find any evidence of personality-congruent processing bias in clinically depressed patients.

This personality-congruent processing bias appears more evident in highly sociotropic than highly autonomous individuals. Thus highly sociotropic individuals appear to selectively process self-referent information related to interpersonal concerns. However, the encoding and retrieval bias for interpersonal material in the nondepressed highly sociotropic person may primarily take the form of an evenhanded processing of positive and negative interpersonal material or even a selective bias for positive sociotropic information. It is only when a dysphoric or depressed state is present that we find a shift toward processing negatively valenced social stimuli. Also, the processing bias toward interpersonal material may be most apparent with cognitive tasks involving elaboration, judgment, and recall, and least evident with more rudimentary attentional processes. We also suggested that experimental cognitive processing tasks may be differentially sensitive to personality-congruent processing effects, with tasks that focus on facilitative information processing possibly more sensitive to the biasing effects of personality vulnerability dimensions like sociotropy and autonomy than tasks that assess information processing interference effects.

The evidence for selective attention, encoding, and retrieval of achievement-related information in the highly autonomous individual is less consistent, though Roxborough et al. (1996) reported stronger congruence effects with currently depressed autonomous than sociotropic patients. Gupta-Rogers (1998) also found stronger interference effects of personality-congruent trait adjectives for the independent (autonomous) women given a sad mood induction. Thus the findings for autonomy may be somewhat less consistent than for sociotropy, but this may reflect the more heterogeneous nature of this construct. Also, the positive findings for autonomy by Roxborough et al. and Gupta-Rogers warrant more research on the information processing effects of autonomy.

Two issues about the congruent processing hypothesis are worth noting. First, these few studies show that individual differences in information processing will not be evident unless a priming manipulation is introduced to activate the latent dysfunctional schemas that are hypothesized to predispose to depression. Either a direct mood induction or presentation of a stressor that is congruent with core schemas or personality suborganization is essential for activating the latent cognitive structures that may direct the information processing apparatus. Unprimed studies on nonclinical samples provide at best a weak test of the congruent processing hypothesis.

Second, too few studies have examined the congruent processing hypothesis to indicate the exact nature of the selective processing effects of cognitive-personality vulnerability. It is likely that personality primarily affects the later, more elaborative stages of information processing such as comprehension, judgment and recall, but not enough studies have been conducted to determine precisely how cognitive vulnerability factors affect information processing. Although it is less likely that the biasing effects of personality will be found in more automatic, preconscious attentional processes, the findings of Gupta-Rogers (1998) suggest that this may still be a worthwhile area in which to investigate the personality-congruent processing hypothesis.

RELATIONSHIP HYPOTHESIS

> Cognitive structures and content that predispose for depression are associated with a characteristic interpersonal style that affects the quality and nature of social relations with significant others.

The importance of interpersonal processes and the social context in understanding the pathogenesis of depression is undeniable. Severe life events involving loss, particularly within valued or close interpersonal relationships through death, divorce, or loss of commitment, are important precipitants to the onset of depression, especially in women (G.W. Brown, Bifulco, & Harris, 1987; Finlay-Jones & Brown, 1981; Kendler et al., 1995; C. Lloyd, 1980; Shrout et al., 1989). In addition, there is considerable empirical evidence that for women, in particular, a significant reduction in extramarital social support and integration (Andrews & Brown, 1988; Billings, Cronkite, & Moos, 1983; Billings & Moos, 1985), as well as disturbances in marital satisfaction, support, and adjustment are important sequelae of depressive symptoms and disorder (Barnett & Gotlib, 1988c; Coyne, Burchill, & Stiles, 1991; Gotlib & Hammen, 1992; Monroe et al., 1986). Stader and Hokanson (1998) found that elevations in interpersonal stress and dependency were evident one day preceding the onset of relatively intense but short-lived depressive symptoms in undergraduates. Studies by Hammen and others have shown that dysfunctional relationship beliefs, poorer interpersonal skills, and even depression itself contribute to the increased incidence of negative interpersonal problems in the lives of depressed individuals, especially depressed women (Hammen, 1991; Pianta & Egeland, 1994). In a more recent study, occurrence of interpersonal loss or conflict and the presence of dysfunctional attitudes and beliefs about adult relationships derived from early attachments (i.e., attachment cognitions) predicted the onset of interview-based general symptoms including depression in senior high school women (Hammen et al., 1995).

As discussed in Chapter 7 under the selective processing hypothesis, not only are the judgments, evaluations and recall of social information more negatively biased in depression, but there is also evidence of poorer social functioning with the depressed. Hoehn-Hyde et al. (1982), for example, found that depressed women were significantly more negative in their ratings of videotaped interactions in which they imagined that actors' comments were directed toward them than were nondepressed controls. The researchers concluded, however, that this difference was due to the control group biasing their ratings of the self-directed negative interactions in a positive direction. Also it would appear that the remitted depressed group did not differ significantly from the control group in their ratings of the social interactions. However, Lunghi (1977) found that depressed patients evaluated their real-life and hypothetical relationships more negatively than nonpsychiatric controls, and that significant reductions in depressive symptoms were not associated with a change in how depression-prone individuals evaluated their interpersonal relationships. Thus it is not clear whether negative social perception is a concomitant of depression, or whether a tendency to perceive, recall, and evaluate one's relationships in a biased negative manner is a vulnerability marker for depression. If social cognition is shown to be related to a predisposition for depression, then we might expect a link between the cognitive vulnerability constructs proposed by the cognitive model and particular social cognition variables.

Several psychological theories of depression have recognized the importance of interpersonal processes in depression. Coyne has argued that the interpersonal environment of the depressed is most negative because depressed individuals create a negative mood in others, thereby increasing the likelihood that they will be the target of rejection, hostility, and criticism (Coyne, Burchill, et al., 1991). Empirical support for Coyne's interactional model has been very mixed and depends on whether one examines long- or short-term relationships and whether actual depressed persons or simulated depressed targets are employed (for reviews, see Marcus & Nardone, 1992; Segrin & Dillard, 1992). Safran (1990) proposed a self-perpetuating *cognitive-interpersonal* cycle in which the maladaptive working models or schemas of interpersonal relationships held by vulnerable individuals guide their perception of the social world and lead to interpersonal plans, strategies, and behaviors whose social consequences merely reinforce the maladaptive interpersonal schemas. Blatt's concept of anaclitic depression (Blatt, 1974) is characterized by excessive dependency needs that stem from early childhood loss and separations resulting in an anxious insecure attachment (Blatt & Zuroff, 1992).

Gotlib and Hammen (1992) proposed a cognitive-interpersonal model of depression that explains vulnerability in terms of the acquisition of negative schemas about the self and others. As a result of difficult early childhood experiences, negative schemas are acquired that cause the formation of goals and propositions about what is needed to attain self-worth. This in turn leads to the development of interpersonal skills and motives that may cause the individual to enter into dysfunctional relationships, and acquire poor conflict resolution strategies and skills for attaining gratification and support. Gotlib and Hammen proposed that cognitive vulnerability to depression in many individuals is interpersonally based on dependency needs and goals so that stressful interpersonal events are more likely to be interpreted as a threat to self-worth. Thus cognitive-interpersonal schemas predispose to depression by biasing the individual's interpretation of interpersonal experiences and contributing to the acquisition of dysfunctional interpersonal skills and motives. However, early childhood experiences are considered crucial in the formation of dysfunctional cognitive-interpersonal schemas:

> Based on this theoretical formulation, we speculate that attachment difficulties and/or other adverse early experiences result in negative cognitive schemata or working models, and in personality characteristics involving elevated dependency needs, both of which may serve to increase the risk of subsequent depression. (Gotlib & Hammen, 1992, p. 250)

The cognitive model described in this book also recognizes an important role for interpersonal processes in understanding the etiology and maintenance of depression. A. Beck et al. (1979) proposed a reciprocal interaction model to account for the effects of the social environment on the maintenance and persistence of depression. Individuals developing depressive symptoms may withdraw from significant relationships, which then elicits rejection and criticisms from others. Depression-prone persons interpret these experiences negatively, which intensifies their self-rejection and self-criticism, leading to further social withdrawal and isolation. In this way, an external vicious cycle operates that may place the depressed individual beyond the emotional support and acceptance of others.

A. Beck (1987) also suggested that environmental factors may be critical in the onset of depression. A series of aversive interactions in a valued relationship could produce maladaptive coping responses in the depression-prone individual which is associated with further negative behavior by the partner. This negative interactional cycle could contribute to the eventual development of a depressive state. Leahy and Beck (1988) suggested that the maladaptive schema that predispose to depression may have been learned through early childhood relationship difficulties with the parent in the form of loss, rejection, imitation of dysfunctional thinking, or labeling. By proposing the sociotropic construct, with its emphasis on social dependency needs, as an important personality constellation that can predispose to depression (A. Beck, 1983), the cognitive model recognizes that the quality and nature of valued interpersonal relationships may play an important role in the pathogenesis of depressive symptoms and disorders.

Given the importance of relationships in the onset and maintenance of depression, we suggest two ways in which cognitive vulnerability may interact with interpersonal functioning in depression (Barnett & Gotlib, 1988c). First, core schemas and predepressive personality suborganization will influence how we relate to others or our behavioral interactional style. For example, the highly sociotropic person will tend to seek out close and confiding relationships. Their interpersonal style with others will be oriented toward maintaining their approval and acceptance. There will be little tolerance for loss, rejection, or abandonment of valued relationships (A. Beck, 1983). Thus the interpersonal style of the highly sociotropic person is consistent with Horney's (1945) description of the "moving toward people" neurotic style. The highly autonomous, on the other hand, evidences a cooler, more distant approach to interpersonal relationships. Here we see greater emotional detachment toward others, and an avoidance of close and confiding relationships. The autonomous person tends to be less sensitive and understanding of the needs of others and often prefers solitude to the company of significant others. Autonomous individuals are more self-oriented than other-oriented, and so their interpersonal style is similar to Horney's (1945) depiction of the "moving away from people" or detached neurotic style.

Cognitive vulnerability will affect not only how we relate to others, or our interpersonal behavioral style, but it will also influence the quality of our interpersonal relationships. Highly sociotropic persons will find their valued relationships less personally satisfying, more intense, and more demanding because of their reliance on relationships with significant others to meet basic needs of self-worth. They will also seek a more extensive social support network. On the other hand, the close and intimate relationships of the highly autonomous person will be less satisfying and fulfilling for the person trying to relate to the autonomous person because of the ambivalence, distance, and detachment they encounter in the relationship. Autonomous persons will tend to be more satisfied with their valued relationships as long as significant others do not demand more emotional intensity or a closer relationship with a higher degree of personal commitment. Autonomous individuals will be satisfied with a narrow social network characterized by relatively few valued relationships.

EMPIRICAL SUPPORT FOR THE RELATIONSHIP HYPOTHESIS

As in our previous hypothesis, very few studies have directly investigated the link between dysfunctional attitudes, sociotropy, autonomy, and relationship variables. In their self-worth contingency model of depression, Dance and Kuiper (1987) proposed that cognitively vulnerable individuals evaluate their personal performance and self-worth on the basis of rigid and excessive dysfunctional attitudes resulting in unrealistic contingencies for evaluating self-worth. These dysfunctional attitudes may also be the basis on which vulnerable persons judge their role performance in social contexts, thereby increasing the opportunity for negative self-evaluations. Swallow and Kuiper (1988) suggested that under threats to self-worth, vulnerable individuals may be more likely to rely on dysfunctional social comparison processes (e.g., comparing one's self to "advantaged" individuals) for evaluating personal performance and self-worth. This would increase the likelihood that one would conclude that their social performance in a particular situation was inadequate.

In one study, Swallow and Kuiper (1987) found that students scoring high on the DAS rated themselves as less similar to others as dysphoric levels increased, whereas no such relationship between dysphoria and similarity ratings existed among the low DAS scorers. Kuiper et al. (1987, Study 1) found that elevated scores on the DAS were significantly related to increased levels of public self-consciousness or the degree to which individuals perceive themselves as social objects. In a second study, Kuiper et al. found that high DAS scores in students were related to greater subjective discomfort and lower response probability for assertive behavior, lower satisfaction with their social relationships, and a lower level of perceived social skills. Also when depressed, vulnerable individuals rated a significant decrease in perceived popularity; whereas low DAS scorers, when depressed, did not exhibit a decrease in perceived popularity ratings. A measure of social support availability indicated that nondepressed vulnerable individuals do not restrict their range of social support but do tend to produce lower satisfaction ratings to an equivalent number of social relationships relative to the lower DAS scoring group.

Rudolph, Hammen, and Burge (1995, Study 1) found that elementary school age children with relatively more negative maternal schemas (assessed by ratings and incidental recall of mother-relevant trait adjectives) had significantly lower perceptions of maternal acceptance and family support, and expected more negative maternal responses. In a second study reported by Rudolph et al. (1995, Study 2), children with negative representations of mother/family and peers, as indicated by self-report belief and relationship appraisal measures, were observed to have lower levels of social competence, less adaptive affect regulation, more conflictual dyadic transactions, and more negative peer responses in an experimental conflict-negotiation task. They also had less positive status in their peer group than children with more positive cognitive representations of family and peers. These studies suggest that cognitive vulnerability to depression, as indicated by high scores on belief scales or information processing tasks, may be associated with negative evaluation of personal social information. This negative social processing bias could be the cognitive mechanism by which depressotypic schemas contribute to the maladaptive interpersonal style and unfulfilling personal relationships predicted by the relationship hypothesis.

A few studies have investigated whether sociotropy and autonomy are associated with particular interpersonal styles. One approach to interpersonal styles that has captured the interest of depression researchers is the notion of adult attachment styles. Zuroff and Fitzpatrick (1995, Study 1) administered the PSI, the Adult Attachment Inventory (a self-report measure of adult attachment), and a romantic relationship satisfaction scale to 160 undergraduates. Sociotropy was associated with anxious attachment (i.e., concerns about maintaining closeness and avoiding separation from valued relationships), whereas autonomy was related to avoidant attachment (i.e., detachment, distrust, and discomfort with close relationships). In a second study reported in Zuroff and Fitzpatrick, a different measure of adult attachment styles revealed that the avoidant interpersonal style of the autonomous was related to a fear of close relationships (i.e., "If I get too close, I might get hurt") rather than an indifferent or dismissive approach to others. In a study involving 184 undergraduates, we also found a significant correlation between the Sociotropy Scale of the Revised SAS and anxious attachment ($r = .48$) and a significant negative correlation between SAS Solitude and close attachment ($r = -.42$).[3] Close attachment refers to one's level of comfort with close or intimate relationships. The SAS Independence scale showed no relationship with any of the attachment styles. These findings, then, replicate those reported by Zuroff and Fitzpatrick who used a different measure, the PSI, to assess sociotropy and autonomy.

[3] This study was supported by a research grant (no. 410-92-0427) from the Social Sciences and Humanities Research Council of Canada awarded to David A. Clark.

Although there may be some overlap in the concepts of adult attachment and sociotropy/autonomy, the secure, anxious/ambivalent, and avoidant adult attachment styles proposed by Hazen and Shaver (1987) are rooted in Bowlby's notions of early childhood attachments. As a result, attachment constructs are framed primarily in terms of interpersonal motives, whereas sociotropy and autonomy are conceptualized from a more cognitive-behavioral perspective. As well, the moderate correlations found between the SAS and attachment measures suggests that the concepts are not entirely overlapping but instead represent different aspects of distinct interpersonal orientations or ways of relating. These results also are supportive of the relationship hypothesis, indicating that sociotropy and autonomy may influence individuals' relational styles which in turn might contribute to their vulnerability to depression. Others have also suggested that some convergence may be evident between the vulnerability concepts of sociotropy and autonomy, and distinct relationship or attachment styles (Blatt & Maroudas, 1992; Gotlib & Hammen, 1992).

Cognitive vulnerability constructs not only may be associated with distinct social processing and interpersonal styles, but may directly affect the quality and extent of social relationships. Zuroff and Fitzpatrick (1995, Study 1) found that PSI Sociotropy was slightly correlated with ratings of love ($r = .24$) and distrust ($r = -.20$) but not with satisfaction ($r = -.07$) or self-disclosure ($r = -.13$) in one's most important current romantic relationship. PSI Autonomy, on the other hand, had a low but significant association with less satisfaction, trust, and self-disclosure to romantic partner. Recently, we collected ratings on relationship satisfaction and personality on 136 undergraduates who indicated that they were currently involved in an exclusive dating relationship.[4] Correlational analysis revealed that the Revised Sociotropy Scale was associated with less satisfaction with the dating relationship ($r = -.25$), higher ratings on how badly one would feel about themselves if there was a breakup in the relationship ($r = .28$), and greater level of conflict or disagreement with one's dating partner ($r = .24$). These correlations held even when SAS Solitude, which correlated with Sociotropy ($r = .33$), was controlled. Although Solitude showed the same associations with relationship variables, these correlations were no longer significant when controlling for Sociotropy. SAS Independence was not correlated with any of the relationship satisfaction variables. These initial findings suggest that sociotropy may be related to greater emotional closeness in

---

[4] This study was supported by a research grant (no. 410-92-0427) from the Social Sciences and Humanities Research Council of Canada awarded to David A. Clark.

intimate relationships but our preliminary findings indicate that this may not lead to greater relationship satisfaction. In fact, the concerns about relationship breakup and its impact on one's self-worth may mitigate against the positive benefits that could derive from a closer emotional attachment to one's romantic partner.

Flett, Hewitt, et al. (1997) found that frequency of negative social interactions as measured by the Inventory of Negative Social Interactions (INSI; Lakey, Tardiff, & Drew, 1994) was correlated with PSI Sociotropy ($r = .31$) and Autonomy ($r = .35$) among female but not male students. Furthermore, main effects of sociotropy, autonomy, and frequency of negative social interactions were predictive of scores on self-reported depressive symptoms, but the interaction of personality and negative interaction was not significant. In a study involving 167 undergraduates, we failed to find a significant correlation between the Revised SAS Sociotropy or Independence scales and INSI scores, although SAS Solitude correlated ($r = .32$) with the INSI Total Score.[5] Flett, Hewitt, et al. found that both sociotropy and autonomy were associated with a tendency to experience more negative social interactions. It is possible that this relationship occurs for different reasons in the two personality orientations. Highly sociotropic persons may perceive more negative social interactions with others because they are sensitive to even minute instances of disapproval or criticism, whereas highly autonomous individuals may experience negative social interactions because of their defensive separation and preference for solitude (Flett, Hewitt, et al., 1997), a suggestion consistent with our findings with the Solitude Scale of the Revised SAS. In our psychometric studies of the Revised SAS (D.A. Clark et al., 1995), we found that sociotropy and independence were generally unrelated to perceived emotional loneliness in romantic or family relationships or the perceived extent of one's social network as measured by the Social and Emotional Loneliness Scale. However, the SAS Solitude Scale showed a low correlation with romantic ($r = .21$) and family ($r = .28$) emotional loneliness, and a moderate relationship with perceived inadequacy in one's social network ($r = .37$).

Bieling and Alden (1998) published a study that provides probably the most direct, important test of the relationship hypothesis. Undergraduate women ($n = 180$) classified as dysphoric or nondysphoric and sociotropic or autonomous participated in a standardized interpersonal task involving a confederate who helped the participant plan life changes that would enhance her level of activity and fitness. Confederates adopted either a

[5] This study was supported by a research grant (no. 410-92-0427) from the Social Sciences and Humanities Research Council of Canada awarded to David A. Clark.

controlling or nondirective role in their interaction with subjects. After the interpersonal task, subjects and confederates completed Likert-type ratings involving their perceptions of the interpersonal interaction, their partner's behavior, and degree of interpersonal liking or rejection assessed in terms of whether the respondent would like to engage in future activities with the target person. Multivariate and univariate analyses of variance revealed that the sociotropic women were significantly more concerned about maintaining interpersonal relatedness (e.g., concern about partner's evaluation, dependency on partner for help with the task), whereas the autonomous women tended ($p = .06$) to be more concerned about self-definition issues (e.g., control issues, setting standards for the task, degree of orientation to task goals). In addition, the sociotropic participants perceived that the confederate was significantly more supportive and approving, and they liked the confederate more than did the autonomous subjects. Finally, analysis of confederates' liking for participants (the extent that they would like to engage in future activities with target) indicated a significant Personality × Dysphoria interaction that was attributable to significantly lower likability ratings by confederates for the autonomous dysphoric than the sociotropic dysphoric individuals. These findings, then, support predictions derived from the relationship hypothesis. Sociotropy and autonomy were shown to differentially affect the interpersonal concerns, perceived quality and satisfaction with the interaction, and degree of acceptance (liking) or rejection associated with a brief social exchange with a stranger (i.e., confederate). As predicted by the relationship hypothesis, although sociotropic persons had more concerns or insecurities about acceptance by the confederate and maintaining the interaction, a higher level of warmth, acceptance, and satisfaction characterized the social interaction of the sociotropic women. The autonomous individuals were more task- or goal-oriented but they were also less well liked by the confederates. Supplementary analyses carried out on an additional sample of students who were nondysphoric and had moderate personality scores revealed that they were better liked by the confederates than dysphoric students or individuals with elevated personality scores.

Summary

The cognitive model recognizes that interpersonal and social factors are important in the pathogenesis of depression. According to the relationship hypothesis, cognitive vulnerability influences social perception and evaluative processes and in this way affects one's interpersonal behavioral style and the quality and character of these relationships with significant others. In fact, the social perception, behavior, and quality of relationships may moderate the relationship between cognitive vulnerability and the onset of depression. Because interpersonal strain, conflict, or loss are often precipitating factors in depression, the impact of cognitive vulnerability factors on interpersonal information processing and behavior may be one of the most important avenues by which cognitive vulnerability leads to depression.

Research on the association between latent maladaptive beliefs or predepressive personality and interpersonal variables has only recently appeared in the empirical literature. Studies by Kuiper and colleagues indicated that nondepressed vulnerable individuals, as defined by high scores on the DAS, evaluated their social performance and relationships more negatively, had lower relationship satisfaction ratings, and tended to engage in different social comparison processes than nonvulnerable individuals. Moreover, there is some evidence that the relationship between negative social interactions or experiences and dysphoria may be mediated by the presence of dysfunctional attitudes and low self-esteem. Lakey et al. (1994, Study 1) found that scores on the DAS correlated with frequency of negative social interactions ($r = .25$) in a college student sample and that the relationship between frequency of negative social interactions and distress was no longer apparent when self-esteem, control beliefs, and dysfunctional attitudes were controlled. Also negative social interactions were only weakly related to perceived and enacted social support, nor did they account for the relationship between social support and distress.

At this point, little is known about how maladaptive beliefs and negative self-evaluative schemas may affect interpersonal processes and experiences, which, in turn, will affect the development of depression. What are the critical social cognitive processes that account for the relationship between dysfunctional self-evaluative attitudes and negative interpersonal variables in predicting depression? Do maladaptive depressotypic schemas directly lead to an increased frequency of negative social experiences, which then predicts psychological distress, or is this relationship mediated by level of social support or presence of negative social cognitive processing? Do latent dysfunctional attitudes lead to negative social evaluative processing and distress only when activated by a triggering event? Is the interpersonal behavior of the vulnerable person most important in depression, or is the negative self-evaluation that results from difficulties in the interpersonal realm most influential in the pathogenesis of depression? Do specific dysfunctional beliefs, such as "need for approval" or "perfectionism," have unique and distinct effects on social processing and behavior? We are only just beginning to explore how negative emotional states like depression may be affected by the relationship between latent dysfunctional schemas on the one hand, and negative social cognitive processing, behavior and experiences on the other.

The cognitive model suggests more specific predictions between the predepressive personality suborganization and relationship factors in predicting depression. Highly sociotropic individuals will seek close emotional relationships, but valued interpersonal relationships will be more conflict-ridden and less satisfying because the basis of their self-worth is dependent on the gaining the approval and support of others. Thus anxious attachment is the interpersonal style or motivation of the sociotropic person, with a cognitive processing bias for any stimuli that might signal that a valued relationship is threatened. The highly sociotropic person will find loss, rejection, or abandonment particularly distressing and so will go to great lengths to avoid these experiences. The autonomous individual, on the other hand, will be oriented toward seeking more distant, emotionally detached relationships and so may be more satisfied with fairly superficial relationships with significant others. Their interpersonal style will be more avoidant and egocentric and they may show a certain degree of cognitive bias against interpersonal stimuli because of their relative insensitivity to interpersonal cues.

In our review of the empirical literature on the SAS and relationship variables, we found that high sociotropy was associated with an anxious attachment style, greater emotional closeness in relationships but possibly less personal satisfaction, and, to a lesser extent, a higher frequency of negative interpersonal experiences, although this last finding was not always evident. Thus there is some preliminary empirical support for the predictions of the relationship hypothesis with respect to sociotropy. In our discussion of the congruence hypothesis, we noted that sociotropic individuals may show a selective processing bias for social information. Furthermore, Bieling and Alden (1998) found that highly sociotropic female undergraduates were more concerned about maintaining social relatedness and the acceptance of others during a social interaction, although the interaction itself was characterized by a higher degree of warmth, acceptance, and satisfaction. However we are only beginning to explore how this selective social processing bias may affect the quality of the sociotropic person's relationships, and whether social cognitive processing mediates the relationship between sociotropy and psychological distress. Also, are sociotropic individuals hypersensitive to negative interpersonal information signifying loss or rejection? The critical question of how these variables may predispose to depression remains unanswered.

In a study of interpersonal sensitivity, defined as an excessively high sensitivity to the behavior and feelings of others (Boyce & Parker, 1989), it was found that high interpersonal sensitivity significantly predicted an increase in depressive symptoms at 6 months in 140 nondepressed primiparous women. In our study involving 167 undergraduates, we found that the Interpersonal Sensitivity Measure (Boyce & Parker, 1989) correlated highly with the Revised SAS Sociotropy scale ($r = .76$) but not the Solitude ($r = .19$) or the Independence ($r = -.16$) subscales. The correlation with the Interpersonal Sensitivity Separation Anxiety subscale was also strong ($r = .53$), which suggests that the fears of abandonment are important in sociotropy. More research is needed that directly focuses on how the relationship correlates of sociotropy may predict depression onset in cognitively vulnerable individuals.

The interpersonal features of autonomy are even less well understood than they are for sociotropy. It appears that autonomy is related to an avoidant attachment style due to a fear of close relationships. Contrary to our prediction, autonomy may be related to less relationship satisfaction, although this finding remains unclear. Considerable research is needed on the interpersonal correlates of autonomy. Bieling and Alden found that highly autonomous women were more task- or goal-oriented in their social interaction with a confederate, and that the dysphoric autonomous subjects were rated as less liked by confederates than dysphoric sociotropic women. In our own research, we found it useful to separate autonomy into two factors, solitude and independence. It is the solitude dimension that may have the greatest relevance for interpersonal relatedness and distress. This is only speculative, however, and whether autonomy is predictive of depression because of its impact on interpersonal functioning is a question for future research.

DIFFERENTIAL COPING HYPOTHESIS

> Maladaptive coping responses and compensatory strategies will play a more significant role in depression when personality-event congruence is present than when personality-event incongruence is present.

Until recently, the cognitive theory did not elaborate on the role of coping strategies in the pathogenesis of depression. In expanding and elaborating cognitive theory and therapy to deal first with anxiety and then personality disorders, however, it became necessary to introduce the concept of *behavioral strategies*, or "relatively enduring [behavioral patterns] that are typical of certain 'personality types'" (A. Beck, Freeman, et al. 1990, p. 25; A. Beck et al., 1985). These behavioral strategies serve the basic biological goals of survival and reproduction, and so may be adaptive or maladaptive depending on the current situation. Behavioral strategies or patterns are linked to our attitudes and beliefs, and in certain cases can become exaggerated, for example, in personality disorders where a "specific strategy representative of a particular disorder would flow logically from this characteristic attitude" (A. Beck, Freeman, et al., 1990, p. 26). From this perspective, then, we would expect that particular behavioral strategies may become manifest when the depressotypic attitudes, self-schema, and personality suborganization of the primal loss mode are activated by congruent life stressors.

It is obvious from later writings that these behavioral strategies fall under the rubric of *compensatory strategies*. J.S. Beck (1995) noted that certain compensatory strategies develop in response to the activation of core dysfunctional beliefs. In his most recent formulation of the cognitive model, A. Beck (1996) noted that *these motivational-behavioral response patterns are derived from the behavioral and motivational schemas of the primal modes and will be elicited in a fairly automatic and involuntary fashion by congruent stressful situations.* The response styles or compensatory strategies relevant to depression are maladaptive, automatic responses that are linked to the self-schema system and personality organization of the individual. They are designed to address basic goals of the individual such as survival, independence, sociability, intimacy, and mastery, and they are triggered when situations threaten the basic goals of the individual. For example, in the depression-prone highly sociotropic individual, an automatic compensatory strategy in response to loss of a relationship might be to seek emotionally closer and more intimate connections with friends or family by trying to please them (i.e., "If I please others, then they will accept me"). The compensatory strategy of depression-prone highly autonomous individuals facing loss of control and dependency might be to automatically increase social distance from others and throw themselves even further into their work believing, "If I work harder, then I can avoid disappointment and failure." Whether a compensatory strategy is adaptive, maladaptive, appropriate, or excessive will depend on the personality suborganization and self-schematic structures from which they are derived.

Cognitive theory also recognizes a second level of coping, referred to as *coping style*, which, like compensatory strategies, is linked to self-schemas and personality and is elicited by congruent stressors. However, one's coping style is much more conscious, voluntary, and effortful than the automatic compensatory strategies. It requires the perception of a problem and considerable cognitive effort. *Coping style refers to the intentional deliberate problem-solving strategies we may use to deal with a difficult life circumstance.* Sociotropic persons might deliberately use whatever interpersonal skills they have to seek out new friendships when faced with the loss of a valued relationship, whereas the autonomous person may consciously and intentionally engage in task-oriented problem-solving to deal with a potential failure situation.

Based on this conceptualization, the differential coping hypothesis proposes that individuals are more likely to exhibit maladaptive compensatory strategies and coping responses to highly significant negative life events that match their dysfunctional schemas and predepressive personality organization. Thus a highly sociotropic individual who is confronted with the prospect of losing a valued intimate relationship will be more likely to exhibit maladaptive compensatory and coping responses, thereby increasing the risk of depression than a person who is low on sociotropy. On the other hand, the autonomous person faced with a situation of reduced mastery or independence may have greater difficulty coping with this situation than someone who is less autonomous. As noted, sociotropic and autonomous individuals, when faced with a congruent life experience, may exhibit certain characteristic maladaptive compensatory strategies and coping responses. In this way, coping could increase risk for depression with the occurrence of congruent life experiences. On the other hand, if vulnerable individuals could mobilize more adaptive coping responses, then this might weaken the cognitive diathesis-stress relationship to depression.

Mathews and MacLeod (1994) concluded from their review of information processing studies using Stroop color-naming interference or memory recall that although individuals vulnerable to emotional disorders may selectively process emotionally threatening material, especially in the presence of stressful events, this bias can be altered by invoking a type of controlled avoidance coping strategy. Vulnerable individuals might override their involuntary propensity to process the threatening aspects of a situation by purposively inhibiting the selective attention to and processing of threatening stimuli. The authors speculated, however, that this controlled inhibition of negative information processing bias may only be possible in low to moderately stressful situations, and is likely to fail under severe stress because of the attentional resource demands the strategies would place on the individual.

EMPIRICAL SUPPORT FOR DIFFERENTIAL COPING
IN PERSONALITY VULNERABILITY

Because the distinction between automatic compensatory strategies and conscious, effortful coping responses was only recently proposed, published studies have yet to investigate the validity of this distinction or the existence of compensatory strategies. However, a few studies have investigated the relationship between dysfunctional attitudes or personality vulnerability, stress, more deliberate coping style, and negative affect or depression. One aspect of coping style that has received some attention in the cognitive-clinical literature is perceived level of social support. The social support one can mobilize when faced with adverse life circumstances can be viewed as a deliberate coping strategy.

Kuiper et al. (1987, Study 2) failed to find a significant relationship between DAS scores and perceived availability of social support, even though the latter was negatively related to BDI depression. Based on a depressed inpatient sample, Norman et al. (1988) found that a high cognitive dysfunction group (elevated DAS and Cognitive Bias Questionnaire scores) had significantly lower perceived social support and poorer overall social adjustment than a low cognitive dysfunction depressed group, even though the two groups did not differ significantly in number of negative life events. Whisman et al. (1995) found that clinically depressed patients with high hopelessness depression symptoms had significantly more cognitive and social dysfunction than low hopelessness symptom patients even though the level of hopelessness was not associated with number of negative life events. These results suggest that an elevation in dysfunctional attitudes may be associated with poorer coping responses, especially within the interpersonal or social realm. However, the relationship between dysfunctional attitudes, stress, and coping style in the pathogenesis of depression has not been subjected to sufficient empirical investigation to draw any conclusions at this time.

Three studies were found that assessed the coping responses of sociotropic and autonomous individuals. S. Reynolds and Gilbert (1991) assessed personality, coping responses, and BDI depression in 50 men who had been unemployed for at least 6 months. Regression analysis revealed a significant interaction between SAS Autonomy and activity level (i.e., number of hours spent away from the family home) in the prediction of BDI scores. Highly autonomous active men had significantly lower BDI depression scores than less active autonomous men. There was no significant interaction between SAS Sociotropy and perceived availability of social support. This is one of the few studies to show that an adaptive coping style (staying active) can actually reduce susceptibility to depression in vulnerable individuals.

Based on A. Beck's (1983) description of the sociotropic and autonomous personality constellations, A. Butler (1993) hypothesized that sociotropic individuals may be more likely to use passive distraction and support-seeking coping strategies and less likely to use task-oriented coping across all types of stressful situations. On the other hand, highly autonomous persons may be more inclined to use task-oriented coping and less inclined to seek social support when under stress. People who are high on both sociotropy and autonomy might be in a state of high emotional tension and so more likely to use emotion-oriented coping responses. To test these predictions, groups of currently depressed, previously depressed, and never-depressed students were selected based on their scores on three self-report depression measures. Participants in the currently and previously depressed groups were classified into sociotropic, autonomous, and mixed high personality subtypes according to median splits on the PSI Sociotropy and Autonomy Total Scales, and coping was assessed with the Coping Inventory for Stressful Situations (Endler & Parker, 1990).

Between-group comparisons revealed significant differences for the currently depressed and previously depressed subgroups. The highly sociotropic students reported significantly more social support seeking than the autonomous group, although this difference was more likely attributable to the autonomous groups' disinclination to engage in support-seeking behaviors. Currently but not previously depressed sociotropic individuals also reported significantly higher levels of distraction. The autonomous students had significantly higher task-oriented coping than the sociotropic types in the currently depressed but not the previously depressed subsample. For the mixed high group, emotion-oriented coping was significantly higher in the previously depressed but not the currently depressed group. A. Butler (1993) concluded from his within-subject correlational analysis that elevated levels of sociotropy are associated with a tendency to seek social support, whereas autonomy is associated with a tendency to rely on task-oriented coping. The between-group analyses suggest that the depressed sociotropic person's lack of task-oriented coping is due to the presence of depressed mood, whereas the disinclination for social support seeking is evident with highly autonomous individuals regardless of their mood state. Only the mixed high sociotropic and autonomous students showed elevated emotion-oriented coping in the previously depressed groups. These results, then, indicate that different coping styles may characterize different personality vulnerabilities, but whether these coping styles are mood state-dependent or not will depend on which particular personality-coping match is under consideration.

We examined the relationship between negative life events, personality vulnerability, and coping style in 176 undergraduates who completed measures at Time 1 and then again 3 months later at Time 2 (D.A. Clark & Steer, 1996). As part of the study, individuals completed appraisal ratings on the single most distressing life event that occurred over the past 3 months as well as the Cope Scale (Carver, Scheier, & Weintraub, 1989).

Even though high SAS Sociotropy and presence of a single negative inter-personal event was a significant predictor of increase in BDI scores at Time 2, these students scored significantly higher than others on the adaptive subscales of the Cope, while not differing significantly on the maladaptive coping subscales.

SUMMARY

Too little research on differential coping styles in cognitive and personality vulnerabilities to depression has been done to draw any substantive conclusions. There is some evidence that different intentional coping styles may characterize sociotropy and autonomy, but the stability of these response styles across time, situations, and mood state is unknown. It is also likely that the presence of a congruent life stressor will greatly influence whether adaptive or maladaptive coping responses are evoked. The relationship between dysfunctional attitudes and coping style also remains uncharted by depression researchers. Furthermore, no published studies have yet examined the role of more automatic compensatory strategies in personality vulnerability to depression. Research is needed to identify the range of compensatory strategies that may be associated with sociotropy and autonomy, and measures must be developed that can reliably assess the more automatic compensatory strategies as distinct from conscious coping styles. Until this basic research is done, it would be premature to test the role of compensatory strategies or coping style in a full cognitive diathesis-stress research design.

SYMPTOM SPECIFICITY HYPOTHESIS

The predepressive personality suborganization associated with the primal loss mode will influence depressive symptom presentation such that sociotropy is associated with symptoms of deprivation and autonomy with symptoms of defeat and self-depreciation.

The predisposing personality vulnerabilities and maladaptive self-schematic structures of the primal loss mode not only are contributory factors in the onset and recurrence of depressive symptoms and disorders, but also play a role in determining the form and expression of the depression. A. Beck (1983) proposed that personality vulnerabilities can influence symptom presentation during the depressive episode. For patients who are highly sociotropic, a state of deprivation will predominate with prominent symptom features involving requests for help, loss of gratification, crying, concern about personal and social attractiveness, lability of mood, anxiety, passive modes of suicide attempts, and heightened sadness and loneliness. For the highly autonomous individuals depression will center on defeat or failure and so involve symptoms of anhedonia, self-criticalness, withdrawal, and loss of interest in others, inability to cry, active modes of suicide attempts, hostility, and concern about personal effectiveness. A reactive or anxious form of depression is shown by the highly sociotropic person, whereas the characteristic depression of the autonomous is consistent with the description of endogenous depression.

Cognitive theory is not the only psychological model of depression to postulate that different personality vulnerabilities will be characterized by a distinct depressive symptom presentation. Blatt (1974) described two types of depression that are direct expressions of dependent and self-critical personality configurations. Anaclitic or the dependent form of depression is characterized by feelings of helplessness, fears of abandonment, and wishes to be cared for, loved, and protected by others. The introjective or self-critical depression is characterized by intense feelings of inferiority, guilt, worthlessness, and a sense that one must compensate for having failed to attain one's self-standards and expectations (Blatt & Maroudas, 1992; Blatt & Zuroff, 1992). Although Blatt's depressive types do not map perfectly onto the sociotropic and autonomous depressions described in A. Beck (1983), nevertheless there is broad agreement that two types of depression are rooted in personality, the one focusing on helplessness and dependency and the other involving inferiority, guilt, and self-criticism (Blatt & Zuroff, 1992).

A competing viewpoint is that a nonspecific relationship exists between cognitive and personality vulnerabilities on the one hand, and depressive symptoms on the other. This could be referred to as the *symptom nonspecificity hypothesis*. The view is that depressed patients more or less express a similar symptom presentation, but that personality factors may have an impact more generally on the severity of symptoms (Persons, Burns, Perloff, & Miranda, 1993). Thus the difference is a matter of degree rather than kind. Coyne and Whiffen (1995), for example, argued that sociotropy/dependency and self-criticism might be saturated with neuroticism, which in turn might account for their relationship with the depressive experience. Moderately high correlations have been found between sociotropy and negative affect (D.A. Clark & Beck, 1991; Jolly et al., 1996). If the pathogenic nature of sociotropy can be traced to a single basic variable like neuroticism or negative affectivity, then sociotropy might be associated with greater symptom severity but not a distinct symptom profile. With these considerations in mind, we next consider the empirical status of symptom specificity.

EMPIRICAL STATUS OF PERSONALITY SYMPTOM SPECIFICITY

Most of the studies on symptom specificity have relied on a priori symptom composites based on items from depression symptom measures like the BDI. The symptom composites are constructed from items that are thought to reflect the sociotropic and autonomous clinical features described by A. Beck (1983). For example, Robins, Block, and Peselow (1989) created a sociotropic symptom composite by summing over BDI items assessing sad mood, crying, decision-making difficulty, negative body image, and somatic concerns, and Hamilton Depression Rating Scale items dealing with sad mood, psychic anxiety, and somatic anxiety and then subtracted the BDI hopelessness and disinterest in people items from the total. The autonomous symptom composite consisted of BDI items dealing with hopelessness, perceived failure, loss of enjoyment, guilt, punishment, self-dislike, self-reproach and irritability, and the Hamilton Depression item of guilt, with the BDI crying item subtracted from the total. In at least one study, a measure was specially constructed to assess the sociotropic and autonomous symptoms postulated in the cognitive model. A third approach has been to utilize exploratory statistical procedures like cluster analysis to search for patterns of symptom covariation that might conform to the symptom composites proposed by the cognitive model. Because these approaches to symptom assessment may not produce comparable results, we consider the empirical support for symptom specificity separately for each type of study.

Most of the studies investigating personality symptom specificity have relied on creating symptom composites from standard self-report depression measures. There has not always been consistency across studies about which items should be included in the sociotropic or autonomous symptom composites. In the first empirical study of symptom specificity based on 65 clinically depressed patients, Robins, Block, Peselow, and Klein (1986) concluded that SAS Sociotropy correlated primarily with symptom items of the BDI and Hamilton Depression Scale dealing with anxious depression, whereas SAS Autonomy correlated primarily with the endogenous symptoms of depression (i.e., weight loss, psychomotor retardation). However, the correlation coefficients between symptom items and personality were all low and many of the symptom items that represented core features of the sociotropic and autonomous symptom type failed to correlate with their predicted personality dimension.

In a later study based on the creation of symptom composites, Robins et al. (1989) found that SAS Sociotropy specifically correlated with its predicted symptom composite, whereas SAS Autonomy did not correlate with the autonomous symptom composite. Robins et al. (1995) found that both SAS Sociotropy and Autonomy scales correlated significantly with their predicted symptom composites and were uncorrelated with their nonpredicted composites in a sample of dysphoric students. However, the difference between the predicted and nonpredicted correlations did not reach statistical significance. In their most recent study involving depressed patients, Robins et al. (1997) derived symptom composites from the BDI, Hamilton Depression Scale, and SCL-90-R items on both theoretical and empirical grounds. PSI Sociotropy showed the predicted differential correlations with the empirically derived sociotropic symptom composite but not with the theoretically derived composite. PSI Autonomy, on the other hand, was more highly correlated with both the theoretical and empirical autonomous symptom composite. Although these results appear to provide strong support for the symptom specificity hypothesis, especially for autonomy, the empirically derived symptom scores were calculated by summing over the symptom items that correlated most highly with PSI Sociotropy and Autonomy, respectively. This introduces a confound into the research design because the symptom composite can no longer be considered independent from the personality measure.

In support of symptom specificity for autonomy, Peselow, Robins, Sanfilipo, Block, and Fieve (1992) found that a significantly greater proportion (90.7%) of a high autonomy-low sociotropy depressed patient group had endogenous depressive symptoms than did a high sociotropy-low autonomous depressed group (19.3%). Likewise in a sample of 20 patients with *DSM-III-R* major depression, Scott et al. (1996) found that SAS Autonomy scores were significantly higher in those with endogenous depression, and that a significant correlation was evident between SAS Autonomy and pretreatment cortisol levels ($r = .65$).

Jolly et al. (1996) found that PSI Sociotropy and Autonomy correlated significantly with both sociotropic and autonomous symptom composites that were derived from BDI and SCL-90-R items. Furthermore, PSI Sociotropy and Autonomy did not account for a significant amount of variance in their predicted symptom composites beyond variance accounted for by negative and positive affect, respectively. Although these results failed to support the symptom specificity hypothesis, they indicated that high negative affect is related to both sociotropic and autonomous symptoms, whereas low positive affect is more specifically related to autonomous symptoms. In a study of 80 depressed elderly patients, Allen, Ames, Layton, Bennetts, and Kingston (1997) found that PSI Sociotropy was a significant unique predictor of sociotropic but not autonomous symptoms, whereas PSI Autonomy failed to emerge as a significant predictor of its expected symptom composite.

Persons, Miranda, and Perloff (1991) investigated symptom specificity in 59 depressed patients using the Achievement (i.e., Perfectionism) and Dependency (i.e., Need for Social Approval) subscales of the DAS. Sociotropic and autonomous symptom composites were derived from BDI items. Ordered probit analyses revealed that DAS Achievement was significantly related to autonomous but not sociotropic symptoms, whereas DAS Dependency was unrelated to either type of depressive symptom. In a second study involving 293 outpatients, Persons et al. (1993) found that Achievement Beliefs, as measured by items developed by David Burns, were significantly related to autonomous symptoms but this relationship was not significantly stronger than the relationship between Dependency Beliefs and autonomous symptoms. Symptom specificity was more evident with the Dependency Beliefs where a strong relationship was found with sociotropic symptoms, and this relationship tended to be stronger than the association of Achievement Beliefs with sociotropic symptoms. However, a high correlation ($r = .73$) was found between the sociotropic and autonomous symptom composites, prompting Persons et al. (1993) to question whether there may be an upper limit to symptom specificity which precludes a strong version of the hypothesis given the considerable overlap between the two symptom clusters.

As can be seen from a review of the preceding studies, there is considerable inconsistency in whether personality-symptom specificity can be demonstrated. It is possible that the reliance on standard depressive symptom measures is inappropriate because the items may not accurately map onto the sociotropic and autonomous symptom features described by A. Beck (1983). To address this problem, Robins and Luten (1991) specifically constructed a self-report measure to assess the 19 clinical features described in the cognitive model. PSI Sociotropy was uniquely related to the sociotropic symptom composite and PSI Autonomy was uniquely related to the autonomous symptoms. For both personality scales, the correlation with the predicted symptom composite was significantly greater than the correlation with the unpredicted composite. In this study, we see the strongest and most consistent support for the symptom specificity hypothesis. It would appear that better results are obtained when items are used that accurately represent the theoretical clinical features described in A. Beck (1983).

A final group of studies utilized exploratory statistical procedures to determine whether symptom patterns could be empirically derived that corresponded to the sociotropic and autonomous symptom clusters postulated by the cognitive model. Haslam conducted analyses on pretreatment symptom measures and subsamples of the outpatient data set of the Philadelphia Center for Cognitive Therapy. In the first study, Haslam and Beck (1993) utilized a categorization algorithm developed for artificial intelligence to find optimal clusters of BDI symptoms in 400 consecutive outpatients with major depression. Of the four symptom subtypes that emerged from this analysis, two had some resemblance to the depressive symptom types described in A. Beck (1983). One subtype showed marked elevations on vegetative symptoms and so conformed to a melancholic or endogenous depression, whereas the other subtype bore some resemblance to a neurotic or anxious depression. In a second study involving 531 outpatients with major depression, Haslam and Beck (1994) used taxometric analysis to determine whether systematic patterns of BDI and SAS item covariation could be detected that corresponded to sociotropic and autonomous symptom profiles. Analysis failed to reveal coherent and discrete sociotropic and autonomous depressive symptom subtypes, although the sociotropic but not the autonomous personality indicators did form a coherent entity. Once again, there was evidence of a discrete endogenous depressive subtype. Overall, though, there was no evidence of discrete patterns of sociotropic or autonomous depressive symptoms. Furthermore, Haslam and Beck concluded that the sociotropic and autonomous personalities were better conceptualized as dimensions than as types.

In two final unpublished studies, Haslam and Beck (1995a) conducted a principal components analysis on the intake BDI scores of 400 outpatients. Two components consisted of anhedonic or negative symptoms and endogenous or melancholic symptoms, whereas a third component consisted of BDI items representing reactive or anxious depressive symptoms. SAS Sociotropy correlated ($r = .35$) with the anxious or neurotic component of the BDI but had very weak correlations with the anhedonic ($r = .11$) and endogenous ($r = .07$) components. SAS Autonomy failed to correlate with any of the BDI components. Moreover, self-criticism, as a primary item in the anxious depression component, was distinctively associated with sociotropy. This suggests that the emphasis on perfectionism/self-critical items in PSI Autonomy may be misplaced and so cause a confound with the sociotropy construct. In the second study (Haslam & Beck, 1995b), canonical correlation analysis revealed two dimensions of BDI symptoms, one that corresponded to negative cognitions and self-criticism and the other that less clearly corresponded to an endogeneity dimension. Correlations with the six SAS subscales revealed that the sociotropic subscales of "Concern about Disapproval" and "Pleasing Others" were associated with the self-criticism canonical function, whereas the third sociotropic subscale "Concern about Separation" was associated with the endogenous function. The three SAS Autonomy subscales had weaker and inconsistent associations with the endogenous function. These findings suggest that sociotropic and autonomous symptom patterns may be discernible in the BDI, but the covariations bear at best a rough approximation to the clinical features postulated by A. Beck (1983).

In a recent study conducted by our own research group, cluster analysis was performed on the six SAS subscales of 2,067 outpatients of the Philadelphia Center for Cognitive Therapy (D.A. Clark, Steer, et al., 1997). Hierarchical and nonhierarchial cluster analyses resulted in four reliable personality subtypes—Independence, Dependence, Individualistic Achievement, and Low Scoring. Stepwise discriminant function analysis on 21 BDI, 21 BAI, 24 Hamilton Depression, and 14 Hamilton Anxiety items failed to reveal that a distinct symptom pattern was associated with the four personality clusters. However, the Dependent (i.e., sociotropic) and Independent (i.e., autonomous) clusters were characterized by a significant elevation in general symptom severity. Robins et al. (1997) also experimented with cluster analysis on the PSI Sociotropic and Autonomous Subscales of 103 outpatients with major depression. Four personality clusters were identified although there was no indication that these were naturally occurring groups. The mixed high Sociotropy/Autonomy group scored significantly higher than other groups on both the empirically derived and theoretically based sociotropic and autonomous symptom composites. The authors concluded that cluster analysis added no new information beyond what is obtained with a dimensional approach to sociotropy and autonomy. Because cluster analysis did not yield highly discrete personality groups, the authors recommended dimensional over categorical approaches in personality vulnerability research.

A final issue that deserves mention is the recent research on the relationship between personality vulnerabilities to depression and Axis II personality disorders. Beck, Freeman, et al. (1990) proposed a link between personality dimensions and personality disorders, with the latter viewed as exaggerated, excessive and inappropriate expressions of normal personality organization. Based on PSI scores and Axis II diagnoses derived from the Personality Disorder Examination and the SCID of 138 outpatients, Ouimette, Klein, Anderson, Riso, and Lizardi (1994) found that PSI Sociotropy was associated with avoidant, dependent, and histrionic personality diagnoses, whereas PSI Autonomy was associated with paranoid, borderline, and self-defeating Axis II disorders. In our own cluster analysis study (D.A. Clark et al., 1997), the Dependent (sociotropic) group had a significantly higher proportion of Dependent and Avoidant personality disorders, and the Individualistic Achievement (autonomous) cluster had a significantly lower prevalence of Dependent personality disorder diagnoses. Overall, then, there may be some relationship between the sociotropic and autonomous personality styles and Axis II personality disorders, but too few studies have addressed this issue to draw firm conclusions about the relationship.

Summary

Numerous studies have investigated the relationship between sociotropic and autonomous personality vulnerability and depression symptom presentation. The evidence for the symptom specificity hypothesis is rather mixed. Generally, there is evidence that highly sociotropic individuals may present with a more anxious, reactive, or neurotic depression with prominent symptoms of self-deprivation, and that the autonomous individual may be more likely to experience an endogenous type of depression with symptoms of self-defeat and failure. However, contrary to prediction, self-criticism appears to be more characteristic of sociotropic rather than autonomous depression, or at the very least, it is a clinical feature found in both types of depression.

There are several reasons why the empirical support for the symptom specificity hypothesis has not been more consistent. First, the reliance on symptom composites based on standard symptom measures of depression has resulted in a weak test of the hypothesis. The items of standard depression measures were not constructed with sociotropic and autonomous clinical features in mind and so these symptom composites do not map well onto the theoretical sociotropic and autonomous symptom types proposed by A. Beck (1983). Second, there has not been perfect agreement across studies on which symptom items from standard measures represents sociotropic or autonomous symptom features. Consequently even though the same symptom measures may be used in different studies, the actual items that comprise the sociotropic and autonomous composites may differ, making it difficult to generalize across studies.

A third reason for the inconsistent support for the symptom specificity hypothesis is the overlap that may be apparent between the sociotropic and autonomous symptom profiles. Persons et al. (1993) noted a high correlation between the sociotropic and autonomous symptom composites, and exploratory statistical approaches have failed to find reliable and distinct symptom configurations that match the clinical descriptions of A. Beck (1983). If the sociotropic and autonomous symptom patterns are overlapping or highly related constructs, distinct personality-symptom covariations will be difficult to detect. And finally, sociotropy is saturated with neuroticism and negative affectivity. Consequently, sociotropy also predicts general symptom severity in a fairly nonspecific fashion. However, this is not entirely inconsistent with the cognitive model because increased emotionality and reactivity are considered prominent features of sociotropic depression (A. Beck, 1983). At the very least, the strong links between heightened sociotropy and increased general symptom severity and intensity will make

personality-symptom specificity more difficult to detect in highly sociotropic patients. To overcome some of these difficulties, we suggest
that specific measures be developed that more fully and completely assess the clinical features of the sociotropic and autonomous symptom
patterns proposed by the cognitive model. It is noteworthy that the
strongest support for the symptom specificity hypothesis is found in a
study by Robins and Luten (1991) where a special sociotropic and autonomous symptom measure was constructed.

DIFFERENTIAL TREATMENT HYPOTHESIS

The predepressive personality suborganization of the primal loss mode
will influence attitudes and response to treatment such that sociotropic individuals are more responsive to interpersonally and emotionally engaging interventions, whereas autonomous persons are more responsive to
less personal and more problem-focused interventions.

The final cognitive vulnerability hypothesis we consider is the differential
treatment hypothesis. According to A. Beck (1983), sociotropy and autonomy will affect individuals' preference and responsiveness to either different types of intervention for depression or to different aspects of the same
treatment. Highly sociotropic persons, with their emphasis on dependency,
close attachments to others and desire to please, will prefer interventions
that emphasize support, helping, and emotional closeness. Sociotropic individuals prefer a closer, more informal relationship with the therapist.
They look to the therapist for help and may depend on the therapist to
solve their personal problems. They will show a strong preference for psychotherapy and so may find treatment termination difficult. Therapeutic
relationship issues may interfere with the treatment process in that the
highly sociotropic person may become either too dependent on the therapist or become preoccupied with receiving the therapist's approval and acceptance. Therapeutic work will need to focus on the sociotropic patient's
dysfunctional beliefs and misinterpretations of rejection, unacceptability,
abandonment, and negative reactions by others.

Highly autonomous individuals, because of their tendency to over-
value independence, personal mastery, and achievement, will prefer a
very different therapeutic style from that used with sociotropic persons.
Autonomous patients may prefer a more formal, detached relationship
with the therapist. Therapy should emphasize a collaborative relationship, with the patient actively engaged with the therapist in setting the
agenda, homework assignments, and topics for each therapy session.
Thus autonomous persons will respond better to a therapeutic style that

maintains patients' personal control, freedom, and sense of accomplishment. Goal-directed, task-focused, and problem-oriented intervention is preferred over more introspective, relational, and emotive therapies. Issues involving demoralization, defeat, failure, and incompetence should be a primary focus of therapy, with treatment oriented toward restoring the autonomous person's sense of competency and accomplishment in life. Given this hypothesized preference for a more impersonal intervention as well as the association of autonomy with endogenous depressive symptoms, Peselow et al. (1992) predicted that autonomy would be associated with a better response to antidepressant drug treatment than sociotropy.

Blatt and Maroudas (1992) noted that, in comparative psychotherapy, researchers have focused little attention on gaining a better understanding of how individuals with different personalities respond to different types of intervention. Unlike most psychological theories of depression, the cognitive model addresses this issue through the differential treatment hypothesis. However, few studies have examined the effects of dysfunctional attitudes, biased information processing, or the predepressive personality dimensions of sociotropy and autonomy on preference and response to depression treatment. This is truly unfortunate for the clinician because this hypothesis is highly relevant to how we approach the treatment of depression. Despite the paucity of research, the following studies have directly or indirectly examined the empirical basis of this hypothesis.

EMPIRICAL STATUS OF THE DIFFERENTIAL TREATMENT HYPOTHESIS

One of the first studies to examine differential treatment response with sociotropy and autonomy was conducted by Peselow et al. (1992). Response to pharmacotherapy was investigated in 217 depressed outpatients who completed the SAS and were assessed for presence of endogenous symptoms according to Research Diagnostic Criteria (Spitzer, Endicott, & Robins, 1978). Patients were classified into high sociotropy or high autonomy, mixed high or mixed low groups based on median splits on the SAS. Correlational analysis revealed that high SAS Autonomy was associated with better symptom improvement to active drug treatment, whereas high SAS Sociotropy was associated with poorer symptom improvement to medication. There was no significant correlation between endogenous symptoms and change in depressive symptoms. Further analysis in terms of absolute response or nonresponse to medication versus placebo treatment conditions revealed a significant group difference, with the high autonomy/low sociotropy group showing the highest response rate to active drug treatment (74.1%), whereas the low autonomy/high sociotropy group had the lowest response rate (38.5%). In addition, only the high autonomy/low sociotropy patients showed a significantly better response to drugs over the placebo condition. These findings suggest that autonomous personality is associated with a better response to drug treatment of depression and that sociotropy is associated with a poorer response to medication. Although these results are entirely consistent with the differential treatment hypothesis, it is interesting that the mixed high autonomous/high sociotropy group's response to medication was not clearly superior. It is evident that differential response to medication is dependent not only on the presence of autonomous traits but also on the relative absence of sociotropic characteristics. Scott et al. (1996) recently reported findings consistent with Peselow et al. (1992). Higher SAS Autonomy but not Sociotropy scores predicted lower symptom severity at 3 months and recovery from depression at 6 months in patients receiving medication treatment for depression.

Moore and Blackburn (1996) found that treatment responders showed a small but significant decrease in SAS Sociotropy but not in SAS Autonomy, and that this reduction was evident whether patients received cognitive therapy or medication. The researchers did not examine whether SAS Sociotropy or Autonomy influenced responsiveness to medication or cognitive therapy. Although these results are only indirectly relevant to the differential treatment hypothesis, we might expect that SAS Sociotropy, for example, would show greater change with cognitive therapy if, in fact, personality does have an impact on response to treatment. The question of whether sociotropy and autonomy are associated with differential response to cognitive therapy or medication, then, remains a matter for further investigation.

Based on the differential treatment effects of personality proposed by the cognitive model (A. Beck, 1983), Zettle, Haflich, and Reynolds (1992) hypothesized that depressed sociotropic individuals should benefit more from group cognitive therapy and autonomous individuals would respond better to individual cognitive therapy. Twenty-two depressed women were randomly assigned to either individual or group cognitive therapy. Both forms of cognitive therapy produced a significant reduction in depressive symptoms. Because of small cell sizes, the relationship between personality and treatment format was analyzed in terms of matches versus mismatches. Analysis revealed that patients who had a match between their personality and treatment format (i.e., sociotropic persons who received group cognitive therapy and autonomous individuals who received individual cognitive therapy) showed greater pretreatment to posttreatment reductions in depressive symptoms than the patients who had a mismatch between their personality and treatment format. Although these results must be considered tentative because of small sample sizes, they are, nonetheless, consistent with the differential treatment hypothesis.

Finally, three studies have been published on the National Institute of Mental Health (NIMH) Treatment of Depression Collaborative Research Program (TDCRP; Elkin et al., 1989) in which the relationship between various patient variables and response to different treatments was examined. Imber et al. (1990) investigated whether there might be mode-specific or differential treatment effects associated with measures designed to assess process and outcome variables that are specific to the rationale and procedures of particular treatment modalities (e.g., whether cognitive measures show greater change with cognitive therapy). Analysis of seven mode-specific outcome variables revealed that only one had a significant differential treatment effect. The Need for Social Approval factor of the DAS predicted significantly better outcome in the cognitive therapy completer sample but not in the interpersonal psychotherapy or pharmacotherapy treatment groups. If we assume that DAS Need for Social Approval assesses beliefs representative of the sociotropic personality orientation, than this finding is entirely consistent with the differential treatment hypothesis. Imber et al., however, concluded that mode-specificity was not generally supported in their findings, suggesting that core common processes appear to operate across different treatment approaches.

In a second study based on the TDCRP data set, Sotsky et al. (1991) found that lower pretreatment scores on the DAS predicted lower depression severity at termination for patients receiving cognitive therapy or pharmacotherapy with clinical management than for individuals in the placebo with clinical management condition. The authors concluded that the presence of less perfectionistic and socially dependent attitudes is associated with better response to either cognitive therapy or imipramine. Although these results indicate a relationship between patient characteristics or attitudes and treatment response, they are more consistent with Imber et al.'s (1990) finding of treatment-mode nonspecificity. Because the purpose of this study was to examine patient characteristics that might predict treatment response, a more specific analysis of the Need for Social Approval and Perfectionism subscales of the DAS was not reported. Thus these results are not directly relevant for the differential treatment hypothesis.

In a third study based on TDCRP data, Blatt et al. (1995) once again investigated whether pretreatment DAS Need for Approval and Perfectionism scores predicted treatment response in the four different treatment conditions. High DAS Perfectionism was associated with significantly poorer response across all four treatment modalities, whereas DAS Need for Approval had a consistent but marginal positive relationship to treatment outcome. There was no evidence of differential responsiveness to the four treatment modalities for either the DAS Need for Approval or Perfectionism subscales. This reanalysis was not supportive of the differential treatment hypothesis, even though perfectionism predicted a poorer treatment response more generally. The three TDCRP studies indicate that patient characteristics and attitudes may be predictive of response to treatment, but that the evidence for a more specific matching between personality or attitudes and response to different modes of treatment for depression is rather weak and inconsistent. However, the TDCRP studies did not assess sociotropic and autonomous personality dimensions and so one must be cautious in extrapolating their findings to the differential treatment hypothesis.

SUMMARY

Compared with the other hypotheses of the cognitive model, the differential treatment hypothesis has the most direct implication for clinical practice and treatment of depression. If empirically supported, the hypothesis indicates that clinicians should assess predepressive personality vulnerabilities and then tailor their interventions to the dominant personality orientation of the patient. The efficacy of depression treatment for any particular individual may depend on the success of matching treatment processes and procedures to the personality characteristics of the individual. At the broader level, however, it is not clear whether treatment mode specificity or nonspecificity may be the order of the day. Analysis of the TDCRP data suggests that treatment mode nonspecificity may be more apparent than treatment mode specificity. If common core processes operate across various treatment approaches, then it may prove difficult to find subtle differential treatment effects with personality.

Despite a high level of clinical relevance, to our knowledge no studies have specifically tested the full predictions of the differential treatment hypothesis. There is some indication that highly autonomous persons may show a better response to pharmacotherapy, and that sociotropic individuals may have a better response to group cognitive therapy. However, with the exception of a couple of studies that have tested implications of the differential treatment hypothesis in terms of these general treatment factors (i.e., medication vs. psychotherapy, group vs. individual psychotherapy), no research has examined whether sociotropic individuals respond better to a personal, more emotionally intense, and introspective psychotherapy, whereas the autonomous respond better to a more impersonal, problem-focused, and collaborative psychotherapy. Furthermore, no studies have investigated whether therapy that deals with achievement- and mastery-related issues is more effective for autonomous individuals, and interventions that focus on interpersonal and relationship issues are more efficacious with the depressed sociotropic person. Until these core predictions are empirically tested, we must await judgment on the empirical status of the differential treatment hypothesis.

CONCLUSION

In this chapter, we have discussed the theoretical and empirical basis of the more tentative hypotheses derived from the cognitive vulnerability level of the cognitive theory of depression. Although these hypotheses are not as central to cognitive vulnerability as the stability, onset, and relapse hypotheses reviewed in the previous chapters, nevertheless they represent predictions that deal with salient concepts of cognitive vulnerability. As we have seen, these hypotheses have not received enough research attention for us to offer any firm conclusions about their empirical status. Having said this, a few studies were found that provided at least some preliminary evidence suggesting that each of these hypotheses are worthy of further consideration by cognitive-clinical researchers.

The *self-evaluation hypothesis* predicted that a stronger relationship would be evident between cognitive and personality vulnerability constructs, and negative self-evaluation in persons predisposed to depression than in nonvulnerable individuals. Although both the DAS Total Score and SAS Autonomy Total Scores do not appear to be significantly correlated with negative self-evaluation and self-esteem measures, SAS Sociotropy was found to correlate with negative self-evaluation. These results, however, are tentative because studies have not included a priming manipulation, which is necessary to provide an adequate test of the hypothesis. We would not expect vulnerable but nondepressed individuals to show negative self-evaluation unless the latent cognitive vulnerability constructs were activated or primed by a triggering stimulus. In addition, it is unclear whether the negative self-evaluation of the vulnerable is global or whether it is more specific to the particular content domain of the predepressive personality vulnerability.

The *congruent processing hypothesis* refers to the possibility of heightened selectivity for processing information congruent with vulnerability schemas and personality. Unprimed studies have found some evidence that selective processing of interpersonal information is associated with sociotropy, although it is unclear whether this is evident as an even-handed processing of positive and negative interpersonal material, or whether there is an enhanced processing of positive social information. Evidence that autonomy is associated with enhanced processing of achievement-related material has not been consistently demonstrated. Nunn et al. (1997) failed to find personality congruent processing in either sociotropic or autonomous depressed patients. Once again a priming manipulation is probably necessary before biased valenced processing of stimuli is evident. There also is some initial evidence that different personality dimensions may not influence exactly the same features of information processing, although it is likely that personality differences will have their greatest impact in directing the more controlled, elaborative, and strategic processes of the cognitive apparatus.

Social and interpersonal factors play an important role in the pathogenesis of depression. The *relationship hypothesis* posits that vulnerability schemas and predepressive personality suborganization will influence social perceptions, interpersonal behavioral styles, and the quality of social experiences. Sociotropic persons will tend to perceive and evaluate interpersonal experiences in terms of their impact on self-worth, and they will seek close and confiding relationships but will often feel dissatisfied and discouraged with their relations with others because of their lack of self-gratification. Autonomous individuals, on the other hand, will perceive relationships more in terms of meeting instrumental needs rather than self-worth contingencies; they will be more distant, detached, and isolated from others; and although they will feel more satisfied with their interpersonal relations, those who interact with them may find the relationship less satisfying. Sociotropic individuals appear to exhibit an anxious attachment style with a higher frequency of negative interpersonal experiences and, possibly, less (or more in some studies) personal satisfaction in relationships. The interpersonal correlates of autonomy are less well understood. Autonomy may be related to a fear of close relationships and, contrary to expectation, less personal satisfaction in relationships. Also recent studies from our own lab suggest that solitude is a more specific feature of autonomy that has particular relevance for interpersonal relatedness and distress.

The *differential coping hypothesis* states that predepressive individuals will be less able to cope with experiences that are congruent with their vulnerability schemas and personality suborganization. To date, very few studies have even tangential data relevant to this hypothesis. There is some suggestive evidence that sociotropy may be associated more with an emotion-focused coping style, whereas autonomy may be associated with task-oriented coping. However, these differential coping styles may be greatly affected by whether the individual is confronting a vulnerability-congruent or incongruent life experience.

The *symptom specificity hypothesis* has been the subject of considerably more research attention because this hypothesis was proposed in earlier writings on the cognitive model (A. Beck, 1983). Two distinct findings can be discerned from this literature. First, there is some evidence of a differential symptom pattern, with sociotropy associated with a more anxious, reactive, and emotive type of depressive experience, whereas autonomy seems more related to an endogenous type of depression. A finding that seems to contradict psychological theories on vulnerability to depression, especially Blatt's model, is that self-criticism is more characteristic of sociotropy or interpersonal dependency, than autonomy or a self-definitional orientation. A. Beck stated that self-criticism would be apparent in the depressive experiences of both personality orientations, with the autonomous person self-critical for past deficiencies and the sociotropic individual self-critical over being socially undesirable. A second trend found in this literature is that SAS Sociotropy may show broad and nonspecific effects on depression in terms of greater symptom severity and distress because it may be saturated with items that reflect negative affectivity or neuroticism. Future studies are needed to sort out the general and specific effects of sociotropy, and autonomy for that matter, on the clinical presentation of depression.

Finally, the *differential treatment hypothesis,* though having direct relevance for clinical practice, has received very little research attention. The cognitive model predicts that depressed sociotropic individuals will be more responsive to psychotherapy that is introspective, personal, interpersonally focused, and deals with emotional issues, whereas the depressed autonomous individual will be more responsive to treatment that is less personal, more detached, problem-focused, and collaborative. Despite a paucity of research, there is some evidence at a more general level that autonomous depressed individuals may respond better to pharmacotherapy and that depressed sociotropic persons may show the best response to group cognitive psychotherapy. However, the more general question of whether treatment mode-specific effects can be detected remains uncertain in light of the TDCRP findings. As with all the vulnerability hypotheses discussed in this chapter, the empirical work on this hypothesis is only in its infancy. However, the early returns from the laboratory suggest that further research on differential treatment, as well as the other five vulnerability hypotheses, is entirely warranted and may, in fact, lead to very useful insights into the pathogenesis and treatment of depression.

CHAPTER 11

Cognitive Theory of Depression: Overview and Future Directions

IT HAS been 35 years since the first publication of a cognitive theory of depression and its accompaniment system of psychotherapy (A. Beck, 1963, 1964, 1967). In the intervening time, cognitive theory as well as therapy has been subjected to intense empirical scrutiny, and has gone through many theoretical and clinical iterations as it has been applied to an increasing number of clinical problems. While the psychological problems addressed by the theory have expanded in range and complexity, so have the criticisms. The primary contention is that cognitive theory is not a scientific theory of depression but rather a conceptualization born out of clinical observation (Blaney, 1977; Coyne & Gotlib, 1983; Rachman, 1997; Teasdale, 1996; Teasdale & Barnard, 1993; Williams et al., 1997). Cognitive theory is criticized as being too imprecise, its concepts too cumbersome, and its account too inaccurate to provide a viable explanation for depression. Some reviewers have also concluded that the cognitive theory of depression has not been supported by empirical investigation (e.g., Coyne & Gotlib, 1983; Teasdale & Barnard, 1993), especially in terms of cognitive constructs as predisposing or vulnerability factors.

Our aim here has been to present a comprehensive and critical evaluation of the empirical status of cognitive theory of depression, and to ascertain whether Beck's cognitive formulation meets the standards of a scientific theory of depression. In Chapter 2, we presented a historical account of the origins of cognitive theory. Contrary to statements that appear in the literature, the historical record shows that the cognitive theory of depression arose from both the clinical observations and early experimental work of Beck and colleagues. In Chapter 3, we presented the theoretical assumptions of the cognitive model, followed by a description of the theory itself in Chapter 4. As specified in Chapters 5 through 10, hypotheses derived from the cognitive model of depression have been subjected to varying levels of empirical investigation. If Beck's cognitive theory is too imprecise and its language too commonsensical to provide an adequate expression for working hypotheses (Teasdale, 1996), how can we account for the voluminous level of empirical research reviewed in this text addressing the hypotheses of cognitive theory? On the contrary, the heuristic value of the assumptions, specifications, and hypotheses that comprise the cognitive theory of depression are a witness to its scientific status.

The scientific credibility of a theory does not rest entirely on the precision of its terms or the heuristic value of its hypotheses. Instead, a scientific theory of depression must also account for important aspects of the phenomenon under question, and it must be consistent with critical findings from laboratory investigations of depressive phenomena. As a theory of clinical disturbance, a strong psychological theory of depression should ultimately make a significant contribution to treatment innovation and practice. The cognitive model has made a significant contribution to the treatment of depression as described in previous publications and documented in reviews of outcome studies (A. Beck et al., 1979; J.S. Beck, 1995; DeRubeis & Crits-Christoph, 1998; Dobson, 1989; Hollon & Beck, 1994). Chapters 5 through 10 focused on a review of all the extant empirical research on the cognitive approach to depression. Our conclusion is that the scientific foundations of cognitive theory are firmly established; they are documented in the hundreds of studies evaluated in the preceding chapters, although the empirical status of specific hypotheses within cognitive theory are not all equally supported in the research literature.

In this concluding chapter, we summarize and evaluate the scientific status of cognitive theory of depression. In Chapter 1, we proposed the characteristics that any credible theory of depression must take into account. In the first section of this chapter, we explore the adequacy of cognitive theory in light of these core features. In a second section, we summarize the empirical status of the cognitive model at both the descriptive and vulnerability levels of conceptualization. In the third section, we conclude this book by offering some final thoughts on the contribution of the experimental information processing paradigm for testing the core meaning representation that forms the cognitive basis of clinical depression.

COGNITIVE THEORY AND
DEPRESSIVE PHENOMENA

As noted in Chapter 1, clinical depression is a complex state involving disturbances in mood, cognition, behavior, motivation, and somatic functioning. *DSM-IV* (APA, 1994) considers depressed mood or dysphoria and loss of interest or pleasure core features of depressive disorders. The emphasis on the subjective or cognitive symptoms of depression, such as feelings of worthlessness, guilt, and hopelessness are afforded secondary status in the diagnostic criteria. The complex mutlifactorial nature of depression is acknowledged within the cognitive model by postulating the activation of the primal loss mode (see Chapter 4). This symbolic representation of loss involves memory for the cognitive-conceptual, affective, physiological, behavioral, and motivational aspects of the biopsychosocial systems of the organism. Thus activation of the primal loss mode in depression will be expressed in terms of symptomatic disturbance across the domains of psychological functioning. However, the cognitive model diverges from the standard psychiatric nomenclature of depression by positing cognitive dysfunction as the core symptom feature of the disorder. This view on the primacy of the negative self-referent cognitive phenomena in depression (i.e., the cognitive triad) is expressed in the negativity and primacy hypotheses of the model (see Chapter 6). As discussed earlier, primacy does not imply causality. It is not that a negative view of self, world, and future causes depression, but rather negative cognitive phenomena are such a core feature of the depressive experience that they have a significant influence on the manifestation of other depressive symptoms.

A second cardinal feature of clinical depression noted in Chapter 1 is the recognition that the symptom presentation of depression is quite heterogeneous in terms of severity, chronicity, and clinical profile. According to the cognitive model, a similar core cognitive disturbance is manifest regardless of the subtype of depression. Thus whether the experience of depression occurs within the context of major depression, bipolar disorder, dysthymia, minor depression, or even mixed anxiety-depression matters little in terms of the activation of negative cognitive structures and processes. As long as depressed affect is present, this is understood in terms of the activation of latent schemas and modes reflecting a sense of personal loss, failure, and deprivation. Differences in the severity and duration of depressive symptoms will depend on the strength of activation and dominance over the information processing system of the primal loss mode. As well, differences in depressive symptom presentation may reflect partial or selective activation of schemas of the loss mode. Whatever the exact symptom array displayed by a particular individual, if depressed affect is present, then the model assumes that cognitive-conceptual schemas representing loss of personal resources have been activated.

A third issue that has been hotly debated is whether depressive phenomena should be conceptualized from a dimensional (continuity) or categorical (discontinuous) perspective. In Chapter 1, we offered a rather extensive discussion of this issue and concluded that a stronger case can be made for the dimensional rather than the categorical nature of depressive mood, symptoms, and disorders. The cognitive model assumes a dimensional perspective, viewing psychopathology in terms of extreme, excessive, or deficient forms of cognitive, emotional, and behavioral functioning. We have expressed this viewpoint in Assumption 11 of the cognitive theory (see Chapter 3). In addition, we consider cognitive-clinical research conducted on dysphoric nonclinical individuals of some relevance to the cognitive dysfunction seen in more severely depressed clinical samples. Although we agree with Flett, Vredenburg, et al. (1997) that continuity may be evident in some spheres of depression and discontinuity in other spheres, we did not find in our review of the empirical literature any *consistent* evidence of a cognitive disturbance in clinical depression that was not manifest in an attenuated form in dysphoric nonclinical individuals. The negative perceptual, evaluative, judgmental, and recall biases found in clinically depressed samples have also been reported in nonclinical dysphoric groups. Thus we conclude that there is broad empirical support for considering the cognitive disturbance evident in clinical depressive disorders as also apparent in a weaker, attenuated form in milder nonclinical depressed states.

A fourth feature noted in Chapter 1 was the high degree of comorbidity evident between depression and other psychological disorders, especially anxiety. The cognitive theory recognizes that the complex major stressors that precipitate psychological distress may activate different systems of meaning representation such as the loss and threat modes. For example, the loss of a spouse through death or divorce will not only trigger cognitive structures representing personal loss but also schemas involving threat and personal vulnerability (i.e., fears of loneliness, future financial problems). The concurrent activation of loss and threat schemas will be manifest as a comorbid depression/anxiety. However, the cognitive model also asserts that different psychopathological and emotional states can be distinguished by their unique cognitive "signature" or profile. This is expressed in terms of the content specificity hypothesis (see Chapter 5). This hypothesis has received considerable empirical support indicating that measures of cognitive content may be useful in arriving at a differential diagnosis and assessment of mixed clinical conditions.

Another characteristic of depression discussed in Chapter 1 concerns the high relapse and recurrence rates that have been noted for individuals who suffer from episodes of clinical depression. In fact, one of the most important challenges facing research and treatment in depression is to understand the factors linked to relapse and to discover more effective means to lower unacceptably high recurrence of depressive episodes. The cognitive theory conceptualizes depressive relapse and recurrence in terms of a diathesis-stress model (see Chapter 7). The existence of latent depressogenic schemas and a predepressive personality suborganization places individuals at higher risk for future depressive episodes by increasing their sensitivity to a wider range of triggering life experiences. In fact, repeated activation of negative self-referent depressogenic structures may increase one's risk for future depressive episodes by lowering the activation threshold for these schemas so that a less intense and wider range of diverse circumstances can trigger primal loss representation. In addition, the cognitive theory asserts that depressive episodes will persist as long as the underlying dysfunctional schemas remain activated. This view is expressed in terms of the severity/persistence hypothesis (see Chapter 6) and has received some support in the empirical literature. In summary, the cognitive model understands the persistence and susceptibility to depressive relapse in terms of hypervalent cognitive structures (schemas) that become increasingly sensitive to a wider range of negative life experiences.

A final feature of depressive disorders presented in Chapter 1 concerns the significant decrements in physical, psychological, social and economic functioning associated with a depressive episode. In Chapter 4, we noted that depression very much involves the cognitive structures and processes implicated in the representation of the self. In fact, the faulty information processing that characterizes depression is confined almost exclusively to self-referent stimuli. In depression, the self is primarily represented within dysfunctional modes involving loss, threat, and victimization. Thus depression is characterized by the activation of core self-schemas involving themes of failure, helplessness, unlovability, rejection, unworthiness, contempt, and depravity, to name but a few. The more severe the depression, the more extreme and dominant the negative self-constructs. It is little wonder that pervasive deficits in psychosocial functioning would be evident in the depressed state. The dominance of negative self-referent thinking and the relative inaccessibility of more constructive modes of thinking will stifle any attempts to deal effectively in one's social, occupational, or familial environment.

From the foregoing discussion, it is evident that the cognitive model can provide a credible explanation for important aspects of depression. In this sense, it meets Teasdale and Barnard's (1993) criteria that an applied science be evaluated in terms of its ability to account for what is known about a concrete "real-world" problem. Obviously, there are other important features of depression that Beck's cognitive theory must take into consideration such as gender differences, age trends, biological and genetic vulnerabilities, developmental antecedents, personality factors, and the social context. It is beyond the scope of this book to deal with the application of the cognitive theory to each of these issues. However, given the capability of the cognitive model to deal with the core features of depression raised in Chapter 1, we see no reason why the theory cannot be used as a basis for understanding other important features of the depressive experience.

COGNITIVE THEORY OF DEPRESSION: EMPIRICAL STATUS

Even if a theory employs precise terminology and accounts for known aspects of a real-world problem, the acid test of its scientific merit surely rests with its ability to account for findings obtained from laboratory experiments of hypotheses derived from the theory. In this section, we provide an overview of the empirical support for the cognitive theory described in Chapter 4. Because of the breadth of this literature, we will divide our summary into two subsections, one dealing with the descriptive hypotheses of cognitive theory, and the other focusing on the vulnerability hypotheses of the model.

DESCRIPTIVE HYPOTHESES OF COGNITIVE THEORY

Hypotheses at the descriptive level refer to the organization and function of the structures, processes, and products that constitute the cognitive basis of depression. These hypotheses assert that negative cognition is an integral part of depressive phenomenology (A. Beck, 1987), and that the activation of certain core cognitive structures and processes is an important concomitant of depression (Haaga et al., 1991). The descriptive hypotheses argue for a cognitive conceptualization or understanding of depression. Although some reviewers have asserted that the specification of the cognitive "architecture" of depression is merely a statement of the obvious (i.e., "depressed people think depressive thoughts"; Coyne & Gotlib, 1986), it must be remembered that Beck's original thesis (A. Beck, 1963) that faulty or disordered thought processes may be more crucial to understanding depression than affective and motivational characteristics was considered a radical reconceptualization of depression at that time. The conclusion reached from our review of the relevant research in Chapters 5 to 7 was that fairly strong and consistent empirical support is evident for most of the descriptive hypotheses of cognitive theory (see reviews by Ackermann-Engel & DeRubeis, 1993; Gotlib & Hammen, 1992; Gotlib & McCabe, 1992; Haaga et al., 1991, for similar conclusion). In fact, the rationale for a cognitive therapy of depression is predicated on the centrality of cognitive disturbance in depression as expressed by the descriptive hypotheses of the theory. Having argued for the importance of the cognitive conceptualization at the descriptive level, we now consider the empirical status of the specific hypotheses.

Negative Cognition in Depression

In Chapter 5, we reviewed empirical support for the negativity, exclusivity, and content-specificity hypotheses which all dealt with evidence of a cognitive disturbance at the phenomenological level of depression. Numerous studies in support of the *negativity hypothesis* have shown that during clinical and nonclinical depressed states, there is a significant elevation in negative thought content about the self, future and, possibly to a lesser extent, personal world. Furthermore, this heightened negative self-referent thinking during depression cannot be discounted as a tautology resulting from item overlap between measures of cognition and depressive symptoms. However, we noted in Chapter 5 that the vast majority of studies on the negativity hypothesis have relied on retrospective cognition inventories and so more research is needed to verify these findings using concurrent production methods of cognitive assessment (e.g., think aloud, thought listing, thought sampling). In addition, studies are needed using finer-grained measures of the cognitive triad to determine the relative importance of negative thinking about the self, world, and future in depressive phenomenology. We also noted that negative thought content may be influenced by sample characteristics so that more specific measures may be needed for special populations of depressed individuals such as children, adolescents, chronic medically ill patients, and individuals from different cultural and ethnic backgrounds.

Moderate empirical support has been found for a significant decline or exclusion of positive self-referent thinking in depression. The *exclusivity hypothesis* refers to a significant decline rather than an absolute exclusion of positive self-referent thinking in depression. Although reductions in positive self-referent thinking are associated with depression, it is apparent that "nonpositive thinking" is not as potent a defining feature of the depressive experience as the elevation in negative self-referent thinking. Furthermore, a low rate of positive cognitions may be less specific to depression than a high rate of negative thinking. It is also unclear whether rates of positive self-referent thinking should be conceptualized in terms of a coping mechanism, an indicator of depression severity, or a core feature of the depressive experience. Another issue that has not been settled in the research literature is whether it is the absolute level of positive cognitions that is important in psychopathological states, or the ratio of positive to negative cognitions, as specified in the States-of-Mind Model (R. Schwartz, 1986, 1997). Whatever the outcome of this debate, measures of depressive cognitions should include items that assess both positive and negative aspects of self-referent thinking to provide a more complete assessment of cognitive disturbance in depression.

One of the core descriptive hypotheses of cognitive theory that has received considerable research attention is the *content-specificity hypothesis.* Strong empirical support for cognitive content-specificity has been found with both group comparison and correlational studies showing that loss and failure beliefs and cognitions are more strongly related to depression than to anxiety. These findings indicate that a cognitive profile involving themes of personal loss and deprivation may be distinct to depression. In fact, measures of depressotypic cognitions have been shown to discriminate depression from other psychopathological states, especially anxiety, thereby demonstrating their usefulness in the differential diagnosis of comorbid states. However, many issues remain for further investigation including whether cognitive content-specificity is less apparent in anxious thinking, in mild less distressed samples, or in children and adolescents. Also, research is needed on cognitive content-specificity using thought production methodologies and experimental information processing procedures, as well as in comparing the cognitive profile of depression with other psychological disorders besides anxiety. Finally, the relationship between negative cognitive content and the symptoms of anxiety and depression remains a matter of debate, with some research suggesting that more specific negative cognitions are linked to a common higher order negative affect dimension (Byrant & Baxter, 1997; D.A. Clark, Steer, et al., 1994; Jolly & Kramer, 1994; Mineka et al., 1998), whereas other studies suggest a greater level of distinctiveness, that is, a nonhierarchical relationship between anxious and depressive cognitive and noncognitive symptoms (Joiner, 1996; Joiner et al., 1996).

The Role of Negative Cognition in Depression

Chapter 6 reviewed the empirical literature relevant to three more descriptive hypotheses, primacy, universality, and severity/persistence, that focus on the role or function of negative cognition and faulty information processing in depressive disorders. The *primacy hypothesis* asserts that negative cognition and biased information processing have a significant influence on the behavioral, affective, somatic, and motivational symptoms of depression. This assertion is derived from the cognitive theory of depression (see Chapter 4), where it was argued that the cognitive-conceptual schemas representing personal loss and negative evaluation have strong links to schemas representing the affective, somatic, behavioral, and motivational features of depression. Strong empirical support was found for the primacy hypothesis in that the generation of negative self-referent thinking is associated with an increase in other symptoms and features of depressed mood. The strongest evidence for the influence of negative cognition on the concomitants of depression comes from Velten mood induction, psychophysiological, and central cortical studies. In the Velten mood induction studies, individuals who read and actively process negative self-referent evaluative statements show brief increases in subjective, behavioral, motivational, and psychophysiological features that mimic the symptom presentation found in mild to moderate clinical depression. Furthermore, the production of negative cognition in nondepressed individuals has been associated with corrugator facial muscle increases, startle reflex potentiation, changes in the endogenous components of ERPs, and increased cerebral blood flow activity in the lateral orbitofrontal and decreased activity in the rostral medial prefrontal cortex. Because many of these changes have been shown to be physiological concomitants of negative emotional states like depression, we conclude that negative cognition can influence the physiological indicators of depressed mood, and possibly depressive disorders.

Other issues remain for further investigation. More research is needed on whether a reduction in the frequency or belief in specific negative thoughts leads to reductions in other depressive symptoms. The few studies that have examined this question suffer from such serious methodological weaknesses that it is difficult to draw any firm conclusions from their findings. Another question concerns whether clinically depressed patients instructed to focus on their negative self-referent thoughts show a corresponding increase in depressive symptoms. A third area for further investigation is whether the production of negative cognitions has a significant impact on the core symptoms of diagnosable depression such as loss of interest and pleasure, loss of energy, and poor motivation. A final issue that might shed further light on the primacy of cognition is to investigate the distinctive characteristics of individuals who do not show criterion mood shifts during induction procedures. Are these individuals simply not complying with experimental instructions, or are they somehow more invulnerable to depression by being less affected by the production of negative self-referent thinking? In a related vein, the findings of Gilboa and Gotlib (1997) and the studies on the mood-state dependent hypothesis (Miranda & Gross, 1997; Persons & Miranda, 1992; see Chapter 8) suggest that heightened sensitivity or responsiveness to mood induction procedures might be an indicator of increased vulnerability to depression.

The *universality hypothesis* states that heightened negative cognition and faulty information processing are evident in all subtypes of depression. We conclude from our review that there is only preliminary empirical support for the universality hypothesis because too few studies have investigated negative thinking and information processing in other subtypes of depression such as dysthymia, bipolar depression, or major depression with endogenous features. Most of the research on the cognitive concomitants of depression has focused on nonpsychotic, unipolar major depression. Furthermore, we were very skeptical of studies that claim that only 40% to 50% of episodically depressed patients show prominent negative self-referent thinking or biased processing of negative material. Little is known about why some individuals with diagnosable depression score low on measures of negative cognition. Is it because (a) they suffer from very mild states of depression (i.e., they also score low on depressive symptom measures); (b) they have been misdiagnosed as having depression; (c) the cognition measures lack sensitivity to their personal negative cognitive content; (d) they lack awareness of their thought content; or (e) their questionnaire responses are confounded by response bias, self-presentational style, or defensiveness? Whatever the case, more research is needed to understand why a minority of depressed patients score low on measures of negative cognition.

According to the *severity/persistence hypothesis,* depressive states will persist as long as dysfunctional beliefs and the faulty information processing are active. Moreover, the more severe and extensive the negative cognition, the more severe the depressive state. Generally, there is strong empirical support for this contention. There appears to be a linear relationship between the level of symptom severity and the frequency, intensity, and pervasiveness of negative self-referent cognition in depression. In addition, elevated levels of negative cognition are associated with greater persistence of and poorer recovery from depression. At this point, however, we have not identified which cognitive indicators may be most predictive of the persistence of depression. Is it the frequency of negative self-referent cognitions, endorsement of dysfunctional beliefs, selective processing of negative self-referent stimuli, degree of mood-congruent recall bias, negative attributional style, or some other cognitive variable? This research could have treatment implications by suggesting cognitive processes linked to the persistence of depression that should be the target of intervention.

Selective Information Processing in Depression

The selective processing, schema activation, and primal processing hypotheses discussed in Chapter 7 in many ways represent the most central hypotheses of the cognitive theory at the descriptive level. These three hypotheses refer to the cognitive structures and processes that characterize the faulty information processing organization in depression. As a result, a very large research literature has addressed these core tenets of the model. Our overall conclusion is that there is strong empirical support for the selective processing, schema activation, and primal processing hypotheses. In Chapter 7, however, we posed four questions about biased information processing in depression that provided a framework for discussing the substantive findings that emerged from our review of this literature.

First, a consistent finding from the experimental information processing studies is that the bias for processing negative information in depression is specific to emotive material relevant to personal concerns. Depressed individuals cannot be distinguished from the nondepressed in their processing of impersonal or neutrally valenced stimuli. Thus the faulty information processing in depression is not a generalized cognitive problem but rather is confined to the processing of self-referent information.

Second, the negativity bias in depression is not equally apparent in all structures and processes of the information processing system. Experimental information processing studies employing such tasks as Stroop color-naming, multistimulus detection, and dichotic listening have provided evidence of attentional bias for negative emotion-congruent information, although less evidence was found for this bias in the preconscious attentional processing of perceptually based material. Stronger empirical support for a selective attentional bias in depression was apparent in studies that investigated the more elaborative and integrative tacit cognitive processes involved in conceptually based tasks, indicating that the processing bias in depression involves sustained attention to negative self-referent material and reduced attentional processing (possibly even avoidance) of positive self-referent information. Moreover, the negativity bias described in the *selective processing hypothesis* is most consistently evident in the more integrative, elaborative, and strategic cognitive processes that are integral to making evaluations, judgments, and inferences of emotion-relevant material (see also Williams et al., 1997, for similar conclusion). We reviewed numerous studies that found evidence of a negativity bias in the perception and recall of interpersonal and task performance feedback, self-evaluation, causal attributions, and expectancies of future success or failure. Biases in these complex cognitive tasks reflect the activation of negative self-referent schematic content and structures.

We also found studies that supported the *schema activation hypothesis,* showing that depressed individuals have enhanced recall of negative mood-congruent autobiographical memories, endorse more negative belief statements and trait adjectives, and respond more negatively to idiographic self-scenarios and sentence stem completions of belief statements than do nondepressed persons. Empirical support for schema activation was also found in the modified Stroop priming task, primed lexical decision and, to a lesser extent, the emotional priming task. In these studies, depressed individuals showed greater priming or relatedness effects for negative self-referent prime-target word pairs than nondepressed individuals. These results suggest that the negative self-referent schemas of the depressed may be more highly elaborated than the negative self-schemas of the nondepressed.

Third, a robust and consistent finding across numerous information processing studies on selective processing and schema activation is that depressed individuals can be differentiated from the nondepressed in how they process self-referent information. Certainly, we found little evidence that depressed individuals actually process self-referent information more accurately than the nondepressed, as stated in the "depressive realism" literature. However, the distinct processing bias in depression did not consistently emerge as a selective processing bias for negative material. Often, the primary difference between groups was a reduced processing of positive self-referent information in depressed or dysphoric groups compared with nondepressed controls.

Several factors may determine whether enhanced negativity and/or reduced positivity (i.e., evenhandedness) characterizes the depressive processing bias evident in a particular cognitive task. As noted in Chapter 7, the negativity bias should be more apparent in experiments that use cognitive tasks that clearly trigger negative schematic processing. Certain cognitive processes, such as the recall of self-referent information, may also be more sensitive to negativity bias in depression, whereas other cognitive processes, such as the attentional processing or encoding of material, may be more prone to elicit evenhanded processing. However, the key factor affecting selective processing bias is the severity of the depression. In nondepressed individuals, one finds a processing bias for positive self-referent material, but with the onset of a mild depressive or dysphoric state, we see a reduced processing of positive material and a slight increase in the processing of negative stimuli so that an evenhandedness is evident in self-referent information processing. As the depression deepens and becomes more severe, the shift in selective processing becomes even more extreme so that there is now a demonstrable selective processing of negative self-referent material. Although some studies of clinically depressed patients have reported evenhanded processing, the most consistent evidence for an enhanced negativity bias in depression comes from studies that used clinically depressed patients. This suggests that severity of depression may be an important factor in determining whether evenhandedness or enhanced negativity emerges in the processing of self-referent information in experimental cognitive tasks.

A fourth issue addressed in Chapter 7 is whether the negative processing bias in depression involves automatic, preconscious as well as more strategic and effortful cognitive processes. From a review of the empirical literature relevant to the *primal processing hypothesis*, we concluded there was strong evidence that negative self-referent processing in depression can occur unintentionally and involuntarily. There was limited support for the notion that negative self-referent processing in depression is more rapid or requires minimal processing capacity. There is evidence of preconscious processing in depression that occurs with later more integrative processes but not with earlier perceptual processing. Also, automatic processing in depression may be more evident in conceptually driven tasks, such as the conceptual implicit memory task of P. Watkins et al. (1996), than in perceptually driven cognitive tasks. It is evident from this research that the selective processing of negative self-referent material in depression involves a considerable degree of automatic information processing that can occur at the encoding, retrieval, and elaborative stages of information processing. Furthermore, there is considerable evidence reviewed throughout Chapter 7 that controlled and effortful cognitive processes are also involved in the biased information processing in depression. The relative contribution of automatic or strategic processes at any moment will depend on the input material and the specific cognitive processes involved. We must await the results of future studies that include measures of both automatic and effortful processing to determine the relative importance of these two characteristics of information processing in the cognitive organization of the depressed.

VULNERABILITY HYPOTHESES OF COGNITIVE THEORY

As noted in Chapters 8 through 10, Beck's cognitive theory recognizes a second level of conceptualization in which cognitive structures and personality suborganizations function as predisposing or vulnerability factors in the pathogenesis and maintenance of depression. The central tenet of cognitive vulnerability is that depressotypic self-referent schemas involving beliefs of failure, rejection, and unworthiness remain latent until activated by a congruent negative life experience (A. Beck, 1967, 1987). Once the negative self-schemas of the primal loss mode are activated, they tend to dominate the information processing system in episodic depression until deactivated by a treatment intervention or some other experience that ameliorates the depressive state. In the same fashion, the maladaptive features of the sociotropic and autonomous personality suborganization of the depression-prone individual will not play a *contributory role* in episodic depression until triggered by a congruent life stressor. Unlike the depressotypic schemas that remain latent in the nondepressed state, however, excessive and maladaptive aspects of one's personality can be expected to exert a continuing influence on the vulnerable person's general psychological and emotional functioning even in the absence of a triggering event.

As previously discussed, Beck's cognitive theory does not claim that negative cognitive structures *cause* depression. Rather, depression results from the combined influence of multiple factors within the biological, genetic, familial, developmental, personality, and social domains. Negative cognitive structures, however, will contribute to the pathogenesis of depression. Even within this more restricted understanding, some reviewers have concluded that there is limited empirical support for the existence of enduring, predisposing cognitive factors that significantly contribute to increased risk for depression (Ackermann-Engel & DeRubeis, 1993; Barnett & Gotlib, 1988c; Coyne & Gotlib, 1983; Coyne & Whiffen, 1995; Gotlib & Hammen, 1992; Haaga et al., 1991; Teasdale & Barnard, 1993; Williams et al., 1997). From our own review of the empirical literature, we arrive at a different set of conclusions. We believe there is sufficient empirical support to warrant continued research on the vulnerability hypotheses of cognitive theory. Although the empirical support of the vulnerability hypotheses may not be as firm as the support for the descriptive hypotheses, this is due in part to the limited number of studies that have examined many of the vulnerability hypotheses, especially the secondary hypotheses reviewed in Chapter 10. In addition, we noted methodological shortcomings with many of the existing studies (see Chapter 9) such that it could be argued that the vulnerability level of the cognitive model has not been adequately tested. Having acknowledged the rather tentative nature of the cognitive vulnerability research, in the following sections we offer some preliminary observations on the empirical status of cognitive predisposition to depression and suggest possible future directions for research at this level of conceptualization.

Stability Hypothesis

According to cognitive theory, the depressotypic schemas that predispose to depression remain latent until activated by a congruent life stressor. The stability hypothesis recognizes that these latent negative self-referent beliefs will remain consistent across time, situations, and mood states, but must be primed to become accessible. The early studies that purported to test for the endurance of dysfunctional beliefs or negative information processing beyond episodic depression in vulnerable individuals (e.g., individuals with remitted depression) did not include a priming manipulation. As a result, most of these studies failed to find evidence of elevated levels of dysfunctional beliefs in remitted depression. As noted, many reviewers concluded from this that the cognitive factors of depression emphasized in the cognitive model are simply concomitants of depression and so have no enduring or predisposing qualities. However, these findings are entirely consistent with the predictions of the cognitive model. Unprimed dysfunctional schemas will remain latent and so inaccessible in remitted depression.

More recent research in which depression-prone individuals are exposed to a priming manipulation such as negative mood induction, semantically paired words, or a congruent life stressor have shown evidence of the persistence of negative schematic constructs and beliefs beyond episodic depression. Although the majority of these priming studies have relied on the activation of dysfunctional schemas in depression-prone individuals by use of sad mood induction procedures, we believe that cognitive priming is the mechanism by which these procedures lead to increased accessibility to negative cognitive content in depression-prone individuals. Instructions to reflect on negative self-referent statements or recall negative life memories are explicit in mood induction procedures like the Velten or autobiographical memory recall, and so raise the likelihood that a type of "cognitive induction" is responsible for eliciting the sad mood state. Whatever the exact mechanisms in standard mood induction procedures, considerably more research is needed that uses life experiences and direct cognitive stimuli to prime depressotypic schemas.

Another limitation of the research on the stability hypothesis has been the over-reliance on elevations in the DAS Total Score as the primary indicator of dysfunctional schema activation. Research is needed to determine whether a greater level of stability may be evident with the DAS subscales or even selected individual items. This is because a more sensitive and fine-grained assessment of core idiosyncratic dysfunctional beliefs in depression-prone individuals is possible at the level of individual items or subscales. Also, idiographic measures of schema content that enable one to focus on specific individualized core self-schema content may produce evidence for greater stability of latent cognitive content in vulnerable individuals than more generalized nomothetic retrospective self-report questionnaires. As noted in Chapter 8, one might expect more supportive findings for the stability hypothesis from studies using information processing tasks than from studies that rely on self-report questionnaires because the information processing tasks do not require participants to consciously self-report schema content that in asymptomatic depression-prone individuals is latent and inactive. From our review of the experimental information processing studies on recovered depressed samples, however, the limited evidence that has emerged for biased processing in these studies has not been more supportive of the stability hypothesis than what has been reported in the research using self-report belief questionnaires. Finally, the few studies that have investigated temporal stability in measures of the predepressive personality have tended to find greater evidence for stability, as predicted by cognitive theory. However, future researchers must distinguish between the maladaptive and adaptive aspects of sociotropy and autonomy to ensure that they are targeting the predepressive aspects of personality (e.g., Bieling et al., 1998).

Diathesis-Stress Hypotheses

In Chapter 9, we presented two vulnerability hypotheses—*depression onset* and *depression relapse/recurrence*,—that adopt a diathesis-stress perspective to describe cognitive predisposition to the onset and recurrence of depressive episodes. In each hypothesis, the cognitive diathesis or predisposition to depression onset or relapse is conceptualized in terms of latent dysfunctional self-referent schemas and maladaptive sociotropic or autonomous personality features that become activated when high-risk individuals are exposed to a negative life stressor that matches the underlying maladaptive schemas and personality suborganization. Thus the person who depends on the love, approval, and acceptance of others for self-worth (i.e., maladaptive social dependency schemas or excessively high sociotropic personality features involving fear of rejection) is more likely to become depressed when exposed to external events that involve a loss of social resources, nurturance, and acceptance from others. Individuals who base their sense of worth on self-determination, mastery, and achievement (i.e., maladaptive achievement schemas or excessively high autonomous personality features involving solitary desire for control) will be at higher risk for depression when exposed to external events involving interference or loss of valued personal goals, achievement, and control.

We concluded from our review in Chapter 9 that there is some empirical support for the depression onset hypothesis. Cross-sectional studies, which are an indirect test of diathesis-stress, have found more evidence of an association between depression severity and the interaction of SAS Sociotropy with negative interpersonal events than between SAS Autonomy and negative achievement events. However, the more direct test of the hypothesis is provided by prospective studies on nonclinical samples that investigate whether a match between cognitive diathesis (maladaptive beliefs or personality) and life stress leads to a greater increase in depressive mood, symptoms, or disorders over a specified follow-up period than when there is a mismatch between the diathesis and life stressor. These prospective studies have provided more supportive evidence of a specific congruence between autonomy and negative achievement events. However, findings for congruence between sociotropy and negative interpersonal events have been less consistent: two prospective studies showed a significant personality-event congruence effect; two studies found no significant interaction effect; and a fifth study reported that sociotropy interacted with both negative interpersonal and achievement events. The best conclusion we can reach at this time is that there is some evidence that cognitive-personality/life event congruence may confer greater risk for depression but the findings across studies are inconsistent. The strongest evidence for a cognitive predisposition to depression onset comes from the preliminary findings of the Temple-Wisconsin Cognitive Vulnerability to Depression Project where high-risk students who evidenced dysfunctional attitudes and a negative attributional style but had no prior history of depressive episodes showed a significantly greater incidence of *DSM-III-R* major depression over a 2½-year follow-up period than did low-risk students (Alloy & Abramson, 1997).

In Chapter 9, we discussed many factors that may affect the strength of the cognitive diathesis-stress relationship. It may be that personality or dysfunctional attitude/life event congruence plays a more prominent role in triggering depressive reactions in women than in men. Also the diathesis-stress congruence effect may be stronger in prospective studies that screen participants to ensure that all individuals are initially asymptomatic for depression at Time 1. It is also important that researchers ensure that their measures assess the dysfunctional or maladaptive aspects of cognitive-personality diathesis. For example, the discrepant findings for life event congruence with autonomy may be due to the use of the SAS Autonomy Total Score, which includes a mixture of adaptive and maladaptive features. More supportive results may be obtained with SAS autonomy raw scores or specific subscales that focus exclusively on the dysfunctional features of autonomy.

In a similar vein, we concluded in Chapter 9 that evidence of greater risk of depressive relapse for individuals showing a match between cognitive diathesis (elevated scores on DAS or SAS subscales) and negative life stressors was rather fragile and inconsistent. Nevertheless, the results are sufficiently encouraging to warrant further research on cognitive diathesis-stress in remitted depressed samples. Of particular note is the study by Segal et al. (1998) showing that increased accessibility to dysfunctional attitudes during a dysphoric mood induction was a significant predictor of relapse in remitted depressives. Segal and his colleagues also found that depressed patients treated with medication showed a significant increase in their endorsement of dysfunctional beliefs during the sad mood induction manipulation, whereas patients treated with cognitive therapy showed no such increase in DAS scores. These findings not only suggest that presence of latent cognitive structures (i.e., dysfunctional attitudes), when activated, predict increase risk for depressive relapse, but they also indicate that cognitive therapy but not pharmacotherapy can decrease a depression-prone individual's cognitive susceptibility to depression. This may be one explanation for the lower relapse and recurrence rates that have been reported in controlled clinical trials of cognitive therapy.

A lengthy discussion was presented on the methodological improvements that could be made in cognitive diathesis-stress research to provide a better test of the depression onset and relapse/recurrence hypotheses. Two issues are worth repeating. In the future, researchers need to pay closer attention to sampling characteristics. Sample sizes need to be large enough to provide adequate statistical power, all participants should be asymptomatic for depression at Time 1, and there must be a moderate level or distribution of both the diathesis and the stressor within the sample to test for interaction effects. A second issue is the assessment of stressors. It is unlikely that independent raters can unambiguously categorize events as either interpersonal or achievement in nature. Most events involve a mixture of both concerns, which will obscure the diathesis-stress relationship. A more accurate test of these hypotheses would include the patients' appraisals so that one can determine which aspects of an event is most distressing to them. The cognitive diathesis-stress hypotheses would predict that depression-prone sociotropic individuals would be most responsive to the negative interpersonal aspects of events, whereas the autonomous would be most sensitive to the negative achievement and control aspects of situations. A great deal of more refined research is needed to test the depression onset and relapse/recurrence hypotheses.

Secondary Vulnerability Hypotheses

Chapter 10 presented more tentative hypotheses dealing with aspects of cognitive vulnerability that may affect the pathogenesis and course of depression. Because most of these hypotheses have only recently come to the attention of researchers, it would be premature to comment on their empirical support. Rather, we will briefly present some speculations on the status of each hypothesis and suggest possible directions for future research.

The *self-evaluation hypothesis* predicts that the dysfunctional schemas and maladaptive personality features that predispose to depression will be associated with negative self-evaluations, perceptions, and judgments in areas congruent with the underlying vulnerability. For example, self-evaluations of the sociotropic person are more likely to be influenced by self-referent information in the interpersonal domain; whereas the self-evaluations of the autonomous individual are more likely to be influenced by self-referent information dealing with issues of independence, achievement, and control. For depression-prone individuals, negative self-evaluations will more likely be generated in response to negative or ambiguous self-referent information that matches their underlying cognitive vulnerability. As noted, the critical research on the relationship between cognitive vulnerability measures like the DAS or SAS, and indices of self-evaluative or self-perception has not been done. There is some evidence of a relationship between SAS Sociotropy and negative self-evaluation. However, studies are needed that incorporate special priming strategies to activate latent dysfunctional schemas and maladaptive personality features, that present nondepressed vulnerable and nonvulnerable groups with positive and negative content-specific self-referent information, and that measure the effects of these manipulations on individuals' self-appraisals.

The *congruent processing hypothesis* proposes that maladaptive schemas and personality suborganization will influence the cognitive apparatus such that information congruent with underlying vulnerability will be selectively processed and elaborated over incongruent information. Thus highly sociotropic individuals, for example, will show heightened sensitivity to the processing of interpersonal information, whereas the autonomous will show enhanced processing of achievement and control information. The few studies that examined personality-congruent processing bias tended to find more evidence of an association between sociotropy and selectivity for interpersonal material than for autonomy and enhanced selection of achievement-related information, although inconsistencies were evident across the studies. One finding that was clear in this research is that a priming manipulation must be included if one is to elicit a personality-congruent negativity processing bias in depression-prone individuals.

The next two vulnerability hypotheses discussed in Chapter 10, the *relationship* and *differential coping* hypotheses, are recent additions to Beck's cognitive theory of depression and so relevant studies are just starting to emerge. According to cognitive theory, we would expect latent dysfunctional schemas, when activated, and maladaptive personality features to influence interpersonal style, quality of relationships, and coping strategies. It is predicted that highly sociotropic individuals will seek close emotional relationships (i.e., anxious attachment style), and will evidence more emotion-focused and maladaptive coping to negative interpersonal events. The highly autonomous individual will tend to maintain distant and detached relationships with others (i.e., avoidant attachment style), and will evidence a more task-oriented coping style except when confronted with an important negative achievement event at which time the autonomous person will show poor coping responses. We noted that there is some preliminary evidence to support the differential patterns of interpersonal style and coping responses of highly sociotropic or autonomous individuals.

The final two vulnerability hypotheses discussed in Chapter 10 were first introduced by A. Beck (1983) and deal with the influence of predepressive personality on the course of depression. Research on the *symptom specificity hypothesis* found evidence of a differential symptom pattern in depressed sociotropic and autonomous individuals. Depressed sociotropic patients tend to show a more anxious, reactive and emotive type of depressive experience, whereas depressed autonomous individuals exhibit more endogenous depressive symptoms. However, self-criticism may be more characteristic of the depressions of sociotropic than autonomous depressed patients, and SAS Sociotropy may also have broader effects on symptom severity because of a higher concentration of items that tap into negative affectivity or neuroticism.

Insufficient research has been conducted on the *differential treatment hypothesis* to allow any conclusions to be drawn on its empirical status. The study by Peselow et al. (1992) suggests that depressed patients with high autonomy and low sociotropy show a significantly better response to pharmacotherapy than the low autonomy/high sociotropy patient group. There is also some preliminary evidence in keeping with our conceptualization that depressed sociotropic patients are more responsive to group cognitive therapy than autonomous patients who receive group cognitive treatment. However, the critical research has not been done to determine whether depressed sociotropic patients respond better to a supportive, helping, and emotionally close therapeutic style, whereas depressed autonomous individuals respond best to a more structured, detached, and goal-directed form of psychotherapy.

CONCLUSION

A number of years ago Ingram and Kendall (1986) challenged cognitive-clinical researchers to adapt the conceptual and experimental methodologies of cognitive psychology to the study of depression. At that time, research on the cognitive basis of depression had largely overlooked developments in experimental cognitive and social psychology. Ingram and Kendall reasoned that the concepts and methodologies of the experimental information processing paradigm would provide a finer-grained analysis of the cognitive structures, processes, and mechanisms in depression, thereby generating more specific, less ambiguous testable hypotheses. As a result, structured, more controlled laboratory experiments could be designed to disentangle the intertwined processes of the cognitive organization so that less ambiguous interpretations could be made of findings on the relationship between cognition and emotion. In the end, the experimental cognitive approach would provide a firmer scientific foundation for a cognitive theory of depression. This view on the merits of the experimental cognitive-processing approach for understanding emotional disorders has been repeated by others, including ourselves, over the intervening years (Dalgleish & Watts, 1990; Gelder, 1997; Gotlib et al., 1997; Mathews, 1997; Williams et al., 1997).

From our review of the empirical research on the cognitive basis of depression, it is abundantly clear that a great deal of information processing research has been conducted since Ingram and Kendall's (1986) commentary. Moreover, there can be little question that this research has provided new insights into the cognitive structures and processes that characterize the faulty information processing in depression. Beck's cognitive theory has been clarified, refined, and elaborated in large part due to the findings from experimental information processing research. In our own review, we placed the strongest weight on findings from laboratory research because one can often arrive at less ambiguous interpretations of the results. This has put cognitive theory and therapy on a firmer scientific foundation. In this closing section, however, we point out a potential shortcoming with experimental cognitive-processing approaches that needs to be addressed if this research is to continue its contribution to an understanding of the psychopathology of depression.

How well do the tightly controlled, precise, but artificially induced tacit cognitive processes studied in the laboratory setting map onto the type of information processing clinicians observe with depressed individuals in the therapy session? Williams et al. (1997) argued that there is a tension (or should we say trade-off) between the use of artificial materials in the laboratory that allow one to make relatively unambiguous interpretations of results and the more uncontrolled naturalistic research in which results cannot be interpreted as clearly. Is it possible, however, that researchers have missed the mark with regard to the critical cognitive processes in depression by their greater concern for specification and control?

We have emphasized here that the cognitive disturbance in depression occurs at the level of "personalized meaning." A depressed person puts the most negative construction on matters that are valued within the self domain. This means that only certain aspects of the self and one's experience may elicit negative processing, and this processing bias is most likely to occur in areas that matter most to the individual. For example, a person may be clinically depressed after suffering a severe financial loss. This event becomes the focus and catalyst that activates schemas of personal loss and failure. However, the individual may readily admit that he has not failed in everything. The person may recognize he has musical talent, is a good worker, is loved by his family, and is quite athletic. However, what matters most to this person and his sense of personal value is this failure in finance. The activated dysfunctional schemas and faulty information processing that occurs in depression must always be understood within a *context*. The biased or faulty meaning about the self that characterizes depression is always contextualized, and it is this contextual element that may be missing in many experimental information processing studies. The challenge for future experimental research on the cognitive basis of depression is to maintain the precision and specification of past research while developing more ecologically valid and powerful experimental methodologies that effectively tap into the core critical negative self-referent cognitive content and biased negative processes that are so often apparent in the suffering of depressed patients seeking relief from their distress.

We have argued that the cognitive theory of depression developed by Beck and colleagues meets all the criteria of a scientific theory of depression. It originated from both clinical observation and experimental research, it describes important features of clinical depression, it has generated specific testable hypotheses that have been subjected to intense empirical scrutiny, and it can account for the major findings from laboratory and naturalistic studies of cognitive phenomena in depression. The theory has also spawned a treatment approach that is now recognized as an established, empirically validated treatment for depression (DeRubeis & Crits-Christoph, 1998). Whether the cognitive formulation remains an established scientific theory of depression must be judged not by personal opinion but by the quality and outcome of its empirical research, and the utility and effectiveness of its derived treatment perspective.

References

Abramson, L.Y., & Alloy, L.B. (1981). Depression, nondepression, and cognitive illusions: A reply to Schwartz. *Journal of Experimental Psychology: General, 110,* 436–447.

Abramson, L.Y., Alloy, L.B., & Hogan, M.E. (1997). Cognitive/personality subtypes of depression: Theories in search of disorders. *Cognitive Therapy and Research, 21,* 247–265.

Abramson, L.Y., Alloy, L.B., Hogan, M.E., & Whitehouse, W.G. (1997). *Depressogenic cognitive style and the prospective development of depression.* Paper presented at the annual meeting of the Association for the Advancement of Behavior Therapy, Miami Beach, FL.

Abramson, L.Y., Alloy, L.B., & Metalsky, G.I. (1988). The cognitive depression onset theories of depression: Toward an adequate evaluation of the theories' validities. In L.B. Alloy (Ed.), *Cognitive processes in depression* (pp. 3–30). New York: Guilford Press.

Abramson, L.Y., Metalsky, G.I., & Alloy, L.B. (1989). Hopelessness depression: A theory-based subtype of depression. *Psychological Review, 96,* 358–372.

Abramson, L.Y., Seligman, M.E.P., & Teasdale, J. (1978). Learned helplessness in humans: Critique and reformulation. *Journal of Abnormal Psychology, 87,* 49–74.

Ackermann, R., & DeRubeis, R.J. (1991). Is depressive realism real? *Clinical Psychology Review, 11,* 565–584.

Ackermann-Engel, R.A., & DeRubeis, R.J. (1993). The role of cognition in depression. In K.S. Dobson & P.C. Kendall (Eds.), *Psychopathology and cognition* (pp. 91–106). San Diego: Academic Press.

Akiskal, H.S. (1983). Dysthymic disorder: Psychopathology of proposed chronic depressive subtypes. *American Journal of Psychiatry, 140,* 11–20.

Akiskal, H.S., & McKinney, W.T. (1975). Overview of recent research in depression: Integration of ten conceptual models into a comprehensive clinical frame. *Archives of General Psychiatry, 32,* 285–301.

Albersnagel, F.A. (1988). Velten and musical mood induction procedures: A comparison with accessibility of thought associations. *Behaviour Research and Therapy, 26,* 76–96.

Alford, B.A., & Beck, A.T. (1997). *The integrative power of cognitive therapy.* New York: Guilford Press.

Alford, B.A., & Gerrity, D.M. (1995). The specificity of sociotropy-autonomy personality dimensions to depression vs. anxiety. *Journal of Clinical Psychology, 51*, 190–195.

Alford, B.A., Lester, J.M., Patel, R.J., Buchanan, J.P., & Giunta, L.C. (1995). Hopelessness predicts future depressive symptoms: A prospective analysis of cognitive vulnerability and cognitive content specificity. *Journal of Clinical Psychology, 51*, 331–339.

Allen, N.B., Ames, D., Layton, T., Bennetts, K., & Kingston, K. (1997). The relationship between sociotropy/autonomy and patterns of symptomatology in the depressed elderly. *British Journal of Clinical Psychology, 36*, 121–132.

Allen, N.B., Horne, D.J., & Trinder, J. (1996). Sociotropy, autonomy, and dysphoric emotional responses to specific classes of stress: A psychophysiological evaluation. *Journal of Abnormal Psychology, 105*, 25–33.

Alloy, L.B., & Abramson, L.Y. (1979). Judgment of contingency in depressed and nondepressed students: Sadder but wiser? *Journal of Experimental Psychology: General, 108*, 441–485.

Alloy, L.B., & Abramson, L.Y. (1988). Depressive realism: Four theoretical perspectives. In L.B. Alloy (Ed.), *Cognitive processes in depression* (pp. 223–265). New York: Guilford Press.

Alloy, L.B., & Abramson, L.Y. (1996). *The Temple-Wisconsin cognitive vulnerability to depression (CVD) project: Conceptual background, design, and methods.* Unpublished manuscript, Department of Psychology, Temple University, Philadelphia, PA.

Alloy, L.B., & Abramson, L.Y. (1997). *The Temple-Wisconsin cognitive vulnerability to depression project: Psychopathology and implications for prevention.* Paper presented at the annual meeting of the American Psychological Association, San Francisco.

Alloy, L.B., Abramson, L.Y., Metalsky, G.I., & Hartlage, S. (1988). The hopelessness theory of depression: Attributional aspects. *British Journal of Clinical Psychology, 27*, 5–21.

Alloy, L.B., Abramson, L.Y., Murray, L.A., Whitehouse, W.G., & Hogan, M.E. (1997). Self-referent information processing in individuals at high and low cognitive risk for depression. *Cognition and Emotion, 11*, 539–568.

Alloy, L.B., Abramson, L.Y., & Viscusi, D. (1981). Induced mood and the illusion of control. *Journal of Personality and Social Psychology, 41*, 1129–1140.

Alloy, L.B., & Ahrens, A.H. (1987). Depression and pessimism for the future: Biased use of statistically relevant information in predictions for self versus others. *Journal of Personality and Social Psychology, 52*, 366–378.

Alloy, L.B., Hartlage, S., & Abramson, L.Y. (1988). Testing the cognitive diathesis-stress theories of depression: Issues of research design, conceptualization and assessment. In L.B. Alloy (Ed.), *Cognitive processes in depression* (pp. 31–73). New York: Guilford Press.

Alloy, L.B., Just, N., & Panzarella, C. (1997). Attributional style, daily life events, and hopelessness depression: Subtype validation by prospective variability and specificity of symptoms. *Cognitive Therapy and Research, 21*, 321–344.

Alloy, L.B., Kelly, K.A., Mineka, S., & Clements, C.M. (1990). Comorbidity of anxiety and depressive disorders: A helplessness-hopelessness perspective. In J. Maser & R.C. Cloninger (Eds.), *Comorbidity of mood and anxiety disorders* (pp. 499–543). Washington, DC: American Psychiatric Press.

Alloy, L.B., Lipman, A.J., & Abramson, L.Y. (1992). Attributional style as a vulnerability factor for depression: Validation by past history of mood disorders. *Cognitive Therapy and Research, 16,* 391–407.

Ambrose, B., & Rholes, W.S. (1993). Automatic cognitions and the symptoms of depression and anxiety in children and adolescents: An examination of the content specificity hypothesis. *Cognitive Therapy and Research, 17,* 289–308.

American Psychiatric Association. (1994). *Diagnostic and statistical manual of mental disorders* (4th ed.). Washington, DC: American Psychiatric Association.

Andersen, S.M. (1990). The inevitability of future suffering: The role of depressive predictive certainty in depression. *Social Cognition, 8,* 203–228.

Andersen, S.M., Spielman, L.A., & Bargh, J.A. (1992). Future-event schemas and certainty about the future: Automaticity in depressives' future-event predictions. *Journal of Personality and Social Psychology, 63,* 711–723.

Andrews, B., & Brown, G.W. (1988). Social support, onset of depression and personality: An exploratory analysis. *Social Psychiatry and Psychiatric Epidemiology, 23,* 99–108.

Angst, J. (1986). The course of affective disorders. *Psychopathology, 19,* 47–52.

Baker, K.D., Nenneyer, R.A., & Barris, B.P. (1997). Cognitive organization of sociotropic and autonomous inpatient depressives. *Journal of Cognitive Psychotherapy: An International Quarterly, 11,* 279–297.

Baker, S.C., Frith, C.D., & Dolan, R.J. (1997). The interaction between mood and cognitive function studied with PET. *Psychological Medicine, 27,* 565–578.

Bandura, A. (1969). *Principles of behavior modification.* New York: Holt, Rinehart & Winston.

Bandura, A. (1971). *Social learning theory.* Morristown, NJ: General Learning Press.

Bargh, J.A., Chaiken, S., Govender, R., & Pratto, F. (1992). The generality of the automatic attitude activation effect. *Journal of Personality and Social Psychology, 62,* 893–912.

Bargh, J.A., & Tota, M.E. (1988). Context-dependent automatic processing in depression: Accessibility of negative constructs with regard to self but not others. *Journal of Personality and Social Psychology, 54,* 925–939.

Barlow, D.H., Chorpita, B.F., & Turovsky, J. (1996). Fear, panic, anxiety and disorders of emotion. In D.A. Hope (Ed.), *Nebraska symposium on motivation* (Vol. 43, pp. 251–328). Lincoln: University of Nebraska Press.

Barnett, P.A., & Gotlib, I.H. (1988a). Dysfunctional attitudes and psychosocial stress: The differential prediction of future psychological symptomatology. *Motivation and Emotion, 12,* 251–270.

Barnett, P.A., & Gotlib, I.H. (1988b). *Personality and depression: New scales and a model of relationships.* Paper presented at the annual convention of the Canadian Psychological Association, Montreal.

Barnett, P.A., & Gotlib, I.H. (1988c). Psychosocial functioning and depression: Distinguishing among antecedents, concomitants, and consequences. *Psychological Bulletin, 104,* 97–126.

Barnett, P.A., & Gotlib, I.H. (1990). Cognitive vulnerability to depressive symptoms among men and women. *Cognitive Therapy and Research, 14,* 47–61.

Baron, R.M., & Kenny, D.A. (1986). The moderator-mediator variable distinction in social psychological research: Conceptual, strategic, and statistical considerations. *Journal of Personality and Social Psychology, 51,* 1173–1182.

Barraclough, B., Bunch, J., Nelson, B., & Sainsbury, P. (1974). A hundred cases of suicide: Clinical aspects. *British Journal of Psychiatry, 125,* 355–373.

Barrett, J.E., Barrett, J.A., Oxman, T.E., & Gerber, P.D. (1988). The prevalence of psychiatric disorders in a primary care practice. *Archives of General Psychiatry, 45,* 1100–1106.

Bartelstone, J.H., & Trull, T.J. (1995). Personality, life events, and depression. *Journal of Personality Assessment, 64,* 279–294.

Baxter, L.R., Phelps, M.E., Mazziotta, J.C., Schwartz, J.M., Gerner, R.H., Selin, C.E., & Sumida, R.M. (1985). Cerebral metabolic rates of glucose in mood disorders. *Archives of General Psychiatry, 42,* 441–447.

Baxter, L.R., Schwartz, J.M., Phelps, M.E., Mazziotta, J.C., Guze, B.H., Selin, C.E., Gerner, R.H., & Sumida, R.M. (1989). Reduction of prefrontal cortex glucose metabolism common to three types of depression. *Archives of General Psychiatry, 46,* 243–250.

Bazin, N., Perruchet, P., De Bonis, M., & Féline, A. (1994). The dissociation of explicit and implicit memory in depressed patients. *Psychological Medicine, 24,* 239–245.

Beaudet, M.P. (1996). Depression. *Health Reports: Statistics Canada, 7,* 11–24.

Bech, P. (1992). Symptoms and assessment of depression. In E.S. Paykel (Ed.), *Handbook of affective disorders* (2nd ed., pp. 3–13). New York: Guilford Press.

Beck, A.T. (1961). A systematic investigation of depression. *Comprehensive Psychiatry, 2,* 163–170.

Beck, A.T. (1963). Thinking and depression: 1. Idiosyncratic content and cognitive distortions. *Archives of General Psychiatry, 9,* 324–333.

Beck, A.T. (1964). Thinking and depression: 2. Theory and therapy. *Archives of General Psychiatry, 10,* 561–571.

Beck, A.T. (1967). *Depression: Causes and treatment.* Philadelphia: University of Pennsylvania Press.

Beck, A.T. (1970). Cognitive therapy: Nature and relation to behavior therapy. *Behavior Therapy, 1,* 184–200.

Beck, A.T. (1971). Cognition, affect, and psychotherapy. *Archives of General Psychiatry, 24,* 495–500.

Beck, A.T. (1976). *Cognitive therapy of the emotional disorders.* New York: New American Library.

Beck, A.T. (1983). Cognitive therapy of depression: New perspectives. In P.J. Clayton & J.E. Barrett (Eds.), *Treatment of depression: Old controversies and new approaches* (pp. 265–290). New York: Raven Press.

Beck, A.T. (1985a). Cognitive therapy, behavior therapy, psychoanalysis, and pharmacotherapy: A cognitive continuum. In M.J. Mahoney & A. Freeman. *Cognition and psychotherapy* (pp. 325–347). New York: Plenum Press.

Beck, A.T. (1985b). Cognitive therapy. In H.I. Kaplan & B.J. Saddock (Eds.), *Comprehensive textbook of psychiatry/IV* (4th ed.) (Vol. 2, pp. 1432–1438). Baltimore: Williams & Wilkins.

Beck, A.T. (1987). Cognitive models of depression. *Journal of Cognitive Psychotherapy: An International Quarterly, 1,* 5–37.

Beck, A.T. (1988). *Cognitive therapy of depression: A personal reflection.* The Malcolm Miller Lecture in Psychotherapy, University of Aberdeen, Department of Mental Health. Aberdeen, UK: Scottish Cultural Press.

Beck, A.T. (1991). Cognitive therapy: A 30-year retrospective. *American Psychologist, 46,* 368–375.

Beck, A.T. (1995). The descent of man: An evolutionary perspective on major depression. *Newsletter of the Society for Research in Psychopathology, 3,* 3–6.

Beck, A.T. (1996). Beyond belief: A theory of modes, personality, and psychopathology. In P.M. Salkovskis (Ed.), *Frontiers of cognitive therapy* (pp. 1–25). New York: Guilford Press.

Beck, A.T. (in press). Cognitive aspects of personality disorders and their relation to syndromal disorders: A psychoevolutionary approach. In C.R. Cloninger (Ed.), *Personality and psychopathology.* Washington, DC: American Psychiatric Press.

Beck, A.T., Brown, G., Berchick, R.J., Stewart, B., & Steer, R. (1990). Relationship between hopelessness and ultimate suicide: A replication with psychiatric outpatients. *American Journal of Psychiatry, 147,* 190–195.

Beck, A.T., Brown, G., Steer, R.A., Eidelson, J.I., & Riskind, J.H. (1987). Differentiating anxiety and depression: A test of the cognitive content-specificity hypothesis. *Journal of Abnormal Psychology, 96,* 179–183.

Beck, A.T., Brown, G., Steer, R.A., & Weissman, A.N. (1991). Factor analysis of the dysfunctional attitude scale in a clinical population. *Psychological Assessment: A Journal of Consulting and Clinical Psychology, 3,* 478–483.

Beck, A.T., & Clark, D.A. (1988). Anxiety and depression: An information processing perspective. *Anxiety Research, 1,* 23–36.

Beck, A.T., & Clark, D.A. (1997). An information processing model of anxiety: Reconsidering the role of automatic and strategic processes. *Behaviour Research and Therapy, 35,* 49–58.

Beck, A.T., & Emery, G. (with Greenberg, R.L.). (1985). *Anxiety disorders and phobias: A cognitive perspective.* New York: Basic Books.

Beck, A.T., & Epstein, N. (1982). *Cognitions, attitudes and personality dimensions in depression.* Paper presented at the annual meeting of the Society for Psychotherapy Research, Smugglers Notch, VT.

Beck, A.T., Epstein, N., Harrison, R.P., & Emery, G. (1983). *Development of the sociotropy-autonomy scale: A measure of personality factors in psychopathology.* Unpublished manuscript, Center for Cognitive Therapy, University of Pennsylvania Medical School, Philadelphia.

Beck, A.T., Freeman, A., & Associates. (1990). *Cognitive therapy of personality disorders.* New York: Guilford Press.

Beck, A.T., Guth, D., Steer, R.A., & Ball, R. (1997). Screening for major depression disorders in medical inpatients with the Beck Depression Inventory for primary care. *Behaviour Research and Therapy, 35,* 785–791.

Beck, A.T., & Hurvich, M.S. (1959). Psychological correlates of depression: I. Frequency of "masochistic" dream content in a private practice sample. *Psychosomatic Medicine, 21,* 50–55.

Beck, A.T., Kovacs, M., & Weissman, A. (1975). Hopelessness suicidal behavior: An overview. *Journal of the American Medical Association, 234,* 1146–1149.

Beck, A.T., Riskind, J.H., Brown, G., & Steer, R.A. (1988). Levels of hopelessness in *DSM-III* disorders: A partial test of content specificity in depression. *Cognitive Therapy and Research, 12,* 459–469.

Beck, A.T., & Rush, A.J. (1988). Cognitive therapy. In H.I. Kaplan & B.J. Sadock (Eds.), *Comprehensive textbook of psychiatry* (Vol. 5). Baltimore: Williams & Wilkins.

Beck, A.T., Rush, A.J., Shaw, B.F., & Emery, G. (1979). *Cognitive therapy of depression.* New York: Guilford Press.

Beck, A.T., Steer, R.A., & Epstein, N. (1992). Self-concept dimensions of clinically depressed and anxious outpatients. *Journal of Clinical Psychology, 48,* 423–432.

Beck, A.T., Steer, R.A., Epstein, N., & Brown, G. (1990). Beck Self-Concept Test. *Psychological Assessment: A Journal of Consulting and Clinical Psychology, 2,* 191–197.

Beck, A.T., & Ward, C.H. (1961). Dreams of depressed patients: Characteristic themes in manifest content. *Archives of General Psychiatry, 5,* 462–467.

Beck, A.T., Ward, C.H., Mendelson, M., Mock, J., & Erbaugh, J. (1961). An inventory for measuring depression. *Archives of General Psychiatry, 4,* 561–571.

Beck, A.T., Ward, C.H., Mendelson, M., Mock, J., & Erbaugh, J. (1962). Reliability of psychiatric diagnoses: 2. A study of consistency of clinical judgments and ratings. *American Journal of Psychiatry, 119,* 351–357.

Beck, A.T., & Weishaar, M. (1989). Cognitive therapy. In A. Freeman, K.M. Simon, L.E. Beutler, & H. Arkowitz (Eds.), *Comprehensive handbook of cognitive therapy* (pp. 21–36). New York: Plenum Press.

Beck, A.T., Weissman, A., Lester, D., & Trexler, L. (1974). The measurement of pessimism: The hopelessness scale. *Journal of Consulting and Clinical Psychology, 42,* 861–865.

Beck, A.T., Wright, F.W., Newman, C.F., & Liese, B. (1993). *Cognitive therapy of substance abuse.* New York: Guilford Press.

Beck, J.S. (1995). *Cognitive therapy: Basics and beyond.* New York: Guilford Press.

Beck, R., Perkins, T.S., & Wilson, S. (1993). *Cognitive specificity, negative affectivity, depression and anxiety: Is integration possible?* Paper presented at the annual meeting of the Association for the Advancement of Behavior Therapy, Atlanta.

Beckham, E.E., & Leber, W.R. (Eds.). (1985). *Handbook of depression: Treatment, assessment, and research.* Homewood, IL: Dorsey Press.

Beckham, E.E., Leber, W.R., Watkins, J.T., Boyer, J.L., & Cook, J.B. (1986). Development of an instrument to measure Beck's cognitive triad: The Cognitive Triad Inventory. *Journal of Consulting and Clinical Psychology, 54,* 566–567.

Beidel, D.C., & Turner, S.M. (1986). A critique of the theoretical bases of cognitive-behavioral theories and therapy. *Clinical Psychology Review, 6,* 177–197.

Belsher, G., & Costello, C.G. (1988). Relapse after recovery from unipolar depression: A critical review. *Psychological Bulletin, 104,* 84–96.

Bemporad, J. (1985). Long-term analytic treatment of depression. In E.E. Beckham & W.R. Leber (Eds.), *Handbook of depression: Treatment, assessment, and research* (pp. 82–99). Homewood, IL: Dorsey Press.

Bergin, A.E., & Lambert, M.J. (1978). The evaluation of therapeutic outcomes. In S.L. Garfield & A.E. Bergin (Eds.), *Handbook of psychotherapy and behavior change: An empirical analysis* (2nd ed., pp. 139–189). New York: Wiley.

Bieling, P.J., & Alden, L.E. (1998). Cognitive-interpersonal patterns in dysphoria: The impact of sociotropy and autonomy. *Cognitive Therapy and Research, 22,* 161–178.

Bieling, P.J., & Olshan, S. (1998). *The Sociotropy-Autonomy Scale: A review of the literature.* Unpublished manuscript, Department of Psychiatry, University of Pennsylvania.

Bieling, P.J., Olshan, S., Brown, G.K., & Beck, A.T. (1998). *The Sociotropy-Autonomy Scale: Structure and implications.* Unpublished manuscript, Department of Psychiatry, University of Pennsylvania.

Bifulco, A., Brown, G.W., Moran, P., Ball, C., & Campbell, C. (1998). Predicting depression in women: The role of past and present vulnerability. *Psychological Medicine, 28,* 39–50.

Billings, A.G., Cronkite, R.C., & Moos, R.H. (1983). Social-environmental factors in unipolar depression: Comparisons of depressed patients and nondepressed controls. *Journal of Abnormal Psychology, 92,* 119–133.

Billings, A.G., & Moos, R.H. (1985). Life stressors and social resources affect posttreatment outcomes among depressed patients. *Journal of Abnormal Psychology, 94,* 140–153.

Blackburn, I.M. (1996). Cognitive vulnerability to depression. In P.M. Salkovskis (Ed.), *Frontiers of cognitive therapy* (pp. 250–265). New York: Guilford Press.

Blackburn, I.M., & Eunson, K.M. (1989). A content analysis of thoughts and emotions elicited from depressed patients during cognitive therapy. *British Journal of Medical Psychology, 62,* 23–33.

Blackburn, I.M., Jones, S., & Lewin, R.J.P. (1986). Cognitive style in depression. *British Journal of Clinical Psychology, 25,* 241–251.

Blackburn, I.M., Roxborough, H.M., Muir, W.J., Glabus, M., & Blackwood, D.H.R. (1990). Perceptual and physiological dysfunction in depression. *Psychological Medicine, 20,* 95–103.

Blackburn, I.M., & Smyth, P. (1985). A test of cognitive vulnerability in individuals prone to depression. *British Journal of Clinical Psychology, 24,* 61–62.

Blaney, P.H. (1977). Contemporary theories of depression: Critique and comparison. *Journal of Abnormal Psychology, 86,* 203–223.

Blaney, P.H. (1986). Affect and memory: A review. *Psychological Bulletin, 99,* 229–246.

Blaney, P.H., & Kutcher, G.S. (1991). Measures of depressive dimensions: Are they interchangeable? *Journal of Personality Assessment, 56,* 502–512.

Blatt, S.J. (1974). Levels of object representation in anaclitic and introjective depression. *Psychoanalytic Study of the Child, 24,* 107–157.

Blatt, S.J., & Bers, S.A. (1993). Commentary. In Z.V. Segal & S.J. Blatt (Eds.), *The self in emotional distress: Cognitive and psychodynamic perspectives* (pp. 164–170) New York: Guilford Press.

Blatt, S.J., & Maroudas, C. (1992). Convergences among psychoanalytic and cognitive-behavioral theories of depression. *Psychoanalytic Psychology, 9,* 157–190.

Blatt, S.J., Quinlan, D.M., Pilkonis, P.A., & Shea, M.T. (1995). Impact of perfectionism and need for approval on the brief treatment of depression: The National Institute of Mental Health Treatment of Depression Collaborative Research Program revisited. *Journal of Consulting and Clinical Psychology, 63,* 125–132.

Blatt, S.J., & Zuroff, D.C. (1992). Interpersonal relatedness and self-definition: Two prototypes for depression. *Clinical Psychology Review, 12,* 527–562.

Blazer, D., Swartz, M., Woodbury, M., Manton, K.G., Hughes, D., & George, L.K. (1988). Depressive symptoms and depressive diagnoses on a community population: Use of a new procedure for analysis of psychiatric classification. *Archives of General Psychiatry, 45,* 1078–1084.

Borden, J.W., Lister, S.C., Powers, K.A., Logsdon, D.J., & Turner, L.C. (1993). *Self-focused attention: Commonalities across pathologies and predictors.* Paper presented at the annual meeting of the Association for the Advancement of Behavior Therapy, Atlanta.

Boyce, P., & Parker, G. (1989). Development of a scale to measure interpersonal sensitivity. *Australian and New Zealand Journal of Psychiatry, 23,* 341–351.

Boyd, J.H., & Weissman, M.M. (1981). Epidemiology of affective disorders: A reexamination and future directions. *Archives of General Psychiatry, 38,* 1039–1046.

Bradley, B.P., & Mathews, A. (1983). Negative self-schemata in clinical depression. *British Journal of Clinical Psychology, 22,* 173–181.

Bradley, B.P., & Mathews, A. (1988). Memory bias in recovered clinical depressives. *Cognition and Emotion, 2,* 235–245.

Bradley, B.P., Mogg, K., & Lee, S.C. (1997). Attentional biases for negative information in induced and naturally occurring dysphoria. *Behaviour Research and Therapy, 35,* 911–927.

Bradley, B.P., Mogg, K., Millar, N., Bonham-Carter, C., Fergusson, E., Jenkins, J., & Parr, M. (1997). Attentional biases for emotional faces. *Cognition and Emotion, 11,* 25–42.

Bradley, B.P., Mogg, K., & Williams, R. (1994). Implicit and explicit memory for emotional information in non-clinical subjects. *Behaviour Research and Therapy, 32,* 65–78.

Bradley, B.P., Mogg, K., & Williams, R. (1995). Implicit and explicit memory for emotion-congruent information in clinical depression and anxiety *Behaviour Research and Therapy, 33,* 755–770.

Brady, E.U., & Kendall, P.C. (1992). Comorbidity of anxiety and depression in children and adolescents. *Psychological Bulletin, 111,* 244–255.

Brent, D.A., Kupfer, D.J., Bromet, E.J., & Dew, M.A. (1988). The assessment and treatment of patients at risk for suicide. In A.J. Frances & R.E. Hales (Eds.), *Review of psychiatry* (pp. 353–385). Washington, DC: American Psychiatric Press.

Breslow, R., Kocsis, J., & Belkin, B. (1981). Contribution of the depressive perspective of memory function in depression. *American Journal of Psychiatry, 138,* 227–229.

Brewer, D., Doughtie, E.B., & Lubin, B. (1980). Induction of mood and mood shift. *Journal of Clinical Psychology, 36,* 215–225.

Brewin, C.R. (1985). Depression and causal attributions: What is their relation? *Psychological Bulletin, 98,* 297–309.

Brewin, C.R. (1988). *Cognitive foundations of clinical psychology.* Hove and London: Erlbaum.

Brewin, C.R., Hunter, E., Carroll, F., & Tata, P. (1996). Intrusive memories in depression: An index of schema activation? *Psychological Medicine, 26,* 1271–1276.

Brittlebank, A.D., Scott, J., Williams, J.M.G., & Ferrier, I.N. (1993). Autobiographical memory in depression: State or trait marker? *British Journal of Psychiatry, 162,* 118–121.

Broadhead, W.E., Blazer, D.G., George, L.K., & Tse, C.K. (1990). Depression, disability days, and days lost from work in a prospective epidemiologic survey. *Journal of the American Medical Association, 264,* 2524–2528.

Bronisch, T., & Hecht, H. (1990). Major depression with and without a coexisting anxiety disorder: Social dysfunction, social integration, and personality features. *Journal of Affective Disorders, 20,* 151–157.

Brown, D.H., & Johnson, E.A. (1998). *Influence of dysfunctional attitudes versus mood on depressive thinking.* Poster presented at the annual conference of the Canadian Psychological Association, Edmonton, Alberta.

Brown, G.P., Hammen, C.L., Craske, M.G., & Wickens, T.D. (1995). Dimensions of dysfunctional attitudes as vulnerabilities to depressive symptoms. *Journal of Abnormal Psychology, 104,* 431–435.

Brown, G.W. (1989). Life events and measurement. In G.W. Brown & T.O. Harris (Eds.), *Life events and illness* (pp. 3–45). New York: Guilford Press.

Brown, G.W., Bifulco, A., & Harris, T.O. (1987). Life events, vulnerability and onset of depression: Some refinements. *British Journal of Psychiatry, 150,* 30–42.

Brown, G.W., Bifulco, A., Harris, T., & Bridge, L. (1986). Life stress, chronic subclinical symptoms and vulnerability to clinical depression. *Journal of Affective Disorders, 11,* 1–19.

Brown, G.W., & Harris, T.O. (1978). *Social origins of depression: A study of psychiatric disorder in women.* London: Tavistock.

Brown, G.W., & Harris, T.O. (1989). Depression. In G.W. Brown & T.O. Harris (Eds.), *Life events and illness* (pp. 49–93). New York: Guilford Press.

Brown, J.D., & Siegel, J.M. (1988). Attributions for negative life events and depression: The role of perceived control. *Journal of Personality and Social Psychology, 54,* 316–322.

Brown, T.A., & Barlow, D.H. (1992). Comorbidity among anxiety disorders: Implications for treatment and *DSM-IV. Journal of Consulting and Clinical Psychology, 60,* 835–844.

Bruch, M.A. (1997). Positive thoughts or cognitive balance as a moderator of the negative life events-dysphoria relationship: A reexamination. *Cognitive Therapy and Research, 21,* 25–38.

Bryant, F.B., & Baxter, W.J. (1997). The structure of positive and negative automatic cognition. *Cognition and Emotion, 11,* 225–258.

Buchwald, A.M. (1977). Depressive mood and estimates of reinforcement frequency. *Journal of Abnormal Psychology, 86,* 443–446.

Buchwald, A.M., & Rudick-Davis, D. (1993). The symptoms of major depression. *Journal of Abnormal Psychology, 102,* 197–205.

Buchwald, A.M., Strack, S., & Coyne, J.C. (1981). Demand characteristics and the Velten mood induction procedure. *Journal of Consulting and Clinical Psychology, 49,* 478–479.

Burgess, E., Dorn, L.D., Haaga, D.A.F., & Chrousos, G. (1996). Sociotropy, autonomy, stress, and depression in Cushing syndrome. *Journal of Nervous and Mental Disease, 184,* 362–367.

Burgess, E., & Haaga, D.A.F. (1994). The Positive Automatic Thoughts Questionnaire (ATQ-P) and the Automatic Thoughts Questionnaire–Revised (ATQ–PR): Equivalent measures of positive thinking? *Cognitive Therapy and Research, 18,* 15–23.

Burns, D.D., & Eidelson, R.J. (1998). Why are depression and anxiety correlated? A test of the tripartite model. *Journal of Consulting and Clinical Psychology, 66,* 461–473.

Burns, D.D., Shaw, B.F., & Croker, W. (1987). Thinking styles and coping strategies of depressed women: An empirical investigation. *Behaviour Research and Therapy, 25,* 223–225.

Butler, A.C. (1993). *Sociotropy/autonomy: Differential coping styles and depression in college students*. Unpublished manuscript, Beck Institute for Cognitive Therapy and Research, Philadelphia, PA.

Butler, A.C., Hokanson, J.E., & Flynn, H.A. (1994). A comparison of self-esteem lability and low trait self-esteem as vulnerability factors in depression. *Journal of Personality and Social Psychology, 66*, 166–177.

Butler, G., & Mathews, A. (1983). Cognitive processes in anxiety. *Advances in Behaviour Research and Therapy, 5*, 51–62.

Byrne, A., & MacLeod, A.K. (1997). Attributions and accessibility of explanations of future events in anxiety and depression. *British Journal of Clinical Psychology, 36*, 505–520.

Cacioppo, J.T., & Petty, R.E. (1981). Social psychological procedures for cognitive response assessment: The thought-listing technique. In T.V. Merluzzi, C.R. Glass, & M. Genest (Eds.), *Cognitive assessment* (pp. 309–342). New York: Guilford Press.

Cacioppo, J.T., von Hippel, W., & Ernst, J.M. (1997). Mapping cognitive structures and processes through verbal content: The thought-listing technique. *Journal of Consulting and Clinical Psychology, 65*, 928–940.

Calhoon, S.K. (1996). Confirmatory factor analysis of the Dysfunctional Attitude Scale in a student sample. *Cognitive Therapy and Research, 20*, 81–91.

Canadian Mental Health Association. (1995). *Depression: An overview of the literature* (Catalogue No. H39-301/1995E). Ottawa, Ontario: Publications/Communications Health Canada.

Cane, D.B., Olinger, L.J., Gotlib, I.H., & Kuiper, N.A. (1986). Factor structure of the Dysfunctional Attitude Scale in a student population. *Journal of Clinical Psychology, 42*, 307–309.

Cantor, N. (1990). From thought to behavior: "Having" and "doing" in the study of personality and cognition. *American Psychologist, 45*, 735–750.

Cappeliez, P. (1993). The relationship between Beck's concepts of sociotropy and autonomy and the NEO-Personality Inventory. *British Journal of Clinical Psychology, 32*, 78–80.

Carney, R.M., Hong, B.A., O'Connell, M.F., & Amado, H. (1981). Facial electromyography as a predictor of treatment outcome in depression. *British Journal of Psychiatry, 138*, 485–489.

Carver, C.S., Scheier, M.F., & Weintraub, J.K. (1989). Assessing coping strategies: A theoretically based approach. *Journal of Personality and Social Psychology, 56*, 267–283.

Casper, R.C., Redmond, E., Katz, M.M., Schaffer, C.B., Davis, J.M., & Koslow, S.H. (1985). Somatic symptoms in primary affective disorders: Presence and relationship to the classification of depression. *Archives of General Psychiatry, 42*, 1098–1104.

Cautela, J.R. (1967). Covert sensitization. *Psychological Reports, 20*, 459–468.

Chartier, G.M., & Ranieri, D.J. (1989). Comparison of two mood induction procedures. *Cognitive Therapy and Research, 13*, 275–282.

Chodoff, P. (1972). The depressive personality: A critical review. *Archives of General Psychiatry, 27*, 666–673.

Christensen, L., & Duncan, K. (1995). Distinguishing depressed from nondepressed individuals using energy and psychosocial variables. *Journal of Consulting and Clinical Psychology, 63*, 495–498.

Chung, G., Tucker, D.M., West, P., Potts, G.F., Liotti, M., Luu, P., & Hartry, A.L. (1996). Emotional expectancy: Brain electrical activity associated with an emotional bias in interpreting life events. *Psychophysiology, 33,* 218–233.

Clark, D.A. (1984). *Psychophysiological, behavioural, and self-report investigations into cognitive-affective interaction within the context of potentially aversive ideation.* Doctoral dissertation, Institute of Psychiatry, University of London, London, England.

Clark, D.A. (1986). Cognitive-affective interaction: A test of the "specificity" and "generality" hypotheses. *Cognitive Therapy and Research, 10,* 607–623.

Clark, D.A. (1988). The validity of measures of cognition: A review of the literature. *Cognitive Therapy and Research, 12,* 1–20.

Clark, D.A. (1992). Depressive, anxious and intrusive thoughts in psychiatric inpatients and outpatients. *Behaviour Research and Therapy, 30,* 93–102.

Clark, D.A. (1995). Perceived limitations of standard cognitive therapy: A consideration of efforts to revised Beck's theory and therapy. *Journal of Cognitive Psychotherapy: An International Quarterly, 9,* 153–172.

Clark, D.A., & Beck, A.T. (1989). Cognitive theory and therapy of anxiety and depression. In P.C. Kendall & D. Watson (Eds.), *Anxiety and depression: Distinctive and overlapping features* (pp. 379–411). San Diego: Academic Press.

Clark, D.A., & Beck, A.T. (1991). Personality factors in dysphoria: A psychometric refinement of Beck's Sociotropy-Autonomy Scale. *Journal of Psychopathology and Behavioral Assessment, 13,* 369–388.

Clark, D.A., & Beck, A.T. (1997). El estado de la cuestion en la teoria y la terapia cognitiva. In I. Caro (Ed.), *Manual de psicoterapias cognitivas* (pp. 119–129). Barcelona: Paidos.

Clark, D.A., Beck, A.T., & Beck, J.S. (1994). Symptom differences in major depression, dysthymia, panic disorder, and generalized anxiety disorder. *American Journal of Psychiatry, 151,* 205–209.

Clark, D.A., Beck, A.T., & Brown, G. (1989). Cognitive mediation in general psychiatric outpatients: A test of the content-specificity hypothesis. *Journal of Personality and Social Psychology, 56,* 958–964.

Clark, D.A., Beck, A.T., & Brown, G.K. (1992). Sociotropy, autonomy, and life event perceptions in dysphoric and nondysphoric individuals. *Cognitive Therapy and Research, 16,* 635–652.

Clark, D.A., Beck, A.T., & Stewart, B. (1990). Cognitive specificity and positive-negative affectivity: Complementary or contradictory views on anxiety and depression? *Journal of Abnormal Psychology, 99,* 148–155.

Clark, D.A., Cook, A.C., & Snow, D. (1998). Depressive symptom differences in hospitalized medically ill, depressed psychiatric inpatients and nonmedical controls. *Journal of Abnormal Psychology, 107,* 38–48.

Clark, D.A., & Oates, T. (1995). Daily hassles, major and minor life events, and their interaction with sociotropy and autonomy. *Behaviour Research and Therapy, 33,* 819–823.

Clark, D.A., Purdon, C.L., & Beck, A.T. (1997). *Sociotropy, autonomy and life event vulnerability to depressive symptoms: A three month prospective study.* Unpublished manuscript, Department of Psychology, University of New Brunswick, Canada.

Clark, D.A., & Steer, R.A. (1996). Empirical status of the cognitive model of anxiety and depression. In P.M. Salkovskis (Ed.), *Frontiers of cognitive therapy* (pp. 75–96). New York: Guilford Press.

Clark, D.A., Steer, R.A., & Beck, A.T. (1994). Common and specific dimensions of self-reported anxiety and depression: Implications for the cognitive and tripartite models. *Journal of Abnormal Psychology, 103*, 645–654.

Clark, D.A., Steer, R.A., Beck, A.T., & Ross, L. (1995). Psychometric characteristics of revised sociotropy and autonomy scales in college students. *Behaviour Research and Therapy, 33*, 325–334.

Clark, D.A., Steer, R.A., Beck, A.T., & Snow, D. (1996). Is the relationship between anxious and depressive cognitions and symptoms linear or curvilinear? *Cognitive Therapy and Research, 20*, 135–154.

Clark, D.A., Steer, R.A., Haslam, N., Beck, A.T., & Brown, G.K. (1997). Personality vulnerability, psychiatric diagnoses, and symptoms: Cluster analyses of the Sociotropy-Autonomy Scales. *Cognitive Therapy and Research, 21*, 267–283.

Clark, D.C., Cavanaugh, S.V., & Gibbons, R.D. (1983). The core symptoms of depression in medical and psychiatric patients. *Journal of Nervous and Mental Disease, 171*, 705–713.

Clark, D.M. (1983). On the induction of depressed mood in the laboratory: Evaluation and comparison of the Velten and musical procedures. *Advances in Behaviour Research and Therapy, 5*, 27–49.

Clark, D.M. (1986). A cognitive approach to panic. *Behaviour Research and Therapy, 24*, 461–470.

Clark, D.M., & Teasdale, J.D. (1982). Diurnal variation in clinical depression and accessibility of memories of positive and negative experiences. *Journal of Abnormal Psychology, 91*, 87–95.

Clark, D.M., & Teasdale, J.D. (1985). Constraints on the effects of mood on memory. *Journal of Personality and Social Psychology, 48*, 1595–1608.

Clark, D.M., Teasdale, J.D., Broadbent, D.E., & Martin, M. (1983). Effect of mood on lexical decisions. *Bulletin of the Psychonomic Society, 21*, 175–178.

Clark, L.A. (1989). The anxiety and depressive disorders: Descriptive psychopathology and differential diagnosis. In P.C. Kendall & D. Watson (Eds.), *Anxiety and depression: Distinctive and overlapping features* (pp. 83–129). San Diego: Academic Press.

Clark, L.A., & Watson, D. (1989). *Psychometric issues relevant to a potential DSM-IV category of mixed anxiety-depression.* Review for the *DSM-IV* subgroup on GAD and Mixed Anxiety-Depression.

Clark, L.A., & Watson, D. (1991a). General affective dispositions in physical and psychological health. In C.R. Synder & D.R. Donaldson (Eds.), *Handbook of social and clinical psychology: The health perspective* (pp. 221–245). New York: Plenum Press.

Clark, L.A., & Watson, D. (1991b). A tripartite model of anxiety and depression: Psychometric evidence and taxometric considerations. *Journal of Abnormal Psychology, 100*, 316–336.

Clark, L.A., Watson, D., & Mineka, S. (1994). Temperament, personality, and the mood and anxiety disorders. *Journal of Abnormal Psychology, 103*, 103–116.

Clark, L.A., Watson, D., & Reynolds, S. (1995). Diagnosis and classification of psychopathology: Challenges to the current system and future directions. *Annual Review of Psychology, 46*, 121–153.

Clifford, P.I., & Hemsley, D.R. (1987). The influence of depression on the processing of personal attributes. *British Journal of Psychiatry, 150*, 98–103.

Cofer, D.H., & Wittenborn, J.R. (1980). Personality characteristics of formerly depressed women. *Journal of Abnormal Psychology, 89,* 309–314.

Coleman, R.E. (1975). Manipulation of self-esteem as a determinant of mood of elated and depressed women. *Journal of Abnormal Psychology, 84,* 693–700.

Compas, B.E., Ey, S., & Grant, K.E. (1993). Taxonomy, assessment, and diagnosis of depression during adolescence. *Psychological Bulletin, 114,* 323–344.

Conway, M., Howell, A., & Giannopoulos, C. (1991). Dysphoria and thought suppression. *Cognitive Therapy and Research, 15,* 153–166.

Cook, E.W., Hawk, L.W., Davis, T.L., & Stevenson, V.E. (1991). Affective individual differences and startle reflex modulation. *Journal of Abnormal Psychology, 100,* 5–13.

Cook, M.L., & Peterson, C. (1986). Depressive irrationality. *Cognitive Therapy and Research, 10,* 293–298.

Coryell, W., Endicott, J., & Keller, M.B. (1991). Predictors of relapse into major depressive disorder in a nonclinical population. *American Journal of Psychiatry, 148,* 1353–1358.

Coryell, W., Endicott, J., & Keller, M.B. (1992). Major depression in a nonclinical sample: Demomgraphic and clinical risk factors for first onset. *Archives of General Psychiatry, 49,* 117–125.

Coryell, W., Endicott, J., Winokur, G., Akiskal, H., Solomon, D., Loen, A., Mueller, T., & Shea, T. (1995). Characteristics and significance of untreated major depressive disorder. *American Journal of Psychiatry, 152,* 1124–1129.

Coryell, W., Scheftner, W., Keller, M., Endicott, J., Maser, J., & Klerman, G. (1993). The enduring psychosocial consequences of mania and depression. *American Journal of Psychiatry, 150,* 720–727.

Coryell, W., & Winokur, G. (1992). Course and outcome. In E.S. Paykel (Ed.), *Handbook of affective disorders* (2nd ed., pp. 89–108). New York: Guilford Press.

Costello, C.G. (1972). Depression: Loss of reinforcers or reinforcer effectiveness. *Behavior Therapy, 3,* 240–247.

Coulehan, J.L., Schulberg, H.C., Block, M.R., & Zettler-Segal, M. (1988). Symptom patterns of depression in ambulatory medical and psychiatric patients. *Journal of Nervous and Mental Diseases, 176,* 284–288.

Cox, B.J., Borger, S.C., Enns, M.W., & Parker, J.D.A. (1997). *Analogue or artificial depression: An empirical analysis.* Poster presented at the annual meeting of the Canadian Psychological Association, Toronto.

Cox, B.J., Swinson, R.P., Kuch, K., & Reichman, J.T. (1993). Self-report differentiation of anxiety and depression in an anxiety disorders sample. *Psychological Assessment, 5,* 484–486.

Coyne, J.C. (1989). Thinking postcognitively about depression. In A. Freeman, K.M. Simon, L.E. Beutler, & H. Arkowitz (Eds.), *Comprehensive handbook of cognitive therapy* (pp. 227–244). New York: Plenum Press.

Coyne, J.C. (1994a). Possible contributions of "cognitive science" to the integration of psychotherapy. *Journal of Psychotherapy Integration, 4,* 401–416.

Coyne, J.C. (1994b). Self-reported distress: Analog or ersatz depression? *Psychological Bulletin, 116,* 29–45.

Coyne, J.C., Burchill, S.A.L., & Stiles, W.B. (1991). An interactional perspective on depression. In C.R. Synder & D.R. Forsyth (Eds.), *Handbook of social and clinical psychology: The health perspective.* New York: Pergamon Press.

Coyne, J.C., & Calarco, M.M. (1995). Effects of the experience of depression: Application of focus groups and survey methodologies. *Psychiatry, 58,* 149–163.

Coyne, J.C., & Downey, G. (1991). Social factors in psychopathology. *Annual Review of Psychology, 42,* 401–425.

Coyne, J.C., Gallo, S.M., Klinkman, M.S., & Calarco, M.M. (1998). Effects of recent and past major depression and distress on self-concept and coping. *Journal of Abnormal Psychology, 107,* 86–96.

Coyne, J.C., & Gotlib, I.H. (1983). The role of cognition in depression: A critical appraisal. *Psychological Bulletin, 94,* 472–505.

Coyne, J.C., & Gotlib, I.H. (1986). Studying the role of cognition in depression: Well-trodden paths and cul-de-sacs. *Cognitive Therapy and Research, 10,* 695–705.

Coyne, J.C., Schwenk, T.L., & Smolinski, M. (1991). Recognizing depression: A comparison of family physician ratings, self-report, and interview measures. *Journal of the American Board of Family Practitioners, 4,* 207–215.

Coyne, J.C., & Whiffen, V.E. (1995). Issues in personality as diathesis for depression: The case of sociotropy-dependency and autonomy-self-criticism. *Psychological Bulletin, 118,* 358–378.

Craighead, W.E. (1990). There's a place for us: All of us. *Behavior Therapy, 21,* 3–23.

Craighead, W.E., Hickey, K.S., & DeMonbreun, B.G. (1979). Distortion of perception and recall of neutral feedback in depression. *Cognitive Therapy and Research, 3,* 291–298.

Crandell, C.J., & Chambless, D.L. (1986). The validation of an inventory for measuring depressive thoughts: The Crandell Cognitions Inventory. *Behaviour Research and Therapy, 24,* 403–411.

Crewdsen, N., & Clark, D.A. (1997). *The measurement of subjective well-being in nonclinical populations.* Unpublished manuscript, Department of Psychology, University of New Brunswick, Fredericton, New Brunswick, Canada.

Cross-National Collaborative Group. (1992). The changing rates of major depression: Cross-national comparisons. *Journal of the American Medical Association, 268,* 3098–3105.

Crowson, J.J., & Cromwell, R.L. (1995). Depressed and normal individuals differ both in selection and in perceived tonal quality of positive-negative messages. *Journal of Abnormal Psychology, 104,* 305–311.

Crum, R.M., Cooper-Patrick, L., & Ford, D.E. (1994). Depressive symptoms among general medical patients: Prevalence and one-year outcome. *Psychosomatic Medicine, 56,* 109–117.

Csikszentmihalyi, M., & Larson, R. (1987). Validity and reliability of the experience-sampling method. *Journal of Nervous and Mental Disease, 175,* 526–536.

Dalgleish, T., Cameron, C.M., Power, M.J., & Bond, A. (1995). The use of an emotional priming paradigm with clinically anxious subjects. *Cognitive Therapy and Research, 19,* 69–89.

Dalgleish, T., & Watts, F.N. (1990). Biases of attention and memory in disorders of anxiety and depression. *Clinical Psychology Review, 10,* 589–604.

Dance, K.A., & Kuiper, N.A. (1987). Self-schemata, social roles, and a self-worth contingency model of depression. *Motivation and Emotion, 11,* 251–268.

Davey, G. (1992). Classical conditioning and the acquisition of human fears and phobias: A review and synthesis of the literature. *Advances in Behaviour Research and Therapy, 14,* 29–66.

Davidson, R.J. (1992). Emotion and affective styles: Hemispheric substrates. *Psychological Science, 3*, 39–43.

Davidson, R.J. (1993). Cerebral asymmetry and emotion: Conceptual and methodological conundrums. *Cognition and Emotion, 7*, 115–138.

Davis, H. (1979). Self-reference and the encoding of personal information in depression. *Cognitive Therapy and Research, 3*, 97–110.

Davison, G.C., Vogel, R.S., & Coffman, S.G. (1997). Think-aloud approaches to cognitive assessment and the articulated thoughts in simulated situations paradigm. *Journal of Consulting and Clinical Psychology, 65*, 950–958.

Deardorff, W.W., & Funabiki, D. (1985). A diagnostic caution in screening for depressed college students. *Cognitive Therapy and Research, 9*, 277–284.

Dember, W.N. (1974). Motivation and the cognitive revolution. *American Psychologist, 29*, 161–168.

DeMonbreun, B.G., & Craighead, W.E. (1977). Distortion of perception and recall of positive and neutral feedback in depression. *Cognitive Therapy and Research, 1*, 311–329.

Dennard, D.O., & Hokanson, J.E. (1986). Performance on two cognitive tasks by dysphoric and nondysphoric students. *Cognitive Therapy and Research, 10*, 377–386.

Denny, E.B., & Hunt, R.R. (1992). Affective valence and memory in depression: Dissociation of recall and fragment completion. *Journal of Abnormal Psychology, 101*, 575–580.

Dent, J., & Teasdale, J.D. (1988). Negative cognition and the persistence of depression. *Journal of Abnormal Psychology, 97*, 29–34.

Depression Guideline Panel. (1993). *Depression in primary care: Volume 1. Detection and diagnosis* (Clinical Practice Guideline No. 5, AHCPR Publication No. 93-0550). Rockville, MD: Agency for Health Care Policy and Research.

Depue, R.A., & Monroe, S.M. (1978a). Learned helplessness in the perspective of the depressive disorders: Conceptual and definitional issues. *Journal of Abnormal Psychology, 87*, 3–20.

Depue, R.A., & Monroe, S.M. (1978b). The unipolar-bipolar distinction in the depressive disorders. *Psychological Bulletin, 85*, 1001–1029.

Depue, R.A., & Monroe, S.M. (1986). Conceptualization and measurement of human disorder in life stress research: The problem of chronic disturbance. *Psychological Bulletin, 99*, 36–51.

Derry, P.A., & Kuiper, N.A. (1981). Schematic processing and self-reference in clinical depression. *Journal of Abnormal Psychology, 90*, 286–297.

DeRubeis, R.J., & Crits-Christoph, P. (1998). Empiricaly supported individual and group psychological treatments for adult mental disorders. *Journal of Consulting and Clinical Psychology, 66*, 37–52.

Di Nardo, P.A., & Barlow, D.H. (1990). Syndrome and symptom co-occurrence in the anxiety disorders. In J.D. Maser & C.R. Cloninger (Eds.), *Comorbidity of mood and anxiety disorders* (pp. 205–230). Washington, DC: American Psychiatric Press.

Dimberg, U. (1982). Facial reactions to facial expressions. *Psychophysiology, 19*, 643–646.

Dimberg, U. (1990). Facial electromyography and emotional reactions. *Psychophysiology, 27*, 481–494.

Diverty, B., & Beaudet, M.P. (1997). Depression: An untreated disorder? *Health Reports: Statistics Canada, 8*, 9–18.

Dixon, N.F., & Lear, T.E. (1962). Perceptual regulation and mental disorder. *Journal of Mental Science, 108,* 356–361.

Dobson, K.S. (1985). An analysis of anxiety and depression scales. *Journal of Personality Assessment, 49,* 522–527.

Dobson, K.S. (1989). A meta-analysis of the efficacy of cognitive therapy for depression. *Journal of Consulting and Clinical Psychology, 57,* 414–419.

Dobson, K.S., & Block, L. (1988). Historical and philosophical bases of the cognitive-behavioral therapies. In K.S. Dobson (Ed.), *Handbook of cognitive-behavioral therapies* (pp. 3–38). New York: Guilford Press.

Dobson, K.S., & Breiter, H.J. (1983). Cognitive assessment of depression: Reliability and validity of three measures. *Journal of Abnormal Psychology, 92,* 107–109.

Dobson, K.S., & Franche, R.L. (1989). A conceptual and empirical review of the depressive realism hypothesis. *Canadian Journal of Behavioural Science, 21,* 419–433.

Dobson, K.S., & Pusch, D. (1995). A test of the depressive realism hypothesis in clinically depressed subjects. *Cognitive Therapy and Research, 19,* 179–194.

Dobson, K.S., & Shaw, B.F. (1986). Cognitive assessment with major depressive disorders. *Cognitive Therapy and Research, 10,* 13–29.

Dobson, K.S., & Shaw, B.F. (1987). Specificity and stability of self-referent encoding in clinical depression. *Journal of Abnormal Psychology, 96,* 34–40.

Doerfler, L.A., & Aron, J. (1995). Relationship of goal setting: Self-efficacy, and self-evaluation in dysphoric and socially anxious women. *Cognitive Therapy and Research, 19,* 725–738.

Dohr, K.B., Rush, A.J., & Bernstein, I.H. (1989). Cognitive biases and depression. *Journal of Abnormal Psychology, 98,* 263–267.

Doost, H.T., Taghavi, M.R., Moradi, A.R., Yule, W., & Dalgleish, T. (1997). The performance of clinically depressed children and adolescents on the modified Stroop paradigm. *Personality and Individual Differences, 23,* 753–759.

Dow, M.G., & Craighead, W.E. (1987). Social inadequacy and depression: Overt behavior and self-evaluation processes. *Journal of Social and Clinical Psychology, 5,* 99–113.

Dozois, D.J.A., Dobson, K.S., & Tait, R. (1995). *Possible self-complexity and sociotropic/autonomous personality in depression.* Paper presented at the annual conference of the Canadian Psychological Association, Charlottetown, Canada.

Ducharme, J., & Bachelor, A. (1993). Perception of social functioning in dysphoria. *Cognitive Therapy and Research, 17,* 53–70.

Duer, S., Schwenk, T.L., & Coyne, J.C. (1988). Medical and psychosocial correlates of self-reported depressive symptoms in family practice. *Journal of Family Practice, 27,* 609–614.

Dunbar, G.C., & Lishman, W.A. (1984). Depression, recognition-memory and hedonic tone: A signal detection analysis. *British Journal of Psychiatry, 144,* 376–382.

Dunkley, D.M., Blankstein, K.R., & Flett, G.L. (1997). Specific cognitive-personality vulnerability styles in depression and the five-factor model of personality. *Personality and Individual Differences, 23,* 1041–1053.

Dunning, D., & Story, A.L. (1991). Depression, realism, and the overconfidence effect: Are the sadder wise when predicting future actions and events? *Journal of Personality and Social Psychology, 61,* 521–532.

Dworkin, R.H., & Goldfinger, S.H. (1985). Processing bias: Individual differences in the cognition of situations. *Journal of Personality, 53,* 480–501.

Dyck, M.J. (1992). Subscales of the Dysfunctional Attitude Scale. *British Journal of Clinical Psychology, 31,* 333–335.

Dyer, J.A.T., & Kreitman, N. (1984). Hopelessness, depression, and suicidal intent in parasuicide. *British Journal of Psychiatry, 144,* 127–133.

Dykman, B.M. (1996). Negative self-evaluations among dysphoric college students: A difference in degree or kind? *Cognitive Therapy and Research, 20,* 445–464.

Dykman, B.M. (1997). A test of whether negative emotional priming facilitates access to latent dysfunctional attitudes. *Cognition and Emotion, 11,* 197–222.

Dykman, B.M. (1998). Integrating cognitive and motivational factors in depression: Initial tests of a goal-orientation approach. *Journal of Personality and Social Psychology, 74,* 139–158.

Dykman, B.M., Abramson, L.Y., Alloy, L.B., & Hartlage, S. (1989). Processing of ambiguous and unambiguous feedback by depressed and nondepressed college students: Schematic biases and their implications for depressive realism. *Journal of Personality and Social Psychology, 56,* 431–445.

Dykman, B.M., Horowitz, L.M., Abramson, L.Y., & Usher, M. (1991). Schematic and situational determinants of depressed and nondepressed students' interpretation of feedback. *Journal of Abnormal Psychology, 100,* 45–55.

Dykman, B.M., & Johll, M. (1998). Dysfunctional attitudes and vulnerability to depressive symptoms: A 14 week longitudinal study. *Cognitive Therapy and Research, 22,* 337–352.

D'Zurilla, T.J., & Goldfried, M.R. (1971). Problem-solving and behavior modification. *Journal of Abnormal Psychology, 78,* 107–126.

Eastman, C. (1976). Behavioral formulations of depression. *Psychological Review, 83,* 277–291.

Eaves, G., & Rush, A.J. (1984). Cognitive patterns in symptomatic and remitted unipolar major depression. *Journal of Abnormal Psychology, 93,* 31–40.

Edelman, R.E., Ahrens, A.H., & Haaga, D.A.F. (1994). Inferences about the self, attributions, and overgeneralization as predictors of recovery from dysphoria. *Cognitive Therapy and Research, 18,* 551–566.

Eich, E., Macaulay, D., & Lam, R.W. (1997). Mania, depression, and mood dependent memory. *Cognition and Emotion, 11,* 607–618.

Ekman, P. (1994). Strong evidence for universals in facial expressions: A reply to Russell's mistaken critique. *Psychological Bulletin, 115,* 268–287.

Ekman, P., Friesen, W.V., & Ellsworth, P. (1982). What emotion categories or dimensions can observers judge from facial behavior. In P. Ekman (Ed.), *Emotion in the human face* (2nd ed.). Cambridge, England: Cambridge University Press.

Ekman, P., Levenson, R.W., & Friesen, W.V. (1983). Autonomic nervous system distinguishes among emotions. *Science, 221,* 1208–1210.

Elkin, I., Shea, M.T., Watkins, J.T., Imber, S.D., Sotsky, S.M., Collins, J.F., Glass, D.R., Pilkonis, P.A., Leber, W.R., Docherty, J.P., Fiester, S.J., & Parloff, M.B. (1989). NIMH treatment of depression collaborative research program: General effectiveness of treatments. *Archives of General Psychiatry, 46,* 971–983.

Elliott, C.L., & Greene, R.L. (1992). Clinical depression and implicit memory. *Journal of Abnormal Psychology, 101,* 572–574.

Ellis, A. (1962). *Reason and emotion in psychotherapy.* Secaucus, NJ: Lyle Stuart.

Ellis, A. (1977). The basic clinical theory of rational-emotive therapy. In A Ellis & R. Grieger (Eds.), *Handbook of rational-emotive therapy* (pp. 3–34). New York: Springer.

Ellis, A. (1989). The history of cognition in psychotherapy. In A. Freeman, K.M. Simon, L.E. Beutler, & H. Arkowitz (Eds.), *Comprehensive handbook of cognitive therapy* (pp. 5–19). New York: Plenum Press.

Emmons, R.A. (1986). Personal strivings: An approach to personality and subjective well-being. *Journal of Personality and Social Psychology, 51*, 1058–1068.

Emmons, R.A. (1991). Personal strivings, daily life events, and psychological and physical well-being. *Journal of Personality, 59*, 453–472.

Emmons, R.A. (1992). *Personal striving coding manual.* Unpublished manuscript, Department of Psychology, University of California, Davis, CA.

Endler, N.S., Cox, B.J., Parker, J.D.A., & Bagby, R.M. (1992). Self-reports of depression and state-trait anxiety: Evidence for differential assessment. *Journal of Personality and Social Psychology, 63*, 832–838.

Endler, N.S., & Parker, J.D. (1990). Multidimensional assessment of coping: A critical evaluation. *Journal of Personality and Social Psychology, 58*, 844–854.

Enns, M.W., & Cox, B.J. (1997). Personality dimensions and depression: Review and commentary. *Canadian Journal of Psychiatry, 42*, 274–284.

Epstein, N., Schlesinger, S.E., & Dryden, W. (1988). Concepts and methods of cognitive-behavioral family treatment. In N. Epstein, S.E. Schlesinger, & W. Dryden (Eds.), *Cognitive-behavioral therapy with families* (pp. 5–48). New York: Brunner/Mazel.

Epstein, S. (1984). Controversial issues in emotion theory. In P. Shaver (Ed.), *Review of personality and social psychology: Emotions, relationship and health* (Vol. 5, pp. 64–88). Beverly Hills, CA: Sage.

Epstein, S. (1994). Integration of the cognitive and the psychodynamic unconscious. *American Psychologist, 49*, 709–724.

Eysenck, H.J. (1952a). The effects of psychotherapy: An evaluation. *Journal of Consulting Psychology, 16*, 319–324.

Eysenck, H.J. (1952b). *The scientific study of personality.* London: Routledge & Kegan Paul.

Eysenck, H.J. (1966). *The effects of psychotherapy.* New York: International Science Press.

Eysenck, H.J. (1997). Personality and experimental psychology: The unification of psychology and the possibility of a paradigm. *Journal of Personality and Social Psychology, 73*, 1224–1237.

Eysenck, H.J., & Rachman, S. (1965). *The causes and cures of neurosis.* San Diego, CA: Robert R. Knapp.

Eysenck, H.J., Wakefield, J.A., & Friedman, A.F. (1983). Diagnosis and clinical assessment: The DSM-III. *Annual Review of Psychology, 34*, 167–193.

Eysenck, M.W., & Calvo, M.G. (1992). Anxiety and performance: The processing efficiency theory. *Cognition and Emotion, 6*, 409–434.

Fabrega, H., Mezzich, J.E., Mezzich, C., & Coffman, G.A. (1986). Descriptive validity of DSM-III depressions. *Journal of Nervous and Mental Disease, 174*, 573–584.

Fairbrother, N., & Moretti, M. (1998). Sociotropy, autonomy, and self-discrepancy: Status in depressed, remitted depressed, and control participants. *Cognitive Therapy and Research, 22*, 279–296.

Fairburn, C.G., Jones, R., Peveler, R.C., Carr, S.J., Solomon, R.A., O'Connor, M.E., Burton, J., & Hope, R.A. (1991). Three psychological treatments for bulimia nervosa: A comparative trial. *Archives of General Psychiatry, 48,* 463–469.

Fechner-Bates, S., Coyne, J.C., & Schwenk, T.L. (1994). The relationship of self-reported distress to depressive disorders and other psychopathology. *Journal of Consulting and Clinical Psychology, 62,* 550–559.

Feldman, L.A. (1993). Distinguishing depression and anxiety in self-report: Evidence from confirmatory factor analysis in nonclinical and clinical samples. *Journal of Consulting and Clinical Psychology, 61,* 631–638.

Fennell, M.J.V. (1997). Low self-esteem: A cognitive perspective. *Behavioural and Cognitive Psychotherapy, 25,* 1–25.

Fennell, M.J.V., & Campbell, E.A. (1984). The cognitions questionnaire: Specific thinking errors in depression. *British Journal of Clinical Psychology, 23,* 81–92.

Fennell, M.J.V., & Teasdale, J.D. (1984). Effects of distraction on thinking and affect in depressed patients. *British Journal of Clinical Psychology, 23,* 65–66.

Ferguson, T.J., Rule, B.G., & Carlson, D. (1983). Memory for personally relevant information. *Journal of Personality and Social Psychology, 44,* 251–261.

Fester, C.B. (1973). A functional analysis of depression. *American Psychologist, 28,* 857–870.

Finkel, C.B., Glass, C.R., & Merluzzi, T.V. (1982). Differential discrimination of self-referent statements by depressives and nondepressives. *Cognitive Therapy and Research, 6,* 173–183.

Finlay-Jones, R., & Brown, G.W. (1981). Types of stressful events and the onset of anxiety and depressive disorders. *Psychological Medicine, 11,* 803–815.

Fisher, S. (1989). The vulnerability of the depressed to life events: Sadder and tougher. *Advances in Behaviour Research and Therapy, 11,* 272–286.

Fitzgerald, J.M., Slade, S., & Lawrence, R.H. (1988). Memory availability and judged frequency of affect. *Cognitive Therapy and Research, 12,* 379–390.

Flett, G.L., Hewitt, P.L., Garshowitz, M., & Martin, T.R. (1997). Personality, negative social interactions, and depressive symptoms. *Canadian Journal of Behavioural Science, 29,* 28–37.

Flett, G.L., Vredenburg, K., & Krames, L. (1997). The continuity of depression in clinical and nonclinical samples. *Psychological Bulletin, 121,* 395–416.

Flint, A.J. (1994). Epidemiology and comorbidity of anxiety disorders in the elderly. *American Journal of Psychiatry, 151,* 640–649.

Fogarty, S.J., & Hemsley, D.R. (1983). Depression and the accessibility of memories: A longitudinal study. *British Journal of Psychiatry, 142,* 232–237.

Frances, A.J., Widiger, T.A., & Fyer, M.R. (1990). The influence of classification methods on comorbidity. In J.D. Maser & C.R. Cloninger (Eds.), *Comorbidity of mood and anxiety disorders* (pp. 41–59). Washington, DC: American Psychiatric Press.

Franche, R.L., & Dobson, K. (1992). Self-criticism and interpersonal dependency as vulnerability factors to depression. *Cognitive Therapy and Research, 16,* 419–435.

Freeman, P., & Genest, M. (1995). *Sex differences in the personality-event congruence model of vulnerability to depression.* Paper presented at the annual conference of the Canadian Psychological Association, Charlottetown, Prince Edward Island, Canada.

Fresco, D.M. (1991). *Cognitive styles in the subsyndromal mood disorders.* Unpublished honor's thesis, Department of Psychology, Temple University, Philadelphia, PA.

Freud, S. (1950). Mourning and melancholia. In *Collected Papers* (Vol. 4, pp. 152–172). London: Hogarth Press and the Institute of Psychoanalysis. (Original work published 1917)

Frijda, N.H. (1987). Emotion, cognitive structure, and action tendency. *Cognition and Emotion, 1,* 115–143.

Frost, R.O., Graf, M., & Becker, J. (1979). Self-devaluation and depressed mood. *Journal of Consulting and Clinical Psychology, 47,* 958–962.

Gable, S.L., & Nezlek, J.B. (1998). Level and instability of day-to-day psychological well-being and risk for depression. *Journal of Personality and Social Psychology, 74,* 129–138.

Ganellen, R.J. (1988). Specificity of attributions and overgeneralization in depression and anxiety. *Journal of Abnormal Psychology, 97,* 83–86.

Gara, M.A., Woolfolk, R.L., Cohen, B.D., Goldston, R.B., Allen, L.A., & Novalany, J. (1993). Perception of self and other in major depression. *Journal of Abnormal Psychology, 102,* 93–100.

Garber, J., & Hollon, S.D. (1991). What can specificity designs say about causality in psychopathology research? *Psychological Bulletin, 110,* 129–136.

Garber, J., & Robinson, N.S. (1997). Cognitive vulnerability in children at risk for depression. *Cognition and Emotion, 11,* 619–635.

Garber, J., Weiss, B., & Shanley, N. (1993). Cognitions, depressive symptoms, and development in adolescents. *Journal of Abnormal Psychology, 102,* 47–57.

Gelder, M. (1997). The scientific foundations of cognitive behaviour therapy. In D.M. Clark & C.G. Fairburn (Eds.), *Science and practice of cognitive behaviour therapy* (pp. 27–46). Oxford, England: Oxford University Press.

Genest, M., & Turk, D. (1981). Think-aloud approaches to cognitive assessment. In T.V. Merluzzi, C.R. Glass, & M. Genest (Eds.), *Cognitive assessment* (pp. 234–263). New York: Guilford Press.

George, M.S., Ketter, T.A., Parekh, P.I., Horwitz, B., Herscovitch, P., & Post, R.M. (1995). Brain activity during transient sadness and happiness in healthy women. *American Journal of Psychiatry, 152,* 341–351.

Gerrig, R.J., & Bower, G.H. (1982). Emotional influences on word recognition. *Bulletin of the Psychonomic Society, 19,* 197–200.

Gilbert, P. (1992). *Depression: The evolution of powerlessness.* New York: Guilford Press.

Gilbert, P., & Reynolds, S. (1990). The relationship between the Eysenck Personality Questionnaire and Beck's concepts of sociotropy and autonomy. *British Journal of Clinical Psychology, 29,* 319–325.

Gilboa, E., & Gotlib, I.H. (1997). Cognitive biases and affect persistence in previously dysphoric and never-dysphoric individuals. *Cognition and Emotion, 11,* 517–538.

Gilboa, E., Roberts, J.E., & Gotlib, I.H. (1997). The effects of induced and naturally occurring dysphoric mood on biases in self-evaluation and memory. *Cognition and Emotion, 11,* 65–82.

Glass, C.R., & Arnkoff, D.B. (1983). Think cognitively: Selected issues in cognitive assessment and therapy. In P.C. Kendall (Ed.), *Advances in cognitive-behavioral research and therapy* (Vol. 1, pp. 35–71). New York: Academic Press.

Glass, C.R., & Arnkoff, D.B. (1997). Questionnaire methods of cognitive self-statement assessment. *Journal of Consulting and Clinical Psychology, 65,* 911–927.

Goethe, J.W., Fischer, E.H., & Wright, J.S. (1993). Severity as a key construct in depression. *Journal of Nervous and Mental Disease, 181,* 718–724.

Gold, J.R. (1990). Levels of depression. In B.B. Wolman & G. Stricker (Eds.), *Depression disorders: Facts, theories and treatment methods* (pp. 203–228). New York: Wiley.

Goldberg, D.P., Bridges, K., Duncan-Jones, P., & Grayson, D. (1987). Dimensions of neuroses seen in primary-care settings. *Psychological Medicine, 17,* 461–470.

Goldberg, J.F., Harrow, M., & Grossman, L.S. (1995). Course and outcome in bipolar affective disorder: A longitudinal follow-up study. *American Journal of Psychiatry, 152,* 379–384.

Goldberg, J.O., Segal, Z.V., Vella, D.D., & Shaw, B.F. (1989). Depressive personality: Millon Clinical Multiaxial Inventory profiles of sociotropic and autonomous subtypes. *Journal of Personality Disorders, 3,* 193–198.

Goldstein, R.B., Black, D.W., Nasrallah, A., & Winokur, G. (1991). The prediction of suicide. Sensitivity, specificity, and predictive value of a multivariate model applied to suicide among 1906 patients with affective disorders. *Archives of General Psychiatry, 48,* 418–422.

Gong-Guy, E., & Hammen, C. (1980). Causal perceptions of stressful events in depressed and nondepressed outpatients. *Journal of Abnormal Psychology, 89,* 662–669.

Gotlib, I.H. (1983). Perception and recall of interpersonal feedback: Negative bias in depression. *Cognitive Therapy and Research, 7,* 399–412.

Gotlib, I.H. (1984). Depression and general psychopathology in university students. *Journal of Abnormal Psychology, 93,* 19–30.

Gotlib, I.H., & Cane, D.B. (1987). Construct accessibility and clinical depression: A longitudinal investigation. *Journal of Abnormal Psychology, 96,* 199–204.

Gotlib, I.H., & Cane, D.B. (1989). Self-report assessment of depression and anxiety. In P.C. Kendall & D. Watson (Eds.), *Anxiety and depression: Distinctive and overlapping features* (pp. 131–169). San Diego: Academic Press.

Gotlib, I.H., & Hammen, C.L. (1992). *Psychological aspects of depression: Toward a cognitive-interpersonal integration.* Chichester, England: Wiley.

Gotlib, I.H., Kurtzman, H.S., & Blehar, M.C. (1997). Cognition and depression: Issues and future directions. *Cognition and Emotion, 11,* 663–673.

Gotlib, I.H., Lewinsohn, P.M., & Seeley, J.R. (1995). Symptoms versus a diagnosis of depression: Differences in psychosocial functioning. *Journal of Abnormal Psychology, 63,* 90–100.

Gotlib, I.H., & McCabe, S.B. (1992). An information-processing approach to the study of cognitive functioning in depression. In E.F. Walker, B.A. Cornblatt, & R.H. Dworkin (Eds.), *Progress in experimental personality and psychopathology research* (Vol. 15, pp. 131–161). New York: Springer.

Gotlib, I.H., & McCann, C.D. (1984). Construct accessibility and depression: An examination of cognitive and affective factors. *Journal of Personality and Social Psychology, 47,* 427–439.

Gotlib, I.H., McLachlan, A.L., & Katz, A.N. (1988). Biases in visual attention in depressed and nondepressed individuals. *Cognition and Emotion, 2,* 185–200.

Gotlib, I.H., & Meltzer, S.J. (1987). Depression and the perception of social skills in dyadic interaction. *Cognitive Therapy and Research, 11*, 41–54.

Gouaux, C., & Gouaux, S. (1971). The influence of induced affective states on the effectiveness of social and nonsocial reinforcers in an instrumental learning task. *Psychonomic Science, 22*, 341–343.

Graf, P., & Schacter, D.L. (1985). Implicit and explicit memory for new associations in normal and amnesic subjects. *Journal of Experimental Psychology: Learning, Memory and Cognition, 11*, 501–518.

Green, S.B. (1991). How many subjects does it take to do a regression analysis? *Multivariate Behavioral Research, 26*, 499–510.

Greenberg, M.S., & Alloy, L.B. (1989). Depression versus anxiety: Processing of self- and other-referent information. *Cognition and Emotion, 3*, 207–223.

Greenberg, M.S., & Beck, A.T. (1989). Depression versus anxiety: A test of the content-specificity hypothesis. *Journal of Abnormal Psychology, 98*, 9–13.

Greenberg, M.S., Vazquez, C.V., & Alloy, L.B. (1988). Depression versus anxiety: Differences in self- and other-schemata. In L.B. Alloy (Ed.), *Cognitive processes in depression* (pp. 109–142). New York: Guilford Press.

Greenberg, P.E., Stiglin, L.E., Finkelstein, S.N., & Berndt, E.R. (1993). The economic burden of depression in 1990. *Journal of Clinical Psychiatry, 54*, 405–426.

Grove, W.M., & Andreasen, N.C. (1992). Concepts, diagnosis and classification. In E.S. Paykel (Ed.), *Handbook of affective disorders* (2nd ed., pp. 25–41). New York: Guilford Press.

Grove, W.M., Andreasen, N.C., Young, M., Endicott, J., Keller, M.B., Hirschfeld, R.M.A., & Reich, T. (1987). Isolation and characterization of a nuclear depressive syndrome. *Psychological Medicine, 17*, 471–484.

Gruen, R.J., Folkman, S., & Lazarus, R.S. (1988). Centrality and individual differences in the meaning of daily hassles. *Journal of Personality, 56*, 743–761.

Gupta-Rogers, R. (1998). *The nature of specificity and temporal stability of emotional information processing in sociotropic and independent individuals.* Doctoral dissertation, Department of Psychology, University of New Brunswick, Fredericton, New Brunswick, Canada.

Haack, L.J., Metalsky, G.I., Dykman, B.M., & Abramson, L.Y. (1996). Use of current situational information and causal inference: Do dysphoric individuals make "unwarranted" causal inferences? *Cognitive Therapy and Research, 20*, 309–331.

Haaga, D.A.F. (1992). Catastrophizing, confounds, and depression: A comment on Sullivan and D'Eon (1990). *Journal of Abnormal Psychology, 101*, 206–207.

Haaga, D.A.F., Ahrens, A.H., Schulman, P., Seligman, M.E.P., DeRubeis, R.J., & Minarik, M.L. (1995). Metatraits and cognitive assessment: Application to attributional style and depressive symptoms. *Cognitive Therapy and Research, 19*, 121–142.

Haaga, D.A.F., & Beck, A.T. (1995). Perspectives on depressive realism: Implications for cognitive therapy of depression. *Behaviour Research and Therapy, 33*, 41–48.

Haaga, D.A.F., Dyck, M.J., & Ernst, D. (1991). Empirical status of cognitive theory of depression. *Psychological Bulletin, 110*, 215–236.

Halbach Mofitt, K., Singer, J.A., Nelligan, D.W., Carlson, M.A., & Vyse, S.A. (1994). Depression and memory narrative type. *Journal of Abnormal Psychology, 103*, 581–583.

Hamilton, E.W., & Abramson, L.Y. (1983). Cognitive patterns and major depressive disorder: A longitudinal study in a hospital setting. *Journal of Abnormal Psychology, 92,* 173–184.

Hammen, C.L. (1985). Predicting depression: A cognitive-behavioral perspective. In P.C. Kendall (Ed.), *Advances in cognitive-behavioral research and therapy* (Vol. 4, pp. 29–71). New York: Academic Press.

Hammen, C.L. (1988a). Depression and cognitions about personal stressful life events. In L.B. Alloy (Ed.), *Cognitive processes in depression* (pp. 77–108). New York: Guilford Press.

Hammen, C.L. (1988b). Self-cognitions, stressful events, and the prediction of depression in children of depressed mothers. *Journal of Abnormal Child Psychology, 16,* 347–360.

Hammen, C.L. (1991). Generation of stress in the course of unipolar depression. *Journal of Abnormal Psychology, 100,* 555–561.

Hammen, C.L., Adrian, C., & Hiroto, D. (1988). A longitudinal test of the attributional vulnerability model in children at risk for depression. *British Journal of Clinical Psychology, 27,* 37–46.

Hammen, C.L., Burge, D., Burney, E., & Adrian, C. (1990). Longitudinal study of diagnosis in children of women with unipolar and bipolar affective disorder. *Archives of General Psychiatry, 47,* 1112–1117.

Hammen, C.L., Burge, D., Daley, S.E., Davila, J., Parley, B., & Rudolph, K.D. (1995). Interpersonal attachment cognitions and prediction of symptomatic responses to interpersonal stress. *Journal of Abnormal Psychology, 104,* 436–443.

Hammen, C.L., & Cochrane, S.D. (1981). Cognitive correlates of life stress and depression in college students. *Journal of Abnormal Psychology, 90,* 23–27.

Hammen, C.L., Ellicott, A., & Gitlin, M. (1989). Vulnerability to specific life events and prediction of course of disorder in unipolar depressed patients. *Canadian Journal of Behavioural Science, 21,* 377–388.

Hammen, C.L., Ellicott, A., & Gitlin, M. (1992). Stressors and sociotropy/autonomy: A longitudinal study of their relationship to the course of bipolar disorder. *Cognitive Therapy and Research, 16,* 409–418.

Hammen, C.L., Ellicott, A., Gitlin, M., & Jamison, K.R. (1989). Sociotropy/autonomy and vulnerability to specific life events in patients with unipolar depression and bipolar disorders. *Journal of Abnormal Psychology, 98,* 154–160.

Hammen, C.L., Marks, T., Mayol, A., & Mayo, R. (1985). Depressive self-schemas, life stress, and vulnerability to depression. *Journal of Abnormal Psychology, 94,* 308–318.

Hammen, C.L., Mayol, A., Mayo, R., & Marks, T. (1986). Initial symptom levels and the life-event-depression relationship. *Journal of Abnormal Psychology, 95,* 114–122.

Hammen, C.L., Miklowitz, D.J., & Dyck, D.G. (1986). Stability and severity parameters of depressive self-schema responding. *Journal of Social and Clinical Psychology, 4,* 23–45.

Harrell, T.H., Chambless, D.L., & Calhoun, J.F. (1981). Correlational relationships between self-statements and affective states. *Cognitive Therapy and Research, 5,* 159–173.

Harrell, T.H., & Ryon, N.B. (1983). Cognitive-behavioral assessment of depression: Clinical validation of the Automatic Thoughts Questionnaire. *Journal of Consulting and Clinical Psychology, 51,* 721–725.

Harter, S. (1990). Developmental differences in the nature of self-representations: Implications for the understanding, assessment, and treatment of maladaptive behavior. *Cognitive Therapy and Research, 14*, 113–142.

Hartlage, S. (1990). *Automatic processing of attributional inferences in depressed and cognitively depression-prone individuals.* Unpublished doctoral dissertation, Northwestern University, Evanston, IL.

Hartlage, S., Alloy, L.B., Vázquez, C., & Dykman, B. (1993). Automatic and effortful processing in depression. *Psychological Bulletin, 113*, 247–278.

Hasher, L., Rose, K.C., Zacks, R.T., Sanft, H., & Doren, B. (1985). Mood, recall, and selectivity effects in normal college students. *Journal of Experimental Psychology: General, 114*, 104–118.

Haslam, N., & Beck, A.T. (1993). Categorization of major depression in an outpatient sample. *Journal of Nervous and Mental Disease, 181*, 725–731.

Haslam, N., & Beck, A.T. (1994). Subtyping major depression: A taxometric analysis. *Journal of Abnormal Psychology, 103*, 686–692.

Haslam, N., & Beck, A.T. (1995a). *Sociotropy, autonomy, and depressive symptoms: A canonical analysis: Sociotropy, autonomy, and depressive symptoms: A canonical analysis.* Unpublished manuscript, New School for Social Research, New York.

Haslam, N., & Beck, A.T. (1995b). *Sociotropy, autonomy, and symptom dimensions in depression.* Unpublished manuscript, New School for Social Research, New York.

Hawton, K. (1992). Suicide and attempted suicide. In E.S. Paykel (Ed.), *Handbook of affective disorders* (2nd ed., pp. 635–650). New York: Guilford Press.

Hays, R.D., Wells, K.B., Sherbourne, C.D., Rogers, W., & Spritzer, K. (1995). Functioning and well-being outcomes of patients with depression compared with chronic general medical illnesses. *Archives of General Psychiatry, 52*, 11–19.

Hazen, C., & Shaver, P. (1987). Romantic love conceptualized as an attachment process. *Journal of Personality and Social Psychology, 52*, 511–524.

Hecht, H., von Zerssen, D., & Wittchen, H.U. (1990). Anxiety and depression in a community sample: The influence of comorbidity on social functioning. *Journal of Affective Disorders, 18*, 137–144.

Hedlund, S., & Rude, S.S. (1995). Evidence of latent depressive schemas in formerly depressed individuals. *Journal of Abnormal Psychology, 104*, 517–525.

Heimberg, R.G., Bruch, M.A., Hope, D.A., & Dombeck, M. (1990). Evaluating the states of mind model: Comparison to an alternative model and effects of method of cognitive assessment. *Cognitive Therapy and Research, 14*, 543–557.

Heimberg, R.G., Klosko, J.S., Dodge, C.S., Shadick, R., Becker, R.E., & Barlow, D.H. (1989). Anxiety disorders, depression, and attributional style: A further test of the specificity of depressive attributions. *Cognitive Therapy and Research, 13*, 21–36.

Heimberg, R.G., Vermilyea, J.A., Dodge, C.S., Becker, R.E. & Barlow, D.H. (1987). Attributional style, depression, and anxiety: An evaluation of the specificity of depressive attributions. *Cognitive Therapy and Research, 11*, 537–550.

Held, B.S. (1995). *Back to reality: A critique of postmodern theory in psychotherapy.* New York: Norton.

Held, B.S. (1996). Constructivism in psychotherapy: Truth and consequences. *Annals of the New York Academy of Sciences, 775*, 198–206.

Heller, W., Etienne, M.A., & Miller, G.A. (1995). Patterns of perceptual asymmetry in depression and anxiety: Implications for neuropsychological models of emotion and psychopathology. *Journal of Abnormal Psychology, 104*, 327–333.

Heller, W., & Nitschke, J.B. (1997). Regional brain activity in emotion: A framework for understanding cognition in depression. *Cognition and Emotion, 11*, 637–661.

Herbert, J.D., Nelson-Gray, R.O., & Herbert, D.L. (1989). *The role of irrational schema in depression.* Poster presented at the annual meeting of the Association for the Advancement of Behavior Therapy, Washington, DC.

Hertel, P.T., & Hardin, T.S. (1990). Remembering with and without awareness in a depressed mood: Evidence of deficits in initiative. *Journal of Experimental Psychology: General, 119*, 45–59.

Hewitt, P.L., & Flett, G.L. (1991). Dimensions of perfectionism in unipolar depression. *Journal of Abnormal Psychology, 100*, 98–101.

Hewitt, P.L., & Flett, G.L. (1993). Dimensions of perfectionism, daily stress, and depression: A test of the specific vulnerability hypothesis. *Journal of Abnormal Psychology, 102*, 58–65.

Hewitt, P.L., Flett, G.L., & Ediger, E. (1996). Perfectionism and depression: Longitudinal assessment of a specific vulnerability hypothesis. *Journal of Abnormal Psychology, 105*, 276–280.

Higgins, E.T. (1987). Self-discrepancy: A theory relating self and affect. *Psychological Review, 94*, 319–340.

Higgins, E.T., Klein, R., & Strauman, T. (1985). Self-concept discrepancy theory: A psychological model for distinguishing among different aspects of depression and anxiety. *Social Cognition, 3*, 51–76.

Higgins, E.T., Strauman, T., & Klein, R. (1986). Standards and the process of self-evaluation: Multiple affects from multiple stages. In R. Sorrentino & E.T. Higgins (Eds.), *Handbook of motivation and emotion: Foundations of social behavior* (pp. 23–63). New York: Guilford Press.

Hill, A.B., & Dutton, F. (1989). Depression and selective attention to self-esteem threatening words. *Personality and Individual Differences, 10*, 915–917.

Hill, A.B., & Knowles, T.H. (1991). Depression and the "emotional" Stroop effect. *Personality and Individual Differences, 12*, 481–485.

Hiroto, D.S., & Seligman, M.E.P. (1975). Generality of learned helplessness in man. *Journal of Personality and Social Psychology, 31*, 311–327.

Hirschfeld, R.M. (1994). Major depression, dysthymia, and depressive personality disorder. *British Journal of Psychiatry, 165* (Suppl. 26), 23–30.

Hirschfeld, R.M., Klerman, G.L., Clayton, P.J., & Keller, M.B. (1983). Personality and depression: Empirical findings. *Archives of General Psychiatry, 40*, 993–998.

Hirschfeld, R.M., Klerman, G.L., Lavori, P., Keller, M.B., Griffith, P., & Coryell, W. (1989). Premorbid personality assessments of first onset of major depression. *Archives of General Psychiatry, 46*, 345–350.

Hoberman, H.M., & Lewinsohn, P.M. (1985). The behavioral treatment of depression. In E.E. Beckham & W.R. Leber (Eds.), *Handbook of depression: Treatment, assessment, and research* (pp. 39–81). Homewood, IL: Dorsey Press.

Hoehn-Hyde, D., Schlottmann, R.S., & Rush, A.J. (1982). Perception of social interactions in depressed psychiatric patients. *Journal of Consulting and Clinical Psychology, 50*, 209–212.

Hollon, S.D., & Beck, A.T. (1994). Cognitive and cognitive-behavioral therapies. In S.L. Garfield & A.E. Bergin (Eds.), *Handbook of psychotherapy and behavior change* (4th ed., pp. 428–466). New York: Wiley.

Hollon, S.D., & Kendall, P.C. (1980). Cognitive self-statements in depression: Development of an Automatic Thoughts Questionnaire. *Cognitive Therapy and Research, 4,* 383–395.

Hollon, S.D., Kendall, P.C., & Lumry, A. (1986). Specificity of depressotypic cognitions in clinical depression. *Journal of Abnormal Psychology, 95,* 52–59.

Horney, K. (1945). *Our inner conflicts: A constructive theory of neurosis.* New York: Norton.

Horowitz, M., Wilner, N., & Alvarez, W. (1979). Impact of event scale: A measure of subjective stress. *Psychosomatic Medicine, 41,* 209–218.

Horwath, E., Johnson, J., Klerman, G.L., & Weissman, M.M. (1992). Depressive symptoms as relative and attributable risk factors for first-onset major depression. *Archives of General Psychiatry, 49,* 817–823.

Howell, A., & Conway, M. (1992). Mood and the suppression of positive and negative self-referent thoughts. *Cognitive Therapy and Research, 16,* 535–555.

Hull, J.G., & Mendolia, M. (1991). Modeling the relations of attributional style, expectancies, and depression. *Journal of Personality and Social Psychology, 61,* 85–97.

Hurlburt, R.T. (1979). Random sampling of cognitions and behavior. *Journal of Research in Personality, 13,* 103–111.

Hurlburt, R.T. (1997). Sampling thinking in the natural environment: An indespensible tool for understanding human functioning. *Journal of Consulting and Clinical Psychology, 65,* 941–949.

Ilardi, S.S., Craighead, W.E., & Evans, D.D. (1997). Modeling relapse in unipolar depression: The effects of dysfunctional cognitions and personality disorders. *Journal of Consulting and Clinical Psychology, 65,* 381–391.

Imber, S.D., Pilkonis, P.A., Sotsky, S.M., Elkin, I., Watkins, J.T., Collins, J.F., Shea, M.T., Leber, W.R., & Glass, D.R. (1990). Mode-specific effects among three treatments for depression. *Journal of Consulting and Clinical Psychology, 58,* 352–359.

Ingram, R.E. (1984a). Information processing and feedback: Effects of mood and information favorability on the cognitive processing of personally relevant information. *Cognitive Therapy and Research, 8,* 371–386.

Ingram, R.E. (1984b). Toward an information-processing analysis of depression. *Cognitive Therapy and Research, 8,* 443–478.

Ingram, R.E. (1989). Unique and shared cognitive factors in social anxiety and depression: Automatic thinking and self-appraisal. *Journal of Social and Clinical Psychology, 8,* 198–208.

Ingram, R.E. (1990a). Attentional nonspecificity in depressive and generalized anxious affective states. *Cognitive Therapy and Research, 14,* 25–35.

Ingram, R.E. (1990b). Self-focused attention in clinical disorders: Review and a conceptual model. *Psychological Bulletin, 107,* 156–176.

Ingram, R.E., Atkinson, J.H., Slater, M.A., Saccuzzo, D.P., & Garfin, S.R. (1990). Negative and positive cognition in depressed and nondepressed chronic-pain patients. *Health Psychology, 9,* 300–314.

Ingram, R.E., Bernet, C.Z., & McLaughlin, S.C. (1994). Attentional allocation processes in individuals at risk for depression. *Cognitive Therapy and Research, 18,* 317–332.

Ingram, R.E., Fidaleo, R.A., Friedberg R., Shenk, J.L., & Bernet, C.Z. (1995). Content and mode of information processing in major depressive disorder. *Cognitive Therapy and Research, 19,* 281–293.

Ingram, R.E., Johnson, B.R., Bernet, C.Z., Dombeck, M., & Rowe, M.K. (1992). Vulnerability to distress: Cognitive and emotional reactivity to chronically self-focused individuals. *Cognitive Therapy and Research, 16,* 451–472.

Ingram, R.E., & Kendall, P.C. (1986). Cognitive clinical psychology: Implications of an information processing perspective. In R.E. Ingram (Ed.), *Information processing approaches to clinical psychology* (pp. 3–21). Orlando, FL: Academic Press.

Ingram, R.E., Kendall, P.C., Siegle, G., Guarino, J., & McLaughlin, S.C. (1995). Psychometric properties of the Positive Automatic Thoughts Questionnaire. *Psychological Assessment, 7,* 495–507.

Ingram, R.E., Kendall, P.C., Smith, T.W., Donnell, C., & Ronan, K. (1987). Cognitive specificity in emotional disorders. *Journal of Personality and Social Psychology, 53,* 734–742.

Ingram, R.E., Lumry, A.E., Cruet, D., & Sieber, W. (1987). Attentional processes in depressive disorders. *Cognitive Therapy and Research, 11,* 351–360.

Ingram, R.E., Miranda, J., & Segal, Z.V. (1998). *Cognitive vulnerability to depression.* New York: Guilford Press.

Ingram, R.E., Partridge, S., Scott, W., & Bernet, C.Z. (1994). Schema specificity in subclinical syndrome depression: Distinctions between automatically versus effortfully encoded state and trait depressive information. *Cognitive Therapy and Research, 18,* 195–209.

Ingram, R.E., & Reed, M.R. (1986). Information encoding and retrieval processes in depression: Findings, issues, and future direction. In R.E. Ingram (Ed.), *Information processing approaches to clinical psychology* (pp. 132–150). Orlando, FL: Academic Press.

Ingram, R.E., Slater, M.A., Atkinson, J.H., & Scott, W. (1990). Positive automatic cognition in major affective disorder. *Psychological Assessment: A Journal of Consulting and Clinical Psychology, 2,* 209–211.

Ingram, R.E., & Wisnicki, K.S. (1988). Assessment of positive automatic cognitions. *Journal of Consulting and Clinical Psychology, 56,* 898–902.

Izard, C.E. (1990). Facial expressions and the regulation of emotions. *Journal of Personality and Social Psychology, 58,* 487–498.

Izard, C.E. (1994). Innate and universal facial expressions: Evidence from developmental and cross-cultural research. *Psychological Bulletin, 115,* 288–299.

James, W. (1948). *The principles of psychology.* New York: World. (Original work published 1890)

Johnson, J., Weissman, M.M., & Klerman, G.L. (1992). Service utilization and social morbidity associated with depressive symptoms in the community. *Journal of the American Medical Association, 267,* 1478–1483.

Johnson, J.G., Han, Y.-S., Douglas, C.J., Johannet, C.M., & Russell, T. (1998). Attributions for positive life events predict recovery from depression among psychiatric inpatients: An investigation of the Needles and Abramson model of recovery from depression. *Journal of Consulting and Clinical Psychology, 66,* 369–376.

Johnson, M.H., & Magaro, P.A. (1987). Effects of mood and severity on memory processes in depression and mania. *Psychological Bulletin, 101,* 22–40.

Joiner, T.E. (1996). A confirmatory factor-analytic investigation of the tripartite model of depression and anxiety in college students. *Cognitive Therapy and Research, 20,* 521–539.

Joiner, T.E., Catanzaro, S.J., & Laurent, J. (1996). Tripartite structure of positive and negative affect, depression, and anxiety in child and adolescent psychiatric inpatients. *Journal of Abnormal Psychology, 105,* 401–409.

Joiner, T.E., & Wagner, K.D. (1995). Attributional style and depression in children and adolescents: A meta-analytic review. *Clinical Psychology Review, 15,* 777–798.

Jolly, J.B., Dyck, M.J., Kramer, T.A., & Wherry, J.N. (1994). Integration of positive and negative affectivity and cognitive content-specificity: Improved discrimination of anxious and depressive symptoms. *Journal of Abnormal Psychology, 103,* 544–552.

Jolly, J.B., Dyck, M.J., Kramer, T.A., & Wherry, J.N. (1996). The relations between sociotropy and autonomy, positive and negative affect and two proposed depression subtypes. *British Journal of Clinical Psychology, 35,* 91–101.

Jolly, J.B., & Dykman, R.A. (1994). Using self-report data to differentiate anxious and depressive symptoms in adolescents: Cognitive content specificity and global distress? *Cognitive Therapy and Research, 18,* 25–37.

Jolly, J.B., & Kramer, T.A. (1994). The hierarchical arrangement of internalizing cognitions. *Cognitive Therapy and Research, 18,* 1–14.

Jolly, J.B., & Wiesner, D.C. (1996). Psychometric properties of the Automatic Thoughts Questionnaire-Positive with inpatient adolescents. *Cognitive Therapy and Research, 20,* 481–498.

Jones, G.E., & Johnson, H.J. (1978). Physiological responding during self-generated imagery of contextually complete stimuli. *Psychophysiology, 15,* 439–446.

Jones, G.E., & Johnson, H.J. (1980). Heart rate and somatic concomitants of mental imagery. *Psychophysiology, 17,* 339–347.

Kammer, D., Behrmann, G., Siemer, J., & Feld, T.R. (1986). *Depressive information processing during failure: Monitoring the achievement-related cognitions of depressed versus nondepressed inpatients.* Unpublished manuscript, Universitat Bielefeld, Bielefeld, Germany.

Karel, M.J. (1997). Aging and depression: Vulnerability and stress across adulthood. *Clinical Psychology Review, 17,* 847–879.

Katon, W., & Roy-Byrne, P.P. (1991). Mixed anxiety-depression. *Journal of Abnormal Psychology, 100,* 337–345.

Katz, P.P., & Yelin, E.H. (1993). Prevalence and correlates of depressive symptoms among persons with rheumatoid arthritis. *Journal of Rheumatology, 20,* 790–796.

Keitner, G.I., & Miller, I.W. (1990). Family functioning and major depression: An overview. *American Journal of Psychiatry, 147,* 1128–1137.

Keller, M.B. (1994). Depression: A long-term illness. *British Journal of Psychiatry, 165*(Suppl. 26), 9–15.

Keller, M.B., Klein, D.N., Hirschfeld, R.M.A., Kocsis, J.H., McCullough, J.P., Miller, I., First, M.B., Holzer, C.P., Keitner, G.I., Marin, D.B., & Shea, T. (1995). Results of the DSM-IV mood disorders field trial. *American Journal of Psychiatry, 152,* 843–849.

Keller, M.B., Shapiro, R.W., Lavori, P.W., & Wolfe, N. (1982). Relapse in major depressive disorder: Analysis with the life table. *Archives of General Psychiatry, 39*, 911–915.

Kelly, G.A. (1955). *The psychology of personal constructs* (Vols. 1–2). New York: Norton.

Kendall, P.C. (1985). Toward a cognitive-behavioral model of child psychopathology and a critique of related interventions. *Journal of Abnormal Child Psychology, 13*, 357–372.

Kendall, P.C. (1992). Healthy thinking. *Behavior Therapy, 23*, 1–11.

Kendall, P.C., & Clarkin, J.F. (1992). Introduction to special section: Comorbidity and treatment implications. *Journal of Consulting and Clinical Psychology, 60*, 833–834.

Kendall, P.C., & Hollon, S.D. (1981). Assessing self-referent speech: Methods in the measurement of self-statements. In P.C. Kendall & S.D. Hollon (Eds.), *Assessment strategies for cognitive-behavioral interventions* (pp. 85–118). New York: Academic Press.

Kendall, P.C., Howard, B.L., & Hays, R.C. (1989). Self-referent speech and psychopathology: The balance of positive and negative thinking. *Cognitive Therapy and Research, 13*, 583–598.

Kendler, K.S., & Karkowski-Shuman, L. (1997). Stressful life events and genetic lability to major depression: Genetic control of exposure to the environment? *Psychological Medicine, 27*, 539–547.

Kendler, K.S., Kessler, R.C., Neale, M.C., Heath, A.C., & Eaves, L.J. (1993). The prediction of major depression in women: Toward an integrated etiologic model. *American Journal of Psychiatry, 150*, 1139–1148.

Kendler, K.S., Kessler, R.C., Walters, E.E., MacLean, C., Neale, M.C., Heath, A.C., & Eaves, L.J. (1995). Stressful life events, genetic liability, and onset of an episode of major depression in women. *American Journal of Psychiatry, 152*, 833–842.

Kendler, K.S., Walters, E.E., & Kessler, R.C. (1997). The prediction of length of major depression episodes: Results from an epidemiological sample of female twins. *Psychological Medicine, 27*, 107–117.

Kessler, R.C., Foster, C.L., Saunders, W.B., & Stang, P.E. (1995). Social consequences of psychiatric disorders: I. Educational attainment. *American Journal of Psychiatry, 152*, 1026–1032.

Kessler, R.C., McGonagle, K.A., Zhao, S., Nelson, C.B., Hughes, M., Eshleman, S., Wittchen, H., & Kendler, K.S. (1994). Lifetime and 12-month prevalence of *DSM-III-R* psychiatric disorders in the United States: Results of the national comorbidity survey. *Archives of General Psychiatry, 51*, 8–19.

Khouri, P.J., & Akiskal, H.S. (1986). The bipolar spectrum reconsidered. In T. Millon & G. Klerman (Eds.), *Contemporary directions in psychopathology* (pp. 457–471). New York: Guilford Press.

Klein, D.C., & Seligman, M.E.P. (1976). Reversal of performance deficits and perceptual deficits in learned helplessness and depression. *Journal of Abnormal Psychology, 85*, 11–26.

Klein, D.N., Clark, D.C., Dansky, L., & Margolis, E.T. (1988). Dysthymia in the offspring of parents with primary unipolar affective disorder. *Journal of Abnormal Psychology, 97*, 265–274.

Klein, D.N., Riso, L.P., Donaldson, S.K., Schwartz, J.E., Anderson, R.L., Ouimette, P.C., Lizardi, H., & Aronson, T.A. (1995). Family study of early-onset dysthymia: Mood and personality disorders in relatives of outpatients with dysthymia and episodic major depression and normal controls. *Archives of General Psychiatry, 52,* 487–496.

Klein, D.N., Taylor, E.B., Dickstein, S., & Harding, K. (1988). Primary early-onset dysthymia: Comparison with primary nonbipolar nonchronic major depression on demographic, clinical, familial, personality, and socioenvironmental characteristics and short-term outcome. *Journal of Abnormal Psychology, 97,* 387–398.

Klein, M. (1948). A contribution to the psychogenesis of manic-depressive states. In *Contributions to psycho-analysis 1921–1945* (pp. 282–310). London: Hogarth Press and the Institute of Psychoanalysis.

Klerman, G.L., & Weissman, M.M. (1989). Increasing rates of depression. *Journal of the American Medical Association, 261,* 2229–2235.

Klieger, D.M., & Cordner, M.D. (1990). The Stroop task as measure of construct accessibility in depression. *Personality and Individual Differences, 11,* 19–27.

Klinger, E. (1975). Consequences of commitment to and disengagement from incentives. *Psychological Review, 82,* 1–25.

Kocsis, J.H., & Frances, A.J. (1987). A critical discussion of *DSM-III* dysthymic disorder. *American Journal of Psychiatry, 144,* 1534–1542.

Koenig, L.J., Ragin, A.B., & Harrow, M. (1995). Accuracy and bias in depressives' judgments for self and other. *Cognitive Therapy and Research, 19,* 505–517.

Kovacs, M., & Beck, A.T. (1978). Maladaptive cognitive structures in depression. *American Journal of Psychiatry, 135,* 525–533.

Kovacs, M., & Beck, A.T. (1979). Cognitive-affective processes in depression. In C.E. Izard (Ed.), *Emotions in personality and psychopathology* (pp. 417–442). New York: Plenum Press.

Krantz, S.E., & Gallagher-Thompson, D. (1990). Depression and information valence influence depressive cognition. *Cognitive Therapy and Research, 14,* 95–108.

Krantz, S.E., & Hammen, C. (1979). Assessment of cognitive bias in depression. *Journal of Abnormal Psychology, 88,* 611–619.

Krantz, S.E., & Liu, C. (1987). The effect of mood and information valence on depressive cognition. *Cognitive Therapy and Research, 11,* 185–196.

Kuiper, N.A., & Derry, P.A. (1982). Depressed and nondepressed content self-reference in mild depressives. *Journal of Personality, 50,* 67–80.

Kuiper, N.A., & Olinger, L.J. (1986). Dysfunctional attitudes and a self-worth contingency model of depression. In P.C. Kendall (Ed.), *Advances in cognitive-behavioral research and therapy* (Vol. 5, pp. 115–142). New York: Academic Press.

Kuiper, N.A., Olinger, L.J., MacDonald, M.R., & Shaw, B.F. (1985). Self-schema processing of depressed and nondepressed content: The effects of vulnerability to depression. *Social Cognition, 3,* 77–93.

Kuiper, N.A., Olinger, L.J., & Martin, R.A. (1988). Dysfunctional attitudes, stress, and negative emotions. *Cognitive Therapy and Research, 12,* 533–547.

Kuiper, N.A., Olinger, L.J., & Swallow, S.R. (1987). Dysfunctional attitudes, mild depression, views of self, self-consciousness, and social perceptions. *Motivation and Emotion, 11,* 379–401.

Kuyken, W., & Brewin, C.R. (1994). Intrusive memories of childhood abuse during depressive episodes. *Behaviour Research and Therapy, 32,* 525–528.

Kuyken, W., & Brewin, C.R. (1995). Autobiographical memory functioning in depression and reports of early abuse. *Journal of Abnormal Psychology, 104,* 585–591.

Kwon, S.-M., & Oei, T.P.S. (1992). Differential causal roles of dysfunctional attitudes and automatic thoughts in depression. *Cognitive Therapy and Research, 16,* 309–328.

Lakey, B., & Ross, L.T. (1994). Dependency and self-criticism as moderators of interpersonal and achievement stress: The role of initial dysphoria. *Cognitive Therapy and Research, 18,* 581–599.

Lakey, B., Tardiff, T.A., & Drew, J.B. (1994). Negative social interactions: Assessment and relations to social support, cognition, and psychological distress. *Journal of Social and Clinical Psychology, 13,* 42–62.

Lam, D.H., Brewin, C.R., Woods, R.T., & Bebbington, P.E. (1987). Cognition and social adversity in the depressed elderly. *Journal of Abnormal Psychology, 96,* 23–26.

Lang, P.J., Bradley, M.M., & Cuthbert, B.N. (1990). Emotion, attention, and the startle reflex. *Psychological Review, 97,* 377–395.

LaPointe, K.A., & Harrell, T.H. (1978). Thoughts and feelings: Correlational relationships and cross-situational consistency. *Cognitive Therapy and Research, 2,* 311–322.

Larsen, R.J., & Diener, E. (1987). Affect intensity as an individual difference characteristic: A review. *Journal of Research in Personality, 21,* 1–39.

Laurent, J., & Stark, K.D. (1993). Testing the cognitive content-specificity hypothesis with anxious and depressed youngsters. *Journal of Abnormal Psychology, 102,* 226–237.

Lazarus, R.S. (1977). Cognitive and coping processes in emotion. In A. Monat & R.S. Lazarus (Eds.), *Stress and coping: An anthology* (pp. 145–158). New York: Columbia University Press.

Lazarus, R.S. (1989). Constructs of the mind in mental health and psychotherapy. In A.R. Freeman, K.M. Simon, L.E. Beutler, & H. Arkowitz (Eds.), *Comprehensive handbook of cognitive therapy* (pp. 99–121). New York: Plenum Press.

Lazarus, R.S. (1991). Cognition and motivation in emotion. *American Psychologist, 46,* 352–367.

Lazarus, R.S., & Folkman, S. (1984). *Stress, appraisal, and coping.* New York: Springer.

Lazarus, R.S., & Folkman, S. (1986). Cognitive theories of stress and the issue of circularity. In M.H. Appley & R. Trumbull (Eds.), *Dynamics of stress: Physiological, psychological and social perspectives* (pp. 63–80). New York: Plenum Press.

Lazarus, R.S., Kanner, A., & Folkman, S. (1980). Emotions: A cognitive-phenomenological analysis. In R. Plutchik & H. Kellerman (Eds.), *Emotion: Theory, research and experience* (Vol. 1, pp. 189–217). New York: Academic Press.

Lazarus, R.S., & Smith, C.A. (1988). Knowledge and appraisal in the cognition-emotion relationship. *Cognition and Emotion, 2,* 281–300.

Leahy, R.L., & Beck, A.T. (1988). Cognitive therapy of depression and mania. In A. Georgotas & R. Cancro (Eds.), *Depression and mania* (pp. 517–537). New York: Elsevier Science.

Leber, W.R., Beckham, E.E., & Danker-Brown, P. (1985). Diagnostic criteria for depression. In E.E. Beckham & W.R. Leber (Eds.), *Handbook of depression: Treatment, assessment, and research* (pp. 343–371). Homewood, IL: Dorsey Press.

Lecci, L., Karoly, P., Briggs, C., & Kuhn, K. (1994). Specificity and generality of motivational components in depression: A personal project analysis. *Journal of Abnormal Psychology, 103,* 404–408.

Lefebvre, M.F. (1981). Cognitive distortion and cognitive errors in depressed psychiatric and low back pain patients. *Journal of Consulting and Clinical Psychology, 49,* 517–525.

Lennox, S.S., Bedell, J.R., Abramson, L.Y., & Foley, F.W. (1990). Judgment of contingency: A replication with hospitalized depressed, schizophrenic and normal samples. *Journal of Social Behavior and Personality, 5,* 189–204.

Lepore, S.J. (1997). Expressive writing moderates the relation between intrusive thoughts and depressive symptoms. *Journal of Personality and Social Psychology, 73,* 1030–1037.

Levenson, R.W. (1992). Autonomic nervous system differences among emotions. *Psychological Science, 3,* 23–27.

Leventhal, H. (1985). A perceptual motor theory of emotions. In A.H. Tuma & J. Maser (Eds.), *Anxiety and the anxiety disorders* (pp. 271–290). Hillsdale, NJ: Erlbaum.

Lewinsohn, P.M. (1974). A behavioral approach to depression. In R.J. Friedman & M.M. Katz (Eds.), *The psychology of depression: Contemporary theory and research* (pp. 157–185). New York: Wiley.

Lewinsohn, P.M. (1975). The behavioral study and treatment of depression. In M. Hersen, R.M. Eisler & P.M. Miller (Eds.), *Progress in behavior modification* (Vol. 1, pp. 19–64). New York: Academic Press.

Lewinsohn, P.M., Hoberman, H.M., & Rosenbaum, M. (1988). A prospective study of risk factors for unipolar depression. *Journal of Abnormal Psychology, 97,* 251–264.

Lewinsohn, P.M., Hoberman, H.M., Teri, L., & Hautzinger, M. (1985). An integrative theory of depression. In S. Reiss & R. Bootzin (Eds.), *Theoretical issues in behavior therapy* (pp. 331–359). New York: Academic Press.

Lewinsohn, P.M., Rohde, P., Seeley, J.R., & Hops, H. (1991). Comorbidity of unipolar depression: I. Major depression with dysthymia. *Journal of Abnormal Psychology, 100,* 205–213.

Lewinsohn, P.M., & Rosenbaum, M. (1987). Recall of parental behavior by acute depressives, remitted depressives, and nondepressives. *Journal of Personality and Social Psychology, 52,* 611–619.

Lewinsohn, P.M., Steinmetz, J.L., Larson, D.W., & Franklin, J. (1981). Depression-related cognitions: Antecedent or consequence? *Journal of Abnormal Psychology, 90,* 213–219.

Lightbody, S.L., & McCabe, S.B. (1997). *Information processing and personality: A test of the congruency hypothesis.* Poster presented at the annual meeting of the Canadian Psychological Association, Toronto.

Lightsey, O.R. (1994). Positive automatic cognitions as moderators of the negative life event-dysphoria relationship. *Cognitive Therapy and Research, 18,* 353–365.

Linville, P.W. (1985). Self-complexity and affective extremity: Don't put all your cognitive eggs in one basket. *Social Cognition, 3,* 94–120.

Lishman, W.A. (1974). The speed of recall of pleasant and unpleasant experiences. *Psychological Medicine, 4,* 212–218.

Lloyd, C. (1980). Life events and depressive disorder reviewed: II. Events as precipitating factors. *Archives of General Psychiatry, 37,* 541–548.

Lloyd, G.G., & Lishman, W.A. (1975). Effect of depression on the speed of recall of pleasant and unpleasant experiences. *Psychological Medicine, 5,* 173–180.

Loeb, A., Beck, A.T., & Diggory, J. (1971). Differential effects of success and failure on depressed and nondepressed patients. *Journal of Nervous and Mental Disease, 152,* 106–114.

Loewenstein, D.A., & Hokanson, J.E. (1986). The processing of social information by mildly and moderately dysphoric college students. *Cognitive Therapy and Research, 10,* 447–460.

Logan, G.D. (1988). Toward an instance theory of automatization. *Psychological Review, 95,* 492–527.

Lonigan, C.J., Carey, M.P., & Finch, A.J. (1994). Anxiety and depression in children and adolescents: Negative affectivity and the utility of self-reports. *Journal of Consulting and Clinical Psychology, 62,* 1000–1008.

Lovibond, P.F., & Lovibond, S.H. (1995). The structure of negative emotional states: Comparison of the Depression Anxiety Stress Scales (DASS) with the Beck Depression and Anxiety Inventories. *Behaviour Research and Therapy, 33,* 335–343.

Lundh, L.-G. (1988). Cognitive therapy and the analysis of meaning structures. In C. Perris, I.M. Blackburn & H. Perris (Eds.), *Cognitive psychotherapy: Theory and practice* (pp. 44–61). Berlin: Springer-Verlag.

Lunghi, M.E. (1977). The stability of mood and social perception measures in a sample of depressive in-patients. *British Journal of Psychiatry, 130,* 598–604.

Luten, A.G., Ralph, J.A., & Mineka, S. (1997). Pessimistic attributional style: Is it specific to depression versus anxiety versus negative affect? *Behaviour Research and Therapy, 35,* 703–719.

Lykken, D., & Tellegen, A. (1996). Happiness is a stochastic phenomenon. *Psychological Science, 7,* 186–189.

Lyness, J.M., Caine, E.D., Conwell, Y., King, D.A., & Cox, C. (1993). Depressive symptoms, medical illness, and functional status in depressed psychiatric in-patients. *American Journal of Psychiatry, 150,* 910–915.

MacDonald, M.R., & Kuiper, N.A. (1985). Efficiency and automaticity of self-schema processing in clinical depressives. *Motivation and Emotion, 9,* 171–184.

MacDonald, M.R., Kuiper, N.A., & Olinger, L.J. (1985). Vulnerability to depression, mild depression, and degree of self-schema consolidation. *Motivation and Emotion, 9,* 369–379.

MacLeod, A.K., & Byrne, A. (1996). Anxiety, depression, and the anticipation of future positive and negative experiences. *Journal of Abnormal Psychology, 105,* 286–289.

MacLeod, A.K., & Cropley, M.L. (1995). Depressive future-thinking: The role of valence and specificity. *Cognitive Therapy and Research, 19,* 35–50.

MacLeod, A.K., Pankhania, B., Lee, M., & Mitchell, D. (1997). Parasuicide, depression and the anticipation of positive and negative future experiences. *Psychological Medicine, 27,* 973–977.

MacLeod, C., Mathews, A., & Tata, P. (1986). Attentional bias in emotional disorders. *Journal of Abnormal Psychology, 95,* 15–20.

MacLeod, C., & Rutherford, E.M. (1991). Anxiety and the selective processing of emotional information: Mediating roles of awareness, trait, and state vulnerability, and personal relevance of stimulus material. *Behaviour Research and Therapy, 30,* 479–491.

MacLeod, C., Tata, P., & Mathews, A. (1987). Perception of emotionally valenced information in depression. *British Journal of Clinical Psychology, 26,* 67–68.

Macpherson, F.D. (1989). *Content analysis of dysfunctional thinking in anxiety and depression.* Paper presented at the World Congress of Cognitive Therapy, Oxford, England.

Mahoney, M.J. (1974). *Cognition and behavior modification.* Cambridge, MA: Ballinger.

Mahoney, M.J. (1977). Reflections on the cognitive-learning trend in psychotherapy. *American Psychologist, 32,* 5–13.

Mahoney, M.J. (1989). Holy epistemology! Construing the constructions of the constructivists. *Canadian Psychology, 30,* 187–188.

Mahoney, M.J. (1991). *Human change processes: The scientific foundations of psychotherapy.* New York: Basic Books.

Mahoney, M.J. (1993). Introduction to special section: Theoretical developments in the cognitive psychotherapies. *Journal of Consulting and Clinical Psychology, 61,* 187–193.

Mahoney, M.J., & Arnkoff, D.B. (1978). Cognitive and self-control therapies. In S.L. Garfield & A.E. Bergin (Eds.), *Handbook of psychotherapy and behavior change: An empirical analysis* (2nd ed., pp. 689–722). New York: Wiley.

Malouff, J.M., & Schutte, N.S. (1986). Development and validation of a measure of irrational beliefs. *Journal of Consulting and Clinical Psychology, 54,* 860–862.

Mandler, G. (1982). *Mind and emotion.* Malabar, FL: Krieger.

Marcus, D.K., & Nardone, M.E. (1992). Depression and interpersonal rejection. *Clinical Psychology Review, 12,* 433–449.

Markus, H. (1977). Self-schemata and processing information about the self. *Journal of Personality and Social Psychology, 35,* 63–78.

Markus, H. (1990). Unresolved issues of self-representation. *Cognitive Therapy and Research, 14,* 241–253.

Markus, H., & Wurf, E. (1987). The dynamic self-concept: A social psychological perspective. *Annual Review of Psychology, 38,* 299–337.

Martin, M. (1985). Neuroticism as predisposition toward depression: A cognitive mechanism. *Personality and Individual Differences, 6,* 353–365.

Martin, M. (1990). On the induction of mood. *Clinical Psychology Review, 10,* 669–697.

Martin, M., & Clark, D.M. (1986a). On the response bias explanation of selective memory effects in depression. *Cognitive Therapy and Research, 10,* 267–270.

Martin, M., & Clark, D.M. (1986b). Selective memory, depression, and response bias: An unbiased response. *Cognitive Therapy and Research, 10,* 275–278.

Martin, M., Ward, J.C., & Clark, D.M. (1983). Neuroticism and the recall of positive and negative personality information. *Behaviour Research and Therapy, 21,* 495–503.

Maser, J.D., & Cloninger, C.R. (1990). Comorbidity of anxiety and mood disorders: Introduction and overview. *Comorbidity of mood and anxiety disorders* (pp. 3–12). Washington, DC: American Psychiatric Press.

Master, S., & Gershman, L. (1983). Physiological responses to rational-emotive self-verbalizations. *Journal of Behavior Therapy and Experimental Psychiatry, 14,* 289–296.

Matheny, K., & Blue, F. (1977). The effects of self-induced mood states on behavior and physiological arousal. *Journal of Clinical Psychology, 33,* 936–940.

Mathews, A. (1997). Information-processing biases in emotional disorders. In D.M. Clark & C.G. Fairburn (Eds.), *Science and practice of cognitive behaviour therapy* (pp. 47–66). Oxford, England: Oxford University Press.

Mathews, A., & MacLeod, C. (1994). Cognitive approaches to emotion and emotional disorders. *Annual Review of Psychology, 45,* 25–50.

Mathews, A., Ridgeway, V., & Williamson, D.A. (1996). Evidence for attention to threatening stimuli in depression. *Behaviour Research and Therapy, 34,* 695–705.

Matt, G.E., Vázquez, C., & Campbell, W.K. (1992). Mood-congruent recall of affectively toned stimuli: A meta-analytic review. *Clinical Psychology Review, 12,* 227–255.

Matthews, G., & Southall, A. (1991). Depression and the processing of emotional stimuli: A study of semantic priming. *Cognitive Therapy and Research, 15,* 283–302.

Matthews, G.R., & Antes, J.R. (1992). Visual attention and depression: Cognitive biases in the eye fixations of the dysphoric and the nondepressed. *Cognitive Therapy and Research, 16,* 359–371.

May, J.R., & Johnson, H.J. (1973). Physiological activity to internally elicited arousal and inhibitory thoughts. *Journal of Abnormal Psychology, 82,* 239–245.

Mayo, P.R. (1983). Personality traits and the retrieval of positive and negative memories. *Personality and Individual Differences, 4,* 465–471.

McCabe, S.B., & Gotlib, I.H. (1993). Attentional processing in clinically depressed subjects: A longitudinal investigation. *Cognitive Therapy and Research, 17,* 359–377.

McCabe, S.B., & Gotlib, I.H. (1995). Selective attention and clinical depression: Performance on a deployment-of-attention task. *Journal of Abnormal Psychology, 104,* 241–245.

McDermut, J.F., & Haaga, D.A.F. (1994). Cognitive balance and specificity in anxiety and depression. *Cognitive Therapy and Research, 18,* 333–352.

McDermut, J.F., Haaga, D.A.F., & Bilek, L.A. (1997). Cognitive bias and irrational beliefs in major depression. *Cognitive Therapy and Research, 21,* 459–476.

McNally, R.J. (1994). *Panic disorder: A critical analysis.* New York: Guilford Press.

McNally, R.J. (1995). Automaticity and the anxiety disorders. *Behaviour Research and Therapy, 33,* 747–754.

McNeal, E.T., & Cimbolic, P. (1986). Antidepressants and biochemical theories of depression. *Psychological Bulletin, 99,* 361–374.

Meichenbaum, D.H. (1977). *Cognitive-behavior modification: An integrative approach.* New York: Plenum Press.

Meichenbaum, D.H. (1993). Changing conceptions of cognitive behavior modification: Retrospect and prospect. *Journal of Consulting and Clinical Psychology, 61,* 202–204.

Meites, K., Lovallo, W., & Pishkin, V. (1980). A comparison of four scales of anxiety, depression and neuroticism in questionnaires. *Journal of Clinical Psychology, 36,* 427–431.

Mendelson, M. (1990). Psychoanalytic views on depression. In B.B. Wolman & G. Stricker (Eds.), *Depressive disorders: Facts, theories and treatment* (pp. 22–37). New York: Wiley.

Metalsky, G.I., Halberstadt, L.J., & Abramson, L.Y. (1987). Vulnerability to depressive mood reactions: Toward a more powerful test of the diathesis-stress and causal mediation components of the reformulated theory of depression. *Journal of Personality and Social Psychology, 52,* 386–393.

Metalsky, G.I., & Joiner, T.E. (1992). Vulnerability to depressive symptomatology: A prospective test of the diathesis-stress and causal mediation components of the hopelessness theory of depression. *Journal of Abnormal Psychology, 63,* 667–675.

Metalsky, G.I., & Joiner, T.E. (1997). The Hopelessness Depression Symptom Questionnaire. *Cognitive Therapy and Research, 21,* 359–384.

Metalsky, G.I., Joiner, T.E., Hardin, T.S., & Abramson, L.Y. (1993). Depressive reactions to failure in a naturalistic setting: A test of the hopelessness and self-esteem theories of depression. *Journal of Abnormal Psychology, 102,* 101–109.

Miller, D.T., & Moretti, M.M. (1988). The causal attributions of depressives: Self-serving or self-disserving? In L.B. Alloy (Ed.), *Cognitive processes in depression* (pp. 266–286). New York: Guilford Press.

Miller, G.A. (1996). How we think about cognition, emotion, and biology in psychopathology. *Psychophysiology, 33,* 615–628.

Miller, I.W., & Norman, W.H. (1986). Persistence of depressive cognitions within a subgroup of depressed inpatients. *Cognitive Therapy and Research, 10,* 211–224.

Miller, W.R., & Seligman, M.E.P. (1975). Depression and learned helplessness in man. *Journal of Abnormal Psychology, 84,* 228–238.

Mineka, S., & Sutton, S.K. (1992). Cognitive bias and the emotional disorders. *Psychological Science, 3,* 65–69.

Mineka, S., Watson, D., & Clark, L.A. (1998). Comorbidity of anxiety and unipolar mood disorders. *Annual Review of Psychology, 49,* 377–412.

Minkoff, K., Bergman, E., Beck, A.T., & Beck, R. (1973). Hopelessness, depression, and attempted suicide. *American Journal of Psychiatry, 130,* 455–459.

Mintz, J., Mintz, L.I., Arruda, M.J., & Hwang, S.S. (1992). Treatments of depression and the functional capacity to work. *Archives of General Psychiatry, 49,* 761–768.

Miranda, J. (1992). Dysfunctional thinking is activated by stressful life events. *Cognitive Therapy and Research, 16,* 473–483.

Miranda, J., & Gross, J.J. (1997). Cognitive vulnerability, depression, and the mood-state dependent hypothesis: Is out of sight out of mind? *Cognition and Emotion, 11,* 585–605.

Miranda, J., & Persons, J.B. (1988). Dysfunctional attitudes are mood-state dependent. *Journal of Abnormal Psychology, 97,* 76–79.

Miranda, J., Persons, J.B., & Byers, C.N. (1990). Endorsement of dysfunctional beliefs depends on current mood state. *Journal of Abnormal Psychology, 99,* 237–241.

Mischel, W., & Shoda, Y. (1995). A cognitive-affective system theory of personality: Reconceptualizing situations, dispositions, dynamics, and invariance in personality structure. *Psychological Review, 102,* 246–268.

Mitchell, S., & Campbell, E.A. (1988). Cognitions associated with anxiety and depression. *Personality and Individual Differences, 9*, 837–838.

Mogg, K., Bradley, B.P., & Williams, R. (1995). Attentional bias in anxiety and depression: The role of awareness. *British Journal of Clinical Psychology, 34*, 17–36.

Mogg, K., Bradley, B.P., Williams, R., & Mathews, A. (1993). Subliminal processing of emotional information in anxiety and depression. *Journal of Abnormal Psychology, 102*, 304–311.

Mogg, K., Mathews, A., May, J., Grove, M., Eysenck, M., & Weinman, J. (1991). Assessment of cognitive bias in anxiety and depression using a colour perception task. *Cognition and Emotion, 5*, 221–238.

Mongrain, M., & Zuroff, D.C. (1989). Cognitive vulnerability to depressed affect in dependent and self-critical college women. *Journal of Personality Disorders, 3*, 240–251.

Monroe, S.M. (1982). Assessment of life events: Retrospective vs. concurrent strategies. *Archives of General Psychiatry, 39*, 606–610.

Monroe, S.M., Bromet, E.J., Connell, M.M., & Steiner, S.C. (1986). Social support, life events, and depressive symptoms: A 1-year prospective study. *Journal of Consulting and Clinical Psychology, 54*, 424–431.

Monroe, S.M., & Simons, A.D. (1991). Diathesis-stress theories in the context of life stress research: Implications for the depressive disorders. *Psychological Bulletin, 110*, 406–425.

Moore, R.G., & Blackburn, I.M. (1993). Sociotropy, autonomy and personal memories in depression. *British Journal of Clinical Psychology, 32*, 460–462.

Moore, R.G., & Blackburn, I.M. (1994). The relationship of sociotropy and autonomy to symptoms, cognition and personality in depressed patients. *Journal of Affective Disorders, 32*, 239–245.

Moore, R.G., & Blackburn, I.M. (1996). The stability of sociotropy and autonomy in depressed patients undergoing treatment. *Cognitive Therapy and Research, 20*, 69–80.

Moore, R.G., Watts, F.N., & Williams, J.M.G. (1988). The specificity of personal memories in depression. *British Journal of Clinical Psychology, 27*, 275–276.

Moretti, M.M., Segal, Z.V., McCann, C.D., Shaw, B.F., Miller, D.T., & Vella, D. (1996). Self-referent versus other-referent information processing in dysphoric, clinically depressed, and remitted depressed subjects. *Personality and Social Psychology Bulletin, 22*, 68–80.

Moretti, M.M., & Shaw, B.F. (1989). Automatic and dysfunctional cognitive processes in depression. In J.S. Uleman & J.A. Bargh (Eds.), *Unintended thought: The limits of awareness, intention, and control* (pp. 383–421). New York: Guilford Press.

Morris, S.J. (1996). Processing strategies used by dysphoric individuals: Self-derograting, non-self-enhancing or schematic? *Cognitive Therapy and Research, 20*, 213–233.

Moss, D.P. (1992). Cognitive therapy, phenomenology, and the struggle for meaning. *Journal of Phenomenological Psychology, 23*, 87–102.

Muran, J.C., & Segal, Z.V. (1993). *Self-scenarios: The development of an idiographic measure of personal constructs.* Paper presented at the annual meeting of the Association for the Advancement of Behavior Therapy, San Francisco.

Muran, J.C., Segal, Z.V., & Samstag, L.W. (1994). Self-scenarios as a repeated measures outcome measurement of self-schemas in short-term cognitive therapy. *Behavior Therapy, 25*, 255–274.

Myers, J.F., Lynch, P.B., & Bakal, D.A. (1989). Dysthymic and hypomanic self-referent effects associated with depressive illness and recovery. *Cognitive Therapy and Research, 13*, 195–209.

Myers, J.K., & Weissman, M.M. (1980). Use of a self-report symptom scale to detect depression in a community sample. *American Journal of Psychiatry, 137*, 1081–1084.

Nasby, W. (1994). Moderators of mood-congruent encoding: Self-/other-reference and affirmative/nonaffirmative judgment. *Cognition and Emotion, 8*, 259–278.

Nasby, W. (1996). Moderators of mood-congruent encoding and judgment: Evidence that elated and depressed moods implicate distinct processes. *Cognition and Emotion, 10*, 361–377.

Needles, D.J., & Abramson, L.Y. (1990). Positive life events, attributional style, and hopelessness: Testing a model of recovery from depression. *Journal of Abnormal Psychology, 99*, 156–165.

Neimeyer, R.A. (1993). An appraisal of constructivist psychotherapies. *Journal of Consulting and Clinical Psychology, 61*, 221–234.

Nelson, R.E., & Craighead, W.E. (1977). Selective recall of positive and negative feedback, self-control behaviors, and depression. *Journal of Abnormal Psychology, 86*, 379–388.

Nietzel, M.T., & Harris, M.J. (1990). Relationship of dependency and achievement/autonomy to depression. *Clinical Psychology Review, 10*, 279–297.

Nix, G., Watson, C., Pyszczynski, T., & Greenberg, J. (1995). Reducing depressive affect through external focus of attention. *Journal of Social and Clinical Psychology, 14*, 36–52.

Nolen-Hoeksema, S. (1987). Sex differences in unipolar depression: Evidence and theory. *Psychological Bulletin, 101*, 259–282.

Norman, W.H., Miller, I.W., & Dow, M.G. (1988). Characteristics of depressed patients with elevated levels of dysfunctional cognitions. *Cognitive Therapy and Research, 12*, 39–52.

Norman, W.H., Miller, I.W., & Klee, S.H. (1983). Assessment of cognitive distortion in a clinically depressed population. *Cognitive Therapy and Research, 7*, 133–140.

Nunn, J.D., Mathews, A., & Trower, P. (1997). Selective processing of concern-related information in depression. *British Journal of Clinical Psychology, 36*, 489–503.

Oatley, K., & Johnson-Laird, P.N. (1987). Towards a cognitive theory of emotion. *Cognition and Emotion, 1*, 29–50.

Olinger, L.J., Kuiper, N.A., & Shaw, B.F. (1987). Dysfunctional attitudes and stressful life events: An interactive model of depression. *Cognitive Therapy and Research, 11*, 25–40.

Oliver, J.M., & Baumgart, E.P. (1985). The Dysfunctional Attitudes Scale: Psychometric properties and relation to depression in an unselected adult population. *Cognitive Therapy and Research, 9*, 161–167.

Oliver, J.M., Maier, M., Ross, M.J., & Wiener, R.L. (1990). *Cognitive vulnerability to depression as revealed by vulnerability markers: Their relations to each other and personality diatheses to depression.* Unpublished manuscript, St. Louis University, St. Louis, MO.

Oliver, J.M., & Simmons, M.E. (1984). Depression as measured by the DSM-III and the Beck Depression Inventory in an unselected adult population. *Journal of Consulting and Clinical Psychology, 52,* 892–898.

Ollendick, T.H., & Yule, W. (1990). Depression in British and American children and its relation to anxiety and fear. *Journal of Consulting and Clinical Psychology, 58,* 126–129.

Orton, I.K., Beiman, I., LaPointe, K., & Lankford, A. (1983). Induced states of anxiety and depression: Effects on self-induced affect and tonic psychophysiological response. *Cognitive Therapy and Research, 7,* 233–244.

Ouimette, P.C., Klein, D.N., Anderson, R., Riso, L.P., & Lizardi, H. (1994). Relationship of sociotropy/autonomy and dependency/self-criticism to *DSM-III-R* personality disorders. *Journal of Abnormal Psychology, 103,* 743–749.

Pardo, J.V., Pardo, P.J., & Raichle, M.E. (1993). Neural correlates of self-induced dysphoria. *American Journal of Psychiatry, 150,* 713–719.

Parrott, W.G. (1991). Mood induction and instructions to sustain moods: A test of the subject compliance hypothesis of mood congruent memory. *Cognition and Emotion, 5,* 41–52.

Parrott, W.G., & Sabini, J. (1990). Mood and memory under natural conditions: Evidence for mood incongruent recall. *Journal of Personality and Social Psychology, 59,* 321–336.

Parry, G., & Brewin, C.R. (1988). Cognitive style and depression: Symptom-related, event-related or independent provoking factor? *British Journal of Clinical Psychology, 27,* 23–35.

Paykel, E.S. (1979). Recent life events in the development of the depressive disorders. In R.A. Depue (Ed.), *The psychobiology of the depressive disorders: Implications for the effects of stress* (pp. 245–262). New York: Academic Press.

Paykel, E.S. (Ed.). (1992). *Handbook of affective disorders* (2nd ed.). New York: Guilford Press.

Paykel, E.S., & Cooper, Z. (1992). Life events and social stress. In E.S. Paykel (Ed.), *Handbook of affective disorders* (2nd ed., pp. 149–170). New York: Guilford Press.

Peacock, E.J., & Wong, P.T.P. (1990). The Stress Appraisal Measure (SAM): A multidimensional approach to cognitive appraisal. *Stress Medicine, 6,* 227–236.

Pepper, C.M., Klein, D.N., Anderson, R.L., Riso, L.P., Ouimette, P.C., & Lizardi, H. (1995). *DSM-III-R* Axis II comorbidity in dysthymia and major depression. *American Journal of Psychiatry, 152,* 239–247.

Perris, C. (1988). Intensive cognitive-behavioral psychotherapy with patients suffering schizophrenic psychotic or post-psychotic syndromes: Theoretical and practical aspects. In C. Perris, I.M. Blackburn, & H. Perris (Eds.), *Cognitive psychotherapy: Theory and practice* (pp. 324–375). Berlin: Springer-Verlag.

Perris, C. (1992). Bipolar-unipolar distinction. In E.S. Paykel (Ed.), *Handbook of affective disorders* (2nd ed., pp. 57–75). New York: Guilford Press.

Persons, J.B., & Burns, D.D. (1985). Mechanisms of action of cognitive therapy: The relative contributions of technical and interpersonal interventions. *Cognitive Therapy and Research, 9,* 539–551.

Persons, J.B., Burns, D.D., Perloff, J.M., & Miranda, J. (1993). Relationships between symptoms of depression and anxiety and dysfunctional beliefs about achievement and attachment. *Journal of Abnormal Psychology, 102,* 518–524.

Persons, J.B., & Miranda, J. (1992). Cognitive theories of vulnerability to depression: Reconciling negative evidence. *Cognitive Therapy and Research, 16,* 485–502.

Persons, J.B., Miranda, J., & Perloff, J.M. (1991). Relationships between depressive symptoms and cognitive vulnerabilities of achievement and dependency. *Cognitive Therapy and Research, 15,* 221–235.

Persons, J.B., & Rao, P.A. (1985). Longitudinal study of cognitions, life events, and depression in psychiatric inpatients. *Journal of Abnormal Psychology, 94,* 51–63.

Pervin, L.A. (1994). A critical analysis of current trait theory. *Psychological Inquiry, 5,* 103–113.

Peselow, E.D., Robins, C., Block, P., Barouche, F., & Fieve, R.R. (1990). Dysfunctional attitudes in depressed patients before and after clinical treatment and in normal control subjects. *American Journal of Psychiatry, 147,* 439–444.

Peselow, E.D., Robins, C.J., Sanfilipo, M.P., Block, P., & Fieve, R.R. (1992). Sociotropy and autonomy: Relationship to antidepressant drug treatment response and endogenous-nonendogenous dichotomy. *Journal of Abnormal Psychology, 101,* 479–486.

Peterson, C., Raps, C.S., & Villanova, P. (1985). Depression and attributions: Factors responsible for inconsistent results in the published literature. *Journal of Abnormal Psychology, 94,* 165–168.

Peterson, C., & Seligman, M.E.P. (1984). Causal explanations as a risk factor for depression: Theory and evidence. *Psychological Review, 91,* 347–374.

Peterson, C., & Seligman, M.E.P. (1985). The learned helplessness model of depression: Current status of theory and research. In E.E. Beckham & W.R. Leber (Eds.), *Handbook of depression: Treatment, assessment, and research* (pp. 914–939). Homewood, IL: Dorsey Press.

Peterson, C., Semmel, A., von Baeyer, C., Abramson, L.Y., Metalsky, G.I., & Seligman, M.E.P. (1982). The Attributional Style Questionnaire. *Cognitive Therapy and Research, 6,* 287–300.

Phillips, K.A., Gunderson, J.G., Hirschfeld, R.M., & Smith, L.E. (1990). A review of the depressive personality. *American Journal of Psychiatry, 147,* 830–837.

Pianta, R.C., & Egeland, B. (1994). Relation between depressive symptoms and stressful life events in a sample of disadvantaged mothers. *Journal of Consulting and Clinical Psychology, 62,* 1229–1234.

Piccinelli, M., & Wilkinson, G. (1994). Outcome of depression in psychiatric settings. *British Journal of Psychiatry, 164,* 297–304.

Pietromonaco, P.R., & Markus, H. (1983). The nature of negative thoughts in depression. *Journal of Personality and Social Psychology, 48,* 799–807.

Pilon, D.J. (1989). *The Sociotropy-Autonomy Scale in a university population: An overview.* Paper presented at the World Congress of Cognitive Therapy, Oxford.

Plumb, M.M., & Holland, J. (1977). Comparative studies of psychological function in patients with advanced cancer: I. Self-reported depressive symptoms. *Psychosomatic Medicine, 39,* 264–276.

Polivy, J. (1981). On the induction of emotion in the laboratory: Discrete moods or multiple affect states? *Journal of Personality and Social Psychology, 41,* 803–817.

Polivy, J., & Doyle, C. (1980). Laboratory induction of mood states through the reading of self-referent mood statements: Affective changes or demand characteristics? *Journal of Abnormal Psychology, 89,* 286–290.

Popper, K.R. (1959). *The logic of scientific discovery.* New York: Basic Books.

Powell, M., & Hemsley, D.R. (1984). Depression: A breakdown in perceptual defence? *British Journal of Psychiatry, 145,* 358–362.

Power, M.J., & Brewin, C.R. (1990). Self-esteem regulation in an emotional priming task. *Cognition and Emotion, 4,* 39–51.

Power, M.J., Brewin, C.R., Stuessy, A., & Mahony, T. (1991). The emotional priming task: Results from a student population. *Cognitive Therapy and Research, 15,* 21–31.

Pretzer, J.L., & Beck, A.T. (1996). A cognitive theory of personality disorders. In J.F. Clarkin (Ed.), *Major theories of personality disorder.* New York: Guilford Press.

Pyszczynski, T., & Greenberg, J. (1987). Self-regulatory perseveration and the depressive self-focusing style: A self-awareness theory of reactive depression. *Psychological Bulletin, 102,* 122–138.

Pyszczynski, T., Holt, K., & Greenberg, J. (1987). Depression, self-focused attention, and expectancies for positive and negative future life events for self and others. *Journal of Personality and Social Psychology, 52,* 994–1001.

Rachman, S.J. (1971). *The effects of psychotherapy.* Oxford, England: Pergamon Press.

Rachman, S. (1981). Unwanted intrusive cognitions: Part I. *Advances in Behaviour Research and Therapy, 3,* 89–99.

Rachman, S. (1997). The evolution of cognitive behaviour therapy. In D.M. Clark & C.G. Fairburn (Eds.), *Science and practice of cognitive behaviour therapy* (pp. 3–26). Oxford, England: Oxford University Press.

Rado, S. (1928). The problem of melancholia. *International Journal of Psychoanalysis, 9,* 420–438.

Raimy, V. (1975). *Misunderstandings of the self.* San Francisco: Jossey-Bass.

Randolph, J.L., & Dykman, B.M. (1998). Perceptions of parenting and depression-proneness in the offspring: Dysfunctional attitudes as a mediating mechanism. *Cognitive Therapy and Research, 22,* 377–400.

Rapp, S.R., Parisi, S.A., Walsh, D.A., & Wallace, C.E. (1988). Detecting depression in elderly medical inpatients. *Journal of Consulting and Clinical Psychology, 56,* 509–513.

Reda, M.A., Carpiniello, B., Secchiaroli, L., & Blanco, S. (1985). Thinking, depression, and antidepressants: Modified and unmodified depressive beliefs during treatment with amitriptyline. *Cognitive Therapy and Research, 9,* 135–143.

Regier, D.A., Burke, J.D., & Burke, K.C. (1990). Comorbidity of affective and anxiety disorders in the NIMH Epidemiologic Catachment Area Program. In J.D. Maser & C.R. Cloninger (Eds.), *Comorbidity of mood and anxiety disorders* (pp. 113–122). Washington, DC: American Psychiatric Press.

Rehm, L.P. (1977). A self-control model of depression. *Behavior Therapy, 8,* 787–804.

Reiser, B.J., Black, J.B., & Abelson, R.P. (1985). Knowledge structures in the organization and retrieval of autobiographical memories. *Cognitive Psychology, 17,* 89–137.

Resnik, H.L.P. (1980). Suicide. In H.I. Kaplan, A.M. Freeman, & B.J. Sadock (Eds.), *Comprehensive textbook of psychiatry* (3rd ed., Vol. 2). Baltimore: Williams & Wilkins.

Reynolds, M., & Salkovskis, P.M. (1992). Comparison of positive and negative intrusive thoughts and experimental investigation of the differential effects of mood. *Behaviour Research and Therapy, 30,* 273–281.

Reynolds, S., & Gilbert, P. (1991). Psychological impact of unemployment: Interactive effects of vulnerability and protective factors on depression. *Journal of Counseling Psychology, 38,* 76–84.

Rholes, W.S., Riskind, J.H., & Lane, J.W. (1987). Emotional states and memory biases: Effects of cognitive priming and mood. *Journal of Personality and Social Psychology, 52,* 91–99.

Rholes, W.S., Riskind, J.H., & Neville, B. (1985). The relationship of cognitions and hopelessness to depression and anxiety. *Social Cognition, 3,* 36–50.

Riemann, B.C., & McNally, R.J. (1995). Cognitive processing of personally relevant information. *Cognition and Emotion, 9,* 325–340.

Rimm, D.C., & Litvak, S.G. (1969). Self-verbalization and emotional arousal. *Journal of Abnormal Psychology, 74,* 181–187.

Riskind, J.H. (1989). The mediating mechanisms in mood and memory: A cognitive-priming formulation. In D. Kuiken (Ed.), Mood and memory: Theory, research, and applications [Special issue]. *Journal of Social Behavior and Personality, 4,* 173–184.

Riskind, J.H., Moore, R., Harman, B., Hohmann, A.A., Beck, A.T., & Stewart, B. (1991). The relation of generalized anxiety disorder to depression in general and dysthymic disorder in particular. In R.M. Rapee & D.H. Barlow (Eds.), *Chronic anxiety: Generalized anxiety disorder and mixed anxiety-depression* (pp. 153–171). New York: Guilford Press.

Riskind, J.H., & Rholes, W.S. (1984). Cognitive accessibility and the capacity of cognitions to predict future depression: A theoretical note. *Cognitive Therapy and Research, 8,* 1–12.

Riskind, J.H., Rholes, W.S., & Eggers, J. (1982). The Velten mood induction procedure: Effects on mood and memory. *Journal of Abnormal Psychology, 30,* 146–147.

Riskind, J.H., & Steer, R.A. (1984). Do maladaptive attitudes "cause" depression: Misconceptions of cognitive theory. *Archives of General Psychiatry, 41,* 1111.

Roberts, J.E., & Gotlib, I.H. (1997). Temporal variability in global self-esteem and specific self-evaluation as prospective predictors of emotional distress: Specificity in predictors and outcome. *Journal of Abnormal Psychology, 106,* 521–529.

Roberts, J.E., & Kassel, J.D. (1996). Mood-state dependence in cognitive vulnerability to depression: The roles of positive and negative affect. *Cognitive Therapy and Research, 20,* 1–12.

Roberts, J.E., & Kassel, J.D. (1997). Labile self-esteem, life stress, and depressive symptoms: Prospective data testing a model of vulnerability. *Cognitive Therapy and Research, 21,* 569–589.

Roberts, J.E., Kassel, J.D., & Gotlib, I.H. (1995). Level and stability of self-esteem as predictors of depressive symptoms. *Personality and Individual Differences, 19,* 217–224.

Roberts, J.E., & Monroe, S.M. (1992). Vulnerable self-esteem and depressive symptoms: Prospective findings comparing three alternative conceptualizations. *Journal of Personality and Social Psychology, 62,* 804–812.

Roberts, J.E., & Monroe, S.M. (1994). A multidimensional model of self-esteem in depression. *Clinical Psychology Review, 14,* 161–181.

Robins, C.J. (1985). *Construct validation of the Sociotropy-Autonomy Scale: A measure of vulnerability to depression.* Paper presented at the annual meeting of the Eastern Psychological Association, Boston.

Robins, C.J. (1986). *Effects of simulated social rejection and achievement failure on mood as a function of sociotropic and autonomous personality characteristics.* Unpublished manuscript, Department of Psychology, New York University.

Robins, C.J. (1988). Attributions and depression: Why is the literature so inconsistent? *Journal of Personality and Social Psychology, 54,* 880–889.

Robins, C.J. (1990). Congruence of personality and life events in depression. *Journal of Abnormal Psychology, 99,* 393–397.

Robins, C.J., Bagby, R.M., Rector, N.A., Lynch, T.R., & Kennedy, S.H. (1997). Sociotropy, autonomy, and patterns of symptoms in patients with major depression: A comparison of dimensional and categorical approaches. *Cognitive Therapy and Research, 21,* 285–300.

Robins, C.J., & Block, P. (1988). Personal vulnerability, life events, and depressive symptoms: A test of a specific interactional model. *Journal of Personality and Social Psychology, 54,* 847–852.

Robins, C.J., & Block, P. (1989). Cognitive theories of depression viewed from a diathesis-stress perspective: Evaluations of the models of Beck and of Abramson, Seligman, and Teasdale. *Cognitive Therapy and Research, 13,* 297–313.

Robins, C.J., Block, P., & Peselow, E.D. (1989). Relations of sociotropic and autonomous personality characteristics to specific symptoms in depressed patients. *Journal of Abnormal Psychology, 98,* 86–88.

Robins, C.J., Block, P., & Peselow, E.D. (1990a). Cognition and life events in major depression: A test of the mediation and interaction hypotheses. *Cognitive Therapy and Research, 14,* 299–313.

Robins, C.J., Block, P., & Peselow, E.D. (1990b). Endogenous and non-endogenous depressions: Relations of life events, dysfunctional attitudes and event perceptions. *British Journal of Clinical Psychology, 29,* 201–207.

Robins, C.J., Block, P., Peselow, E.D., & Klein, R. (1986). *Relationship of sociotropic and autonomous personality styles to specific symptoms in depressed patients.* Paper presented at the annual meeting of the Eastern Psychological Association, New York.

Robins, C.J., & Hayes, A.M. (1993). An appraisal of cognitive therapy. *Journal of Consulting and Clinical Psychology, 61,* 205–214.

Robins, C.J., Hayes, A.M., Block, P., Kramer, R.J., & Villena, M. (1995). Interpersonal and achievement concerns and the depressive vulnerability and symptom specificity hypotheses: A prospective study. *Cognitive Therapy and Research, 19,* 1–20.

Robins, C.J., Ladd, J., Welkowitz, J., Blaney, P.H., Diaz, R., & Kutcher, G. (1994). The Personal Style Inventory: Preliminary validation studies of new measures of sociotropy and autonomy. *Journal of Psychopathology and Behavioral Assessment, 16,* 277–300.

Robins, C.J., & Luten, A.G. (1991). Sociotropy and autonomy: Differential patterns of clinical presentation in unipolar depression. *Journal of Abnormal Psychology, 100,* 74–77.

Robinson, J.A. (1976). Sampling of autobiographical memory. *Cognitive Psychology, 8,* 578–595.

Robinson, R.G. (1995). Mapping brain activity associated with emotion. *American Journal of Psychiatry, 152,* 327–329.

Roediger, H.L. (1990). Implicit memory: Retention without remembering. *American Psychologist, 45,* 1043–1056.

Roediger, H.L., & McDermott, K.B. (1992). Depression and implicit memory: A commentary. *Journal of Abnormal Psychology, 101,* 587–591.

Roemer, L., & Borkovec, T.D. (1994). Effects of suppressing thoughts about emotional material. *Journal of Abnormal Psychology, 103,* 467–474.

Rogers, T., & Craighead, W.E. (1977). Physiological responses to self-statement valence and discrepancy. *Cognitive Therapy and Research, 1,* 99–119.

Rohde, P., Lewinsohn, P.M., & Seeley, J.R. (1990). Are people changed by the experience of having an episode of depression? Further test of the scar hypothesis. *Journal of Abnormal Psychology, 99,* 264–271.

Rohde, P., Lewinsohn, P.M., & Seeley, J.R. (1991). Comorbidity of unipolar depression: II. Comorbidity with other mental disorders in adolescents and adults. *Journal of Abnormal Psychology, 100,* 214–222.

Rose, D.T., Abramson, L.Y., Hodulik, C.J., Halberstadt, L., & Leff, G. (1994). Heterogeneity of cognitive style among depressed inpatients. *Journal of Abnormal Psychology, 103,* 419–429.

Roseman, I.J. (1984). Cognitive determinants of emotion: A structural theory. In P. Shaver (Ed.), *Review of personality and social psychology: Emotions, relationship and health* (Vol. 5, pp. 11–36). Beverly Hills, CA: Sage.

Ross, S.M., Gottfredson, D.K., Christensen, P., & Weaver, R. (1986). Cognitive self-statements in depression: Findings across clinical populations. *Cognitive Therapy and Research, 10,* 159–166.

Roth, D., & Rehm, L.P. (1980). Relationships among self-monitoring processes, memory, and depression. *Cognitive Therapy and Research, 4,* 149–157.

Roxborough, H.M., Blackburn, I.M., & Glabus, M. (1996). *Psychophysiological and personality correlates of information processing biases in depression.* Unpublished manuscript, Department of Psychiatry, University of Newcastle, Newcastle upon Tyne, U.K.

Rude, S.S., & Burnham, B.L. (1993). Do interpersonal and achievement vulnerabilities interact with congruent events to predict depression? Comparison of DEQ, SAS, DAS and combined scales. *Cognitive Therapy and Research, 17,* 531–548.

Rude, S.S., & Burnham, B.L. (1995). Connectedness and neediness: Factors of the DEQ and SAS dependency scales. *Cognitive Therapy and Research, 19,* 323–340.

Rude, S.S., Krantz, S.E., & Rosenhan, D.L. (1988). Distinguishing the dimensions of valence and belief consistency in depressive and nondepressive information processing. *Cognitive Therapy and Research, 12,* 391–407.

Rudolph, K.D., Hammen, C., & Burge, D. (1995). Cognitive representations of self, family, and peers in school-age children: Links with social competence and sociometric status. *Child Development, 66,* 1385–1402.

Ruehlman, L.S., West, S.G., & Pasahow, R.J. (1985). Depression and evaluative schemata. *Journal of Personality, 53,* 46–92.

Ruiz-Caballero, J.A., & González, P. (1994). Implicit and explicit memory bias in depressed and nondepressed subjects. *Cognition and Emotion, 8,* 555–569.

Ruiz-Caballero, J.A., & González, P. (1997). Effects of level of processing on implicit and explicit memory in depressed mood. *Motivation and Emotion, 21,* 195–209.

Rush, A.J., Beck, A.T., Kovacs, M., & Hollon, S. (1977). Comparative efficacy of cognitive therapy and imipramine in the treatment of depressed outpatients. *Cognitive Therapy and Research, 1,* 17–37.

Rush, A.J., & Weissenburger, J.E. (1994). Melancholic symptom features and DSM-IV. *American Journal of Psychiatry, 151,* 489–498.

Rush, A.J., Weissenburger, J., & Eaves, G. (1986). Do thinking patterns predict depressive symptoms? *Cognitive Therapy and Research, 10,* 225–236.

Russell, J.A. (1991). In defense of a prototype approach to emotion concepts. *Journal of Personality and Social Psychology, 60,* 37–47.

Russell, P.L., & Brandsma, J.M. (1974). A theoretical and empirical integration of the rational-emotive and classical conditioning theories. *Journal of Consulting and Clinical Psychology, 42,* 389–397.

Safran, J.D. (1990). Towards a refinement of cognitive therapy in light of interpersonal theory: I. Theory. *Clinical Psychology Review, 10,* 87–105.

Safran, J.D., & Segal, Z.V. (1990). *Interpersonal process in cognitive therapy.* New York: Basic Books.

Safran, J.D., Segal, Z.V., Hill, C., & Whiffen, V. (1990). Refining strategies for research on self-representations in emotional disorders. *Cognitive Therapy and Research, 14,* 143–160.

Sahin, N., Ulusoy, M., & Sahin, N. (1992). *Exploring the sociotropy-autonomy dimensions in a sample of Turkish psychiatric inpatients.* Paper presented at the World Congress of Cognitive Therapy, Toronto.

Sanderson, W.C., Beck, A.T., & Beck, J. (1990). Syndrome comorbidity in patients with major depression or dysthymia: Prevalence and temporal relationships. *American Journal of Psychiatry, 147,* 1025–1028.

Santor, D.A., Ramsay, J.O., & Zuroff, D.C. (1994). Nonparametric item analyses of the Beck Depression Inventory: Evaluating gender item bias and response option weights. *Psychological Assessment, 6,* 255–270.

Santor, D.A., Zuroff, D.C., Ramsay, J.O., Cervantes, P., & Palacios, J. (1995). Examining scale discriminability in the BDI and CES-D as a function of depressive severity. *Psychological Assessment, 7,* 131–139.

Sanz, J. (1996). Memory bias in social anxiety and depression. *Cognition and Emotion, 10,* 87–105.

Sanz, J., & Avia, M.D. (1994). Cognitive specificity in social anxiety and depression: Self-statements, self-focused attention, and dysfunctional attitudes. *Journal of Social and Cognitive Psychology, 13,* 105–137.

Schacter, D.L. (1990). Introduction to "Implicit memory: Multiple perspectives." *Bulletin of the Psychonomic Society, 28,* 338–340.

Schlenker, B.R., & Britt, T.W. (1996). Depression and the explanation of events that happen to self, close others, and strangers. *Journal of Personality and Social Psychology, 71,* 180–192.

Schrader, G., Gibbs, A., & Harcourt, R. (1986). Dysfunctional attitudes in former psychiatric inpatients. *Journal of Nervous and Mental Disease, 174,* 660–663.

Schroeder, R.M. (1994). *The relationship between depression, cognitive distortion, and life stress among African-American college students.* Doctoral dissertation, School of Education in Counseling Psychology, University of North Carolina at Chapel Hill, NC.

Schuele, J.G., & Wiesenfeld, A.R. (1983). Autonomic response to self-critical thought. *Cognitive Therapy and Research, 7,* 189–194.

Schulberg, H.C., Saul, M., McClelland, M., Ganguli, M., Christy, W., & Frank, R. (1985). Assessing depression in primary medical and psychiatric practices. *Archives of General Psychiatry, 42*, 1164–1170.

Schwartz, G.E., Ahern, G.L., & Brown, S.L. (1979). Lateralized facial muscle response to positive and negative emotional stimuli. *Psychophysiology, 16*, 561–571.

Schwartz, G.E., Fair, P.L., Salt, P., Mandel, M.R., & Klerman, G.L. (1976). Facial expression and imagery in depression: An electromyographic study. *Psychosomatic Medicine, 38*, 337–347.

Schwartz, G.E., Fair, P.L., Mandel, M.R., Salt, P., Mieske, M., & Klerman, G.L. (1978). Facial electromyography in the assessment of improvement in depression. *Psychosomatic Medicine, 40*, 355–360.

Schwartz, G.E., Weinberger, D.A., & Singer, J.A. (1981). Cardiovascular differentiation of happiness, sadness, anger and fear following imagery and exercise. *Psychosomatic Medicine, 43*, 343–364.

Schwartz, R.M. (1986). The internal dialogue: On the asymmetry between positive and negative coping thoughts. *Cognitive Therapy and Research, 10*, 591–605.

Schwartz, R.M. (1997). Consider the simple screw: Cognitive science, quality improvement and psychotherapy. *Journal of Consulting and Clinical Psychology, 65*, 970–983.

Schwartz, R.M., & Garamoni, G.L. (1986). A structural model of positive and negative states of mind: Asymmetry in the internal dialogue. In P.C. Kendall (Ed.), *Advances in cognitive-behavioral research and therapy* (Vol. 5, pp. 1–62). New York: Academic Press.

Schwartz, R.M., & Garamoni, G.L. (1989). Cognitive balance and psychopathology: Evaluation of an information processing model of positive and negative states of mind. *Clinical Psychology Review, 9*, 271–294.

Scott, J., Harrington, J., House, R., & Ferrier, N. (1996). A preliminary study of the relationship between personality, cognitive vulnerability, symptom profile and outcome in major depressive disorder. *Journal of Nervous and Mental Disease, 184*, 503–505.

Segal, Z.V. (1988). Appraisal of the self-schematic construct in cognitive models of depression. *Psychological Bulletin, 103*, 147–162.

Segal, Z.V., & Dobson, K.S. (1992). Cognitive models of depression: Report from a consensus development conference. *Psychological Inquiry, 3*, 219–224.

Segal, Z.V., & Gemar, M. (1997). Changes in cognitive organization for negative self-referent material following cognitive behaviour therapy for depression: A primed Stroop study. *Cognition and Emotion, 11*, 501–516.

Segal, Z.V., Gemar, M., Truchon, C., Guirguis, M., & Horowitz, L.M. (1995). A priming methodology for studying self-representation in major depressive disorder. *Journal of Abnormal Psychology, 104*, 205–213.

Segal, Z.V., Gemar, M., & Williams, S. (1998). *Differential cognitive responses to a mood challenge following successful cognitive therapy or pharmacotherapy for unipolar depression.* Unpublished manuscript, Cognitive Behavior Therapy Unit, Clarke Institute of Psychiatry, Toronto, Canada.

Segal, Z.V., Hood, J.E., Shaw, B.F., & Higgins, E.T. (1988). A structural analysis of the self-schema construct in major depression. *Cognitive Therapy and Research, 12*, 471–485.

Segal, Z.V., & Ingram, R.E. (1994). Mood priming and construct activation in tests of cognitive vulnerability to unipolar depression. *Clinical Psychology Review, 14*, 663–695.

Segal, Z.V., & Muran, J.C. (1993). A cognitive perspective on self-representation in depression. In Z.V. Segal & S.J. Blatt (Eds.), *The self in emotional distress: Cognitive and psychodynamic perspectives* (pp. 131–170). New York: Guilford Press.

Segal, Z.V., & Shaw, B.F. (1986a). Cognition in depression: A reappraisal of Coyne and Gotlib's critique. *Cognitive Therapy and Research, 10*, 671–693.

Segal, Z.V., & Shaw, B.F. (1986b). When cul-de-sacs are mentality than reality: A rejoiner to Coyne and Gotlib. *Cognitive Therapy and Research, 10*, 707–714.

Segal, Z.V., Shaw, B.F., & Vella, D.D. (1989). Life stress and depression: A test of the congruency hypothesis for life event content and depressive subtype. *Canadian Journal of Behavioural Science, 21*, 389–400.

Segal, Z.V., Shaw, B.F., Vella, D.D., & Katz, R. (1992). Cognitive and life stress predictors of relapse in remitted unipolar depressed patients: Test of the congruency hypothesis. *Journal of Abnormal Psychology, 101*, 26–36.

Segal, Z.V., & Swallow, S.R. (1994). Cognitive assessment of unipolar depression: Measuring products, processes and structures. *Behaviour Research and Therapy, 32*, 147–158.

Segal, Z.V., & Vella, D.D. (1990). Self-schema in major depression: Replication and extension of a priming methodology. *Cognitive Therapy and Research, 14*, 161–176.

Segal, Z.V., Williams, J.M., Teasdale, J.D., & Gemar, M. (1996). A cognitive science perspective on kindling and episode sensitization in recurrent affective disorder. *Psychological Medicine, 26*, 371–380.

Segrin, C., & Dillard, J.P. (1992). The interactional theory of depression: A meta-analysis of the research literature. *Journal of Social and Clinical Psychology, 11*, 43–70.

Seligman, M.E.P. (1975). *Helplessness: On depression, development, and death.* San Francisco: Freeman.

Seligman, M.E.P. (1978). Comment and integration. *Journal of Abnormal Psychology, 87*, 165–179.

Seligman, M.E.P. (1990). *Learned optimism: How to change your mind and your life.* New York: Pocket Books.

Seligman, M.E.P., & Johnston, J.C. (1973). A cognitive theory of avoidance learning. In F.J. McGuigan & D.B. Lumsden (Eds.), *Contemporary approaches to conditioning and learning* (pp. 69–110). Washington, DC: Winston & Sons.

Seligman, M.E.P., & Maier, S.F. (1967). Failure to escape taumatic shock. *Journal of Experimental Psychology, 74*, 1–9.

Shelton, R.C., Hollon, S.D., Purdon, S.E., & Loosen, P.T. (1991). Biological and psychological aspects of depression. *Behavior Therapy, 22*, 201–228.

Sherbourne, C.D., Wells, K.B., Hays, R.D., Rogers, W., Burnam, M.A., & Judd, L.L. (1994). Subthreshold depression and depressive disorder: Clinical characteristics of general medical and mental health specialty outpatients. *American Journal of Psychiatry, 151*, 1777–1784.

Shrout, P.E., Link, B.G., Dohrenwend, B.P., Skodol, A.E., Stueve A., & Mirotznik, J. (1989). Characterizing life events as risk factors of depression: The role of fateful loss events. *Journal of Abnormal Psychology, 98*, 460–467.

Silverman, J.S., Silverman, J.A., & Eardley, D.A. (1984). Do maladaptive attitudes cause depression? *Archives of General Psychiatry, 41*, 28–30.

Simon, G., Ormel, J., VonKorff, M., & Barlow, W. (1995). Health care costs associ-ated with depressive and anxiety disorders in primary care. *American Journal of Psychiatry, 152,* 352–357.

Simons, A.D., Angell, K.L., Monroe, S.M., & Thase, M.E. (1993). Cognition and life stress in depression: Cognitive factors and the definition, rating, and gen-eration of negative life events. *Journal of Abnormal Psychology, 102,* 584–591.

Simons, A.D., Murphy, G.E., Levine, J.L., & Wetzel, R.D. (1986). Cognitive ther-apy and pharmacotherapy for depression: Sustained improvement over one year. *Archives of General Psychiatry, 43,* 43–48.

Sjolander, S. (1997). On the evolution of reality: Some biological prequisites and evolutionary stages. *Journal of Theoretical Biology, 187,* 595–600.

Slyker, J.P., & McNally, R.J. (1991). Experimental induction of anxious and de-pressed moods: Are Velten and musical procedures necessary? *Cognitive Ther-apy and Research, 15,* 33–45.

Smith, C.A. (1991). The self, appraisal, and coping. In C.R. Synder & D.R. Don-aldson (Eds.), *Handbook of social and clinical psychology: The health perspective* (pp. 116–137). New York: Pergamon Press.

Smith, C.A., & Ellsworth, P.C. (1985). Patterns of cognitive appraisal in emotions. *Journal of Personality and Social Psychology, 48,* 813–838.

Smith, T.W., Ingram, R.E., & Roth, D.L. (1985). Self-focused attention and de-pression: Self-evaluation, affect and life stress. *Motivation and Emotion, 9,* 381–389.

Sobin, C., & Sackeim, H.A. (1997). Psychomotor symptoms of depression. *Ameri-can Journal of Psychiatry, 154,* 4–17.

Somoza, E., Steer, R.A., Beck, A.T., & Clark, D.A. (1994). Differentiating major depression and panic disorders by self-report and clinical rating scales: ROC analysis and information theory. *Behaviour Research and Therapy, 32,* 771–782.

Sotsky, S.M., Glass, D.R., Shea, M.T., Pilkonis, P.A., Collins, J.F., Elkin, I., Watkins, J.T., Imber, S.D., Leber, W.R., Moyer, J., & Oliveri, M.E. (1991). Pa-tient predictors of response to psychotherapy and pharmacotherapy: Find-ings in the NIMH Treatment of Depression Collaborative Research Program. *American Journal of Psychiatry, 148,* 997–1008.

Spangler, D.L., Simons, A.D., Monroe, S.M., & Thase, M.E. (1993). Evaluating the hopelessness model of depression: Diathesis-stress and symptom compo-nents. *Journal of Abnormal Psychology, 102,* 592–600.

Spangler, D.L., Simons, A.D., Thase, M.E., & Monroe, S.M. (1997). Comparison of cognitive models of depression: Relationships between cognitive constructs and cognitive diathesis-stress match. *Journal of Abnormal Psychology, 106,* 395–403.

Spitzer, R., Endicott, J., & Robins, C.J. (1978). Research diagnostic criteria: Rationality and reliability. *Archives of General Psychiatry, 46,* 53–58.

Spitzer, R.L., Williams, J.B.W., Kroenke, K., Linzer, M., deGruy, F.V., Hahn, S.R., Brody, D., & Johnson, J.G. (1994). Utility of a new procedure for diagnosing mental disorders in primary care. The PRIME-MD 1000 Study. *Journal of the American Medical Association, 272,* 1749–1756.

Spivak, G., Platt, J.J., & Shure, M.B. (1976). *The problem-solving approach to adjust-ment.* San Francisco: Jossey-Bass.

Stader, S.R., & Hokanson, J.E. (1998). Psychosocial antecedents of depressive symptoms: An evaluation using daily experiences methodology. *Journal of Ab-normal Psychology, 107,* 17–26.

Steer, R.A., Beck, A.T., Clark, D.A., & Beck, J.S. (1994). Psychometric properties of the Cognition Checklist with psychiatric outpatients and university students. *Psychological Assessment, 6*, 67–70.

Steer, R.A., Clark, D.A., Beck, A.T., & Ranieri, W.F. (1995). Common and specific dimensions of self-reported anxiety and depression: A replication. *Journal of Abnormal Psychology, 104*, 542–545.

Sternberg, R.J. (1996). *Cognitive psychology.* Forth Worth, TX: Harcourt Brace College.

Stiles, T.C., & Gotestam, K.G. (1988a). *Cognitive vulnerability to depression: A longitudinal study.* Unpublished manuscript, University of Trondheim, Norway.

Stiles, T.C., & Gotestam, K.G. (1988b). The role of cognitive vulnerability factors in the development of depression: Theoretical and methodological considerations. In C. Perris, I.M. Blackburn, & H. Perris (Eds.), *Cognitive psychotherapy: Theory and practice* (pp. 120–139). Berlin: Springer-Verlag.

Stiles, T.C., & Gotestam, K.G. (1989). The role of automatic negative thoughts in the development of dysphoric mood: An analogue experiment. *Cognitive Therapy and Research, 13*, 161–170.

Stiles, T.C., Schroder, P., & Johansen, T. (1993). The role of automatic thoughts and dysfunctional attitudes in the development and maintenance of experimentally induced dysphoric mood. *Cognitive Therapy and Research, 17*, 71–82.

Strauman, T.J. (1989). Self-discrepancies in clinical depression and social phobia: Cognitive structures that underlie emotional disorders? *Journal of Abnormal Psychology, 98*, 14–22.

Strauman, T.J. (1992). Self-guides, autobiographical memory, and anxiety and dysphoria: Toward a cognitive model of vulnerability to emotional distress. *Journal of Abnormal Psychology, 101*, 87–95.

Strauman, T.J., & Higgins, E.T. (1993). The self construct in social cognition: Past, present, and future. In Z.V. Segal & S.J. Blatt (Eds.), *The self in emotional distress: Cognitive and psychodynamic perspectives* (pp. 3–40). New York: Guilford Press.

Strickland, B.R., Hale, W.D., & Anderson, L.K. (1975). Effect of induced mood states on activity and self-reported affect. *Journal of Consulting and Clinical Psychology, 43*, 587.

Study results bolster depression screening efforts. (1994, September). *Mental Health Weekly, 4*(37), 1, 4.

Suinn, R.M. (1995). Schizophrenia and bipolar disorder: Origins and influences. *Behavior Therapy, 26*, 557–571.

Sullivan, M.J.L., & D'Eon, J.L. (1990). Relation between catastrophizing and depression in chronic pain patients. *Journal of Abnormal Psychology, 99*, 260–263.

Sutherland, G., Newman, B., & Rachman, S. (1982). Experimental investigations of the relations between mood and intrusive unwanted cognitions. *British Journal of Medical Psychology, 55*, 127–138.

Swallow, S.R., & Kuiper, N.A. (1987). The effects of depression and cognitive vulnerability to depression on judgments of similarity between self and other. *Motivation and Emotion, 11*, 157–167.

Swallow, S.R., & Kuiper, N.A. (1988). Social comparison and negative self-evaluations: An application to depression. *Clinical Psychology Review, 8*, 55–76.

Sweeney, P.D., Anderson, K., & Bailey, S. (1986). Attributional style in depression: A meta-analytic review. *Journal of Personality and Social Psychology, 50*, 974–991.

Talbot, L.M. (1994). *Sociotropy, autonomy, and depression: The influence of attributional style and self-esteem.* Honor's Thesis, Department of Psychology, University of Saskatchewan, Canada.

Tarlov, A.R., Ware, J.E., Greenfield, S., Nelson, E.C., Perrin, E., & Zubkoff, M. (1989). The Medical Outcomes Study. An application of methods for monitoring the results of medical care. *Journal of the American Medical Association, 262,* 925–930.

Taylor, S.E., & Brown, J.D. (1994). Positive illusions and well-being revisited: Separating fact from fiction. *Psychological Bulletin, 11*(6), 21–27.

Teasdale, J.D. (1983). Negative thinking in depression: Cause, effect or reciprocal relationship? *Advances in Behaviour Research and Therapy, 5,* 3–25.

Teasdale, J.D. (1988). Cognitive vulnerability to persistent depression. *Cognition and Emotion, 2,* 247–274.

Teasdale, J.D. (1996). Clinically relevant theory: Integrating clinical insight with cognitive science. In P.M. Salkovskis (Ed.), *Frontiers of cognitive therapy* (pp. 26–47). New York: Guilford Press.

Teasdale, J.D., & Bancroft, J. (1977). Manipulation of thought content as a determinant of mood and corrugator electromyographic activity in depressed patients. *Journal of Abnormal Psychology, 86,* 235–241.

Teasdale, J.D., & Barnard, P.J. (1993). *Affect, cognition and change: remodelling depressive thought.* Hove, UK: Erlbaum.

Teasdale, J.D., & Dent, J. (1987). Cognitive vulnerability to depression: An investigation of two hypotheses. *British Journal of Clinical Psychology, 26,* 113–126.

Teasdale, J.D., & Fennell, M.J.V. (1982). Immediate effects on depression of cognitive therapy interventions. *Cognitive Therapy and Research, 6,* 343–352.

Teasdale, J.D., & Fogarty, S.J. (1979). Differential effects of induced mood on retrieval of pleasant and unpleasant events from episodic memory. *Journal of Abnormal Psychology, 88,* 248–257.

Teasdale, J.D., & Rezin, V. (1978a). The effects of reducing frequency of negative thoughts on the mood of depressed patients-tests of a cognitive model of depression. *British Journal of Social and Clinical Psychology, 17,* 65–74.

Teasdale, J.D., & Rezin, V. (1978b). Effect of thought-stopping on thoughts: Mood and corrugator EMG in depressed patients. *Behaviour Research and Therapy, 16,* 97–102.

Teasdale, J.D., & Russell, M.L. (1983). Differential effects of induced mood on the recall of positive, negative and neutral words. *British Journal of Clinical Psychology, 22,* 163–171.

Teasdale, J.D., Segal, Z., & Williams, J.M.G. (1995). How does cognitive therapy prevent depressive relapse and why should attentional control (mindfulness) training help? *Behaviour Research and Therapy, 33,* 25–39.

Teasdale, J.D., Taylor, M.J., Cooper, Z., Hayhurst, H., & Paykel, E.S. (1995). Depressive thinking: Shifts in construct accessibility or in schematic mental models? *Journal of Abnormal Psychology, 104,* 500–507.

Teasdale, J.D., & Taylor, R. (1981). Induced mood and accessibility of memories: An effect of mood state or of induction variation? *British Journal of Clinical Psychology, 20,* 39–48.

Teasdale, J.D., Taylor, R., & Fogarty, S.J. (1980). Effects of induced elation-depression on the accessibility of memories of happy and unhappy experiences. *Behaviour Research and Therapy, 18,* 339–346.

Tellegen, A. (1985). Structures of mood and personality and their relevance to assessing anxiety, with an emphasis on self-report. In A.H. Tuma & J.D. Maser (Eds.), *Anxiety and the anxiety disorders* (pp. 681–706). Hillsdale, NJ: Erlbaum.

Tennen, H., Hall, J.A., & Affleck, G. (1995). Depression research methodologies in the *Journal of Personality and Social Psychology*: A review and critique. *Journal of Personality and Social Psychology, 68*, 870–884.

Thase, M.E., Simons, A.D., McGeary, J., Cahalane, J.F., Hughes, C., Harden, T., & Friedman, E. (1992). Relapse after cognitive behavior therapy of depression: Potential implications for longer courses of treatment. *American Journal of Psychiatry, 149*, 1046–1052.

Thompson, R., & Genest, M. (1995). *Sociotropy-autonomy and negative event perception.* Paper presented at the annual convention of the Canadian Psychological Association, Charlottetwon, Prince Edward Island, Canada.

Thoresen, C.E., & Mahoney, M.J. (1974). *Behavioral self-control.* New York: Holt, Rinehart and Winston.

Thorpe, G.L., Barnes, G.S., Hunter, J.E., & Hines, D. (1983). Thoughts and feelings: Correlations in two clinical and two nonclinical samples. *Cognitive Therapy and Research, 7*, 565–574.

Thorpe, S.J., & Salkovskis, P.M. (1997). Information processing in spider phobics: The Stroop colour naming task may indicate strategic but not automatic attentional bias. *Behaviour Research and Therapy, 35*, 131–144.

Tripp, D.A., Catano, V., & Sullivan, M.J. (1997). The contributions of attributional style, expectancies, depression and self-esteem in a cognition-based depression model. *Canadian Journal of Behavioural Science, 29*, 101–111.

Turpin, G., & Sartory, G. (1980). Effects of stimulus position in the respiratory cycle of the evoked cardiac response. *Physiological Psychology, 8*, 503–508.

Velten, E. (1968). A laboratory task for induction of mood states. *Behaviour Research and Therapy, 6*, 473–482.

Vestre, N.D., & Caulfield, B.P. (1986). Perception of neutral personality descriptions by depressed and nondepressed subjects. *Cognitive Therapy and Research, 10*, 31–36.

von Hippel, W., Hawkins, C., & Narayan, S. (1994). Personality and perceptual expertise: Individual differences in perceptual identification. *Psychological Science, 5*, 401–406.

Vrana, S.R. (1993). The psychophysiology of disgust: Differentiating negative emotional contexts with facial EMG. *Psychophysiology, 30*, 279–286.

Vrana, S.R., Spence, E.L., & Lang, P.J. (1988). The startle probe response: A new measure of emotion? *Journal of Abnormal Psychology, 97*, 487–491.

Vredenburg, K., Flett, G.L., & Krames, L. (1993). Analogue versus clinical depression: A critical reappraisal. *Psychological Bulletin, 113*, 327–344.

Waikar, S.V., & Craske, M.G. (1997). *Cognitive correlates of depression and anxiety: An examination of the helplessness/hopelessness model.* Manuscript submitted for publication.

Warner, V., Weissman, M.M., Fendrich, M., Wickramaratne, P., & Moreau, D. (1992). The course of major depression in the offspring of depressed parents: Incidence, recurrence, and recovery. *Archives of General Psychiatry, 49*, 795–801.

Watkins, J.T., & Rush, A.J. (1983). Cognitive Response Test. *Cognitive Therapy and Research, 7*, 425–436.

Watkins, P.C., Mathews, A., Williamson, D.A., & Fuller, R.D. (1992). Mood-congruent memory in depression: Emotional priming or elaboration? *Journal of Abnormal Psychology, 101,* 581–586.

Watkins, P.C., Vache, K., Verney, S.P., Mathews, A., & Muller, S. (1996). Unconscious mood-congruent memory bias in depression. *Journal of Abnormal Psychology, 105,* 34–41.

Watson, D., & Clark, L.A. (1984). Negative affectivity: The disposition to experience aversive emotional states. *Psychological Bulletin, 96,* 465–490.

Watson, D., Clark, L.A., & Carey, G. (1988). Positive and negative affectivity and their relation to anxiety and depressive disorders. *Journal of Abnormal Psychology, 97,* 346–353.

Watson, D., & Kendall, P.C. (1989). Common and differentiating features of anxiety and depression: Current findings and future directions. In P.C. Kendall & D. Watson (Eds.), *Anxiety and depression: Distinctive and overlapping features* (pp. 493–508). San Diego: Academic Press.

Watson, D., & Tellegen, A. (1985). Toward a consensual structure of mood. *Psychological Bulletin, 98,* 219–235.

Watson, D., Weber, K., Assenheimer, J.S., Clark, L.A., Strauss, M.E., & McCormick, R.A. (1995). Testing a tripartite model: I. Evaluating the convergent and discriminant validity of anxiety and depression symptom scales. *Journal of Abnormal Psychology, 104,* 3–14.

Weary, G., & Williams, J.P. (1990). Depressive self-presentation: Beyond self-handicapping. *Journal of Personality and Social Psychology, 58,* 892–898.

Wegner, D.M. (1994). Ironic processes of mental control. *Psychological Review, 101,* 34–52.

Wegner, D.M., & Erber, R. (1992). The hyperaccessibility of suppressed thoughts. *Journal of Personality and Social Psychology, 63,* 903–912.

Wegner, D.M., Erber, R., & Zanakos, S. (1993). Ironic processes in the mental control of mood and mood-related thought. *Journal of Personality and Social Psychology, 65,* 1093–1104.

Wegner, D.M., Schneider, D.J., Carter, S.R., & White, T.L. (1987). Paradoxical effects of thought suppression. *Journal of Personality and Social Psychology, 53,* 5–13.

Weingartner, H., Miller, H., & Murphy, D.L. (1977). Mood-state-dependent retrieval of verbal associations. *Journal of Abnormal Psychology, 86,* 276–284.

Weissman, A.N., & Beck, A.T. (1978). *Development and validation of the Dysfunctional Attitude Scale.* Paper presented at the annual meeting of the Association for the Advancement of Behavior Therapy, Chicago.

Weissman, M.M., Bruce, M.L., Leaf, P.J., Florio, L.P., & Holzer, C. (1991). Affective disorders. In L.N. Robins & D.A. Reiger (Eds.), *Psychiatric disorders in America* (pp. 53–81). New York: Free House.

Weissman, M.M., Leaf, P.J., Bruce, M.L., & Florio, L. (1988). The epidemiology of dysthymia in five communities: Rates, risks, comorbidity, and treatment. *American Journal of Psychiatry, 145,* 815–819.

Weissman, M.M., Prusoff, B., & Pincus, C. (1975). Symptom patterns in depressed patients and normals. *Journal of Nervous and Mental Diseases, 160,* 15–23.

Wells, A., & Matthews, G. (1994). *Attention and emotion: A clinical perspective.* Hove, UK: Erlbaum.

Wells, K.B., Burnam, A., Rogers, W., Hays, R., & Camp, P. (1992). The course of depression in adult outpatients: Results from the Medical Outcomes Study. *Archives of General Psychiatry, 49,* 788–794.

Wells, K.B., Golding, J.M., & Burnam, M.A. (1988). Psychiatric disorder in a sample of the general population with and without chronic medical conditions. *American Journal of Psychiatry, 145,* 976–981.

Wells, K.B., Stewart, A., Hays, R.D., Burnam, A., Rogers, W., Daniels, M., Berry, S., Greenfield, S., & Ware, J. (1989). The functioning and well-being of depressed patients: Results from the Medical Outcomes Study. *Journal of the American Medical Association, 262,* 914–919.

Wenzlaff, R.M., & Grozier, S.A. (1988). Depression and the magnification of failure. *Journal of Abnormal Psychology, 97,* 90–93.

Wenzlaff, R.M., Wegner, D.M., & Klein, S.B. (1991). The role of thought suppression in the bonding of thought and mood. *Journal of Personality and Social Psychology, 60,* 500–508.

Wenzlaff, R.M., Wegner, D.M., & Roper, D.W. (1988). Depression and mental control: The resurgence of unwanted negative thoughts. *Journal of Personality and Social Psychology, 55,* 882–892.

Westra, H.A., & Kuiper, N.A. (1997). Cognitive content specificity in selective attention across four domains of maladjustment. *Behaviour Research and Therapy, 35,* 349–365.

Whisman, M.A., Diaz, M.L., & Luboski, J.A. (1993). *Cognitive specificity of major depression and generalized anxiety disorder.* Paper presented at the annual meeting of the Association for Advancement of Behavior Therapy, Atlanta, GA.

Whisman, M.A., Miller, I.W., Norman, W.H., & Keitner, G.I. (1995). Hopelessness depression in depressed inpatients: Symptomatology, patient characteristics, and outcome. *Cognitive Therapy and Research, 19,* 377–398.

Whisman, M.A., & Pinto, A. (1997). Hopelessness depression in depressed inpatient adolescents. *Cognitive Therapy and Research, 21,* 345–358.

White, J., Davison, G.C., Haaga, D.A.F., & White, K. (1992). Cognitive bias in the articulated thoughts of depressed and nondepressed psychiatric patients. *Journal of Nervous and Mental Disease, 180,* 77–81.

Whitman, P.B., & Leitenberg, H. (1990). Negatively biased recall in children with self-reported symptoms of depression. *Journal of Abnormal Child Psychology, 18,* 15–27.

Whittal, M., & Dobson, K.S. (1991). An investigation of the temporal relationship between anxiety and depression as a consequence of cognitive vulnerability to interpersonal evaluation. *Canadian Journal of Behavioural Science, 23,* 391–398.

Wickless, C., & Kirsch, I. (1988). Cognitive correlates of anger, anxiety, and sadness. *Cognitive Therapy and Research, 12,* 367–377.

Williams, J.M.G. (1984). *The psychological treatment of depression: A guide to the theory and practice of cognitive behaviour therapy.* London/New York: Croom Helm/Free Press.

Williams, J.M.G. (1996). Memory processes in psychotherapy. In P.M. Salkovskis (Ed.), *Frontiers of cognitive therapy* (pp. 97–113). New York: Guilford Press.

Williams, J.M.G. (1997). Depression. In D.M. Clark & C.G. Fairburn (Eds.), *Science and practice of cognitive behaviour therapy* (pp. 259–283). Oxford, England: Oxford University Press.

Williams, J.M.G., & Broadbent, K. (1986). Autobiographical memory in suicide attempters. *Journal of Abnormal Psychology, 95,* 144–149.

Williams, J.M.G., & Dritschel, B.H. (1988). Emotional disturbance and the specificity of autobiographical memory. *Cognition and Emotion, 2,* 221–234.

Williams, J.M.G., Healy, D., Teasdale, J.D., White, W., & Paykel, E.S. (1990). Dysfunctional attitudes and vulnerability to persistent depression. *Psychological Medicine, 20,* 375–381.

Williams, J.M.G., Mathews, A., & MacLeod, C. (1996). The emotional Stroop task and psychopathology. *Psychological Bulletin, 120,* 3–24.

Williams, J.M.G., & Nulty, D.D. (1986). Construct accessibility, depression, and the emotional Stroop task: Transient mood or stable structure? *Personality and Individual Differences, 7,* 485–491.

Williams, J.M.G., Watts, F.N., MacLeod, C., & Mathews, A. (1988). *Cognitive psychology and emotional disorders.* Chichester, England: Wiley.

Williams, J.M.G., Watts, F.N., MacLeod, C., & Mathews, A. (1997). *Cognitive psychology and emotional disorders* (2nd ed). Chichester, England: Wiley.

Wilson, A.R., & Krane, R.V. (1980). Change in self-esteem and its effects on symptoms of depression. *Cognition Therapy and Research, 4,* 419–421.

Wilson, G.T. (1978). Cognitive behavior therapy: Paradigm shift or passing phase? In J.P. Foreyt & D.P. Rathjen (Eds.), *Cognitive behavior therapy: Research and application* (pp. 7–32). New York: Plenum Press.

Wilson, G.T., & Fairburn, C.G. (1993). Cognitive treatments for eating disorders. *Journal of Consulting and Clinical Psychology, 61,* 261–269.

Winokur, G., Coryell, W., Keller, M., Endicott, J., & Leon, A. (1995). A family study of manic-depressive (bipolar I) disease: Is it a distinct illness separate from primary unipolar depression? *Archives of General Psychiatry, 52,* 367–373.

Wise, E.H., & Barnes, D.R. (1986). The relationship among life events, dysfunctional attitudes, and depression. *Cognitive Therapy and Research, 10,* 257–266.

Wittchen, H.-U., Knauper, B., & Kessler, R.C. (1994). Lifetime risk of depression. *British Journal of Psychiatry, 165*(Suppl. 26), 16–22.

Witvliet, C.V., & Vrana, S.R. (1995). Psychophysiological responses as indices of affective dimensions. *Psychophysiology, 32,* 436–443.

Wolpe, J. (1958). *Psychotherapy by reciprocal inhibition.* Stanford, CA: Stanford University Press.

Wong, J.L., & Whitaker, D.J. (1994). The stability and prediction of depressive mood states in college students. *Journal of Clinical Psychology, 50,* 715–722.

Young, G.C.D., & Martin, M. (1981). Processing of information about self by neurotics. *British Journal of Clinical Psychology, 20,* 205–212.

Young, M.A., Fogg, L.F., Akiskal, H., Maser, J., Scheftner, W., & Fawcett, J. (1996). Stable trait components of hopelessness: Baseline and sensitivity to depression. *Journal of Abnormal Psychology, 105,* 155–165.

Zettle, R.D., Haflich, J.L., & Reynolds, R.A. (1992). Responsivity to cognitive therapy as a function of treatment format and client personality dimensions. *Journal of Clinical Psychology, 48,* 787–797.

Zimmerman, M., & Coryell, W. (1986). Dysfunctional attitudes in endogenous and nonendogenous depressed inpatients. *Cognitive Therapy and Research, 10,* 339–346.

Zimmerman, M., Coryell, W., Corenthal, C., & Wilson, S. (1986). Dysfunctional attitudes and attribution style in healthy controls and patients with schizophrenia, psychotic depression, and nonpsychotic depression. *Journal of Abnormal Psychology, 95,* 403–405.

Zinbarg, R.E., Barlow, D.H., Liebowtz, M., Street, L., Broadhead, E., Katon, W., Roy-Byrne, P., Lepine, J.P., Teherani, M., Richards, J., Brantley, P.J., & Kraemer, H. (1994). The DSM-IV field trail for mixed anxiety-depression. *American Journal of Psychiatry, 151,* 1153–1156.

Zonderman, A.B., Herbst, J.H., Schmidt, C., Costa, P.T., & McCrae, R.R. (1993). Depressive symptoms as a nonspecific, graded risk for psychiatric diagnoses. *Journal of Abnormal Psychology, 102,* 544–552.

Zurawski, R.M., & Smith, T.W. (1987). Assessing irrational beliefs and emotional distress: Evidence and implications of limited discriminant validity. *Journal of Counseling Psychology, 34,* 224–227.

Zuroff, D.C. (1994). Depressive personality styles and the five-factor model of personality. *Journal of Personality Assessment, 63,* 453–472.

Zuroff, D.C., Colussy, S.A., & Wielgus, M.S. (1983). Selective memory and depression: A cautionary note concerning response bias. *Cognitive Therapy and Research, 7,* 223–232.

Zuroff, D.C., Colussy, S.A., & Wielgus, M.S. (1986). Additional comments on depression, selective memory and response bias. *Cognitive Therapy and Research, 10,* 271–274.

Zuroff, D.C., & Fitzpatrick, D.K. (1995). Depressive personality styles: Implications for adult attachment. *Personality and Individual Differences, 18,* 253–265.

Zuroff, D.C., Igreja, I., & Mongrain, M. (1990). Dysfunctional attitudes, dependency, and self-criticism as predictors of depressive mood states: A 12-month longitudinal study. *Cognitive Therapy and Research, 14,* 315–326.

Zuroff, D.C., & Mongrain, M. (1987). Dependency and self-criticism: Vulnerability factors for depressive affective states. *Journal of Abnormal Psychology, 96,* 14–22.

Author Index

Subject Index